Turbo Pascal® 5.5:
The Complete Reference

Turbo Pascal® 5.5:
The Complete Reference

Stephen K. O'Brien

BORLAND·OSBORNE/McGRAW·HILL

PROGRAMMING SERIES

Berkeley   New York   St. Louis   San Francisco
Auckland   Bogotá   Hamburg   London   Madrid
Mexico City   Milan   Montreal   New Delhi   Panama City
Paris   São Paulo   Singapore   Sydney
Tokyo   Toronto

Osborne **McGraw-Hill**
2600 Tenth Street
Berkeley, California 94710
U.S.A.

For information on translations and book distributors outside of the U.S.A., write to Osborne **McGraw-Hill** at the above address.

A complete list of trademarks appears on page 893.

Turbo Pascal® 5.5: The Complete Reference

 234567890 DOC 89

ISBN 0-07-881501-0

CONTENTS

Turbo Pascal 5.5: The Complete Reference is an indispensable tool for anyone who develops programs in Turbo Pascal version 5.5 and earlier. Experienced and novice programmers alike will want this desktop reference at their fingertips while they work. Author Stephen K. O'Brien provides answers to the most frequently asked questions about programming in Turbo Pascal. As a bonus, he presents routines that will be a welcome addition to any programmer's library.

You can rely on this book both for the thoroughness with which it covers the subject and for the lucidity of the explanations. In particular, there is a new chapter to get you started with the new object oriented language features of Turbo Pascal. All aspects of Turbo Pascal programming—from accessing DOS services to writing terminate- and stay-resident programs—are included. Special attention is paid to telecommunications, a common use of Turbo Pascal, and to interfacing Turbo Pascal with assembly language. The procedures and functions are well written and extremely useful, and even the most complex processes are accompanied by easy-to-understand examples that users can follow to write their own programs.

Stephen K. O'Brien has been programming in Turbo Pascal since its launch by Borland in 1983. Now he provides you with everything you need to know to develop programs in Turbo Pascal efficiently and productively in one concise, easy-to-use volume.

Philippe Kahn
Chief Executive Officer
Borland International, Inc.

About the Book
In This Book
Diskette Offer

If there was ever any doubt, it is now clear that Turbo Pascal is Pascal. Borland's leadership has taken a language limited to the classroom and made it the only serious challenger to C, the reigning monarch. With the version 5.0 debugger and version 5.5 object oriented programming extensions, Turbo Pascal is the most productive compiler you can buy for microcomputer programming. Whether you are just learning about PC programming or are a serious software developer, Turbo Pascal offers every powerful feature you could ask for in one friendly package.

About the Book

This book is intended for all Turbo Pascal programmers, from beginners to experts. It covers all aspects of the compiler, with extensive examples. Both beginners and advanced programmers will find useful information ranging from dynamic allocation to memory-resident programming. Designed primarily as a reference guide, the book provides quick access to concise information on a broad range of topics.

In This Book

Turbo Pascal beginners will appreciate Chapter 1, "A Quick Start to Programming," which introduces programming basics. Chapters 2 through 9 cover all aspects of the Turbo Pascal system, from the integrated development environment to pointers and dynamic memory allocation. Chapters 10 through 18 offer valuable insights into such important programming topics as DOS and BIOS functions, the use of assembly language, and memory-resident programs. The Turbo Pascal toolboxes are covered in Chapters 18 through 22. Here you'll find quick reference guides to the powerful graphics, database, editor, and numerical methods routines the toolboxes offer. Chapter 23 describes how to use the new integrated debugger, which can save you hours of wasted programming time, and Chapter 24 introduces Borland's newest enhancement, object oriented programming.

Turbo Pascal is one of the leading programming environments for personal computers. *Turbo Pascal 5.5: The Complete Reference* is the resource you need to get the most from Borland's premier product.

Diskette Offer

All the programs listed in this book are available on either 5 1/4- or 3 1/2-inch disks. The source code is written for version 5.5 of the compiler. To order your disk, send $35.00 in check or money order along with the form on the following page.

Order Form

Please send me the disk that accompanies *Turbo Pascal 5.5: The Complete Reference*. My payment of $35.00 in check or money order is enclosed.

Name_____

Address_____

City _____ State _____ ZIP_____

Disk size   [ ] 5 1/4-inch   [ ] 3 1/2-inch

Solo Flight Software, Inc., 217 East 85th Street, Suite 194, New York, New York 10028

This is solely the offering of Stephen K. O'Brien, Solo Flight Software, Inc. Osborne/McGraw-Hill takes no responsibility for the fulfillment of this offer.

A Quick Start to Programming

**O
N
E**

If you are using Turbo Pascal for the first time, this chapter is for you. In it you will discover the fundamentals of the Turbo Pascal system and, at the same time, write and run your first programs. Do not be too concerned about understanding everything presented in this chapter; even simple programming concepts take time to sink in. Just take your time, get comfortable with the system, try the sample programs, and experiment on your own.

A Simple Turbo Pascal Program

The best way to begin is by writing your first program. To start Turbo Pascal, make sure you are logged in to the drive and directory in which the TURBO.EXE file resides. At the DOS prompt, type **TURBO** and press ENTER.

On your screen, you see the Turbo Pascal integrated development environment. At the top of the screen is the main menu, which gives you access to all of Turbo Pascal's features. Below the main menu is the Edit window, in which you will type your programs. And below the Edit window is the Watch window, which is used in debugging programs.

To write your first program, press F10 to activate the main menu and then press E (for **Edit**). Now the cursor will appear in the Edit window, ready for you to begin typing in the following Turbo Pascal program, which will display one line of text on your computer's screen:

```
Program Prog1;
Begin
WriteLn('This is my first program.');
ReadLn;
End.
```

If you make a typing mistake, use the arrow keys on the numeric keypad to position the cursor at the error, press DEL to delete the error, and then type the correct letters.

Once you have completely typed the program, press F10 again to activate the main menu. Then press R to select the Run menu, and press R again to run your program. Turbo Pascal will now execute the program you just wrote—your monitor will show this message:

```
This is my first program.
```

When you are ready to return to the integrated development environment, press ENTER.

While it is small, this program contains elements common to all Turbo Pascal programs. It has a program heading, **Program Prog1**, which identifies the program. It also has a program block that starts with **Begin** and terminates with **End**, as shown in Figure 1-1.

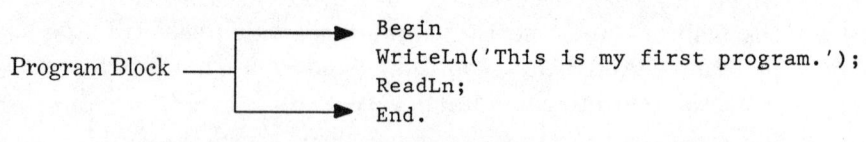

Figure 1-1.   A short program block

A Turbo Pascal program always starts execution at the first **Begin** statement of the main program block and continues until it reaches the final **End** statement. (A program will also stop when it encounters the **Halt** command or a fatal error, but these are exceptions.)

The program block in the example just given contains only two statements.

```
WriteLn('This is my first program.');
ReadLn;
```

The **WriteLn** statement displays the string, and **ReadLn** makes the computer wait until you press ENTER. If you run a program in the integrated development environment (IDE), you can use the **ReadLn** statement to stop a program before the screen switches back to the editor screen. When in the IDE, you can always view the output screen by pressing ALT-F5.

WriteLn is a Turbo Pascal standard procedure that displays numbers and strings of characters to the screen, prints them on a printer, or writes them to a disk file. It also adds two special characters, carriage return and line feed (ASCII codes 13 and 10), to the end of the line. These special characters, often referred to in programming shorthand as CR/LF, signal that the end of a line of text has been reached, and that any additional text should start on the next line.

Inside the parentheses of the **WriteLn** statement are the items to be printed. While in this case the **WriteLn** procedure prints only one line, it is capable of printing more than one item at a time. Figure 1-2 shows an example of a **WriteLn** statement that prints three separate strings.

A *string* is any combination of characters that is enclosed in single quotation marks. In the example **WriteLn** procedure, commas separate one string from another. Note that the second string consists of two blank characters, thus creating a space between the first and third strings. When this statement is executed, the result looks like the following.

```
This is one string.  This is another string.
```

Like **WriteLn**, the procedure **Write** also displays strings and
numbers; but **Write** does not add CR/LF characters to the end
of the line. When you use **Write**, the cursor remains on the same
line as the information written, while **WriteLn** moves the cursor
to the beginning of the next line.

Adding Variables to a Program

Programs that merely write messages are not very interesting.
To be truly useful, a program must process data, and that
requires the use of *variables;* places in your computer's memory
that hold values, such as numbers or strings.

To define a variable, you must give it a name and a type.
You can give a variable almost any name you want, but it is best
to choose a name that describes the information the variable
holds. For example, you might call a variable that holds the
name of a customer **CustomerName** and define it as follows:

```
L 1-5 Var
         CustomerName : String[50];
```

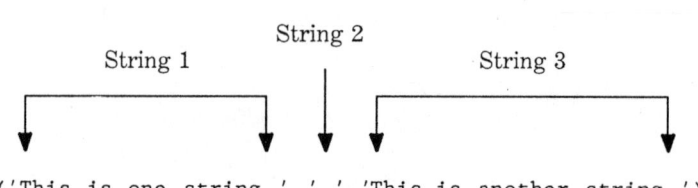

Figure 1-2.   A WriteLn statement with multiple strings

CustomerName, the name of the variable, is also referred to as the variable identifier because it identifies by name the location in memory where the value is stored. **String [50]** identifies the variable as a string and indicates that the length of this string cannot exceed 50 characters.

Var is a Turbo Pascal *reserved word* that indicates the beginning of variable declarations. There are many other reserved words in Turbo Pascal, such as **Integer, Begin, End,** and so on. (Appendix D contains a complete list of Turbo Pascal reserved words.) Reserved words are central to the Turbo Pascal language, and therefore, you cannot redefine them. These examples illustrate illegal attempts to use reserved words as variable identifiers:

```
Var
  Begin : Integer;
  Real  : String[50];
```

Integer and *Real* variables can hold numbers; *char* variables can hold single characters; *String* variables can hold groups of characters; and *Boolean* variables contain true/false indicators. While they are designed for different purposes, these variable types share one common characteristic—their values can be changed (or varied) in a program by using an *assignment statement*.

Assignment statements set variables to particular values. For example, the statement

```
CustomerName := 'John Doe';
```

takes the group of characters "John Doe" and stores them in the string variable **CustomerName**. Note that the assignment statement uses the **:=** operator, which is known as the *assignment operator*.

Variables and Input

The assignment statement is just one way to set the value of a variable; the **ReadLn** procedure is another. But unlike assignment statements, **ReadLn** gets its value from a source outside the program, such as the person using the program or a disk file. When a program encounters a **ReadLn** statement, it stops and waits until the user types in the data and presses ENTER. **ReadLn** then takes the input and assigns it to a variable named in the **ReadLn** statement. For example, the Pascal input statement **ReadLn(CustomerName)** waits for the user to type in a string of characters, accepts a string, and stores it in the variable **CustomerName**.

The following sample program demonstrates how **ReadLn** obtains input and stores it in variables.

```
Program Prog2;

Uses CRT;

Var
  i : Integer;
  s : String[20];

Begin
ClrScr;

Write('Enter a number: ');
ReadLn(i);
WriteLn('Your number is ',i);

Write('Enter a string: ');
ReadLn(s);
WriteLn('Your string is ',s);

ReadLn;
End.
```

Now, go back into the Turbo Editor and type in the program just listed. You will notice that this program is somewhat more complicated than the first one. For one thing, the program includes the following declaration:

```
Uses CRT;
```

CRT is a Turbo Pascal *standard unit*. Units contain data declarations, procedures, and functions that are designed for specific purposes. The routines in the CRT unit, for example, apply primarily to the use of the video display screen. If you want to use the procedures and functions in a unit, you must include the **Uses** statement at the beginning of your program.

Now that you have typed in the program, start it as you did the first program (select the **Run** option from the Run menu). When the program starts, the **ClrScr** command (from the CRT unit) clears the screen, and the program displays **Enter a number:** on your monitor. Type the number **9** and press ENTER. The program now displays **Your number is 9**, skips one line on the screen, and displays **Enter a string:**. Type in **ABC** and press ENTER. The program now displays **Your string is ABC**. The program used the **ReadLn** statement to obtain a number and a string from the user.

Prog2 uses two variables: **i**, an integer, and **s**, a string. Integers are numerical values with no decimal place and can range in value from 32,767 down to $-32,768$. The string variable **s** is defined as **String[20]**, which means that it can hold up to 20 characters. (The maximum number of characters a string can hold is 255.)

The example program just given uses a common, if crude, method of getting input from the user. First, the program prompts the user for input by asking for a number. The prompt **Enter a number:** is displayed by using the **Write** procedure, as opposed to **WriteLn**, because **Write** places the cursor directly after the prompt message. This tells the user that the program is waiting for input.

The next statement, **ReadLn(i);**, waits for the user to type a valid integer and press ENTER. The program assigns whatever the user types to the integer variable **i**. The last statement confirms the input by displaying both a message and the contents of **i**.

If the **ReadLn** statement detects an error in the input, it notifies you and halts the program. For example, run **Prog2** again, but when it asks for a number, type **ABC** and press ENTER. Turbo Pascal detects an *input/output error* and displays this message:

```
Runtime error 106 at 0000:0041
```

Error 106 indicates an invalid numeric format. In short, Turbo Pascal was expecting a number, and it got something else, **ABC**, which is not a valid integer. The value 0000:0041 is the location in the program at which the error occurred. If you are running the program from within the integrated development environment, Turbo Pascal will automatically locate the error in the source code and bring that part of the program into the editor.

Prog2 also demonstrates the use of the **WriteLn** statement when used with no parameters. When executed, this statement simply writes a CR/LF combination to the computer monitor, which places the cursor on the first position of the next line.

Simple Turbo Pascal Arithmetic

The following example program demonstrates how arithmetic is used in Turbo Pascal programs and introduces another data type called **Real**. Like **Integer** variables, **Real** variables are numbers; unlike **Integers**, they can have decimal places. They can also be much larger than **Integers**: the maximum value for an **Integer** variable is 32,767, while for a **Real** variable it is 1.0E38, or a 1 with 38 zeros after it.

```
Program Prog3;
Uses CRT;
Var
  Number1,
  Number2,
  AddResult,
  SubResult,
  MultResult,
  DivResult   : Real;

Begin
ClrScr;

Write('Enter a number: ');
ReadLn(number1);
Write('Enter another number: ');
ReadLn(number2);

AddResult  := Number1 + Number2;
SubResult  := Number1 - Number2;
```

```
MultResult := Number1 * Number2;
DivResult  := Number1 / Number2;

WriteLn;
WriteLn('Number1 + Number2 = ',AddResult);
WriteLn('Number1 - Number2 = ',SubResult);
WriteLn('Number1 * Number2 = ',MultResult);
WriteLn('Number1 / Number2 = ',DivResult);

WriteLn;

WriteLn('Number1 + Number2 = ',AddResult:10:3);
WriteLn('Number1 - Number2 = ',SubResult:10:3);
WriteLn('Number1 * Number2 = ',MultResult:10:3);
WriteLn('Number1 / Number2 = ',DivResult:10:3);

WriteLn;
Write('Press ENTER...');
ReadLn;
End.
```

Prog3 asks the user to enter two numbers, which are assigned to **Real** variables **Number1** and **Number2** and then used in four arithmetic operations: addition, subtraction, multiplication, and division. After performing the computations, **Prog3** writes out the results in two different formats: scientific and decimal.

Scientific notation, used only for **Real** variables, is a shorthand way of expressing large values. For example, the result of the following calculation:

$$5342168903247 \times 24729234798734$$

expressed in scientific notation, would be 1.3210774914E + 26. The first part of the number (1.3210774914) contains the significant digits; the second part (E + 26) is the power of 10 to which the first part is raised. In other words, the number 1.3210774914E + 26 can be expressed as 1.3210774914 times 10 to the 26th power.

Scientific notation is the default format for the value of **Real** variables in Turbo Pascal. You can, however, also write **Real** values in decimal format. For example, in the statement

```
WriteLn('Number1 + Number2 = ', AddResult:10:3);
```

the variable **AddResult** is followed by the format specification :10:3, which tells Turbo Pascal to print the **Real** variable right-justified in a field that is 10 spaces wide and allows 3 decimal places. If the resulting number were equal to 5, the number would be displayed as shown in Figure 1-3.

If the number printed requires more than the 10 spaces allocated, the program prints the entire number, taking as many spaces as needed.

Repeating Statements with Loops

A loop is a mechanism that allows you to repeat a statement or group of statements. Turbo Pascal provides several ways of creating loops. The program shown here demonstrates two of them, the For-Do loop and the Repeat-Until loop.

```
Program Prog4;
Uses CRT;
Var
  NumberArray : Array [1..5] Of Integer;
  Average : Real;
  i : Integer;

Begin
ClrScr;

(*******************)
(* The For-Do Loop *)
(*******************)
For i := 1 To 5 Do
  Begin
  Write('Enter a number: ');
  ReadLn(NumberArray[i]);
  End;

Average := 0;
i := 1;

(************************)
(* The Repeat-Until Loop *)
(************************)

  Repeat
  Average := Average + NumberArray[i];
  i := i + 1;
  Until i > 5;
```

```
Average := Average / 5;
WriteLn('The average is: ',Average:0:2);

ReadLn;
End.
```

You need three elements to write a loop: a starting point, an ending point, and an integer variable, which is used as a counter. In the For-Do loop definition

```
For i := 1 To 5 Do
```

i is the counter, 1 is the starting point, and 5 is the ending point. When the loop starts, the program sets **i** to 1. Each time the loop repeats, the value of **i** is incremented by one; after the fifth time through the loop, **i** is equal to 6. Since 6 is greater than the ending point specified in the For-Do loop, the loop ends, and the program proceeds with the first statement that follows the For-Do loop block.

The example program also demonstrates a second type of loop, known as the Repeat-Until loop. Compared with For-Do loops, Repeat-Until loops require a little more work; you, not Turbo Pascal, must initialize the value of the counter, increment its value, and test the value to terminate the loop. For all this work, Repeat-Until loops do have advantages. For one thing, you do not need to know before you write the loop how many times it will execute. Repeat-Until loops repeat until the condition specified in the **Until** line is satisfied. You can also increment the counter by any amount you like. Another advantage is

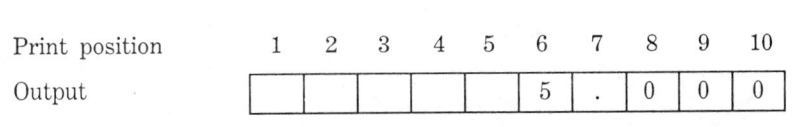

Print position	1	2	3	4	5	6	7	8	9	10
Output						5	.	0	0	0

Figure 1-3.   Formatted numeric output

that you can test for more than one condition at the same time, as is shown in this example:

```
Repeat
i := i + 1;
j := j + 1;
Until (i > 100) Or (j = 50);
```

If either of the tests in the **Until** statement is found to be true, the program exits the Repeat-Until loop. Loop structures are fundamental to all aspects of computer programming. You will find many uses for them as your programming skills grow.

Using Disk Files

Eventually, you will write programs that need to store and retrieve data from disk files. Turbo Pascal makes using disk files easy, as this program demonstrates.

```
Program Prog5;
Uses CRT;
Var
   i,j : Integer;
   f : Text;
   r : Real;

Begin
ClrScr;

Assign(f,'SQUARES.DAT');
Rewrite(f);

For i := 1 To 20 Do
  WriteLn(f,Sqr(i):10);

Reset(f);
For i := 1 To 20 Do
  Begin
  ReadLn(f,j);
  WriteLn(i:4,' squared is ',j:4);
  End;
```

```
Close(f);

WriteLn;
Write('Press ENTER...');
ReadLn;
End.
```

Prog5 creates a text file and fills it with the squares of the first 20 positive integers. The program then rereads this file and writes the values to the screen.

Prog5 introduces the Turbo Pascal reserved word **Text**, a type of disk file that holds mainly words and sentences, although a text file can also hold numbers. **Prog5** declares the file identifier **f** to be of type **Text**. This file identifier is then used in the familiar **ReadLn** and **WriteLn** statements to direct input and output to disk files rather than to the screen.

Before you use a file variable, you must first assign it, by name, to a disk file. Do this with the **Assign** command:

```
Assign (f, 'SQUARES.DAT');
Rewrite(f);
```

The **Assign** command links the file variable **f** with the physical file SQUARES.DAT. The **Rewrite** statement prepares the file to accept data. If the physical file SQUARES.DAT does not exist, the **Rewrite** command creates it. If the file does exist, **Rewrite** destroys the contents of the file. Once a file has been rewritten, it is ready to receive output. In **Prog5**, output is written to file **f** with this statement:

```
WriteLn(f,Sqr(i):10);
```

This is the same **WriteLn** procedure used in earlier program examples, but this time the first parameter is the file variable **f**, which tells Turbo Pascal that everything written by this statement goes to this file.

While **Rewrite** prepares a file for writing, **Reset** prepares it for reading. Once the file is reset, the **ReadLn** statement can be used to read data from it, as demonstrated here:

```
ReadLn(f,j);
```

This statement reads an integer from **Text** file **f** and stores that integer in **j**. While Turbo Pascal supports different types of files, **Text** files (like those used in the example just given) are the easiest for beginning programmers because they can be used for input and output in much the same way as the keyboard and monitor are used.

One last note on using files concerns the importance of closing disk files. When a disk file is closed, two things happen. First, if the file is being used for output, any data residing in buffers is flushed to the disk. If your program ends without closing an output file, you risk losing any buffered data that has not yet been written to disk. Second, closing a file frees a file handle. When you start your computer, DOS reserves a fixed number of file handles. The default number of file handles is 8, although you can expand this to up to 20 by adding the line

    FILES = 20

to your CONFIG.SYS file. Turbo Pascal always claims the first five file handles for its standard input and output devices. This means that you may have as few as three file handles available to your program. Since every open file uses a file handle, you could be limited to only three open disk files at one time. If your program uses a lot of different disk files, take care to close unused files so that your program will not use up all the available file handles.

As you read through this book, you will find in-depth discussions of the programming concepts introduced in this chapter, as well as information on many advanced topics. Turbo Pascal offers a number of powerful features that may take some time to grasp fully. Read, experiment, have fun, and you will become an accomplished programmer before you know it.

The Turbo Pascal
Programming System

Getting Started
The File Menu
The Run Menu
The Compile Menu
The Options Menu
The Debug Menu
The Break/watch Menu

One of the reasons Turbo Pascal is so enjoyable to use is its integrated development environment (IDE). Once you are in the Turbo Pascal IDE, you can edit, compile, run, and debug your programs without having to go back to the DOS prompt. Borland pioneered the concept of the IDE and, through constant refinement, has produced the most efficient programming system available.

With the introduction of Turbo Pascal 5.5, the IDE now offers even more options, including integrated debugging facilities. A welcome addition is the Watch window, which allows you to see the values of variables as your program runs. This chapter covers the Turbo Pascal 5.5 user interface in detail and explains how each function is used.

Getting Started

To start Turbo Pascal, type **TURBO** at the DOS prompt and press ENTER. Turbo Pascal enters the integrated development environment, shown in Figure 2-1. At the top of the screen is the main menu, which contains seven choices: **File, Edit, Run, Compile, Options, Debug,** and **Break/watch**. To select one of these options, you can either highlight the option using F10 and the arrow keys and then press ENTER or type the first letter of the option (for example, press F for **File**).

15

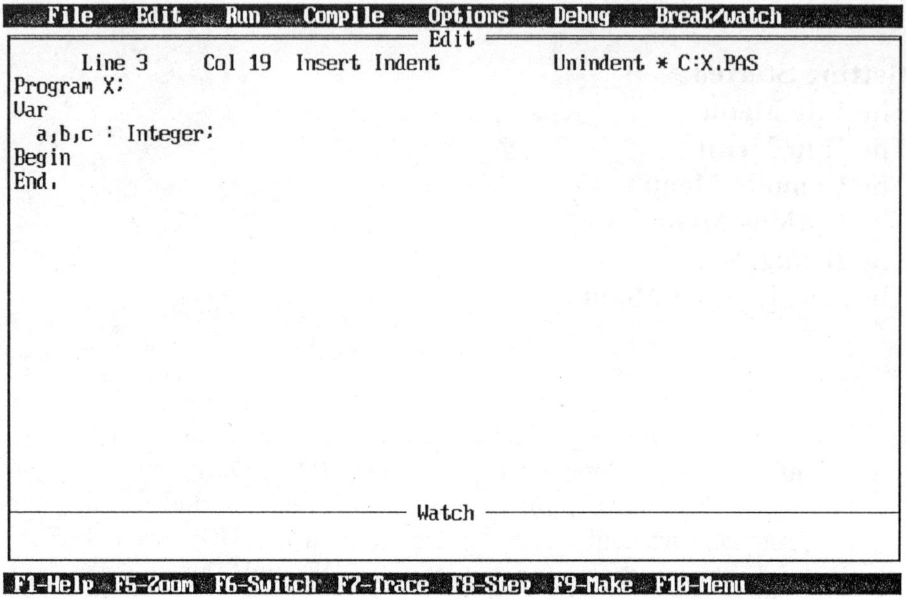

```
 File   Edit   Run   Compile   Options   Debug   Break/watch
                             Edit
    Line 3      Col 19   Insert Indent          Unindent * C:X.PAS
Program X;
Var
  a,b,c : Integer;
Begin
End,




                             Watch

 F1-Help  F5-Zoom  F6-Switch  F7-Trace  F8-Step  F9-Make  F10-Menu
```

Figure 2-1.   The Turbo Pascal 5.5 main menu

In the Turbo Pascal integrated development environment, the screen is divided into two sections—the Edit window and the Watch window. Program source code is entered and edited in the Edit window, which activates the Turbo Pascal editor. The editor is like a simple word processor that you can use to write your programs.

Once you have typed your program into the Edit window, you can use the Watch window to examine your program as it executes. A detailed discussion of the Watch window appears later in this chapter.

The File Menu

The **File** menu is the first selection on the main menu. From this menu you can load source files, change the logged disk and directory, activate the DOS shell, and more. The File menu contains nine choices: **Load, Pick, New, Save, Write to, Directory, Change dir, OS shell,** and **Quit.**

The Edit Selection

Selecting **Edit** brings you into the Edit window and activates the Turbo Pascal editor. The highlight on the menu will disappear and a cursor will appear in the Edit window. To return to the main menu from the Edit window, simply press the F10 key.

The top of the Edit window is a status line that gives you information about the editor. The elements of the status line are summarized here.

Line n
: This displays the line number, in the current source file, on which the cursor is located

Col n
: This displays the column number in which the cursor is located

Insert
: When this indicator is visible, any characters typed will be inserted in the existing text. When it is not visible, typing will overwrite existing text. You can toggle this feature with the CTRL-V key combination

Indent
: This indicator signals that the auto-indent feature is active. When you press ENTER, the auto-indent feature causes the cursor to return to the beginning of the previous line in the source file. When auto-indent is not active, pressing ENTER causes the cursor to return to the first column. You can toggle this feature with the CTRL-OI key combination

Tab
: This indicates that the Tab mode is active. In the Tab mode, pressing the TAB key generates a tab character (^I) and moves the cursor right by a fixed number of spaces. When Tab mode is inactive, pressing the TAB key produces space characters until the cursor is aligned with the beginning of the word to the right of the cursor on the previous line in the editor. You can toggle this option with CTRL-OT

Fill   The Fill feature, which works only when the
                Tab mode is on, causes Turbo Pascal to begin
                each line with a combination of tab and space
                characters such that the total number of char-
                acters used is the fewest possible. This option is
                toggled with CTRL-OF

Unindent   When you press the BACKSPACE key when un-
                indent is active, Turbo Pascal moves the cursor
                backward until it is aligned with the first out-
                dented line found in a line above the current
                one

The Run Menu

From the Run menu you can execute a program just as you
would from the DOS prompt, or step through a program one line
at a time. The Run menu includes **Run, Program reset, Go to
cursor, Trace into, Step over,** and **User screen.**

The Compile Menu

You will use the Compile menu to compile units and complete
programs. The choices on this menu include **Compile, Make,
Build, Destination, Find error, Primary file,** and **Get info.**

The Options Menu

With the Turbo Pascal Options menu, you can choose from a
wide range of features that give you complete control over both
the compiler and the programming environment. The selections
on the Options menu include **Compiler, Linker, Environment,
Directories,** and **Parameters.** Two additional selections on the
Options menu, **Save options** and **Retrieve options,** respectively,
let you save option settings in a disk file and retrieve option
settings saved previously.

The Debug Menu

The **Debug** option, introduced in Turbo Pascal 5.5, provides features needed to use either the integrated debugger built into Turbo Pascal or a stand-alone debugger. The options on this menu are **Evaluate, Call stack, Find procedure, Integrated debugging, Standalone debugging, Display swapping,** and **Refresh display.**

Note: **Call stack** and **Find procedure** only operate once you have compiled a program.

Debugging is of two types: integrated and stand-alone. When you turn on **Integrated debugging** in the Debug menu, Turbo Pascal generates debugging information that can be used only while you are in the integrated development environment. If you want to debug a program outside the integrated development environment (using the Turbo Debugger or another product) you must turn on **Standalone debugging**, which causes Turbo Pascal to attach debugging information to the .EXE program file.

The Break/watch Menu

You will appreciate the power of the Break/watch menu when you want to debug a program. One of the easiest ways to debug a program is to watch how the values of key variables change from one point in a program to another. With the features on the Break/watch menu — **Add watch, Delete watch, Edit watch, Remove all watches, Toggle breakpoint, Clear all breakpoints, View next breakpoint** — you can watch one or more variables, set break points within a program, and truly control every aspect of program execution.

The Main Menu Hot Keys

When you are in the Turbo Pascal integrated development environment, seven hot keys are displayed at the bottom of the screen. While Turbo Pascal supports other hot keys, these are the most important. They are as follows.

F1-Help   This opens a Help window that can tell you nearly everything you need to know about the Turbo Pascal integrated development environment

F5-Zoom   Turbo Pascal normally displays both the Edit and Watch windows. When you press F5, the currently active window expands to use the entire screen. Pressing F5 again restores the split screen

F6-Switch   The F6 key allows you to toggle between the Edit window and the Watch window

F7-Trace   When you press F7, Turbo Pascal will compile the current program and start executing one line at a time. This is known as tracing through a program

F8-Step   Step is much like Trace, except that when you step through a program, Turbo Pascal executes procedure and function calls in one step

F9-Make   The **Make** function compiles the current program, checking to make sure that all units are up to date. A unit is considered up to date when the date and time of the .TPU file is more recent than the date and time of any source file upon which the .TPU file depends

F10-Menu   When you press F10, the main menu becomes active

The File Menu

The features in the File menu let you load a file into the Turbo editor, change directory, or execute a DOS command without leaving the Turbo Pascal integrated development environment. The File menu is shown in Figure 2-2.

Load

The **Load** option is used to read a file from disk and place it in the Turbo editor. You can also call the **Load** function directly by

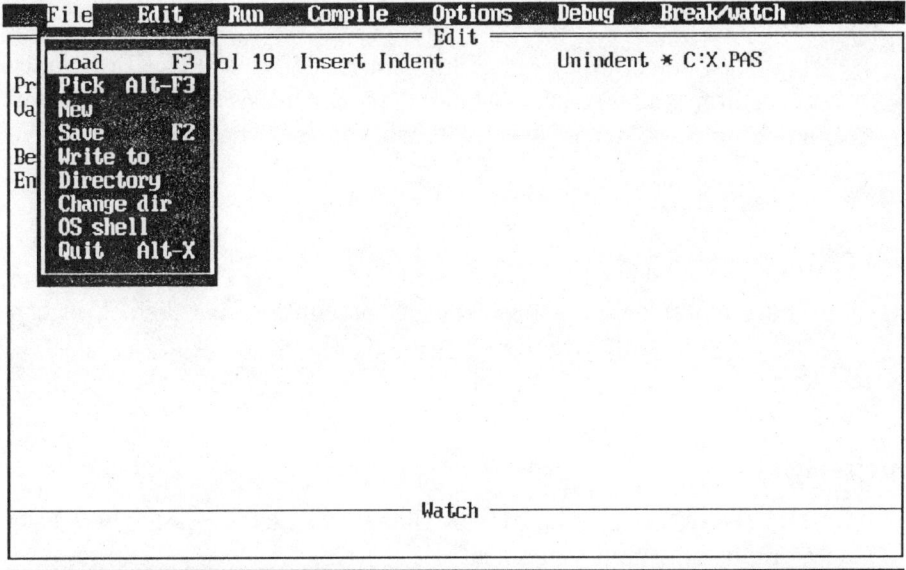

Figure 2-2.   The File menu

pressing the F3 key. When you select the **Load** function, Turbo
Pascal will ask you which file you wish to load. You can specify a
complete filename or use the DOS wildcard characters (* and ?)
to specify a range of files.

　　If you use the wildcard characters, Turbo Pascal will display a Directory window with all directory entries that match
your specification. To load a file from the Directory window, use
the arrow keys to highlight the name you want, and then press
ENTER.

Pick

As you edit different files, Turbo Pascal remembers the previous
eight files you worked with and stores their names on a Pick list.
When you select **Pick** from the File menu, Turbo Pascal displays
the names of the last eight files used. (You can call the **Pick**
function directly by pressing ALT-F3). Use the arrow keys to select
the file you want, and then press ENTER to load the file into the
editor. The Pick facility is a great aid when you are making
editing changes to several different files.

New

The **New** selection on the File menu tells Turbo Pascal to empty the editor and set the file name to NONAME.PAS. When you save the file, Turbo Pascal will ask you for a new filename.

Save

The **Save** selection stores the editor contents to disk. You can call this function directly by pressing the F2 key.

Write to

The **Write to** selection writes the current contents of the editor to a filename that you specify.

Directory

The **Directory** function operates just like the **Load** function.

Change dir

To change the logged disk or directory, choose the **Change dir** option. When you select this function, you can either edit the current directory and path or enter an entirely new one.

OS shell

The **OS shell** function temporarily suspends Turbo Pascal, clears the screen, and displays the DOS prompt, from which you can run other programs or DOS commands. You must remember, however, that Turbo Pascal is still resident, so your computer will not have as much memory as it would normally. To return to Turbo Pascal from the OS shell, simply type **Exit** at the DOS prompt.

Quit

When you want to exit the Turbo Pascal integrated development environment, select **Quit** or press ALT-X to return to DOS.

The Run Menu

The options on the Run menu (Figure 2-3) are used to execute a program from within the Turbo integrated development environment. Most of the selections are used for debugging programs by executing portions and then stopping.

Run

The **Run** selection on the Run menu is used to execute a program from within the Turbo integrated development environment. You can also select this option by pressing CTRL-F9. When you select **Run**, Turbo Pascal will execute the program currently

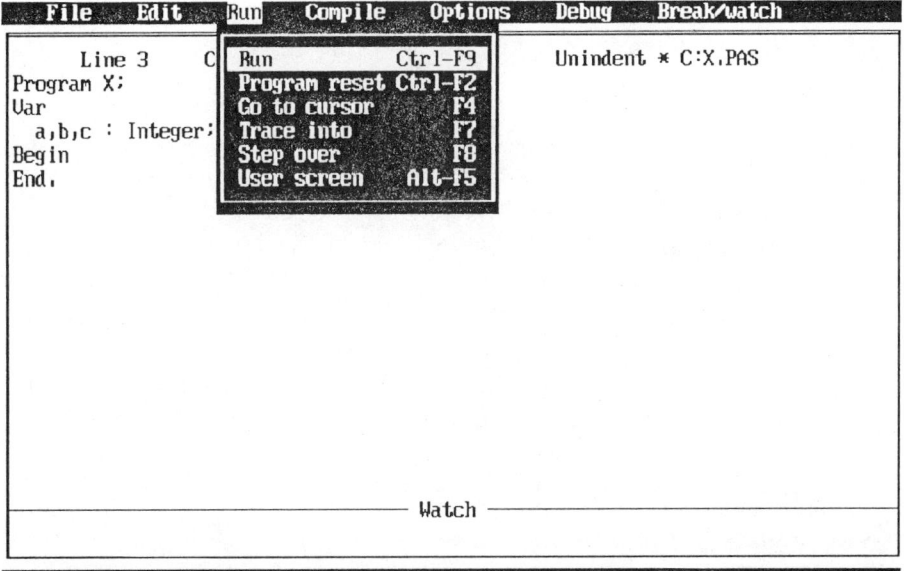

Figure 2-3.   The Run menu

in the editor (or the file currently specified as the primary file). The program will run normally until it encounters a run-time error or a break point that you have set.

Program reset

While debugging a program, you might want to reset the program to start from the beginning. To do this, simply select **Program reset** or press CTRL-F2. The **Program reset** function closes all open files and returns the program pointer to the first statement in the program.

Go to cursor

The **Go to cursor** option is perhaps the most useful addition to Turbo Pascal 5.5. To use this feature, place the cursor on any line in a program, and then select **Go to cursor** from the Run menu (or just press F4). Turbo Pascal will execute your program normally, but when it encounters the line on which you placed the cursor, it stops the program and returns you to the editor. At that point you can continue debugging or reset the program and start from the beginning.

Trace into

Trace into is a powerful new feature of Turbo Pascal. When you select **Trace into** (or press F7), Turbo Pascal will begin executing your program one line at a time. Each time you press F7, Turbo will execute one more line. When Turbo encounters a procedure or function call, it jumps to the source code for that routine and continues to execute one line at a time. With this feature you can see how your program works, line by line, from start to finish.

Step over

The **Step over** feature works much like **Trace into**, except that when using **Step over**, Turbo will execute procedure and function calls in one step. You can also initiate the **Step over** feature by pressing F8. Use this feature when you want to execute a procedure or function without seeing the process line by line.

User screen

When you are debugging in Turbo Pascal, you cannot see what your program is displaying on the screen. If you want to see what your program is displaying (from the user's point of view), use the **User screen** selection or press ALT-F5.

The Compile Menu

The Compile menu (Figure 2-4) contains the commands you need to create linkable object modules or complete executable programs. You can specify a primary file, get information about a compiled program, and more.

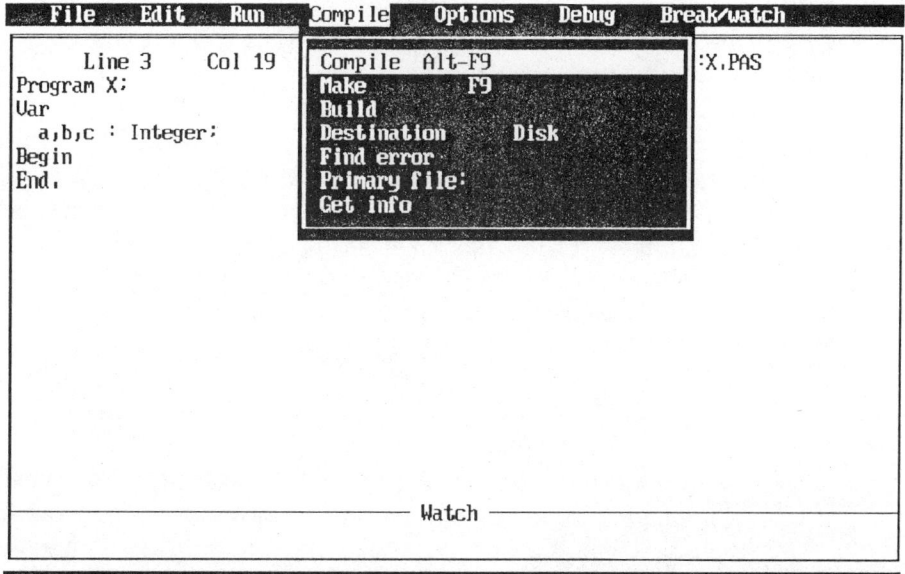

Figure 2-4.   The Compile menu

Compile

When you select the **Compile** feature from the Compile menu, Turbo Pascal compiles the source file that is currently loaded in the editor. If the source file is a unit, Turbo Pascal creates a file with the .TPU extension. Program files, on the other hand, are compiled to executable code that is stored either in memory or on disk in an .EXE file. If the source file in the editor uses any other units, those units must be compiled first. You can call the **Compile** feature by pressing ALT-F9.

Make

The **Make** feature invokes a compilation process that is rather complicated. Like the **Compile** feature, the **Make** option compiles the source file that is currently loaded in the editor, unless a file has been named as a primary file, in which case **Make** will start compiling the primary file regardless of the file currently in the editor. For example, if TEST1.PAS is currently in the editor and TEST2.PAS is named as the primary file, then the **Make** process will begin compiling TEST2.PAS while TEST1.PAS remains in the editor.

Not only does **Make** compile the primary file, but it also compiles every unit used by the primary file *if the unit is not current*. A current unit is one whose source code file (.PAS) has a date stamp that precedes the object code file (.TPU). The **Make** feature compiles units only when the .TPU file is missing or is not current. The Turbo Pascal **Make** feature also checks the time stamps for include files and external object files, to make sure that the Turbo Pascal object file is up to date. You can call the **Make** feature by pressing F9.

Build

The **Build** feature operates just like **Make**, except that all units are recompiled whether or not they are out of date. For example, when developing a program, you might have **Range checking** turned on. When your program is final, however, you want to turn **Range checking** off to maximize speed. To do this, you will change the setting of the global compiler directive (assuming the units don't have their own) and use the **Build** feature to recompile all the units. The new units will reflect the changed compiler directive.

Destination

When compiling, making, or building a program, you can store the resulting executable code either on disk (in a file with the .EXE extension) or in memory. Compiling to memory is faster than to disk, but requires more memory and does not create a permanent copy of the executable code.

Find error

Sometimes, while a program is being run from the DOS prompt, the program will encounter a run-time error that looks like this:

Runtime error 200 at 0000:0099.

Code 200 is the run-time error caused by division by zero. The numbers 0000:0099 are the address (segment) and offset, at which the error occurred. To locate the error, you select the **Find error** feature from the Compile menu, and enter the address. Turbo Pascal will locate the error in the source code and display the location on the screen. Note that to use the **Find error** feature, you must have **Debug information** (in the Options/Compiler menu) turned on and **Integrated debugging** enabled (in the Debug menu) when your program is compiled.

Primary file

When no file is specified as the primary file, the **Make** and **Build** process will begin with the file that is in the editor. Once you specify a primary file, however, the **Make** or **Build** process will always begin with that file, no matter what file is in the editor. This feature is particularly useful when you are working on a program with multiple source files.

Get info

After you have compiled a program, you can get information
about it by selecting **Get info**, which opens the Information
window (see Figure 2-5). The Information window tells you how
much memory your program requires, the memory available to
run the program, the number of lines compiled in your program,
and more.

The Options Menu

Turbo Pascal offers many options that let you customize your
programs and programming environment. The Options menu
(Figure 2-6) gives you complete control over these options so
that the Turbo Pascal compiler, linker, and environment work
the way you want them to.

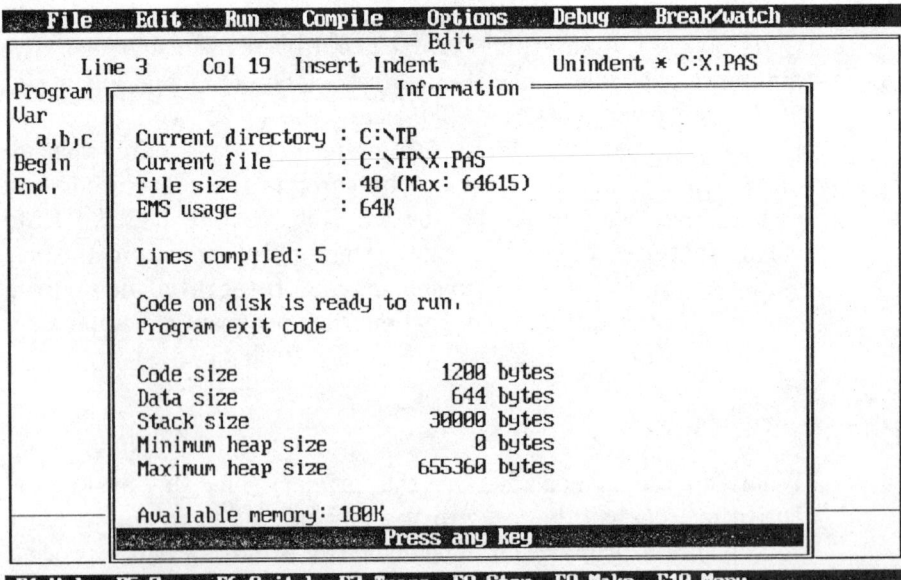

Figure 2-5.   The Information window

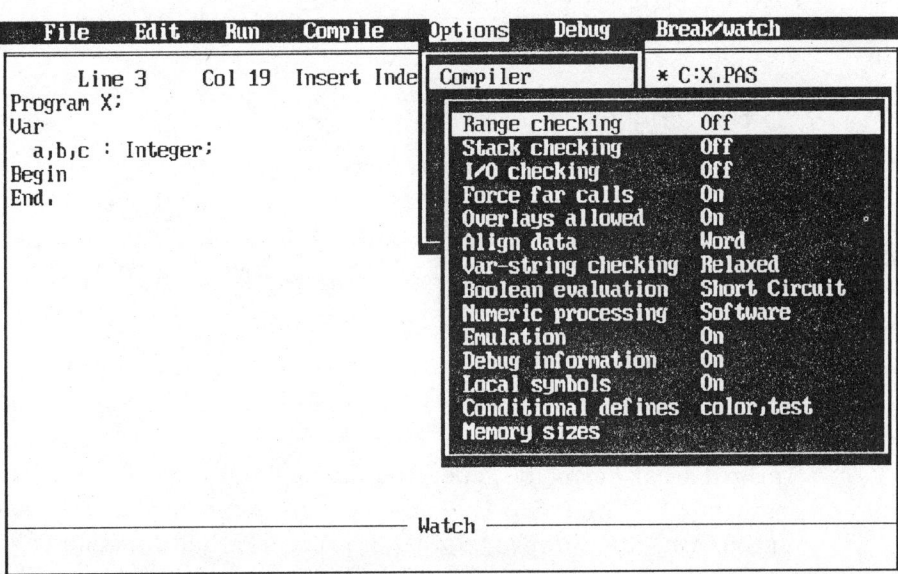

Figure 2-6.   The Options menu

Figure 2-7.   The Options/Compiler menu

Compiler

The Compiler menu (Figure 2-7), the first choice on the Options menu, lets you set various options that change the way Turbo Pascal compiles a program.

Range checking

When **Range checking** is enabled, Turbo Pascal will check for all out-of-bounds conditions on arrays, strings, and assignments to scalar-type variables. When an out-of-range condition is detected, Turbo Pascal generates a run-time error.

Stack checking

When **Stack checking** is enabled, Turbo Pascal checks the amount of memory available on the stack before executing a procedure or function. Insufficient space on the stack produces a run-time error.

I/O checking

Enabling **I/O checking** causes Turbo Pascal to check for errors after every input or output process. An error with **I/O checking** generates a run-time error. When **I/O checking** is disabled, you can check for I/O errors yourself by examining the value of the global variable **IOResult**.

Force far calls

Turbo Pascal normally generates far calls only when an intersegment (a call outside the current code segment) jump is required. You can, however, force all procedure and function calls to be far calls, even when the jump is intrasegment (inside the current code segment).

Overlays allowed

Turbo Pascal 5.5 supports overlays. To overlay a unit, you must activate the **Overlays allowed** option before you compile the unit.

Align data

Turbo Pascal can align data in two ways: by byte and by word. Aligning data by word means that all variables are located on word boundaries (even addresses). The computer's microprocessor accesses memory on word boundaries faster than it accesses data not found on word boundaries. Thus, aligning data by word can make your program run faster. Aligning data by word requires more memory, however, because bytes must be appended to variables in order for all variables to align on word boundaries. If you are more concerned about conserving memory than about speed, align data by byte.

Var-string checking

When **Var-string checking** is enabled, Turbo Pascal checks every instance in which a string is passed as a **Var** parameter. If the declaration of the string being passed does not match the declaration of the parameter, Turbo Pascal generates a compile error. Disabling **Var-string checking** can hide potentially dangerous programming errors.

Boolean evaluation

In Turbo Pascal, Boolean expressions can be evaluated using two options—**Complete** or **Short Circuit**. Complete evaluation means that every condition in the Boolean expression is evaluated before a result is produced. In many cases, however, the result of the expression is certain before the entire expression is evaluated. Under short-circuit evaluation, a result is returned as soon as the overall result of the expression is assured. For example, consider the following Boolean expression:

    If (x < 1) and (x < 5) Then . . .

There is never a need to evaluate the second half of the expression because if the first half is true, the second half will also be true. Under short-circuit evaluation, the second half of the equation would never be tested.

Numeric processing

When you set **Numeric processing** to 8087/80287, you can take advantage of the extended set of floating-point data types supported by Turbo Pascal (**Single, Double, Extended,** and **Comp**). When **Numeric processing** is set to **Software**, you can use only the standard floating-point data type (**Real**). Note that the impact of **Numeric processing** depends on whether **Emulation** is enabled. When **Emulation** is enabled, Turbo Pascal will use the 8087 or 80287 *if it is available*; otherwise, Turbo will emulate the math coprocessor. When **Emulation** is disabled, however, your program will run only when the 8087 or 80287 chip is present.

Emulation

When **Emulation** is turned on, Turbo Pascal is capable of generating code that performs calculations to the same precision as the 8087 or 80287 math coprocessor chips. When **Emulation** is turned off, the computer must have the coprocessor chip to produce high-precision calculations.

Debug information

When **Debug information** is on, Turbo Pascal generates the code needed to allow step-by-step debugging both internally and in the Standalone mode.

Local symbols

Local symbols are the names and types of variables and constants that are local in scope. A variable or constant is *local* in scope if it is declared within a procedure or function or if it is declared within the implementation section of a unit.

Activating the **Local symbols** option does several things. First, it tells Turbo Pascal to generate information needed by the integrated debugger that allows you to examine and change the values of local variables. This information is appended to the .EXE program file.

Conditional defines

Many programmers use conditional compilation directives to make their programming easier. Programmers control these directives, which include or exclude portions of code, by defining compiler directive constants. These constants can be defined in the program itself or in the **Conditional defines** section of the Options/Compiler menu.

Memory sizes

The **Memory sizes** window (Figure 2-8), the last choice on the Options/Compiler menu, lets you set the amount of memory your program will use for its heap and stack. Note that the heap is defined as a minimum and maximum amount. If you set a minimum heap limit, Turbo Pascal will check to see if that much memory is available before your program begins. If you set a maximum heap limit, Turbo Pascal will grab no more than that amount of memory for your program.

Linker

From the Linker window (Figure 2-9), which pops up when you select **Linker** from the Options menu, you can select the type of map file Turbo Pascal should produce and specify where the link buffer should be. Turbo Pascal can produce three types of map files: Segments, Publics, and Detailed.

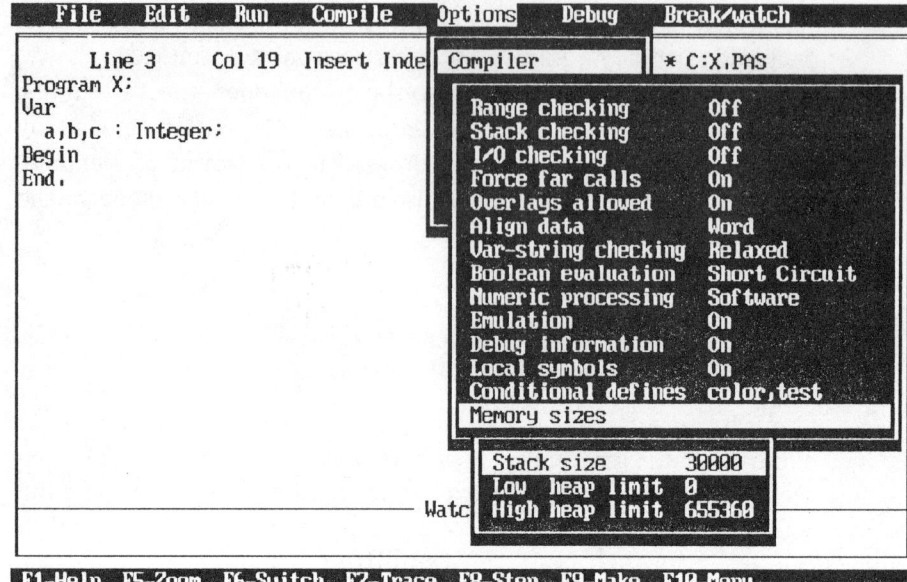

Figure 2-8.   The Memory sizes window

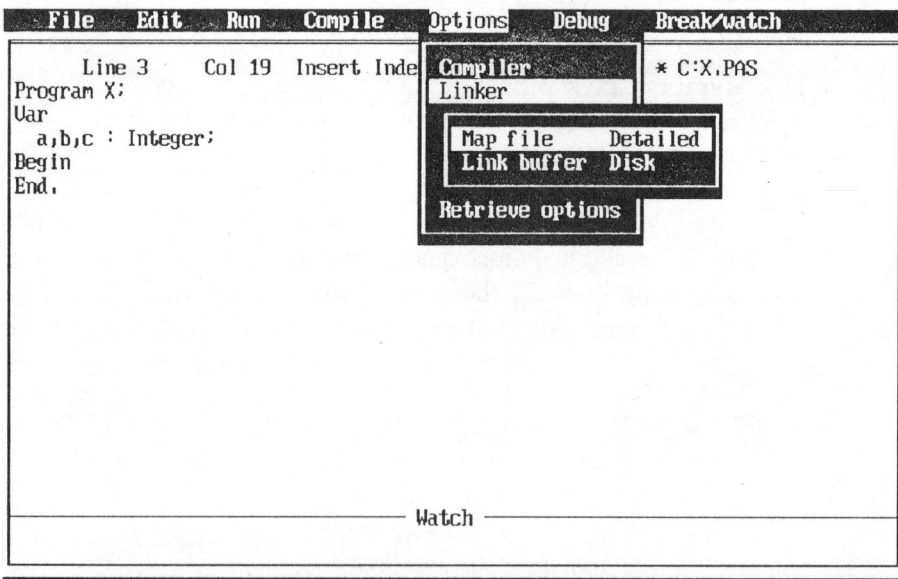

Figure 2-9.   The Options/Linker menu

The Segments map file contains only the location, size, and name of each segment created by Turbo Pascal. A typical program uses several code segments, one data segment, one stack segment, and one heap segment.

The Publics map file contains all the segment information and adds the memory location of every public procedure, function, and variable.

Finally, the Detailed map file contains all the Segments and Publics information plus line number information that links specific memory locations to specific source code lines. For large programs, the detailed map file can be quite large.

The location of the link buffer depends on how much memory your program needs—putting the link buffer in memory speeds things up, but requires more RAM. For large programs, you may have to assign the link buffer to disk.

Environment

The **Environment** menu (Figure 2-10), the third choice on the Options menu, contains features that you can use to customize the Turbo integrated development environment.

Config auto save

All the settings you make in the Turbo integrated development environment can be saved to a configuration file so that you do not have to reset everything each time you start Turbo Pascal. When you enable **Config auto save**, Turbo Pascal automatically saves the current configuration for you, so you do not lose any changes you made during your programming session.

Edit auto save

When you use the **Run** or **OS shell** option, you risk losing your edited code if you should crash the computer. To avoid this

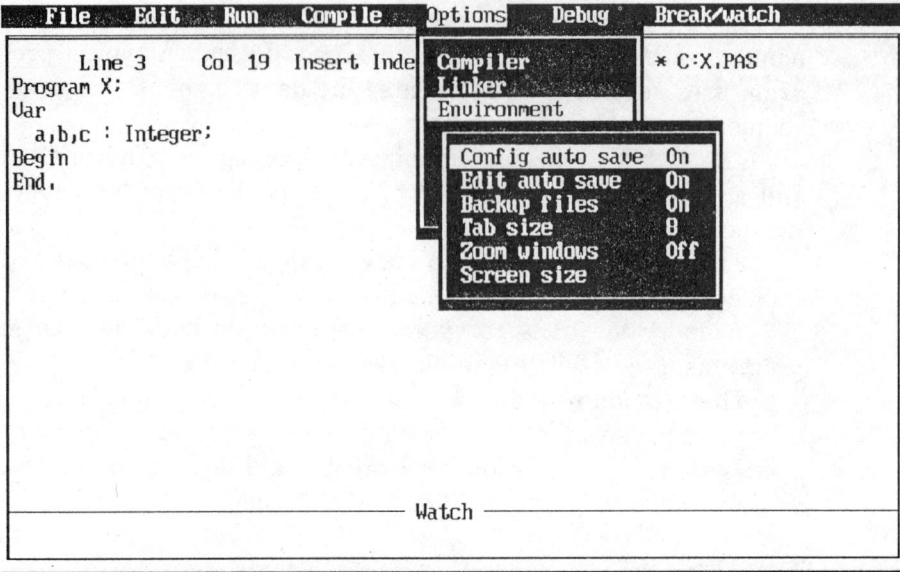

Figure 2-10. The Options/Environment menu

risk, you can enable **Edit auto save,** which saves your edited file to disk every time you use the **Run** or **OS shell** options.

Backup files

When **Backup files** is enabled, Turbo Pascal automatically places the next-most-recent copy of a file into a file with the .BAK extension.

Tab size

While Turbo Pascal normally sets tab stops at eight spaces, you can use the **Tab size** option to change this to a value from 2 to 16.

Zoom windows

When **Zoom windows** is enabled, Turbo Pascal devotes the entire screen to either the Edit window or the Watch window.

When **Zoom windows** is disabled, Turbo Pascal splits the screen, with the Edit window above the Watch window.

Screen size

Turbo Pascal supports the 25-line standard display, the 43-line EGA text display, and the 50-line VGA text display. You can select the display you want with the **Screen size** option.

Directories

The **Directories** window, the fourth item on the Options menu, lets you tell Turbo Pascal where to look for files that don't exist in the current directory. Consider the settings shown in Figure 2-11. **Include directories** is set to D:\INCLUDE. This means that if Turbo Pascal cannot find an include file in the current directory, it will continue to search first in D:\INCLUDE and

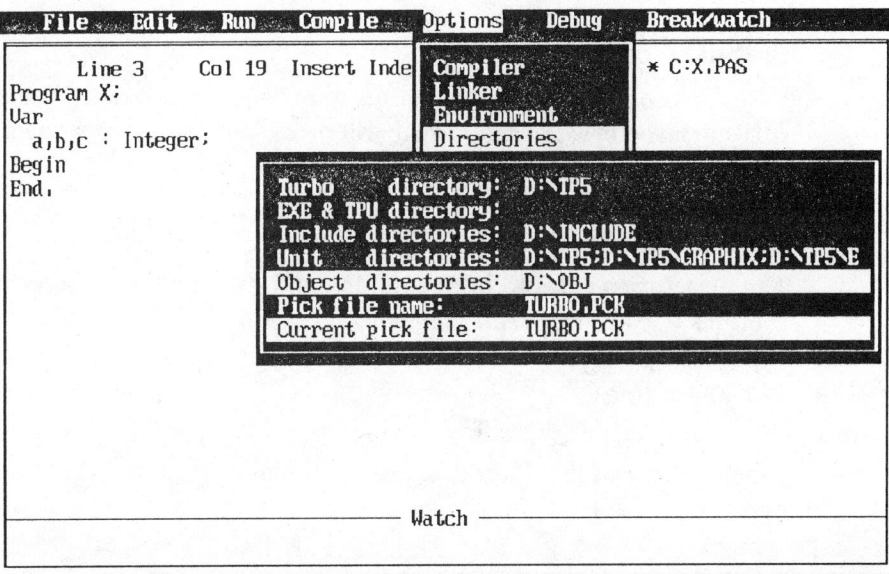

Figure 2-11.   The Options/Directories menu

then in D:\MISC. The **EXE & TPU directory** choice has no setting— if Turbo cannot find a .TPU file in the current directory, it stops looking.

The Directories window also lets you name a pick file, which is used to hold the names of the most recently edited files. Maintaining a pick file is useful when your programs consist of multiple source files.

Turbo directory

This entry tells Turbo Pascal where to find the TURBO.HLP and TURBO.TP files.

EXE & TPU directory

This entry is the directory in which Turbo Pascal will store any .EXE, .TPU or .MAP files.

Include directories

Turbo Pascal will search the directories named here if it cannot find an include file in the current directory.

Unit directories

If your program calls for a unit that does not exist in the current directory, Turbo Pascal will search in directories specified under **Unit directories**.

Object directories

The directories entered here contain .OBJ files used for external routines declared in your programs.

Pick file name

This option lets you define a pick file with a name that you choose. You can maintain separate pick files for use with specific programs or sets of files.

Current pick file

This entry simply tells you which pick file is currently in use.

Parameters

Many programs require command-line parameters in order to operate correctly. You can use the **Parameters** option to store a command line in memory. Then, when you run a program from the integrated development environment, Turbo Pascal will pass your command line to the program as if it had been entered at the DOS prompt.

Save options

Once you have set all your options the way you want them, you can save the configuration by selecting the **Save options** choice. The options are saved in a disk file that you name. You can create different options files for specific situations.

Retrieve options

Once you have stored options in a disk file, you can use **Retrieve options** to read in an options file and set the compiler and environment options appropriately.

The Debug Menu

The Debug menu (Figure 2-12) contains functions that you will find useful when testing a program for errors. From this menu you can evaulate equations that use variables in the program, alter the value of variables to test the effect of the change, find the source-code location where a function is defined, and more.

Evaluate

The Evaluate window serves two useful purposes. First, it is a powerful calculator that can use variables from a program in expressions. Take for example, the Evaluate window shown in

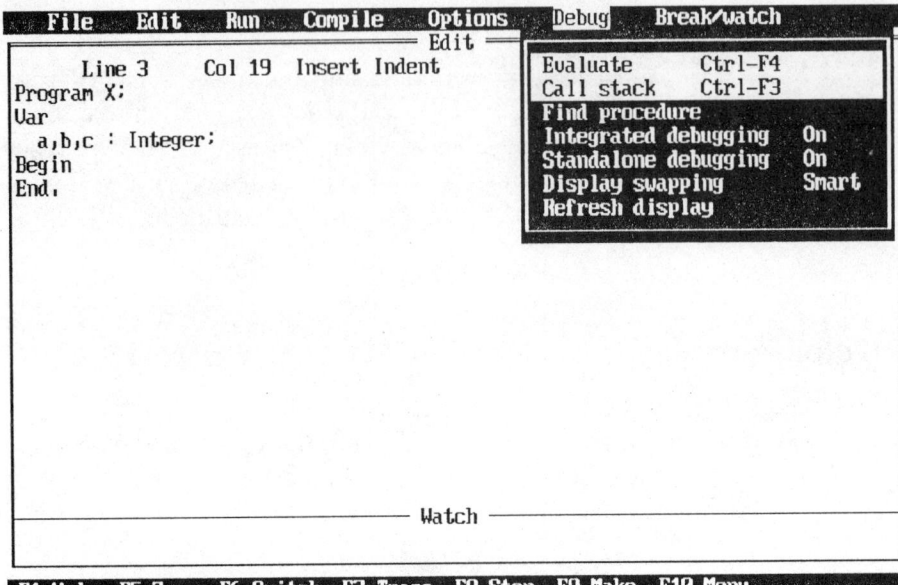

Figure 2-12.   The Debug menu

Figure 2-13. The program has executed the loop just one time. In the Evaluate window, you have entered the expression $(z*i)$ **Shl 4**. At this point in the program, **z** is equal to 2 and **i** is equal to 1, so that the result of the entire equation is 32, the value that appears in the Result window. By using the Evaluate window, you can test the validity of expressions before their results are used by other parts of the program.

The second use of the Evaluate window is to give variables new values. Consider the situation shown in Figure 2-14, in which execution has stopped at the end of the first loop. At this point, **z** would normally have a value of 2 (which you can see in the Watch window). You can change the value of **z** by calling up the Evaluate window, typing **z** in the **Evaluate** box, entering the new value, 6, in the **New value** box, and pressing ENTER. The value of **z** has now been changed from 2 to 6. (The value in the Watch window is not updated until you escape from the Evaluate window.)

```
  File   Edit   Run   Compile   Options   Debug   Break/watch
══════════════════════════════ Edit ══════════════════════════
       Line 12     Col 23    Insert Indent        Unindent    C:X.PAS
Program Test;
Var                         ┌─────────────── Evaluate ─────────────┐
   i,z : Integer;           │ (z*i) Shl 4                          │
   a : Array [1..300] of    └──────────────────────────────────────┘
                            ┌──────────────── Result ──────────────┐
Begin                       │ 32                                   │
z := 1;                     └──────────────────────────────────────┘
FillChar(a,SizeOf(a),0)     ┌─────────────── New value ────────────┐
For i := 1 To 300 Do        │                                      │
   Begin                    └──────────────────────────────────────┘
   z := z + 1;
   a[i] := (z*i) Shl 4;
   End;
End.



───────────────────────────── Watch ──────────────────────────
•z: 2
 i: 1
──────────────────────────────────────────────────────────────
 F1-Help  F7-Trace  F8-Step  F10-Menu  TAB-Cycle  <─┘-Evaluate
```

Figure 2-13.   The Evaluate window

```
  File   Edit   Run   Compile   Options   Debug   Break/watch
══════════════════════════════ Edit ══════════════════════════
       Line 12     Col 1     Insert Indent        Unindent    C:X.PAS
Program Test;
Var                         ┌─────────────── Evaluate ─────────────┐
   i,z : Integer;           │ z                                    │
   a : Array [1..300] of    └──────────────────────────────────────┘
                            ┌──────────────── Result ──────────────┐
Begin                       │ 6                                    │
z := 1;                     └──────────────────────────────────────┘
FillChar(a,SizeOf(a),0)     ┌─────────────── New value ────────────┐
For i := 1 To 300 Do        │ 3                                    │
   Begin                    └──────────────────────────────────────┘
   z := z + 1;
   a[i] := (z*i) Shl 4;
   End;
End.



───────────────────────────── Watch ──────────────────────────
•z: 2
 i: 1
──────────────────────────────────────────────────────────────
 F1-Help  F7-Trace  F8-Step  F10-Menu  TAB-Cycle  <─┘-Modify
```

Figure 2-14.   Changing a variable's value in the Evaluate window

The ability to evaluate expressions and change the values of variables is important because it allows you to simulate a wide range of situations without repeatedly recompiling the entire program.

Call stack

While debugging a program, you might find yourself deep inside a procedure and wonder how you got there. The **Call stack** function is a quick way of tracing the sequence of procedure and function calls that led to your current position. Consider the program in Figure 2-15, which consists of a main program (**TestCallStack**) and three procedures (**a**, **b**, and **c**). While tracing through the program, you stop at the statement **WriteLn('Procedure C');** and wonder what procedures preceded your current procedure. When you select the **Call stack**

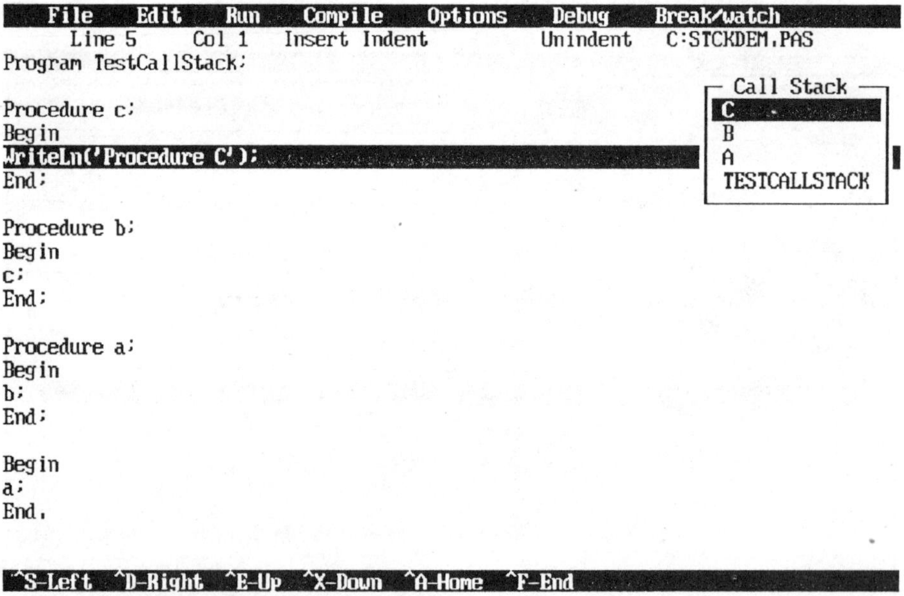

```
   File    Edit    Run    Compile    Options    Debug    Break/watch
      Line 5      Col 1    Insert Indent              Unindent    C:STCKDEM.PAS
Program TestCallStack;
                                                           ┌─ Call Stack ─┐
Procedure c;                                               │ C          · │
Begin                                                      │ B            │
WriteLn('Procedure C');                                    │ A            │
End;                                                       │ TESTCALLSTACK│
                                                           └──────────────┘
Procedure b;
Begin
c;
End;

Procedure a;
Begin
b;
End;

Begin
a;
End.

 ^S-Left  ^D-Right  ^E-Up  ^X-Down  ^A-Home  ^F-End
```

Figure 2-15.   The Call Stack window

function, a window pops up that shows you that **Procedure c,** the current procedure, was preceded by **Procedure b, Procedure a,** and the main program itself. While this example is relatively simple, you can appreciate how this feature can help unravel programming problems caused by circuitous logic.

Find function

If you have ever written a large program with many procedures and functions, you know how hard it is to remember how each works. The **Find function** feature helps by quickly locating the source code where a procedure or function was defined. Now you can check out a procedure or function in just seconds, even when your source code consists of thousands of lines in 20 different units.

Integrated debugging

If you wish to perform debugging while in the integrated development environment, you must enable **Integrated debugging.** (You must also enable **Debug information** in the Options/Compiler menu.) Enabling **Integrated debugging** tells Turbo Pascal to add debugging code to object modules.

Standalone debugging

You can use Borland's stand-alone debugger to debug programs from outside the integrated development environment.

Display swapping

When you are debugging a program, you see only the Edit and Watch windows—the display that the user would see is hidden. To keep your program's screen output from interfering with the Edit and Watch windows, Turbo Pascal uses screen swapping. For a split second, Turbo switches from the Edit window to the output screen, executes the line of code, and returns to the Edit window. The process is too fast for you to see what your program wrote to the screen. To see what the display screen looks like, press ALT-F5.

Turbo Pascal provides three types of screen swapping— **Smart, Always,** and **None.** When **Display swapping** is set to **None,** Turbo Pascal will not swap the display as you trace through a program. This feature removes the annoying flash you see on your display as it is swapped, allowing your program to write over the Edit and Watch windows. When a program overwrites your display, you can restore it by using the **Refresh display** feature. At the other extreme, you can set screen swapping to **Always,** which means that Turbo Pascal will swap screens with every statement, even when your program is not writing to the screen.

In between **Always** and **None** is **Smart** screen swapping, which means that Turbo Pascal will swap screens only when the code affects the screen, or a procedure or function is called.

Refresh display

If, while debugging, your program's output overwrites the Edit or Watch windows, you can clean things up by selecting the **Refresh display** feature, which simply updates the entire screen.

The Break/watch Menu

The Break/watch menu (Figure 2-16) contains the debugging tools that will change the way you program with Turbo Pascal. With this menu you can add variables to the Watch window and see how their values change as the program progresses.

Add watch

Use **Add watch** to add a variable to the Watch window. After you have added a variable to the Watch window, its value will

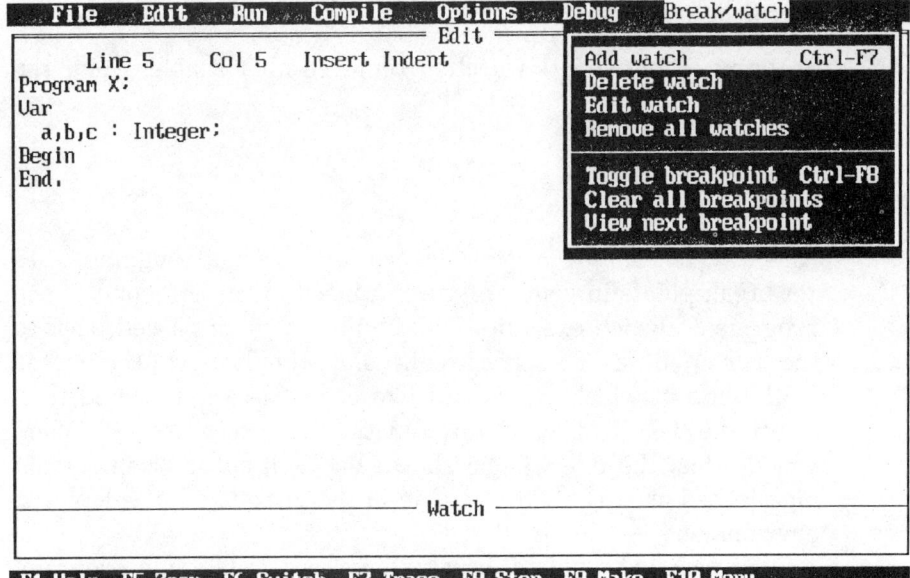

Figure 2-16.   The Break/watch menu

appear and change as your program executes. You can call **Add watch** directly by pressing CTRL-F7.

Delete watch

You can delete a variable from the Watch window by using the **Delete watch** function. This function removes the last variable that was added to the Watch window.

Edit watch

The **Edit watch** function lets you change the definition of a variable in the Watch window. Before you edit a Watch variable, you must mark it (the marked variable is the one with the dot to the left). To mark a variable, press F6 to activate the Watch window, and then use the UP and DOWN ARROW keys to highlight the variable you want to make active. At this point, you can edit the highlighted variable simply by pressing ENTER. Alternatively, you can press F6 to return to the Edit window, and then select **Edit watch** from the Break/watch menu.

Remove all watches

Selecting **Remove all watches** removes all variables from the Watch window.

Toggle breakpoint

One way to control program execution during debugging is to set break points in your program. A break point is a point in the program at which execution halts and control is passed back to the Turbo editor. To set a break point, simply move the cursor to the line at which you would like execution to stop, and then select the **Toggle breakpoint** function (or press CTRL-F8). When you do this, the line will be shown highlighted and will remain highlighted as long as you remain in the integrated development environment.

You can set as many break points as you like in a program, depending on how many places you want to halt execution. Once you hit a break point, you can continue to run the program or use the tracing and stepping features on the Run menu. To clear a break point, simply place the cursor on the line that contains the break point, and select **Toggle breakpoint**, which removes both the highlight and the break point.

Clear all breakpoints

If you wish to remove all break points from a program at one time, select the **Clear all breakpoints** function.

View next breakpoint

The **View next breakpoint** function locates the position of the next break point, loads the appropriate file, and positions the cursor on the line containing the break point.

Fundamental Concepts of Turbo Pascal Programming

Pascal Control Structures and Goto-less Programming
Turbo Pascal and Standard Pascal
Strong Typing of Variables in Pascal
Type Casting
Procedures and Functions
Functions Versus Procedures

Two of the most widely used programming languages today, Pascal and BASIC, started out as teaching tools. There the similarity between the two languages ends. Comparing the two will help you understand what Pascal is all about.

In the early 1970s, a major movement in programming began. Known as *structured programming,* this approach stressed breaking a program down into manageable pieces and then assembling those pieces into a program with a coherent, logical flow.

Pascal, developed by Niklaus Wirth, was designed to teach structured programming skills to future programmers. By enforcing a strict set of rules regarding the declaration of variables, program structure, and flow of control, Pascal steered the aspiring programmers toward good programming habits. In addition, Pascal provided a wide range of programming tools that made writing good, clear code much easier than was possible with COBOL or FORTRAN.

BASIC, on the other hand, was developed as an easy-to-learn language for nonprogrammers. It lets nontechnical people quickly learn to write simple programs. Unfortunately, BASIC encourages poor programming habits and unreadable code. It is significant that many new versions of BASIC resemble Pascal.

Pascal Control Structures and Goto-less Programming

Contemporary students of programming, who are generally taught structured programming from the outset, might be surprised at just how pervasive the **Goto** command was and, to a great extent, still is. This simple command allows programmers to jump anywhere within a program regardless of consistency in the program flow. Debugging and maintaining programs full of **Goto**s is very difficult.

Structured programming, sometimes known as "**Goto**-less programming," sought to eliminate the **Goto** command by providing a rich set of program control structures. Pascal, a direct result of the structured programming philosophy, provided these control structures, which both increased program readability and helped eliminate unforeseen errors created by unstructured program flow. As a result, by learning to program in Pascal, students were almost forced into learning good programming habits.

Turbo Pascal and Standard Pascal

While standard Pascal had many strong points, it was never fully developed for use in commercial applications. It lacked useful input and output functions and sorely needed string types. Nonetheless, this version of Pascal was considered the standard for the world.

Borland recognized both the strengths and the weaknesses of standard Pascal and updated the language substantially. The result is a rich language that provides the programmer with the logical structure of standard Pascal plus an extensive set of tools.

In making these additions, Borland broke away from the Pascal standard, a move that prompted criticism from some quarters. Despite this, Turbo Pascal and its extensions have become the standard international microcomputer Pascal.

Strong Typing of Variables in Pascal

Pascal is often called a *strong-typed language*. This means that you cannot mix different types of variables. In assignment statements, the values on the right must be compatible in type with the corresponding variable on the left. For example, if the variable **i** is defined as an integer, the following statement would be illegal:

    i := 1.0 + 2;

The value **1.0** is a real value and cannot be used in an assignment statement for an integer because using a real value to evaluate an integer variable goes against the properties of a strong-typed language. Observing the strong-typing rules helps avoid errors in programming. Turbo Pascal is less picky about strong typing than standard Pascal, but you still have to follow these rules:

• A **Real** cannot be used directly in an assignment statement for an **Integer** or **Byte**. The **Real** must first be converted to an **Integer** by using the **Trunc** or **Round** standard functions.

• An array can be assigned to another array only when the two have the same range and type.

• A variable that is passed to a procedure (or function) must be defined as the same type as the variable defined in the procedure heading. This rule can be relaxed for **String** variables by using the {**$V −**} compiler directive.

Strong typing as implemented in Turbo Pascal is relatively unrestrictive, yet it still helps programmers avoid unnecessary errors.

Type Casting

While strong typing has its advantages, there are times when a programming problem can be solved best by relaxing type checking. This can be done with type casting, a technique in which a variable of one type is temporarily treated as another type. For example, you cannot normally assign a character variable to an integer variable because the types are incompatible. You can, however, use the following type cast to achieve the same result:

```
i := Integer(c);
```

where **i** is an integer variable and **c** is a character variable. This statement treats the binary value of **c** as if it were an integer value. The program below demonstrates more ways to use the type cast technique:

```
Program TestTypeCast;
Uses CRT;
Var
  i : Integer;
  w : Word;
  c : Char;
  b : Boolean;
  p : Pointer;
  r : Real;
  s : String;

Begin
ClrScr;

c := 'A';
WriteLn('c = ',c);

(* Convert character to integer *)
i := Integer(c);
WriteLn('i = ',i);

(* Convert integer to boolean *)
b := Boolean(i);
WriteLn('b = ',b);

(* Convert pointer value to real *)
p := @c;
```

```
r := Real(p^);
WriteLn('r = ',r);

(* Convert pointer value to a string *)
s := String(p^);
Writeln('s = ',s);

ReadLn;
End.
```

Note how the pointer variable is interpreted as both a **Real** variable and a **String** variable. When used with type casts, pointers are particularly powerful, since they can take on any data type.

Procedures and Functions

The logic of modular programming states that it is easier to write a good program if you break it down into small chunks. In Pascal, these chunks are called *procedures* or *functions*. Modular programs are easier to write and maintain because each procedure and function can be written and tested independently of the main program. Once you are sure it is functioning correctly, you can integrate it into the main program with confidence. In addition, Pascal allows you to pass variables into the function or procedure, further increasing the modularity of the program.

Defining Procedures in Pascal

To define a procedure in Pascal, you need at least two things: a name for the procedure and a block of code. The example shown here presents a simple procedure definition that provides both ingredients.

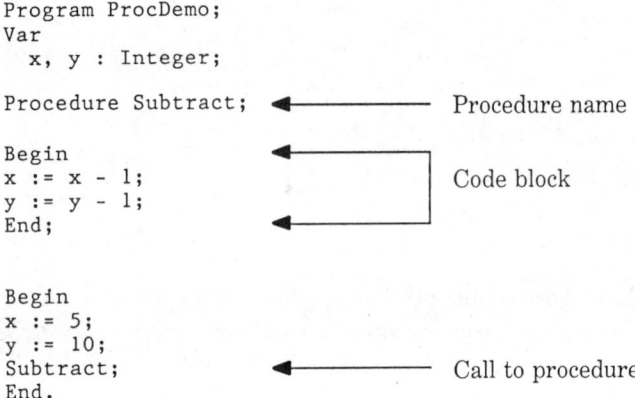

```
Program ProcDemo;
Var
  x, y : Integer;

Procedure Subtract;          ◄────────── Procedure name

Begin                        ◄──────┐
x := x - 1;                         │    Code block
y := y - 1;                         │
End;                         ◄──────┘


Begin
x := 5;
y := 10;
Subtract;                    ◄────────── Call to procedure
End.
```

The Pascal reserved word **Procedure** tells the compiler that a procedure is about to be defined. The next identifier is the name of the procedure, **Subtract**. When you want to execute a procedure in your program, you will call it by the name you gave it in the procedure definition.

The procedure **Subtract** decrements the value of variables **x** and **y** by 1. In the example, **x** and **y** are initialized to 5 and 10, respectively. Upon returning from **Subtract**, **x** is equal to 4 and **y** is equal to 9. Note that **Subtract** can use variables **x** and **y** because they are *global variables*—variables that are declared at the main program level and can be used by any procedure in the program.

Passing Parameters to a Procedure

The preceding example works for global variables **x** and **y** only. If you want to decrement any other pair of variables, you are out of luck. You can expand the usefulness of this procedure by defining parameters. Then you can use the same procedure for any two-integer variables. The following example shows the revised procedure with the **Subtract** parameters.

```
Program ProcDemo2;
Var
  q, w, x, y : Integer;
```

```
(**************************************************)

Procedure Subtract(a : Integer; Var b : Integer);
Begin
a := a - 1;
b := b - 1;
End;

(**************************************************)

Begin
x := 5;
y := 10;
q := 1;
w := 4;
Subtract(x,y);
Subtract(q,w);
End.
```

Note that the procedure name is now followed by a list of two parameters—**a** and **b**—both of which are integers. When **Subtract** is called, the program passes two integer values to the procedure. In the statement **Subtract(x,y)**, **x** supplies the value for parameter **a**, and **y** supplies the value for parameter **b**. Thus, **x** and **y** are the parameters being passed to the procedure. Once inside the procedure, **a** takes the value of **x**, and **b** takes the value of **y**. The same logic applies to the second call to **Subtract**, where **q** and **w** are passed as parameters.

While the procedure **Subtract** decrements each parameter by one, the effect on **x** will be different than on **y**. In the procedure definition, parameter **b** is preceded by the Pascal reserved word **Var**, while **a** is not. Parameters preceded by **Var** are called *reference parameters;* those without it are called *value parameters.*

Reference Parameters

When a variable is passed to a procedure as a reference parameter, changes made to that variable within the procedure remain even after the procedure has ended. Changes to reference parameters are permanent because Turbo Pascal passes to the procedure not the variable's value, but the variable's address in memory. In other words, the variable inside the procedure and the variable passed to the procedure as a reference parameter share the same address. Therefore, a change in the former is reflected in the latter.

In the preceding example, the global variable **y**, with a value of 10, is passed to the procedure as parameter **b**. The procedure subtracts 1 from **b**, giving a value of 9. When the procedure ends, **y** is passed back to the main program, where it retains the value of 9.

In short, the reference parameter and the actual variable passed to the procedure are the same; that is, they share the same position in memory. Therefore, any change made to the reference parameter is stored as a permanent change in the actual variable.

Value Parameters

Value parameters are different from reference parameters. When a value parameter is passed to a procedure, a temporary copy of the variable is placed in memory. Within the procedure, only the copy is used. When the value of the parameter is changed, it only affects the temporary storage; the actual variable outside the procedure is never touched.

In the preceding illustration, **a** is a value parameter because it is not preceded by the reserved word **Var**. When the program starts, it initializes **x** to 5. Upon calling **Subtract**, the program makes a copy of **x** in temporary storage and passes the copy to the procedure. Within **Subtract**, parameter **a** refers to the temporary storage location, not to the actual location of **x**. Therefore, when **a** is decremented, only the value in temporary storage is affected. At the end of the procedure, the value in temporary storage is discarded, and the global variable **x** retains the original value of 5.

Functions Versus Procedures

Both procedures and functions provide modularity to your programs. Both are self-contained blocks of code and both can accept data through parameters. The difference between functions and procedures, illustrated by the following examples, is in how they return values.

```
Procedure Square(x : Real; Var x2 : Real);
Begin
x2 := x * x;
End;

Function Square(x : Real) : Real;
Begin
Square := x * x;
End;
```

The procedure **Square** passes two parameters. The first parameter, **x**, is the number to be squared, and the second, **x2**, is the result. The procedure multiplies parameter **x** by itself and assigns the result to the parameter **x2**. Because **x2** is a reference parameter, its new value is retained when the procedure ends.

The function **Square** produces basically the same result as the procedure. However, the function does not store the result in a parameter, but passes it back through the function itself. To clarify the difference, examine how the two would be used in a program.

Using the Procedure **Square**,

Square(x, x2);
or
Square(x, x2);
if x2 > 100 then . . .

Using the Function **Square**,

x2 := Square(x);
or
if Square(x) > 100 then . . .

A function can (and must) be used in an assignment, comparison, or arithmetic expression. Another way of looking at it is that functions are like variables whose value depends on the parameters you pass to them.

Procedures, on the other hand, cannot be used in assignment, comparison, or arithmetic expressions. At most, a procedure can return a variable that can be used in expressions.

Both functions and procedures have their strong points. Functions are generally preferred when one clearly identifiable result is desired. In the preceding example, a function makes more sense than a procedure since obtaining the squared value is the objective. A procedure, rather than implying a specific result, performs an operation that may return many or no results. In the end, experience is the best guide in deciding between functions and procedures.

Passing Parameters of Different Types

The variables that you pass to a procedure or function must match the type declaration of their respective parameters. If, for example, a parameter is declared to be an **Integer**, you cannot pass a **Real** type through it. A procedure declaration that includes the standard Turbo Pascal scalars follows.

```
Procedure Example (i : Integer;
                   r : Real;
                   b : Boolean;
                   x : Byte);
```

User-defined types, such as **String**s, can also be used to define parameters, as follows:

```
Program ProcDemo3;
Type
  Str255 = String[255];
  Str80 = String[80];

Var
  St1 : Str255;
  St2 : Str80;

(****************************************************)

Procedure Blank(Var s : Str255);
Begin
s := '';
End;
```

```
(**************************************************)

Begin
Blank(St1); (* legal *)
{
Blank(St2); (* not legal *)
}
End.
```

Note that the parameter **s** is defined by using the type definition supplied by the user. Note also that you can pass strings to the procedure as reference parameters only if the parameter and the variable have been defined as the same string type. In the example just given, variable **St2** cannot be passed as a parameter because it is defined as **String[80]**, while the procedure heading defines the parameter as **String[255]**. This is an example of Pascal's strong typing.

You can override Turbo Pascal's strict checking on string reference parameters by using the {$V−} compiler directive, which turns off string-type checking. With the {$V−} compiler directive disabled, Turbo Pascal allows you to pass any type of string variable through any type of string parameter. Compiler directives are discussed in detail in Chapter 4.

Passing Set Parameters

Sets, another type of user-defined type, follow the same rules that apply to strings. An example of a set used as a parameter is shown in the following illustration:

```
Program ProcDemo4;
Type
  CharSet = Set Of Char;

Var
  Ch : Char;
  UpCaseChar : CharSet;

(**************************************************)

Function TestChar(Ch : Char; TestSet : CharSet) : Boolean;
Begin
TestChar := Ch In TestSet;
End;
```

```
(***************************************************)
Begin
Ch := 'A';
UpCaseChar := ['A'..'Z'];
If TestChar(Ch,UpCaseChar) Then WriteLn(Ch);
End.
```

The user-defined type **CharSet** is used to define a parameter in
TestChar. When the function is called, the variable **UpCase-
Char** is passed to the function as parameter **TestSet**.

Passing Untyped Parameters

Parameters defined using a data type (such as **Real, Integer,**
and so on) are appropriately called *typed parameters*. Turbo
Pascal also allows you to use *untyped parameters*. The advantage of untyped parameters is that you can pass variables of any
type of data into them—**Strings, Reals, Integers, Booleans,**
and any other data type are all legal.

How is it that an untyped parameter can accept any data
type? To understand this, think about typed parameters. When
you define a typed parameter, you tell Turbo Pascal what type of
data to expect. Thus, Turbo Pascal can easily determine if a
mismatch exists between the variable type and the parameter
type. When you use untyped parameters, however, the procedure or function has no idea what it is you are passing to it. The
procedure accepts whatever is passed to it and expects the
programmer to know how to handle it. Because of this, untyped
parameters must be used carefully. Consider the example shown
here:

```
Procedure Example(Var x);
Var
  y : Integer Absolute x;
Begin
WriteLn(y);   (* Legal: y is of type Integer *)
WriteLn(x);   (* Illegal: x has no type *)
End;
```

Parameter **x** (a reference parameter) has no type associated with it. Therefore, **x** is an untyped parameter. The reserved word **Var** is necessary because all untyped parameters must be reference parameters.

While **x** is clearly a parameter, it cannot be used directly by the procedure. Why not? The procedure does not know what **x** is, so it cannot handle the parameter.

Instead of using **x**, you must declare a variable in the procedure that is *Absolute* at **x**. This means that the variable you declare will reside at exactly the same address as **x**. In the example, **y** is defined as an **Integer** variable that is located at the same place in memory as **x**. Now you can use variable **y** in place of **x**.

When this procedure is called, any type of variable can be passed to this procedure, and the procedure will treat the variable as an integer. What does that mean? Suppose you pass a string into the procedure. Since **y** is an integer, and an integer is two bytes long, the procedure will take the first two bytes of the string and treat them as an integer value. Of course, the integer value will have absolutely no relation to the value of the string. If you pass a string with the value "TEXT" into the procedure, the integer value will be 21,500 — a totally arbitrary value.

So why use untyped parameters? In certain and very few instances, untyped parameters are useful. One example, a procedure that compares two variables to see if they are equal, is shown in the following illustration:

```
{$V-}
Program CompareData;
Var
  i1,i2 : Integer;
  r1,r2 : Real;
  s1,s2 : String;

(**************************************************)

Function Compare(Var x,y; kind : Char) : Integer;
Var
  aString : String[255] Absolute x;
  bString : String[255] Absolute y;

  aReal : Real Absolute x;
  bReal : Real Absolute y;
```

```
      aInteger : Integer Absolute x;
      bInteger : Integer Absolute y;

Begin
  Case kind Of

  'R' : (* Real *)
    Begin
    If aReal > bReal Then
      Compare := 1
    Else If aReal < bReal Then
      Compare := -1
    Else
      Compare := 0;
    End;

   'I' : (* Integer *)
    Begin
    If aInteger > bInteger Then
      Compare := 1
    Else If aInteger < bInteger Then
      Compare := -1
    Else
      Compare := 0;
    End;

   'S' : (* String *)
    Begin
    If aString > bString Then
      Compare := 1
    Else If aString < bString Then
      Compare := -1
    Else
      Compare := 0;
    End;

  End; (* of case *)
End;

(*************************************************)

Begin
rl := 10000.0;
r2 := -33.0;
WriteLn(Compare(rl,r2,'R'));

il := 100;
i2 := 200;
WriteLn(Compare(il,i2,'I'));

sl := 'Xavier';
s2 := 'Smith';
WriteLn(Compare(sl,s2,'S'));

End.
```

This example passes two variables at a time into the function **Compare**. The variables are passed as untyped parameters and are subsequently redefined as **Real**, **Integer**, and **String** variables. The third parameter, **kind**, is a character denoting the type of the first two parameters. An **S** indicates **String**, **R** indicates **Real**, and **I** indicates **Integer**.

By checking the value of **kind**, the procedure knows whether to compare **String**s, **Real**s, or **Integer**s. The final result, then, is a generalized procedure that can compare any two variables of type **Integer**, **Real**, or **String**. The only restriction is that you must tell the procedure what type of variable you are comparing.

Passing Literal Values

In the examples so far, only variables have been passed as parameters to functions. You can also pass literal values, such as a number or a string, to a procedure, but only as value parameters. The example here shows how the numeric literal 3.0 is passed to the function **Square**. The function performs just as it would if a variable had been passed to it.

```
Function Square(x : Real) : Real;
Begin
Square := x * x;
End;

Begin
WriteLn(Square(3.0));
End.
```

String literals are groups of characters enclosed in single quotation marks. The following example illustrates how a string literal is passed to a procedure:

```
Program StringTest;

(**********************************************)

Procedure WriteUpCase(st : String);
Var
  i : Integer;
Begin
```

```
For i := 1 To Length(st) Do
  st[i] := UpCase(st[i]);
WriteLn(st);
End;

(**********************************************)

Begin
WriteUpCase('This is a string literal');
End.
```

This procedure takes the string passed to it, converts it to all uppercase characters, and writes it out. In the preceding example, the string passed is a literal, but the procedure would accept a string variable as well. Note, however, that you can pass literal values and string literals to value parameters only, not to reference parameters.

Procedures and the Scope of Variables

In BASIC and some other programming languages, all variables are *global,* that is, all variables can be referred to at any point throughout the program. Pascal supports global variables, but also provides local variables. These are variables that exist within a limited portion of the program, also known as the *scope of a variable.* By limiting the scope of variables, unwanted side effects are eliminated.

The scope of a variable is determined by the block in which it is declared, as illustrated in Figure 3-1. Because it is defined within the program block, variable **x** is global in scope, meaning it can be accessed throughout the program. The variable **y**, defined within **Procedure A**, is limited in scope and can only be referred to within the scope of **Procedure A**.

Finally, variable **z**, defined within **Procedure B**, is even more limited in scope: it can only be referred to within the scope of **Procedure B**. Therefore, **Procedure B** can use variables **x**, **y**, and **z**; and **Procedure A** can use both variable **x** and variable **y**, but not variable **z**. The main program, the most limited of all, can refer only to variable **x**.

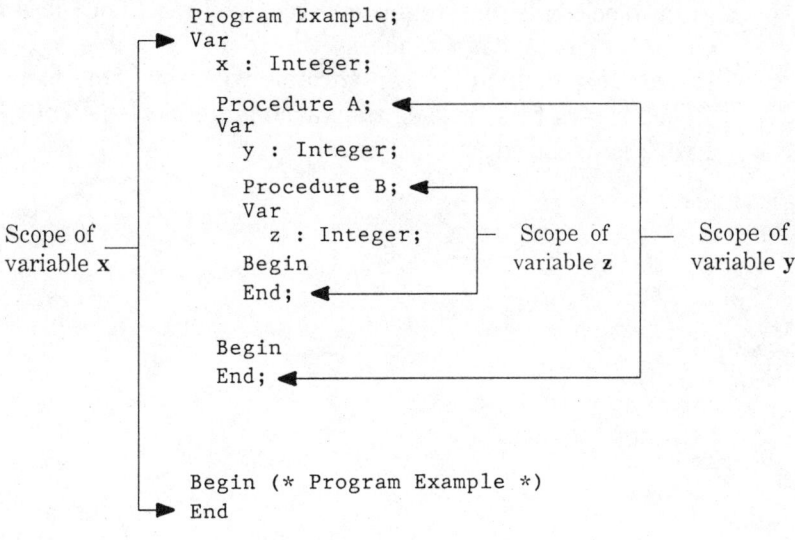

Figure 3-1.   Determining the scope of a variable

Variables at different levels can share the same name. However, giving variables the same name limits the scope of one of the two. This is demonstrated in the program listed here:

```
Program DoubleName;
Var
  x : Integer;

  Procedure Proc1;
  Var
    x : String[20];

    Procedure Proc2;
    Begin
    x := 'Bill';
    End;

  Begin
  x := 'Jones';
  End;

Begin
x := 1;
End.
```

This program contains two variables named **x**. In the program block, **x** is an integer variable, while in **Proc1** it is a string variable. **Proc1** cannot access the global variable **x** because it has already defined its own variable with the same name. When **Proc2** refers to **x**, it uses the variable defined in **Proc1** because **Proc2** is declared within **Proc1**.

Turbo Pascal Program Structure

The Program Heading
The Data Section
The Code Section
More on Program Blocks
Include Files
Overlays
Summary

A place for everything and everything in its place. This saying accurately describes Pascal, an orderly language consisting of well-defined sections, each of which serves a specific purpose. The major sections of a Pascal program are the *program heading,* the *data section,* and the *code section,* whose components are shown in Figure 4-1.

The Program Heading

The first two lines in a Turbo Pascal program generally consist of the *program name* and the *compiler directives.* Both are optional, but for the sake of program documentation, it is preferable to include them.

As the first line in the program, the *program heading* does no more than identify the name of the program and whether it will be using input, output, or both. A typical program heading follows.

Program ProgName(Input,Output);

Note that Turbo Pascal allows you to add a parameter list after the program name. This is a holdover from standard Pascal, in which such parameters were required, and is ignored by Turbo Pascal.

The second line of the program contains the *compiler directives,* which can play an active and vital role in Turbo Pascal programs, controlling various types of error checking and input/output control. Although beginners can often ignore compiler directives entirely, more advanced programmers must understand how to use these options to get the most out of Turbo Pascal.

Compiler Directives

The Turbo Pascal compiler offers many options that you can use to make programming and debugging easier. These options, which perform tasks such as error checking, are called compiler directives because they direct the compiler in its work. Compiler directives can be broadly classified into three groups: *switch directives, parameter directives,* and *conditional directives.*

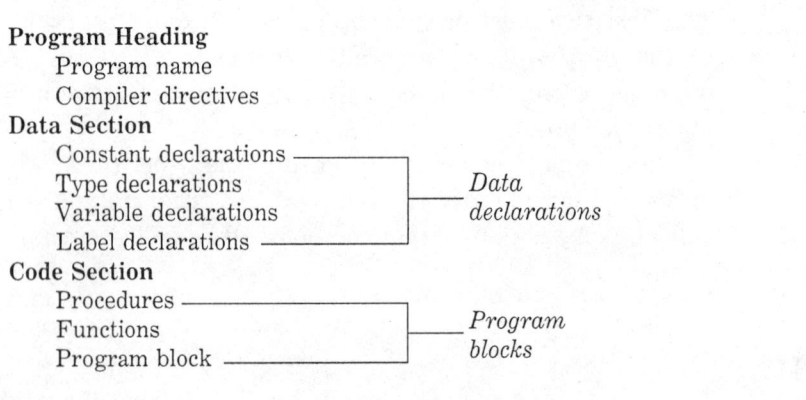

Program Heading
    Program name
    Compiler directives
Data Section
    Constant declarations ─┐
    Type declarations   ├─ *Data*
    Variable declarations   │   *declarations*
    Label declarations ─────┘
Code Section
    Procedures ─────┐
    Functions   ├─ *Program*
    Program block ───┘   *blocks*

Figure 4-1.   The structure of a Turbo Pascal program

Switch Directives

Switch directives turn on or off Turbo Pascal's special features, such as input/output error checking, stack checking, and data alignment. They are called switch directives because they can have only two conditions: on or off.

Switch directives are identified by single letters (uppercase or lowercase). For example, the **S** directive controls stack checking, **R** sets up range checking, **I** specifies input/output error checking, and so on. The format for enabling or disabling a compiler directive is a dollar sign followed by the directive and either a plus sign (to enable) or a minus sign (to disable); these characters are enclosed in comment delimiters (either parentheses with asterisks or braces). The following are examples of valid compiler directive statements:

```
(*$I-*)

{$i-}

{$s+,v-,r+,a+}
```

The first two statements are the same; both disable input/output error checking. As you can see from the examples, either type of comment delimiter (braces or parentheses with asterisks) can be used; the case of the directive (upper or lower) is unimportant. The third example specifies four compiler directives at once. It enables **Stack-Overflow Checking**, disables **Var-String Checking**, and enables **Range Checking** and **Align Data by Word**. Note that in this statement, the dollar sign appears before the first directive only.

Turbo Pascal lets you set compiler directives in two ways. The easiest way is to set the directives from the Options/Compiler menu. The directive settings in this menu become the global default values for all programs and units. In other words, Turbo Pascal will use the settings in the Options/Compiler menu for all compiler directives not specified in the source code.

Switch directives are of two types: global and local. Global directives, as the name implies, affect the compilation of an entire program, from beginning to end, and must be declared at the very beginning of your program or unit (before the first

Uses, Label, Const, Type, Procedure, Function, or **Begin** keyword). Local directives can appear at any point in a program and only affect that portion of the program which follows the directive. For example, you can turn on range checking, a local directive, at the beginning of a procedure and then turn it off at the end of the procedure.

Align Data (Global)

The 8086 family of microprocessors can access memory faster when data are aligned on even-numbered addresses, also known as *word boundaries*. When the **Align Data** compiler directive is active ({$A+}, Turbo Pascal makes sure that every variable and typed constant larger than one byte begins at an even address. Aligning data on word boundaries makes data access faster, but also increases the amount of memory required for data storage because "dead" bytes are inserted where necessary to make sure that variables begin on word boundaries. If you are concerned about the amount of memory your program requires, you may want to disable this directive ({$A−}).

Boolean Evaluation (Local)

Turbo Pascal supports two types of Boolean evaluation—complete and short-circuit. To understand the difference between the two, consider the following example:

```
If (a < b) And (b > c) Then
  Begin
  .
  .
  .
  End;
```

The preceding Boolean statement consists of two separate tests connected with **And.** Under complete Boolean evaluation, Turbo Pascal will test both comparisons before branching. But, if **a** is greater than or equal to **b**, there is really no need to test if **b** is greater than **c**. Under short-circuit evaluation, Turbo Pascal will only test so far as is necessary to determine the result of the entire expression. Under certain circumstances, short-circuit evaluation can speed up a program appreciably. To turn on short-circuit evaluation, use {$B −}; to select complete evaluation, use {$B +}.

Debug Information (Global)

Enabling the **Debug Information** directive ({$D +}), instructs Turbo Pascal to generate information needed to match executable instructions to locations in source files. This is the information that allows you to step through a program one line at a time or to locate the source of a run-time error when it occurs. Turbo Pascal adds debugging information to the end of .TPU files, making the files larger than they otherwise would be. This does not, however, affect the speed of the executable code.

Disabling this directive will gain you very little (for example, a little extra disk space, slightly shorter compile time) at the cost of not being able to step through a program. Generally speaking, **Debug Information** should always be enabled.

Emulation (Global)

The 8087 math coprocessor chip offers significant computational advantages over the 8088/8086. Unfortunately, not every computer has the 8087 installed. When enabled, the **Emulation** compiler directive gives you access to the 8087's data types whether or not the math chip is present.

Let's say you are distributing a statistics program that requires the mathematical precision of the 8087. But you also want to sell the program to people without the coprocessor installed. When **Emulation** is enabled, Turbo Pascal checks to see if the 8087 chip is installed. If it is, your program will use the power of the math chip; if not, your program will perform all the 8087 computations using the main microprocessor. Naturally, your computations will take much longer without the 8087 chip. Even so, it is better to have one program that everyone can use than to have separate versions for 8087 and non-8087 machines.

Unless you are going to need extremely precise mathematical results, you are better off leaving **Emulation** disabled.

Force Far Calls (Local)

Turbo Pascal supports multiple code segments—one code segment for each unit and an additional one for the main program. Function and procedure calls that take place within a unit or program file are known as *intrasegment* or *near* calls because the code that executes the call and the called procedure both reside in the same code segment. When, however, a statement in one unit calls a procedure in another unit, this is an *intersegment* or *far* call because the call crosses code segment boundaries.

Near calls require less work than far calls because the code segment does not change. Far calls, by virtue of the fact that more than one code segment is involved, require more work and execute more slowly. Fortunately, Turbo Pascal is smart enough to know when to use a near call and when to use a far call. There are, however, times when you will want to override Turbo's judgment and force a procedure to be called as a far call, even though it would normally be considered a near call.

The circumstances under which you would need to force a far call are generally very advanced and uncommon. Suffice it to say that when necessary, you can force a procedure to be a far call by enabling the **F** compiler directive as demonstrated here:

```
Program TestFarCall;

(*******************************************)

{$F+}Procedure FarCall;{$F-}
Begin
End;

(*******************************************)

Begin
FarCall; { This would normally be a near call }
End.
```

The procedure **FarCall** is clearly in the same code segment as the call made at the end of the program, which means that the procedure would be executed as a near call. The **F** compiler directive alters the situation by forcing the procedure to be a far call.

Input/Output Checking (Local)

The **I** compiler directive, which is used to check for I/O errors in your program, is enabled with the statement {$I +}. Perhaps the most common type of Turbo Pascal error, I/O errors are also among the most dangerous. Undetected, they can produce unpredictable results in a program that appears to be operating normally.

When **Input/Output Checking** is enabled, an I/O error produces a run-time error and halts your program. However, enabling the **I** compiler directive is not the best way to handle I/O errors. A more effective method is to disable the **I** directive with the statement {$I −} and trap I/O errors yourself. Techniques for trapping I/O errors are covered in Chapter 9, "Input/Output Considerations."

Local Symbol Information (Global)

Local Symbol Information refers to information about variables and constants that are local to a unit or procedure. Normally, Turbo Pascal does not save information about these symbols, making it impossible to view or change their values in a debugging session. By enabling the **Local Symbol Information** compiler directive, {$L +}, Turbo Pascal generates and saves information about all local variables so that you can use them as you debug your program.

The Local Symbol Information compiler directive works with the Debug Information directive in the following ways. When **Debug Information** is disabled ({$D −,L −} or {$D −,L +}), Turbo Pascal saves no information for debugging purposes and the **L** compiler directive has no effect. When **D** is enabled but **L** is disabled ({$D +,L −}), Turbo Pascal stores debugging information only for global variables and constants. When both **D** and **L** are enabled ({$D+,L+}), Turbo Pascal saves debugging information for both global and local symbols.

Numeric Processing (Global)

Turbo Pascal offers two types of floating-point numeric processing: Normal mode and 8087 mode. The Normal mode supports the 6-byte **Real** data type and does not use the 8087 match coprocessor, even if it is available. The 8087 mode offers four additional floating-point data types as well as access to the power of the 8087 math chip. Use the {$N−} compiler directive to select the Normal mode and {$N+} to select the 8087 mode.

The **N** compiler directive is used in conjuction with the **E** (Emulation) compiler directive. When both are enabled ({$N+,E+}), your program can use the 8087 mode even when the math chip is not installed. If the chip is installed, your program will use it for floating-point operations; if not, your program will use emulation routines that provide the same level of precision, but at a lower speed. When **Emulation** is not enabled in the 8087 mode, ({$N+,E−}), your program will run only on machines with the math chip installed.

Overlay Code Generation (Global)

If you want to include a unit in an overlay file, you must enable the **Overlay Code Generation** compiler directive ({$O+}). This tells Turbo Pascal to generate the code necessary to manage this unit as an overlay. Note, however, that enabling the **O** compiler directive does not require you to overlay the unit, it only makes overlaying possible. On the other hand, you cannot overlay a unit unless you have enabled the **O** compiler directive.

Range Checking (Local)

Most data types in Turbo Pascal have limitations. For example, a byte cannot hold a value greater than 255. An array of five elements cannot hold a sixth element. A string defined as **String[20]** cannot hold 21 characters. Any attempt to violate these limitations creates a range error—a value or condition that does not fit within the limits of the variable.

When **Range Checking** is enabled ({$R+}), Turbo Pascal generates code that checks that all indexing and assignments are within proper range. When a range error is found, Turbo Pascal generates a run-time error and halts the program. If, on the other hand, **Range Checking** is disabled, all out-of-bounds assignments and indexing operations go unreported. The results could be disastrous.

Range errors never occur in a properly functioning program, but they can be common during early stages of program development. To protect yourself against them, always enable the **R** compiler directive while developing a program and then disable it when compiling the final version.

One final point about **Range Checking**: when enabled, it significantly increases the size of your compiled program and slows its execution. If you find your program poking along where it should be flying, make sure that you did not inadvertently leave **Range Checking** enabled somewhere in your program.

Stack-Overflow Checking (Local)

When your program calls a procedure or function, Turbo Pascal allocates memory from the stack for local variables. Enabling the **Stack-Overflow Checking** compiler directive ({$S+}) tells Turbo Pascal to generate the code needed to make sure that enough memory is available on the stack to hold these local variables. If there is not enough memory, your program will terminate with a run-time error. If the **S** compiler directive is disabled ({$S−}), no checking will be done, and your computer will probably crash when it runs out of stack memory. Stack checking takes time and increases your program's executable code, so you should only enable the **S** directive when you are developing and debugging your program.

Var-String Checking (Local)

When **Var-String Checking** is enabled, Turbo Pascal performs strict type checking on string parameters passed to procedures and functions. To understand how **Var-String Checking** works and why it is important, consider the following program:

```
Program TestVarStr;
Type
  Str30 = String[30];
Var
  S : String[20];

(**************************************************)

Procedure ChangeS(Var S : Str30);
Var
  i : Integer;
Begin
For i := 1 To 30 Do
  s[i] := Chr(Ord(s[i]) + 1);
End;

(**************************************************)

Begin
s := 'abc';
ChangeS(s);
WriteLn(s);
ReadLn;
End.
```

In this program, **S**, a variable declared to be **String[20]**, is passed to procedure **ChangeS** whose parameter type is **String[30]**. If **Var-String Checking** were enabled ({$V+}), this program would not compile because the variable type and the parameter type do not match. You might think that forcing string variables to match procedure parameters is unnecessary, but consider what could happen.

In the preceding program, procedure **ChangeS** alters each character in a 30-character string. The variable **S**, however, is declared to be only 20 characters long. What happens when **ChangeS** tries to modify 30 characters when the variable has only 20? The answer is that the program will alter memory beyond the limit of string **S**. In short, you will be trashing memory and not know it. By now you should realize just how important **Var-String Checking** is and how insidious **Var-string** errors can be if they go undetected. If you do decide to disable **Var-String Checking**, make certain that there is no chance that your program will create undesired havoc.

Parameter Directives

Unlike switch directives, parameter directives do not have clearly defined on/off states. Instead, these directives indicate names of files that are to be used during compilation and the size of memory to be allocated to the program.

Include File (Local)

An *include file* is a source file that is compiled as part of another source file. The **I** directive is used followed by the name of the file with the source code. If you do not specify a file extension for the **I** directive, Turbo Pascal will assume the .PAS extension.

To understand how this works, look at the following listing. The procedure **ProcA** is contained in a file named MAININC. PAS. The main program file uses the Include compiler directive to insert the code in MAININC.PAS into the program. Include files are normally used when a program becomes too large to fit into the Turbo Pascal editor in one piece or when you wish to make changes to a program as a whole by changing values in the include file.

```
(* Contents of file MAININC.PAS *)
Procedure ProcA;
Begin
WriteLn('ProcA');
End;

(* Program using MAININC.PAS *)
Program Main;
{$I MainInc}
Begin
ProcA;
ReadLn;
End.
```

Link Object File (Local)

If you write routines in assembler for use in your Pascal programs, you will need to link the assembler object files with your

Pascal program. This is done with the Link Object File compiler directive (**L**) followed by the name of the object file.

Memory Allocation Sizes (Global)

The Memory Allocation Sizes (**M**) compiler directive gives you complete control over the amount of memory your program uses for its stack and heap. The directive is followed by three numbers, separated by commas, representing the amount of memory for the stack, and the minimum and maximum memory sizes for the heap. For example, the directive {**$M** 30000,1000,5000} allocates 30,000 bytes to the stack and a minimum of 1000 and a maximum of 5000 to the heap. The amount of memory you allocate to the stack must be from 1024 to 65520. The heap can have from 0 to 655360 bytes allocated to it.

Overlay Unit Name (Local)

The Overlay Unit Name compiler directive (**O**) is followed by the name of a unit and instructs Turbo Pascal to include that unit in the overlay file. The unit named in this directive must be compiled with the {**$O+**} compiler directive to allow it to be overlaid. The Overlay Unit Name compiler directive must be placed after the program **Uses** clause, as shown here:

```
Program OvrTest;
Uses
  Unit1,
  Unit2,
  Unit3;

{$O Unit1}
{$O Unit2}
```

In this program's declaration section, **Unit1** and **Unit2** are named to be included in the overlay file; **Unit3** will not be overlaid.

Conditional Compilation

Turbo Pascal's conditional compilation directives allow you to maintain different versions of a program in the same source file.

By changing certain definitions, you can compile some sections of code and hide others. At the heart of conditional compilation is the *condition symbol*, a symbol defined by you to control the conditional compilation process. The program listed here demonstrates how the conditional symbol is defined and used to control compilation.

```
Program ConditionExample;

{$DEFINE TEST} (* Define symbol *)

{$IFDEF TEST}  (* If symbol defined, do this... *)
{$R+,S+}

{$ELSE}        (* If symbol not defined, do this... *)
{$R-,S-}

{$ENDIF}       (* End of conditional compilation. *)

Begin
{$UNDEF TEST}  (* Undefine the symbol *)

{$IFDEF TEST}  (* If symbol defined, do this... *)

WriteLn('TEST DEFINED');

{$ELSE}        (* If symbol not defined, do this... *)

WriteLn('TEST NOT DEFINED');

{$ENDIF}       (* End of conditional compilation. *)

ReadLn;
End.
```

The program begins by defining the symbol TEST. The first use of TEST enables the **R** and **S** compiler directives if TEST is defined (as it is in this case) and disables them if TEST is not defined. After the **Begin** keyword, TEST is undefined, a process that nullifies the previous **{$DEFINE TEST}** directive. Since TEST is no longer defined, the line **WriteLn('TEST NOT DEFINED');** is compiled. The conditional compilation directives offered by Turbo Pascal are described next.

DEFINE

Use this directive to define a conditional symbol. Any code that depends on the symbol defined will be compiled, *but only in the* *file in which the **DEFINE** directive appears.* Consider the case of a program that uses a main source file, an include file, and a unit file. In each file, conditional compilation directives are used. If you use the **DEFINE** directive in the main source file, and not in the include and unit files, only the main source file will be affected; the other files will compile without the **DEFINE** directive. The only way to globally define a compilation symbol is to use the **Conditional defines** feature on the Options/Compiler menu.

UNDEF

This directive negates the **DEFINE** directive. Once a symbol has been used with **UNDEF**, any code that depends on that symbol will not be compiled.

IFDEF

This directive instructs Turbo Pascal to compile code if a named conditional symbol is defined.

IFNDEF

This directive instructs Turbo Pascal to compile code if a named conditional symbol is *not* defined.

IFOPT

You can also control compilation based on another compilation directive. For example, you can compile code only when the **R** compile directive is enabled by writing {**IFOPT R +**}.

ELSE

Use this directive after any of the IF. . . directives (**IFDEF, IFNDEF, IFOPT**) as a branch when the first condition is untrue.

ENDIF

This directive marks the end of a conditional compilation sequence. All code appearing after the **ENDIF** statement will be compiled regardless of conditional symbols.

Using compiler directives effectively is an important step in becoming a productive programmer. You must understand how to use these directives to get the most out of Turbo Pascal.

The Data Section

In Turbo Pascal global variables, constants, labels, and user-defined data types are declared directly following the program heading and global compiler directives. Local variables are declared within procedures and functions, but follow the same basic rules.

Constant Definitions

Many programs have certain values that never change, such as the number of days in a week, or if they do change, they change for the program as a whole. Using constant identifiers for these constant values simplifies your programs and makes them easier to maintain; for a change to be reflected throughout a program, you need only change the value of the constant.

The Turbo Pascal reserved word **Const** signals the beginning of a constant-definition block. (Reserved words are those used solely by Turbo Pascal; they cannot be defined by users as identifiers.)

You have two choices of constants in Turbo Pascal: *untyped* and *typed*. An untyped constant is declared with the following syntax: an identifier followed by an equal sign, a literal value (numeric or text), and a semicolon, as shown in this example:

```
CONST
      DaysPerWeek = 7;
      HoursPerDay = 24;
      Message = 'Good Morning';
```

These constants are called untyped because you do not specify their type definition.

Typed constants are defined similarly, except that the type definition is inserted between the identifier and the equal sign, as shown in the following example.

```
CONST
     DaysPerWeek : Integer = 7;
     Message : String[20] = 'Good Morning';
     Interest : Real = 0.14;
```

If you are concerned about code space, you should use typed constants rather than untyped constants. Untyped constants take up more space because the constant identifier is replaced by the literal value when the program is compiled. In the preceding example of untyped constants, Turbo Pascal would replace every identifier **Message** with the string literal 'Good Morning'.

Typed constants, on the other hand, are defined in the data segment one time and take up only as much space as the data type requires. Anytime your program uses a typed constant, it refers to that single copy.

Another characteristic of typed constants is that you can change their values. In a sense, typed constants are not constants at all, but are initialized variables. If you want to be absolutely certain that a constant's value remains the same throughout a program, use an untyped constant.

Type Definitions

In the type-definition block, denoted by the Turbo Pascal reserved word **Type**, you can define your own data types and later use them to declare variables. The general form for type definitions is an identifier followed by an equal sign, the data type, and a semicolon, as shown here:

```
Type
  PayType = (Salary,HourlyRate);
  Customer = Record
    Name : String[30];
```

```
        Age : Integer;
        Income : Real;
        End;
    MaxString = String[80];
    NameList = Array [1..100] Of String[30];
```

The first data type, **PayType**, is an enumerated scalar with two legal values. The second, **Customer**, is a **Record** data type containing three fields. **MaxString** denotes a string variable with 80 characters, and **NameList** is an array of 100 strings, each 30 characters long. The ability to create customized data types is one of Pascal's most powerful features and is discussed throughout this book.

Variable Declarations

Variables are areas in memory that you name. To begin a variable-declaration block, type the reserved word **Var** followed by the variable identifier (the name you give the variable), a colon, and the data type (for example, **Var i : Integer;**).

You can declare variables by using standard Turbo Pascal data types (for example, **Boolean**, **Real**, **Integer**) or user-defined data types created in the **Type** section. The format for variable declarations is nearly the same as that used for **Type** definitions, but the identifier is followed by a colon rather than an equal sign.

```
    Var
        i, j, k : Integer;
        x, y, z : Real;
        BeyondLimit : Boolean;
        Ad : AdType;

    Book : Record
        Title : String[20];
        TotPages : Integer;
        Text : Array [1..10000] Of String[20];
        End;
```

The declaration of the variable **Book** uses the **Record** type that allows you to group more than one data element into a single variable.

Label Declarations

Labels are used to mark points in a program. By using the **Goto** statement together with a label, you can force the program flow to jump from place to place. Many programmers consider the use of the **Goto** statement bad programming technique because it leads to messy, unstructured programs. To keep you from abusing the **Goto** statement, Turbo Pascal limits the scope of a label to a single procedure block.

The label-declaration block begins with the reserved word **Label**. The declarations themselves consist simply of identifiers that are separated by commas and terminate with a semicolon, as shown here.

```
Label
    EndOfProgram, NextStep;
```

When used in your program, the label is followed by a colon (for example, **EndOfProgram:**). Statements following the label are executed whenever a **Goto** statement branches to that label. The following program demonstrates a valid use of a label and **Goto** statement.

```
Program GoToTest;
Var
  i,j : Integer;
  a : Array [1..100,1..100] Of Integer;

(*******************************************************)

Function Found : Boolean;
Label JumpOut;
Begin
For i := 1 To 100 Do
  Begin
  For j := 1 To 100 Do
    Begin
    If a[i,j] < 0 Then
      Begin
```

```
        Found := True;
        Goto JumpOut;
        End;
      End;
    End;
Found := False;

JumpOut:
End;


(**************************************************)


Begin
FillChar(a,sizeof(a),0);
a[50,50] := -1;
WriteLn(Found);
ReadLn;
End.
```

The function **Found** searches through a matrix of integers looking for a negative value. If a negative value is found, the function
should return TRUE, if not, FALSE. In cases where you need
to break out of a nested loop, the **Goto** command is a good
choice because avoiding **Goto** would significantly increase the
complexity of the routine.

The Code Section

The third major part of a Turbo Pascal program is the code
section. It is the largest portion of the program and contains the
step-by-step instructions that make the program work.

The code section always contains a program block and often
contains procedures and functions. Blocks, delimited by the
Turbo Pascal reserved words **Begin** and **End**, contain the instructions that assign values to variables, create logical branching,
call other procedures and functions, and so on. In Turbo Pascal,
the part of the program that executes first, the program block, is
defined at the end of the program, as shown in Figure 4-2.

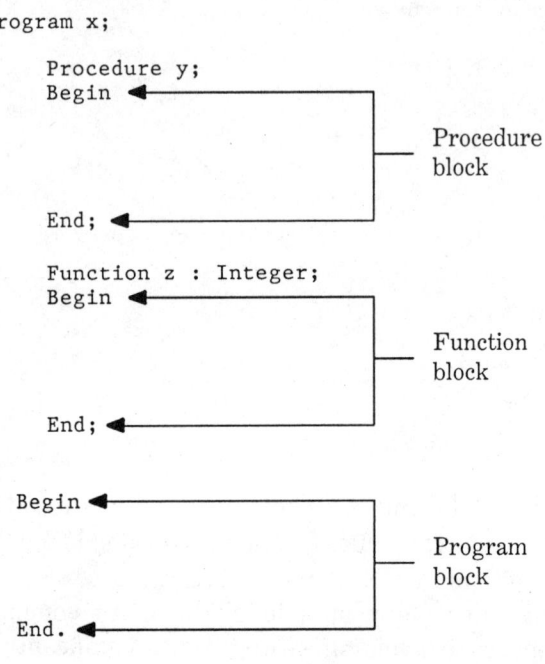

Figure 4-2.   Organization of the code section

The program in Figure 4-3, which computes the weekly pay for a group of employees, demonstrates all the fundamental characteristics of a Turbo Pascal program. The program heading and the compiler directives are at the top. The data section defines constants and data types and declares variables and labels. Procedures and functions are defined in the code section.

At the heart of this program is the user-defined record type **EmployeeType**. This record, containing basic information about an employee, defines the array **Employee**. This array contains 60 elements, each of which is a record of type **EmployeeType**. A customized data type (the constant **Employees**) defines the array. If the number of employees changes, all you need to do is change the definition of this constant.

The main program block in Figure 4-3 consists of a loop
that executes once for every employee. Each iteration, or execution, of the loop calls the procedure **CalcPay**, which calculates
the pay for the employee. When the procedure ends, the main
program block tests to make sure that the result, **TotalPay**, is
not less than zero, since clearly no one should (or could) be paid
a negative amount. If the result is less than zero, the program
jumps to the **EndOfProgram** label and terminates. If, however,
the amount of **TotalPay** is in the correct range, the program

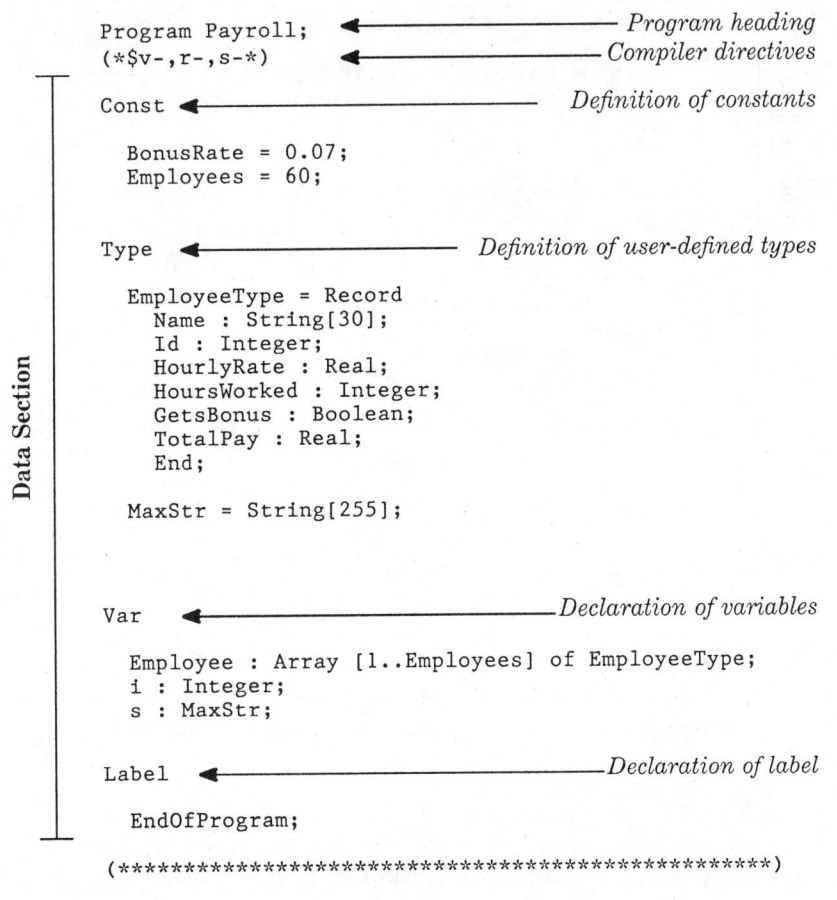

```
Program Payroll;                                      ← ———————— Program heading
(*$v-,r-,s-*)                                         ← ———————— Compiler directives

Const ←——————————————————————————— Definition of constants

  BonusRate = 0.07;
  Employees = 60;


Type ←——————————————————— Definition of user-defined types

  EmployeeType = Record
    Name : String[30];
    Id : Integer;
    HourlyRate : Real;
    HoursWorked : Integer;
    GetsBonus : Boolean;
    TotalPay : Real;
    End;

  MaxStr = String[255];



  Var ←——————————————————————————Declaration of variables

  Employee : Array [1..Employees] of EmployeeType;
  i : Integer;
  s : MaxStr;

Label ←———————————————————————Declaration of label

  EndOfProgram;

(*************************************************)
```

Data Section

Figure 4-3.   A typical Turbo Pascal program

Code Section

```
Procedure CalcPay(Var Employee : EmployeeType)

  Function CalcBonus(Pay : Real) : Real;
  Begin
  CalcBonus := Pay + (Pay * BonusRate);
  End;
Begin
Employee.TotalPay := Employee.HoursWorked *
                     Employee.HourlyRate;

If Employee.GetsBonus then
  Employee.TotalPay := CalcBonus(Employee.TotalPay);
End;

(***************************************************)

  Procedure WriteReport (Employee : EmployeeType);
  Begin
  Writeln('Name:       ',Employee.name)
  Writeln('Total Pay: ',Employee.TotalPay:0:2);
  Writeln;
  End;

(***************************************************)


Begin
For i := 1 To Employees Do
  Begin
  CalcPay(Employee[i];
  If Employee[i].TotalPay < 0 then
    Begin
    Writeln('Error: Total pay less than zero');
    Goto EndOfProgram;
    End;
  WriteReport(Employee[i]);
  End;


EndOfProgram:
End.
```

Main program block

Figure 4-3.   A typical Turbo Pascal program (*continued*)

calls the procedure **WriteReport**, which writes the employee's name and the total amount paid.

More on Program Blocks

Pascal is known as a block-structured language, that is, a language in which every statement in a program belongs to a specific block of code. A simple program can consist of only one block, as shown here:

```
Program Sample;
Begin
WriteLn('Hello');
End.
```

The program block is the lowest level in the program: it is the foundation upon which you can build more layers. In the preceding example, the entire program exists at the program-block level. When you add procedures and functions to a program, you add more levels, as shown in Figure 4-4. This program consists

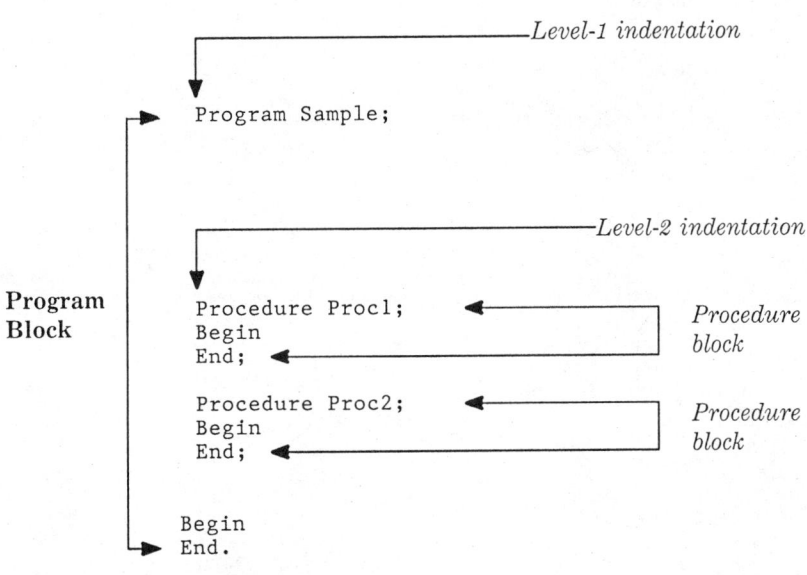

Figure 4-4.   Adding levels to a Turbo Pascal program

of three blocks—one program block and two procedure blocks—but has only two levels. Because both procedures are nested within the program block, they are both level-2 procedures, as the indentation suggests.

By nesting procedures within other procedures, you can add even more levels to the program. In Figure 4-5, for example, procedure **Proc1A** is nested inside procedure **Proc1** to form a third level in the program.

Nesting procedures creates "privacy" among procedures. A procedure that is nested inside another is private to that procedure. Keeping procedures private can decrease programming errors by limiting the use of a procedure to a specific section of your program.

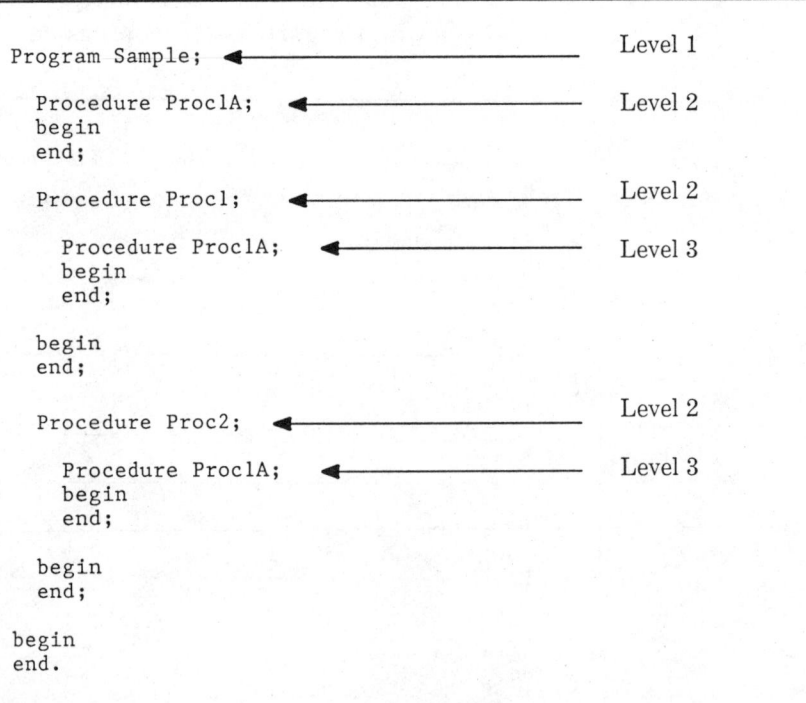

Figure 4-5.   Nesting procedures within procedures

Procedural Scope

Note that Figure 4-5 contains three procedures named **Proc1A**: the first is at level 2; the other two are at level 3, nested within the procedures **Proc1** and **Proc2**.

Although these three procedures have the same name, each is treated as a distinct entity. A call to **Proc1A** in the program block executes the level-2 procedure, while calls made within **Proc1** and **Proc2** refer to their respective nested procedures.

Two rules govern the scope of procedures:

- A program may call a procedure within the block where it is declared and within any subblock nested in that block.

- The exception to Rule 1 occurs when the program declares another procedure of the same name in a higher-level subblock.

In Figure 4-5, the level-2 procedure **Proc1A** would normally extend its scope into **Proc1** and **Proc2**. But because the program declares the same procedure name in **Proc1** and **Proc2**, the scope of the level-2 procedure is limited to the first level.

Procedural Precedence

In some languages (notably C), the order in which you declare procedures makes no difference. In Turbo Pascal, a language far more orderly than C, you cannot call procedures until you have declared them. (The only exception to this is when you use **FORWARD** declarations, which are discussed in the next section.) For example, in Figure 4-5, **Proc2** can call **Proc1**, but **Proc1** cannot call **Proc2**.

The rule of procedural precedence is based on the logic that a complex idea is best built from simple ideas. In other words, a program should be built from small, simple procedures that are combined to form increasingly complex procedures. A programmer should see a continual evolution from the beginning to the end of a Turbo Pascal program, culminating in the program block, which may well consist of only a few procedure calls.

Forward Declarations

While procedural precedence enforces a desirable order in a program, there are times when you simply need to refer to a procedure before you declare it. For these cases, Turbo Pascal provides the *FORWARD declaration*, which informs the compiler that a procedure exists before it specifies what the procedure does. A **FORWARD** declaration consists of the normal procedure heading followed by the word **FORWARD** and a semicolon. The body of the procedure is declared later, at which point only the name of the procedure, and not the entire program heading, is declared. The following listing shows an example of a **FORWARD**-declared procedure.

```
Program Endless_Loop;
Var
  i : Integer;

  Procedure Step2(i : Integer); FORWARD;

  Procedure Step1(i : Integer);
  Begin
  i := i + 1;
  WriteLn(i);
  Step2(i);
  End;

  Procedure Step2;
  Begin
  i := i + 1;
  WriteLn(i);
  If i > 100 Then Halt;
  Step1(i);
  End;

Begin
i := 1;
Step1(i);
End.
```

In this case, **Step2** and **Step1** both call each other—something not allowed by procedure precedence, but overcome by the **FORWARD** declaration of **Step2**.

Include Files

The Turbo Pascal editor cannot hold more than 62K of text at any time. If your program exceeds this limit, you have to break it into pieces by storing it in multiple files. When you compile the program, the Include File directive pulls all the pieces together from these multiple files. The Include File directive is also useful when you have standard libraries of frequently used routines.

To include a file in a Pascal program, type a left parenthesis or brace followed by an asterisk, **$I**, the name of the file to be used, another asterisk, and a right parenthesis or brace. For example, the sample directive **(*$I PROCS.INC*)** tells Turbo Pascal to read the include file PROCS.INC as if the text were written in the program. Another example of how to include a file is shown in Figure 4-6.

Here, the main program file (MAIN.PAS) makes a call to the procedure **ListFiles**, yet **ListFiles** is defined not in the file MAIN.PAS but in the file PROCS.INC. The include statement in MAIN.PAS tells the compiler to read in PROCS.INC at that point and use its code as part of the program.

Include file is PROCS.INC

```
Procedure ListFiles;
Var
  i : Integer;
Begin
End;
```

Main program file is MAIN.PAS

```
Program Main;
(*$I Procs.Inc*)
Begin
ListFiles;
End.
```

Figure 4-6.   Using an include file

Overlays

To support overlays, Turbo Pascal supplies a standard unit aptly named **OVERLAY**. By including this unit in your program's **Uses** clause, you can overlay your program's units to minimize the amount of memory your program requires. Using overlays is quite easy as long as you follow some simple rules.

- Enable the Force Far Calls compiler directive for the program and all units.

- Name the **OVERLAY** unit first in your program's **Uses** clause.

- Compile overlaid units with the {$O+} compiler directive.

- List the overlaid units using the {$O *filename*} compiler directive.

- Make sure that your program initializes the overlay before any statements execute, including initialization sections of overlaid units.

The use of overlays is best described by example. The following listing includes the code for two units (**Ovr1** and **Ovr2**) and a main program **TestOvr**. Both the units are to be overlaid and, therefore, include the {$O+,F+} compiler directive.

```
{$O+,F+}
Unit Ovr1;
Interface
Procedure Message1;
Implementation

Procedure Message1;
Begin
WriteLn('Message 1');
End;

End.

(************************************)

{$O+,F+}
Unit Ovr2;
```

```
Interface

Procedure Message2;

Implementation

Procedure Message2;
Begin
WriteLn('Message 2');
End;

End.

(***********************************)

{$O+,F+}
Program TestOvr;
Uses Overlay,
     Ovr1,
     Ovr2;

{$O Ovr1}
{$O Ovr2}

Begin
OvrInit('TESTOVR.OVR');
Message1;
Message2;
ReadLn;
End.
```

The program declares the **OVERLAY** unit as the first unit in
the **Uses** clause and also declares the units to be overlaid using
the {$O *filename*} directive. The first line of the program per-
forms the necessary initialization of the overlay.

As you can see, the overlay process is extremely simple.
Complications arise, however, when the overlaid units contain
initialization code. Consider the following listings, which are
similar to the previous unit, except that initialization code has
been added to the units to be overlaid. Turbo Pascal always
executes initialization code before it executes the first statement
in the main program. This means that the overlaid units will
execute before the overlay manager is initialized. How can you
overcome this problem?

```
{$O+,F+}
Unit Ovr1;
```

```
Interface

Procedure Message1;

Implementation
Var
  s : String;

Procedure Message1;
Begin
WriteLn(s);
End;

Begin
s := 'Message 1';
End.

(***********************************)

{$O+,F+}
Unit Ovr2;

Interface

Procedure Message2;

Implementation
Var
  s : String;

Procedure Message2;
Begin
WriteLn(s);
End;

Begin
s := 'Message 2';
End.

(***********************************)

{$O+,F+}
Unit OvrStart;
Interface
Uses Overlay;

Implementation

Begin
OvrInit('TESTOVR.OVR');
If OvrResult = OvrNotFound Then
  Begin
  WriteLn('File TESTOVR.OVR not found.');
  Halt;
  End;
End.
```

```
(***********************************)

{$O+,F+}
Program TestOvr;
Uses Overlay,
     OvrStart,
     Ovr1,
     Ovr2;

{$O Ovr1}
{$O Ovr2}

Begin
Message1;
Message2;
ReadLn;
End.
```

Fortunately, the answer is not so difficult. Instead of initializing the overlay manager in your main program, place the initialization code in a unit and include this unit in the **Uses** clause *before* any of the overlaid units. This ensures that the overlay manager will be installed before any of the overlaid files execute.

The Turbo Pascal overlay system includes five routines for initializing the overlay manager and controlling the program's use of memory. When they execute, these routines set the global variable **OvrResult** to indicate if any problems occurred. The Overlay unit defines the following constants to help you interpret the value of **OvrResult**:

```
Const
  OvrOk           =  0; (* No error *)
  OvrError        = -1; (* Nonspecific error *)
  OvrNotFound     = -2; (* Overlay file not found *)
  OvrNoMemory     = -3; (* Not enough memory *)
  OvrIOError      = -4; (* Error reading .OVR file *)
  OvrNoEMSDriver  = -5; (* EMS driver not loaded *)
  OvrNoEMSMemory  = -6; (* Insufficient EMS memory *)
```

Your program should take care to test the value of **OvrResult** every time you use one of the five overlay routines.

OvrInit

This procedure initializes the overlay manager and prepares overlaid units for use. **OvrInit** takes a single string parameter containing the name of the overlay file, which is usually the name of the main program file with the .OVR suffix. This procedure is called only once and must be called before any of the overlaid units.

OvrInitEMS

While overlays save memory, they slow down your program due to frequent disk reads. The Turbo Pascal overlay manager is capable of loading the entire overlay file into expanded memory, which greatly reduces access time to overlaid procedures. To load an overlay into expanded memory, simply execute the procedure **OvrInitEMS**. If the computer has enough expanded memory available, the overlay file will be loaded into it; if not, the overlay will execute from disk as it normally would.

OvrSetBuf

When you initiate **OvrInit**, the overlay manager captures the minimum amount of memory needed to run the overlaid procedures. You can expand this amount of memory with **OvrSetBuf**, a procedure that takes a **LongInt** parameter which represents the size, in bytes, of the overlay buffer you wish to use. For example, the statement **OvrSetBuf(100000)** reserves 100,000 bytes for use as an overlay buffer. The size of the buffer must be at least as large as the minimum buffer size and less than **MemAvail**. Also, **OvrSetBuf** must be called only when the heap is clear of dynamic variables.

OvrGetBuf

This function returns a **LongInt** representing the current size of the overlay buffer. You can use this value as a guide when increasing the size of the buffer with **OvrSetBuf**.

OvrClearBuf

This procedure removes all overlaid units from the overlay buffer. Doing this ensures that any subsequent call to an overlaid procedure will require a disk read. You will normally never need to clear the overlay buffer. One circumstance where you might is when you want to reclaim, for other purposes, the memory used by the overlay buffer.

Turbo Pascal's program structure is straightforward and logical, but requires the programmer to understand the concepts of structured programming. Some programmers see this imposition of structure as a limitation, an unnecessary attempt to tell them how to program. In time, however, you will come to appreciate the strict nature of Turbo Pascal and will learn from it good programming habits that apply to any language.

Turbo Pascal Data Types

Standard Data Types
Constants in Turbo Pascal
Sets
User-Defined Data Types

**F
I
V
E**

Turbo Pascal provides programmers with a rich set of data types, each of which serves a specific purpose. **Byte** and **Short-Int** variables are used for small, unsigned, and signed numbers, respectively; **Integer** and **LongInt** for numbers without decimal places; **Real** for numbers with decimal places; **Boolean** for true and false conditions; **char** for characters; and **String** for concatenated characters. This chapter discusses the standard data types offered by Turbo Pascal and how they can be used.

Standard Data Types

A variable of type **Byte** occupies one byte. A **Byte** is an unsigned numeric value that can range from 0 to 255. In arithmetic expressions, a **Byte** variable can be assigned a value from an **Integer** or **LongInt** variable as long as the value does not exceed the byte's numeric range.

Like **Byte** variables, **Integer** variables hold numerical values that have no decimal places. Because they are two bytes (16 bits) long, **Integers** can range in value from −32,768 to 32,767. The **Word** data type is two bytes long, like **Integer**, but is unsigned, giving it a range of 0 to 65,535. **LongInt** variables occupy four bytes in memory and have a range of $-2,147,483,648$ to $2,147,483,647$.

For numbers with fractional portions, or with magnitudes that exceed $2,147,483,647$ (the maximum value of **LongInt**), Turbo Pascal provides the **Real** data type, also known as the **floating-point** type. A **Real** variable requires six bytes of storage and can range in value from $2.9 \times 10E-39$ to $1.7 \times 10E38$. Because of their complex structure, arithmetic operations involving **Reals** take far longer to execute than do operations on **Integers** or **Bytes,** which are stored in their binary numerical equivalents.

A common problem encountered with **Real** variables is the overflow condition. This occurs when you try to assign too large a number to a **Real** variable and causes a run-time error in the program. You will find, however, that this is not always true. For example, if 1 is added to a **Real** variable with the maximum value of $1.7 \times 10E38$, the value remains unchanged and no execution error is detected. Even though an overflow condition logically should exist, the program does not detect one. This is because a **Real** can store only 11 to 12 significant digits. That means that adding small numbers to a large **Real** value will not change the value of the **Real**.

On the other hand, an overflow condition can occur unexpectedly. If a **Real** variable with the maximum value of $1.7 \times 10E38$ is multiplied by 1.0, the value should not change and there should be no overflow error. Even so, Turbo Pascal detects an overflow condition and halts execution.

Admittedly, you are unlikely to encounter such extreme conditions regularly; in most cases you will never come close to the limit of **Real**s in Turbo Pascal.

Char

Like the **Byte** type, the **char** (character) data type occupies one byte of storage in memory. Unlike the **Byte** variable, however, a **char** variable cannot be used directly in arithmetic expressions.

It is used instead for manipulating and comparing text, as well as in string-assignment statements.

String

The **String** data type stores text information. A **String** variable can be from 1 to 255 characters long, but it occupies one byte more than its defined length. For example, if a **String** variable is declared to be 10 characters long (S : **String[10]**;), the variable occupies 11 bytes in memory. This is because the first byte in every **String** variable keeps track of the length of the string currently stored in the variable (and so is called the *length byte*). If a 10-character **String** variable contains the word "HELLO", the first byte in memory holds the binary value 5, indicating that the variable contains five characters. In this case, the last five bytes of the variable are ignored by Turbo Pascal's string-manipulation procedures. The memory allocated to the **String** variable would look like this:

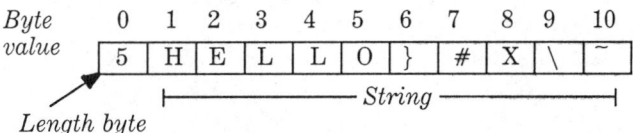

Note that the first byte is not the character "5" but the number 5 in binary (00000101) and that the last five bytes contain random data.

Maintaining a length byte requires quite a bit of overhead. As a result, string-manipulation statements tend to be among the slowest in Turbo Pascal. Yet the alternative implementation of strings, such as in C, is even less efficient. In C, the character array (the equivalent of the Pascal **String** type) has no length byte. Consequently, any time a program needs to know the length of a string, it has to calculate it by counting every character until a delimiter is reached.

Turbo Pascal allows you to define variables as type **String** without any specified length. In this case, the **String** will be given the maximum length of 255 characters.

8087 Data Types

In addition to the **Byte, Integer, Word, LongInt,** and **Real** data types, Turbo Pascal supports four other numerical data types: **Single, Double, Extended,** and **Comp.** The **Single** data type is a "short **Real**" in the sense that it requires only 4 bytes of storage and has only 7 to 8 significant digits. The **Double** data type is a "long **Real**," requiring eight bytes and giving 15 to 16 significant digits. And for those who need the ultimate in precision, there is the "really, really long **Real**," the **Extended** data type, which uses ten bytes and provides 19 to 20 significant digits with a range in value of $3.4 \times 10E-4932$ to $1.1 \times 10E4932$.

The 8087 data types also include the **Comp** type, which is not floating-point. This data type uses 8 bytes, contains 19 to 20 significant digits, and ranges from $-(2 \times 10E63) + 1$ to $(2 \times 10E63) -1$. This data type can be useful for calculations requiring large integer values.

With Turbo Pascal's range of numerical data types, you should be able to select the one that precisely fits your needs. And best of all, Turbo Pascal's Emulation mode gives you access to them whether or not your computer has the 8087 math coprocessor installed.

Constants in Turbo Pascal

Turbo Pascal does not initialize variables when a program starts up. As a result, there is no way of telling what value a variable has until you assign one.

Constants, on the other hand, are assigned values specified by the programmer when the program starts. To illustrate the importance of constants, consider the example of a program that computes interest on loans. The program uses a fixed interest rate of 7%, which appears about 100 times within the program. At the same time, a variable interest rate of 7% also appears frequently in the program. To change all the fixed-rate values from 7% to 8% would require checking each occurrence of the number 7, deciding if the number is a fixed or a variable rate, and changing the value manually.

If, on the other hand, a constant named **FixedRate** (or some other appropriate name) is declared, changing the value throughout the program would be accomplished simply by changing the declaration.

Untyped and Typed Constants

Turbo Pascal provides two types of constants, untyped and typed. Untyped constants are true constants in that Turbo Pascal does not allow their value to be altered. Typed constants, on the other hand, can change in value (just as variables can).

To understand how typed constants got their name, consider the sample declarations shown here.

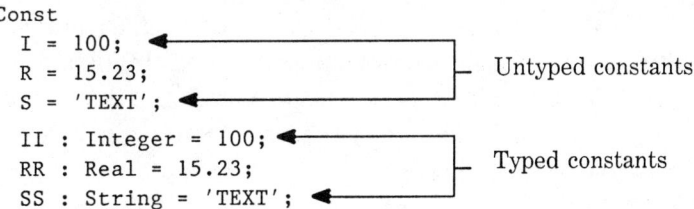

```
Const
   I = 100;                         ─┐
   R = 15.23;                        ├─ Untyped constants
   S = 'TEXT';                      ─┘

   II : Integer = 100;              ─┐
   RR : Real = 15.23;                ├─ Typed constants
   SS : String = 'TEXT';            ─┘
```

A definition of a typed constant contains the type declaration (for example, **Integer**, **Real**, **String**) and can be used in assignment statements. Untyped constants cannot be used in assignment statements, as is shown here.

```
Const
   S : String[4] = 'TEXT';
Begin                              Correct
S := 'AAAA';
End.

Const
   S = 'TEXT';
Begin                              Incorrect
S := 'AAAA';
End.
```

Since Turbo Pascal provides both constants and variables, what is the intrinsic value of a typed constant? Some programmers prefer to initialize all variables to specific values when a program starts. This avoids the unpredictable results that can occur when a variable is not properly assigned.

One difference between typed and untyped constants concerns their use as parameters to a procedure. Either constant can be passed as a value parameter without any difficulty; however, only a typed constant can be passed by reference.

Sets

In Turbo Pascal, a *set* is a group of related numbers or characters. Sets are primarily used to see if a character or number belongs to the set. For example, you might define a set that consists of the capital letters from A to Z and then use the set to check if other characters in the program are included in it. If a character is included in the set, you know it is uppercase. A discussion of numeric and character sets follows.

Numeric Sets

Numeric sets can consist only of integers (actually byte values). The sets include any integers from 0 to 255; such numbers as −1 and 256 exceed the range established by Turbo Pascal. Here are two examples of numeric set definitions.

Zero_Through_Nine : Set of 0 .. 9;

FullRange : Set of Byte;

In the first line, Zero_Through_Nine can include any combination of integers (byte values) from 0 to 9, but the number 10 cannot be included because it is outside the range of the set.

In the second line, no range is specified for the set FullRange; the definition specifies only that the set consists of bytes. Later in the program, the programmer can define FullRange to be any numeric subset with a statement such as this:

FullRange := [0..9];

Now, the set FullRange has the same elements as

Zero_Through_Nine.

Character Sets

Character sets can consist only of characters. Like numeric sets, the maximum range of character sets is from 0 (00h) to 255 (FFh). The major difference between numeric sets and character sets is that character sets can be directly compared with character variables. Here are two examples of character-set definitions:

UpperCase : Set of 'A'..'Z';
AllChars : Set of Char;

The set UpperCase can include any combination of uppercase characters from "A" (ASCII code 65) to "Z" (ASCII code 90). Thus, the character "a" (ASCII code 97) could not be included in this set.

The second set, AllChars, is defined as a "Set of Char." This means that this set can include any combination of characters from 0 to 255.

Sets of User-Defined Elements

Lastly, a set can consist of elements defined by the user. These elements are neither numeric nor character and must be listed individually. The maximum number of elements allowed is 255. Here is an example of a user-defined set:

Ingredients : Set of (eggs, milk, butter, flour);

All operations on sets of user-defined elements follow the same rules as all other sets.

Sets and Memory Allocation

Sets can use a maximum of 32 bytes of storage — the equivalent of 256 individual bits. This is what limits the scope of a set to the range 0 to 255. If your set has only a few elements, it uses only a few bytes, and allocating the full 32 bytes would be wasteful.

Therefore, sets are automatically reduced in size. For example, a set defined as follows

X : 1 .. 5;

needs only one byte, so Turbo Pascal allocates just one byte for the set. The values in the byte are allocated as follows:

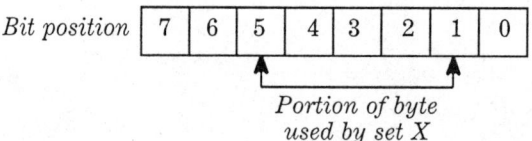

Bit position

Portion of byte used by set X

The arrows indicate the part of the byte used to store the set. When an element is present in a set, the appropriate bit is turned on (that is, set to 1). To illustrate how the memory would represent the presence of elements in a set, consider the following set assignment:

X := [1 .. 3,5];

This statement assigns the elements 1, 2, 3, and 5 to set X. In memory, this assignment creates the following bit pattern:

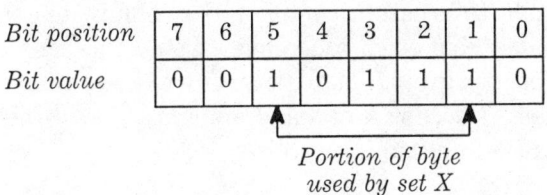

Portion of byte
used by set X

The ones in the bit value portion of this illustration indicate the presence of an element in the set. They are found in the 1, 2, 3, and 5 positions of the byte, which correspond precisely to the assignment statement.

Since Turbo Pascal needs only one byte to store set X, the remaining 31 bytes are used for other purposes. Only three bits of memory (the 0, 6, and 7 positions) are wasted. To further illustrate the storage of sets, consider the following set definition:

X : Set of 7..8;

This set comprises only two elements, but requires two bytes of storage. Why? Because the set straddles a byte boundary, as shown in this illustration:

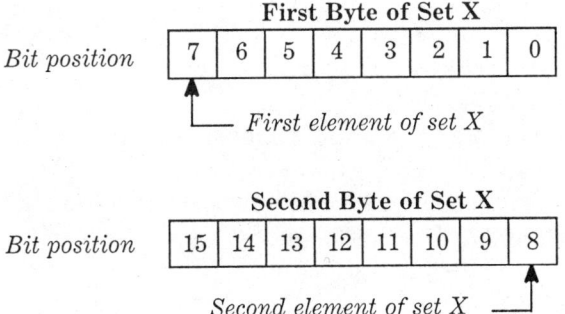

The first element (7) is in the first byte, while the second element (8) is in the second byte. Two bytes are used (but 14 of the 16 bits are ignored), and 30 bytes are used for other purposes.

It is possible to create a compiler that eliminates this kind of wasted memory, but such a compiler would increase the size of the compiled programs and slow down execution. Wisely, Borland decided to accept a minimal amount of waste in return for faster execution and smaller code.

User-Defined Data Types

One of the most powerful aspects of Turbo Pascal is its ability to define customized data types. By tailoring data structures to a program's specific algorithms, you can increase your program's readability and simplify its maintenance. User-defined data types fall into one of three categories: user-defined scalars, records, and arrays.

User-Defined Scalar Type

A user-defined scalar (or enumerated scalar) requires one byte of memory and can have up to 256 elements. The power of user-defined scalars is that the programmer names the values, allowing easier programming and debugging. The following are examples of enumerated scalars:

```
Income : (High, Moderate, Low);
Sex : (Male, Female);
Occupation : (Doctor, Teacher, Other);
```

The following code excerpt demonstrates the readability of user-defined scalars:

```
If Occupation = Doctor Then
     Income := High
```

```
Else If Occupation = Teacher Then
Income := Moderate
Else
Income := Low;
```

Without user-defined scalars, the programmer must develop coding schemes to represent the values (for example, 1 = Doctor, 2 = Teacher, 3 = Other). When the number of coded variables is large, it is difficult to keep track of the meanings of different values.

Each element of a user-defined scalar equates to a byte value according to its position in the enumerated set, with the first element having a value of 0. In the preceding examples of enumerated sets, the high income has the value 0, while low income has the value 2. To determine the current value of **Income**, use the Turbo Pascal standard function **Ord**. If **Income** is currently High, then the statement **Ord(Income)** returns the value 0; if it is Low, it returns 2. If you wish, you can assign this value to a numeric variable, as is done next, where the variable **i** will be equal to 1 after the assignment statement:

```
Var
  i : Integer;
  Color : (Black, Brown, Blue, Green, Red, Yellow, White);
Begin
Color := Brown;
i := Ord(Color);
End.
```

While transforming a user-defined scalar to a numeric value is easy, the opposite is untrue. In the following example, the statement **Color := i** is illegal:

```
Var
  i : Integer;
  Color : (Black, Brown, Blue, Green, Red, Yellow, White);
Begin
i := 1;
Color := i;
End.
```

To resolve this illegal statement simply, you can use the Turbo Pascal standard function **Fillchar**, which is discussed in greater detail in Appendix E. The following example shows one way to assign a numeric value (**Integer** or **Byte**, not **Real**) to an enumerated set.

```
Var
  i : Integer;
  Color : (Black, Brown, Blue, Green, Red, Yellow, White);
Begin
i := 1;
FillChar(color,1,i);
End.
```

Records

A record is a combination of other data types into a new data type. This example exhibits a typical record definition:

```
Var
  Customer : Record
    Name : String[30];
    Address : String[60];
    Age : Integer;
    Income : Real;
    Married : Boolean;
    End;
```

Using records has two advantages. First, all data elements for a single record are logically connected to each other. This makes it easier to keep track of things. Second, some operations, such as assignments and file operations, can be performed on an entire record, eliminating the need to refer to each element in the record.

Using records in assignment statements is straightforward. You can access elements in a record in two ways: by explicit reference or implicit reference using the reserved word **With**, as shown in Figure 5-1. The statement

Rec1.b := 1;

```
Program X;
Uses CRT;
Var
  Rec1, Rec2. : Record
    a : String[20];
    B : Integer;
    c : Real;
    End;

Begin
ClrScr;

Rec1.a := 'sss';                ◄─────────────┐
Rec1.b := 1;                                  │
Rec1.c := 123.23;               ◄─────────────┤
                                              │         These segments do
With Rec1 Do                    ◄──────────┐  │            exactly the
  Begin                                    │  │            same thing
    a := 'sss';                            │  │
    b := 1;                                │  │
    c := 123.23;                           └──┘
    End;                        ◄──────────┘

Rec2 := Rec1;                   ◄──────────────────────   Record-to-record
                                                          block assignment
With Rec2 Do                    ◄──────────┐
  Begin                                    │
    WriteLn(a);                            │              Output using the
    WriteLn(b);                            │              **With** option
    WriteLn(c);                            │
    End;                        ◄──────────┘

WriteLn;
Write('Press ENTER ...');
ReadLn;
End.
```

Figure 5-1.   Using the With statement with records

is an example of explicit reference because both the record name and the element name, separated by a period, appear in the assignment. In an implicit reference, using the reserved word **With**, you do not need to repeat the record name in each assignment statement. The assignment statement

Rec2 := Rec1;

assigns every element in Rec1 to the corresponding element in Rec2.

Implicit references can be nested so that one **With** statement refers to more than one record, as shown in Figure 5-2. The statement

With Rec2, Rec1 Do

allows the programmer to reference elements in both records implicitly. Problems can arise, however. In Figure 5-2, Rec1 and Rec2 both have an element "a". This ambiguous reference does not tell Turbo Pascal which record element is being referred to. Thus, the compiler assumes that the ambiguous element belongs to the last record that contains that element. In Figure 5-2, the assignment statement

a := a;

assumes that both elements are from Rec1. In short, it assumes that the statement means

Rec1.a := Rec1.a;

Variant Records

Turbo Pascal allows programmers to produce what are known as *variant records*. Variant records are records that permit different types of data to be stored in the same memory location; they are a combination of a record type and the Turbo Pascal logical operator **Case**. Variant records are explored more fully in Chapter 6 under the general discussion of the **Case** operator.

Arrays

Any data type, whether standard or user defined, can be extended into an *array*. An array is a variable that repeats a data type a specified number of times. To define an array, follow this general format:

Variable Name :
      Array [lower limit .. upper limit] of Data Type;

```
Program X;
Uses CRT;
Var
  Rec1 : Record
    a : String[20];
    b : Integer;
    c : Real;
    End;

  Rec2 : Record
    a : String[20];
    r1, r2 : Real;
    End;

Begin
ClrScr;

With Rec1 Do
  a := 'sss';
  b := 1;
  c := 123.23;
  End;

With Rec2 Do
  Begin
  a := 'xxx';
  r1 := 20.0;
  r2 := 10.0;
  End;

With Rec2, Rec1 Do
  Begin
  a := a;
  c := r1 * r2;
  End;

With Rec2 Do
With Rec1 Do
  Begin
  a := a;
  c := r1 * r2;
  End;

With Rec1 Do
  Begin
  WriteLn(a);
  WriteLn(b);
  WriteLn(c);
  End;

WriteLn;
Write('Press ENTER ...');
ReadLn;
End.
```

These segments do exactly the same thing

Figure 5-2.   Nested With statements

The lower limit and the upper limit are any legal integer values in which the upper limit is greater than the lower limit.

Arrays are usually used when a program includes a list of recurring elements. For example, to hold a year's worth of stock prices, define the array as follows:

Price : Array [1 .. 365] of Real;

To refer to a specific price, indicate which element in the array you want. For example, to set the price on the tenth day in the year, you would use

Price[10] := 34.50;

The lower limit on an array does not have to be 1. It makes more sense to start the array at a value that corresponds to the context of your data. If you were measuring the conductivity of a metal with a temperature range of $-100°$ to $+100°$ C, you would define the array as

Conductivity : Array [−100 .. 100] of Real;

The range of the array now matches the functional range of temperatures (assuming that the measurements will be taken at whole-number intervals).

Another example of an array that matches its data is one that stores the average income of people age 35 to 65. An array defined as

Average Income : Array [35 .. 65] of Real;

would do the trick.

Multidimensional Arrays

Any arrays defined to have more than one dimension are considered to be *multidimensional arrays*, although they rarely exceed three dimensions. Two-dimensional arrays, sometimes called *matrices,* are quite common, especially in multivariate statistics. For example, when measuring the conductivity of a metal, the following two-dimensional arrays could be used, assuming that the temperature intervals are not whole numbers:

Temp _ Conductivity : Array [1 .. 200,1 .. 2] of Real;

The best way to think about this array is to visualize a table of columns and rows: the first dimension in the array (1 .. 200) provides the rows, and the second dimension (1 .. 2) provides the columns. Going row by row, all you need to do is put the temperatures in one column and the matching conductivity ratings in another, as shown in Table 5-1.

To assign a value in a multidimensional array, specify both dimensions, as shown in the following two statements:

Temp _ Conductivity[1,1] := −99.34;
Temp _ Conductivity[1,2] := 12.3;

	1 Temperature	2 Conductivity
1	− 99.34	12.3
2	− 97.76	12.2
3	− 96.01	11.9
.		
.		
.		
200	99.01	2.9

Table 5-1.   Sample Temperature and Conductivity Readings

To refer to the first pair of observations, specify both the row and the column. In this example, the first temperature reading is "Temp_Conductivity[1,1]," while the corresponding conductivity rating is "Temp_Conductivity[1,2]."

Substitute for Multidimensional Arrays

The examples of multidimensional arrays should make one thing clear—it is hard to keep track of what values are in which column. There is simply no clue given in the array itself. Because it is preferable to deal with variables that have meaningful names, Turbo Pascal provides an alternative to multidimensional arrays: arrays of records. The following example shows why these arrays are better than the multidimensional ones:

```
Observation : Array [1..200] Of Record
  Temperature : Real;
  Conductivity : Real;
  End;
```

Arrays of records create clear definitions; it is immediately apparent that the **Record** definition in the preceding illustration defines a series of observations consisting of temperatures and conductivities. These can be referred to by name in the following manner:

Observation[1].Temperature
Observation[1].Conductivity

Whenever you use multidimensional arrays, consider the possibility that you may be able to substitute an array of a record type that does the job, yet improves program clarity.

Arithmetic and Logic in Turbo Pascal

Arithmetic in Turbo Pascal
Logical Operators

Intelligence and number-crunching power are characteristics long associated with computers, an association reinforced by the names of such computer languages as FORTRAN (from Formula Translator) and ALGOL (from Algorithmic Logic). Pascal continues in this vein: it is named after Blaise Pascal, a 17th-century mathematician, and provides powerful arithmetic functions and extensive logic commands.

Arithmetic in Turbo Pascal

Turbo Pascal arithmetic is based on the concept of an expression or equation. An expression consists of a combination of identifiers, numeric values and functions, and operators, all of which result in a specific numeric value. If that sounds too complicated, consider this well-known expression:

$$2 + 2$$

This has all the elements of a mathematical expression—numeric values and an operator (the plus sign)—but it is not a Pascal statement. In Pascal, a mathematical expression must be part of either an assignment statement or a logical statement. A numerical assignment statement computes a value from an expression and stores the value in a numeric variable. An example of an arithmetic assignment statement is

Result := 2 + 2;

When this statement is executed, Turbo Pascal calculates the right-hand side of the statement and assigns the result in the variable **Result**.

An arithmetic expression in a logical statement is similar, except that the expression does not result in a numerical value but in a TRUE or FALSE condition. For example, the logical statement

If Result = (2 + 2) Then . . .

does not change the value in the variable **Result**. Rather, Turbo Pascal adds the two numbers and compares them to the value that is already in **Result**. In this case, if **Result** is equal to 4, then the expression is TRUE; if NOT, it is FALSE. Logical structures are discussed more fully later in this chapter.

Note that the assignment operator in Pascal is :=, while the logical operator is =. This might seem to be a trivial distinction, but there is a rationale behind it: an assignment statement does not imply equality. In arithmetic, a statement such as X = X + 1 is simply incorrect. In Pascal, however, the statement **X := X + 1** is perfectly legal. Remember, this assignment statement does not say, "X is equal to X + 1"; it says, "Take the value of X + 1 and assign it to the variable X."

Integer and Real Expressions

In Turbo Pascal, arithmetic expressions result in either an **Integer** value or a **Real** value. For an expression to yield an **Integer** result, two conditions must be met. First, all the operands in the expression must be integers (or floating-point variables converted to integers with the **Trunc** or **Round** functions). Second, if division is performed, the **Div** operator must be used instead of the **/** character.

Any expression that is not an **Integer** expression is, by default, a **Real** expression. Even if an expression has 50 **Integer** operands and only 1 **Real** operand, the expression results in a **Real** value. The following illustration shows examples of both **Integer** and **Real** expressions:

```
Program Math1;
Var
  i,j,k : Integer;
  x,y,z : Real;

Begin

j := 2;

i := 1 + j;
j := 3 Div i;                     ◄─┐  Integer expressions
k := (i + j) Div (3 * j);         ◄─┘

WriteLn(i,' ',j,' ',k);

j := 2;

x := 1.0 + j;
y := 3 / i;                       ◄─┐  Real expressions
z := (i + j) Div (3 * j);         ◄─┘
WriteLn(x:2:2,' ',y:2:2,' ',z:2:2);
WriteLn;
Write('Press ENTER...');
ReadLn;
End.
```

Hierarchy of Arithmetic Operators

The order of precedence dictates that multiplication and division are performed before addition and subtraction and that any operation in parentheses is done first. Turbo Pascal follows these rules: it has four hierarchical levels of arithmetic operators, as shown here:

Level 1: Unary Minus, Unary Plus   ◄─── *Highest priority*
Level 2: Parentheses
Level 3: Multiplication, Division
Level 4: Addition, Subtraction   ◄─── *Lowest priority*

A *unary minus* is the sign that directly precedes a number and indicates that the number is negative. For example, the minus sign in the number −3 is a unary minus. When used in arithmetic expressions, the unary minus can lead to statements such as

Result := 1 − −3

in which case, **Result** is equal to 4.

Turbo Pascal also supports the unary plus. While the unary plus has absolutely no impact on the value of the number, the fact that it is supported means that a statement such as

Result := 1 − +2

is perfectly legal. Please note, however, that the unary plus operator is not an indicator of absolute value (the absolute value of a negative number is its positive equivalent). If a unary plus precedes a variable with a negative value, the variable remains negative.

The second level in the hierarchy of Turbo Pascal arithmetic operators is parentheses. Following the order of precedence, operations within parentheses are executed before operations outside parentheses. To clarify this rule, consider the following two expressions:

A := 3 * 4 + 5;
A := 3 * (4 + 5);

In the first case, the multiplication operator takes precedence, so that 3 * 4 is evaluated first, yielding 12, and 5 is added to 12 for a final result of 17. In the second case, the operation within the parentheses takes precedence over the multiplication operator, so that 4 + 5 is evaluated first, yielding 9, and 9 is multiplied by 3 for a final result of 27.

You should use parentheses to increase clarity, even when they are not strictly necessary. For example, the following two expressions yield the same result, yet the parentheses in the latter make it more readable.

```
r := a + b * c * d + x + y / r;
r := a + (b * c * d) + x + (y / r);
```

Integer Versus Real Arithmetic

The last two levels in the hierarchy of arithmetic operators are multiplication and division (level 3) and addition and subtraction (level 4). Here Turbo Pascal's strong typing forces a separation between integer arithmetic and real arithmetic.

Integer Arithmetic

The rules of integer arithmetic apply when an expression is assigned to an **Integer** variable. All operators in an integer expression must be either **Integer**s or **Real**s converted to **Integer**s using the Turbo Pascal standard functions **Round** or **Trunc**. The program shown next provides examples of both legal and illegal integer arithmetic statements.

```
Program IntegerMath;
Var
   i,j,k : Integer;
   x,y,z : Real;

Begin

(* Legal Statements*)

i := 10 + j;
j := i Div k;
k := j + Round(x) + Trunc(y/z);
WriteLn('i = ',i);
WriteLn('j = ',j);
WriteLn('k = ',k);
WriteLn;
Write('Press ENTER...');
ReadLn;

(* Illegal Statements*)

{
i := 10.0 + j;
j := i / k;
k := j + x + y / z;
}

End.
```

Note that numeric literals are not allowed to have decimal places in integer expressions.

Round and **Trunc** are Turbo Pascal standard functions that convert real values into integer values, but in slightly different ways. The **Round** function rounds a real value to the nearest integer. If the decimal portion is below 0.5, the real value is rounded down; otherwise, it is rounded up. For example, the result of **Round**(10.49) is the integer value **10**, while **Round**(10.5) returns the value **11**.

The **Trunc** standard function truncates a real value, chopping off any decimal places. Therefore, the result of **Trunc**(10.99) is **10**. With the **Round** and **Trunc** standard functions, you can freely mix **Real**s within **Integer** expressions. However, it is important that the value of the **Real** does not exceed the limits of an **Integer**.

Special Integer Operators

The integer-division operator **Div** is replaced by the slash character for floating-point arithmetic. The following integer operators, however, have no counterpart for floating-point operations: **Mod, And, Or, Xor, Shl, Shr.**

The **Mod** operator returns the remainder of integer division. For example, 7 **Div** 2 yields 3; the remainder of 1 is lost. The **Mod** operator, however, discards the dividend and returns the remainder. Therefore, 7 **Mod** 2 returns 1.

The remaining integer operators—**And, Or, Xor, Shl,** and **Shr**—are familiar to anyone who has used Assembler. These are also known as *bit-manipulation operators* since they are usually used not for arithmetic but to alter the values of specific bits in a byte or integer variable. To understand how these operators work, it is necessary to know what a byte and integer look like in memory.

A byte consists of eight bits, each bit capable of storing one of two values: 0 and 1. Because bits can store only two numbers, they are base-two numbers. Consider the equivalent binary and decimal numerical values in Table 6-1. (Binary numbers are typically indicated by a lowercase "b" appended to the digits.)

Decimal	Binary
0	00000000b
1	00000001b
2	00000010b
3	00000011b
10	00001010b
100	01100100b
255	11111111b

Table 6-1.   Binary and Decimal Equivalents

Note that the highest value a byte can hold is 255.

Integers consist of two bytes. As a result, their numerical range extends far beyond the limit of 255 that a single byte can hold. The largest possible two-byte integer value is 65,535, or 11111111 11111111b. In Turbo Pascal, however, the left-most bit in an integer determines the sign of the number; 0 indicates a positive number, 1 a negative number. As a result, the largest integer value in Turbo Pascal is 32,767, or 01111111 11111111b, and the smallest integer value is −32,768, or 11111111 11111111b. For simplicity, the bit-manipulation operators are illustrated with byte values rather than integers; the general concepts apply equally to both.

The And, Or, and Xor Operators

The **And**, **Or**, and **Xor** operators compare each bit in two different byte variables and return a third byte variable as the result. The value of the resulting byte depends on the type of the comparison.

The **And** operator compares each bit in two bytes one by one and stores the result in a third byte. If the comparison finds both bits are on, the corresponding bit in the third byte is also turned on (that is, set to a value of 1). If the bits compared are not both on, the corresponding bit in the third byte is turned off.

Figure 6-1 gives an example of the **And** command. Byte1 is

```
PROGRAM AndOperator;
VAR
   Byte1, Byte2, Byte3 : BYTE;
BEGIN
Byte1 := 77;
Byte2 := 62;
Byte3 := Byte1 AND Byte2;
WriteLn (Byte3);
END.
```

Bit position	7	6	5	4	3	2	1	0
Byte1	0	1	0	0	1	1	0	1
And	↓	↓	↓	↓	↓	↓	↓	↓
Byte2	0	0	1	1	1	1	1	0
Gives	↓	↓	↓	↓	↓	↓	↓	↓
Byte3	0	0	0	0	1	1	0	0

Figure 6-1. Bit manipulation using the And operator

ANDed with Byte2, yielding Byte3. Bit 0 in Byte1 is on, but it is off in Byte2. Because only one, and not both, of these bits is on, bit 0 in Byte3 is turned off. Bit position 2 is different in that it is on in both Byte1 and Byte2. Therefore, bit 2 in Byte3 is turned on.

Like the **And** operator, the **Or** operator compares each bit in two bytes and stores the result in a third byte. However, the bit in the third byte is turned on if the comparison finds either bit or both bits in Byte1 and Byte2 are on. The corresponding bit in the third byte is turned off only if both of the bits compared are off.

In Figure 6-2, Byte1 is **OR**ed with Byte2, yielding Byte3. Bit 0 in Byte1 is on, but in Byte2 it is off. Because the **Or** operator requires only one of the bits to be on, bit 0 in Byte3 is turned on. In this example, the only bit position that fails the **Or** test is bit 7. Because bit 7 is off in both Byte1 and Byte2, bit 7 in Byte3 is also turned off.

```
PROGRAM OrOperator;
VAR
   Byte1, Byte2, Byte3 : BYTE;
BEGIN
Byte1 := 77;
Byte2 := 62;
Byte3 := Byte1 OR Byte2;
WriteLn (Byte3);
END.
```

Bit position	7	6	5	4	3	2	1	0
Byte1	0	1	0	0	1	1	0	1
Or	↓	↓	↓	↓	↓	↓	↓	↓
Byte2	0	0	1	1	1	1	1	0
Gives	↓	↓	↓	↓	↓	↓	↓	↓
Byte3	0	1	1	1	1	1	1	1

Figure 6-2.   Bit manipulation using the Or operator

The **Xor** comparison is TRUE if one bit, and only one bit, is on between two bytes. If both bits are on or both bits are off, the comparison fails and the corresponding bit in the third byte is turned off.

In Figure 6-3, Byte1 is **XOR**ed with Byte2. Bit 0 is on in Byte1 and off in Byte2. Because only one of the bits is on, the comparison is TRUE, and bit 0 in Byte3 is turned on. On the other hand, bits 2 and 7 are turned off in Byte3 because bit 2 is on in both Byte1 and Byte2 and bit 7 is off in both bytes.

The Shl and Shr Operators

As their names suggest, the operators **Shift-left (Shl)** and **Shift-right (Shr)** shift the bits in a byte left or right. A byte can be shifted left or right a maximum of eight times, at which point all the bits are set to zero. When a byte is shifted left by 1, each bit in the byte moves one position to the left. The left-most bit is

```
PROGRAM XorOperator;
VAR
  Byte1, Byte2, Byte3 : BYTE;
BEGIN
Byte1 := 77;
Byte2 := 62;
Byte3 := Byte1 XOR Byte2;
WriteLn (Byte3);
END.
```

Bit position	7	6	5	4	3	2	1	0
Byte1	0	1	0	0	1	1	0	1
Xor	↓	↓	↓	↓	↓	↓	↓	↓
Byte2	0	0	1	1	1	1	1	0
Gives	↓	↓	↓	↓	↓	↓	↓	↓
Byte3	0	1	1	1	0	0	0	1

Figure 6-3.   Bit manipulation using the Xor operator

lost, and a zero appears in the right-most position, as follows:

```
{$R-}
Program ShiftLeft;
Var
  i : Byte;

Begin
i := 255;      (* i equals 11111111b *)
WriteLn('i = ',i);
i := i Shl 1;  (* i equals 11111110b *)
WriteLn('i = ',i);
i := i Shl 1;  (* i equals 11111100b *)
WriteLn('i = ',i);
i := i Shl 1;  (* i equals 11111000b *)
WriteLn('i = ',i);
i := i Shl 1;  (* i equals 11110000b *)
WriteLn('i = ',i);
i := i Shl 1;  (* i equals 11100000b *)
WriteLn('i = ',i);
i := i Shl 1;  (* i equals 11000000b *)
WriteLn('i = ',i);
i := i Shl 1;  (* i equals 10000000b *)
WriteLn('i = ',i);
i := i Shl 1;  (* i equals 00000000b *)
WriteLn('i = ',i);

WriteLn;
Write('Press ENTER...');
```

```
ReadLn;
End.
```

Shift-right (**Shr**) operates in the same way as **Shift-left**, but it works in the opposite direction. When a byte is shifted to the right, the right-most bit is lost and the left-most bit is set to zero.

While they are considered arithmetic in nature, bit-manipulation operators are not often used for computations. More often, they test or set specific bit values. The following listing contains several procedures that use these bit-manipulation operators.

```
Program BinaryDemo;
Uses CRT;
Type
  Binstr = String[8];
Var
  i : Integer;
  b : Byte;

(*******************************************************)

Function Binary(b : Byte) : Binstr;
{
This function accepts a byte parameter and returns
a string of eight ones and zeros indicating the binary
form of the byte.
}
Var
  i : Integer;
  bt : Byte;
  s : Binstr;
Begin
bt := $01;
s := '';
For i := 1 To 8 Do
  Begin
  If (b And bt) > 0 Then
    s := '1' + s
  Else
    s := '0' + s;
  {$R-}
  bt := bt Shl 1;
  {$R+}
  End;
Binary := s;
End;

(*******************************************************)
```

```
Procedure SetBit(Position, Value : Byte;
                 Var ChangeByte : Byte);
{
This procedure sets a particular bit in the byte ChangeByte
to either 1 or 0. The bit is specified by Position, which
can range from 0 to 7.
}
Var
   bt : Byte;
Begin
bt := $01;
bt := bt Shl Position;
If Value = 1 Then
   ChangeByte := ChangeByte Or bt
Else
   Begin
   bt := bt Xor $FF;
   ChangeByte := ChangeByte And bt;
   End;
End;

(*******************************************************)

Function BitOn(Position, TestByte : Byte) : Boolean;
{
This function tests if a bit in TestByte is turned on
(equal to one). The bit to test is indicated by the parameter
Position, which can range from 0 (right-most bit) to 7
(left-most bit). If the bit indicated by Position is
turned on, then BitOn returns TRUE.
}
Var
   bt : byte;
Begin
bt := $01;
bt := bt Shl Position;
BitOn := (bt And TestByte) > 0;
End;

(*******************************************************)

Begin
ClrScr;
WriteLn;
WriteLn('Demonstrate binary conversion.');
Write('Enter a number (0 - 255): ');
ReadLn(b);
WriteLn('Binary equivalent is: ',binary(b));
WriteLn;
Write('Press ENTER...');
ReadLn;

ClrScr;
WriteLn;
WriteLn('Demonstrate SetBit procedure.');
WriteLn;
```

```
b := 0;
For i := 0 To 7 Do
  Begin
  SetBit(i,1,b);
  WriteLn(binary(b));
  End;

For i := 0 To 7 Do
  Begin
  SetBit(i,0,b);
  WriteLn(binary(b));
  End;
WriteLn;
Write('Press ENTER...');
ReadLn;

ClrScr;
WriteLn;
Write('Enter a number (0 - 255): ');
ReadLn(b);
WriteLn('Binary value is ',binary(b));
If BitOn(0,b) Then
  WriteLn('Bit 0 is on.')
Else
  WriteLn('Bit 0 is off.');
WriteLn;
Write('Press ENTER...');
ReadLn;
End.
```

Procedure **Binary** converts a byte value into a string of ones and zeros that represent the bits. Procedure **SetBit** turns on or off any individual bit in a byte. The last procedure, the Boolean function **BitOn**, tests whether a particular bit in a byte is turned on.

Real Arithmetic

An arithmetic expression yields a floating-point result under two conditions: when the expression contains any floating-point operands and when division is executed with the slash (*/*) operator. Floating-point operands are any identifiers defined as **Real** or any numeric literal with decimal places (for example, 10.2). The following program, which comprises examples of both integer and floating-point expressions, highlights the small differences between the two expression types.

```
{$N-,E-}
Program Math1;
Uses CRT;
Var
  i,j,k : Integer;
  x,y,z : Real;

Begin
ClrScr;
i := 1;
k := 3;
z := 3.324;

j := i Div k; (* integer expression *)
x := i / k;   (* floating-point expression *)
WriteLn('Integer math.  i Div k = ',j);
WriteLn('Real math.     i / k   = ',x:0:4);
WriteLn;

j := i + 3;   (* integer expression *)
x := i + 3.0; (* floating-point expression *)
WriteLn('Integer math.  i + 3 = ',j);
WriteLn('Real math.     i + 3.0 = ',x:0:4);
WriteLn;

j := i + k;   (* integer expression *)
x := i + z;   (* floating-point expression *)
WriteLn('Integer math.  i + k = ',j);
WriteLn('Real math.     i + z = ',x:0:4);
WriteLn;
WriteLn;


x := 10 * 10;
WriteLn('Valid conversion to real.  10 * 10 =   ',x:0:2);
WriteLn;

i := 10000;
j := 10000;
x := i * j;
WriteLn('i = 10000');
WriteLn('j = 10000');
WriteLn('Invalid conversion to real.  i * j = ',x:0:2);
WriteLn;

i := 10000;
j := 10000;
x := 1.0 * i * j;
WriteLn('i = 10000');
WriteLn('j = 10000');
WriteLn('Valid conversion to real.  1.0 * i * j = ',x:0:2);
WriteLn;
Write('Press ENTER...');
ReadLn;
End.
```

The preceding listing points out a potential source of error in programs. Consider the assignment statement

```
x := 10 * 10;
```

The right side of the statement, which is an integer expression, is evaluated as an integer before being converted into a floating-point value.

A problem arises when the result of the integer expression exceeds the maximum integer value of 32,767. In the following statements

```
i := 10000;
j := 10000;
x := i * j;
```

the integer expression overflows the maximum integer value before being converted to a **Real**. As a result, **x** is incorrectly assigned the value −7936. To eliminate this error, include a floating-point operand in the expression. The expression is then evaluated as a floating-point expression.

In the preceding program listing, the solution is to multiply the expression by 1.0. This forces the expression to be evaluated as a floating-point value, thereby producing the correct result.

Arithmetic Functions

Turbo Pascal provides a rich set of standard arithmetic functions that give easy access to complex computations. These are as follows:

Abs(num) Returns the absolute value of the number passed as a parameter. The value passed can be either **Integer** or **Real**, and the value returned will match the type of the parameter: If **num** is an **Integer**, then **Abs** returns an **Integer**.

Arctan(num) Returns the arctangent of **num**. **Num** can be either **Real** or **Integer**, but the result is **Real**.

Cos(num)   Returns the cosine of **num**, where **num** is either **Real** or **Integer**, and the result is **Real**.

Exp(num)   Computes the exponential of **num**. **Num** is **Real** or **Integer**; the result is **Real**. When using standard **Reals** (no emulation or 8087), **Exp** produces an overflow error when **num** is greater than 88 or less than −88.

Frac(num)   This is the fractional part of **num**. **Num** can be **Real** or **Integer**, although **Integers** always return a value of zero. The result is **Real**. When using standard **Reals** (no emulation or 8087), **Frac** returns zero for any number raised to 1.0E10 power.

Hi(num)   Returns an **Integer** whose high-order byte is zero and whose low-order byte contains the high-order byte of **num**. **Num** must be of type **Integer**.

Int(num)   Returns the nonfractional portion of **num**. **Num** may be either **Real** or **Integer**. If **num** is **Integer**, the function does not change the value, but it does produce a **Real**.

Lo(num)   Returns an **Integer** whose high-order byte is zero and whose low-order byte contains the low-order byte of **num**. **Num** must be of type **Integer**.

Ln(num)   Calculates the natural logarithm of **num**. **Num** can be either **Real** or **Integer**, but it must be greater than zero.

Ord(var)   Returns the relative value of any scalar, including type **Char**. The result is of type **Integer**.

Pred(num)   Returns the value of the **Integer**-type **num** decremented by one. The result is of type **Integer**.

Random   Returns a random value than one but greater than or equal to 0. The result is of type **Real**.

Random(num) Computes a random number from an **Integer**-type **num**. The random number will be of type **Integer**, and its value will be greater than or equal to zero but less than **num**.

Round(num)   Returns the value of **num**, rounded to the nearest whole number. **Num** is **Real**, while the result is of type **Integer**.

Sin(num)   Computes the sine of **num**. **Num** can be **Real** or **Integer**; the result is **Real**.

Sqr(num)   Returns the square of **num**. **Num** can be **Real** or **Integer**; the result is **Real**. When using standard **Real**s (no emulation or 8087), an overflow error will occur when **num** exceeds 1.0E18.

Sqrt(num)   Computes the square root of **num**. **Num** can be **Real** or **Integer**; the result is **Real**.

Succ(num)   Returns the value of the **Integer**-type **num** incremented by one. The result is of type **Integer**.

Trunc(num)   Returns the value of **num** with the decimal portion removed. **Num** is **Real**, and the result is **Integer**.

You can also write your own numeric functions. The following listing contains two valuable numerical functions; the first computes the cumulative normal probability density function of a number and the second raises a number to a power.

```
{$N+,E+}

Program NumberFunctions;
Uses CRT;

{$IFOPT N+}
Type
  Float = Double;
{$ELSE}
  Float = Real;
{$ENDIF}
```

```
(***********************************************)

Function n(x : Float) : Float;
(* Computes the Cumulative Normal *)
(* Probability Density Function    *)
Var
  x2, t, y1, y2, y3, y4, y5, z, R : Float;

Begin
y1 := 1.0/(1.0+(0.2316419*Abs(x)));
y2 := y1*y1;
y3 := y2*y1;
y4 := y3*y1;
y5 := y4*y1;
x2 := x*x;

z := 0.3989423 * Exp(-x2/2.0);

R := (1.330274*y5) -
     (1.821256*y4) +
     (1.781478*y3) -
     (0.356538*y2) +
     (0.3193815*y1);

t := 1.0 - (z*R);

If x > 0 Then
  n := t
Else
  n := 1-t;
End;

(*****************************************************)

Function X_To_Y(x, y : Float) : Float;
Var
  r : Float;

Begin
r := y*Ln(x);
X_To_Y := Exp(r);
End;

(*****************************************************)

Begin
ClrScr;
WriteLn('3 to power of 2 is: ',X_To_Y(3, 2):0:4);
WriteLn;
WriteLn('Cumulative normal probability of 1.96 = ',
        n(1.96):0:4);
WriteLn;
Write('Press ENTER...');
ReadLn;
End.
```

Notice the use of conditional compilation in this example program. If the {N+} directive is present (activating the 8087 mode), the data type **Float** represents a **Double** data type. If, however, the {$N+} is not present, the **Float** type is declared to be a standard **Real**. This use of conditional compilation lets you choose the degree of numerical precision throughout a program simply by changing a compiler directive.

Logical Operators

Turbo Pascal supports the following logical operators:

=	Equal to
< >	Not equal to
<	Less than
>	Greater than
< =	Less than or equal to
> =	Greater than or equal to
Not	Negation of condition
Case	Multiple comparison

Strictly speaking, **Case** is a statement and not an operator. Yet it is so closely allied with the logical operators discussed in this section that it makes sense to include it here.

Logical operators are generally used in **If-Then** statements, which test to determine whether adjacent statements should be executed. This is an example of an **If-Then** statement:

```
If a > b Then
  WriteLn('A is greater than B');
```

In this example, **a** and **b** are **Integer** variables. If **a** equals 5 and **b** equals 2, then the test a > b will be TRUE, and the line following the statement will execute.

The **Not** operator negates the result of a logical test. For example, if **a > b** is evaluated as TRUE, then **Not a > b** will be FALSE. For any test using the **Not** operator, there is an equivalent test without it. For example, **Not a > b** is the same as **a <= b**.

An **If-Then** statement can control the execution of more than one statement by using **Begin** and **End** to create a block of code. In the following example, if **a** is greater than **b**, all the statements between the **Begin** and **End** statements will execute:

```
If a > b Then
  Begin
  WriteLn('A is greater than B');
  b := a;
  End;
```

The **If-Then** statement can be extended with the Turbo Pascal reserved word **Else**. If the condition tested fails, the program executes the code following the **Else** clause, as shown in this example:

```
If a > b Then
  Begin
  WriteLn('A is greater than B');
  b := a;
  End
Else
  Begin
  WriteLn('A is not greater than B');
  a := b;
  End;
```

Note that the statement preceding the **Else** clause is not terminated with a semicolon. Turbo Pascal considers the **Else** clause to be a continuation of one long statement, so a semicolon indicating the end of a statement is inappropriate.

To create *multiple-condition branching,* you can give an **If-Then** statement more than one **Else** clause. This is useful when you test a variable against many possible values.

```
If a = 1 Then
  Begin
  WriteLn('A equals 1');
  End
```

```
Else If a = 2 Then
   Begin
   WriteLn('A equals 2');
   End
Else If a = 3 Then
   Begin
   WriteLn('A equals 3');
   End
Else If a = 4 Then
   Begin
   WriteLn('A equals 4');
   End;
```

Case Operator

An alternative to multiple **Else-If** statements is the **Case** statement, which is specifically designed to handle tests that require multiple conditions. A typical **Case** statement looks like this:

```
Case a of

1 :     WriteLn('a equals 1');

2..4 : Begin
        WriteLn('a is between 2 and 4');
        WriteLn('Case statements can specify ranges.');
        End;

5 :     WriteLn('a equals 5');

Else Begin
        WriteLn('a is not between 1 and 5');
        WriteLn('The case statement supports the Else clause');
        End;

End;
```

Case statements are easier to read than extended **If-Then-Else** statements and are more flexible because they allow you to specify a range of values, such as $2..4$.

Note, however, that because it uses only simple data types, the **Case** statement is more restrictive than the **If-Then** statement. Therefore, you cannot use **Real** or **String** data types with the **Case** statement.

Using the Case Operator in Variant Records

Declaring **Record** data types is discussed in Chapter 5. This section discusses how the **Case** operator can be used within the **Record** data type to create what is called a *variant record*.

Variant records are intended to conserve space as well as create data structures that more precisely reflect the entities they represent. For example, consider the use of the variant record in the following listing:

```
Program VariantRecord;
Uses CRT;
Type
  VehicleType = (Car, Boat, Plane);
  VehicleRec = Record
    IDnumber : Integer;
    Price    : Real;
    Weight   : Real;

    Case Kind : VehicleType Of
    Car : (MilesPerGallon : Integer;
           Odometer : Real);

    Boat : (Displacement : Real;
            Length : Integer);

    Plane : (Engines : Integer;
             Seats : Integer);

  End;

Var
  Vehicle : VehicleRec;

Begin
ClrScr;

Vehicle.IDnumber := 123;
Vehicle.Price := 12000;
Vehicle.Weight := 1200;
Vehicle.Kind := Car;
Vehicle.MilesPerGallon := 21;
Vehicle.Odometer := 75000.0;

With Vehicle Do
  Begin
    Case Kind Of

    Car:
      Begin
      WriteLn('Kind = Car');
      WriteLn('Miles per gallon = ',MilesPerGallon);
```

```
      WriteLn('Odometer = ',Odometer:0:1);
      End;

   Boat:
     Begin
     WriteLn('Kind = Boat');
     WriteLn('Displacement = ',Displacement);
     WriteLn('Length = ',Length);
     End;

   Plane:
     Begin
     WriteLn('Kind = Plane');
     WriteLn('Engines = ',Engines);
     WriteLn('Seats = ',Seats);
     End;

   End;
  End;
WriteLn;
Write('Press ENTER...');
ReadLn;
End.
```

Notice how the record contains separate sections pertaining to different types of transportation. Because of this flexibility, variant records can cover broad classes of categorical data, yet still retain specific detailed information.

The fields under Car, Boat, and Plane comprise a total of four **Integers** and two **Reals**—20 bytes in total. But the variant portions of the records share the same memory. Since the largest single block of memory used by a variant portion of the record is eight bytes (a **Real** and an **Integer**), only eight bytes are allocated to the variant part of the record.

The field named Kind is known as the *tag field*. The tag field helps keep track of which part of the variant record is in use. When a tag field is used, the variant record is known as a *discriminated union* because the tag field can discriminate which portion of the variant record should be used.

Another type of variant record is the *free union*, or a variant record that does not have a tag field. COBOL programmers will feel at home with free unions because they resemble COBOL's redefined fields.

The following program example presents an example of a free-union variant record.

```
Program FreeUnion;
Uses CRT;
Type
  CharByte = Record
    Case Integer Of
    1 : (Characters : Array [1..10] Of Char);
    2 : (Numbers : Array [1..10] Of Byte);
    End;

Var
  CB : CharByte;
Begin
ClrScr;
With CB Do Characters[1] := 'A';
With CB Do
  WriteLn('Numeric value of character A is: ',Numbers[1]);
WriteLn;
Write('Press ENTER...');
ReadLn;
End.
```

Notice that the variant record definition has no tag field; only a data type, **Integer**, is specified. The lack of a tag field means no tag value is stored and that you can refer to any of the variant elements without restriction.

This example program is special because the variant record defines one array in two different ways. The 10-byte array in one line is defined as an array of characters, while in the next line it is defined as an array of bytes. Since these arrays share the same memory (because they are the variant part of the record), you can refer to the elements in the arrays as either characters or numbers. This is demonstrated in the program block. Notice where a character is assigned to the first element in the array using the identifier **Characters**, and then the element is written out as a number using the identifier **Numbers**.

Program Control Structures

Condition Statements
Decision Making and Conditional Branching
Conditional Branching with the Case Statement
Repetitive Control Structures
Unstructured Branching

This chapter discusses the various control structures Pascal provides, the ways they are used, and their good and bad points.

The least complicated Turbo Pascal program starts at the first **Begin** statement of the program block, executes each statement in order, and stops when it hits the final **End** statement. This straightforward program structure is illustrated in the following program:

```
Program PayRoll;
Uses CRT;
Var
  TotalPay,
  HourlyRate,
  HoursWorked : Real;

Begin
ClrScr;
Write('Enter your hourly rate: ');
ReadLn(HourlyRate);
Write('Enter the number of hours you worked: ');
ReadLn(HoursWorked);
TotalPay := HourlyRate * HoursWorked;
WriteLn('Your total pay is: $',TotalPay:0:2);
WriteLn;
Write('Press ENTER...');
ReadLn;
End.
```

Programming tasks can rarely be expressed in such simple terms, however. The preceding program, for example, does not take into account that people often work more than 40 hours per week, entitling them to overtime pay.

You can express additional complexity by using *control structures*. Control structures give programs the ability to act differently under different situations. Adding a control structure (in this case, the **If-Then** statement) to the preceding program gives it the ability to compute overtime pay:

```
Program PayRoll2;
Uses CRT;
Var
  TotalPay,
  HourlyRate,
  HoursWorked,
  OvertimeHours : Real;

Begin
ClrScr;
Write('Enter your hourly rate: ');
ReadLn(HourlyRate);
Write('Enter the number of hours you worked: ');
ReadLn(HoursWorked);

OvertimeHours := 0.0;
If (HoursWorked > 40.0) Then
  Begin
  OvertimeHours := HoursWorked - 40.0;
  HoursWorked := 40.0;
  End;

TotalPay := (HourlyRate * HoursWorked) +
            (1.5 * HourlyRate * OvertimeHours);

WriteLn('Your total pay is: $',TotalPay:0:2);
WriteLn;
Write('Press ENTER...');
ReadLn;
End.
```

Here, the **If-Then** statement tests whether an individual put in any overtime by comparing the number of hours worked to 40. If the number of hours is greater than 40, overtime pay is clearly due. The expanded equation includes the calculation of overtime pay at 1.5 times the standard rate.

Condition Statements

All Turbo Pascal control structures, with the major exception of the **Goto** statement, have one thing in common: they do something based on the evaluation of a *condition statement.* A condition statement, also known as a *Boolean statement,* is any expression that results in either a true or false condition. In **For-Do** statements, explained later in this chapter, the condition is implied, but for all other control structures (**If-Then, While-Do, Repeat-Until**), the condition statement is explicitly defined.

Condition statements can consist of direct comparisons:

```
age > 12
name = 'Jones'
x < y
```

or they can include calculations:

```
x > (y * 12)
(x-15) <> (y * 12) + Sqr(z)
```

or they might have multiple conditions:

```
(age > 12) And (name = 'Jones');
```

All Boolean expressions have a common element: they have a left side that is compared with a right side using a logical operator. Logical operators were discussed briefly in Chapter 6, but are presented here again:

>	Greater than
<	Less than
>=	Greater than or equal to
<=	Less than or equal to
=	Equal to
<>	Not equal to

These operators can be used to compare any two expressions when the operands are compatible. For example, it is illegal to compare a **Real** with a **String**, or a **String** with an **Integer**. You can, however, mix **Reals**, **Integers**, and **Byte**s in Boolean expressions because they are all numeric types.

Simple Boolean expressions, those that use only one operator, are easy to understand. For example, the Boolean expression (**i** > 0) is clearly understood to mean "**i** is greater than 0." Complications arise, however, when you combine multiple expressions with the **And** or **Or** operators. The following program illustrates the kind of unexpected results that can occur:

```
Program IntegerOr;
Uses CRT;
Var
   i,j : Integer;

Begin
ClrScr;
i := 9;
j := -47;
WriteLn('i Or j > 0  = ',i Or j > 0);
WriteLn;
WriteLn('(i > 0) Or (j > 0)  = ',(i > 0) Or (j > 0));
WriteLn;
Write('Press ENTER...');
ReadLn;
End.
```

This program writes out the result of two Boolean expressions. Both expressions are legal and appear to test if either **i** or **j** is greater than zero. Since **i** is assigned a value greater than zero, you might expect both expressions to be true. Appearances can be deceiving, however: the result of the first Boolean expression is false.

To understand why the first expression is false, you must understand Turbo Pascal's hierarchy of operators. Arithmetic operators (**+**, **−**, *****, **/**, **Div**) are always executed before logical operators (**And**, **Or**, **Xor**). The **And** and **Or** operators, however, can serve as either arithmetic or logical operators, depending on how they are used. In the preceding example, the **Or** operator is positioned between two integers, which tells Turbo Pascal to treat it as an arithmetic **Or**. When **i** equals 9 and **j** equals −47, the arithmetic result of **i Or j** is −39. Since −39 is less than 0, the result of the Boolean expression is false.

The program's second Boolean expression, on the other hand, separates the tests of **i** and **j** into two distinct Boolean expressions and clarifies the separation with parentheses. (In general, parentheses make Boolean expressions more readable and less prone to error.) In this case, the **Or** operator is treated as a logical operator. First **i** is compared with 0, which results in TRUE. Then **j** is compared with 0, resulting in FALSE. Finally, the two results are combined with the **Or** operator, giving an overall true result.

The Not Operator

The **Not** operator negates a Boolean expression. If the result is TRUE, the **Not** operator reverses the result to FALSE. For example, (10 > 0) is TRUE, but **Not** (10 > 0) is FALSE.

While the **Not** operator can be useful, it is never required. For every Boolean expression that uses the **Not** operator, there is an equivalent expression that does not. For example, the expression **Not (age > 65)** can be replaced by the expression (**age** <= 65). The **Not** operator sometimes increases the readability of a Boolean expression, but it is better to avoid it because it unnecessarily complicates a Boolean expression and thus increases the possibility of introducing errors in your program.

Boolean Functions in Control Structures

If a control statement requires an especially complex Boolean expression or if the same Boolean expression is used in many control statements throughout your program, you should create a Boolean function that contains the expression. Using the Boolean function in place of the expression decreases your coding and reduces errors. For example, the following program uses the Boolean function **Qualifies** to determine whether a potential site for a store is a good candidate.

```
Program SiteEvaluation;
Uses CRT;
Var
  CarsPerHour,
  PopulationDensity,
  TaxRate,
  LandCostPerSquareFoot,
  LaborCostPerHour : Real;

(***************************************************)

Function Qualifies : Boolean;
Begin
Qualifies := (CarsPerHour > 1000) And
             (PopulationDensity > 5000) And
             (TaxRate < 0.10) And
             (LandCostPerSquareFoot < 150) And
             (LaborCostPerHour < 6.50)
End;

(***************************************************)

Begin
ClrScr;
Write('Enter number of cars per hour: ');
ReadLn(CarsPerHour);
Write('Enter population density per square mile: ');
ReadLn(PopulationDensity);
Write('Enter Tax Rate: ');
ReadLn(TaxRate);
Write('Enter land cost per square foot: ');
ReadLn(LandCostPerSquareFoot);
Write('Enter labor cost per hour: ');
ReadLn(LaborCostPerHour);
WriteLn;
If Qualifies Then
  WriteLn('Good site!')
Else
  WriteLn('Forget it.');
WriteLn;
Write('Press ENTER...');
ReadLn;
End.
```

The following Boolean expression is complex:

```
(CarsPerHour > 1000) And
(PopulationDensity > 5000) And
(TaxRate < 0.10) And
(LandCostPerSquareFoot < 150) And
(LaborCostPerHour < 6.50)
```

By isolating it in a function, you can substitute the identifier **Qualifies** wherever the full Boolean statement would normally go. This reduces the possibility of error (and the amount of typing) and makes it easier to modify the program since all changes can be done in the function itself; these modifications are automatically reflected throughout the program.

Decision Making and Conditional Branching

Based on information it receives, a program can choose between different courses of action. However, if you want your program to make decisions, you must specifically tell it what information it will use, how to evaluate the information, and what course of action to follow. This type of programming is often called *conditional branching* because programs that use this method branch in different directions based on a condition (that is, the evaluation of data).

The If-Then Statement

The simplest form of conditional branching is the **If-Then** statement, which causes a program to execute a block of code if a condition is true. This process is described schematically in Figure 7-1.

The first thing an **If-Then** statement does is to evaluate the information provided to it in the form of a Boolean statement. If, for example, the Boolean statement is (**Age** > 21), the information is contained in the variable **Age**, which is compared with the test value 21.

The evaluation produces one of two possible results — true or false. If the statement is true, the program executes the block of code that immediately follows the **If-Then** statement. If the result is false, the program skips the block. Consider the following example.

```
Program TestAge;
Uses CRT;
Var
  Age : Integer;

Begin
ClrScr;
Write('Enter Age: ');
ReadLn(Age);
If (Age >= 21) Then
  WriteLn('This person is not a minor.');
WriteLn;
Write('Press ENTER...');
ReadLn;
End.
```

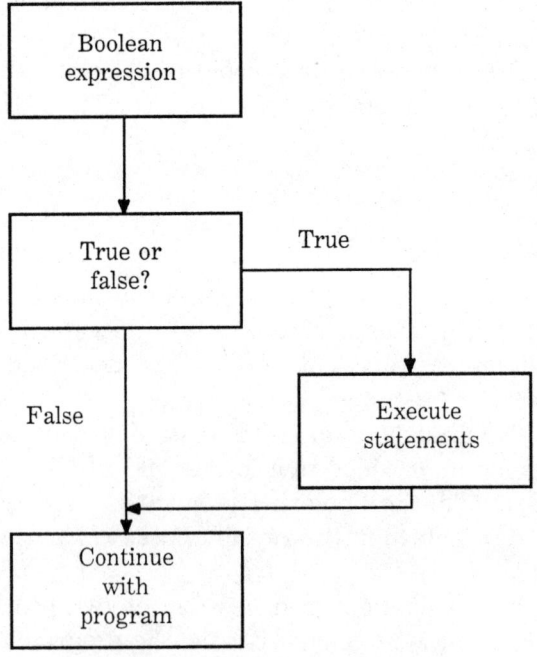

Figure 7-1.   Flowchart of If-Then statement

The program asks the user to enter a number (an age), and then the **If-Then** statement tests to see if **Age** is greater than or equal to 21. If the result of the test is true, the program executes the statement

WriteLn('This person is not a minor');

The program executes the second **WriteLn** statement regardless of the result of the **If-Then** statement. In this example, only one statement follows the **If-Then** test. If you want to conditionally execute more than one statement, use **Begin** and **End** to indicate what statements are included. For example, the expanded version of **TestAge**, shown here, writes two lines when **Age** is greater than or equal to 21:

```
Program TestAge;
Uses CRT;
Var
  Age : Integer;

Begin
ClrScr;
Write('Enter Age: ');
ReadLn(Age);
If (Age >= 21) Then
  Begin
  WriteLn('This person is not a minor.');
  WriteLn('This person is ',Age,' years old.');
  End;
WriteLn;
Write('Press ENTER...');
ReadLn;
End.
```

The **Begin** and **End** statements tell Turbo Pascal to execute both of the enclosed **WriteLn** statements when **Age** is greater than or equal to 21. Although the **Begin** and **End** statements are not required when only one statement is to be executed conditionally, you might want to include them for the sake of program clarity and consistency.

The If-Then-Else Statement

The **If-Then** statement provides just one branch, which executes when the Boolean statement is true. Many times, a program requires two branches: one that executes if true, the other if false. This situation is shown in Figure 7-2, where a program executes different blocks of code depending on the outcome of an evaluation.

To express this situation in Turbo Pascal code, you must use the control structure of an **If-Then-Else** statement. This statement works as follows: if an evaluation is true, the block of code that follows the **Then** statement executes; if false, the block of code that follows the **Else** statement executes. In either case, when the selected block of code terminates, program control skips to the end of the **If-Then-Else** statement, as depicted here:

```
Program TestAge;
Uses CRT;
Var
  Age : Integer;

Begin
ClrScr;
Write('Enter Age: ');
ReadLn(Age);
If (Age >= 21) Then
  Begin
  WriteLn('This person is not a minor.');
  WriteLn('This person is ',Age,' years old.');
  End
Else
  Begin
  WriteLn('This person is a minor.');
  WriteLn('This minor is ',Age,' years old.');
  End;
WriteLn;
Write('Press ENTER...');
ReadLn;
End.
```

As in the earlier examples, the following statements are executed when **age** is greater than or equal to 21:

```
WriteLn('This person is not a minor');
WriteLn('This person is ',Age,' years old');
```

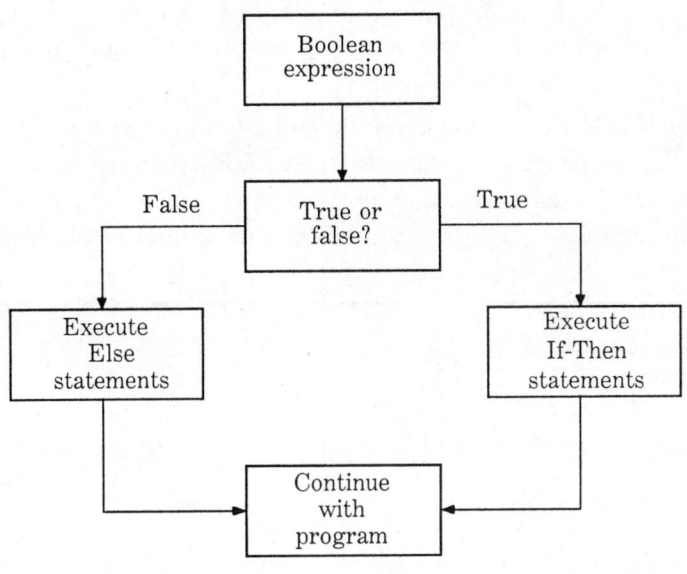

Figure 7-2.   Flowchart of If-Then-Else statement

If **age** is less than 21, the program executes these two statements:

    WriteLn('This person is a minor');
    WriteLn('This minor is ',age,' years old');

When writing code that uses **If-Then-Else** statements, do not terminate the **End** that precedes the **Else** with a semicolon. Turbo Pascal considers the entire **If-Then-Else** structure to be one continuous statement, and semicolons appear only at the end of a statement.

Extending the If-Then-Else Statement

The **If-Then** structure provides one branch, and the **If-Then-Else** structure provides two. But what happens when you need to express a series of conditions? In such cases, you can extend

If-Then-Else with the **Else-If** statement. **Else-If** statements allow you to chain Boolean statements, giving your program the ability to multiple branch (see Figure 7-3). The key element of this figure is the path that the program takes when it finds the first Boolean expression to be false. Instead of executing a block of code, the program evaluates a second Boolean expression; it is here that the **Else-If** statement comes into play. If this expression is also false, the program executes the final block of code.

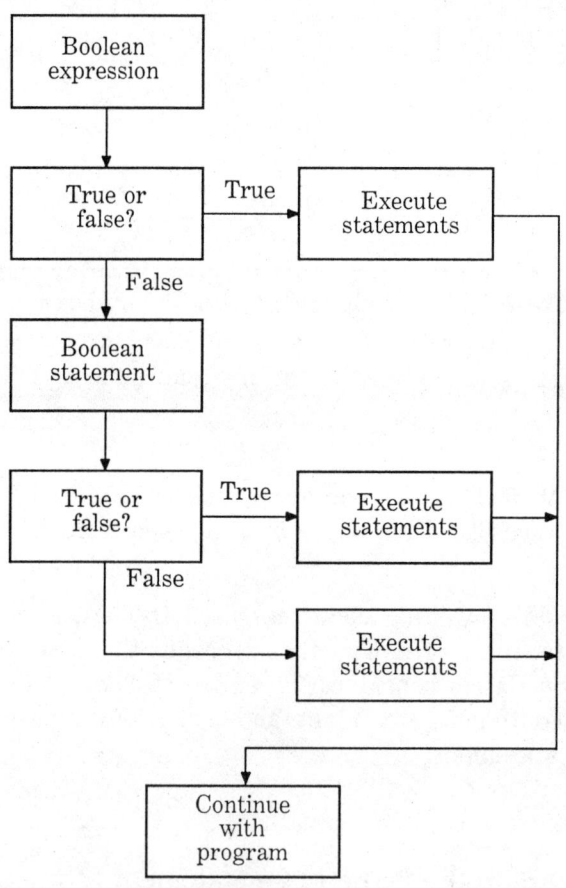

Figure 7-3.   Multiple branching

The following sample program demonstrates how **Else-If** can create multiple branches:

```
Program PrintGradeMessage;
Uses CRT;
Var
   Grade : Char;

Begin
ClrScr;
Write('Enter your Grade: ');
ReadLn(Grade);
Grade := UpCase(Grade);

If Grade = 'A' then
   WriteLn('Excellent.')
Else If Grade = 'B' Then
   WriteLn('Getting there.')
Else If Grade = 'C' Then
   WriteLn('Not too bad.')
Else If Grade = 'D' Then
   WriteLn('Just made it.')
Else If Grade = 'F' Then
   WriteLn('Summer school!')
Else
   WriteLn('That''s not a Grade.');
WriteLn;
Write('Press ENTER...');
ReadLn;
End.
```

This program asks the user to enter a grade (A, B, C, D, or F) and prints a message that comments on the grade entered. The program's five Boolean expressions result in a total of six branches. (The sixth branch is the statement that follows the final **Else**.)

As you can see by now, the **If-Then-Else** structure is extremely powerful, allowing you to build a tremendous amount of intelligence into your programs.

Nested If-Then Statements

One way to allow your program to consider two or more separate conditions before embarking on a course of action is to nest the **If-Then** statements. Figure 7-4 depicts the flow of a nested **If-Then** statement.

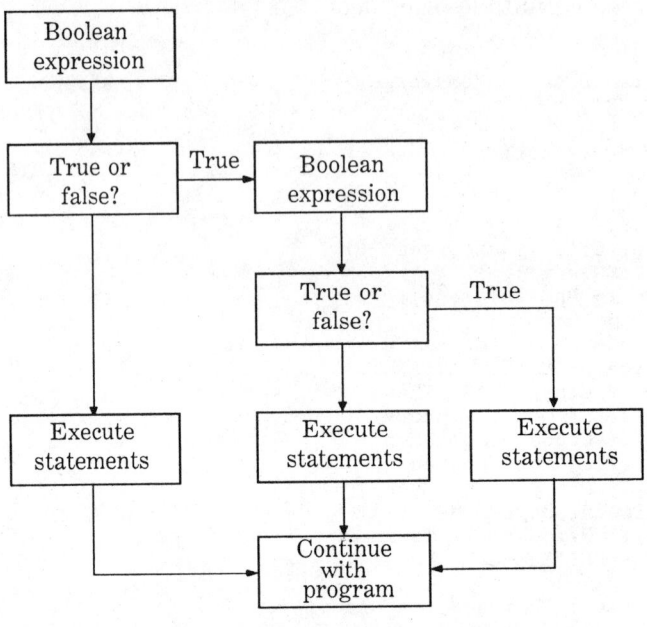

Figure 7-4.   Nested If-Then statements

A nested **If-Then** statement can produce very complex branching schemes. Consider this problem: you are running a game of chance using a box full of black and white marbles. A player takes two marbles from the box at random, and, depending on the combination of colors chosen, he or she is paid at the following rate:

First Marble	Second Marble	Payoff
White	White	0:1
White	Black	2:3
Black	White	1:1
Black	Black	2:1

If the first marble is white and the second is white, the gambler loses everything. If white is first and black is second, he or she loses two-thirds of the bet. If black is followed by white, the gambler breaks even. Two black marbles doubles the bet.

To code this game in Turbo Pascal, use the **If-Then-Else** statement, as shown here:

```
Program BetTest;
Uses CRT;
Var
  FirstMarble,
  SecondMarble : (black,white);
  i   : Integer;
  Bet : Real;

Begin
ClrScr;
  Repeat

  i := Random(2);
  FillChar(FirstMarble,1,i);

  i := Random(2);
  FillChar(SecondMarble,1,i);

  Write('Enter amount of bet (zero to quit): ');
  ReadLn(Bet);
  If Bet = 0 Then Halt;

  If (FirstMarble = white) And (SecondMarble = white) Then
    Begin
    Bet := Bet * 0.0;
    WriteLn('First Marble is White; Second Marble is White');
    End
  Else If (FirstMarble = white) And (SecondMarble = black) Then
    Begin
    Bet := Bet * (2 / 3);
    WriteLn('First Marble is White; Second Marble is Black');
    End
  Else If (FirstMarble = black) And (SecondMarble = white) Then
    Begin    Bet := Bet * 1.0;
    WriteLn('First Marble is Black; Second Marble is White');
    End
  Else (* (FirstMarble = black) And (SecondMarble = black) *)
    Begin
    Bet := Bet * 2.0;
    WriteLn('First Marble is Black; Second Marble is Black');
    End;
  WriteLn('You get $',Bet:0:2,' back.');
  WriteLn;
  WriteLn;
  Until i > 100;
End.
```

The program explicitly refers to each of the four possible combinations of black and white marbles. It will work just fine, but it could be coded more efficiently in this format:

```
If (FirstMarble = white) Then
  Begin

  (*****************************************)
  (* Beginning of nested If-Then statement. *)
  (*****************************************)

  If (SecondMarble = white) Then
    Begin
    Bet := Bet * 0.0;
    WriteLn('First Marble is White; Second Marble is White');
    End
  Else (* SecondMarble = black *)
    Begin
    Bet := Bet * (2 / 3);
    WriteLn('First Marble is White; Second Marble is Black');
    End
  End
Else (* FirstMarble = black *)
  Begin

  (*****************************************)
  (* Beginning of nested If-Then statement. *)
  (*****************************************)

  If SecondMarble = white) Then
    Begin
    Bet := Bet * 1.0;
    WriteLn('First Marble is Black; Second Marble is White');
    End
  Else (* SecondMarble = black *)
    Begin
    Bet := Bet * 2.0;
    WriteLn('First Marble is Black; Second Marble is Black');
    End;
  End;
End;
```

The preceding program's first-level **If-Then** statement tests for the color of the first marble, and its second-level, or nested, statement tests the color of the second marble. Rather than testing both marbles in each **If-Then** statement, the nested **If-Then** structure separates the tests.

The first example evaluates up to three Boolean statements before it finds the correct branch. Since each Boolean statement contains two comparisons, the program may execute as many as six comparisons before coming to a result.

If you use nested **If-Then** statements, however, you do not need to test more than two comparisons at any time. Thus, your program does less work and gives results more quickly than it would otherwise. While the time saved by the sample program is too small to be noticeable, it can be significant in programs with nested **If-Then** statements that are repeated many times.

Conditional Branching with the Case Statement

If you often use simple data types (that is, no **Real** or **String**) in your programs, you can use the Turbo Pascal **Case** statement in place of the **If-Then** statement. **Case** provides a logical and clear structure for multiple branching. Here is a typical use of the **Case** statement:

```
Program CaseExample;
Uses CRT;
Var
  Number1,
  Number2  : Real;
  Operator : Char;
  St,St1,St2 : String[80];
  p,
  Code : Integer;

(***************************************************)

Procedure Compute;
Begin
St1 := '';
St2 := '';
p := 1;

Write('Enter a formula with two numbers (e.g. 1+2): ');
ReadLn(St);

(* Pick up the first number *)

While (St[p] = ' ') And (p <= Length(St)) Do
```

```
  p := p + 1;
While (St[p] in ['1'..'9','.']) And (p <= length(St)) Do
  Begin
  St1 := St1 + St[p];
  p := p + 1;
  End;

(* Pick up the Operator *)

While (St[p] = ' ') And (p <= Length(St)) Do
  p := p + 1;
Operator := St[p];
  p := p + 1;

(* Pick up the second number *)

While (St[p] = ' ') And (p <= Length(St)) Do
  p := p + 1;
While (St[p] in ['1'..'9','.']) And (p <= Length(St)) Do
  Begin
  St2 := St2 + St[p];
  p := p + 1;
  End;

(* Convert number strings to reals *)

Val(St1,Number1,Code);
Val(St2,Number2,Code);

(* Perform computations *)

  Case Operator Of
  '+' : WriteLn('Answer is: ',Number1 + Number2:0:3);
  '-' : WriteLn('Answer is: ',Number1 - Number2:0:3);
  '*' : WriteLn('Answer is: ',Number1 * Number2:0:3);
  '/' : WriteLn('Answer is: ',Number1 / Number2:0:3);
  End;

End;

(*****************************************************)

Begin
ClrScr;

  Repeat
  Compute;
  Until St = '';

End.
```

This program asks for a string that contains a simple formula (for example, 1 + 2). It extracts the numbers and the operator from the string, converts the extracted strings into **Real** values, and then uses the **Case** statement to perform the correct calculation.

An especially powerful feature of the **Case** statement is its ability to interpret ranges, as shown here:

```
Program CaseWithRanges;
Uses CRT;
Var
  Key : Char;

Begin
ClrScr;
  Repeat
  WriteLn;
  Write('Press a Key (q to quit): ');
  Key := ReadKey;
  WriteLn;
  If Key = 'q' then halt;

    Case Key of

    'A'..'Z' :
      WriteLn('You pressed an uppercase letter');

    'a'..'z' :
      WriteLn('You pressed a lowercase letter');

    '0'..'9' :
      WriteLn('You pressed a numeric key');

    Else
       Begin
       WriteLn('You pressed an unknown key');
       WriteLn('Try again');
       End;

    End;
  Until False;
End.
```

When the user of this program presses a key, the **Char** variable **Key** stores the character. The **Case** statement then evaluates the character according to the ranges specified; if the character falls between "A" and "Z," the program knows it must be an uppercase letter. The last statement in the **Case** structure is preceded by **Else**, which provides a default branch for variables that do not fit into any of the specified categories. Any time a character is not in one of the ranges A..Z, a..z, or 0..9, the program executes the statement that follows **Else**.

Repetitive Control Structures

Most programs require a method of repeating a block of code. One way is simply to write as many statements as you need, as in the program in Figure 7-5, which reads in five numbers and writes out the sum.

All those **ReadLn** statements are not only inefficient, but they also produce a very limited program, one that must have five numbers entered, no more, no less. To improve this program, you can use one of Turbo Pascal's three looping control structures.

```
Program NoLoop;
Uses CRT;
Var
  Numbers : Array [1..5] OfReal;
  Sum : Real;

Begin
ClrScr;
Write('Enter a number: ');
ReadLn(Numbers[1]);
Write('Enter a number: ');
ReadLn(Numbers[2]);
Write('Enter a number: ');
ReadLn(Numbers[3]);
Write('Enter a number: ');
ReadLn(Numbers[4]);
Write('Enter a number: ');
ReadLn(Numbers[5]);

Sum := Numbers[1] + Numbers[2] + Numbers[3] +
       Numbers[4] + Numbers[5];

WriteLn('The sum is: ',Sum:0:2);
WriteLn;
Write('Press ENTER...');
ReadLn;
End.
```

Figure 7-5.   A program without looping structures

For-Do Loop

The For-Do loop is a particularly powerful looping structure. Nearly every programming language provides some form of this structure, but Turbo Pascal's implementation of it is superior to that of most other languages.

When coding a For-Do loop, you must specify a starting point, an ending point, and a **scalar** variable to be used as a counter. A typical For-Do loop statement might look like this:

```
For i := 1 To 100 Do
    Begin
    {
    Statements
    }
    End;
```

The first time Turbo Pascal executes this For-Do loop, it sets i equal to 1 and executes the block of code following the loop statement. When it has executed the last statement in the block, it increases i by one. When i exceeds the upper limit (in this case, 100), the loop terminates, and control passes to the next line in the program. But as long as i is less than or equal to 100, Turbo Pascal continues to execute the block of code.

Figure 7-6 shows an updated version of the program in Figure 7-5. Adding For-Do loops to a program substantially reduces the amount of code needed.

Repeat-Until Loop

While the For-Do loop clearly improves the program, it still must read five numbers, and no more or no less than five numbers, to run properly. You can eliminate this restriction by using the Repeat-Until loop.

Following is the general format for the Repeat-Until loop.

```
Repeat
{
Statements
}
Until (Boolean condition);
```

The word **Repeat** tells Turbo Pascal to execute statements until it reaches the **Until** instruction. Turbo Pascal then evaluates the Boolean expression or function in the **Until** instruction, and if it is not true, the program goes back to the **Repeat** instruction and continues executing the block of code.

The main advantage of the Repeat-Until loop is that it does not require you to specify a set number of iterations in advance: it continues to repeat until the Boolean expression is true.

```
Program ForDoLoop;
Uses CRT;
Var
  i : Integer;
  Numbers : Array [1..5] Of Real;
  Sum : Real;

Begin
ClrScr;
For i := 1 To 5 Do
  Begin
  Write('Enter a number: ');
  ReadLn(Numbers[i]);
  End;

Sum := 0;
For i := 1 To 5 Do
  Sum := Sum + Numbers[i];

WriteLn('The sum is: ',Sum:0:2);
WriteLn;
Write('Press ENTER...');
ReadLn;
End.
```

Figure 7-6.   A program with For-Do loops

The following sample program is a refined version of the previous example. This program allows you to enter from zero to five numbers, which are then summed:

```
Program RepeatUntilLoop;
Uses CRT;
Var
  i : Integer;
  Numbers : Array [1..5] Of Real;
  Sum : Real;

Begin
ClrScr;
Sum := 0;
i := 0;

  Repeat
  Write('Enter a Number: ');
  i := i + 1;
  ReadLn(Numbers[i]);
  Until (i = 5) Or (Numbers[i] = 0);

For i := 1 To i Do
  Sum := Sum + Numbers[i];

WriteLn('The sum is: ',sum:0:2);
WriteLn;
Write('Press ENTER...');
ReadLn;

End.
```

In this example, the Repeat-Until loop terminates under two conditions: when i equals five or the number entered is zero. For example, if you enter the numbers 1, 3, and 0, the program exits from the Repeat-Until loop without asking for the fourth and fifth numbers. The For-Do loop that calculates the sum is the same as the one in the previous program, but in this program the upper limit is set to the **Integer** variable i, which counts the number values the user enters. Therefore, the For-Do loop executes once for each number entered.

While-Do Loop

The While-Do loop is similar to the Repeat-Until loop, except the While-Do loop tests a Boolean condition *before* it executes any statements in a block. The following code shows the sample program with a While-Do loop:

```
Program WhileDoLoop;
Uses CRT;
Var
  i : Integer;
  Numbers : Array [1..5] Of Real;
  Sum : Real;

Begin
ClrScr;
Sum := 0;
i := 1;
Write('Enter a Number: ');
ReadLn(Numbers[i]);

While (Numbers[i] <> 0) And (i < 5) Do
  Begin
  Write('Enter a Number: ');
  i := i + 1;
  ReadLn(Numbers[i]);
  End;

For i := 1 To i Do
  Sum := Sum + Numbers[i];

WriteLn('The sum is: ',sum:0:2);
WriteLn;
Write('Press ENTER...');
ReadLn;
End.
```

If the While-Do loop finds that the Boolean expression is not true, Turbo Pascal does not execute the block of code that follows the While-Do block.

Unstructured Branching

The term *unstructured branching* describes what happens when a program jumps directly from one point to another. This process is also known as *direct transfer* or *unconditional branching*. The latter term is misleading because unstructured branching can and usually is used with a Boolean condition statement. Turbo Pascal allows unstructured branching through the **Goto** statement, which is used with a *label identifier*. The label identifier marks the position in the program to which control is to be transferred.

Labels are declared with the Turbo Pascal reserved word **Label**, followed by the label identifiers, which are separated by commas and terminated with a semicolon.

```
Label
   Point1,
   Point2;
```

You can place the label identifiers in the program at locations to which you wish to transfer control. To do this, simply type the label identifier followed by a colon, as shown here:

```
i := 1;
WriteLn(i);
Point1:
b := j / 3;
```

To execute a **Goto** statement, simply specify the label to which the code is to branch. For example, the instruction

```
Goto Point1;
```

tells Turbo Pascal to skip directly to the point in the program where the label Point1 is located. The following program shows an example of unstructured branching:

```
Program GoToExample;
Uses CRT;
Var
  i : Integer;
  ch : Char;

Label
  Retry,
  Stop,
  DoLoop,
  Next,
  Male,
  Female;
```

```
Begin
ClrScr;
Retry:
Write('What is your sex: ');
ReadLn(ch);
ch :=UpCase(ch);
If Not (ch In ['F', 'M']) Then
  GoTo Retry;

If ch = 'M' Then
  GoTo Male
Else
  GoTo Female;

Male:
  WriteLn('Sex is Male');
  GoTo DoLoop;

Female:
  WriteLn ('Sex is Female');

DoLoop:
i := 1;

Next:
i := i + 1;
If I > 10 Then
  GoTo Stop;
WriteLn('i = ',i);
GoTo Next;

Stop:
WriteLn;
Write('Press ENTER...');
ReadLn;
End.
```

As discussed earlier, the Pascal language was developed to do away with the **Goto** statement. Turbo Pascal supports the **Goto** statement, but with one major restriction that keeps it from being misused: Turbo Pascal will not let you transfer control to a label that is outside the current program block. In other words, you can jump to a point within a program or procedure block, but you cannot jump from one procedure into another. With this restriction, you can learn to use the **Goto** statement fairly safely.

While the **Goto** statement is never strictly necessary, there are a number of situations where it can yield a more elegant solution to a problem than using other control structures. Consider the following program. In it, a three-dimensional array is searched until an element with the value of 1 is found. The first approach uses the **Goto** statement, while the second uses the **While-Do** statement. The former is easier to understand and executes more efficiently.

```
Program TestGoTo;
Uses CRT;
Label Found;
Var
  i,j,k : Integer;
  m : Array [1..25, 1..25, 1..25] Of Byte;

Begin
ClrScr;
FillChar(m,SizeOf(m),0);
m[20,20,20] := 1;

(* Using GoTo *)

For i := 1 To 25 Do
For j := 1 To 25 Do
For k := 1 To 25 Do
If m[i,j,k] = 1 Then
  GoTo Found;
Found:
  WriteLn('Found at: ',i,',',j,',',k);

(* Avoiding GoTo *)

i := 1;
j := 1;
k := 1;
While (i <= 25) And (m[i,j,k] <> 1) Do
  Begin
  While (j <= 25) And (m[i,j,k] <> 1) Do
    Begin
    While (k <= 25) And (m[i,j,k] <> 1) Do
      k := k + 1;
    If (m[i,j,k] <> 1) Then
      Begin
      k := 1;
      j := j + 1;
      End;
    End;
  If (m[i,j,k] <> 1) Then
    Begin
    j := 1;
    i := i + 1;
    End;
  End;
WriteLn('Found at: ',i,',',j,',',k);
```

```
WriteLn;
Write('Press ENTER...');
ReadLn;
End.
```

Given the **Goto** command's drawbacks, when does it make sense to use it? One rule is to use **Goto** when the point to which the program jumps is close to the **Goto** statement that branches to it. Here is an example of a program with a valid use of a **Goto** statement:

```
Program MathError;
Uses CRT;
Var
  Numbers1,
  Numbers2,
  Numbers3 : Array [1..3] Of Real;

(**********************************************)

Procedure Divide;
Var
  i : Integer;
Label
  DivideEnd;

Begin
For i := 1 To 3 Do
  Begin
  If Numbers2[i] = 0 Then
    Begin
    WriteLn('Error: Division by zero');
    GoTo DivideEnd;
    End;
  Numbers3[i] := Numbers1[i] / Numbers2[i];
  WriteLn(Numbers3[i]:0:2);
  End;
DivideEnd:
End;

(**********************************************)

Begin
ClrScr;
Numbers1[1] := 1;
Numbers1[2] := 2;
Numbers1[3] := 3;

Numbers2[1] := 5;
Numbers2[2] := 2;
Numbers2[3] := 0;
```

```
Divide;
WriteLn;
Write('Press ENTER...');
ReadLn;
End.
```

This program relies on three arrays of integers. The procedure **Divide** divides the elements in one array by the elements in another and assigns the result to an element in a third array. Whenever you divide in Turbo Pascal, you risk a run-time error if the divisor is zero, so the program first tests the divisor to see if it is zero, in which case the **Goto** statement is used to branch to the end of the procedure. This is a valid use of the **Goto** statement because not only is the distance between the **Goto** statement and the label small, but also the logic behind the statement is clear. Nonetheless, the following structure is an example of more elegant and precise code:

```
i := 0;
  Repeat
  i := i + 1;
  If (Numbers2[i] <> 0) Then
    Numbers3[i] := Numbers1[i] Div Numbers2[i]
  Else
    WriteLn('Error: Division by zero');
  Until (i = 100) Or (Numbers2[i] = 0);


For i := 1 To 100 Do
  Begin
  If (Numbers2[i] = 0) Then
    Begin
    WriteLn('Error: Division by zero');
    Exit;
    End;
  Numbers3[i] := Numbers1[i] Div Numbers2[i];
  End;
```

The first routine uses the Repeat-Until loop to provide both a means to increment **i** and to exit if the divisor is found to be zero. The second routine uses **Exit**, a standard Turbo Pascal function. Strictly speaking, **Exit** is an unconditional branching statement because it ignores the normal path of execution for the block of code.

Turbo Pascal offers both structured and unstructured methods for creating clear, concise applications. This variety of tools makes programming in Turbo Pascal especially rewarding, allowing you to develop a personal programming style while encouraging you to learn good programming habits.

Pointers and Dynamic Memory Allocation

Turbo Pascal Memory Allocation
The Heap and Pointers
Using Pointers with Complex Data Types
Using the @ Operator

Turbo Pascal uses different parts, or segments, of your computer's memory for different purposes. Some segments hold the instructions your computer executes, while the others store data. Each of these segments performs a specific role, and you must understand these roles and how the segments work before you can master advanced programming concepts.

Turbo Pascal Memory Allocation

Turbo Pascal divides your computer's memory into four parts—the code segment, the data segment, the stack segment, and the heap. Programs that use units have a code segment for each unit as well as for the main program. All programs, however, have only one data segment, which contains typed constants and global variables.

Although the data segment is clearly dedicated to data storage, data also can be stored in other locations. The stack and heap hold dynamic data, allocating memory as it is needed. While the stack is critically important, its operation is controlled automatically by Turbo Pascal—you can't do much with the stack yourself. The heap, on the other hand, is especially important for advanced programming techniques. This chapter discusses the role of the heap and how you can use *dynamic allocation* in your programs.

DOS Memory Mapping Conventions

The first step in understanding how Turbo Pascal manages memory is to learn something about the internal workings of your microcomputer. A computer has a certain amount of RAM (random access memory). Let's say yours has 640 kilobytes. A kilobyte represents 1024 bytes, so your 640K computer really has a total of 655,360 bytes of RAM.

When your program first starts, it sets up a segment that holds the program's instructions (the code segment or segments), a segment to hold the program's data (the data segment), and a segment to hold temporary data (the stack segment). As the instructions in the code segment execute, they manipulate data in both the data segment and the stack segment.

How does the program know at which byte these three segments begin? For that matter, how does a program locate any particular byte in memory? By using addresses. Every byte has an *address,* a 20-bit value that uniquely identifies that location. When a program needs to access a particular byte, it uses the address to find the byte's location in memory.

If a computer's address consisted of a single word (two bytes), it could not address more than 64K (65,536 bytes) of RAM. This was the case for the early 8-bit microprocessors.

The advent of 16-bit processors, particularly the Intel 8086/88 family, ushered in a new memory-addressing scheme, known as *segmented addressing.* Segmented addressing combines two word values—a segment and an offset—to form a 20-bit address. Think of segments as blocks on a street and offsets as the houses on each block.

Each segment holds 64K of RAM. The 8086/88 processors have 16 segments, resulting in 1,048,560 bytes (1 *megabyte*) of addressable memory. However, DOS limits the amount of memory your computer can use to 640K.

Segments and Offsets

Turbo Pascal provides two standard functions, **Seg** and **Ofs**, that make it easy to explore memory addressing on your PC. **Seg** provides the segment in which a variable resides, and **Ofs** provides its offset. The following program uses these functions to display the addresses of four variables:

```
Program Addresses;
Uses CRT;
Type
  StType = String[10];
Var
  i : Word;
  s : String[5];
  r : Real;
  c : Char;

Type
  St4 = String[4];

(**********************************************)

Function IntToHex(i : Word) : St4;
Var
 HexStr : String[8];
 b : Array [1..2] Of Byte Absolute i;
 bt : Byte;

(**********************************************)

Function Translate(b : Byte) : Char;
Begin
If b < 10 Then
  Translate := Chr(b + 48)
Else
  Translate := Chr(b + 55);
End;

(**********************************************)

Begin
HexStr := '';
HexStr := HexStr + Translate(b[2] Shr 4);
HexStr := HexStr + Translate(b[2] And 15);
HexStr := HexStr + Translate(b[1] Shr 4);
HexStr := HexStr + Translate(b[1] And 15);
IntToHex := HexStr;
End;
```

```
(***********************************************)
Begin
ClrScr;
WriteLn('Word:    ',IntToHex(Seg(i)),':',IntToHex(Ofs(i)));
WriteLn('String:  ',IntToHex(Seg(s)),':',IntToHex(Ofs(s)));
WriteLn('Real:    ',IntToHex(Seg(r)),':',IntToHex(Ofs(r)));
WriteLn('Char:    ',IntToHex(Seg(c)),':',IntToHex(Ofs(c)));
WriteLn;
Write('Press ENTER...');
ReadLn;
End.
```

This program defines four variables of different types and then displays the addresses of each of the variables. For example, the statement **Seg(i)** finds the segment of variable **i**, while **Ofs(i)** returns the offset.

The function **IntToHex** accepts a word parameter and returns the hexadecimal value as a string of four characters. Segments and offsets are customarily shown in hexadecimal format.

When you run the previous program, your screen will show the following messages, though you will see different numbers because your computer may be configured differently.

```
Word:   68BB:003C
String: 68BB:003E
Real:   68BB:0044
Char:   68BB:004A
```

As you can see, all the variables, which are global, have the same segment. (Global variables all reside in the data segment.) Furthermore, the distance between offsets exactly matches the number of bytes needed to store each variable type. For example, a word starts at offset 3Ch and requires two bytes of storage; the next variable in line (a **String**) starts at offset 3Eh.

Turbo Pascal typed constants are stored in the data segment, while untyped constants exist in the code segment. Actually, untyped constants simply become part of the computer code. For this reason, untyped constants do not have addresses.

Variables that are declared in procedures and functions are stored on the stack, a dynamic data storage area. When a program calls a procedure, Turbo Pascal allocates space on the stack for the procedure's local variables. As Turbo Pascal adds variables to the stack, the stack grows downward in memory. When the procedure ends, Turbo Pascal discards these variables and frees the memory to be used again.

The fourth segment in Turbo Pascal memory, the heap, is a dynamic data area that you control. The heap allows efficient use of memory because it eliminates the need to preserve all the data structures throughout a program; instead, you can create a variable on the heap at one point, remove it from the heap at another, and then reuse the space for another variable at still another place.

The following program demonstrates how data can exist in any of the four Turbo Pascal segments:

```
Program Segments;
Uses CRT;
Type
  StType = String[80];
Var
  r1,r2 : Real;
  x : Word;
  p : ^Word;

Type
  St4 = String[4];

(***********************************************)

Function IntToHex(i : Word): St4;
Var
  HexStr : String[8];
  b : Array [1..2] Of Byte Absolute i;
  bt : Byte;

(***********************************************)

Function Translate(b : byte) : Char;
Begin
If b < 10 Then
  Translate := Chr(b + 48)
Else
  Translate := Chr(b + 55);
End;

(***********************************************)
```

```
Begin
HexStr := '';
HexStr := HexStr + Translate(b[2] Shr 4);
HexStr := HexStr + Translate(b[2] And 15);
HexStr := HexStr + Translate(b[1] Shr 4);
HexStr := HexStr + Translate(b[1] And 15);
IntToHex := HexStr;
End;

(**********************************************)

Procedure ShowCodeSegment;
Begin
WriteLn;
WriteLn('The code segment is ',IntToHex(cseg));
End;

(**********************************************)

Procedure ShowDataVariable;
Begin
WriteLn;
WriteLn('The location of global variable x is ',
        IntToHex(seg(x)),':',
        IntToHex(ofs(x)));

WriteLn('This is in the data segment.');
End;

(**********************************************)

Procedure ShowStackVariable;
Var
  i : Word;
Begin
WriteLn;
WriteLn('The location of variable i is ',
        IntToHex(seg(i)),':',
        IntToHex(ofs(i)));

Writeln('This is in the stack segment.');
End;

(**********************************************)

Procedure ShowHeapVariable;
Begin
WriteLn;
WriteLn('The location of pointer variable p is ',
        IntToHex(seg(p^)),':',
        IntToHex(ofs(p^)));

WriteLn('This is on the heap.');
End;

(**********************************************)
```

```
Begin
ClrScr;
WriteLn('Addresses are shown in the format Segment:Offset.');
New(p);
ShowCodeSegment;
ShowDataVariable;
ShowHeapVariable;
ShowStackVariable;
WriteLn;
Write('Press ENTER...');
ReadLn;
End.
```

When you run this program, your terminal will display output that looks something like this:

Addresses are shown in the format Segment:Offset.

The code segment is 67A9

The location of global variable x is 691E:0048
This is in the data segment.

The location of pointer variable p is 709C:0000
This is on the heap.

The location of variable i is 6949:7524
This is in the stack segment.

Each of the four variables in this example resides in a different segment. The first location, that of the code segment, is 67A9h. The variable **x** is located in the data segment (691Eh). Pointer variable **p**, placed on the heap with the statement **New(p)**, is located in segment 709Ch.

The last variable listed is a local variable declared within a procedure. All local variables get stored on the stack, and in this example the stack segment begins at 6949h.

Figure 8-1 provides a schematic diagram of Turbo Pascal's memory. The lines separating the segments are matched with the hexadecimal values from the sample program. The code segment occupies lowest memory followed by the data and stack

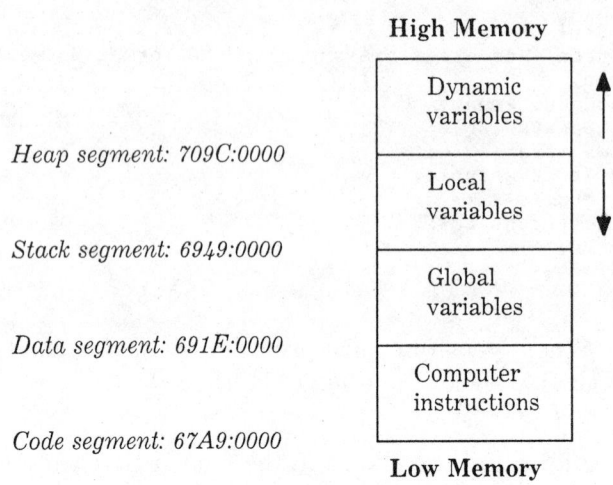

Figure 8-1. Turbo Pascal memory allocation

segments. The heap occupies all the high memory that is left over, up to the maximum you set with the **M** compiler directive. The diagram also demonstrates that the stack grows downward and the heap grows upward.

The Heap and Pointers

Most variables you declare in Turbo Pascal are static, that is, memory is allocated to them from the time the program starts until it ends. The heap, on the other hand, uses dynamic data types known as *pointers*. Pointer variables are dynamic because you can create them and dispose of them while a program is running. In short, different pointer variables can use and reuse memory on the heap.

Using pointer variables on the heap offers two main advantages. First, it expands the total amount of data space available to a program. The data segment is limited to 64 kilobytes, but the heap is limited only by the amount of RAM in your computer.

The second advantage of using pointer variables on the heap is that it allows your program to run with less memory. For example, a program might have two very large data structures, but only one of them is used at a time. If these data structures are declared globally, they reside in the data segment and occupy memory at all times. However, if these data structures are defined as pointers, they can be put on the heap and taken off as needed, thus reducing your program's memory requirements.

The Pointer Variable

A pointer variable does not hold data in the same way that other variables do. Instead, it holds the address that points to a variable located on the heap. Suppose you have a pointer variable named **px** that holds the address of an **Integer**. Now, you can use **px** to point to the **Integer**, but **px** itself is not the **Integer**. If you are confused, this example, which demonstrates the simple use of a pointer variable, may help. The following program listing demonstrates the simple use of a pointer variable:

```
Program PointerDemo;
Uses CRT;
Var
  i : ^Integer;
  j : Integer Absolute i;

(**********************************************)

Type
  St4 = String[4];
Function IntToHex(i : Word) : St4;
Var
 HexStr : String[8];
 b : Array [1..2] Of Byte Absolute i;
 bt : Byte;

(**********************************************)
```

```
Function Translate(b : Byte) : Char;
Begin
If b < 10 Then
  Translate := Chr(b + 48)
Else
  Translate := Chr(b + 55);
End;

(*********************************************)

Begin
HexStr := '';
HexStr := HexStr + Translate(b[2] Shr 4);
HexStr := HexStr + Translate(b[2] And 15);
HexStr := HexStr + Translate(b[1] Shr 4);
HexStr := HexStr + Translate(b[1] And 15);
IntToHex := HexStr;
End;

(*********************************************)

Begin
ClrScr;
New(i);
i^ := 100;
WriteLn('The value of i is: ',IntToHex(j));
WriteLn('The value that i points to is: ',i^);
Dispose(i);
WriteLn;
Write('Press ENTER...');
ReadLn;
End.
```

The ^ placed before the data type in the definition tells Turbo Pascal to define **i** as a pointer variable:

    i : ^Integer;

When the program starts, the heap is a blank slate. Before you can use pointer **i**, you must use the statement **New(i)** to tell Turbo Pascal to assign an address on the heap to the pointer **i**. **Dispose(i)**, which appears near the end of the program, is the opposite of **New(i)**. **Dispose** effectively takes a variable off the heap, allowing memory to be used for other variables.

Once you place it on the heap, you can use the variable in **Assignment** and **Arithmetic** statements by adding the ^ symbol to the identifier:

    i^ := 100;

The ˆ tells Turbo Pascal that you are referring to the variable on the heap and not to the pointer itself. What would happen if the statement were **i := 100**? This statement changes the value of the pointer, not the value of the variable on the heap. Now, **i** points to memory location 100 rather than to its proper location.

When you run the preceding program, your terminal displays the following messages:

The value of i is: 0000
The value that i points to is: 100

The first line displays the address that the pointer is holding. In this case the address is 0000, indicating that this variable is the first to be placed on the heap. The second line is the value of **iˆ**, the variable at address 0000 on the heap.

New and Dispose

When you allocate and dispose of dynamic variables, what actually happens in the heap? Figure 8-2 describes the process of allocation and deallocation. In the figure, Turbo Pascal declares four pointer variables: one **Integer**, one **Real**, and two **String**s, one 5 and the other 10 bytes long. The columns represent memory on the heap. Turbo Pascal always allocates memory on the heap in exact amounts. Thus, when the program executes the statement **New(i)**, the heap provides 2 bytes, just enough to store the **Integer** variable.

In the second column, Turbo Pascal allocates a string of 10 characters to the heap. Because this string requires 11 bytes of storage (10 characters plus the length byte), Turbo Pascal allocates 11 bytes on the heap. In short, the heap always provides as many bytes of memory as are necessary to contain the data structure put on the heap.

The third column in Figure 8-2 shows the additional allocation of a **Real** variable, requiring 5 bytes of memory. The next

```
Type
  St10 = String[10];
Var
  i : ^Integer;
  r : ^Real;
  s10 : ^St10;
  w : ^Word;
```

New(i)   New(s10)   New(r)   Dispose(i)   New(w)

i	i	i	-	w
-	s10	s10	s10	s10
-	s10	s10	s10	s10
-	-	r	r	r

Figure 8-2.   Dynamic allocation using New and Dispose

column demonstrates the impact of the **Dispose** statement. When Turbo Pascal disposes **i**, the 2-byte chunk that **i** was using is released for use by other dynamic variables. This creates a "hole" in the heap. To use this portion of memory again, the data structure must fit into this hole. If not, Turbo Pascal must allocate memory elsewhere on the heap.

In the fifth column, Turbo Pascal allocates a **word** variable to the heap. Because this variable fits into the hole left by **i**, Turbo Pascal reuses that memory.

Using **New** and **Dispose** requires careful planning and rigorous testing. One common error is to reallocate the same variable on the heap. For example, the two following statements

```
New(i);
New(i);
```

both allocate an **Integer** on the heap, but only one of the **Integer**s can be accessed as a variable. You not only cannot access the first **Integer**, you cannot even get rid of it. Since the **i** pointer points to the second **Integer**, it cannot be used to **Dispose** the first variable. Always make sure that each **New** is matched by a **Dispose**.

Mark and Release

Turbo Pascal offers an alternative to using **New** and **Dispose** to dynamically allocate memory: **Mark** and **Release**. Instead of leaving holes in the heap the way **New** and **Dispose** do, **Mark** and **Release** lop off an entire end of the heap from a particular point onward. This process is demonstrated in the following program:

```
Program HeapRelease;
Uses CRT;
Type
   Atype = Array [1..100] Of Char;
Var
   HeapTop : ^Word;
   a1,a2,a3 : ^Atype;

Begin
ClrScr;
Mark(HeapTop);

WriteLn('Initial free memory: ',MemAvail);
WriteLn;
WriteLn('---------------');
WriteLn;

New(a1);
WriteLn('Free memory after allocating a1: ',MemAvail);
New(a2);
WriteLn('Free memory after allocating a2: ',MemAvail);
New(a3);
WriteLn('Free memory after allocating a3: ',MemAvail);
WriteLn;
WriteLn('---------------');
WriteLn;

Release(HeapTop);
WriteLn('Free memory after release: ',MemAvail);
WriteLn;
Write('Press ENTER...');
ReadLn;
End.
```

This program allocates three pointer variables—**a1**, **a2**, and **a3**—and uses the **MemAvail** standard function to display the amount of free memory left over. **MemAvail** returns the total amount of memory in bytes available on the heap returns. For example, if **MemAvail** returns a value of 20, that means there are 20 bytes of memory left on the heap for use in dynamic allocation.

The previous program uses a pointer variable named **HeapTop** to keep track of the point from which you release memory. The statement **Mark(HeapTop)** stores the current address of the top of the heap to the pointer **HeapTop**. The program calls **Mark(HeapTop)** prior to placing any variables on the heap. As a result, when it calls **Release(HeapTop)**, it deallocates all the variables on the heap, freeing the memory for another use. Running the program results in the following messages:

```
Initial free memory: 195632

--------------

Free memory after allocating a1: 195532
Free memory after allocating a2: 195432
Free memory after allocating a3: 195332

--------------

Free memory after release: 195632
```

As you can see, each time a variable is placed on the heap, the amount of available memory decreases. When **Release(HeapTop)** is called at the end of the program, the amount of free memory reverts to the initial amount. If you had marked the **HeapTop** pointer after **a1** was allocated, only the memory for **a2** and **a3** would be released.

Note that **Dispose** and **Release** are incompatible methods of recovering memory. You can choose to use one or the other, but never use both in the same program.

GetMem and FreeMem

A third method of dynamic memory allocation is **GetMem** and **FreeMem**. These are much like **New** and **Dispose** in that they allocate and deallocate memory one variable at a time. The special value of **GetMem** and **FreeMem** is that you can specify how much memory you want to allocate regardless of the type of variable you are using. For example, you can allocate 100 bytes to an **Integer** with the statement

```
GetMem(i,100);
```

Variables allocated with **GetMem** are deallocated with **FreeMem**, as shown by the following:

```
GetMem(i,20);
i := x + y;
WriteLn(i);
FreeMem(i,20);
```

The number of bytes specified in the **FreeMem** statement must match that in the **GetMem** statement. Do not use **Dispose** in place of **FreeMem**; if you do, the heap will become hopelessly unsynchronized.

Using Pointers with Complex Data Types

Since the heap is generally used to access large data spaces, pointer variables are generally used with large, complex data structures. Defining a complex data structure as a pointer is a two-step process.

```
Type

  CustPtr = ^CustRec;

  CustRec = Record
    Name : String[25];
    Address : String[30];
    City: String[30];
    State: String[2];
    Zip: String[5];
    End;

Var

  Cust : CustPtr;
```

Here, the statement **CustPtr = ^CustRec;** defines **CustPtr** as a pointer to **CustRec**. Note that **CustRec** has not yet been defined. Declaring pointers is the one case in which Turbo Pascal allows you to refer to a data structure before it is defined. The variable **Cust** is then defined as type **CustPtr**.

Linked Lists

The easy way to manage a list is to define an array. One problem with arrays, however, is that you always have to allocate enough space for the maximum possible number of elements. As a result, you either define very large arrays and waste memory or define small arrays and limit the power of your program. Pointers provide an alternative to arrays—*linked lists.*

Data items in a linked list have pointers that keep track of the order of the list. *Singly linked lists* use one pointer that points to the record that comes next. *Doubly linked lists* have pointers in both directions, so that each data item is linked to the one before it and the one after it.

Figure 8-3 shows the structure of a singly linked list. Each record contains data and a pointer. The pointers indicate which record comes next in the list. The pointer of the last record is set to Nil, indicating there are no more records in the list.

To change the order of the list, only the pointer values need to be changed. In Figure 8-3, the pointer in Data 1 is changed to

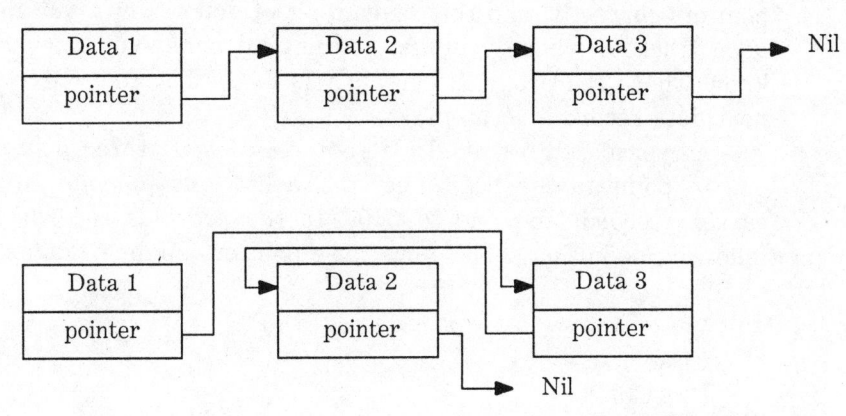

Figure 8-3.   A singly linked list

point to Data 3, and Data 3 is made to point to Data 2. Now, the pointer in Data 2 points to Nil, indicating that this is the last record in the list.

Building a linked list in a Turbo Pascal program requires considerable effort. Even so, it is a skill worth learning since many advanced sorting and searching routines use linked lists to increase their speed and maximize memory usage.

A data item in a singly linked list must have a *forward-referencing pointer* that tells Turbo Pascal where it can find the next data item in the list. The following record definition includes a forward-referencing pointer named **Next**:

```
CustPtr = ^CustRec;
CustRec = Record
  Name    : String[20];
  Address : String[40];
  City    : String[20];
  State   : String[2];
  Next    : CustPtr;
  End;
```

CustPtr points to the record **CustRec**. The record **Cust-Rec**, in turn, contains a field named Next, which is defined as **CustPtr**.

You, not Turbo Pascal, are responsible for maintaining pointers correctly, and this takes a bit of doing. First, you must keep track of where your list begins and ends. You must also know where the program currently is in the list and where the next data record is located.

A typical singly linked list requires at least three pointers: one to point to the beginning of the list, one to point to the current record, and one to point to the previous record. The following definition shows how these pointers might be defined:

```
Var
FirstCust,
PrevCust,
CurrentCust : CustPtr;
```

If you want to process the list sequentially from beginning to end, you must know the location of the first link in the list. **PrevCust**, which points to the link preceding the current link, makes the pointer called **Next** point to the next record.

A new link in a linked list must be connected to the previous link. The very first link, however, has no previous link and is, therefore, an exception. How does a program know if it is creating the first link or some other link? When the program begins, you must initialize the pointer **FirstCust** to Nil:

```
FirstCust := Nil;
```

The procedure that creates new links tests **FirstCust** to see if it is equal to Nil. If it is, the program knows this is the first link in a linked list and processes it appropriately. The following program segment demonstrates how these pointers create a linked list.

```
If FirstCust = Nil Then
  Begin
  New(CurrentCust);
  FirstCust := CurrentCust;
  CurrentCust^.Next := Nil;
  End
Else
  Begin
```

```
PrevCust := CurrentCust;
New(CurrentCust);
PrevCust^.Next := CurrentCust;
CurrentCust^.Next := Nil;
End;
```

The **If-Then-Else** statement checks to see if this is the first link in the list (**FirstCust = Nil**). If so, the program creates a **CurrentCust** record and sets **FirstCust** equal to **CurrentCust**. It sets the Next field in **CurrentCust** equal to Nil because there is no next link in the chain at this time.

The second time through, **FirstCust** is not equal to Nil since it was previously set equal to **CurrentCust**. Therefore, the program skips to the **Else** branch, where it sets the pointer **PrevCust** equal to **CurrentCust** and creates a new **CurrentCust**. At this time, the program is using all three position pointers: **CurrentCust** points to the newly created link, **PrevCust** points to the preceding link, and **FirstCust** points to the first link in the list. After it creates the new **CurrentCust**, the program sets the Next field in **PrevCust** to point to the new link. The elements of these lists are linked by the connection of one record to another with a pointer field.

The following program shows how a singly linked list creates and manipulates a list of customer names and addresses:

```
Program SimpleLink;
Uses CRT;
Type
  CustPtr = ^CustRec;
  CustRec = Record
    Name : String[20];
    Address : String[40];
    City : String[20];
    State : String[2];
    Next : CustPtr;
    End;
Var
  FirstCust,
  PrevCust,
  CurrentCust : CustPtr;
  ch : Char;

(**************************************)

Procedure AddRecord;

(**************************************)
```

```
Procedure EnterData;
Begin
With CurrentCust^ Do
  Begin
  Write('Enter customer name: ');
  ReadLn(Name);
  Write('Enter address: ');
  ReadLn(Address);
  Write('Enter city: ');
  ReadLn(City);
  Write('Enter state: ');
  ReadLn(State);
  End;
End;

(***************************************)

Begin
ClrScr;
If FirstCust = Nil Then
  Begin
  New(CurrentCust);
  EnterData;
  FirstCust := CurrentCust;
  CurrentCust^.Next := Nil;
  End
Else
  Begin
  PrevCust := CurrentCust;
  New(CurrentCust);
  EnterData;
  PrevCust^.Next := CurrentCust;
  CurrentCust^.Next := Nil;
  End;
End;

(***************************************)

Procedure ListRecords;
Var
  Cust : CustPtr;
Begin
Cust := FirstCust;
While Cust <> Nil Do
  Begin
  With Cust^ Do
    WriteLn(Name,', ',Address,', ',City,', ',State);
  Cust := Cust^.Next;
  End;
WriteLn;
Write('Press ENTER...');
ReadLn;
End;

(***************************************)
```

```
Begin
FirstCust := Nil;

  Repeat
  ClrScr;
    Repeat
    Write('A)dd a customer, L)ist customers, Q)uit: ');
    ch := ReadKey;
    If ch = #0 Then
       ch := ReadKey;
    WriteLn;
    ch := Upcase(ch);
    Until ch In ['A','L','Q'];

  If ch = 'A' Then
     AddRecord
  Else If ch = 'L' Then
     ListRecords;

  Until ch = 'Q';
End.
```

The procedure **ListRecords** demonstrates how to process a linked list sequentially. The essential parts of the code are as follows:

```
CurrentCust := FirstCust;
While CurrentCust <> Nil Do
  Begin
  (* Statements *)
  CurrentCust := CurrentCust^.Next;
  End;
```

The procedure sets pointer **CurrentCust** equal to **First-Cust**, the first item in the list. Next, a While-Do loop repeats a block of code until the pointer **CurrentCust** is Nil, indicating that the program has reached the end of the list. Within the block of code, the last statement

CurrentCust := CurrentCust^.Next;

causes **CurrentCust** to point to the next item in the list.

Even a cursory review of the previous program illustrates the added complexity of using a linked list instead of a standard array. Every time the program needs a new record, it must create it and set up all the appropriate links. And if you want to move backward through a singly linked list, you simply cannot do it.

Doubly Linked Lists

Doubly linked lists maintain links in both directions, allowing you to process the list backward or forward. This requires another pointer field (**Prev**) in the record definition, as follows:

```
CustRec = Record
  Name : String[20];
  Address : String[40];
  City : String[20];
  State : String[2];
  Prev,
  Next : CustPtr;
  End;
```

The **Prev** pointer keeps track of the link preceding the current one, while the **Next** pointer keeps track of the next link.

While they are more powerful than singly linked lists, doubly linked lists require you to write even more code. Compare the doubly linked list in Figure 8-4 with the singly linked list in Figure 8-3. Adding the *backward-referencing pointer* doubles the number of linkages to maintain.

Doubly linked lists require position pointers to keep track of both the beginning and the end of the list. When a new link is created, you must keep track of the location of the first record,

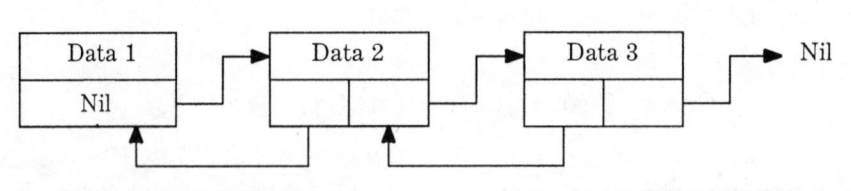

Figure 8-4.   A doubly linked list

the last record, the current record, and the record prior to the current record. The following program segment illustrates this process:

```
If FirstCust = Nil Then
  Begin
  New(CurrentCust);
  CurrentCust^.Next := Nil;
  CurrentCust^.Prev := Nil;
  FirstCust := CurrentCust;
  LastCust := CurrentCust;
  End
Else
  Begin
  PrevCust := LastCust;
  New(CurrentCust);
  EnterData;
  PrevCust^.Next := CurrentCust;
  CurrentCust^.Next := Nil;
  CurrentCust^.Prev := PrevCust;
  LastCust := CurrentCust;
  End;
```

When **FirstCust** is equal to Nil, the program creates the first element in the linked list and sets its pointers, **Prev** and **Next**, to Nil. The other position pointers, **FirstCust**, **LastCust**, and **PrevCust**, are set equal to **CurrentCust**.

The next time through, the program branches to the **Else**, where it sets **PrevCust** equal to **LastCust** before creating the new link. When it creates the new link, the program sets the **Prev** pointer to **PrevCust** and the **Next** pointer in **PrevCust** to **CurrentCust**. This establishes the double link that allows processing in either direction.

The following program uses doubly linked lists to manage a list of names and addresses. Two features to pay attention to are the ability to sort the list and to write out the list in reverse order.

```
Program DoubleLink;
Uses CRT;
Type
  CustPtr = ^CustRec;
  CustRec = Record
    Name : String[20];
    Address : String[40];
    City : String[20];
```

```
      State : String[2];
      Prev,
      Next : CustPtr;
      End;
Var
  FirstCust,
  LastCust,
  PrevCust,
  CurrentCust : CustPtr;
  ch : Char;

(*************************************)

Procedure AddRecord;

(*************************************)

Procedure EnterData;
Begin
With CurrentCust^ Do
  Begin
  Write('Enter customer name: ');
  ReadLn(Name);
  Write('Enter address: ');
  ReadLn(Address);
  Write('Enter city: ');
  ReadLn(City);
  Write('Enter state: ');
  ReadLn(State);
  End;
End;

(*************************************)

Begin
ClrScr;
If FirstCust = Nil Then
  Begin
  New(CurrentCust);
  EnterData;
  CurrentCust^.Next := Nil;
  CurrentCust^.Prev := Nil;
  FirstCust := CurrentCust;
  LastCust := CurrentCust;
  End
Else
  Begin
  PrevCust := LastCust;
  New(CurrentCust);
  EnterData;
  PrevCust^.Next := CurrentCust;
  CurrentCust^.Next := Nil;
  CurrentCust^.Prev := PrevCust;
  LastCust := CurrentCust;
  End;
End;
```

```
(*************************************)

Procedure ListRecords;
Var
  ch : Char;

(*************************************)

Procedure ListForwards;
Begin
CurrentCust := FirstCust;
While CurrentCust <> Nil Do
  Begin
  With CurrentCust^ Do
    WriteLn(Name,', ',Address,', ',City,', ',State);
  CurrentCust := CurrentCust^.Next;
  End;
End;

(*************************************)

Procedure ListBackwards;
Begin
CurrentCust := LastCust;
While CurrentCust <> Nil Do
  Begin
  With CurrentCust^ Do
    WriteLn(Name,', ',Address,', ',City,', ',State);
  CurrentCust := CurrentCust^.Prev;
  End;
End;

(*************************************)

Begin
  Repeat
  Write('F)orwards or B)ackwards, Q)uit: ');
  ch := ReadKey;
  If ch = #0 Then
    ch := ReadKey;
  WriteLn;
  ch := upcase(ch);
  Until (ch In ['F','B','Q']);

If ch = 'F' Then
  ListForwards
Else If ch = 'B' Then
  ListBackwards;
WriteLn;
Write('Press ENTER...');
ReadLn;
End;

(*************************************)
```

```pascal
Procedure SortRecords;
Var
  NextRec,FarCust : CustPtr;
  SortDone : Boolean;

Begin

  Repeat
  CurrentCust := FirstCust;
  PrevCust := Nil;
  SortDone := True;

  While CurrentCust^.Next <> Nil Do
    Begin
    NextRec := CurrentCust^.Next;

    If CurrentCust^.Name > NextRec^.Name Then
      Begin
      SortDone := False;

      If NextRec^.Next <> Nil Then
        Begin
        FarCust := NextRec^.Next;
        FarCust^.Prev := CurrentCust;
        End
      Else
        FarCust := Nil;

      If CurrentCust^.Prev = Nil Then
        Begin
        FirstCust := NextRec;
        PrevCust := Nil;
        End
      Else
        Begin
        PrevCust := CurrentCust^.Prev;
        PrevCust^.Next := NextRec;
        End;

      CurrentCust^.Next := FarCust;
      CurrentCust^.Prev := NextRec;

      NextRec^.Next := CurrentCust;
      NextRec^.Prev := PrevCust;

      CurrentCust := FirstCust;
      End
    Else
      CurrentCust := CurrentCust^.Next;
    End;

  Until SortDone;

LastCust := CurrentCust;
WriteLn;
```

```
Write(''Sort completed. Press ENTER...');
ReadLn;
End;

(************************************)

Begin
FirstCust := Nil;

  Repeat
  ClrScr;
    Repeat
    Write('A)dd a customer, L)ist customers, S)ort, Q)uit: ');
    ch := ReadKey;
    If ch = #0 Then
      ch := ReadKey;
    WriteLn;
    ch := Upcase(ch);
    Until ch In ['A','L','S','Q'];

  If ch = 'A' Then
    AddRecord
  Else If ch = 'L' Then
    ListRecords
  Else If ch = 'S' Then
    SortRecords;

  Until ch = 'Q';
End.
```

Dynamic memory allocation is a powerful tool. It allows you to expand your program's data space while opening the door to linked lists and other dynamic data structures. But there is a price to pay. Linked lists maximize the efficient use of memory, but impose considerable overhead and require much more time to develop. In the end, dynamic data structures are best used when the benefits they provide are certain to outweigh the costs of developing and using them. Such programs include database applications that benefit from using as much memory as possible, but must be able to run on computers that have small amounts of memory.

Using the @ Operator

When performing address operations, it is often necessary to assign the address of a variable or procedure to a pointer. This is accomplished with the @ operator, which returns the address of the identifier that follows it. For example, if **A** is an **Integer**, then **@A** is the memory address of the **Integer** variable. The following code demonstrates how you might use the @ operator with a pointer variable:

```
Program AddressTest;
Type  B_Type = Array [1..2] Of Byte;
Var
  i : Word;
  b : ^B_Type;

Begin
i := $FFFF;
b := @i;
WriteLn(b^[1],' ',b^[2]);
WriteLn;
Write('Press ENTER...');
ReadLn;
End.
```

In this example, **b** is a pointer to an array of two bytes, and **i** is a word variable. The program initializes **i** to FFFFh and then assigns the address of **i** to pointer **b**. Now, using the pointer variable, it is possible to treat the two bytes in the word variable as separate entities. This chapter gives only a hint at the usefulness of pointers and dynamic allocation. While it is a difficult topic to master, the rewards can be great in terms of program efficiency and flexibility.

Turbo Pascal Files

File Handling Concepts
Turbo Pascal Text Files
Disk Files and Buffers
Typed Files
Untyped Files
Erasing and Renaming Files

A computer that does not store programs and data is little more than a powerful calculator. People who bought early microcomputers without disk drives soon found this out—when they turned their computers off, their work disappeared. Of course, your computer does have at least a floppy disk drive and possibly a hard disk drive. This allows you to take advantage of Turbo Pascal's powerful disk file operations. Learning to use disk files is vital to producing useful programs, and Turbo Pascal helps by supporting three basic types of disk files: *text*, *typed*, and *untyped*. This chapter discusses how you create and use these kinds of files.

File Handling Concepts

All Turbo Pascal files, regardless of type, share common characteristics. First, all files are used for either input or output. Input is when a program takes data from a file and uses it in the program; output stores the results of a program in a file or sends the results to a *device* such as a terminal or printer. As you will see, it is also possible for a file to be used for both input and output.

Files can be stored on floppy disks and hard disk drives. There are, of course, other storage media (tape, optical disks, RAM disks, and so on), but they are less common. DOS requires that every file have a name of one to eight characters. Filenames can also include a three-letter *extension* that usually helps describe the contents of a file. For example, the Turbo Pascal program file is named TURBO.EXE. The .EXE filename extension tells DOS that this is a program file that can be executed from the DOS prompt. Turbo Pascal source files (the files you create with the Turbo Pascal editor) generally have the .PAS filename extension (for example, PROG1.PAS).

If a file is stored in a DOS directory, the directory path is also part of the filename. If, for example, the file PROG1.PAS is in the Turbo directory on drive C:, the full description or *pathname* of the filename is C:\TURBO\PROG1.PAS. DOS filename conventions are discussed in detail in the DOS user's manual. You should be thoroughly familiar with these conventions before using Turbo Pascal files.

Turbo Pascal Text Files

Text files consist of lines that are terminated by a carriage return and linefeed (CR/LF) and which contain characters, words, and sentences, as shown in Figure 9-1. The CR/LF

File Name: TEXT.DAT

Line 1 → This is an example of a line of text.[CR/LF]
Line 2 → Every line in a text file ends with a[CR/LF]
Line 3 → carriage return and linefeed.[CR/LF]
Line 4 → [CR/LF]
Line 5 → Even empty lines, like the one above.[CR/LF]
Line 6 → 50 12.23 0.23 40343 332324[CR/LF]

Figure 9-1.   A typical text file

combination (ASCII codes 10 and 13) is known as a delimiter. A delimiter marks the end of some element, such as a field, record, or in this case, the end of a line.

You can tell if a file consists of text by using the DOS **Type** command. For example, your Turbo Pascal disk comes with a text file called README. If you enter **TYPE README** at the DOS prompt and press ENTER, the file is displayed on the screen in a readable form. If, on the other hand, you try to display a nontext file (such as TURBO.EXE) in the same way, you will see only gibberish.

Text-File Identifiers

Before you work with text files, you must declare a *text-file identifier* in your program. Text-file identifiers are declared just like variable identifiers, except that the Turbo Pascal reserved word **Text** is used. An example of a text-file declaration is as follows:

```
Program TextFile;
Var
      TxtFile : Text;
```

In this illustration, **TxtFile** is a variable identifier of type **Text**. Before using **TxtFile** for input or output, you must assign it to a disk file. A typical **Assign** statement looks like this:

```
Assign(TxtFile,'TEXT.DAT');
```

Once **TxtFile** is assigned to TEXT.DAT, the disk file is never referred to by name again: all file operations refer to the identifier **TxtFile**.

After you assign a file identifier to a disk file, prepare the disk file with one of three Turbo Pascal commands—**Reset**, **Rewrite**, or **Append**. **Reset** opens the disk file and prepares it as an input file. Only input commands can be used on a file that has been reset. Any attempt to write to a **Reset** text file generates an I/O (input/output) error.

The **Reset** command also positions the *file pointer*, a counter that keeps track of a program's position in a file, at the beginning of the file. This causes all input to start at the very beginning of the file and move forward from there.

An attempt to *Reset* a file that does not exist generates an I/O error. You can override the I/O error, if desired, by disabling the **I** compiler directive with the statement {$I –}.

Rewrite and **Append** both prepare a text file for output, but they function in different ways. When an existing file is prepared with **Rewrite**, its contents are erased and the file pointer is placed at the beginning of the file. If the file identifier is assigned to a nonexisting file, the **Rewrite** command creates a file with the name given in the **Assign** statement. The **Append** command, on the other hand, preserves the contents of a file and positions the file pointer at the very end of the file. As a result, any data added to the file is appended to what is already there.

As with the **Reset** statement, should you attempt to use **Append** on a file that does not exist, Turbo Pascal generates an I/O error.

When you are finished using a file for either input or output, you must close the file. The **Close** command performs this task and performs several other tasks in the process. **Close** makes sure that all data in temporary buffers is stored to disk. This is known as *flushing the buffer* and is discussed in detail later in this chapter.

The **Close** command also frees up a DOS *file handle*. A file handle is a mechanism that DOS provides to programs that helps manage file operations. When you **Reset** or **Rewrite** a file, DOS allocates a file handle to Turbo Pascal. Because DOS limits the number of file handles, you cannot have more than 15 Turbo Pascal files open at one time. Closing files keeps the supply of file handles plentiful. Finally, the **Close** command updates the DOS file directory to reflect the file's size, time, and date.

Once closed, a file cannot be used for input or output until it is opened again with **Reset**, **Rewrite**, or **Append**. The link between the file identifier and the disk file, however, remains in force even after the file is closed. Therefore, to reopen a file, it is not necessary to repeat the **Assign** command. This process is illustrated in Figure 9-2.

```
Program FileTime;
Var
   TxtFile : Text;

Begin
Assign(TxtFile,'TEXT.DAT');     ◄─────── Links TxtFile to the file TEXT.DAT

Reset(TxtFile);    ◄─────────────────── Prepares TxtFile to be read

Rewrite(TxtFile); ◄──────────────────── Prepares TxtFile to be written to

Close(TxtFile);   ◄──────────────────── Closes TxtFile, updates DOS directory


Append(TxtFile); ◄───────────────────── Reopens TxtFile for additional output


Close(TxtFile); ◄────────────────────── Final closing ensures
                                         that all output is saved
End.
```

Figure 9-2.   Opening text files

Reading Strings from Text Files

Once a text file is reset, you can extract information from it with the **Read** and **ReadLn** procedures. Examples of text-file input can be seen in the following program, in which the disk file TEXT.DAT is linked to the file identifier **TxtFile**.

```
Program Text1;
Var
   TxtFile : Text;
   s : String[80];

Begin
Assign(TxtFile,'TEXT.DAT');
Reset(TxtFile);

ReadLn(TxtFile,s);
WriteLn(s);

Read(TxtFile,s);
WriteLn(s);
Close(TxtFile);
End.
```

Subsequently, **TxtFile** is prepared for reading with the **Reset** command. The first input operation in this program example is the statement

ReadLn(TxtFile,s);

which tells Turbo Pascal to read characters from the current line in the file and place them into the string variable s. After the characters are read, the file pointer skips any remaining characters on the line and moves to the beginning of the next line in the file.

When reading in a string from a text file with the **ReadLn** procedure, three possible situations can occur:

- There are exactly enough characters left in the line to fill the string to its maximum length.

- There are not enough characters left in the line to fill the string to its maximum length.

- There are more characters left in the line than are needed to fill the string to its maximum length.

In the first two cases, Turbo Pascal reads in all the characters left in the line, assigns them to s, and then moves the file pointer to the beginning of the next line. The string length is set equal to the number of characters read.

In the third case, Turbo Pascal reads in as many characters as necessary to fill the **String** variable and then moves the file pointer to the next line. Any characters between the end of the string and the end of the line are discarded.

The **Read** procedure operates much like the **ReadLn** procedure, but after it reads in a string, **Read** places the file pointer just after the last character read; it does not move the file pointer to the beginning of the next line. If the **Read** procedure encounters a CR/LF (or just a simple carriage return), indicating the end of the line has been reached, it stops reading characters and also does not advance the file pointer until a **ReadLn** procedure is used.

Reading Multiple Strings per Line

A single **ReadLn** procedure can read in several strings at one time. For example, the statement

ReadLn(TxtFile,s1,s2,s3)

reads characters from the current line and fills the **String** variables **s1**, **s2**, and **s3** in order. If the line being read is

This is a line of characters

and the **String** variables are all of type **String[5]**, the **Strings** would be assigned values as follows:

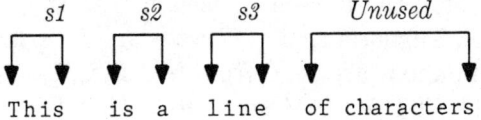

Reading Numbers from Text Files

Text files can store not only words and sentences, but also numeric data. Numbers, however, are not stored in their binary form but as characters. For example, in RAM, the **Integer** value 20,545 is stored as two bytes with a binary value of 0101000001000001. But in a text file, the number is stored as the characters 2, 0, 5, 4, 5, requiring a total of five bytes. When reading the number 20,545 from a text file, Turbo Pascal translates the number from a string of characters into binary integer format.

As it reads a number from a text file, Turbo Pascal skips the blank characters in a line until it finds a nonblank character. It then reads in characters until it encounters either another nonblank character or a CR/LF. When the characters are read in, Turbo Pascal combines the characters into an alphanumeric string and converts the string into either an **Integer** or a **Real** value, depending on the type of variable being used. If the

11	27.53	6.4144900000E + 02
21	50.83	1.1843390000E + 03
31	74.13	1.7272290000E + 03
41	97.43	2.2701190000E + 03
51	120.73	2.8130090000E + 03
61	144.03	3.3558990000E + 03
71	167.33	3.8987890000E + 03
81	190.63	4.4416790000E + 03
91	213.93	4.9845690000E + 03
101	237.23	5.5274590000E + 03

Figure 9-3.   TEST.DAT, a numeric text file

conversion is successful, the number is assigned to the variable; if it is not successful, Turbo Pascal generates an I/O error.

To learn how numbers are read from text files, examine the numeric text file TEST.DAT in Figure 9-3. This file contains three columns of numbers. The first column is **Integer**s, the second **Real** numbers in decimal format, and the third **Real** numbers in scientific notation. You can read the three numbers on each line of the file by employing the following statements:

```
Read(TxtFile,i);
Read(TxtFile,r1);
ReadLn(TxtFile,r2);
```

or by using the equivalent single statement:

```
ReadLn(TxtFile,i,r1,r2);
```

Turbo Pascal assigns the first number found in a line to the **Integer** variable **i** and the next two numbers to **Real** variables **r1** and **r2**.

The following program contains a routine that reads the numerical file TEST.DAT and calculates the average of each column of figures.

```
Program ComputeAverages;
Var
  f : Text;

  i,count : Integer;

  imean,
  r1,r2,
  r1mean,
  r2mean : Real;

Begin
Assign(f,'TEST.DAT');
Reset(f);

count := 0;
imean := 0;
r1mean := 0;
r2mean := 0;

While Not Eof(f) Do
  Begin
  ReadLn(f,i,r1,r2);
  WriteLn(i:10,' ',r1:10:3,' ',r2:10:3);

  count := count + 1;
  imean := imean + i;
  r1mean := r1mean + r1;
  r2mean := r2mean + r2;
  End;

imean := imean / count;
r1mean := r1mean / count;
r2mean := r2mean / count;

WriteLn;
WriteLn(imean:10:3,' ',r1mean:10:3,' ',r2mean:10:3);
Close(f);
WriteLn;
Write('Press ENTER...');
ReadLn;
End.
```

This program introduces the Turbo Pascal standard function **Eof**, which stands for end-of-file. **Eof** is a Boolean function that is true only when the file pointer is at the end of your file. It can be used to repeat input commands so that an entire file is processed from beginning to end. In the previous example, the statement

While Not Eof(f) Do

tells Turbo Pascal to execute the next block of code until **Eof(f)** returns TRUE, that is, until the last character in the file is read.

The function **Eoln** tests for the end of a line. **Eoln** is true under two conditions: when the file pointer encounters a carriage return and when the file pointer reaches the end of a file. You can use **Eoln** to read each character in a line one by one, as is shown in Figure 9-4. **Eoln** reads the characters in a line and writes them out on separate lines.

SeekEof and SeekEoln

To give you even more control over text files, Turbo Pascal offers **SeekEof** and **SeekEoln**. Like their counterparts **Eof** and **Eoln**, **SeekEof** returns TRUE at the end of a file and **SeekEoln** returns TRUE at the end of a line. These functions have a unique capability to skip over ASCII characters in the range 0

```
Program ReadChar;

Var
  f : Text;
  i : Integer;
  c : Array [1..1000] Of Char;

Begin
Assign(f,'TEST.TXT');
Reset(f);

While Not Eof(f) Do          ◄─── Continue for the entire file
  Begin
  While Not Eoln(f) Do       ◄─── Continue until next carriage return
    Begin
    Read(f,Ch);
    WriteLn(Ch);
    End;
  ReadLn(f);                 ◄─── Skip past the carriage return,
  End;                            to beginning of the next line

Close(f);
End.
```

Figure 9-4.   Reading characters from a text file

to 32 when testing for end-of-file or end-of-line. This range includes the standard ASCII control characters as well as the blank character. Consequently, **SeekEof** returns TRUE even when there are characters left in the file, so long as those characters are blank or control codes.

Errors in Numeric Input

If the format of a number read from a text file is incorrect, the program produces an I/O error. For example, reading the number 50,000 into an **Integer** variable would cause an error because the largest **Integer** allowable is 32,767. Similarly, reading the number 32.1 into an **Integer** variable would cause an error because of the decimal place, which is illegal for **Integer**s. **Real** variables pose fewer restrictions since numbers can be read with or without a decimal place or in scientific notation.

Writing Text Files

A text file can be used for output after being prepared with the **Rewrite** or **Append** procedures, as discussed earlier in this chapter. Once prepared, the **Write** or **WriteLn** procedures output the file. The first parameter in these procedures, the text-file identifier, tells Turbo Pascal where to send the data. It is followed by any number of variable identifiers or literal values to be output. For example, the following statements write the line "Jones 21" to the text file identified as **TxtFile**.

```
Name := 'Jones';
i := 21;
WriteLn(TxtFile,name,' ',i);
```

Write and **WriteLn** normally output values without any special formatting. Adding a colon and a number after the parameter, however, specifies that the value is to be right-justified in a space defined by the number. For example, these statements

```
Name := 'Johnson';
WriteLn(Name)
WriteLn(Name:20);
WriteLn(Name:4);
```

result in the following output:

```
Johnson
            Johnson
Johnson
```

The first **WriteLn** statement is unformatted, so the value is written left-justified. The second statement tells Turbo Pascal to create a field 20 characters wide and to right-justify the value within this field. Since the name "Johnson" is seven characters long, Turbo Pascal right-justifies the name by preceding it with 13 blanks. The third statement is also formatted, but the field width of 4 is less than the length of the value itself. When this occurs, the formatting has no effect. **Integer**s follow the same output formatting as **String**s: a single colon followed by the number of spaces to right-justify the number. **Real**s, however, can be formatted with either one or two parameters. The first parameter determines the width of the field in which the number will be right justified, and the second determines the number of decimal places. The following program demonstrates various formats for **Real** numbers and shows their results:

```
Program RealFormat;
Var
  r : Real;
Begin
r := 123.23;
WriteLn(r);            (* Result: ' 1.2323000000E+02'  *)
WriteLn(r:0);          (* Result: ' 1.2E+02'           *)
WriteLn(r:10);         (* Result: ' 1.2323E+02'        *)
WriteLn(r:10:2);       (* Result: ' 123.23'            *)
WriteLn(r:0:0);        (* Result: ' 123'               *)
WriteLn;
Write('Press ENTER...');
ReadLn;
End.
```

Disk Files and Buffers

Reading from and writing to a disk file are two of the slowest operations a computer performs. The time it takes for a disk drive to locate data seems like years to a microprocessor. Small chunks of memory called *buffers* are set aside for data to be used in disk operations. Buffers speed up processing by reducing the number of disk reads and writes. For example, suppose a program reads five characters from a text file with the following statements:

```
Read(TxtFile,Ch1);
Read(TxtFile,Ch2);
Read(TxtFile,Ch3);
Read(TxtFile,Ch4);
Read(TxtFile,Ch5);
```

If the input is not buffered, the program must go to the disk for each character read. If, however, the program picks up all five characters with the first **Read** statement and stores them in a buffer, the buffer can distribute the characters to the next four **Read** statements without having to access the disk.

Turbo Pascal provides text files with a standard 128-byte buffer. Every time a program reads data from a text file, the buffer is filled with 128 bytes, even if you only ask for 10. Of course, you will never know the extra bytes are in memory since Turbo Pascal takes care of all that for you.

When you process large text files, the standard 128-byte buffer is inadequate. Turbo Pascal allows you to expand a text file's buffer with the **SetTextBuf** procedure, in which you specify a variable to use as the buffer, for example:

```
Var
  f : Text;
  Buffer : Array [1..512] of Byte;
Begin
Assign(f,'TEST.DAT');
SetTextBuf(f, Buffer);
Reset(f);
```

This code assigns a buffer of 512 bytes to text file F, though you could have made the buffer larger. Be careful, however, not to call **SetTextBuf** once you have opened a file, or you will probably lose some data. Also, make sure that the buffer is declared globally; if you use a local buffer, you might lose data if the local variable is discarded.

Flushing a File

When writing to a buffered file, Turbo Pascal actually sends the data to an output buffer. When the buffer is filled, the entire contents are written to the disk at one time.

To force Turbo Pascal to empty an output buffer before it is filled, use the **Flush** procedure. The statement **Flush(f)** forces any data in the **f** buffer to be saved to disk immediately, thus eliminating any possibility that the data will be lost. Closing an output file automatically flushes the output buffer.

Typed Files

Typed files are files that contain data of a particular type, such as **Integer**s, **Real**s, **Record**s, and so on. These valuable files can make your programming easier and more efficient. In fact, typed files provide far faster input and output than do text files.

Unlike text files, which are unstructured, typed files have a rigid structure that is dependent on, and defined by, the type of data they hold. In the following example, the file identifier **f** is declared as a typed file called File of Real.

```
Program TypedFile;
Var
     f : File Of Real;
```

This declaration tells Turbo Pascal that this file will be used to store only **Real** numbers. In fact, this file will store **Real** numbers in the same format in which they are stored in RAM.

Herein lies the reason that typed files are fast: because they bypass all the translation and conversion processes that data undergoes within text files, they can transfer the data directly to memory.

For example, a file that is declared to be of type **Integer** knows that it is to store only **Integer**s; the data within it does not have to be converted into **Integer**s before it can be processed.

Records and Untyped Files

Because they are not made up of lines, as are text files, typed files cannot use the **ReadLn** and **WriteLn** statements. But if typed files are not organized into lines, how are they organized? Untyped files are organized into records, each data item representing one record. The length of a record corresponds to the number of bytes required to store the data type. In the previous example, the file stores numbers of type **Real**. Since a **Real** number requires six bytes in Turbo Pascal, the record length for the file is six bytes: the first six bytes of the file contain the first record (**Real** number), the next six contain the second record, and so on. For **Integer**s, numbers that require just two bytes, an untyped file is organized into two-byte records.

The following program shows how a typed file is declared, used for output, and then used for input:

```
Program RealFile;
Uses CRT;
Var
   r : Real;
   f : File Of Real;
Begin
ClrScr;
Assign(f,'REAL.DAT');
Rewrite(f);

r := 100.234;
Write(f,r);

r := 32.23;
Write(f,r);

r := 9894.40;
```

```
Write(f,r);

Reset(f);

While Not Eof(f) Do
  Begin
  Read(f,r);
  WriteLn(r:0:3);
  End;
WriteLn;
Write('Press ENTER...');
ReadLn;
End.
```

This program writes out three **Real** numbers. Since each **Real** number requires six bytes, the size of the file is 18 bytes. You can confirm this with the **Dir** command at the DOS prompt.

Strings and Typed Files

Typed files can also be of a **String** type, but this is very different from a text file. Even though both are designed to hold strings, the way they store strings is what separates them. Consider the following example:

```
Program OutputCompare;
Type
  Str10 = String[10];
Var
  TxtFile : Text;
  StringFile : File Of Str10;
  s : Str10;

Begin
WriteLn('Rewriting OUTPUT.TXT');
Assign(TxtFile,'OUTPUT.TXT');
Rewrite(TxtFile);

WriteLn('Rewriting OUTPUT.STR');
Assign(StringFile,'OUTPUT.STR');
Rewrite(StringFile);

s := 'ABCD';

WriteLn('Writing to OUTPUT.TXT');
Write(TxtFile,s);
WriteLn('Writing to OUTPUT.STR');
Write(StringFile,s);
WriteLn('Closing files.');
Close(TxtFile);
```

```
Close(StringFile);
WriteLn;
Write('Press ENTER...');
ReadLn;
End.
```

The program declares two files, one Text and the other type File Of Str[10]. Both files are prepared for output, and the string 'ABCD' is written to both. This is where the similarity ends.

In the case of the Text file, Turbo Pascal writes the letters A, B, C, and D and nothing more, as shown here:

A	B	C	D

In the typed file, however, Turbo Pascal stores the string in its full form: the length byte, the legitimate characters in the string (ABCD), and any garbage characters that fill out the remaining six bytes of storage, as shown here:

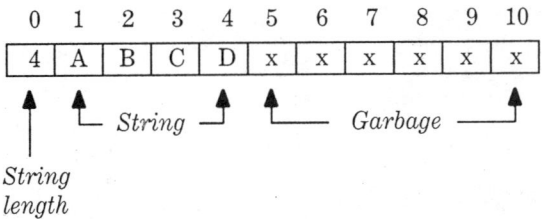

This example demonstrates that **String** files require more space than text files because the **Record** includes the string length byte as well as any garbage bytes.

Typed Files and Speed

The data stored in a typed file has exactly the same form that it has when it is stored in RAM. This fact leads to a tremendous increase in input/output performance when compared to text-file processing. Why? Because every time Turbo Pascal uses a text file, some time is wasted while numbers are converted into characters and back again and strings are stripped of their length byte and any unused bytes. Data from typed files, on the other hand, can be read directly into RAM without any transformation. That means less work for the computer and, as a result, faster processing.

More Complex Typed Files

Just as you can define your own data types, you can also define a file to hold these data types. For example, a record of data type **Customer** with fields Name, Address, and Telephone could be stored in a file as defined in the following program:

```pascal
Program RecordFile;
Uses CRT;
Type
  CustomerRec = Record
    Name : String[30];
    Address : String[40];
    Telephone : String[15];
    End;

Var
  Customer : CustomerRec;
  CustFile : File Of CustomerRec;

(*****************************************************)

Procedure CreateFile;
Var
  i : Integer;
Begin
Assign(CustFile,'CUST.DAT');
Rewrite(CustFile);

With Customer Do
  Begin
  Name       := 'L. M. Quibble';
  Address    := 'New York City';
  Telephone := '(123) 456-7890';
  End;
Write(CustFile,Customer);

With Customer Do
  Begin
  Name       := 'Berlina Flopp';
```

```
        Address   := 'Miami';
        Telephone := '(098) 765-4321';
        End;
    Write(CustFile,Customer);

    With Customer Do
      Begin
      Name      := 'Arthur Brainer';
      Address   := 'Hollywood';
      Telephone := '(111) 222-3333';
      End;
    Write(CustFile,Customer);

    Close(CustFile);
    End;

    (*******************************************************)

    Begin
    ClrScr;
    CreateFile;

    Assign(CustFile,'CUST.DAT');
    Reset(CustFile);

    While Not Eof(CustFile) Do
      Begin
      Read(CustFile,Customer);
      With Customer Do
        Begin
        WriteLn(Name,'  ',Address,' ',Telephone);
        End;
      End;
    Close(CustFile);
    WriteLn;
    Write('Press ENTER...');
    ReadLn;
    End.
```

Because the file is declared to be of the same type as the record **Customer**, it is possible to read and write a complete record at a time. This increases speed because you do not have to read or write each item of the record separately.

Untyped Files

Untyped files are an especially powerful tool provided by Turbo Pascal. While text files assume that a file consists of lines terminated with CR/LF, and typed files assume that a file consists of a particular type of data structure, untyped files make no assumptions about the structure of the data in a file. You can read data from an untyped file into any data type you want.

Because Turbo Pascal makes no assumptions about the format of the data, the transfer from disk to your data structure is immediate. This is why untyped files are used for applications requiring high-speed input and output.

The following example, which copies the contents of one file to another, demonstrates a typical use of untyped files. As you can see, two file identifiers, **SourceFile** and **DestFile**, are declared to be of type **File**. Untyped files get their name from the fact that the reserved word **File** is not followed by a type specification, as is the case with typed files.

```
Program CopyFile;
Uses CRT;
Var
  SourceFile,
  DestFile    : File;
  RecordsRead : Integer;
  Buffer : Array [1..1000] Of Byte;

Begin
ClrScr;
If ParamCount <> 2 Then
  Begin
  WriteLn('CopyFile [FromFile] [ToFile]');
  Halt;
  End;

Assign(SourceFile,ParamStr(1));
{$I-}
Reset(SourceFile,1);
If IOresult <> 0 Then
  Begin
  WriteLn(ParamStr(1),' not found.');
  Halt;
  End;

Assign(DestFile,ParamStr(2));
Rewrite(DestFile,1);

WriteLn('. = 1,000 bytes copied.');

BlockRead(SourceFile,Buffer,SizeOf(Buffer),RecordsRead);

While RecordsRead > 0 Do
  Begin
```

```
Write('.');
BlockWrite(DestFile,Buffer,RecordsRead);
BlockRead(SourceFile,Buffer,SizeOf(Buffer),RecordsRead);
End;

Close(SourceFile);
Close(DestFile);
WriteLn;
Write('Press ENTER...');
ReadLn;
End.
```

Unlike text and typed files, the **Reset** and **Rewrite** statements for untyped files can take a second parameter, the record size. For example, the statement

Reset(SourceFile,1);

prepares the file to be read and specifies that the record length is 1 byte. This makes sense since the data structure is an array of **Bytes**. If the data structure were an array of **Integers**, you could set the record length to 2. While Turbo Pascal does not require you to match the record length to the size of the data type you are using, doing so makes programming easier. Note that if you do not specify a record length in the **Reset** or **Rewrite** statements, Turbo Pascal assigns a default record length of 128 bytes. Reading and writing to untyped files requires two special Turbo Pascal standard procedures, **BlockRead** and **BlockWrite**. In the previous example, the statement

BlockRead(SourceFile,Buffer,SizeOf(Buffer),RecordsRead);

takes four parameters. The file identifier **SourceFile** is first. The second parameter specifies the data structure into which the data will be placed. In the example, the data structure is the array of bytes **Buffer**.

The third parameter specifies the number of records to read. In the example, the record size was set to 1 byte by the **Reset** statement. The data structure **Buffer**, however, is 10,000 bytes in length. To completely fill **Buffer**, then, you have to read in 10,000 records. You could simply write in the number 10,000 as the third parameter, but the Turbo Pascal standard function

SizeOf offers a better alternative. **SizeOf** returns the number of bytes used by a specific data structure. For example, if **i** is an **Integer**, then **SizeOf(i)** returns the value 2 because **Integers** require two bytes of storage. In the example, the statement **SizeOf(Buffer)** returns 10,000 because that is the number of bytes **Buffer** uses. By using the **SizeOf** function, you can change the size of the buffer without having to change **BlockRead** statements.

The fourth and last parameter in the **BlockRead** statement is the **Integer** variable **RecordsRead**. When the **BlockRead** statement executes, it attempts to read in the number of records specified (10,000 in the example). However, if the file pointer is close to the end of the file, you may actually read fewer than 10,000 records. **RecordsRead** tells you exactly how many records were read by the **BlockRead** statement. When **RecordsRead** equals zero, the end of the file has been reached.

BlockWrite operates much the same as **BlockRead**, except that there are only three parameters. The file identifier comes first, followed by the data structure used for the output. The third parameter is the number of records to write to the file. In the example program **CopyFile**, **RecordsRead** specifies the number of records to write because you want to write out exactly what was read in.

Procedures for Typed and Untyped Files

Nontext files (that is, typed and untyped files) are also known as *random access files*, meaning that records in a file can be accessed in nonsequential order. If you want to, you can read the third record first, then the tenth record, and the first record after that. This is done in a two-step process: first position the file pointer at the correct record, and then read the record. This is demonstrated in the following program, which creates a typed data file and then reads the records back in nonsequential order.

```
Program DataBaseFile;
(*$v-*)
Uses CRT;
Type
  MaxStr  = String[255];
  CustRec = Record
```

```
      Name : String[30];
      Age  : Integer;
      Income : Real;
      End;

Var
  Cust : CustRec;
  CustFile : File Of CustRec;

(**********)

Procedure AddRec(NameIn : MaxStr;
                 AgeIn : Integer;
                 IncomeIn : Real);
Begin
With Cust Do
  Begin
  Name := NameIn;
  Age := AgeIn;
  Income := IncomeIn;
  Write(CustFile,Cust);
  End;
End;

(**********)

Procedure DumpRec;
Begin
WriteLn;
With Cust Do
  Begin
  WriteLn('Name:    ',Name);
  WriteLn('Age:     ',Age);
  WriteLn('Income: ',Income:0:0);
  End;
End;

(**********)

Begin
ClrScr;
Assign(CustFile,'CUSTFILE.DAT');
Rewrite(CustFile);

AddRec('Jones',30,23000.0);
AddRec('Adams',65,34000.0);
AddRec('Smith',21,18000.0);

Reset(CustFile);

WriteLn('The number of records in the file is: ',
        FileSize(CustFile));
WriteLn;
Write('Press ENTER...');
ReadLn;
```

```
(*****************************************************************)
(* Write out the contents of the third record in the file.   *)
(* Because the first record in a file is number 0, the third *)
(* record is number 2.                                       *)
(*****************************************************************)

Seek(CustFile,2);
WriteLn;
WriteLn;
WriteLn('This is record number: ',FilePos(CustFile)+1);
Read(CustFile,Cust);
DumpRec;
WriteLn;
Write('Press ENTER...');
ReadLn;

(************************************************************)
(* Write out the contents of the first record in the file. *)
(************************************************************)

Seek(CustFile,0);
WriteLn;
WriteLn;
WriteLn('This is record number: ',FilePos(CustFile)+1);
Read(CustFile,Cust);
DumpRec;
WriteLn;
Write('Press ENTER...');
ReadLn;

(*************************************************************)
(* Write out the contents of the second record in the file. *)
(*************************************************************)

Seek(CustFile,1);
WriteLn;
WriteLn;
WriteLn('This is record number: ',FilePos(CustFile)+1);
Read(CustFile,Cust);
DumpRec;
WriteLn;
Write('Press ENTER...');
ReadLn;

(********************************************)
(* Change the contents of the first record *)
(********************************************)

Seek(CustFile,0);
AddRec('Arnold',32,43000.0);

Seek(CustFile,0);
WriteLn;
WriteLn;
```

```
WriteLn('This is record number: ',FilePos(CustFile)+1);
Read(CustFile,Cust);
DumpRec;
WriteLn;
Write('Press ENTER...');
ReadLn;

Close(CustFile);
End.
```

The **Seek** statement moves the file pointer to the beginning of the third record. Note that the third record is referred to as number 2 in the **Seek** statement because Turbo Pascal typed files begin with record 0. When the file pointer is in place, you can read the record as you normally would. After the **Read** is executed, the file pointer is automatically moved to the beginning of the next record. In this case, the third record is the last record in the file. Any attempt to read beyond the end of the file results in an I/O error.

An example of a nonsequential **Read** is shown by the following two statements:

```
Seek(CustFile,2);
Read(CustFile,Cust);
```

Two other standard functions, **FileSize** and **FilePos**, are also used. **FileSize** returns the total number of records in the file; **FilePos** returns the current position of the file pointer.

An especially powerful feature of random access files is the ability to update records at any point in the file. This is demonstrated at the end of the previous example program (titled **DataBaseFile**), where the information in the first record is changed and then displayed. What is particularly noteworthy is that the **Write** procedure is used without a preceding **Rewrite** statement. This seems to go against the rule that a file must be prepared with **Rewrite** before you can add data to it. For nontext files, the **Rewrite** command is only necessary to create the file. Once the file exists, the **Reset** command allows you to both read and write to the file.

Erasing and Renaming Files

Sophisticated file management requires the ability to rename and erase files without going back to the DOS prompt. Turbo Pascal provides two procedures to do just that. To rename a file, first assign a file to a file variable, then call the **Rename** procedure with the new name specified:

```
Assign(f,'FILE.OLD');
Rename(f,'FILE.NEW');
```

The **Erase** procedure works essentially the same way. Assign the disk file to a file identifier and then call the **Erase** procedure.

```
Assign(f,'FILE.OLD');
Erase(f);
```

The following program provides a simple method for renaming and erasing files. When you start the program, three choices are presented: rename a file, erase a file, or quit.

```
Program FileControl;
Uses CRT;
Var
  Filel : File;
  Name1,
  Name2 : String[255];
  Choice : Char;

Begin
ClrScr;
  Repeat
  Write('R)ename, E)rase, Q)uit: ');
  ReadLn(Choice);

    Case Upcase(Choice) Of
    'R':
      Begin
      Write('Name of file to rename: ');
      ReadLn(Name1);
      Write('New name for the file: ');
      ReadLn(Name2);
      Assign(Filel,Name1);
      Rename(Filel,Name2);
```

```
      End;
   'E':
     Begin
     Write('Name of file to erase: ');
     ReadLn(Name1);
     Assign(File1,Name1);
     Erase(File1);
     End;
   End; (* of case *)

 Until Upcase(Choice) = 'Q';
End.
```

Make a selection by typing **R**, **E**, or **Q** and pressing ENTER. When renaming a file, enter the name of the existing file as well as the new name for the file. Erasing a file requires only that you enter the name of the file to be erased.

General Programming Techniques: Strings, Recursion, and Files

Using Strings in Turbo Pascal
Using Recursion in Turbo Pascal
DOS Devices

A carpenter can build many houses of different shapes and sizes using the same tools and techniques. Like carpenters, programmers use the same tools over and over to perform common programming tasks. A well-stocked programming toolbox is a sure sign of an experienced programmer. This chapter introduces several useful tools that can make your programming easier and better.

Using Strings in Turbo Pascal

The Turbo Pascal **String** data type (which is described in Chapter 5) is a powerful and frequently used data structure. While it is most commonly used to hold words and messages, a string can perform far more interesting tasks.

As you may recall, a string consists of a length byte followed by as many bytes as are defined in the string declaration. For example, **String[4]** declares a 5-byte data type: one length byte followed by four character bytes.

One of the reasons that the **String** type is so powerful is that it can be processed in two different ways: by directly manipulating its individual elements or by using one of the Turbo Pascal standard functions and procedures for strings. Both methods (each of which are discussed in this chapter) have advantages, depending on the circumstances.

Standard Procedures and Functions for Strings

Because they require a great many character manipulations, string-handling procedures are sometimes difficult to write. Turbo Pascal eliminates the need to write these character-by-character manipulations by providing powerful standard functions, making string manipulation an easy job.

Chr

The standard function **Chr** accepts an **Integer** parameter and returns its equivalent ASCII value. For example, because ASCII code 65 represents the character "A," the statement **Chr(65)** returns **A**.

While it is not a **String** procedure, the **Chr** function is frequently used with **String** statements, especially those with unusual characters. For example, the following program writes out a string with a double exclamation point, a character represented by ASCII code 19.

```
Program DoubleExclamation;
Uses CRT;
Var
  s : String[20];
Begin
ClrScr;
s := 'Wow' + Chr(19);
WriteLn(s);
WriteLn;
Write('Press ENTER...');
ReadLn;
End.
```

Upcase

Upcase, another character-level function, accepts a single lowercase alphabetic character from a to z and returns its uppercase equivalent. If the character is not lowercase and alphabetic, **Upcase** returns the character unchanged.

Concat

Concatenation is the combination of several strings into a single string. Turbo Pascal offers two ways to concatenate strings: **Concat** and the **Plus** (+) operator.

The standard function **Concat** accepts any number of strings as parameters and returns them as one string. This program shows how to use this function:

```
Program Concatenate;
Uses CRT;
Var
   s1,s2,s3 : String[80];
Begin
ClrScr;
s1 := 'This is the beginning -';
s2 := '- This is the end.';
s3 := Concat(s1,s2);
WriteLn(s3);
WriteLn;
Write('Press ENTER...');
ReadLn;
End.
```

In this example, strings **s1** and **s2** are passed into **Concat**, where they are combined and assigned to **s3**. When **s3** is written out, the message displayed is

This is the beginning -- This is the end.

Most programmers prefer to use the + operator to concatenate their strings, primarily because it is simpler to use and produces more readable code, as shown here:

```
Program Concat;
Uses CRT;
Var
   s1,s2,s3,s4: String[80];
Begin
ClrScr;
s1 := 'This is ';
```

```
s2 := 'all one ';
s3 := 'sentence.';

s4 := s1 + s2 + s3;
WriteLn(s4);
WriteLn;
Write('Press ENTER...');
ReadLn;
End.
```

The statement

```
    s4 := s1 + s2 + s3;
```

produces the same result as

```
    s4 := Concat(s1,s2,s3);
```

but the **+** operator is cleaner looking and easier to type.

With both **Concat** and the **+** operator, the concatenated string is truncated when the total length of the concatenated strings exceeds the maximum length of the receiving string.

Copy

The standard function **Copy** extracts a substring from a larger string. To use **Copy**, you must know where in the larger string you want to start copying and how many characters you want to copy. For example, the statement **Copy(s,12,3)** tells Turbo Pascal to return three characters from string **s** starting with character 12.

The following program uses the **Copy** function to write a long string as a column ten characters wide.

```
Program DoCopy;
Uses CRT;
Var
  s : String[80];
  i : Integer;

Begin
ClrScr;
s :=
'This is a long line that will be written out in a column.';
i := 1;
```

```
While i < Length(s) Do
  Begin
  WriteLn(Copy(s,i,10));
  i := i + 10;
  End;
WriteLn;
Write('Press ENTER...');
ReadLn;
End.
```

When you run this program, the output looks like this:

```
This is a
long line
that will
be written
 out in a
column.
```

Each line in the output, except the last line, contains ten characters, including blank characters. The last line contains only seven characters because this is all that remained at the end of the sentence. If you attempt to copy beyond the end of the string, you get either a partial result or no characters at all, but Turbo Pascal does not generate an error.

Delete

The **Delete** procedure removes characters from a string. As with **Copy**, you must specify the starting point in the string and the number of characters to delete. For example, the statement **Delete(s,5,3)** tells Turbo Pascal to delete three characters from string s starting at the fifth character.

Insert

The **Insert** procedure inserts a substring into another string. Three parameters are passed into **Insert**: the substring to insert, the string into which the substring will be inserted, and the position of the insertion. For example, the statement **Insert**

(s1,s2,4) tells Turbo Pascal to insert string **s1** into **s2** starting at the fourth character. This sample program illustrates both **Delete** and **Insert**:

```
Program TestInsert;
Uses CRT;
Var
  s1,s2 : String[80];

Begin
ClrScr;
s1 := 'A';
s2 := '1234567890';
WriteLn('Insert ',s1,' into ',s2);
Insert(s1,s2,3);
WriteLn(s2);
WriteLn('Remove ',s1,' from ',s2);
Delete(s2,3,1);
WriteLn(s2);
WriteLn;
Write('Press ENTER...');
ReadLn;
End.
```

This program displays the string '12A34567890', showing that "A" has been inserted into the third character in the string. The statement **Delete(s2,3,1)** then removes the "A" from the string and displays it once again.

Length

The standard function **Length** returns the number of characters currently held in a **String** variable. Thus, if a string **s** is equal to 'This is a string.   ', then **Length(s)** will be equal to 20. The blanks at the end of the string are counted as part of the string.

Pos

When you want to know if one string is contained in another, Turbo Pascal can tell you this with the standard function **Pos**. Consider the following example.

```
Program TestPos;
Uses CRT;
Var
  s : String[80];
Begin
ClrScr;
s := 'This is a test string';
WriteLn('The position of ''test'' in "',s,'" is: ',
        pos('test',s));
WriteLn('The position of ''TEST'' in "',s,'" is: ',
        pos('TEST',s));
WriteLn;
Write('Press ENTER...');
ReadLn;
End.
```

This program displays the following messages:

> The position of 'test' in "s" is: 11
> The position of 'TEST' in "s" is: 0

The first message confirms that the word "test" is located at the 11th character of the larger string. The second message simply shows that **Pos** returns zero when a match is not found.

Str and Val

Str and **Val**, two closely related standard procedures, are frequently used in programs that process numerical input and output. **Str** converts a number into a string, and **Val** converts a string into a number.

Str makes two parameters: a number (**Integer** or **Real**) and a **String** variable. The number can be formatted according to Turbo Pascal conventions. Examples of **Str** statements and their results are shown in Figure 10-1.

The first **Str** statement—**Str(10,s)**—converts an **Integer** to a **String** with no formatting. The statement **Str(10:4,s)**, on the other hand, is formatted as right-justified in a field four spaces wide. The resulting string, therefore, consists of two blank characters before the number 10.

Formatting **Real** numbers is a bit more complicated. When a **Real** number is unformatted, **Str** produces a string in scientific notation. For example, the statement **Str(3.2,s)** sets s

```
Var
  s : String[20];
```

Statement	Result
Str(10,s);	'10'
Str(10:4,s);	' 10'
Str(3.2,s);	' 3.2000000000E + 00'
Str(3.2:0,s);	'3.2E + 00'
Str(3.2:15:3,s);	' 3.200'

Figure 10-1.   Results of the Str procedure

equal to ' 3.2000000000E + 00'. Note that a string begins with a blank character and contains all significant digits. If the number is negative, the leading blank is replaced with a minus sign.

If the **Real** is formatted to a field width of 0 — **Str(3.2:0,s)** — the result is '3.2E + 00'. In this case, only the essential digits are present, and no blanks are added to the string. The final example, **Str(3.2:15:3,s)**, creates a 15-character string with three decimal places: '   3.200'.

The **Val** procedure accepts three parameters: the string to convert into a number, the numeric variable to receive the value, and an **Integer** variable used to flag errors. The following sample program shows how to use the **Val** procedure:

```
Program StringToNumber;
Uses CRT;
Type
  MaxStr = String[20];
Var
  r : Real;
  code : Integer;

(*****************************************)

Procedure WriteNumber(s : MaxStr);
Begin
Val(s,r,code);
If code = 0 Then
  WriteLn(r:0:3)
Else
  WriteLn('Error in numeric conversion');
End;

(*****************************************)
```

```
Begin
ClrScr;
WriteLn('Below is the conversion of 123.23');
WriteNumber('123.23');
WriteLn;
WriteLn('Below is the conversion of s123.23');
WriteLn;
WriteNumber('s123.23');
WriteLn;
Write('Press ENTER...');
ReadLn;
End.
```

At the heart of the sample program is the statement **Val(s,r,code)**, which attempts to convert string **s** into a valid **Real** number. If **s** contains a valid number in the correct format, the conversion will be successful and **code** will set to zero; if **s** contains a nonnumeric character, **code** will be set to a nonzero value.

To be valid for numeric conversions, a string must meet these conditions:

1. It must contain a number in **Integer, Real,** or scientific notation.

2. It must not contain any alphabetic or other characters not used in numeric representation. The "E" used in scientific notation is an exception.

3. It must not contain any trailing blanks—leading blanks are acceptable.

Table 10-1 shows examples of both valid and invalid strings for numeric conversion. As you can see, a string must be in a proper form before it can be converted.

Valid	Invalid	Reason
'12'	'1×2'	String contains nonnumeric character
'3.2E+100'	'3.2E+00 '	String contains a trailing blank character

Table 10-1.   Valid and Invalid Strings for Numeric Conversion

A final point on converting strings to numbers: if you try to convert a string that contains a valid **Real** number (for example, 1.32) into an **Integer**, Turbo Pascal generates an error. The safest approach in such cases is to convert all numeric strings into **Reals** and then convert the **Real** to an **Integer** with the **Round** or **Trunc** functions.

Direct Manipulation of Characters

While the Turbo Pascal string procedures are powerful, they do have limitations. For example, to change a string to all uppercase characters, you must process the string yourself. This is not a difficult task; a string, after all, is nothing more than an array of characters with a length byte in position zero. The following program shows how you can process strings. It contains the function **UpCaseStr**, which accepts a string parameter, changes all lowercase letters to uppercase, and then returns the string.

```
Program UpperCase;
Uses CRT;
Type
  MaxStr = String[255];
Var
  s : MaxStr;

(********************)

Function UpCaseStr(s : MaxStr) : MaxStr;
Var
  i,j : Integer;
Begin
j := ord(s[0]);
For i := 1 To j Do
  s[i] := Upcase(s[i]);
UpCaseStr := s;
End;

(********************)

Begin
ClrScr;
s := 'abc';
WriteLn(s);
WriteLn('Change to upper case.');
WriteLn(UpCaseStr(s));
WriteLn;
Write('Press ENTER...');
```

```
ReadLn;
End.
```

The first statement in the function **UpCaseStr** is

```
j := ord(s[0]);
```

where **s** is defined as **String[255]**. But **s[0]** appears to be outside the range 1..255. How can this be? Whatever their length, all strings have a character at position zero that contains the length of the string. The statement **ord(s[0])** converts that character into its equivalent byte value so that it can be assigned to the **Integer j**. The same thing could have been accomplished with the statement **j := Length(s)**.

The next part of the procedure processes the string from the first character to the last. A character that is referred to individually in a string (for example, **s[2]**) can be substituted for a variable of type **Char** in any expression. Thus, the **Upcase** procedure, which takes a parameter of type **Char**, can accept individual characters from a string.

```
For i := l to j Do
  s[i] := Upcase(s[i]);
```

When all characters in the string are uppercase, the function passes the altered string back to the program.

Manipulating the Length Byte

You can play some tricks with strings by altering the value of the length byte. This lets you lengthen or shorten a string without assigning a new value. For example, consider this block of code:

```
s  := 'ABCDEFG';
s[0] := Chr(3);
WriteLn(s);
```

When the string 'ABCDEFG' is assigned to variable **s**, Turbo Pascal sets the length to ASCII code 7. The next line, however, changes the length byte to ASCII code 3. The **Chr** function is used because Turbo Pascal considers the length byte to be a character. Thus, when the statement **WriteLn(s)** is executed, the output is **ABC**. In Turbo Pascal, changing the length byte changes the string.

On the other hand, changing characters in the string directly does not change the length byte, as illustrated by this code segment:

```
s := 'ABC';
s[4] := 'D';
s[5] := 'E';
WriteLn(s);
```

The first statement assigns the string 'ABC' to the variable and sets the length byte to ASCII code 3. The next two statements change the value in positions 4 and 5 of the string, but this does not affect the length byte. Therefore, the statement **WriteLn(s)** displays **ABC**, not **ABCDE**.

Direct manipulation of strings has many practical uses, such as the creation of strings for special text displays. For example, the following program uses an 80-character string that contains the double horizontal line character (ASCII code 205) to split the screen in half:

```
Program SplitScreen;
Uses CRT;
Type
  MaxStr = String[255];
Var
  Divider : MaxStr;

Begin
ClrScr;
FillChar(Divider,Sizeof(Divider),205);
Divider[0] := Chr(80);

Gotoxy(1,14);
Write(Divider);

Gotoxy(1,7);
Write('This is the upper portion of the screen.');

Gotoxy(1,21);
Write('This is the lower portion of the screen.');
```

```
WriteLn;
Write('Press ENTER...');
ReadLn;
End.
```

The first statement in the procedure,

FillChar(Divider,SizeOf(Divider),205);

fills the entire string, from position 0 to position 255, with the ASCII value 205. To make the string fill one line of the screen, however, the length byte must be 80. Therefore, the length byte is set to 80 with the statement

Divider[0] := Chr(80);

Now the string can be written to the screen, providing an attractive divider. In other places in the program, you might want to use the same string, but in shorter lengths, perhaps only 10 or 20 characters. Just change the length byte according to your needs; you do not have to change the characters because they are already set properly.

Resolving Programming Problems with Strings

Now that you understand how to manipulate **String** variables, you can put them to use. The rest of this section is devoted to some of the more common programming problems that can be resolved by creatively using strings.

A Search and Replace Procedure

From their earliest days, microcomputers have been associated with word processing and text editing. It is not surprising, therefore, that Turbo Pascal provides string procedures that closely resemble the features of a word processor. These procedures allow you to locate a combination of letters in a string, delete that combination, and replace it with another, as shown in the following example.

```
Program SearchAndReplace;
Uses CRT;
Var
  BigString : String[255];
  FindString,
  ReplaceString : String[20];
  i : Integer;

Begin
ClrScr;
FindString := 'Steve';
ReplaceString := 'John';
BigString :=
'Tell Steve to pay me the five dollars he owes me.';

WriteLn(BigString);
i := Pos(FindString,BigString);
Delete(BigString,i,Length(FindString));
Insert(ReplaceString,BigString,i);
WriteLn(BigString);
WriteLn;
Write('Press ENTER...');
ReadLn;
End.
```

This program uses four string procedures: **Pos**, **Delete**, **Insert**, and **Length**. The substring 'Steve' is contained in the larger string starting at the sixth character. Therefore, the statement

$$i := Pos(FindString,BigString);$$

assigns the value 6 to **i**.

Now that you know where in the larger string the substring is located, you can remove it with **Delete**. This is accomplished with the following statement:

$$Delete(BigString,i,Length(FindString));$$

In this case, the substring is the **String** variable **FindString**, which holds the value 'Steve'. The first parameter, **BigString**, contains **FindString**; the second parameter, **i**, indicates the position of **FindString** in **BigString**. Length(FindString), the third parameter, uses the standard function **Length** to tell the program how many characters to delete.

Because **FindString** is equal to 'Steve', **Length(Find-String)** is equal to 5. Thus, the **Delete** statement tells Turbo Pascal to delete five characters from **BigString**, starting with the sixth character.

Finally, the following statement inserts the second substring (**ReplaceString**) in **BigString** at exactly the same position as the other string.

```
Insert(ReplaceString,BigString,i);
```

This tells Turbo Pascal to insert **ReplaceString** into the **BigString** at position **i**.

Now that you know how the program works, you should be able to guess how it will look when it runs. The program first writes out **BigString** in its original form. It then substitutes 'John' for 'Steve' and writes **BigString** out again, as shown here:

```
Tell Steve to pay me the five dollars he owes me.
Tell John to pay me the five dollars he owes me.
```

Thus, by combining four of the string-processing procedures, you are able to perform a rather complex piece of programming with only a few lines of code.

Personalizing Messages

Obviously you cannot write a complete word processing program with these few functions. You can, however, put the search-and-replace principle to some clever uses. For example, suppose you want to add a personal touch to a program by inserting the user's name into some of the messages your computer displays. To do this, you need to know the user's name, in what strings it is to be inserted, and where it goes in those strings.

First, set a general rule: the @ character in a string indicates where the user's name should be placed. If the name is "John," the string 'Hello, @' would become 'Hello, John'. You can place the @ character anywhere you want the name to appear. The following sample program demonstrates how to do this:

```
Program InsertName;
Uses CRT;
Type
  Str255 = String[255];
Var
  Message1,
  Message2,
  Message3 : String[255];
  Name : String[20];

Function WriteMessage(s,Name : Str255) : Str255;
Var
  i : Integer;
Begin
i := Pos('@',s);
If i > 0 Then
  Begin
  Delete(s,i,1);
  Insert(Name,s,i);
  End;
WriteMessage := s;
End;

Begin
Message1 := 'Hello, @';
Message2 := 'This message is unchanged.';
Message3 := 'This message, @, has been changed.';

ClrScr;
Write('Enter your Name: ');
ReadLn(Name);

WriteLn(WriteMessage(Message1,Name));
WriteLn(WriteMessage(Message2,Name));
WriteLn(WriteMessage(Message3,Name));

WriteLn;
Write('Press ENTER...');
ReadLn;
End.
```

One problem with this program is that every time it encounters the @ character in a message, it replaces it with the user's name. For example, in the message 'This is the @ character, @.', you want the first @ to print as is and the second @ to change the individual's name. Unfortunately, **WriteMessage** will change the first @ and leave the second unchanged. Therefore, you should choose a character that will not be used in its literal form in messages.

Error-free Data Entry

Converting strings to numbers has one very important application: checking for errors in numbers entered by a user. For example, the code for a program that asks a user to enter his or her age may look like this:

```
Var
   Age : Integer;
Begin
Write('Enter age: ');
ReadLn(age);
End.
```

The problem with this code is that if a user enters invalid numbers or numbers with spaces, Turbo Pascal generates a run-time error and aborts the program. Avoid this situation by having the user enter the number into a string and then convert the string into a number. If the conversion fails, the user entered an invalid number, and you can ask for input again. The following program illustrates this method:

```
Program EnterNumber;
Uses CRT;
Var
   Age,Code : Integer;
   AgeString : String[10];
Begin
ClrScr;
   Repeat
   Write('Enter your age: ');
   ReadLn(AgeString);
   Val(AgeString,Age,Code);
   If Code <> 0 Then
      Write(^g);            (* Make the computer beep *)
   Until Code = 0;
WriteLn('Your age is : ',Age);
WriteLn;
Write('Press ENTER...');
ReadLn;
End.
```

In this example, when the user enters his or her age into the **String** variable **AgeString**, the program attempts to convert **AgeString** into the **Integer Age**. If the conversion fails, the **Integer** variable **Code** is set to a value other than zero. When this occurs, the program writes the character ^g, which makes the terminal beep, and continues the loop until the user enters a valid number.

Removing Blanks

As mentioned previously, blank characters at the end of a numeric string cause a numeric conversion to fail. The string ' 10 ', for example, cannot be converted to a numeric value unless the blank character at the end is removed. This can be accomplished with the procedure **StripBlanks**, as shown here:

```
Program NoBlanks;
Uses CRT;
Type
  MaxStr = String[255];
Var
  s : MaxStr;
  i,code : Integer;

(*********************************)

Procedure StripBlanks(Var s: MaxStr);
Begin
While (s[Length(s)] = ' ') Do
  Delete(s,Length(s),1);
End;

(*********************************)

Begin
ClrScr;

(* Note: Leading blanks do not *)
(* cause conversion problems.  *)

s := '    20    ';
WriteLn('String = <',s,'>');
StripBlanks(s);
WriteLn('String = <',s,'>');
Val(s,i,code);
WriteLn('Value is: ',i);
WriteLn;
Write('Press ENTER...');
ReadLn;
End.
```

This program passes a string into **StripBlanks** as a reference parameter, so whatever changes are made to the string are retained after the procedure ends. **StripBlanks** consists of a While-Do loop that controls a **Delete** statement:

```
While (s[Length(s)] = ' ') Do
    Delete(s,Length(s),1);
```

This loop removes blanks from the end of a string by repeatedly deleting the last character from the string: the statement s[**Length(s)**] points to the last character in the string, 's'. If the last character is blank, that character is removed with the **Delete** procedure.

These are just a few examples of how strings can be used to solve tricky programming problems. As you program, you will discover many more.

Using Recursion in Turbo Pascal

Recursion is a technique wherein a procedure, in the process of performing its tasks, makes calls to itself. How can a procedure make calls to itself? It is a difficult concept to grasp, even for experienced programmers. Recursion can best be described by the classic example, the *factorial function*. The factorial of **Integer n** is the cumulative product of all **Integers** from 1 to **n**. For example, the factorial of 2 is 1 * 2, while the factorial of 3 is 1 * 2 * 3. The nonrecursive factorial function would be coded as follows:

```
Function Factorial(n : Integer) : Real;
Var
  r : Real;
  i : Integer;
Begin
r := 1;
For i := 2 To n Do
  r := r * i;
Factorial := r;
End;
```

The calculation in this nonrecursive example is straightforward: **r**, originally set equal to 1, is repeatedly multiplied by successive **Integer** values up to and including **n**. Compare this to this recursive version:

```
Function Factorial(n : Integer) : Real;
Begin
If n = 0 Then
  Factorial := 1
Else
  Factorial := n * Factorial(n-1);
End;
```

The recursive version works by repeatedly multiplying **n** by the factorial of the number just preceding it. While the recursive version is more elegant and intellectually appealing, most programmers find the nonrecursive version easier to understand and code. Which is better? That depends on several things.

On the negative side, recursive procedures have a major weak point: each time a procedure calls itself, Turbo Pascal must set up space on the stack for temporary storage. This not only slows a procedure's execution, but also increases the danger of using up the program's stack space, which could cause the program to crash.

On the other hand, some algorithms are so naturally adapted to a recursive structure that forcing them into a nonrecursive form just does not make sense. A good example of such an algorithm is a function that evaluates a mathematical expression stored in a string. The following program shows how the recursive process follows the flow of the underlying algorithm. Study it carefully.

```
Program Calculator;
Uses CRT;
Type
  MaxCompStr = String[255];
Var
  i : Integer;
  Formula : String[80];
  p : Integer;
  Result : Real;
  Error : Boolean;

(********************)
```

```
Function Compute_Formula(Var p : Integer;
                         Strg : MaxCompStr;
                         Var Error : Boolean) : Real;

Var
  r : Real;
  i,
  BreakPoint : Integer;
  Ch : Char;

(********************)

Procedure Eval(Var Formula : MaxCompStr;
                   Var Value : Real;
                   Var BreakPoint : Integer);
Const
  Numbers : Set Of Char = ['0'..'9','.'];
Var
  p,i : Integer;
  Ch : Char;

(********************)

Procedure NextP;
Begin
  Repeat
  p := p+1;
  If p <= Length(Formula) Then
    Ch := Formula[p]
  Else
    Ch := #13;
  Until (Ch <> ' ');
End;

(*****************************************)

Function Expr : Real;
Var
  E : Real;
  Operator : Char;

(*****************************************)

Function SmplExpr : Real;
Var
  S : Real;
  Operator : Char;

(*****************************************)

Function Term : Real;
Var
  T : Real;

(*****************************************)
```

```
Function S_Fact : Real;

(*****************************************)

Function Fct : Real;
Var
  fn : String[20];
  l,start: Integer;
  F : Real;

(*****************************************)

Procedure process_as_number;
Var
  code : Integer;
Begin
Start := p;
  Repeat
  NextP
  Until Not(Ch In Numbers);
If Ch = '.' Then
  Repeat
  NextP
  Until Not(Ch In Numbers);
If Ch = 'E' Then
  Begin
  NextP;
    Repeat
    NextP
    Until Not(Ch In Numbers);
  End;
Val(Copy(Formula, Start, p-Start), F, code);
End;

(*****************************************)

Procedure process_as_new_Expr;
Begin
NextP;
F := Expr;
If Ch = ')' Then
  NextP
Else
  BreakPoint := p;
End;

(*****************************************)

Procedure process_as_standard_Function;

(*****************************************)

Function Fact(I : Integer) : Real;
Begin
If I > 0 Then
  Fact := I*Fact(I-1)
```

```
Else
  Fact := 1;
End;

(*****************************************)

Begin
If Copy(Formula, p, 3) = 'ABS' Then
  Begin
  p := p + 2;
  NextP;
  F := Fct;
  f := Abs(f);
  End
Else If Copy(Formula, p, 4) = 'SQRT' Then
  Begin
  p := p + 3;
  NextP;
  F := Fct;
  f := Sqrt(f);
  End
Else If Copy(Formula, p, 3) = 'SQR' Then
  Begin
  p := p + 2;
  NextP;
  F := Fct;
  f := Sqr(f);
  End
Else If Copy(Formula, p, 3) = 'SIN' Then
  Begin
  p := p + 2;
  NextP;
  F := Fct;
  f := Sin(f);
  End
Else If Copy(Formula, p, 3) = 'COS' Then
  Begin
  p := p + 2;
  NextP;
  F := Fct;
  f := Cos(f);
  End
Else If Copy(Formula, p, 6) = 'ARCTAN' Then
  Begin
  p := p + 5;
  NextP;
  F := Fct;
  f := ArcTan(f);
  End
Else If Copy(Formula, p, 2) = 'LN' Then
  Begin
  p := p + 1;
  NextP;
  F := Fct;
  f := Ln(f);
  End
```

```
Else If Copy(Formula, p, 3) = 'EXP' Then
  Begin
  p := p + 2;
  NextP;
  F := Fct;
  f := Exp(f);
  End
Else If Copy(Formula, p, 4) = 'FACT' Then
  Begin
  p := p + 3;
  NextP;
  F := Fct;
  f := fact(Trunc(f));
  End
Else
  Begin
  BreakPoint := p;
  End;
End;

(*****************************************)

Begin (* process_as_standard_Function *)
If (Ch In Numbers) Then
  process_as_number
Else If (Ch = '(') Then
  process_as_new_Expr
Else
  process_as_standard_Function;
Fct := F;
End; (* process_as_standard_Function *)

(********************)

Begin
If Ch = '-' Then
  Begin
  NextP;
  S_Fact := -Fct;
  End
Else
  S_Fact := Fct;
End;

(********************)

Begin
T := S_Fact;
While Ch = '^' Do
  Begin
  NextP;
  t := Exp(Ln(t)*S_Fact)
  End;
Term := t;
End;
```

```
(********************)

Begin
s := term;
While Ch In ['*', '/'] Do
  Begin
  Operator := Ch;
  NextP;
    Case Operator Of
    '*' : s := s*term;
    '/' : s := s/term;
    End;
  End;
SmplExpr := s;
End;

(********************)

Begin
E := SmplExpr;
While Ch In ['+', '-'] Do
  Begin
  Operator := Ch;
  NextP;
    Case Operator Of
    '+' : e := e+SmplExpr;
    '-' : e := e-SmplExpr;
    End;
  End;
Expr := E;
End;

(********************)

Begin
For i := 1 To Length(Formula) Do
  Formula[i] := Upcase(Formula[i]);
If Formula[1] = '.' Then Formula := '0'+Formula;
If Formula[1] = '+' Then Delete(Formula, 1, 1);
p := 0;
NextP;
Value := Expr;

If Ch = #13 Then
  Error := False
Else
  Error := True;
BreakPoint := p;
End;

(********************)

Begin
Eval(Strg, r, p);
Compute_Formula := r;
End;
```

```
(********************)
Begin
ClrScr;
  Repeat
  Write('Enter Formula: ');
  Read(Formula);
  If Formula <> '' Then
    Begin
    Result := Compute_Formula(p,Formula,Error);
    If Error Then
      Begin
      WriteLn;
      WriteLn('Error!');
      WriteLn(Formula);
      For i := 1 To p-1 Do Write(' ');
      WriteLn('^');
      End
    Else
      WriteLn(' = ',Result:0:2);
    End;
  ReadLn;
  Until Formula = '';
End.
```

When you run this program, you will be asked to enter an equation, which the program stores in a string and passes to the function **Compute_Formula**. This function evaluates the equation through a series of recursive calls. If successful, the result is passed back to the program; if not, the Boolean parameter **Error** is set to TRUE, and the **Integer** parameter **p** indicates the point in the string at which the error was detected.

Coding this same procedure in a nonrecursive manner is possible, but given the nature of the algorithm, which lends itself to the recursive approach, it is undesirable.

DOS Devices

In Turbo Pascal, all input and output are performed using devices such as a keyboard, a monitor, or a disk file. To make things easier, Turbo Pascal lets you treat all devices as files. This allows you to treat all input and output uniformly, making your programming much easier.

All input and output in a program normally are performed using DOS devices. A DOS device is an input or output device that DOS is designed to handle. This includes keyboards, disk drives, and video monitors. Some devices, such as optical disks, tape backup units, mice, and other specialized equipment, are not supported by DOS and require their own *device drivers* to make them work with DOS. Writing device drivers is an advanced topic outside the range of this book, but every programmer should know how to use DOS devices.

The Standard Input and Output Devices

While all input and output in Turbo Pascal are performed through devices, you are not always aware of it. For example, the statement **ReadLn(s)** tells Turbo Pascal to accept input from the *standard input device.* Likewise, the statement **Write Ln(s)** indicates output using the *standard output device.*

The name of the standard output device is CON, as in console, and refers to the video display. The standard input device is also CON, but refers not to the screen, but to the keyboard. The following program demonstrates how the CON device can be used for input and output much like a disk file.

```
Program DeviceTest;
Uses CRT;
Var
  f : Text;
  s : String;
Begin
ClrScr;
Assign(f,'CON');
Rewrite(f);
WriteLn(f,'Output to CON');
WriteLn;

WriteLn('Enter string using ReadLn(s)');
Write('Type a string. Press ENTER when done: ');
ReadLn(s);
WriteLn('>',s);

Assign(f,'CON');
Reset(f);
WriteLn('Enter string from CON using ReadLn(f,s)');
Write('Type a string. Press ENTER when done: ');
ReadLn(f,s);
```

```
WriteLn('>',s);

WriteLn;
Write('Press ENTER...');
ReadLn;
End.
```

Notice that the CON device can be used with the **Reset** or **Rewrite** procedures, just like a disk file. In fact, the standard input and output devices use the same file handles used by disk files.

Printer Devices

DOS supports various printer devices: PRN, LPT1, LPT2, and LPT3. (LPT1 and PRN refer to the same device.) Most people use only one printer, and so use only LPT1 and PRN devices. Naturally, printers are used for output only. If you try to use **Reset** on a printer device, Turbo Pascal will generate an immediate end of file (the **Eof** function will return TRUE).

Turbo Pascal also offers another way to route output to the printer: the **PRINTER** unit. This unit declares a text-file variable name **Lst**, which directs output to the printer. This brief program demonstrates how the LST device is used:

```
Program TestPrt;
Uses Printer;
Begin
WriteLn(Lst,'ABC');
End.
```

Serial Devices

Most computers have serial ports, which they use for printers, modems, local area networks, and other communications purposes. Turbo Pascal supports two DOS serial devices: COM1 and COM2. In addition, Turbo Pascal supports an AUX (for auxiliary) device, which is the same as COM1.

While these devices make it easy to send and receive data through serial ports, they are far too limited for most purposes. Communications programs, for example, usually need to bypass DOS devices and go directly to the serial port.

The NUL Device

Turbo Pascal recognizes one more device; the NUL device. This device is special because it ignores everything you send to it. You might wonder what use such a device could possibly have. Generally, you will use the NUL device when you are programming an output function, but don't actually want to send out any data.

Merging, Sorting, and Searching

Merging
Sorting Methods
Searching Methods

Some programming tasks are so common that over the years standardized, highly efficient algorithms have been developed to take care of them. Searching, sorting, and merging are three of the most common, turning up in nearly every book on computer programming. While entire books have been devoted to these subjects, this chapter touches on only the most practical algorithms and how they are used in Turbo Pascal.

Merging

Merging files refers to the process by which two ordered files are combined to form one large ordered file. For example, a master file of historical transactions might be updated by merging a file of daily transactions into it. Both files must be ordered in the same way (for example, by date or account number); the updated file then becomes the master file that will be updated the next day.

Of course, you could add the daily file to the end of the historical file and sort the whole thing at one time, but sorting takes far longer than merging.

The merge process is straightforward. It starts by reading the first record from each file, after which the program enters a loop. Inside the loop, the program compares the two records and writes the one with the lower value to the newly created file. Another record is then read from the input file.

This process continues until all records in one or both files have been processed. Usually, one of the input files runs out of records before the other. When this occurs, the procedure continues to read records from the remaining file and write them to the newly created file.

This process is illustrated in Figure 11-1, where two input files of integers are merged. File 1 contains three integer

	File 1	File 2
	1	2
	4	3
	6	7
		9

Step 1:	record 1 = 1	record 2 = 2 → Write record 1
Step 2:	Read a new record 1	
Step 3:	record 1 = 4	record 2 = 2 → Write record 2
Step 4:	Read a new record 2	
Step 5:	record 1 = 4	record 2 = 3 → Write record 2
Step 6:	Read a new record 2	
Step 7:	record 1 = 4	record 2 = 7 → Write record 1
Step 8:	Read a new record 1	
Step 9:	record 1 = 6	record 2 = 7 → Write record 1
Step 10:	Read a new record 1 — end of file	
Step 11:	record 1 = EOF	record 2 = 7 → Write record 2
Step 12:	Read a new record 2	
Step 13:	record 1 = EOF	record 2 = 9 → Write record 2
Step 14:	Read a new record 2 — end of file	
Step 15:	Both input files are EOF: Procedure ends	

Figure 11-1.   Merging two sorted files

records—1, 4, and 6—and File 2 contains four integer records—
2, 3, 7, and 9. The procedure reads and compares the first
records from File 1 and from File 2. The record from File 1 is
then written to the merged file because it is lower in value than
the record from File 2.

The procedure then reads a new record from File 1 and
compares it to the record already in Record 2. Record 1 has a
greater value than the value already in Record 2. Therefore,
Record 2 is written to the merged file and another record is
read from File 2.

This process continues until the procedure reaches the end
of File 1, at which point the procedure reads all the records
remaining in File 2 and writes them to the merge file. The
procedure ends when it reaches the end of File 2.

While the merge procedure is simple in concept, it is not so
simple to express in Turbo Pascal. The major complexity is in
determining when a new record is needed from an input file and
when an input file is empty. In the following program, input is
controlled through two Boolean functions, **GetItem1** and
GetItem2:

```
Program MergeTest;
Uses CRT;
Type
  Str80 = String[80];

Var
  File1,
  File2,
  File3 : Str80;

(**************************************)

Procedure Merge(Fname1,Fname2,Fname3 : Str80);
Var
  ok1,ok2 : Boolean;
  f1,f2,f3 : Text;
  i1,i2 : Integer;

(**************************************)

Function GetItem1(Var i : Integer) : Boolean;
Begin
If Not Eof(f1) Then
  Begin
```

```
  ReadLn(f1,i);
  GetItem1 := True;
  End
Else
  GetItem1 := False;
End;


(**************************************)

Function GetItem2(Var i : Integer) : Boolean;
Begin
If Not Eof(f2) Then
  Begin
  ReadLn(f2,i);
  GetItem2 := True;
  End
Else
  GetItem2 := False;
End;


(**************************************)

Begin
Assign(f1,Fname1);
Reset(f1);
Assign(f2,Fname2);
Reset(f2);
Assign(f3,Fname3);
Rewrite(f3);

ok1 := GetItem1(i1);
ok2 := GetItem2(i2);

While ok1 Or ok2 Do
  Begin
  (* If ok1 is true, then a record from File 1 is present. *)
  (* If ok2 is true, then a record from File 2 is present. *)

  If ok1 And ok2 Then       (* records are present *)
    Begin                   (* from both files.    *)
    If i1 < i2 Then
      Begin
      WriteLn(f3,i1);
      ok1 := GetItem1(i1);
      End
    Else
      Begin
      WriteLn(f3,i2);
      ok2 := GetItem2(i2);
      End;
    End
  Else If ok1 Then          (* a record is present from *)
    Begin                   (* the first file only.     *)
```

```
        WriteLn(f3,il);
        okl := GetIteml(il);
        End
      Else If ok2 Then        (* a record is present from *)
        Begin                 (* the second file only.    *)
        WriteLn(f3,i2);
        ok2 := GetItem2(i2);
        End;
      End;

  Close(fl);
  Close(f2);
  Close(f3);
  End;

  (***************************************)

  Begin
  ClrScr;
  Write('Enter name of first file: ');
  ReadLn(Filel);
  Write('Enter name of second file: ');
  ReadLn(File2);
  Write('Enter name of merged file: ');
  ReadLn(File3);
  Merge(filel,file2,file3);
  End.
```

GetItem1 and **GetItem2** read the next record from their respective files. If successful, they return the value TRUE along with the record read; if unsuccessful (that is, if it reaches the end of the file), they return FALSE. By isolating the input process in these two functions, the structure of the merge procedure is simplified.

When the procedure **Merge** begins, the Boolean variables **ok1** and **ok2** are set with **GetItem1** and **GetItem2**. The loop controlled by the statement

    While ok1 Or ok2 Do

executes as long as records are present from either file and terminates when the end is reached for both files.

Three program branches are contained in the **While-Do** loop. The first is executed when input from both files is present. In this case, the procedure compares the two records, the record with the lower value is written to the merge file, and another record is read in.

The two other branches execute when one of the input files reaches its end. When this occurs, the loop continues to read records from the remaining file and write them to the merged file. When the procedure reaches the end of the remaining file, the input files and the merged file are closed and the procedure ends.

Sorting Methods

Although many sorting algorithms have been developed over the years, three are the most frequently used: the bubble sort, the shell sort, and the quick sort.

The *bubble sort* is easy to write but terribly slow. The *shell sort* is moderately fast, but excels in its use of memory resources. The *quick sort,* the fastest of the three, requires extensive stack space for recursive calls. Knowing all three algorithms, and understanding why one is better than another, is important and illustrates the subtleties of good programming.

General Sorting Principles

The sorting algorithms presented in this section compare one element in an array to another, and, if the two elements are out of order, the algorithms switch their order in the array. This process is illustrated in this code segment:

```
If a[i] > a[i+1] Then
  Begin
  temp := a[i];
  a[i] := a[i+1];
  a[i+1] := temp;
  End;
```

The first line of code tests if two elements of the array are out of order. Generally, arrays are in order when the current element is smaller than the next element. If the elements are not properly ordered, that is, when the current element is greater than the next element, their order is switched. The switch requires a temporary storage variable of the same type as that of the elements in the array being sorted.

The main difference between the three sorting algorithms is the method by which array elements are selected for comparison. The comparison method has a tremendous impact on the efficiency of the sort. For example, the bubble sort, which compares only adjacent array elements, may require half a million comparisons to sort an array, while the quick sort requires only three or four thousand.

Bubble Sort

To computer programmers, there are good methods, there are bad methods, and there are kludges. A kludge is a method that works, but slowly and inefficiently. The bubble sort is a good example of a kludge: given enough time, it will sort your data, but you might have to wait a day or two.

The bubble-sort alogorithm is simple: it starts at the end of the array to be sorted and works toward the beginning of the array. The procedure compares each element to the one preceding it. If the elements are out of order, they are switched. The procedure continues until it reaches the beginning of the array.

Because the sort works backward through the array, comparing each adjacent pair of elements, the lowest element will always "float" to the top after the first pass. After the second pass, the second lowest element will "float" to the second position in the array, and so on, until the algorithm has passed through the array once for every element in the array.

This code shows this process in Turbo Pascal:

```
For i := 2 To n Do
For j := n DownTo i Do
  If a[j-1] > a[j] Then
    Switch(a[j],a[j-1]);
```

As you can see, the bubble-sort algorithm is compact; in fact, it is a single Turbo Pascal statement. The bubble sort receives two inputs: **a**, the array to be sorted, and **n**, the number of elements in the array. The inside loop, controlled by the statement

For j := n DownTo i Do

performs all the comparisons in each pass through the array. The outside loop, controlled by the statement

For i := 2 To n Do

Pass	Position in Array									
	1	2	3	4	5	6	7	8	9	10
Start:	91	6	59	0	75	0	48	92	30	83
1	0	91	6	59	0	75	30	48	92	83
2	0	0	91	6	59	30	75	48	83	92
3	0	0	6	91	30	59	48	75	83	92
4	0	0	6	30	91	48	59	75	83	92
5	0	0	6	30	48	91	59	75	83	92
6	0	0	6	30	48	59	91	75	83	92
7	0	0	6	30	48	59	75	91	83	92
8	0	0	6	30	48	59	75	83	91	92
9	0	0	6	30	48	59	75	83	91	92

Figure 11-2.   Sorting an array of integers with the bubble-sort algorithm

determines the number of passes to execute. Notice that **j** executes from the end of the array (**n**) to **i** and that **i** decreases after every pass. Thus, each pass through the array becomes shorter as the bubble sort executes.

An example of how the bubble sort works is shown in Figure 11-2. An array of 10 integers is sorted in order of increasing value. The elements of the array are listed at the end of each pass. A pass consists of one complete execution of the inside **For-Do** loop.

The order of the original array is shown in the row labeled "Start." The values range from 0 to 92, and they are distributed randomly throughout the array. The first pass through the array places the lowest value (0) in the first position in the array, and the number 91 is shifted from the first position into the second position. The other elements are still more or less randomly scattered.

With each step of the bubble sort, the next lowest number takes its proper place in the array, and the higher numbers get shifted to the right. By the end of the eighth pass, the array is completely sorted, yet the sort continues to make one more pass over the array.

The following program contains the bubble-sort algorithm, which takes an **Integer** array and the number of elements in the array as parameters:

```
Program BubbleTest;
Type
   Int_Arr = Array [1..10] Of Integer;
Var
   i : Integer;
   a : Int_Arr;

(*********************************************)

Procedure Bubble(Var a : Int_Arr;
                     n : Integer);
Var
   i,j : Integer;

(*********************************************)

Procedure Switch(Var a,b : Integer);
Var
   c : Integer;
```

```
Begin
c := a;
a := b;
b := c;
End;


(*********************************************)

Begin
For i := 2 To n Do
For j := n DownTo i Do
  If a[j-1] > a[j] Then
    Switch(a[j],a[j-1]);
End;


(*********************************************)

Begin
a[1] := 91;
a[2] := 06;
a[3] := 59;
a[4] := 0;
a[5] := 75;
a[6] := 0;
a[7] := 48;
a[8] := 92;
a[9] := 30;
a[10] := 83;

For i := 1 To 10 Do
  Write(a[i]:4);
WriteLn;

Bubble(a,10);

For i := 1 To 10 Do
  Write(a[i]:4);

WriteLn;
Write('Press ENTER...');
ReadLn;
End.
```

The program begins by assigning random values to array **a**, and displays the values on your terminal. The procedure **Bubble** sorts the array. When the sort is finished, the array is displayed again.

The weakness of the bubble sort is that it compares only adjacent array elements. If the sorting algorithm first compared elements separated by a wide interval, and then focused on progressively smaller intervals, the process would be more efficient. This train of thought led to the development of the shell-sort and quick-sort algorithms.

Shell Sort

The shell sort is far more efficient than the bubble sort. It first puts elements approximately where they will be in the final order and determines their exact placement later. The strength of the algorithm lies in the method it uses to estimate an element's approximate final position.

The key concept in the shell sort is the *gap*, which is the distance between the elements compared. If the gap is 5, the first element is compared with the sixth element, the second with the seventh, and so on. In a single pass through the array, all elements within the gap are put in order. For example, the elements in this array are in order given a gap of 2:

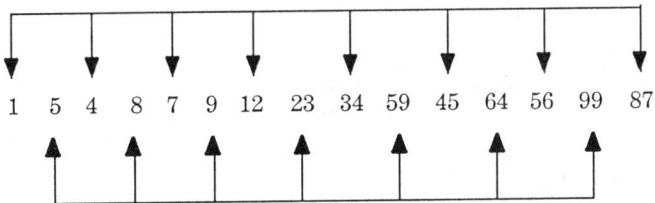

As you can see, the array is nearly completely sorted before the algorithm tests adjacent elements. In the next pass over this array, the gap is reduced to 1, which results in a completely sorted array. The initial value of the gap is arbitrary, although it is common to set it to one half the number of elements in the array (that is, **n div 2**).

The many versions of the shell sort vary in complexity and efficiency. The version presented in this chapter is extremely efficient, requiring few passes to complete the sort.

Unfortunately, there is no simple way to describe how this particular shell algorithm works. Efficient algorithms tend to be more complex than inefficient ones and are therefore harder to express in words. This is why poor algorithms are used so often. Figure 11-3 contains the essential code for the shell-sort algorithm. Review this code as you read the explanation.

The first line in the procedure sets the gap to **n div** 2. The outside loop in the shell sort, controlled by the statement

While (gap > 0) Do

determines the number of passes made through the array. After each pass through the array, the gap is reduced by half for each pass until the gap reaches 0. For example, if there were ten elements in the array, the first gap would be 5, followed by 2, 1, and 0. Because **Integer** division is used, **1 div** 2 results in 0.

In each pass, three variables determine which elements to compare: **i**, **j**, and **k**. The variable **i** points to the far element, and **j** points to the near element. For example, if the **gap** is 5, **i** will equal 6 and **j** will equal 1. Before the comparison, **k** is set equal to **j** + **gap**, which, for the first comparison, equals **i**.

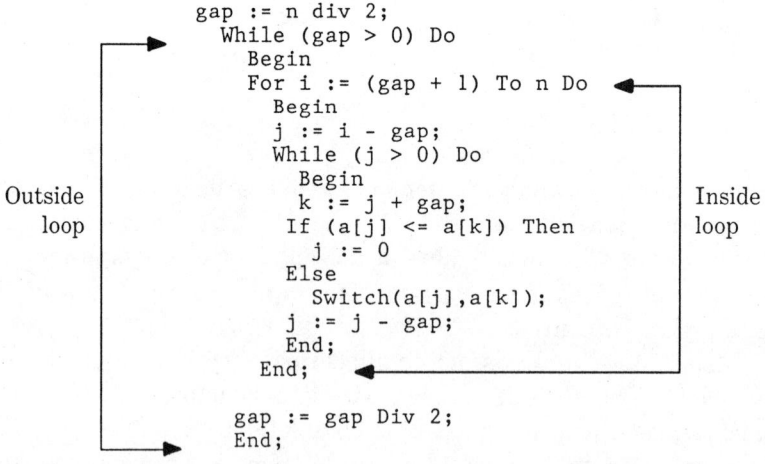

```
                      gap := n div 2;
                        While (gap > 0) Do
                          Begin
                          For i := (gap + 1) To n Do
                            Begin
                            j := i - gap;
                            While (j > 0) Do
                              Begin
                              k := j + gap;
                              If (a[j] <= a[k]) Then
                                j := 0
                              Else
                                Switch(a[j],a[k]);
                              j := j - gap;
                              End;
                          End;

                        gap := gap Div 2;
                        End;
```

Outside loop

Inside loop

Figure 11-3.   The main loops in the shell-sort algorithm

The comparison uses **k** instead of **i** because it may be necessary to backtrack through the array. To backtrack, **j** is reduced by **gap** and **k** is also changed so that a new pair of elements is compared. Because **i** controls the inside loop, it should not be changed in this backtracking process.

Consider the example in Figure 11-4 where a ten-element array is being sorted. At step 1, **gap** is 2, **j** is equal to 6, and **k** is equal to 8. Thus, the sixth and eighth elements in the array will be compared. Since element 6 is 85 and element 8 is 49, the two must be switched, as is shown in step 2.

Next, the algorithm sets **j** equal to **j** − **gap**, in this case 4. Since **j** is greater than zero, the inside loop executes again. Because **j** has been reduced by 2, the fourth and sixth elements are compared. Again, the elements are out of order and need to be switched. As before, **j** is set to **j** − **gap**, or 2, leading to step 3.

Elements 2 and 4 of the array are in the correct order, so rather than switching the elements, the program sets **j** to zero.

Position in Array

	1	2	3	4	5	6	7	8	9	10
Step 1:	19	9	32	63	86	85	87	49	35	86
						↑ j		↑ k		
Step 2:	19	9	32	63	86	49	87	85	35	86
				↑ j		↑ k				
Step 3:	19	9	32	49	86	63	87	85	35	86
		↑ j		↑ k						
Step 4:	19	9	32	49	86	63	87	85	35	86
							↑ j		↑ k	

Figure 11-4.   Sorting an array of integers with the shell-sort algorithm

Now, the result of **j** − **gap** is negative 2. Since this is less than zero, the inner loop is terminated and **i** is incremented. Working downward, **j** is set to **i** − **gap**, or 7, and **k** is set equal to **j** + **gap**, or 9.

In short, **i** keeps track of the overall flow of the algorithm, while **k** backtracks when necessary. This tricky bit of logic increases the efficiency by about 300% over the most simple shell sort.

The following sample program includes the procedure **Shell**, which contains the shell-sort algorithm.

```
Program ShellTest;
Uses CRT;
Type
  Int_Arr = Array [1..10] of Integer;
Var
  i : Integer;
  a : Int_Arr;

(******************************)

Procedure Shell(Var a : Int_arr;
                    n : Integer);
Var
  gap,i,j,k,x : Integer;

(******************************)

Procedure Switch(var a,b : Integer);
Var
  c : Integer;
Begin
c := a;
a := b;
b := c;
End;

(******************************)

Begin
gap := n div 2;
While (gap > 0) Do
  Begin
  For i := (gap + 1) To n Do
    Begin
    j := i - gap;
    While (j > 0) Do
      Begin
      k := j + gap;
      If (a[j] <= a[k]) Then
        j := 0
```

```
      Else
         Begin
         Switch(a[j],a[k]);
         j := j - gap;
         End;
      End;
   End;

 gap := gap Div 2;
 End;
End;

(*********************)

Begin
ClrScr;
a[1]  := 19;
a[2]  := 9;
a[3]  := 32;
a[4]  := 63;
a[5]  := 86;
a[6]  := 85;
a[7]  := 87;
a[8]  := 49;
a[9]  := 35;
a[10] := 86;

For i := 1 To 10 Do
   Write(a[i]:4);
WriteLn;

Shell(a,10);

For i := 1 To 10 Do
   Write(a[i]:4);
WriteLn;
Write('Press ENTER...');
ReadLn;
End.
```

Shell accepts the array to be sorted, including the number of elements in the array, and then returns the array in its sorted form. If you test this program against the bubble sort with an array of 1,000 elements, you will see an amazing difference in the time required to sort the array. Yet as efficient as the shell sort is, the quick sort is two or three times as efficient.

Quick Sort

The queen of all sorting algorithms is the quick sort: this algorithm is widely accepted as the fastest general-purpose sort available.

One of the pleasing aspects of the quick sort is that it sorts things in much the same way people do. It first creates large "piles," and then sorts those piles into smaller and smaller piles, eventually ending up with a completely sorted array.

The quick-sort algorithm begins by estimating a midrange value for the array. If the array consists of numbers 1 through 10, the midpoint could be 5 or 6. The midpoint's exact value is not crucial; the algorithm will work with a midpoint of any value. However, the closer the estimated midpoint is to the true midpoint of the array, the faster the sort will be.

The procedure calculates a midpoint by averaging the first and last elements in the portion of the array being sorted. Once the procedure selects a midpoint, it puts all the elements lower than the midpoint in the lower part of the array, and all the elements higher in the upper part. This is illustrated in Figure 11-5.

Mid-Point	Position in Array									
	1	2	3	4	5	6	7	8	9	10
Step 1: 55	86	3	10	23	12	67	59	47	31	24
Step 2: 35	24	3	10	23	12	31	47	59	67	86
Step 3: 27	24	3	10	23	12	31	47	59	67	86
Step 4: 18	24	3	10	23	12	31	47	59	67	86
Step 5: 11	12	3	10	23	24	31	47	59	67	86
Step 6: 6	10	3	12	23	24	31	47	59	67	86
Step 7: 23	3	10	12	23	24	31	47	59	67	86
Step 8: 72	3	10	12	23	24	31	47	59	67	86
Step 9: 63	3	10	12	23	24	31	47	59	67	86
Final order:	3	10	12	23	24	31	47	59	67	86

Figure 11-5.   The quick-sort algorithm

In step 1, the midpoint is 55, which is the average of 86 and 24. In step 2, the segment being sorted is 24 through 47, leading to a midpoint of 35. Notice that the elements in the segment rarely split evenly around the midpoint. This does not harm the algorithm, but does decrease its efficiency somewhat.

At each step in the process, the quick sort orders the elements of an array segment around the midpoint value. As the segments get smaller and smaller, the array approaches the completely sorted order.

In this program, the procedure **Quick** contains the quick-sort algorithm:

```
Program QuickTest;
Uses CRT;
Type
  Int_Arr = Array [1..10] Of Integer;
Var
  InFile : Text;
  i : Integer;
  a : Int_Arr;

(*****************************)

Procedure Quick(Var item : Int_Arr; count : integer);

(*****************************)

Procedure PartialSort(left, right : Integer;
                      Var a: Int_Arr);
Var
  ii,
  ll,rl,
  i,j,k : Integer;

(*****************************)

Procedure Switch(Var a,b : Integer);
Var
  c : Integer;
Begin
If a <> b Then
  Begin
  c := a;
  a := b;
  b := c;
  End;
End;

(*****************************)
```

```
Begin
k := (a[left] + a[right]) Div 2;
i := left;
j := right;

  Repeat

  While a[i] < k Do
    Inc(i,1);

  While k < a[j] Do
    Dec(j,1);

  If i <= j Then
    Begin
    Switch(a[i],a[j]);
    Inc(i,1);
    Dec(j,1);
    End;
  Until i > j;

If left < j Then
  PartialSort(left,j,a);
If i < right Then
  PartialSort(i,right,a);
End;

(***********************)

Begin
PartialSort(1,count,item);
End;

(***********************)

Begin
ClrScr;
a[1]  := 86;
a[2]  := 3;
a[3]  := 10;
a[4]  := 23;
a[5]  := 12;
a[6]  := 67;
a[7]  := 59;
a[8]  := 47;
a[9]  := 31;
a[10] := 24;

For i := 1 To 10 Do
  Write(a[i]:4);
WriteLn;

Quick(a,10);

For i := 1 To 10 Do
```

```
   Write(a[i]:4);
WriteLn;
Write('Press ENTER...');
ReadLn;
End.
```

The procedure begins by calling the subprocedure **Partial-Sort**, which takes three parameters: the lower bound of the array segment, the upper bound, and the array itself. When first called, the lower bound passed to **PartialSort** is 1, and the upper bound is the number of elements in the array.

PartialSort computes a midpoint and orders the elements in the array segment accordingly. It then calls itself by passing new lower and upper boundaries, thereby focusing on progressively smaller segments of the array. When it reaches the lowest level of the array, the recursion ends, and the procedure passes the sorted array back to the program.

Comparing Sorting Algorithms

The number of comparisons required to sort a list is the universal measure by which all sorting algorithms are judged. The number of comparisons is expressed as a multiple of the number of elements in the list. For example, if you are sorting an array of **n** elements with the bubble sort, the program will have to perform $1/2(n^2 - n)$ comparisons. If **n** is 100, the number of comparisons is 4950.

This benchmark is fine for those with a theoretical bent, but most programmers find it easier to compare sorting methods by measuring the amount of time it takes for each method to sort the same array. Table 11-1 shows the results of tests performed using the bubble-sort, shell-sort, and quick-sort algorithms on arrays with 100, 500, and 1000 random numbers. As the table shows, the bubble sort is a poor algorithm compared to the shell and quick sorts, taking from 6 to 68 times as long to sort an array. Between the shell sort and quick sort, the difference in time is also significant. The shell sort takes twice as long as the quick sort and requires nearly four times as many comparisons.

	Bubble		Shell		Quick	
N	*Time*	*Comparisons*	*Time*	*Comparisons*	*Time*	*Comparisons*
100	0.66	4,950	0.11	849	0.06	232
500	15.88	124,750	0.77	5,682	0.44	1473
1000	63.66	499,500	1.87	13,437	0.93	3254

Table 11-1.   Relative Efficiency of Different Sorting Methods

The only drawback to the quick sort is the amount of space it requires on the stack. Because quick sort is a recursive procedure, space on the stack must be allocated every time the procedure calls itself. If you are concerned about stack space, you might want to use the shell sort: otherwise, use the quick sort.

Searching Methods

In programming, *searching* means finding a particular item within a group of items, for example, finding a particular **Integer** in an array of **Integer**s, finding a person's name in an array of strings, and so forth. The two methods of searching presented here, sequential and binary, accomplish the same end with different means.

Sequential Search

The *sequential search* is so simple it practically needs no explanation. The program simply starts at the beginning of the array to be searched and compares each element with the value you are seeking. The process of finding the number 10 in an array of **Integer**s is shown in Figure 11-6. The search compares x, which is equal to 10, to the first element, then the second, and so on.

Variable x equals 10:

Index	Array	Comparison	Result
1	3	x = 3?	False
2	21	x = 21?	False
3	4	x = 4?	False
4	10	x = 10?	True
5	55		
6	31		
7	9		
8	12		
9	15		Exit from search: Return index value 4

Figure 11-6.   Locating a number with a sequential search

As soon as the value finds a match in the array, it exits from the search process and returns the index of the element found, which in this example is 4.

The following program includes the function **SeqSearch**, which takes three parameters: the value to search for, the array to search through, and the number of elements in the array.

```
Program SequentialSearch;
Type
   Int_Arr = Array [1..100] of Integer;

Var
  a : Int_Arr;
  i,j : Integer;

(*****************************)

Function SeqSearch(x : Integer;
                   a : Int_Arr;
                   n : Integer) : Integer;
Var
  i : Integer;
Begin
```

```
For i := 1 To n Do
If x = a[i] Then
  Begin
  SeqSearch := i;
  Exit;
  End;
SeqSearch := 0;
End;

(*****************************)

Begin
For i := 1 To 100 Do
  a[i] := Random(100);

  Repeat
  Write('Enter a number to search for (0 to exit): ');
  ReadLn(i);
  j := SeqSearch(i,a,100);
  If j = 0 Then
    WriteLn('Number not in list.')
  Else
    WriteLn(i,' is element number ',j);
  WriteLn;
  Until i = 0;
End.
```

When **SeqSearch** finds a matching value, it assigns the value to the function and exits. Because a sequential search processes the array element by element, the order of the list is unimportant—the search works equally well with random lists as with sorted lists.

Binary Search

The *binary search* is one of the most efficient searching methods known and a big improvement over the sequential search. With an array of 100 elements, for example, a sequential search requires an average of 50 comparisons to find a match; the binary search requires at most seven comparisons and as few as four to accomplish the same goal. As the list gets longer, the relative efficiency of the binary search increases.

To perform a binary search, a list must be in sorted order. The search begins by testing the target element against the middle element in the array. If the target element is higher than the middle element, the search continues in the upper half of the list; if the target value is lower than the middle element, the target element is in the lower half.

The binary search process is shown in Figure 11-7. The array is searched for the target value 10. The fifth element, which is equal to 12, is tested first. Since 10 is less than 12, the target value must be in the lower half of the array. The algorithm, therefore, selects element 2—midway between 1 and 4. The value of the second element is 4 (less than 10). The algorithm knows the target value must lie between elements 3 and 4. First, the algorithm tests element 3 and fails. This leaves element 4, which is equal to 10. The binary search now ends, returning a value of 4. Had element 4 been equal to 11, no match would have been found, and the function would have returned a zero.

Because the array in Figure 11-7 is so small, the benefit of the binary search is not fully illustrated. For example, a sequential search of a 1000-element array requires 500 comparisons on average, whereas a binary search requires between 5 and 10 comparisons.

Variable x equals 10:

Index	Array	Comparison	Result
1	3	2	Higher
2	4	3	Higher
3	9	4	Equal
4	10	1	Lower
5	12		
6	15		
7	21		
8	31		
9	55		

Figure 11-7.   Searching a sorted array with the binary search algorithm

The following program uses the function **Bsearch** to perform a binary search on an array of **Integer**s:

```
Program BinarySearch;
Type
  Int_Arr = Array [1..100] Of Integer;

Var
  a : Int_Arr;
  i,j : Integer;

(*****************************)
(*$i quick.inc*)
(*****************************)

Function Bsearch(x : Integer;
                 a : Int_Arr;
                 n : Integer) : Integer;
Var
  high, low, mid : integer;

Begin
low := 1;
high := n;
While high >= low Do
  Begin
  mid := Trunc((high+low) Div 2);
  If x > a[mid] Then
    low := mid + 1
  Else If x < a[mid] Then
    high := mid - 1
  Else
    high := -1;
  End;
If high = -1 Then
  Bsearch := mid
Else
  Bsearch := 0;
End;

(*****************************)

Begin
j := 2;
For i := 1 To 100 Do
  a[i] := Random(200);

Quick(a,100);

  Repeat
  Write('Enter a number to search for: (0 to exit): ');
  ReadLn(i);
  j := Bsearch(i,a,100);
  If j = 0 Then
```

```
  WriteLn('Number not in list.')
 Else
   WriteLn(i,' is element number ',j);
 WriteLn;
 Until i = 0;

End.
```

The program calls for an include file (with (***$i quick.inc***)), which holds the quick sort procedure described earlier in this chapter. The **Binary Search** program also illustrates the correct sequence. Notice that the **Quick** sort procedure is executed before the binary search function is executed.

The main code of the binary search algorithm, contained in the function **Bsearch**, is as follows:

```
low := 1;
high := n;
While high >= low Do
  Begin
  mid := Trunc((high+low) Div 2);
  If x > a[mid] Then
    low := mid + 1
  Else If x < a[mid] Then
    high := mid - 1
  Else
    high := -1;
  End;
If high = -1 Then
  Bsearch := mid
Else
  Bsearch := 0;
```

The variables **low** and **high** keep track of the portion of the array being searched. At the beginning, the program sets **low** equal to 1 and **high** equal to **n**, the number of elements in the array. Thus, the algorithm begins with the entire array.

The binary search loop is controlled by the statement

While high > = low Do

Each time the loop executes, either **high** is decremented or **low** is incremented by 1, bringing the two variables closer to each other. If **low** becomes greater than **high,** the element you are searching for does not exist in the sorted array and **Bsearch** returns zero.

If, at any point, **a[mid]** is equal to the value you are searching for, the program sets **high** equal to −1, causing the loop to terminate and the function to return the value of **mid.**

DOS and BIOS Functions

The 8088 Registers
The DOS Unit
The Register Set
Disk-Drive Services
Video Services
Time and Date Functions
Report Shift Status
The Turbo Pascal DOS Unit

Your PC consists of various physical devices: a keyboard, a monitor, disk drives, a printer, and so on. The *Disk Operating System* (DOS) and *Basic Input Output System* (BIOS) comprise software routines that control these devices, making sure data comes and goes to the right place without errors.

Your Turbo Pascal programs are constantly using DOS and BIOS services for such activities as writing to a disk file, displaying information on the monitor, getting the current time and date, and more. Because Turbo Pascal does all the work for you, you don't normally need to know anything about the DOS and BIOS services that are being called into play. Still, there are two reasons why you should know about these services and how to use them.

First, while Turbo Pascal gives you access to many services, it does not use them all. If you want complete control over your PC, you will have to learn to harness the power of DOS and BIOS services. Second, even if you never need to use these services, learning about them will greatly increase your understanding of personal computers and operating systems.

The 8088 Registers

The 8088 family of microprocessors (which includes the 8086 and 80286) contains a standard set of 14 *registers*, or internal memory locations, that computers use to execute commands. Each register is 16 bits long, which is why the 8088 is called a 16-bit microprocessor. (In Turbo Pascal, a 16-bit chunk of memory is known as a *word*.) The 8088's registers are shown in Figure 12-1.

The first four registers—AX, BX, CX, and DX—are general-purpose areas that temporarily store data used in computations, comparisons, and other operations. Assembly-language programmers use these registers in the same way

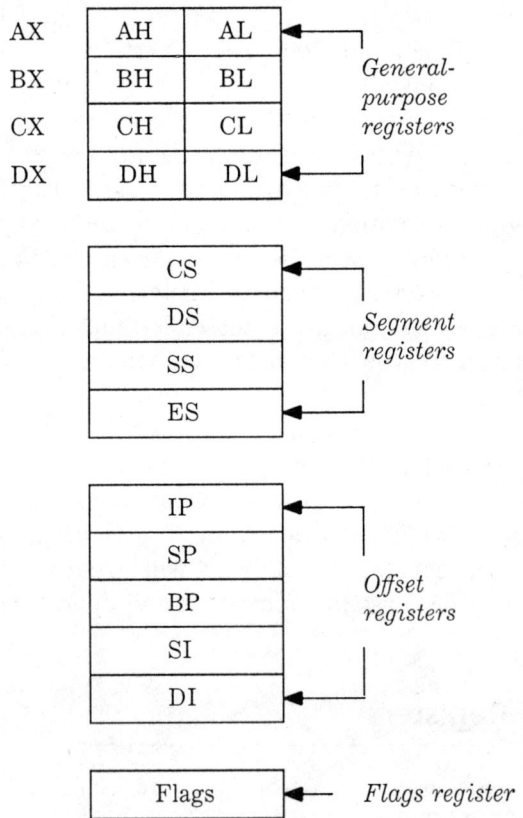

Figure 12-1.   The 8088 CPU registers

Pascal programmers use variables. Each of the general-purpose registers is divided into two one-byte registers; thus AX consists of AH and AL. These general registers are the ones most commonly used to call DOS and BIOS services.

The 8088 also has four segment registers: CS, DS, SS, and ES. CS stores the program's segment, DS contains the data segment, SS holds the stack segment, and ES holds temporary segments for special operations. The CS and SS registers hold critical data that is changed only at great risk to the program's integrity. Therefore, Turbo Pascal does not allow you to access these registers for DOS or BIOS calls, but DS and ES are used occasionally to pass segment addresses.

A memory address consists of a segment and an offset, and the 8088 contains five offset registers: IP, SP, BP, SI, and DI. These are used in conjunction with the segment registers to address specific locations in memory. Turbo Pascal allows access only to SI, DI, and BP; IP and SP are never used in DOS or BIOS calls.

Finally, the Flags register contains information about the status of the instruction last executed. Individual bits in the flag byte indicate specific conditions that result from CPU operations, although not all bits are used. The Flags register is used primarily to identify error conditions. While it can be used in Turbo Pascal, the Flags register is generally not necessary for DOS and BIOS calls, as they usually return error codes in one of the general registers.

The DOS Unit

Turbo Pascal 5.5 provides a standard unit, named DOS, which contains routines that call specific DOS and BIOS services as well as the data structures and procedures you need to call services on your own. With these routines you can get information on files, get a directory listing, set time and date for the system and individual files, and more. This section describes these new procedures and how you use them.

Some of the procedures in the DOS unit require special data types that you use to define variables. The DOS unit also contains two procedures, **MsDos** and **Intr**, that you can use to call specific DOS and BIOS services. Both procedures take a parameter of type **Registers.** With **MsDos, Intr,** and the **Registers** data structure, you can take advantage of all the services provided by DOS and BIOS. Fortunately, Borland has already packed the DOS unit full of easy-to-call procedures for the most commonly used services.

The Register Set

The **Registers** variable is the key to unlocking the power of DOS and BIOS services. This variable, passed to both **MsDos** and **Intr,** includes fields that match most of the 8088's registers:

```
Type
  Registers = Record
    Case Integer Of
    0: (AX,BX,CX,DX,BP,SI,DI,DS,ES,Flags : Word);
    1: (AL,AH,BL,BH,CL,CH,DL,DH : Byte);
    End;
```

The **Registers** data type contains only those CPU registers that are used in BIOS and DOS services. The record has two variant parts: one part consists of **Word** variables representing whole registers; the other part consists of bytes that define the high and low portions of the general registers. For example, the two **Byte** variables **AL** and **AH** refer to the same memory location that contains **AX.** The low-order byte (**AL**) precedes the high-order byte (**AH**) because the 8088 microprocessor stores bytes within words in reverse order. Therefore, if the integer 1 is stored in **AX**, it appears in memory as follows:

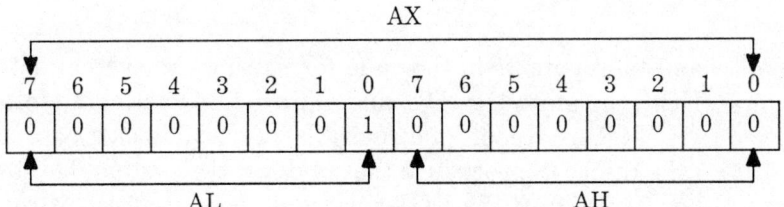

Before you can call **MsDos** or **Intr**, you must set the register-set variable to specific values that tell the computer which service you want and how you want to execute it. For example, to select a DOS service, place the code for the service in the AH register. DOS service **2Bh**, which sets the system date, is shown here:

```
Program SetTime;
Uses DOS, CRT;
Var
   Regs : Registers;

Begin
ClrScr;
FillChar(Regs,SizeOf(Regs),0);
With Regs Do
   Begin
   AH := $2B;
   DH := 12;      (* Month *)
   DL := 31;      (* Date  *)
   CX := 1990;    (* Year  *)
   End;

MsDos(Regs);    (* Call the DOS service *)

If Regs.AL <> 0 Then
   WriteLn('Error!')
Else
   WriteLn('Date has been set.');

WriteLn;
Write('Press ENTER...');
ReadLn;
End.
```

The procedure first initializes the register set to zero with the statement

FillChar(Regs,SizeOf(Regs),0);

and then puts **2Bh**, the code for setting the system date, in AH. Next, registers DH, DL, and CX are filled with date information.

MsDos accepts the register-set variable as a parameter and calls the DOS procedure that updates the system date to December 31, 1990. If the DOS service detects an error, it returns the register set with the error code in AL. The statement

```
If Regs.AL <> 0 Then
  WriteLn('Error!');
```

checks this code; if it is not equal to zero, an error occurs.

While the **MsDos** procedure is used for DOS services, the **Intr** procedure is used for BIOS services. **Intr** accepts two variables: the interrupt number and the register-set variable. For example, the BIOS call that prints the contents of a screen is invoked by setting register AH to 5 and calling interrupt 5, as follows:

```
FillChar(Regs,SizeOf(Regs),0);
Regs.AH := 5;
Intr(5,Regs);
```

The first parameter is the interrupt number. The example above calls interrupt 5, which can be used to do many things. Setting **Regs.AH** to 5, however, specifies the print-screen service (the same service invoked by pressing the SHIFT and PRTSC keys at the same time). In this service, no error indicator is returned in the register set.

The use of DOS and BIOS services greatly increases what you can do with Turbo Pascal, but learning to use them properly takes some time. The remainder of this chapter deals with procedures that incorporate the most useful of the DOS and BIOS services and serve as examples of how to use them.

Disk-Drive Services

The main purpose of the Disk Operating System is to manage your computer's disk drives and files. Fortunately, Turbo Pascal's standard procedures take care of the most difficult disk-related tasks, such as reading and writing files. This section presents several DOS functions not supported by Turbo Pascal that can improve your programs.

Report Free Disk Space

DOS service **36h** indicates how much space is available on a disk. The DL register selects the disk to check; 0 indicates the default drive, 1 indicates drive A, 2 indicates drive B, and so on. After **MsDos** is called, the general-purpose registers contain the following information:

AX	Sectors per allocation cluster
BX	Number of unused clusters
CX	Bytes per sector
DX	Total number of clusters

Using these values, you can easily calculate the total amount of free disk space with the equation

LongInt(AX) * BX * CX.

(The **LongInt** typecast in the equation is necessary to avoid integer overflow.) If an invalid drive is specified, Turbo Pascal returns $FFFF in AX.

The function **FreeDiskSpace**, shown here, reports the number of free bytes for a drive:

```
Program DiskSpace;
Uses CRT, DOS;
Var
  Drive : Char;
```

```
(**********************************************************)
Function FreeDiskSpace(Drive : Char) : LongInt;
Var
  Regs : Registers;
Begin
FillChar(Regs,SizeOf(Regs),0);
With Regs Do
  Begin
  AH := $36;
  DL := Ord(UpCase(Drive)) - 64;
  End;

MsDos(Regs);

With Regs Do
If AX = $FFFF Then
  FreeDiskSpace := -1
Else
  FreeDiskSpace := LongInt(AX)*BX*CX;
End;

(**********************************************************)

Begin
ClrScr;
Write('Which Drive? (A/B/C/D): ');
ReadLn(Drive);
Drive := UpCase(Drive);
WriteLn(FreeDiskSpace(Drive):0,' bytes free.');
WriteLn;
Write('Press ENTER...');
ReadLn;
End.
```

The parameter in the preceding procedure is a character
that indicates which drive to check. To assign the drive number
to DL, the procedure changes the parameter **Drive** to uppercase, converts it into its ASCII value, and subtracts 64. If **drive**
is equal to **a**, it is changed to **A**, which has an ASCII value of 65.
Subtracting 64 from 65 gives 1, which is the correct drive number for DL.

After **MsDos** is called, the procedure checks the AX register. If AX contains $FFFF, an error occurred during the proce-
dure and the function returns the value −1. If no error is indicated, the function computes the amount of free disk space.

Get and Set File Attributes

Disk files can have any of six attributes provided by DOS: *read-only, hidden, system, volume label, subdirectory,* and *archive.* File attributes are contained in a single byte, with individual attributes controlled by bits.

Bit 1 in the attribute byte represents a file's read-only status. Read-only files cannot be changed in any way. DOS blocks any attempt to write over or erase read-only files, just as a write-protect tab protects a floppy disk.

Bit 2 tells you if a file is hidden or not. Hidden files, which often contain sensitive information, are ignored by DOS: they are not listed by the **Dir** command, they cannot be erased or displayed, and so forth. As a result, hidden files are invisible unless the user has a program that can find them. While DOS does not acknowledge hidden files, Turbo Pascal allows them to be used for input or output.

Bit 3 controls the system attribute. System files, like hidden files, are not acknowledged by DOS commands. The system attribute, however, has no real role and is merely a carryover from CP/M.

Bit 4 in the attribute byte toggles the volume label, which is a statement that identifies a floppy disk or hard disk. This is an option set by the user when a disk is formatted.

Bit 5 in the attribute byte indicates that the file is a subdirectory. DOS uses subdirectory files, which contain no data, to keep track of directories and subdirectories.

Bit 6, the archive attribute bit, is turned on when a file is first created. The bit is turned off when the file is copied with the DOS **Backup** command, and it remains off until the file's contents are changed. The archive bit allows you to back up only those files that have changed since the previous backup. Bits 7 and 8 of the attribute byte are not used.

To find what attributes a file has, or to set the attributes you want, use DOS service **43h.** The value in register AL controls which action to execute: 0 to report a file's attributes; 1 to set a file's attributes.

When you report a file's attributes, service **43h** returns the attribute byte in register CL. By testing the individual bits, you can determine the status of each attribute. When setting a file's attributes, you must create an attribute byte and place it in CL prior to calling **MsDos**.

Whether setting or reporting a file's attribute byte, you must load the register set DS:DX with the segment and offset of an *ASCIIZ string* that contains the filename. An ASCIIZ string is an array of letters terminated by a binary zero. You can use a Turbo Pascal string as an ASCIIZ string by adding #0 to it. Turbo Pascal strings, however, have a length byte, while ASCIIZ strings do not. Therefore, you must use the address of the first character in the string to use it as an ASCIIZ string.

In the following procedure, DOS service **43h** sets six Boolean parameters, one for each possible file attribute:

```
Program FileAttributes;
Uses CRT, DOS;
Var
  Fname : String;
  RO, Hidden,
  Sys, Vol,
  SubDir, Arch, Error : Boolean;

(**********************************************************)

Procedure GetFileAttributes( FileName : String;
                             Var RO,
                                 Hidden,
                                 Sys,
                                 Vol,
                                 SubDir,
                                 Arch,
                                 Error : Boolean);
Var
  Regs : Registers;

Begin
FillChar(Regs,SizeOf(Regs),0);
FileName := FileName + #0;

With Regs Do
  Begin
  AH := $43;
  DS := Seg(FileName);
  DX := Ofs(FileName) + 1;
  End;

MsDos(Regs);

Error := (Regs.AL in [2,3,5]);
```

```
RO      := (Regs.CL And $01) > 0;
Hidden  := (Regs.CL And $02) > 0;
Sys     := (Regs.CL And $04) > 0;
Vol     := (Regs.CL And $08) > 0;
SubDir  := (Regs.CL And $10) > 0;
Arch    := (Regs.CL And $20) > 0;
End;


(**********************************************************)

Begin
ClrScr;
Write('Which file?: ');
ReadLn(Fname);

GetFileAttributes(Fname,
                  RO,
                  Hidden,
                  Sys,
                  Vol,
                  SubDir,
                  Arch,
                  Error);

If Error Then
  WriteLn('Error!')
Else
  Begin
  WriteLn(Fname,' has these attributes: ');
  WriteLn('Read only:      ',RO);
  WriteLn('Hidden:         ',Hidden);
  WriteLn('System file:  ',Sys);
  WriteLn('Volume label: ',Vol);
  WriteLn('Subdirectory: ',SubDir);
  WriteLn('Archive:        ',Arch);
  End;

WriteLn;
Write('Press ENTER...');
ReadLn;
End.
```

DOS service **43h** reports error conditions when the file is not found (AL register is 2), the path is not found (AL is 3), or access to the file is denied (AL is 5).

The following procedure sets a file's attribute byte. The procedure accepts four Boolean parameters for four file attributes. It does not include the volume-label and subdirectory attributes, since they cannot be set by this DOS service.

```
Program FileAttributes;
Uses CRT, DOS;
Var
  ch : Char;
  Fname : String;
  RO, Hidden,
  Sys, Arch : Boolean;

(*******************************************************)

Procedure SetFileAttributes( FileName : String;
                             Var RO,
                                 Hidden,
                                 Sys,
                                 Arch : Boolean);

Var
  Regs : Registers;

Begin
FillChar(Regs,SizeOf(Regs),0);
FileName := FileName + #0;

With Regs Do
  Begin
  AH := $43;
  AL := 1;
  DS := Seg(FileName);
  DX := Ofs(FileName) + 1;

  If RO Then
    CL := (CL Or $01);
  If Hidden Then
    CL := (CL Or $02);
  If Sys Then
    CL := (CL Or $04);
  If Arch Then
    CL := (CL Or $20);
  End;

MsDos(Regs);

End;

(*******************************************************)

Begin
ClrScr;
Write('Which file?: ');
ReadLn(Fname);

Write('Set to read only? (Y/N) ');
ReadLn(ch);
RO := UpCase(ch) = 'Y';

Write('Set to hidden (Y/N) ');
ReadLn(ch);
```

```
Hidden := UpCase(ch) = 'Y';

Write('Set to archive (Y/N) ');
ReadLn(ch);
Arch := UpCase(ch) = 'Y';

Write('Set to system file (Y/N) ');
ReadLn(ch);
Sys := UpCase(ch) = 'Y';

SetFileAttributes(Fname,
                  RO,
                  Hidden,
                  Sys,
                  Arch);

WriteLn(Fname,' has been set to these attributes: ');
WriteLn('Read only:     ',RO);
WriteLn('Hidden:        ',Hidden);
WriteLn('System file:   ',Sys);
WriteLn('Archive:       ',Arch);
WriteLn;
Write('Press ENTER...');
ReadLn;
End.
```

It is useful to change a file's attributes to hide files that you want to keep secret or to reveal files that are already hidden or are set to read-only status.

Directory Listing

Displaying a disk directory requires three different DOS services and an understanding of the program segment prefix (PSP) and the disk-transfer area (DTA), which is a part of the PSP.

When a program starts, DOS sets aside the first 256 bytes of memory for its PSP. Because it contains highly technical information, the PSP is normally never touched by the programmer, except for the DTA portion. The DTA is a 128-byte default buffer used for certain DOS operations, such as reading a disk directory, in which case the DTA contains the information shown in Table 12-1.

The filename and its extension constitute the last field in the DTA. The file attribute, time, date, and file size can be read and translated for a more complete directory listing.

Description	Offset	Length
Data used by DOS	0	21
File attribute	21	1
Time stamp of file	22	2
Date stamp of file	24	2
File size in bytes	26	4
Filename and extension	30	13

Table 12-1.   Contents of DTA for a Directory Listing

Before obtaining information from the DTA, you must know its address, which is reported by DOS service **2Fh**. When executed, service **2Fh** places the DTA segment in ES and the DTA offset in BX, as shown here:

```
Regs.AH := $2F;
MsDos(Regs);
DTAseg := Regs.ES;
DTAofs := Regs.BX;
```

The preceding program segment stores the DTA segment in the variable **DTAseg** and the offset in **DTAofs**. These variables are used with the Turbo Pascal standard array **Mem** to extract information from the DTA. For example,

Mem[DTAseg:DTAofs+21]

points to the location of the file-attribute byte in the DTA.

The DOS function **4Eh** searches for the first matching file in the directory and fills the DTA with the file's information. Before **4Eh** is called, however, the registers DS and DX must contain the segment and offset of an ASCIIZ string with the path and filename. This is shown in the following code segment:

```
Mask_In := Mask_In + #0;
With Regs Do
  Begin
  AH := $4E;
  DS := Seg(Mask_In);
```

```
   DX := Ofs(Mask_In) + 1;
   CL := $00;
   End;
MsDos(Regs);

If Regs.AL <> 0 Then Exit;
```

The CL register tells DOS what type of file it should include in its search. If the register is set to zero, DOS locates only standard files. To include hidden or system files in the directory listing, set CL to a value according to the guidelines in Table 12-2.

If CL is set to 16h (the sum of 2h, 4h, and 10h), hidden files, system files, and subdirectories will be included in the directory listing. If the AL register returns with a nonzero value, no file entries matching the file spec were found in the directory.

The program **Directory** uses the procedure **DirList** to create an array of filenames for a file spec entered by the user:

```
Program Directory;
Uses CRT, DOS;
Type
  Dir_Files = Array [1..200] Of String[13];
Var
  FileSpec : String;
  i,
  fc : Integer;
  df : Dir_Files;

(**********************************************)

Procedure DirList( Mask_In : String;
                   Var Name_List : Dir_Files;
                   Var File_Counter : Integer);
Var
  i : Byte;
  Regs : Registers;

  DTAseg,
  DTAofs : Word;

  FileName : String[20];

Begin
FillChar(Regs,SizeOf(Regs),0);
File_Counter := 0;

Regs.AH := $2F;
MsDos(Regs);
With Regs Do
```

```
   Begin
   DTAseg := ES;
   DTAofs := BX;
   End;

FillChar(Regs,SizeOf(Regs),0);
Mask_In := Mask_In + #0;
With Regs Do
   Begin
   AH := $4E;
   DS := Seg(Mask_In);
   DX := Ofs(Mask_In) + 1;
   CL := $00;
   End;
MsDos(Regs);

If Regs.AL <> 0 Then Exit;

i := 1;
   Repeat
   FileName[i] := Chr(Mem[DTAseg:DTAofs+29+i]);
   i := i + 1;
   Until (FileName[i-1] < #32) Or (i > 12);

FileName[0] := Chr(i-1);
File_Counter := 1;
Name_List[File_Counter] := FileName;

   Repeat
   FillChar(Regs,SizeOf(Regs),0);
   With Regs Do
     Begin
     AH := $4F;
     CL := $00;
     End;
   MsDos(Regs);

   If Regs.AL = 0 Then
     Begin
     i := 1;
       Repeat
       FileName[i] := Chr(Mem[DTAseg:DTAofs+29+i]);
       i := i + 1;
       Until (FileName[i-1] < #32) Or (i > 12);

     Inc(File_Counter,1);
     FileName[0] := Chr(i-1);
     Name_List[File_Counter] := FileName;
     End;

   Until Regs.AL <> 0;

End;


(************************************************)
```

```
Begin
ClrScr;
  Repeat
  Write('Enter file spec: ');
  ReadLn(FileSpec);
  If FileSpec <> '' Then
    Begin
    DirList(FileSpec,df,fc);
    For i := 1 To fc Do
      WriteLn(df[i]);
    WriteLn;
    End;
  Until FileSpec = '';
End.
```

The procedure **DirList** accepts the following three parameters: **mask_in**, **name_list**, and **file_counter**. The string parameter **mask_in** contains the file spec to match (for example, test.pas, *.pas, or ???.pas). Filenames that match the file spec are stored in **name_list**, an array of strings. The **Integer file_counter** returns the number of matching filenames **DirList** finds.

Note that DOS service **4Eh** locates only the first file; **4Fh** finds all subsequent files and continues to locate them until register AL contains a nonzero value, which indicates that there are no more matching files in the directory.

Video Services

Most users judge a program almost entirely by its use of video, largely because well-designed and attractive displays make pro-

Attribute to Include	Value of CL
Hidden	$02
System	$04
Volume label	$08
Subdirectory	$10

Table 12-2.   Setting DOS File Attributes with the CL Register

grams easier to use. Unfortunately, Turbo Pascal provides only limited screen-control capabilities. The procedures presented in this section extend your control over the monitor and make possible more sophisticated video displays.

Report Current Video Mode

One fundamental aspect of screen control is determining what type of video adapter the computer has. The major categories are monochrome and color graphics adapter followed by the PCjr and enhanced graphics adapters.

BIOS interrupt **10h** reports the type of video adapter being used and is demonstrated in the function **CurrentVidMode**, shown here:

```
Program VideoMode;
Uses CRT, DOS;

(**********************************************)

Function CurrentVidMode : Char;
Var
  Regs : Registers;
Begin
FillChar(Regs,SizeOf(Regs),0);
Regs.AH := $0F;
Intr($10,Regs);

  Case Regs.AL of
  1..6   : CurrentVidMode := 'C'; (* CGA *)
  7      : CurrentVidMode := 'M'; (* Monochrome *)
  8..10  : CurrentVidMode := 'P'; (* PCjr *)
  13..16 : CurrentVidMode := 'E'; (* EGA *)
  End;

End;

(**********************************************)

Begin
ClrScr;
WriteLn('Current video mode is: ',CurrentVidMode);
WriteLn;
Write('Press ENTER...');
ReadLn;
End.
```

Before the interrupt is called, the function sets the AH register to 0Fh. The interrupt stores the screen width (as the number of characters per line) in AH, the video mode in AL, and the video page number in BH. The procedure determines the video mode by examining AL. If this register is equal to 7, the screen is monochrome and the function returns the letter M. A value from 1 to 6 indicates a color graphics monitor (C), 8 to 10 means PCjr (P), and 13 to 16 is for enhanced graphics (E).

Knowing the type of display is essential when you begin writing information directly to video memory, a topic covered in Chapter 13.

Setting the Cursor Size

At times in a program, it is best not to show the cursor. At other times, a large cursor makes more sense than a small one. Typically, a cursor consists of two scan lines. A color graphics adapter, however, can display a cursor with as many as 8 scan lines, and a monochrome adapter can go up to 14. The more scan lines used, the larger the cursor; if no scan lines are used, the cursor disappears.

To set the cursor size, use BIOS interrupt **10h** with register AH set equal to 1. Put the number of the starting scan line in register CH and the ending scan line in CL. The color graphics adapter uses 8 scan lines (0 to 7); the monochrome adapter uses 14 lines (0 to 13). The lower scan lines appear toward the top of the screen. For example, a small cursor on a color graphics monitor consists of scan lines 6 and 7, the bottom two scan lines.

```
Program Cursor;
Uses DOS, CRT;

(*******************************************************)

Procedure CursorSize(Stype, Size : Char);
Var
  Regs : Registers;
  i : Integer;
Begin
Size := UpCase(Size);
```

```pascal
If UpCase(Stype) = 'M' Then
  i := 6
Else
  i := 0;

Regs.AH := $01;

  Case Size Of
  'O' :
    Begin
    Regs.CH := $20;
    Regs.CL := $20;
    End;
  'B' :
    Begin
    Regs.CH := $0;
    Regs.CL := $7+i;
    End;
  'S' :
    Begin
    Regs.CH := $6+i;
    Regs.CL := $7+i;
    End;
  End;

Intr($10,Regs);
End;

(*****************************************************)

Begin
ClrScr;
WriteLn('Big cursor');
CursorSize('C','B');
WriteLn;
Write('Press ENTER...');
ReadLn;

WriteLn;
WriteLn;
WriteLn('No cursor');
CursorSize('C','O');
WriteLn;
Write('Press ENTER...');
ReadLn;

WriteLn;
WriteLn;
WriteLn('Small cursor');
CursorSize('C','S');
WriteLn;
Write('Press ENTER...');
ReadLn;

End.
```

This procedure sets the cursor size according to the parameters you pass to it. The parameter **stype** can be equal to M for monochrome or C for color graphics. The parameter **size** can take three values: B for big, S for small, or O for off.

If the computer uses a monochrome adapter, the variable **i** is set equal to 6; otherwise it is set to 0. The cursor is turned off by simply setting both CH and CL to 20h, while a large cursor is created by setting CH to 0, and CL to 7 for color-graphics adapters or 13 for monochrome adapters. For a small cursor, CH and CL are set to 6 and 7 for color graphics adapters or 12 and 13 for monochrome adapters.

Read a Character from the Screen

You can read characters from the video screen with BIOS interrupt **10h**. The function **ScreenChar**, as follows, demonstrates how to read characters from the screen with interrupt **10h**.

```
Program ScreenTest;
Uses DOS, CRT;
Var
   s : String;
   i : Integer;

(*******************************************************)

Function ScreenChar : Char;
Var
   Regs : Registers;
Begin
FillChar(Regs,SizeOf(Regs),0);
Regs.AH := 8;
Regs.BH := 0; (* video page *)
Intr($10,Regs);
ScreenChar := Chr(Regs.AL);
End;

(*******************************************************)

Begin
ClrScr;

WriteLn('ABCDE');

s := '';
For i := 1 To 5 Do
   Begin
```

```
    GotoXY(i,1);
    s := s + ScreenChar;
    End;
WriteLn;
WriteLn(s);

WriteLn;
Write('Press ENTER...');
ReadLn;
End.
```

Because **ScreenChar** reads the character at the current cursor position, you must position the cursor correctly before calling the interrupt. Put 8 in register AH and 0 in register BH. The number in register BH selects the video page to be used, but you will most likely use video page 0.

After the interrupt is called, the ASCII code for the character at the cursor position is returned in register AL. **Screen-Char** converts the ASCII code into a character and returns it as the function result.

Time and Date Functions

DOS maintains an internal clock that keeps track of the time and date. When a file is created or changed, DOS uses the clock to stamp the time and date on it. The DOS services shown in Table 12-3 give you control over the system date and time.

DOS Service	Function
2Ah	Report the system date
2Bh	Set the system date
2Ch	Report the system time
2Dh	Set the system time

Table 12-3.   DOS System Time and Date Services

Register	Information
AL	Day of week (0 = Sunday)
CX	Year
DH	Month
DL	Day

Table 12-4.   Contents of Registers After DOS Service 2Ah

Before calling one of these services, specify the appropriate DOS service code in the AH register.

Get the System Date

DOS service **2Ah,** which reports the current system date, puts date information in the registers displayed in Table 12-4.

This is demonstrated in the procedure **GetSystemDate** (as follows), which uses DOS service **2Ah** to report the system date and then formats that date into a string. The date is then passed back to the program.

```
Program Date;
Uses CRT, DOS;
Var
  s : String;

(******************************************************)

Procedure GetSystemDate(Var date : String);
Var
  Regs : Registers;
  st1, st2, st3, st4 : String[10];

Begin
FillChar(Regs,SizeOf(Regs),0);
Regs.AH := $2A;
MsDos(Regs);
With Regs Do
  Begin
    Case AL Of
    0 : st1 := 'Sunday';
    1 : st1 := 'Monday';
    2 : st1 := 'Tuesday';
    3 : st1 := 'Wednesday';
```

```
    4 : st1 := 'Thursday';
    5 : st1 := 'Friday';
    6 : st1 := 'Saturday';
    End;
  Str(CX, st2); (* Year *)
  Str(DH, st3); (* Month *)
  Str(DL, st4); (* Date *)
  End;
If Length(st3) = 1 Then
  st3 := '0' + st3;
If Length(st4) = 1 Then
  st4 := '0' + st4;
date := st1+' '+st3+'-'+st4+'-'+st2;
End;

(********************************************************)

Begin
ClrScr;

GetSystemDate(s);
WriteLn('The date is ',s);

WriteLn;
Write('Press ENTER...');
ReadLn;

End.
```

GetSystemDate uses a **Case** statement to determine the appropriate day of the week. The year, month, and day are converted into strings. (If the day or month consists of a single numeral, the strings are padded with a leading zero.)

Set the System Date

DOS service **2Bh** sets the system date. Before making a call to **MsDos**, you must insert the month in register DH, the day in DL, and the year in CX. The following procedure shows how Turbo Pascal uses this service:

```
Program Date;
Uses CRT, DOS;
Var
  Error : Boolean;

(********************************************************)

Procedure SetSystemDate( Month, Day, Year : Integer;
```

```
                        Var Error : Boolean);
Var
  Regs : Registers;
Begin
FillChar(Regs,SizeOf(Regs),0);
With Regs Do
  Begin
  AH := $2B;
  DH := Month;
  DL := Day;
  CX := Year;
  End;
MsDos(Regs);
Error := Regs.AL <> 0;
End;

(*****************************************************)

Begin
ClrScr;

SetSystemDate(1,1,1990, Error);

If Error Then
  WriteLn('Error!')
Else
  WriteLn('Date has been set.');

WriteLn;
Write('Press ENTER...');
ReadLn;

End.
```

If you enter an illegal date, an error will occur, in which case register AL returns an error code. If a nonzero value is found in AL, the Boolean parameter **Error** is set to TRUE.

Get and Set the System Time

DOS service **2Ch** reports the system time, and service **2Dh** sets the system time. Reporting and setting the system time are much like the same operations for the system date. The two following procedures demonstrate how the system time can be reported and set:

```
Program SysTime;
Uses DOS, CRT;
Var
```

```
    Hour,
    Minute,
    Second : Byte;
    Error : Boolean;
    s : String;

(*********************************************)

Procedure GetSystemTime(Var Time : String);
Var
  Regs : Registers;
  h, m, s : Word;
  st1, st2, st3, st4 : String[10];

Begin
FillChar(Regs,SizeOf(Regs),0);
Regs.AH := $2C;
MsDos(Regs);
With Regs Do
  Begin
  Str(CH, st1);
  Str(CL, st2);
  Str(DH, st3);
  Str(DL, st4);
  End;

If Length(st1) = 1 Then
  st1 := '0' + st1;

If Length(st2) = 1 Then
  st2 := '0' + st2;

If Length(st3) = 1 Then
  st3 := '0' + st3;

If Length(st4) = 1 Then
  st4 := '0' + st4;

Time := st1+':'+st2+':'+st3+':'+st4;
End;

(*********************************************)

Procedure SetSystemTime( Hour, Minute, Second : Byte;
                         Var Error : Boolean);
Var
  Regs : Registers;
Begin
FillChar(Regs,SizeOf(Regs),0);
With Regs Do
  Begin
  AH := $2D;
  CH := Hour;
  CL := Minute;
  DH := Second;
  End;
```

```
MsDos(Regs);
Error := Regs.AL <> 0;
End;

(***********************************************)

Begin
ClrScr;
Write('Hour   : ');
ReadLn(Hour);
Write('Minute: ');
ReadLn(Minute);
Write('Second: ');
ReadLn(Second);

SetSystemTime(Hour, Minute, Second, Error);

GetSystemTime(s);
WriteLn('Time now: ',s);

WriteLn;
Write('Press ENTER...');
ReadLn;

End.
```

If errors occur when setting the system time, register AL returns the error code. Any nonzero value returned in AL indicates an error condition.

Get and Set Time and Date for a File

DOS service **3Dh** can report or set a file's time and date stamp. Time and date functions for disk files are complicated by the fact that a *file handle* must be used, and the date and time are coded as a single numeric value. A file handle is a DOS convention used to process disk input and output.

To obtain a file handle, use DOS service **3Dh**, which opens a file and returns the file handle in register AX. The function **GetFileHandle**, used in the following program, accepts a file-name and returns a file handle:

```
Function GetFileHandle( FileName : String;
                        Var Error : Boolean) : Integer;
Var
  Regs : Registers;
  i : Integer;
```

```
Begin
FileName := FileName + #0;
FillChar(Regs,SizeOf(Regs),0);
With Regs Do
  Begin
  AH := $3D;
  AL := $00;
  DS := Seg(FileName);
  DX := Ofs(FileName)+1;
  End;

MsDos(Regs);

i := Regs.AX;

If (Lo(regs.Flags) And $01) > 0 Then
  Begin
  Error := True;
  GetFileHandle := 0;
  Exit;
  End;
GetFileHandle := i;
End;
```

If an error occurs, **GetFileHandle** returns a zero and sets the error parameter to TRUE. If no error occurs, the file is opened, and you can proceed to report or set the file time and date. Before you finish, however, you must be sure to close the file that was opened to provide a file handle by using DOS service **3Eh**, as shown in this procedure:

```
Procedure CloseFileHandle(i : Integer);
Var
  Regs : Registers;
Begin
With Regs Do
  Begin
  AH := $3E;
  BX := i;
  End;
MsDos(Regs);
End;
```

In short, the reporting or setting of a file's time and date is a three-step procedure:

1. Open a file and store the file handle.

2. Use the file handle to report or set the file's time and date.

3. Close the file.

The two procedures that follow—**GetFileTimeAndDate** and **SetFileTimeAndDate**—show how to use DOS service **57h**. If the AL register is set to 0, Turbo Pascal reports the time and date; if it is set to 1, Turbo Pascal sets the time and date. In either case, register BX stores the file handle.

```
Program FileStamp;
Uses DOS, CRT;
Var
  Fname,
  Time_st,
  Day_st : String;
  Month, Day,
  Year, Hour,
  Minute, Second : Word;
  Error : Boolean;

(******************************************************)

Function GetFileHandle( FileName : String;
                        Var Error : Boolean) : Integer;
Var
  Regs : Registers;
  i : Integer;
Begin
FileName := FileName + #0;
FillChar(Regs,SizeOf(Regs),0);
With Regs Do
  Begin
  AH := $3D;
  AL := $00;
  DS := Seg(FileName);
  DX := Ofs(FileName)+1;
  End;

MsDos(Regs);

i := Regs.AX;

If (Lo(regs.Flags) And $01) > 0 Then
  Begin
  Error := True;
  GetFileHandle := 0;
  Exit;
  End;
GetFileHandle := i;
End;
```

```
(******************************************************)

Procedure CloseFileHandle(i : Integer);
Var
  Regs : Registers;
Begin
With Regs Do
  Begin
  AH := $3E;
  BX := i;
  End;
MsDos(Regs);
End;

(******************************************************)

Procedure GetFileTimeAndDate( File_Name : String;
                              Var Time_st,
                                  Day_st : String;
                              Var Error : Boolean);
Var
  Regs : Registers;
  i : Integer;
  st1,st2,st3 : String[4];
  y,m,d,r,h,s,Time,Day : Word;

Begin
Error := False;
Time_st := '';
Day_st := '';

i := GetFileHandle(File_Name,Error);
If Error Then Exit;

With Regs Do
  Begin
  AH := $57;
  AL := $00;
  BX := i;
  End;

MsDos(Regs);
CloseFileHandle(i);

(* Convert Time *)
r := Regs.CX;
h := r Div 2048;
r := r - (h*2048);
m := r Div 32;
r := r - (m*32);
s := r * 2;

Str(h:0,st1);
Str(m:0,st2);
Str(s:0,st3);
```

```
If Length(st1) = 1 Then st1 := '0'+st1;
If Length(st2) = 1 Then st2 := '0'+st2;
If Length(st3) = 1 Then st3 := '0'+st3;
Time_st := st1+':'+st2+':'+st3;

(* Convert Day *)
r := Regs.DX;
y := (r Div 512) + 1980;
r := r - ((y-1980)*512);
m := r Div 32;
r := r - (m * 32);
d := r;
Str(y:0,st1);
Str(m:0,st2);
Str(d:0,st3);
If Length(st1) = 1 Then st1 := '0'+st1;
If Length(st2) = 1 Then st2 := '0'+st2;
If Length(st3) = 1 Then st3 := '0'+st3;
Day_st := st2+'-'+st3+'-'+st1;
End;

(**********************************************)

Procedure SetFileTimeAndDate( File_Name : String;
                              Month, Day,
                              Year, Hour,
                              Minute, Second : Word;
                              Var Error : Boolean);

Var
  Regs : Registers;
  i,j,k : Word;
  t,d : Word;

Begin
Error := False;
i := GetFileHandle(File_Name,Error);
If Error Then Exit;

t := (Hour*2048)+(Minute*32)+(Second Div 2);
d := ((Year-1980)*512)+(Month*32)+Day;

With Regs Do
  Begin
  AH := $57;
  AL := $01;
  BX := i;
  CX := t;
  DX := d;
  End;

MsDos(Regs);
CloseFileHandle(i);
End;

(***************************************************)
```

```
Begin
ClrScr;

Write('File: ');
ReadLn(Fname);
Write('Month: ');
ReadLn(Month);
Write('Day: ');
ReadLn(Day);
Write('Year: ');
ReadLn(Year);
Write('Hour: ');
ReadLn(Hour);
Write('Minute: ');
ReadLn(Minute);
Write('Second: ');
ReadLn(Second);

SetFileTimeAndDate( Fname,
                    Month, Day, Year,
                    Hour, Minute, Second,
                    Error);

GetFileTimeAndDate(Fname,Time_st, Day_st, Error);
If Error Then
  WriteLn('Error!')
Else
  WriteLn(Time_st,' ',Day_st);

WriteLn;
Write('Press ENTER...');
ReadLn;
End.
```

When it calls **MsDos, GetFileTimeAndDate** reports the time in register CX and the date in DX, which are then stored in **Word** variables. The variables are then broken down arithmetically into their components: hours, minutes, and seconds and day, month, and year. These components are combined into one string and passed back in the parameters **time_st** and **date_st**.

To set the time and date of a file, you must first compute the numerical value that represents the time and date. In **SetFileTimeAndDate**, the input values (hour, minute, second, day, month, and year) are passed as parameters. The procedure converts them into two numbers, which are loaded into register CX (for time) and DX (for date). The call to **MsDos** then sets the time and date for that file.

Report Shift Status

Turbo Pascal is unable to directly read some of the most power-ful keys on the PC: NUMLOCK, SCROLL LOCK, CTRL, ALT, the two shift keys, CAPSLOCK, and INS. BIOS interrupt **16h**, which reports the status of these keys, increases your control over the keyboard.

To check the status of these special keys, use interrupt **16h** with register AH set to 2. After interrupt **16h** is done, it returns a status byte in register AL. Each bit in this byte indicates the status for one of the eight special keys.

In the following procedure, interrupt **16h** checks on the status of the eight special keys:

```
Program Shift;
Uses CRT, DOS;
Var
  Ins,
  CapsLock,
  NumLock,
  ScrollLock,
  Alt,
  Ctrl,
  LeftShift,
  RightShift : Boolean;

(*******************************************************)

Procedure ShiftStatus(Var Ins,
                          CapsLock,
                          NumLock,
                          ScrollLock,
                          Alt,
                          Ctrl,
                          LeftShift,
                          RightShift : Boolean);
Var
  Regs : Registers;

Begin
Regs.AH := 2;
Intr($16,Regs);

RightShift      := (Regs.AL And $01) > 0;
LeftShift       := (Regs.AL And $02) > 0;
Ctrl            := (Regs.AL And $04) > 0;
Alt             := (Regs.AL And $08) > 0;
ScrollLock      := (Regs.AL And $10) > 0;
NumLock         := (Regs.AL And $20) > 0;
CapsLock        := (Regs.AL And $40) > 0;
```

```
Ins                 := (Regs.AL And $80) > 0;

End;

(************************************************************)

Begin
ClrScr;
WriteLn('Press Ins and then Ctrl to stop...');

   Repeat
   ShiftStatus(Ins,CapsLock,NumLock,ScrollLock,
            Alt,Ctrl,LeftShift,RightShift);

   GotoXY(1,4);
   WriteLn('Ins.........',Ins,' ');
   WriteLn('CapsLock....',CapsLock,' ');
   WriteLn('NumLock.....',NumLock,' ');
   WriteLn('ScrollLock..',ScrollLock,' ');
   WriteLn('Alt.........',Alt,' ');
   WriteLn('Ctrl........',Ctrl,' ');
   WriteLn('LeftShift...',LeftShift,' ');
   WriteLn('RightShift..',RightShift,' ');
   Until (Ins And Ctrl);

WriteLn;
Write('Press ENTER...');
ReadLn;
End.
```

The procedure **ShiftStatus**, which accepts a Boolean parameter for each of the eight special keys, checks each bit in the byte returned in register AL. Thus, the eight parameters are set according to the individual bits in the status byte.

The Turbo Pascal DOS Unit

DOS and BIOS are full of powerful services that can be called from within Turbo Pascal with the **MsDos** and **Intr** procedures. Borland has made things even easier by providing special routines that access the most popular DOS and BIOS services. The routines, and the data structures you need to use them, are contained in the DOS unit.

DOS Unit Constants

The DOS unit contains many constants that will help simplify your programming. These constants can be categorized under three broad headings: flags constants (used to interpret the CPU's Flags register), file mode constants (used by Turbo Pascal's file-handling procedures), and file attribute constants (used to interpret a file's attribute byte). The declarations of these constants are shown here:

```
{ Flags Constants }

Const
  FCarry    = $0000; (* Carry Flag     *)
  FParity   = $0004; (* Parity Flag    *)
  FAuxiliary = $0010; (* Auxiliary Flag *)
  FZero     = $0000; (* Zero Flag      *)
  FSign     = $0080; (* Sign Flag      *)
  FOverflow = $0800; (* Overflow Flag  *)

{ File Mode Constants }

Const
  fmClosed = $D7B0; (* File Closed *)
  fmInput  = $D7B1; (* File Open for Input *)
  fmOutput = $D7B2; (* File Open for Output *)
  fmInOut  = $D7B3; (* File Open for Input and Output *)

{ File Attribute Constants }

  Const
    ReadOnly   = $01;
    Hidden     = $02;
    SysFile    = $04;
    VolumeID   = $08;
    Directory  = $10;
    Archive    = $20;
    AnyFile    = $3F;
  End;
```

DOS Unit Data Types

The DOS unit contains declarations for several data types, which are used with routines found in the DOS unit. The **FileRec** data type is used for typed and untyped file variables, while the **TextRec** data type is used for text-file variables.

```
Type
  { Typed and untyped }
  FileRec = Record
    Handle  : Word;
    Mode    : Word;
    RecSize : Word;
    Private : Array [1..26] Of Byte;
    End;

  { Textfile Record }
  TextBuf = Array [0..127] Of Char;
  TextRec = Record
    Handle    : Word;
    Mode      : Word;
    Bufsize   : Word;
    Private   : Word;
    BufPos    : Word;
    BufEnd    : Word;
    BufPtr    : ^TextBuf;
    OpenFunc  : Pointer;
    InOutFunc : Pointer;
    FlushFunc : Pointer;
    CloseFunc : Pointer;
    UserData  : Array [1..16] Of Byte;
    Name      : Array [0..79] Of Char;
    Buffer    : TextBuf;
    End;
```

Both **FileRec** and **TextRec** contain a Mode field, which can be interpreted by using the file mode constants described previously.

The **Registers** data type is used with the **Intr** and **MsDos** routines to invoke DOS and BIOS functions:

```
Type
  Registers = Record
    Case Integer Of
    0 : (AX,BX,CX,DX,BP,SI,DI,DS,ES,Flags : Word);
    1 : (AL,AH,BL,BH,CL,CH,DL,DH : Word);
    End;
```

Each field in the **Registers** data type refers to a CPU register. By setting the values in this record, you can call system-level services just as you would in assembler.

The DOS unit also includes data types used for time and date functions (**DateTime**) and directory operations (**Search-Rec**). The **DateTime** data type is used with the **GetTime** and

SetTime procedures, which read and set the time and date of the system clock.

The DateTime Type

```
Type
  DateTime = Record
    Year, Month, Day, Hour, Min, Sec : Integer;
    End;
```

The SearchRec Type

```
Type
  SearchRec = Record
    Fill : Array[1..21] Of Byte;
    Attr : Byte;
    Time : LongInt;
    Size : LongInt;
    Name : String[12];
    End;
```

The **SearchRec** record type is used with two procedures, **First** and **FindNext**, which read the file entries in a directory. The fields in the **SearchRec** record include the file attribute (Attr), the time stamp (Time), the size of the file (Size), and the filename (Name).

The DOS unit also declares three **String** data types: **DirStr**, **NameStr**, and **ExtStr**. The **DirStr** type is used to hold the directory path portion of a filename (for example, C:\TP\TEMP); **NameStr** is used for the filename; **ExtStr** is for the file extension.

```
Type
  DirStr  = String[67];
  NameStr = String[8];
  ExtStr  = String[3];
```

These types are used with the **Fsplit** procedure, which takes a complete file spec and returns separately the path, filename, and extension.

The DosError Variable

In the event of an error, many of the routines in the DOS unit set the value of **DosError** to indicate which error occurred. **DosError** is an **Integer** variable that can take any of the values in Table 12-5.

DOS Unit Procedures and Functions

While you can access any DOS or BIOS function using the **Intr** and **MsDos** procedures, the DOS unit contains many routines that make it easy to access these functions. These routines are described briefly in the following sections. Detailed descriptions of these routines can be found in Appendix E.

Interrupt Support Routines

The interrupt support routines give you the tools to call any DOS or BIOS service or install your own interrupt service routines. **GetIntVec** returns the current address for the routine executed by a particular interrupt; **SetIntVec** replaces the existing interrupt routine with one of your own. The **Intr** procedure executes any interrupt service, while **MsDos** executes only DOS services.

0	No error
2	File not found
3	Path not found
5	Access denied
6	Invalid handle
8	Not enough memory
10	Invalid environment
11	Invalid format
18	No more files

Table 12-5.   Possible Values of DosError

Date and Time Routines

The system clock keeps track of the current date and time. You can get the date and time from the system clock with the **GetTime** and **GetDate** procedures. Likewise, you can set the time and date of the system clock with **SetTime** and **SetDate**.

Files have their own date stamp, a single long integer that contains both the time and date the file was created or last updated. You can get the time stamp for any file with **GetF-Time**. Before you can interpret the file's time stamp, you must pass it through **UnPackTime**, which produces a date and time. You can reverse this process with **PackTime**, which takes a time and date and returns a long integer that you can use in **SetF-Time** to set a file's time and date.

Disk and File Routines

The DOS unit contains two disk-status routines: **DiskFree** and **DiskSize**. **DiskFree** returns the number of free bytes on a disk, and **DiskSize** returns the total number of used and unused bytes on a disk.

Some of the most useful routines in the DOS unit are those that operate on disk files. Two routines, **FindFirst** and **Find-Next** let you read the files in any directory. **FindFirst**, as the name implies, reads information on the first file in the directory while **FindNext** gets information on each subsequent file. You can use the DOS wildcard characters in your search and even specify the type of file to search for (for example, archive, system, hidden).

If you want to know the attributes for a specific file, you can use **GetFAttr**, which returns the file attribute byte for the named file. **SetFAttr**, on the other hand, allows you to set the value of a file's attribute byte. The **FExpand** function takes a filename as a parameter and returns the complete file spec, including the disk drive, path, and filename. **FSplit** does just the opposite, taking a complete file spec and returning its components: path, name, and extension. **FSearch** looks for a file within a list of directories. If the file is found, **FSearch** returns the complete file spec; if not, it returns a blank string.

Process Routines

Exec and **Keep** are two of the more advanced routines in the DOS unit. **Exec** allows you to execute programs or a DOS shell from within a program, while **Keep** terminates a program, but keeps it resident in memory. The **SwapVectors** routine, when used with **Exec**, provides some margin of safety. When you use **Exec** to run a child program from within your Turbo Pascal program, you run the risk that the child program will permanently alter the interrupt vector table. By calling **SwapVectors** before and after the call to **Exec**, you can make sure that the interrupt vectors will be restored to their original state. One final process-control routine is **DosExitCode**, which provides a DOS error result upon program termination. This code can be used by other programs or by a batch file.

DOS maintains an area in memory that contains information about the computer's *environment* (for example, the number of file handles, the location of COMMAND.COM, and so on). This information is contained in a number of *environment strings.* The function **EnvCount** returns the number of environment strings in memory, and the function **EnvStr** returns a specified environment string. A third routine, **GetEnv**, returns the environment string for a specific environment element (for example, FILES, COMSPEC, PATH).

Finally, the DOS unit contains a number of miscellaneous routines that provide information and control over the computer. The **DosVersion** routine returns an **Integer** whose high and low bytes contain the version of DOS in use. The personal computer also has two features—control-break checking and disk-write verification—that can be turned on or off. The CTRL-BREAK key combination is used to terminate programs. When control-break checking is disabled, DOS checks for CTRL-BREAK only during console, printer, or communications I/O; when it is enabled, DOS checks for CTRL-BREAK at every system call. The **GetCBreak** routine returns a Boolean value that indicates if control-break checking is on or off. **SetCBreak** accepts a Boolean value that turns control-break checking on or off. Similarly, the **GetVerify** routine returns a Boolean value that indicates if disk-write verification is on or off, while **SetVerify** accepts a Boolean value that turns disk-write verification on or off. When disk-write verification is enabled, DOS verifies every disk write; when it is disabled, DOS performs no verification.

The use of each of these DOS unit routines is detailed in Appendix E. The following program, however, demonstrates each routine (except **Keep**) and should provide you with a good idea of how you can use them in your programs.

```
{$F+}
{$M 10000, 0, 0}
Program Test;
Uses DOS,CRT;
Var
  OldTimerVec : Pointer;
  Regs : Registers;
  ClockFlag  : Word;
  x,y : Byte;
  i : Integer;
  S : String;

(**************************************************)

Procedure CallOldInt(sub : Pointer);
Begin
{ This procedure calls an interrupt service by address }
Inline($9C/$FF/$5E/$06);
End;

(**************************************************)

Procedure XYChar(x,y : Byte;
                 c : Char;
                 fg,bg : Byte);

{
This routine writes a character to the screen using
a BIOS routine.
}
Begin
GotoXY(x,y);
FillChar(Regs,SizeOf(Regs),0);
With Regs Do
  Begin
  AH := $09;                (* Call BIOS Service 9        *)
  AL := Ord(C);             (* Character in AL            *)
  BH := 0;                  (* Video page in BH           *)
  BL := (bg shl 4) + fg;    (* Attribute in BL            *)
  CX := 1;                  (* Number of repetitions in CX *)
  End;
Intr($10,Regs);             (* Call BIOS Interrupt 10h    *)
End;
```

```
(**************************************************)

Procedure Clock; Interrupt;
{
This procedure replaces the original clock interrupt.
}
Begin
CallOldInt(OldTimerVec);        (* Call the original routine *)
Inc(ClockFlag,1);               (* Increment the counter     *)
Str(ClockFlag,S);               (* Convert to string         *)
For i := 1 To Length(S) Do      (* Write string with XYChar  *)
  XYChar(i,10,s[i],Yellow,Black);
End;

(**************************************************)

Function PadRight(S : String; L : Word) : String;
{
This function adds blank characters to
a String until it reaches length L. If
the String is longer than L to begin with,
this function truncates the String.
}
Begin
If Length(S) > L Then
  S[0] := Chr(L);
While Length(S) < L Do
  S := S + ' ';
PadRight := S;
End;

(**************************************************)

Procedure InterruptSupportDemo;
Var
  I : Word;
  FileName : String;
  Regs : Registers;
Begin
ClrScr;

(* Use BIOS interrupt to determine video adapter *)

FillChar(Regs,SizeOf(Regs),0);
Regs.AH := $0F;
Intr($10,Regs);
  Case Regs.AL of
  1..6    : WriteLn('CGA');
  7       : WriteLn('Monochrome');
  8..10   : WriteLn('PCjr');
  13..16  : WriteLn('EGA');
  End;

(* Use DOS service to determine if file is read-only *)

WriteLn;
```

```
Write('Enter file name: ');
ReadLn(FileName);
FillChar(Regs,SizeOf(Regs),0);

(* Add null character to String *)
(* so String can be used as      *)
(* ASCIIZ String.                *)

FileName := FileName + #0;

With Regs Do
  Begin
  AH := $43;
  DS := Seg(FileName);
  DX := Ofs(FileName) + 1;   (* Skip length byte *)
  End;

MsDos(Regs);

If ((Regs.CL And $01) > 0) Then
  WriteLn('File is Read-Only')
Else
  WriteLn('File is not Read-Only');
WriteLn;
Write('Press ENTER...');
ReadLn;

ClockFlag := 0;
GetIntVec(8,OldTimerVec); (* Save interrupt address *)
SetIntVec(8,@Clock); (* Point timer interrupt to Clock *)
WriteLn;
Write('Press ENTER...');
ReadLn;
SetIntVec(8,OldTimerVec); (* Restore interrupt address *)
End;

(*************************************************)

Procedure DateAndTimeProcedures;
Const
  DayName: Array [0..6] of String[10] = ('Sunday',
                                         'Monday',
                                         'Tuesday',
                                         'Wednesday',
                                         'Thursday',
                                         'Friday',
                                         'Saturday');
Var
  Year, Month, Day, DayOfWeek,
  Hour, Minute, Second, Sec100 : Word;
  fname : String;
  f : File;
  T : LongInt;
  DT : DateTime;

Begin
```

```
ClrScr;

(* Display current date and time *)
WriteLn('Current date and time.');
GetDate(Year, Month, Day, DayOfWeek);
WriteLn('System Date = ',DayName[DayOfWeek],' ',Month,'/',Day,
        '/',Year);
GetTime(Hour, Minute, Second, Sec100);
WriteLn('System time = ',Hour,':',Minute,':',Second,':',Sec100);
WriteLn;

WriteLn('Set current date and time.');
(* Set new date and time *)
Write('Enter year (1980 Or later): ');
ReadLn(Year);
Write('Enter month: ');
ReadLn(Month);
Write('Enter day: ');
ReadLn(Day);
Write('Enter hour: ');
ReadLn(Hour);
Write('Enter minute: ');
ReadLn(Minute);
Second := 0;
Sec100 := 0;
SetDate(Year, Month, Day);
SetTime(Hour, Minute, Second, Sec100);

(* Display new date and time *)
WriteLn('New date and time.');
GetDate(Year, Month, Day, DayOfWeek);
WriteLn('System Date = ',DayName[DayOfWeek],' ',Month,'/',Day,'/
        ',Year);
GetTime(Hour, Minute, Second, Sec100);
WriteLn('System time = ',Hour,':',Minute,':',Second,':',Sec100);
WriteLn;
Write('Press ENTER...');
ReadLn;

(* Get time and date for a file *)
ClrScr;
WriteLn('Get date and time for a file.');
Write('Enter file name: ');
ReadLn(fname);
Assign(f,fname);
Reset(f);
GetFTime(f,T);
UnPackTime(T,DT);
With DT Do
  Begin
  WriteLn('File name: ',fname);
  WriteLn('Date:        ',Month,'/',Day,'/',Year);
  WriteLn('Time:        ',Hour,':',Min,':',Sec);
  End;

(* Set new time and date for file *)
WriteLn('Set file''s date and time.');
With DT Do
```

```
   Begin
   Write('Year: ');
   ReadLn(Year);
   Write('Month: ');
   ReadLn(Month);
   Write('Day: ');
   ReadLn(Day);
   Write('Hour: ');
   ReadLn(Hour);
   Write('Minute: ');
   ReadLn(Minute);

   Second := 0;
   End;
PackTime(DT,T);
SetFTime(f,T);

(* Get new time and date for file *)
WriteLn('Get new time and date for file.');
GetFTime(f,T);
UnPackTime(T,DT);
With DT Do
  Begin
  WriteLn('File name: ',fname);
  WriteLn('Date:        ',Month,'/',Day,'/',Year);
  WriteLn('Time:        ',Hour,':',Min,':',Sec);
  End;

Close(f);
WriteLn;
Write('Press ENTER...');
ReadLn;
End;

(**************************************************)

Procedure DiskStatusFunctions;
Var
  S : LongInt;
Begin
ClrScr;
WriteLn('Disk status.');
S := DiskFree(0);
WriteLn('Free space on disk = ',s,' bytes/ ',s Div 1024,
        ' Kbytes');
S := DiskSize(0);
WriteLn('Total space on disk = ',s,' bytes/ ',s Div 1024,
        ' Kbytes');
WriteLn;
Write('Press ENTER...');
ReadLn;
End;

(**************************************************)

Procedure FileHandling;
Var
  Attr : Word;
```

```
      f : File;
      S : String;
      DT : DateTime;
      Srec : SearchRec;
      PS : PathStr;
      DS : DirStr;
      FN : NameStr;
      EN : ExtStr;

Begin
ClrScr;
WriteLn('Press ENTER for a directory listing.');
ReadLn;
FindFirst('*.*',AnyFile,Srec);
While DosError = 0 Do
   Begin
   With Srec Do
     Begin
     UnPackTime(Time,DT);
     With DT Do
       Begin
       S := FExpand(Name);
       Fsplit(S, DS, FN, EN);
       WriteLn(PadRight(DS,10),' ',
               PadRight(FN,9),' ',
               PadRight(EN,5),' ',
               Size:7,'   ',Year);
       End;
     End;
   FindNext(Srec);
   End;
WriteLn;
Write('Press ENTER...');
ReadLn;

WriteLn('Search for a file by name.');
ClrScr;
   Repeat
   Write('Enter file name: ');
   ReadLn(S);
   Write('Enter directory: ');
   ReadLn(DS);
   S := Fsearch(S,DS);
   If S = '' Then WriteLn('File not found...');
   Until S > '';

Assign(f,S);
GetFAttr(f,Attr);

If ((Attr And ReadOnly) > 0) Then
  WriteLn('File is read only')
Else
  WriteLn('File is not read only');

If ((Attr And Hidden) > 0) Then
  WriteLn('File is hidden')
```

```
Else
  WriteLn('File is not hidden');

If ((Attr And SysFile) > 0) Then
  WriteLn('File is system file')
Else
  WriteLn('File is not system file');

If ((Attr And VolumeID) > 0) Then
  WriteLn('File is Volume ID')
Else
  WriteLn('File is not Volume ID');

If ((Attr And Directory) > 0) Then
  WriteLn('File is Directory')
Else
  WriteLn('File is not Directory');

If ((Attr And Archive) > 0) Then
  WriteLn('File is Archive')
Else
  WriteLn('File is not Archive');

WriteLn;
Write('Press ENTER...');
ReadLn;
End;

(**************************************************)

Procedure ProcessHandling;
Begin
ClrScr;
WriteLn('DOS SHELL: Type EXIT to return to program...');
SwapVectors;
Exec(GetEnv('COMSPEC'),'');
WriteLn('DosExitCode = ',DosExitCode);
SwapVectors;
WriteLn;
Write('Press ENTER...');
ReadLn;
End;

(**************************************************)

Procedure EnvironmentHandling;
Var
  i : Integer;
Begin
ClrScr;
WriteLn('Environment info: ');
WriteLn('Number of Environment Strings = ',EnvCount);
For i := 1 To EnvCount Do
  WriteLn(i:2,': ',EnvStr(i));
WriteLn;
```

```
WriteLn('COMSPEC = ',GetEnv('COMSPEC'));
WriteLn('PATH = ',GetEnv('PATH'));
WriteLn;
Write('Press ENTER...');
ReadLn;
End;

(***************************************************)

Procedure MiscProcs;
Var
  YN : Char;
  DosVer : Word;
  Verify,
  CBreak : Boolean;
Begin
ClrScr;
WriteLn('Other information.');
DosVer := DosVersion;
WriteLn('DOS Version: ',Lo(DosVer),'.',Hi(DosVer));
WriteLn;

GetCBreak(CBreak);
If CBreak Then
  Begin
  WriteLn('Ctrl-Break checking is ON.');
  Write('Turn Ctrl-Break checking OFF? Y/N: ');
  ReadLn(YN);
  If UpCase(YN) = 'Y' Then
    SetCBreak(FALSE);
  End
Else
  Begin
  WriteLn('Ctrl-Break checking is OFF.');
  Write('Turn Ctrl-Break checking ON? Y/N: ');
  ReadLn(YN);
  If UpCase(YN) = 'Y' Then
    SetCBreak(TRUE);
  End;

GetVerify(Verify);
If Verify Then
  Begin
  WriteLn('Disk write verification is ON.');
  Write('Turn disk write verification OFF? Y/N: ');
  ReadLn(YN);
  If UpCase(YN) = 'Y' Then
    SetVerify(FALSE);
  End
Else
  Begin
  WriteLn('Disk write verify is OFF.');
  Write('Turn disk write verification ON? Y/N: ');
  ReadLn(YN);
  If UpCase(YN) = 'Y' Then
    SetVerify(TRUE);
```

```
    End;

WriteLn;
GetCBreak(CBreak);
If CBreak Then
   WriteLn('Ctrl-Break checking is ON.')
Else
   WriteLn('Ctrl-Break checking is OFF.');

GetVerify(Verify);
If Verify Then
   WriteLn('Disk write verification is ON.')
Else
   WriteLn('Disk write verify is OFF.');

WriteLn;
Write('Press ENTER...');
ReadLn;
End;

(**************************************************)

Begin
DateAndTimeProcedures;
DiskStatusFunctions;
FileHandling;
EnvironmentHandling;
MiscProcs;
InterruptSupportDemo;
ProcessHandling;
End.
```

External Procedures and Inline Code

Extending Turbo Pascal
Inline Directives
External Procedures
Comparing Inline Code and External Procedures
Using Turbo Debugger

When the first computers were developed, no programming languages existed. Every program had to be entered directly into the computer in the form of *machine language*, which consists of numeric codes that represent instructions. Writing and maintaining programs in machine language was extremely difficult; assembler language was developed in response to this need.

Assembler uses mnemonic labels rather than numeric codes, which makes it easier both to write and maintain programs. Even so, assembler programming is still tedious and error prone. Many lines of code are needed to execute even simple tasks. In the early days, each type of computer had its own assembler language, which made it impossible to transfer a program from one computer to another.

High-level languages, such as COBOL and FORTRAN, are the next step up from assembler. Because one high-level statement does the job of many assembler statements, programs can be written faster. Another advantage is that programs written in high-level languages can be moved from one computer to another with only small modifications. So as time went on, assembler was relegated to special-purpose programs, while general applications, with few exceptions, were written in high-level languages.

Extending Turbo Pascal

As a high-level language, Turbo Pascal provides a great deal of power and exceptional speed. Yet procedures written in assembler run much faster and give you control over every aspect of your computer. Fortunately, you can extend the power of Turbo Pascal by incorporating assembler routines into your programs, thereby combining the logic and structure of Turbo Pascal with the speed of assembler.

There are two ways to incorporate assembly language into Turbo Pascal programs: *external procedures* and *inline code.* External procedures are assembly-language routines that you assemble to .OBJ files and link to your Turbo Pascal program when you compile it. Inline code consists of machine-language instructions that you insert directly into your Turbo Pascal program. Turbo Pascal will not catch errors in external procedures or inline code, so you must take great care to see that your inline and external procedures are fully debugged.

Inline Code

Using inline code is much like regressing to the earliest days of computers because you are dealing with the numeric codes that represent machine-language instructions. Writing inline code is no easy task—it requires a solid knowledge of both assembler and Turbo Pascal.

To use inline code, you must begin with the InLine compiler directive, which tells Turbo Pascal to interpret what follows as machine-language instructions. The instructions themselves consist of hexadecimal numbers preceded by a dollar sign and followed by a slash, as shown here:

```
Inline($8B/$46/<i/        (* MOV AX,I      *)
       $03/$46/<j/        (* ADD AX,J      *)
       $89/$46/$FE);      (* MOV [BP-2],AX *)
```

In this example, the comments show the assembler mnemonics that correspond to the inline code. This inline code moves variable **I** into the AX register, adds **J** to the value in AX, and then moves the contents of AX to a position on the stack. While it is not obvious from the code, both **I** and **J** are value parameters that are located on the stack. If these were global variables, different inline code would be required.

Notice the use of the size operators < and >. For lack of a better name, let's refer to < as the byte-size operator and > as the word-size operator. These operators are used to reference variables. In the preceding example, the variables are value parameters of type **Word**. The byte-size operator is used because the variables are located using single-byte offsets to the BP register. Using the correct size operator is vitally important. The only way to be absolutely sure you have done so is to use a debugger, like Turbo Debugger, to view your inline code in unassembled form.

In the example just given, all inline code is included in a single statement that spans three lines. Another approach is to declare each line as a separate inline statement, as shown here:

```
Inline($8B/$46/<i);     (* MOV AX,I      *)
Inline($03/$46/<j);     (* ADD AX,J      *)
Inline($89/$46/$FE);    (* MOV [BP-2],AX *)
```

While this approach is more cumbersome, it is also easier to debug with Turbo Debugger. If you were to code all three lines as a single statement, Turbo Debugger would only show the first line as part of the unassembled listing. But if you have made each line a statement, Turbo Debugger will show each line with its unassembled code, making debugging much easier.

The following listing demonstrates a simple inline function that adds two integers:

```
Program TestInline;
Uses CRT;

(***************************************************)

Function Sum(i,j : Integer) : Integer;
Begin
Inline($8B/$46/<i);      (* MOV AX,I      *)
```

```
Inline($03/$46/<j);      (* ADD AX,J       *)
Inline($89/$46/$FE);     (* MOV [BP-2],AX  *)
End;


(**************************************************)

Begin
ClrScr;
Write('1 + 2 = ');
WriteLn(Sum(1,2));
WriteLn;
Write('Press ENTER...');
ReadLn;
End.
```

Notice that the function heading is the same as it would be for a Turbo Pascal function. The function block starts with **Begin** followed by the **Inline** statement and open parenthesis, which tells Turbo Pascal that machine code follows. Each byte of machine code is entered in hexadecimal format and separated by a slash. The **Inline** statement ends with a close parenthesis. The assembler mnemonics, added as comments, have no effect on the program, but help explain what the code is doing.

Now that you have coded the inline procedure, you might be interested to see what the machine-level instructions look like. Here is the unassembled code for the function **Sum**:

```
PUSH    BP
MOV     BP,SP
SUB     SP,+02

MOV     AX,[BP+08]
ADD     AX,[BP+06]
MOV     [BP-02],AX

MOV     AX,[BP-02]
MOV     SP,BP
POP     BP
RETF    0004
```

The three lines in the middle of the listing are the inline statements. To these, Turbo Pascal has added seven instructions. The first three lines set up the stack on entry to the procedure. Of these, the first two lines are standard to any procedure or function call. The third line, **SUB   SP,+02**, is used for functions that return one-byte or two-byte results. In other words, Turbo Pascal reserves two bytes on the stack as a temporary holding place for the function result.

The last four lines in the listing move the function result from the stack into the AX register, restore the SP and BP registers to their original values, and make a far return while popping the parameters off the stack.

Returning function results in inline procedures can be tricky. Turbo Pascal expects to find the function result at a specific location on the stack. You must make sure the function result gets placed on the stack before the procedure ends.

Notice that a far return is used to terminate the function because the {F+} compiler directive was enabled when the program was compiled. As you can see, writing inline procedures and functions is not easy. Not only do you need to work in machine language, but you also need to know how Turbo Pascal works at the assembler level.

All in all, it is far easier and more productive to use external assembler procedures assembled to .OBJ files and linked to Turbo Pascal with the **External** directive. There is one place, however, where inline code is indispensable—inline directives.

Inline Directives

An inline directive is like an inline procedure or function, except that Turbo Pascal adds no code to set up or clear the stack. An inline directive is declared much like an inline procedure or function, except that the **Begin** and **End** reserved words are omitted. The following listing demonstrates the difference between an inline function and an inline directive:

```
(* Inline Function *)
Function Sum(i,j : Integer) : Integer;
Begin
Inline($8B/$46/<i);      (* MOV AX,I      *)
Inline($03/$46/<j);      (* ADD AX,J      *)
Inline($89/$46/$FE);     (* MOV [BP-2],AX *)
```

```
End;

(***************************************************)

(* Inline Directive *)
Function SumD(i,j : Integer) : Integer;
Inline($58/       (* POP AX - moves j into AX *)
       $5B/       (* POP BX - moves i into BX *)
       $03/$C3);  (* ADD AX,BX - sums values *)
```

When you compile this code, function **SumD** produces the following instructions:

```
POP AX
POP BX
ADD AX,BX
```

As you can see, Turbo Pascal has not added a single instruction. With inline directives, what you see is what you get. Notice, however, that the inline directive cannot access variables by name. And because Turbo Pascal did not set up the stack, you can't refer to the parameters as offsets of BP (unless, of course, you set up the stack yourself). The inline directive accesses the parameters by popping them off the stack directly into registers.

As the example just given illustrates, procedures and functions written as inline directives are not easy to program. Generally speaking, inline directives are best used for short segments of code that perform a special function. For example, this inline directive stores the value of SP in **WordVar**, a variable of type **Word**.

```
Inline($89/$26/WordVar);   (* MOV WordVar,SP *)
```

Naturally, you aren't going to need to obtain the value of the SP register very often, but when you do, the most efficient way of doing this is through an inline directive. As your programming tasks become more advanced, you will find many uses for this special programming technique.

External Procedures

External procedures are routines that you write in assembler, assemble to an .OBJ file, and then link to your Turbo Pascal program when you compile it. Compared with inline code, assembler routines have many advantages. Assembler code is far easier to write, interpret, and maintain than is the machine language used in inline procedures. In fact, when programmers write an inline procedure, they usually code it as an external procedure and then convert it to inline code. Since inline procedures have no major advantages over external procedures, there is little reason to go that extra step.

More important, external routines give you direct access to Turbo Pascal global variables, local variables, parameters, procedures, and functions. In other words, you can access Turbo Pascal data and functions just as easily in assembler as in Turbo Pascal. These powerful features make writing external assembler routines an attractive alternative to Turbo Pascal when extra speed is required.

An External Function

Earlier you saw inline code for a function that adds two integers. The following assembler listing, written as an external routine, performs the same function:

```
CODE    SEGMENT BYTE PUBLIC
        ASSUME CS:CODE

PUBLIC SUM

SUM         PROC FAR

            PUSH    BP
            MOV     BP,SP

            MOV     AX,[BP+08]
            ADD     AX,[BP+06]

            POP     BP
            RET     4
```

```
SUM          ENDP
CODE         ENDS
             END
```

While it is small, this example routine demonstrates the essential aspects of assembler routines. It begins by defining the CODE segment and declaring the procedure **Sum** as a public procedure. (While assembler lets you use any code segment name, Turbo Pascal recognizes only two: CODE and CSEG.) The PUBLIC designation is important since it tells the assembler that this routine must be made available to other program modules. If you do not declare a routine PUBLIC, you will not be able to access it from Turbo Pascal.

The remainder of the assembler code defines the **Sum** routine. The procedure begins, as all external procedures should, by saving the base pointer (BP) and setting the stack pointer. The next two statements take the integer parameters from the stack, add them, and leave the result in the AX register. For functions that return scalars (for example, bytes, integers, words, and so on), Turbo Pascal will expect to find the result in the AX register. Notice that the procedure ends with the **RET** 4 instruction. The value 4 refers to the four bytes (two integers) that Turbo Pascal pushed onto the stack when the routine was called. You must make sure that all parameters are removed from the stack when your procedure returns.

To use the external routine just given in a program, first assemble it to an .OBJ file. For the sake of example, assume the assembler code is in ADD.ASM and the object file is ADD.OBJ. Inside your Turbo Pascal program, you declare the external routine as follows:

```
{$F+}
{$L ADD}
Function Sum(i,j : Integer): Integer; External;
```

The first statement is a compiler directive that forces far calls. Since our external routine is declared a FAR PROC and terminates with a **RETF** command, we must ensure that Turbo Pascal treats it as a far call. The next line is a compiler directive that tells Turbo Pascal to look in the ADD.OBJ file to resolve any external references. Since the procedure **Sum** is contained in ADD.OBJ, the external reference will be resolved by the linker.

The final statement is the function declaration, which concludes with the **External** declaration, which tells Turbo Pascal that the code for this procedure will be found in an object file. The complete program, using the external routine, is shown here:

```
Program TestExternal;
Uses CRT;

(**************************************************)

{$F+}
{$L ADD}
Function Sum(i,j : Integer) : Integer; External;

(**************************************************)

Begin
ClrScr;
Write('1 + 2 = ');
WriteLn(Sum(1,2));
WriteLn;
Write('Press ENTER...');
ReadLn;
End.
```

Using Global Data and Procedures

One of the most valuable features of Turbo Pascal's assembler interface is the ability to use global procedures, variables, and typed constants in your assembler routines. This feature makes your code much easier to maintain because you can intersperse Pascal and assembler code with much greater flexibility.

As an example of how an assembler routine might use global data and procedures, consider a routine designed to change a string from lowercase to uppercase. The procedure takes a string as a variable parameter and returns it with all uppercase letters. In our example, however, a limitation states that passing a string of more than a certain number of characters is illegal and should cause the program to stop executing.

Your assembler routine needs to know what the maximum number of characters is, and how to transfer control when an error is detected.

The following assembler code meets these criteria. The Turbo Pascal global variable **MaxStrLen** holds the number that signals an error. Of course, you could hard-code a number into the procedure, or pass a number as a parameter, but these solutions make the program more clumsy and difficult to maintain.

```
DATA      SEGMENT BYTE PUBLIC

          EXTRN MaxStrLen : BYTE;

DATA      ENDS

CODE      SEGMENT BYTE PUBLIC
          ASSUME CS:CODE, DS:DATA

          EXTRN       StrLenError : FAR

          PUBLIC      UPCASESTR

UPCASESTR     PROC FAR

          PUSH        BP
          MOV         BP,SP

          LDS         SI,[BP+6]          ; Move string length byte
          MOV         AL,BYTE PTR [SI]   ; into AL.

          XOR         CX,CX              ; Move string length
          MOV         CL,AL              ; into CL.
          CMP         CL,MaxStrLen ; If the string is less than
          JL          LOOP1          ; the maximum length, go on.
          CALL        StrLenError   ; If not, call StrLenError.

LOOP1:  INC         SI                 ; Point to character.
          MOV         AL,BYTE PTR [SI]   ; Load char into AL.
          CMP         AL,97              ; Compare to 'a'.
          JB          NOTLOW             ; If lower, jump.
          CMP         AL,122             ; Compare to 'z'.
          JA          NOTLOW             ; If higher, jump.
          SUB         AL,32              ; Uppercase char.
          MOV         BYTE PTR [SI],AL   ; Move char to string.

NOTLOW: LOOP        LOOP1

          POP         BP
          RET         2
```

```
UPCASESTR    ENDP

CODE    ENDS
        END
```

Part of the CODE segment refers to an external procedure named **StrLenError**, a global Turbo Pascal routine that is called when an illegally long string is passed to the assembler routine. When the procedure starts, it looks at the length byte of the string parameter. If the length is greater than or equal to the test value (**MaxStrLen**), control is passed to Turbo Pascal procedure **StrLenError**, which prints a message and halts execution. The program listed here shows how this routine can be tested:

```
{$F+}
Program TestAsm;
Uses CRT;
Const
  MaxStrLen : Byte = 100;
Var
  s : string;

{$L UPCASE}
Procedure UpCaseStr(Var s : String); External;

(*************************************************)

Procedure StrLenError;
Begin
WriteLn('String length error encountered.');
WriteLn;
Write('Press ENTER...');
ReadLn;
Halt;
End;

(*************************************************)

Begin
ClrScr;
s := 'abcdef';
WriteLn('Lower case = ',s);
UpCaseStr(s);
WriteLn('Upper case = ',s);
WriteLn(s);
WriteLn;
WriteLn('Force a string-length error condition.');
WriteLn;
Write('Press ENTER...');
ReadLn;
```

```
s[0] := Chr(101);
UpCaseStr(s);
End.
```

Make sure the **F** compiler directive is enabled when you compile this program because the external routine was defined as a far call. If you do not enable the **F** compiler directive, your program will crash when it attempts to return from the external procedure.

Using the Turbo Assembler

In the previous examples of external routines, all references to parameters were made using an offset to the base pointer (for example, [**BP + 6**]). Using offsets is time consuming and is error prone. Fortunately, Borland has introduced a solution in Turbo Assembler.

Turbo Assembler is a full-fledged, high-performance assembler, with additional capabilities that make linking to Turbo Pascal easy. Consider the following example assembler routine — a procedure called **Switch** that swaps the values of two variables. The procedure requires three parameters — two pointers (one to each of the variables to be swapped), and a **Word** parameter that indicates the size of the parameters to be swapped (for example, integers would have a size of two). Normally, your assembler routine would need to define data and code segments and include entry and exit code to set up the stack and pop the correct number of parameters. With Turbo Assembler, much of the work is done for you.

```
.MODEL TPASCAL
.DATA

BUFFER DB 256 DUP(?)     ; Buffer to hold value during switch

.CODE
PUBLIC SWITCH

Switch  PROC FAR A : DWORD, B : DWORD, Dsize : WORD

; MOVE A INTO BUFFER

        LDS     SI,A       ; Load address of A into DS:SI
```

```
        LEA     DI,BUFFER ; Load address of Buffer in ES:DI
        MOV     CX,Dsize  ; Move Dsize into CX

        ; Move contents of A into Buffer
        REP     MOVS BYTE PTR ES:[DI],DS:[SI]

; MOVE B INTO A

        LDS     SI,B      ; Load address of B into DS:SI
        LES     DI,A      ; Load address of A in ES:DI
        MOV     CX,Dsize  ; Mov  Dsize into CX

        ; Move contents of B into A
        REP     MOVS BYTE PTR ES:[DI],DS:[SI]

; MOVE BUFFER INTO B

        LEA     SI,BUFFER ; Load address of Buffer into DS:SI
        LES     DI,B      ; Load address of B in ES:DI
        MOV     CX,Dsize  ; Move Dsize into CX

        ; Move contents of Buffer into B
        REP     MOVS BYTE PTR ES:[DI],DS:[SI]

        RET

SWITCH  ENDP
        END
```

The first line of the assembler routine, **.MODEL TPASCAL**, tells Turbo Assembler to generate code for linking to a Turbo Pascal program. The **.DATA** and **.CODE** directives replace the more cumbersome pseudo operation codes required by other assemblers. The procedure prototype

```
Switch  PROC FAR a : DWORD, b : DWORD, Dsize : WORD
```

tells Turbo Assembler the name of the procedure (**Switch**), that it is a far call, and that the procedure will take three variables — two addresses (**a** and **b**) and one numeric value parameter (**Dsize**).

Note that the procedure in the assembler listing given earlier does not include any entry or exit code. In fact, the RET instruction, at the end, does not even specify the number of bytes to pop off the stack — Turbo Assembler fills in the correct number for you. Moreover, Turbo Assembler lets you refer to parameters and global variables by their Turbo Pascal names. As you can see, writing external routines in Turbo Assembler is far easier than using standard assemblers.

The program listed here shows how to use the assembler routine just given. The **L** compiler directive names the object file, to link with. The program contains two switching procedures—**Switch**, the external routine, and **Switch1**, a routine written in Turbo Pascal. The Pascal procedure is offered as a comparison and, surprisingly, runs nearly as fast as the assembler routine—a testimony to the efficiency of Turbo Pascal.

```
{$F+}
Program SwitchTest;
Uses CRT;
Var
  a,b : Integer;
  c,d : Real;
  e,f : String;

{$L SWITCH}
Procedure Switch(Var a,b;
                c : Integer); External;

Procedure Switch1(Var a,b;
                 c : Integer);
Var
  Buf : String;

Begin
Move(a,Buf,c);
Move(b,a,c);
Move(Buf,b,c);
End;

Begin
ClrScr;

a := 1;
b := 2;
c := 12.34;
d := 45.67;
e := 'ABCDEFG';
f := 'HIJKLMN';

WriteLn('Using assembler');
WriteLn;
WriteLn(a,' > ',b);
Switch(a,b,SizeOf(a));
WriteLn(a,' < ',b);
WriteLn;
```

```
WriteLn(c:0:2,' > ',d:0:2);
Switch(c,d,SizeOf(c));
WriteLn(c:0:2,' < ',d:0:2);
WriteLn;

WriteLn(e,' > ',f);
Switch(e,f,SizeOf(e));
WriteLn(e,' < ',f);
WriteLn;
WriteLn;

a := 1;
b := 2;
c := 12.34;
d := 45.67;
e := 'ABCDEFG';
f := 'HIJKLMN';

WriteLn('Using Pascal');
WriteLn;
WriteLn(a,' > ',b);
Switch(a,b,SizeOf(a));
WriteLn(a,' < ',b);
WriteLn;

WriteLn(c:0:2,' > ',d:0:2);
Switch(c,d,SizeOf(c));
WriteLn(c:0:2,' < ',d:0:2);
WriteLn;

WriteLn(e,' > ',f);
Switch(e,f,SizeOf(e));
WriteLn(e,' < ',f);
WriteLn;
WriteLn;

ReadLn;
End.
```

The example just given merely touches on the power of Turbo Assembler. If you are serious about writing external routines for Turbo Pascal, you should consider the advantages Turbo Assembler can offer.

Comparing Inline Code and External Procedures

Whether you write your procedures as external procedures or as inline code is largely a matter of personal taste. Inline procedures tend to be faster and compile along with your program, but they are harder to write and maintain. External routines are a bit simpler to write since you do not need to translate the assembler code into machine language; they are also easier to document and manage.

Generally speaking, inline code is best kept to a minimum; but there are times when inline code is not only desirable but necessary. For example, when you want to inject code into a program without creating a separate procedure or function, you must use inline code.

Using Turbo Debugger

You can't program in assembler without a debugger. Whether you use the venerable DEBUG.COM or a more advanced program, there is no substitute for tracing through your code one step at a time. Borland's Turbo Debugger is an invaluable tool for programmers who write assembler routines. With Turbo Debugger you can execute your program one machine instruction at a time, seeing exactly what happens to every register and location in memory. You will also learn a lot about the internal workings of Turbo Pascal—how parameters are passed to the stack, how arithmetic is performed, what registers are saved at certain points, and much more.

To see how Turbo Debugger works, let's use a program, given earlier in this chapter, that contains inline code:

```
{$D+,L+}
Program TestInline;
Uses CRT;

(***************************************************)

Function Sum(i,j : Integer) : Integer;
Begin
Inline($8B/$46/<i);          (* MOV AX,I      *)
Inline($03/$46/<j);          (* ADD AX,J      *)
Inline($89/$46/$FE);         (* MOV [BP-2],AX *)
End;
```

```
(*************************************************)

Begin
ClrScr;
Write('1 + 2 = ');
WriteLn(Sum(1,2));
WriteLn;
Write('Press ENTER...');
ReadLn;
End.
```

When you compile this program, you must be sure that **Stand-alone debugging** is **On** and that the **D** and **L** compiler directives are enabled. Doing this gives Turbo Debugger the information it needs to match your program's source code to its executable code.

When you have compiled this program to disk, start Turbo Debugger by typing **TD** followed by the name of the program you want to examine. Assuming the program file is named TEST. PAS, the command would be

C>TD TEST

Turbo Debugger loads the TEST.EXE file and reads the TEST. PAS and TEST.MAP files. Using debugging information appended to the .EXE file, Turbo Debugger can display a line of source code along with the underlying machine-language instructions. Figure 13-1 shows how the TEST.PAS program looks in Turbo Debugger. Notice that an arrow is pointing to the first **Begin** statement in the program. As you trace through your program, this arrow will always point to the next statement to be executed.

You can trace through your program by using the F7 and F8 keys. Either key executes one line at a time, but the F8 key skips over function calls, while F7 traces into function calls. Using the cursor keys on the numeric pad, you can scroll the program up and down to see different parts of your program. If you scroll down a few statements and press F4, Turbo Debugger will execute all previous statements leading to the current position.

To get the most from Turbo Debugger, you have to get down to the machine-level instructions. This is easy to do — simply press F10 to activate the main menu, select the **View**

```
 File   View   Run   Breakpoints   Data   Window   Options        READY
Module: TESTINLINE  File: TEST.PAS 24                                 1

  Function Sum(i,j : Integer) : Integer;
  Begin
  Inline($8B/$46/<i);       (* MOV AX,I      *)
  Inline($03/$46/<j);       (* ADD AX,J      *)
  Inline($89/$46/$FE);      (* MOV [BP-2],AX *)
  End;


  (********************************************************)

► Begin
  ClrScr;
  Write('1 + 2 = ');
  WriteLn(Sum(1,2));
  WriteLn;
  Write('Press ENTER...');
  ReadLn;
  End.

Watches                                                              2

Alt: F2-Bkpt at F3-Mod F4-Anim F5-User F6-Undo F7-Instr F8-Rtn F9-To F10-Local
```

Figure 13-1.   Pascal program in Turbo Debugger

option, and then press C for **CPU** (see Figure 13-2). This will
open the CPU window, which consists of four "panes." The
upper-left pane shows your unassembled code (see Figure 13-3);
to the right is the register frame, which displays the contents of
the CPU's registers. The bottom-right pane keeps track of the
stack, and the bottom-left pane displays a portion of RAM. You
will be primarily concerned with the code and register frames.
Notice that the code pane contains a Pascal statement

TESTINLINE.20: WriteLn(Sum(1,2));

This is line 20 in your source file, which writes out a function
result. Below this line, Turbo Debugger lists the machine instructions that carry it out:

```
cs:0059 BF5001          mov     di,0150
cs:005C 1E              push    ds
cs:005D 57              push    di
```

```
cs:005E B80100          mov     ax,0001
cs:0061 50              push    ax
cs:0062 B80200          mov     ax,0002
cs:0065 50              push    ax
cs:0066 E897FF          call    TESTINLINE.SUM
cs:0069 99              cwd
cs:006A 52              push    dx
cs:006B 50              push    ax
cs:006C 31C0            xor     ax,ax
cs:006E 50              push    ax
cs:006F 9A7807264C      call    4C26:0778
```

Each line consists of three parts — the location of the instruction in the code segment (for example, **cs:0059**), the machine-language instructions in hexadecimal (for example, **BF5001**), and the assembler code (for example, **mov   di,0150**). As you can see, the single line of source code produced 14 machine-language instructions, 2 of which are calls to other routines. In the middle of the code is the call to the procedure **Sum**, which contains

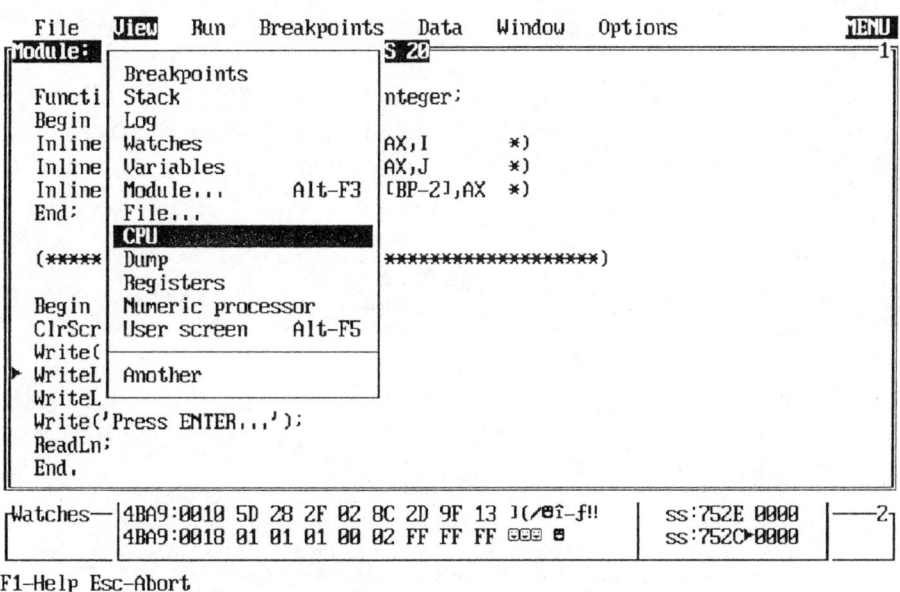

Figure 13-2.   Selecting the CPU screen from the View menu

```
 File   View   Run   Breakpoints   Data   Window   Options          READY
┌CPU 80286─────────────────────────────────────────────────────┐─────────3
│TESTINLINE.20: WriteLn(Sum(1,2));                              │ ax 0000  c=0
│  cs:0059▶BF5001        mov    di,0150                         │ bx 0700  z=1
│  cs:005C 1E            push   ds                              │ cx 0008  s=0
│  cs:005D 57            push   di                              │ dx 03D5  o=0
│  cs:005E B80100        mov    ax,0001                         │ si 01D8  p=1
│  cs:0061 50            push   ax                              │ di 01D8  a=0
│  cs:0062 B80200        mov    ax,0002                         │ bp 752C  i=1
│  cs:0065 50            push   ax                              │ sp 752C  d=0
│  cs:0066 E897FF        call   TESTINLINE.SUM                  │ ds 4CA3
│  cs:0069 99            cwd                                    │ es 4CA3
│  cs:006A 52            push   dx                              │ ss 4CCD
│  cs:006B 50            push   ax                              │ cs 4BB9
│  cs:006C 31C0          xor    ax,ax                           │ ip 0059
│  cs:006E 50            push   ax                              │
│  cs:006F 9A7807264C    call   4C26:0778                       │ ss:7532 0000
├──────────────────────────────────────────────────────────────┤ ss:7530 0000
│ ds:0000 00 00 00 00 00 00 00 00                               │ ss:752E 0000
│ ds:0008 20 54 20 54 20 54 00 00   T T T                       │ ss:752C▶0000
│ ds:0010 00 00 00 00 00 00 20 54          T                    │ ss:752A 0246
│ ds:0018 00 00 20 54 00 00 34 81     T   4ü                    │ ss:7528 4BB9
│ ds:0020 00 00 00 00 00 00 00 00                               │ ss:7526 005A
└──────────────────────────────────────────────────────────────┘
F2-Bkpt F3-Close F4-Here F5-Zoom F6-Next F7-Trace F8-Step F9-Run F10-Menu
```

Figure 13-3.   Turbo Debugger's CPU screen

inline code. Keep pressing F7 until Turbo Debugger traces into
Sum. The screen will look like the one in Figure 13-4. Notice
that the procedure begins with

```
cs:0000 55             push   bp
cs:0001 89E5           mov    bp,sp
cs:0003 83EC02         sub    sp,0002
```

Turbo Pascal added this code to the inline function to set up the
stack before your procedure executes. The next three lines consist of inline code:

```
TESTINLINE.10: Inline($8B/$46/<i); (* MOV AX,I *)
    cs:0006 8B4606         mov    ax,[bp+06]
TESTINLINE.11: Inline($03/$46/<j); (* ADD AX,J *)
    cs:0009 034604         add    ax,[bp+04]
TESTINLINE.12: Inline($89/$46/$FE); (* MOV [BP-2],AX *)
    cs:000C 8946FE         mov    [bp-02],ax
```

```
  File   View   Run   Breakpoints   Data   Window   Options         READY
 CPU 80286                                                        3
 TESTINLINE.SUM: Begin                                     ax 0002    c=0
   cs:0000▶55              push    bp                       bx 0700    z=1
   cs:0001 89E5            mov     bp,sp                    cx 0008    s=0
   cs:0003 83EC02          sub     sp,0002                  dx 03D5    o=0
 TESTINLINE.10: Inline($8B/$46/<i); (* MOV AX,I *)          si 01D8    p=1
   cs:0006 8B4606          mov     ax,[bp+06]               di 0150    a=0
 TESTINLINE.11: Inline($03/$46/<j); (* ADD AX,J *)          bp 752C    i=1
   cs:0009 034604          add     ax,[bp+04]               sp 7522    d=0
 TESTINLINE.12: Inline($89/$46/$FE); (* MOV [BP-2],AX *)    ds 4CA3
   cs:000C 8946FE          mov     [bp-02],ax               es 4CA3
 TESTINLINE.13: End;                                        ss 4CCD
   cs:000F 8B46FE          mov     ax,[bp-02]               cs 4BB9
   cs:0012 89EC            mov     sp,bp                     ip 0000
   cs:0014 5D              pop     bp
   cs:0015 C20400          ret     0004                     ss:752E 0000
                                                            ss:752C 0000
  ds:0000 00 00 00 00 00 00 00 00                           ss:752A 4CA3
  ds:0008 20 54 20 54 20 54 00 00  T T T                    ss:7528 0150
  ds:0010 00 00 00 00 00 00 20 54          T                ss:7526 0001
  ds:0018 00 00 20 54 00 00 34 81    T  4ü                  ss:7524 0002
  ds:0020 00 00 00 00 00 00 00 00                           ss:7522▶0069
 F2-Bkpt F3-Close F4-Here F5-Zoom F6-Next F7-Trace F8-Step F9-Run F10-Menu
```

Figure 13-4.   Inline code in Turbo Debugger

Notice how the inline code compares with the machine instructions in the unassembled lines. By using Turbo Debugger, you can check your inline code to make sure it is doing what you expected.

The procedure ends with code that moves the function result into the AX register, cleans up the stack, and returns to the originating point in the program:

```
cs:000F 8B46FE          mov     ax,[bp-02]
cs:0012 89EC            mov     sp,bp
cs:0014 5D              pop     bp
cs:0015 C20400          ret     0004
```

Inline code is particularly difficult to debug because it consists of nothing but numeric machine instructions. Turbo Debugger lets you see the assembler instructions that your inline statements represent, and executes each statement individually so you can isolate problem areas. But Turbo Debugger is not restricted to use with inline code—it works equally well for external routines and straight Pascal code. It is also a great way to learn about assembler programming. With Turbo Debugger, you can inspect the handiwork of some of the best programmers around.

Turbo Pascal produces extremely efficient code, but there are times when you want or need to do even better. Assembler routines and inline code can make your programs faster and more powerful. Compared with inline code, external routines tend to be easier to develop and maintain. Whichever approach you take, Turbo Assembler will make assembler programming easier, and Turbo Debugger will aid in tracking down errors in your assembler code.

Text Display

Personal Computer Text Display
Using Display Memory
Locating Video Memory
Turbo Pascal Windows

People often judge programs primarily by the quality of their video display. Screen presentation is so important that often programs are successful simply because they "look like" other popular programs. Your computer is capable of producing screen displays that are both attractive and helpful. This chapter discusses these capabilities and how you can control them with Turbo Pascal.

Personal Computer Text Display

Personal computers have two video modes: Text and Graphics (the Graphics mode is covered in Chapter 15). When it is in Text mode, a personal computer can display any of the 256 standard ASCII characters it supports. These characters are locked permanently in the computer's memory, so your PC always knows how to draw them.

To display characters, your computer uses a *video adapter*, which is a circuit board that connects the computer to a monitor. Most computers have either a monochrome adapter or a color graphics adapter (CGA), though enhanced graphics adapters (EGA) and VGA are becoming more common. This chapter focuses on monochrome and color graphics adapters, but the concepts discussed can also apply to the enhanced graphics adapter.

The Video Adapter and Display Memory

Your monitor can display up to 80 characters horizontally and 25 vertically, or a total of 2000 characters in an entire screen. Each character has its own *foreground* and *background color*. The foreground color is the color of the character itself; the background color is the color of the space around the character.

Your computer stores characters and color information in a special part of memory known as the *display memory*. This is what tells your computer which characters and colors to display. Although it is located on the video adapter card, the display memory is considered to be part of RAM. The first byte of the display memory contains the first character on your monitor, which appears in the upper left corner.

Thus, if the first byte in the display memory contains the value 41h (the hexadecimal ASCII value for the letter "A"), the monitor displays the letter "A" in the upper left corner of the monitor. The second byte in display memory, the attribute byte for the first character, contains color and other display information.

This pattern—character, attribute, character, attribute—is repeated for all 2000 characters that appear on the monitor. Thus, the contents of a single screen require 4000 bytes of video memory.

The Attribute Byte

A computer with a color graphics adapter is capable of displaying 16 different colors, each of which consists of up to four elements: blue, red, green, and brightness. The color your computer displays depends on the particular combination of these elements. For example, the color black uses no elements, while light cyan uses the blue, green, and brightness elements. Video adapters also support a blinking element that makes the character flash on and off and has no effect on color.

An attribute byte stores the foreground and background color for the preceding character byte. Figure 14-1 shows how each bit in the attribute byte contributes to the color of the character and its background.

The first three bits (0, 1, and 2) in the attribute byte control a character's foreground color, while the fourth bit (bit 3) adds brightness to the color. You can combine these four elements to create 16 different foreground colors. Bits 4, 5, and 6 determine a character's background color, and bit 7, when on, makes the character blink. Because the background has no brightness element, only eight colors are available for it.

On the monochrome monitor, the attribute byte can create only five display formats: hidden, normal, bright, underlined, and reverse. As with the color graphics adapter, brightness is controlled by bit 3 and blinking is controlled by bit 7.

Characters are hidden when both the foreground and background colors are set to the same color. The brightness and blinking bits have no effect with hidden characters.

To display characters in *reverse video* (dark characters on a light background), set the background color to light gray (white

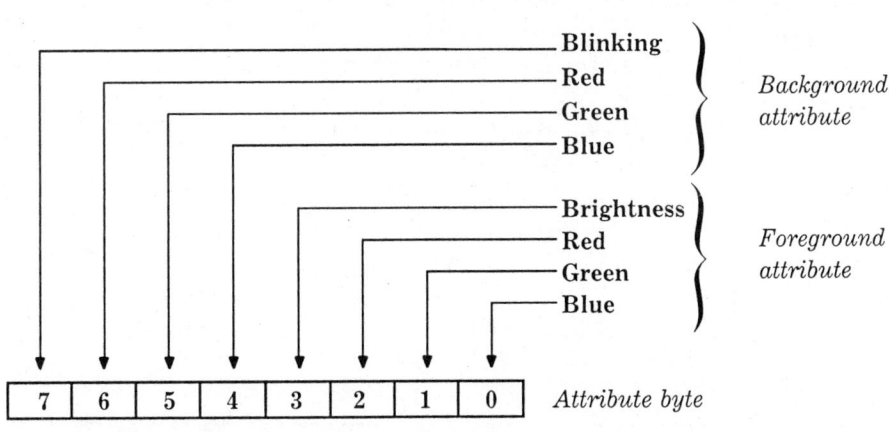

Figure 14-1. Mapping the attribute byte

without brightness) and the foreground color to black. Characters in reverse video cannot be made bright, but they can be made to blink.

Underlining, a specialty of the monochrome adapter, can only be displayed when the foreground is blue. An underlined character can be shown bright and be made to blink, but it cannot be shown in reverse video.

Personal Computer Text Modes

Personal computers support 16 different display modes, and five of these display text. These modes, listed in Table 14-1, control both the size of the characters and the colors in a display. Mode 0, for example, displays large characters (40 per line) in shades of gray.

The first four display modes, 0 through 3, work only with color graphics adapters and enhanced graphics adapters, most of which can switch between the four modes. Mode 7, on the other hand, is used only by the monochrome adapter.

You can change your computer's Text mode with the Turbo Pascal command **TextMode** (see Figure 14-2). This command, which works only with the color graphics adapter (it has no effect on monochrome adapters), can be used with or without parameters. Without parameters, **TextMode** sets the video display to the previous setting. With parameters, it can set the

Mode	Size	Colors	Adapter
0	40 × 25	Shades of gray	CGA,EGA
1	40 × 25	Colors	CGA,EGA
2	80 × 25	Shades of gray	CGA,EGA
3	80 × 25	Colors	CGA,EGA
7	80 × 25	Black and white	Monochrome

Table 14-1. Personal Computer Text Modes

Parameters	Settings
TextMode	Set to previous text mode
TextMode(BW40)	Black and white/40 characters per line
TextMode(BW80)	Black and white/80 characters per line
TextMode(CO40)	Color/40 characters per line
TextMode(CO80)	Color/80 characters per line

**Value of Turbo Pascal
Standard Constants**

BW40 = 0
BW80 = 1
CO40 = 2
CO80 = 3

Figure 14-2.   Turbo Pascal TextMode command

video display to any of the first four modes. Turbo Pascal supplies four standard integer constants for the **TextMode** command; **BW40**, **BW80**, **CO40**, and **CO80**. Note that **TextMode** always clears the screen before changing the mode.

Controlling Color with Turbo Pascal

Turbo Pascal allows you to select the foreground and background colors for your text with the commands **TextColor** and **TextBackground**. The color graphics adapter provides 16 colors to choose from, as shown in Table 14-2. **TextColor**, which sets the foreground color (the color of the character), can use all 16 colors. **TextBackground**, which sets the background color, can use only the dark colors.

Turbo Pascal provides a standard constant called **Blink**, which when added to the foreground color causes the character to blink. Here are some examples of how to use Turbo Pascal's color commands:

```
TextBackground(Blue);

TextColor(Cyan);

TextColor(Cyan+Blink);
```

Dark Colors	Light Colors
0: Black	8: DarkGray
1: Blue	9: LightBlue
2: Green	10: LightGreen
3: Cyan	11: LightCyan
4: Red	12: LightRed
5: Magenta	13: LightMagenta
6: Brown	14: Yellow
7: LightGray	15: White

Table 14-2.   Turbo Pascal Color Identifiers

Once invoked, the new colors take effect with the next characters you display; the characters already on the screen retain their colors.

Using Screen Coordinates

Like a map, your computer monitor has locations that are defined by coordinates. Screen coordinates are commonly referred to as x and y, where x is the column position and y is the row position. (Coordinates are displayed in x:y format.) Thus, the upper left corner of the monitor has coordinate position 1:1, while the lower right corner is at coordinate 80:25.

You can move the cursor to any coordinate location on your monitor with the Turbo Pascal command **GotoXY**. For example, the command **GotoXY(1,10)** positions the cursor at column 1 of row 10. If you want to know the coordinates for the cursor's current position, use the Turbo Pascal functions **WhereX** and **WhereY**. **WhereX** returns an integer that represents the cursor column; **WhereY** does the same for the cursor row.

Turbo Pascal's standard screen commands give you the control you need to create attractive and informative screen displays. The following program demonstrates how to create a simple data-entry routine with all of the commands described thus far: **TextMode, TextColor, TextBackground, GotoXY, WhereX**, and **WhereY**.

```
Program Box;
Uses CRT;
Var
  i, code,
  x, y : Integer;
  s : String[20];

(************************************************)

Procedure DrawBox(x1,y1,x2,y2,fg,bg : Integer);
Var
  i : Byte;
Begin
TextColor(fg);
TextBackground(bg);
For i := (x1+1) To (x2-1) Do
  Begin
  GotoXY(i,y1);
  Write(#205);
  GotoXY(i,y2);
  Write(#205);
  End;

For i := (y1+1) To (y2-1) Do
  Begin
  GotoXY(x1,i);
  Write(#186);
  GotoXY(x2,i);
  Write(#186);
  End;

GotoXY(x1,y1);
Write(#201);
GotoXY(x2,y1);
Write(#187);
GotoXY(x1,y2);
Write(#200);
GotoXY(x2,y2);
Write(#188);
End;

(************************************************)

Procedure GetNumber;
Begin
DrawBox(5,14,35,16,White,Black);
GotoXY(7,15);
Write('Enter a number (1-10): ');
x := WhereX;
y := WhereY;
  Repeat
  GotoXY(x,y);
  s := '     ';
  Write(s);
  GotoXY(x,y);
  ReadLn(s);
```

```
  Val(s,i,code);
  Until ((i > 0) And (i < 11)) And (code = 0);

End;

(************************************************)

Begin
ClrScr;
TextMode(c40);
GetNumber;

ClrScr;
TextMode(c80);
GetNumber;
GotoXY(1,20);
WriteLn;
Write('Press ENTER...');
ReadLn;
End.
```

The procedure **DrawBox** uses standard ASCII graphics characters to draw a rectangle anywhere on the screen. The procedure defines a data-entry portion on the screen.

Using Display Memory

The standard Turbo Pascal command **Write** uses a BIOS interrupt to send characters to the monitor. You can bypass BIOS, however, and write characters directly to display memory. This approach is far faster, but is complicated by vertical retrace, which creates a "snow" effect on CGA adapters. If you want your program to write directly to video memory, you must take special steps to eliminate snow. Fortunately, Turbo Pascal offers an easy solution in the form of the CRT unit. When you use the CRT unit in a program, Turbo Pascal automatically writes directly to video memory without generating snow.

While extremely useful, the video capabilities of the Turbo Pascal CRT unit do have limitations. For example, the CRT unit, even when writing directly to video memory, is still slower than the maximum speed you can get. This chapter provides several assembler routines that give your programs that extra burst of speed. In addition, the **Write** command always moves the cursor to the next position on the screen. So, if you write a character to the lower right corner of the screen, the display scrolls up one line. This makes it impossible to write out entire screens using Turbo Pascal statements. The remainder of this chapter will go into the technical details of your computer's video display and show how you can harness its power for your programs.

Locating Video Memory

Before you can use your computer's display memory, you must know where it is. On a monochrome adapter, the display memory starts at segment B000h, while on the color graphics adapter, it starts at B800h. Because each adapter uses different locations for video memory, you must determine which adapter is in use. One way to determine the adapter in use is through a BIOS interrupt. This technique is demonstrated in Chapter 12, with the **CurrentVidMode** procedure. Another way of obtaining the same information is shown here:

```
Function VidSeg : Word;
Begin
If Mem[$0000:$0449] = 7 Then
  VidSeg := $B000
Else
  VidSeg := $B800;
End;
```

The **VidSeg** function checks the memory location at segment 0000h and offset 0449h, where DOS stores the video adapter code. If the byte at this location is equal to 7, the adapter is monochrome; if not, it is safe to assume the adapter is color graphics.

While this method is more direct than using a BIOS interrupt, it is highly sensitive to IBM-PC compatibility: if your computer stores this information at a different memory address, this approach will not work. Fortunately, most PC manufacturers are careful to maintain the location of the video display type in the same place as the IBM PC does.

Once you know the type of video adapter in use, it is easy to bypass BIOS and write characters directly to the display memory. The program shown here determines the type of adapter used, and then fills the display memory with the letter "A" in white letters on a black background:

```pascal
{$R-,S-}
Program FillScreen;
Uses CRT;
Var
  CharAtt,
  i,j,
  VS   : Word;

(***************************************************)

Function VidSeg : Word;
Begin
If Mem[$0000:$0449] = 7 Then
  VidSeg := $B000
Else
  VidSeg := $B800;
End;

(***************************************************)

Begin
ClrScr;
VS := VidSeg;

j := 0;

(* $41 is the character 'A' *)
(* $70 is White on Black *)

CharAtt := ($70 Shl 4) + $41;

For i := 1 To 2000 Do
  Begin
  MemW[VS:j] := CharAtt; (* Write character and attribute *)
  Inc(j,2);              (* Point to next video character *)
  End;
GotoXY(1,1);
Write('Press ENTER...');
ReadLn;
End.
```

The program uses the function **VidSeg** to store the video display memory segment in the **Integer** variable **VS**. The **For-Do** loop uses the standard array **MemW** to move the character and attribute byte to video memory. Because **MemW** operates on a full word (16 bytes), both the attribute byte and character byte must be combined into a single word. The character is set to 41h, the ASCII code for the letter "A," and the attribute byte is set to 70h, which produces a white letter on a black background. The variable **j** holds the offset in display memory and is incremented by 2 after each character and attribute are written.

With the following procedure, **FastWrite**, you can write strings directly to display memory at specific x and y coordinates, as well as set the color attributes.

```
Procedure FastWrite(x,y : Byte;
                    Var s : String;
                    fg,bg : Byte);

Var
  w : Word;
  i,ColAtr : Byte;

Begin
ColAtr := (bg Shl 4) + fg;      (* create attribute byte *);
w := ((y-1)*80 + (x-1))*2;      (* calculate offset *)

For i := 1 To Length(s) Do
  Begin
  MemW[VS:w] := (ColAtr Shl 8) + Ord(s[i]);
  Inc(w,2);
  End;
End;
```

The procedure first creates the attribute byte (**ColAtr**) by shifting the background color left four bits and adding the foreground color. Next, the procedure computes the starting offset in display memory with the following formula:

$$x := ((y-1)*80 + (x-1)) *2;$$

In each iteration of the loop, the Turbo Pascal array **MemW** sets the character byte and the attribute byte at the same time. The procedure combines them by shifting the color byte to the left eight bits and adding the character byte. Notice that this puts the attribute byte in the high-order portion of the word, yet the attribute byte should be placed after the character byte in display memory. Once again, Intel's backward storage method forces you to think in reverse when operating with words.

Avoiding Vertical Retrace

If you use a CGA video adapter, you will soon find out why avoiding vertical retrace is so important. Try running the following program, which uses the Turbo Pascal **FastWrite** procedure to display a large "V" on your monitor.

```
{$R-}
Program FastWriteDemo;
Uses CRT;
Var
  VS  : Word;
  i,j : Byte;
  s : String;

(***************************************************)

Function VidSeg : Word;
Begin
If Mem[$0000:$0449] = 7 Then
  VidSeg := $B000
Else
  VidSeg := $B800;
End;

(***************************************************)

Procedure FastWrite(x,y : Byte;
                    Var s : String;
                    fg,bg : Byte);

Var
  w : Word;
  i,ColAtr : Byte;

Begin
ColAtr := (bg Shl 4) + fg;      (* create attribute byte *);
w := ((y-1)*80 + (x-1))*2;      (* calculate offset *)

For i := 1 To Length(s) Do
  Begin
  MemW[VS:w] := (ColAtr Shl 8) + Ord(s[i]);
  Inc(w,2);
```

```
    End;
End;

(***************************************************)

Begin
ClrScr;
VS := VidSeg;
s := 'XXXXXXX';
j := 5;

For i := 1 To 25 Do
   Begin
   FastWrite(j,i,s,Yellow,Black);
   Inc(j,1);
   End;

For i := 25 DownTo 1 Do
   Begin
   FastWrite(j,i,s,Yellow,Black);
   Inc(j,1);
   End;
GotoXY(1,24);
Write('Press ENTER...');
ReadLn;
End.
```

When you run this program with a CGA adapter, you will notice some "snow" on your screen. This is caused by the *vertical retrace,* a process that updates your screen from display memory many times per second (each vertical retrace takes approximately 1.25 milliseconds). If you move bytes directly to display memory while a vertical retrace is in progress, you will get snow.

The only way to avoid snow is to write to display memory between vertical retraces; in other words, the program must wait until the retrace has ended and then write the characters to display memory before the next retrace begins. Turbo Pascal is simply not fast enough to do this; you must use an external assembler procedure or inline code.

The following listing is an assembler procedure that writes out a string to video memory without generating snow. The assembler listing uses the special features of the Turbo Assembler, so you must use TASM.EXE to assemble it.

```
.MODEL TPASCAL

.DATA
```

```
VIDTYPE DB ?

.CODE

FastWrite PROC FAR x:BYTE, y:BYTE, s:DWORD, fg:BYTE, bg:BYTE

                PUBLIC        FASTWRITE

FASTSTR:

;----------------------------------------------------------------
; Compute offset into display memory--((y-1)*80 + (x-1)) * 2
;----------------------------------------------------------------
            PUSH    DS
            XOR     BX,BX
            XOR     AX,AX
            MOV     BL,x          ; Get x from stack;
            MOV     AL,y          ; Get y from stack;
            DEC     BX            ; Decrement x and y to get
            DEC     AX            ;   correct offset.
            MOV     CX,0080       ; Multiply y (in AX) by
            MUL     CX            ;   80 (in CX).
            ADD     AX,BX         ; Add x to y;
            MOV     CX,0002       ; Multiply the
            MUL     CX            ;   sum by 2.
            MOV     DI,AX         ; Store starting offset in DI.

;----------------------------------------------------------------
; Create the attribute byte
;----------------------------------------------------------------

            MOV     BL,bg         ; Get the background color.
            MOV     AL,fg         ; Get the foreground color.
            MOV     CL,4          ; Shift the foreground color
            SHL     BX,CL         ;   into the high nybble.
            ADD     BX,AX         ; Add in the foreground.
            XCHG    BL,BH         ; Move into the upper byte.
            MOV     DX,3DAH       ; Load CRT port address in DX.

;----------------------------------------------------------------
; Get the monitor type
;----------------------------------------------------------------

            XOR     AX,AX         ; Assign 0000h to ES.
            MOV     ES,AX

            MOV     AX,0449h      ; Assign offset of
            MOV     SI,AX         ; video type location.

            MOV     AX,ES:[SI]    ; If video type is 7
            CMP     AL,7          ; then monitor is
```

```
                JZ      MONO            ; monochrome.

                MOV     AX,0B800H       ; Load the color
                MOV     ES,AX           ;   segment into ES.
                MOV     VIDTYPE,1
                JMP     CHKSTR          ; Continue.

MONO:
                MOV     AX,0B000H       ; Load the monochrome
                MOV     ES,AX           ;   segment into ES.
                MOV     VIDTYPE,0


;-----------------------------------------------------------
; Load the string and check for zero length
;-----------------------------------------------------------

CHKSTR:         LDS     SI,s    ; Load string address into DS:SI.
                MOV     CL,[SI]   ; Move string length into CL.
                CMP     CL,0      ; If string length is zero,
                JZ      ENDSTR    ;   exit procedure.
                CLD               ; Clear direction flag.

NEXTCHAR:       INC     SI        ; Point to next character.
                MOV     BL,[SI]   ; Move it into BL.
                CMP     VIDTYPE,0 ; If monochrome, don't check
                JE      MOVECHAR  ; for retrace.

WLOW:           IN      AL,DX     ; Get CRT status.
                TEST    AL,1      ; Is retrace off?
                JNZ     WLOW    ; If off, wait for it to start.
                CLI               ; No interrupts, please.

WHIGH:          IN      AL,DX     ; Get CRT status.
                TEST    AL,1      ; Is retrace on?
                JZ      WHIGH     ; If on, wait for it to stop.

MOVECHAR:       MOV     AX,BX   ; Move color and character to AX.
                STOSW           ; Move color & character to screen.
                STI             ; Interrupts are now allowed.

LOOP            NEXTCHAR          ; Done yet?

ENDSTR:         POP     DS
                RET

FASTWRITE       ENDP
CODE            ENDS
                END
```

The **FastWrite** procedure checks the adapter I/O port number 3DAh for a status bit known as the *vertical sync signal*. When this status bit is on, a vertical retrace is in progress. The procedure first checks to see if the monitor is between retraces (the status bit equals 0). If so, the loop repeats until a retrace begins. The procedure then waits for the retrace to end.

As soon as the retrace ends, the procedure moves characters to the display memory. Because the procedure waited until the very end of a retrace, there should be ample time to move the characters before the next retrace begins.

Use TASM, the Turbo Assembler, to assemble this code to an object file (FASTWRIT.OBJ) and declare the external routine as shown in the program listed here:

```
{$R-,F+}
Program FastWriteDemo;
Uses CRT;
Var
  VS  : Word;
  i,j : Byte;
  s : String;

{$L FASTWRIT}
Procedure FastWrite(x,y : Byte;
                    Var s : String;
                    fg,bg : Byte); External;

Begin
ClrScr;
s := 'XXXXXXX';
j := 5;

For i := 1 To 25 Do
  Begin
  FastWrite(j,i,s,Yellow,Black);
  Inc(j,1);
  End;

For i := 25 DownTo 1 Do
  Begin
  FastWrite(j,i,s,Yellow,Black);
  Inc(j,1);
  End;
GotoXY(1,24);
Write('Press ENTER...');
ReadLn;
End.
```

The technique used in **FastWrite** works on most IBM-compatible personal computers and greatly improves the speed of video displays.

Turbo Pascal Windows

Normally, your programs will take advantage of the PC's entire
80×25 video display. There are times, however, when it is desirable to restrict output to just a portion of your monitor, using
the Turbo Pascal command **Window**. For example, the command

Window(10,10,20,15)

restricts your program's display to a 10 by 5 rectangle starting
at column 10 and row 10; the remainder of the display is off
limits to the **Write** command. (Note that the **FastWrite** procedure pays no attention to Turbo Pascal and can write outside the
active window.) When you want to return to the full screen, the
command

Window(1,1,80,25)

returns the monitor to normal operation.

The **Window** command's most useful feature is its ability to
realign the screen coordinates so that they fit the active window;
that is, screen coordinates refer only to the active window, not
to the entire screen. Thus, the command

GotoXY(1,1)

positions the cursor at the upper left corner of the active window, not the entire screen. In fact, Turbo Pascal treats the
window as if it were the entire screen: when text runs off the
bottom of the window, the screen scrolls up one line.

Pop-Up Windows

While useful in its own right, the Turbo Pascal **Window** command is simply not powerful enough to create professional-
looking pop-up windows. The problem is that a Turbo Pascal
window wipes out the portion of the screen it uses. Most people

expect windows to act the way they do in the popular program SideKick; that is, when a window disappears, the text that was on the screen "beneath" the window reappears.

To create true pop-up windows, save the contents of the screen before you open the window and then restore the screen when you close the pop-up window.

To save a screen, define a variable that can store all the information contained in the screen: 2000 characters, 2000 color attributes, and the x and y coordinates of the cursor. The following data structure, **ScreenType**, provides all you need.

```
Type
  ScreenType = Record
    Pos : Array [1..80, 1..25] Of Record
      Ch : Char;
      At : Byte;
      End;
    CursX,
    CursY : Byte;
    End;
```

ScreenType, a nested **Record** data type, stores characters and attributes in the array named **Pos**, which has dimensions that match the coordinates of your monitor. Thus, to refer to the character in column 10 and row 20, you would use the following statement:

Screen.Pos[10,20].Ch

Integer variables **CursX** and **CursY** are used to store the cursor position.

The **ScreenType** variable is quite powerful. You can use it not only to store a screen's contents, but also to change the contents of the variable in memory, and then move it directly to video display, updating an entire video display in one shot.

There are several ways you can use a **ScreenType** variable to save and restore video images. One way to do this is to

declare the variable **Absolute** at the display memory location. If
you have a color graphics adapter, you would use this declaration:

```
Var
     Screen : ScreenType Absolute $B800;
```

Unfortunately, this approach requires you to choose the
offset in advance, which means you can service only one type of
video adapter (unless you define separate screens for monochrome and color). A better approach is to define the screen as a
pointer variable. The program then sets the pointer to the
correct offset in display memory, depending on the adapter in
use. The following program demonstrates this technique:

```
Program WindowPointer;
Uses CRT;

Const
  MaxWin = 5;
Type
  ScreenPtr = ^ScreenType;
  ScreenType = Record
    Pos : Array [1..80, 1..25] Of Record
      Ch : Char;
      At : Byte;
      End;
    CursX, CursY : Integer;
    End;

Var
  Screen : ScreenPtr;

(***************************************************)

Function VidSeg : Word;
Begin
If Mem[$0000:$0449] = 7 Then
  VidSeg := $B000
Else
  VidSeg := $B800;
End;

(***************************************************)

Begin
ClrScr;

Screen := Ptr(VidSeg,$0000);
```

```
Screen^.Pos[1,1].Ch := 'A';

ReadLn;
End.
```

The program begins by clearing the screen and then uses the **Ptr** command to point the **Screen** variable to the correct location in the display memory. Because of this repositioning, any changes made to the variable **Screen** will show up on your monitor.

When you use this method, do not use the **Dispose** command on the **Screen** variable, or Turbo Pascal will try to deallocate memory from the display adapter, most likely crashing your program.

Multiple Logical Screens and Pop-Up Windows

Your program can have as many screen variables as its memory will hold. Screens that are held in memory, and not displayed, are often called *logical* screens to distinguish them from the *physical screen* (the computer monitor). A program can write to a logical screen without disturbing the display on the physical screen. Then, when you want to display the logical screen, simply move its contents into the physical screen.

The use of logical screens is best explained by an example. This program uses one physical screen variable (**Screen**) and three logical screen variables (**Screen1**, **Screen2**, and **Screen3**). By typing **1**, **2**, or **3** on the keyboard, you can display any of the three logical screens.

```
Program FastScreenDemo;
Uses CRT;

Const
  MaxWin = 5;

Type
  ScreenPtr = ^ScreenType;
  ScreenType = Record
    Pos : Array [1..80,1..25] Of Record
      Ch : Char;
      At : Byte;
      End;
    CursX,
```

```
     CursY : Byte;
     End;

Var
   Screen,
   Screen1,
   Screen2,
   Screen3 : ScreenPtr;
   Ch : Char;
   i,j : Byte;

(**********************************************)

Function VidSeg : Word;
Begin
If Mem[$0000:$0449] = 7 Then
   VidSeg := $B000
Else
   VidSeg := $B800;
End;

(**********************************************)

Begin
New(Screen1);
New(Screen2);
New(Screen3);

For i := 1 To 80 Do
For j := 1 To 25 Do
   Begin
   Screen1^.Pos[i,j].Ch := '1';
   Screen2^.Pos[i,j].Ch := '2';
   Screen3^.Pos[i,j].Ch := '3';
   Screen1^.Pos[i,j].At := $07;
   Screen2^.Pos[i,j].At := $07;
   Screen3^.Pos[i,j].At := $07;
   End;

ClrScr;
Screen := Ptr(VidSeg,$0000);

   Repeat
   GotoXY(1,1);
   Write('Press 1,2,3 to change screens or 0 to exit.');

   Ch := ReadKey;
     Case Ch Of
     '1' : Screen^ := Screen1^;
     '2' : Screen^ := Screen2^;
     '3' : Screen^ := Screen3^;
     End;
   Until Ch = '0';

End.
```

Screen, which is superimposed on the display memory, acts as the physical device. The program changes the display memory by setting the physical device variable **Screen** equal to one of the logical screens. The transfer is fast, and the entire screen is updated in one statement. A program can also move the contents of the physical screen to a logical screen with a statement like this:

PhysicalScreen^ := LogicalScreen^;

Manipulating logical screens is the technique you need to create pop-up windows. Before you open a pop-up window, save a copy of the physical screen in a logical screen variable. Then, when you close the window, restore the screen to its original appearance. Thus, your windows seem to pop up from nowhere and, when no longer needed, disappear without a trace.

The following program uses an array of logical screens to create up to five pop-up windows. When you run the program, you will see how windows can overlap without causing problems.

```
(*$R-*)
Program WindowDemo;
Uses CRT;
Const
  MaxWin = 5;
Type
  ScreenType = Record
    Pos : Array [1..80,1..25] Of Record
      Ch : Char;
      At : Byte;
      End;
    CursX,
    CursY : Byte;
    End;

  WindowPtr = ^WindowType;
  WindowType = Record
    Scr : ScreenType;
    WinX1,
    WinY1,
    WinX2,
    WinY2 : Byte;
    End;

Var
  Ch : Char;
  i : Integer;
```

```
    ActiveWin : WindowPtr;
    Windo : Array [0..MaxWin] Of WindowPtr;
    CurrentWindow : Integer;

(**********************************************)

Function VidSeg : Word;
Begin
If Mem[$0000:$0449] = 7 Then
    VidSeg := $B000
Else
    VidSeg := $B800;
End;

(***********************************************)

{$L FASTWRIT}
Procedure FastWrite(x, y : Byte;
                    S : String;
                    bc, fc : Byte); External;

(***********************************************)

Procedure FastBox(x1,y1,x2,y2,fg,bg : Byte);
Var
    i : Byte;
    s : String[1];
Begin
TextColor(fg);
TextBackground(bg);

s := #205;
For i := (x1+1) To (x2-1) Do
    Begin
    FastWrite(i,y1,s,fg,bg);
    FastWrite(i,y2,s,fg,bg);
    End;

s := #186;
For i := (y1+1) To (y2-1) Do
    Begin
    FastWrite(x1,i,s,fg,bg);
    FastWrite(x2,i,s,fg,bg);
    End;

s := #201;
FastWrite(x1,y1,s,fg,bg);
s := #187;
FastWrite(x2,y1,s,fg,bg);
s := #200;
FastWrite(x1,y2,s,fg,bg);
s := #188;
FastWrite(x2,y2,s,fg,bg);
End;

(****************************************)
```

```
Procedure SetUpWindows;
Var
  i : Integer;
Begin
New(ActiveWin);
For i := 0 To MaxWin Do
  New(Windo[i]);

With ActiveWin^ Do
  Begin
  WinX1 := 1;
  WinY1 := 1;
  WinX2 := 80;
  WinY2 := 25;
  With Scr Do
    Begin
    CursX := WhereX;
    CursY := WhereY;
    End;
  End;

ActiveWin := Ptr(VidSeg,$0000);
CurrentWindow := 0;
With Windo[CurrentWindow]^ Do
  Begin
  WinX1 := 1;
  WinY1 := 1;
  WinX2 := 80;
  WinY2 := 25;
  With Scr Do
    Begin
    CursX := 1;
    CursY := 1;
    End;
  End;
End;

(*****************************************)

Procedure OpenWindow;
Begin
If CurrentWindow < MaxWin Then
  Begin
  Windo[CurrentWindow]^.Scr := ActiveWin^.Scr;
  Windo[CurrentWindow]^.Scr.CursX := WhereX;
  Windo[CurrentWindow]^.Scr.CursY := WhereY;

  CurrentWindow := CurrentWindow + 1;
  With Windo[CurrentWindow]^ Do
    Begin
    WinX1 := CurrentWindow * 10;
    WinY1 := CurrentWindow * 2;
    WinX2 := WinX1 + 20;
    WinY2 := WinY1 + 5;
    With Scr Do
```

```
      Begin
      CursX := 1;
      CursY := 1;
      End;
    Window(WinX1,WinY1,WinX2,WinY2);
    FastBox(WinX1-1,WinY1-1,WinX2+1,WinY2+1,Yellow,Black);
    TextColor(Yellow);
    TextBackGround(Black);
    ClrScr;
    End;
  End;
End;

(****************************************)

Procedure CloseWindow;
Begin
If CurrentWindow > 0  Then
  Begin
  Windo[CurrentWindow]^.Scr.CursX := WhereX;
  Windo[CurrentWindow]^.Scr.CursY := WhereY;

  CurrentWindow := CurrentWindow - 1;
  ActiveWin^.Scr := Windo[CurrentWindow]^.Scr;
  With Windo[CurrentWindow]^ Do
    Begin
    Window(WinX1,WinY1,WinX2,WinY2);
    GotoXY(Scr.CursX,Scr.CursY);
    End;
  End;
End;

(****************************************)

Procedure FillWindow;
Var
  Ch : Char;
Begin
Ch := ReadKey;
  Repeat
  Write(Chr(Random(80)+30));
  Delay(20);
  Until KeyPressed;
End;

(****************************************)

Begin
ClrScr;
SetUpWindows;

TextColor(Yellow+Blink);
GotoXY(1,25);
Write('Press any key to open windows...');
GotoXY(1,1);
```

```
TextColor(Yellow);

FillWindow;
For i := 1 To MaxWin Do
  Begin
  OpenWindow;
  FillWindow;
  End;

For i := 1 To MaxWin Do
  Begin
  CloseWindow;
  FillWindow;
  End;
End.
```

When you run **WindowDemo**, CGA users will notice snow on the screen. There is just no way to avoid it with code written in Turbo Pascal. An external procedure written in assembler, however, can eliminate the snow while making the screen update even faster. Listed here are two assembler procedures you can use as external procedures. The first moves a logical screen to video memory. The second moves the screen currently in video memory to a logical screen. In both cases, snow is eliminated. Be sure to use the Turbo Assembler to assemble this listing.

```
.MODEL TPASCAL

.DATA

VIDTYPE DB ?

.CODE

PUBLIC READSCR
PUBLIC WRITESCR

WRITESCR PROC FAR s:DWORD

;-------------------------------------------------------------
; Save registers.
;-------------------------------------------------------------
          PUSH     DS

;-------------------------------------------------------------
; Get the monitor type.
;-------------------------------------------------------------
          XOR      AX,AX       ; Assign 0000h to ES.
```

```
        MOV     ES,AX

        MOV     AX,0449h    ; Assign offset of
        MOV     SI,AX       ; video type location.

        MOV     AX,ES:[SI]  ; If video type is 7
        CMP     AL,7        ; then monitor is
        JZ      MONO1       ; monochrome.

        MOV     AX,0B800H   ; Load the color
        MOV     ES,AX       ;    segment into ES.
        MOV     VIDTYPE,1
        JMP     CONT1       ; Continue.

MONO1:
        MOV     AX,0B000H   ; Load the monochrome
        MOV     ES,AX       ;    segment into ES.
        MOV     VIDTYPE,0


;-------------------------------------------------------------
; Load buffer to screen.
;-------------------------------------------------------------

CONT1:      LDS     SI,s        ; Load buffer address in DS:SI.
            MOV     DI,0        ; Point to start of memory.
            MOV     CX,2000     ; Move 2000 characters.
            CLD                 ; Clear direction flag.

            MOV     DX,3DAh     ; Load CRT port address.

NEXTCHAR1:  CMP     VIDTYPE,0   ; If monochrome, don't check
            JE      MOVECHAR1   ; for retrace.

WLOW1:      IN      AL,DX       ; Get CRT status.
            TEST    AL,1        ; Is retrace off?
            JNZ     WLOW1       ; If off, wait for it to start.
            CLI                 ; No interrupts, please.

WHIGH1:     IN      AL,DX       ; Get CRT status.
            TEST    AL,1        ; Is retrace on?
            JZ      WHIGH1      ; If on, wait for it to end.

MOVECHAR1:  LODSW               ; Get word from buffer to AX.
            STOSW               ; Move word from AX to screen.
            STI                 ; Interrupts are allowed.
            LOOP    NEXTCHAR1   ; Done yet?

ENDSTR1:

;-------------------------------------------------------------
; Restore registers.
;-------------------------------------------------------------

        POP     DS
```

```
                    RET

WRITESCR    ENDP

READSCR  PROC FAR s:DWORD

;------------------------------------------------------------
; Save registers.
;------------------------------------------------------------

                    PUSH    DS

;------------------------------------------------------------
; Get the monitor type
;------------------------------------------------------------

            XOR     AX,AX       ; Assign 0000h to ES.
            MOV     ES,AX

            MOV     AX,0449h    ; Assign offset of
            MOV     SI,AX       ; video type location.

            MOV     AX,ES:[SI]  ; If video type is 7
            CMP     AL,7        ; then monitor is
            JZ      MONO2       ; monochrome.

            MOV     VIDTYPE,1
            MOV     AX,0B800H   ; Load the color
            MOV     DS,AX       ;   segment into DS.
            JMP     CONT2       ; Continue.

MONO2:
            MOV     VIDTYPE,0
            MOV     AX,0B000H   ; Load the monochrome
            MOV     DS,AX       ;   segment into DS.

CONT2:
            LES     DI,s        ; Load buffer address in ES:DI.
            MOV     SI,0        ; Point to start of memory.
            MOV     CX,2000     ; Characters in screen.
            CLD                 ; Clear direction flag.

;------------------------------------------------------------
; Transfer display memory to buffer.
;------------------------------------------------------------

            MOV     DX,3DAh ; Load CRT port address into DX.

NEXTCHAR2:  CMP     ES:VIDTYPE,0 ; If monochrome, don't check
            JE      MOVECHAR2    ; for retrace.

WLOW2:      IN      AL,DX       ; Get CRT status.
```

```
              TEST     AL,1         ; Is retrace off?
              JNZ      WLOW2      ; If off, wait for it to start.
              CLI                   ; No interrupts please.

WHIGH2:       IN       AL,DX        ; Get CRT status.
              TEST     AL,1         ; Is retrace on?
              JZ       WHIGH2       ; If on, wait for it to end.

MOVECHAR2:    LODSW                 ; Move word from screen to AX.
              STOSW                 ; Move AX to buffer.
              LOOP     NEXTCHAR2    ; Done yet?
              STI                   ; Interrupts are allowed.

ENDSTR2:

;------------------------------------------------------------
; Restore registers.
;------------------------------------------------------------

              POP      DS

              RET

READSCR       ENDP

CODE          ENDS

              END
```

The assembler listing just given contains two procedures, **WriteScr** and **ReadScr**. You can use these procedures in the program **WindowDemo** as shown here:

```
(*$R-,F+*)
Program WindowDemo;
Uses CRT;
Const
  MaxWin = 5;
Type
  ScreenType = Record
    Pos : Array [1..80,1..25] Of Record
      Ch : Char;
      At : Byte;
      End;
    CursX,
    CursY : Byte;
    End;

  WindowPtr = ^WindowType;
  WindowType = Record
    Scr : ScreenType;
```

```
        WinX1,
        WinY1,
        WinX2,
        WinY2 : Byte;
        End;

Var
  Ch : Char;
  i : Integer;
  Windo : Array [0..MaxWin] Of WindowPtr;
  CurrentWindow : Integer;

(**********************************************)

Function VidSeg : Word;
Begin
If Mem[$0000:$0449] = 7 Then
  VidSeg := $B000
Else
  VidSeg := $B800;
End;

(**********************************************)

{$L FASTWRIT}
Procedure FastWrite(x, y : Byte;
                    s : String;
                    bc, fc : Byte); External;

{$L FASTSCR}
Procedure WriteScr(Var s : ScreenType); External;
Procedure ReadScr(Var s : ScreenType);  External;

(****************************************)

Procedure FastBox(x1,y1,x2,y2,fg,bg : Byte);
Var
  i : Byte;
  s : String[1];
Begin
TextColor(fg);
TextBackground(bg);

s := #205;
For i := (x1+1) To (x2-1) Do
  Begin
  FastWrite(i,y1,s,fg,bg);
  FastWrite(i,y2,s,fg,bg);
  End;

s := #186;
For i := (y1+1) To (y2-1) Do
  Begin
  FastWrite(x1,i,s,fg,bg);
  FastWrite(x2,i,s,fg,bg);
  End;
```

```
s := #201;
FastWrite(x1,y1,s,fg,bg);
s := #187;
FastWrite(x2,y1,s,fg,bg);
s := #200;
FastWrite(x1,y2,s,fg,bg);
s := #188;
FastWrite(x2,y2,s,fg,bg);
End;

(****************************************)

Procedure SetUpWindows;
Var
  i : Integer;
Begin
For i := 0 To MaxWin Do
  Begin
  New(Windo[i]);
  FillChar(Windo[i]^,SizeOf(Windo[i]^),0);
  End;

CurrentWindow := 0;
With Windo[CurrentWindow]^ Do
  Begin
  WinX1 := 1;
  WinY1 := 1;
  WinX2 := 80;
  WinY2 := 25;
  With Scr Do
    Begin
    CursX := 1;
    CursY := 1;
    End;
  End;
End;

(****************************************)

Procedure OpenWindow;
Begin
If CurrentWindow < MaxWin Then
  Begin
  ReadScr(Windo[CurrentWindow]^.Scr);
  Windo[CurrentWindow]^.Scr.CursX := WhereX;
  Windo[CurrentWindow]^.Scr.CursY := WhereY;

  CurrentWindow := CurrentWindow + 1;
  With Windo[CurrentWindow]^ Do
    Begin
    WinX1 := CurrentWindow * 10;
    WinY1 := CurrentWindow * 2;
    WinX2 := WinX1 + 20;
    WinY2 := WinY1 + 5;
    With Scr Do
```

```
      Begin
      CursX := 1;
      CursY := 1;
      End;
    Window(WinX1,WinY1,WinX2,WinY2);
    FastBox(WinX1-1,WinY1-1,WinX2+1,WinY2+1,Yellow,Black);
    TextColor(Yellow);
    TextBackGround(Black);
    ClrScr;
    End;
  End;
End;

(****************************************)

Procedure CloseWindow;
Begin
If CurrentWindow > 0  Then
  Begin
  Windo[CurrentWindow]^.Scr.CursX := WhereX;
  Windo[CurrentWindow]^.Scr.CursY := WhereY;

  CurrentWindow := CurrentWindow - 1;
  WriteScr(Windo[CurrentWindow]^.Scr);
  With Windo[CurrentWindow]^ Do
    Begin
    Window(WinX1,WinY1,WinX2,WinY2);
    GotoXY(Scr.CursX,Scr.CursY);
    End;
  End;
End;

(****************************************)

Procedure FillWindow;
Var
  Ch : Char;
Begin
Ch := ReadKey;
  Repeat
  Write(Chr(Random(80)+30));
  Delay(20);
  Until KeyPressed;
End;

(****************************************)

Begin
ClrScr;
SetUpWindows;

TextColor(Yellow+Blink);
GotoXY(1,25);
Write('Press any key to open windows...');
GotoXY(1,1);
```

```
TextColor(Yellow);
FillWindow;
For i := 1 To MaxWin Do
  Begin
  OpenWindow;
  FillWindow;
  End;

For i := 1 To MaxWin Do
  Begin
  CloseWindow;
  FillWindow;
  End;
End.
```

Within the program, delete all references to the variable **activewin** and replace the line

ActiveWin^.Scr := Windo[CurrentWindow]^.Scr;

with the line

WriteScr(Windo[CurrentWindow]^.Scr);

and replace

Windo[CurrentWindow]^.Scr := ActiveWin^.Scr;

with the line

ReadScr(Windo[CurrentWindow]^.Scr);

These fast, clean screen procedures make your windows look professional. Now you can spend your time on filling the windows with useful information and tools (calendars, calculators, note pads, and so on) and not on getting the windows started in the first place.

Graphics

FIFTEEN

Your computer's graphics capability is one of its strongest features. Using graphics you can create drawings, charts, multifont text, or anything that can be drawn. But using graphics requires far more work than using the PC's Text mode. You must develop methods for drawing lines and characters and be able to scale them in the proper perspective. What's more, there are now more than ten commonly available graphics adapters comprising more than two dozen different graphics modes. Fortunately, Turbo Pascal provides an exceptionally rich set of graphics routines that can make graphics programming much easier. This chapter covers some of the basics of programming graphics using Turbo.

Graphics Versus Text

Compared with the Graphics mode, the PC's Text mode is easy to use. Displaying information on the screen is as simple as placing ASCII characters in specific memory locations. The text screen is neatly divided into 80 columns and 25 rows, and your computer already knows how to draw the ASCII characters, sparing you most of the headaches.

The Graphics mode requires a completely different orientation. Instead of characters and attribute bytes, you have *pixels*, the smallest picture element on your computer's display. A single character on your computer's screen is made up of many pixels arranged in a pattern that forms a character. In the Graphics mode, you can light pixels anywhere on your display. The program listed here, which demonstrates some fundamental graphics programming techniques, lights pixels at random locations on your screen.

```
Program DemoPixel;
Uses CRT, GRAPH;
Var
  x,y,
  ErrorCode,
  GraphMode,
  GraphDriver : Integer;

Begin
(* Initiate the CGA high resolution mode. *)
GraphDriver := CGA;
GraphMode := CGAhi;
InitGraph(GraphDriver,GraphMode,'D:\TP5');
ErrorCode := GraphResult;
If ErrorCode <> grOK Then
  Begin
  WriteLn('Graphics error: ',GraphErrorMsg(ErrorCode));
  Halt;
  End;

  Repeat
  x := Random(640); (* CGA high resolution coordinates *)
  y := Random(200); (* 640 x 200 *)
  PutPixel(x,y,White);
  Delay(100);
  Until KeyPressed;

CloseGraph;
End.
```

The preceding program not only demonstrates the concept of the pixel, but also highlights some of the difficulties involved in writing graphics programs. The program begins by initializing the Turbo Pascal CGA graphics driver. It does this by specifying the type of adapter and the Graphics mode and then calling

InitGraph. You must also tell **InitGraph** where to look for the .BGI file that corresponds to the adapter. A .BGI file contains information on a specified graphics adapter. This information is needed to draw a graph properly. In the example, this file is found in the D:\TP5 directory.

```
GraphDriver := CGA;
GraphMode := CGAhi;
InitGraph(GraphDriver,GraphMode,'D:\TP5');
```

After calling **InitGraph**, the program calls **GraphResult**, a function that returns a status code. If the code is not equal to **grOK**, you know that an error occurred. (**grOK** is a constant defined in the GRAPH unit and has a value of zero.) If an error is detected, the program passes the error code to the **GraphErrorMsg** function, which then returns a string that describes the error condition.

```
ErrorCode := GraphResult;
If ErrorCode <> grOK Then
  Begin
  WriteLn('Graphics error: ',GraphErrorMsg(ErrorCode));
  Halt;
  End;
```

While checking for graphics errors is not required, it is a good idea. Nearly every graphics procedure and function can produce serious errors when used improperly. Always remember, though, to store the value of **GraphResult** in a variable because once the function is called, it will thereafter return the value 0 until another error occurs.

Specifying the display adapter in your program is fine if you know in advance what adapter will be used. If you're wrong, however, the program won't run. Notice also that the screen coordinate limits (640 and 200) are hard-coded into the program. If your computer uses a graphics adapter that has a different coordinate system, the program will not work properly. To make a graphics program truly useful, it must be able to run on any graphics adapter and, ideally, would use that adapter's advanced features as much as possible.

Graphics Adapters and Coordinate Systems

Your graphics screen consists of pixels ordered in horizontal and vertical lines. This is true of all computer graphics modes; the major difference is the size of the pixel. In CGA's Low-resolution mode, the pixels are quite large, so only 320 fit horizontally and 200 fit vertically. The VGA adapter, a relatively new video display controller, has a High-resolution mode with pixels so small that 640 fit horizontally and 480 fit vertically. The smaller the pixel, the more pixels per image, and the higher the quality of the graphic display.

Each adapter has one or more graphics modes, and each mode has an associated coordinate system. The coordinate system for high-resolution CGA graphics is 320 × 200, as shown in Figure 15-1. Graphics coordinates begin at position (0,0), which is located at the upper left corner of the screen. The right-most pixel is number 319 and the bottom-most is number 199. By referring to pixels by coordinates, you can light the pixels you want for your graphic image.

Now you can see why it is so important to know what graphics adapter is installed and which mode is active. Screen

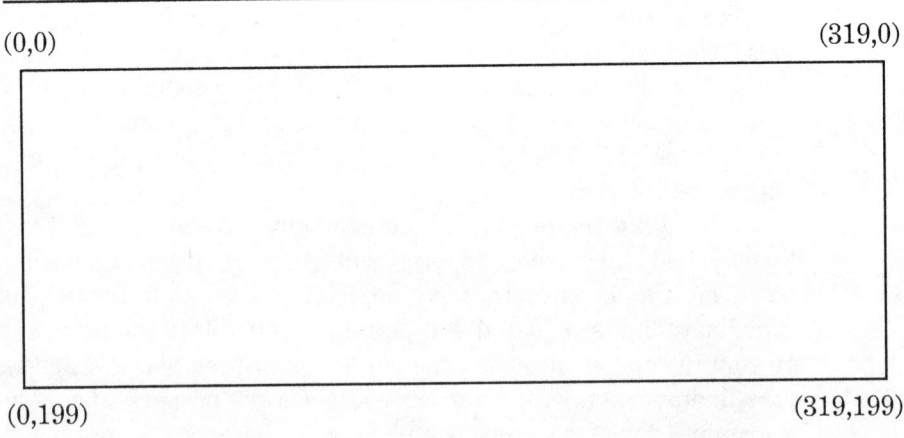

Figure 15-1.   CGA high-resolution coordinates

coordinate systems vary from adapter to adapter and from mode to mode. For example, the CGA adapter supports High- and Low-resolution modes, each having different coordinate systems. If you want to light a pixel at the lower right corner of the screen, you must know what the screen coordinates are. Fortunately, Turbo Pascal provides the answer with two GRAPH unit functions, **GetMaxX** and **GetMaxY**, which return the maximum x and y coordinates for the active graphics display adapter and mode. Here is the program given earlier, but updated to be used on any graphics adapter:

```
Program DemoPixel2;
Uses CRT, GRAPH;
Var
   MaxX,
   MaxY,
   x,y,
   ErrorCode,
   GraphMode,
   GraphDriver : Integer;

Begin
GraphDriver := Detect;
InitGraph(GraphDriver,GraphMode,'D:\TP5');
ErrorCode := GraphResult;
If ErrorCode <> grOK Then
   Begin
   WriteLn('Graphics error: ',GraphErrorMsg(ErrorCode));
   Halt;
   End;

MaxX := GetMaxX;
MaxY := GetMaxY;

   Repeat
   x := Random(MaxX)+1;
   y := Random(MaxY)+1;
   PutPixel(x,y,White);
   Delay(100);
   Until KeyPressed;

CloseGraph;
End.
```

This program, while simple in function, demonstrates how complicated even simple graphics programs can be. Given the rich set of tools that the Turbo Pascal graphics unit provides, the possibilities could fill a book on their own. The remainder of this chapter will touch on the important aspects of graphics programming and how to use the basics of the GRAPH unit.

The GRAPH Unit

The GRAPH unit is by far the most complex of all the units supplied by Borland. It contains more than 50 procedures, over 20 functions, and scores of constants, variables, and data types. What's more, Borland includes drivers for all the major graphics adapters and fonts for drawing a wide range of character styles. If you are serious about graphics programming, the GRAPH unit alone is worth the price of the Turbo Pascal compiler.

Drawing Lines

A fundamental task in graphics is drawing a line between two points. The GRAPH unit provides a **Line** procedure that does this. Still, you may find it useful to understand how such a routine works because, as you do more complicated graphics programming, you will probably decide to write your own specialized graphics routines.

Drawing horizontal or vertical lines is easy—you simply hold one coordinate value fixed and plot pixels along the other coordinate. Once you begin to slant the line, however, the process becomes much more complicated. Somehow, you must determine which pixels to light. This is done with an algorithm that computes one coordinate given a value of the other coordinate.

Graphics systems based on algorithms (as opposed to fixed bit maps) are the basis of nearly all graphics and provide a great deal of flexibility because an algorithm need not be tied to a particular scaling factor. This means that you can use the same algorithm to draw a small box or a large box, a circle or an ellipse, a thick line or a thin line. The algorithm for drawing a straight line is fairly straightforward, though somewhat complicated.

The straight-line algorithm is based on the algebraic equation for a straight line:

$$Y = a + bX$$

where **Y** is the vertical coordinate, **X** is the horizontal coordinate, **a** is a constant factor, and **b** is the slope of the line. Once you have determined the value of **a** and **b**, drawing the line is easy.

To compute **a** and **b**, you need two coordinate pairs. In the code extract shown here, x1:y1 and x2:y2 are pairs of coordinates representing points on the graphics screen.

```
dx := (x2 - x1);
dy := (y2 - y1);
If dx <> 0 Then
  b := dy / dx
Else
 b := 0;
a := y1 - x1*b;
```

The **b** variable is defined as the difference between the x coordinates divided by the difference between the y coordinates. If **x1** equals **x2**, then **b** is defined as zero. Once **b** is calculated, **a** is easily calculated using one of the two coordinate pairs.

With **a** and **b** both defined, the algorithm is complete. To draw the line, you need only trace along the x axis, compute the corresponding y coordinate, and plot the pixel. One problem with this approach, however, is that lines will become very sparse when the range between the x coordinates is small compared to the range of the y coordinates. To compensate for this, the line-drawing procedure must compare the distances between the vertical coordinates and between the horizontal coordinates. If the gap between the y coordinates is greater than the gap between the x coordinates, tracing should move along the vertical axis. The complete line-drawing process is contained in the procedure **PlotLine**, in the following program:

```
Program LineDemo;
Uses CRT, GRAPH;
Var
  MaxX,
  MaxY,
  ErrorCode,
  GraphMode,
  GraphDriver : Integer;

(*******************************************************)

Procedure PlotLine(x1, y1, x2, y2, color : Integer);
Var
  a,b   : Real;
  dx,dy,
  x,y,i : Integer;

(*******************************************************)

Procedure Switch(var x,y : Integer);
Var
  t : Word;
Begin
t := x;
x := y;
y := t;
End;

(*******************************************************)

Begin

If Abs(x1-x2) > Abs(y1-y2) Then
  Begin
  (* Gap between x's is greater than y's.
     Trace horizontally*)
  If x1 > x2 Then
    Begin
    Switch(x1,x2);
    Switch(y1,y2);
    End;

  dx := (x2 - x1);
  dy := (y2 - y1);
  If dx <> 0 Then
    b := dy / dx
  Else
   b := 0;
  a := y1 - x1*b;
  For x := x1 to x2 do
```

```
      Begin
      y := Round(a+x*b);
      PutPixel(x,y,color);
      End;
   End
Else
   Begin
   (* Gap between y's is greater than x's.
      Trace vertically. *)
   If y1 > y2 Then
      Begin
      Switch(y1,y2);
      Switch(x1,x2);
      End;

   dx := (x2 - x1);
   dy := (y2 - y1);

   If dx <> 0 Then
      b := dy / dx
   Else
    b := 0;
   a := y1 - x1*b;

   For y := y1 to y2 do
      Begin
      If b <> 0 Then
        x := Round((y-a)/b)
      Else
        x := 0;
      PutPixel(x,y,color);
      End;
   End;
End;

(****************************************************)

Begin
GraphDriver := Detect;
InitGraph(GraphDriver,GraphMode,'D:\TP5');
ErrorCode := GraphResult;
If ErrorCode <> grOK Then
   Begin
   WriteLn('Graphics error: ',GraphErrorMsg(ErrorCode));
   Halt;
   End;

MaxX := GetMaxX;
MaxY := GetMaxY;

   Repeat
   PlotLine(Random(MaxX),
            Random(MaxY),
            Random(MaxX),
            Random(MaxY),
            White);
```

```
Until KeyPressed;

CloseGraph;
End.
```

This program draws lines between random points on the computer screen (see Figure 15-2). To stop the program, simply press any key.

If drawing a straight line is difficult, as the program just given demonstrates, imagine the difficulty in writing complete graphics routines for drawing polygons, ellipses, pie charts, and, perhaps most difficult, text characters. The GRAPH unit is a tremendous asset to all graphics programmers.

Circles, Lines, and Patterns

With the GRAPH unit's procedures you can create extremely complex graphics with relative ease, controlling color, shape, and size. **Line** and **Circle** are two important procedures: most common graphics, such as bar charts, pie charts, histograms, and polygons, are combinations of lines and circles.

The procedure **Line** takes four parameters in the form of coordinate pairs. The statement

```
Line(MaxX Div 2, 0, MaxX Div 2, MaxY);
```

draws a line that runs down the center of the screen, from top to bottom. Using **MaxX Div 2** to determine the center of the horizontal axis makes the statement independent of the coordinate system in use.

The procedure **Circle** takes three parameters. The first two form a coordinate pair that determines the center of the circle, while the third parameter is the radius of the circle in horizontal pixels — **Circle** computes the appropriate number of vertical pixels to maintain the proper proportions. The ratio of vertical to horizontal pixels is known as the *aspect ratio*. Each graphics driver has an aspect ratio that determines the scaling of graphic images. While Turbo Pascal allows you to alter the aspect ratio, you will probably never need to do so.

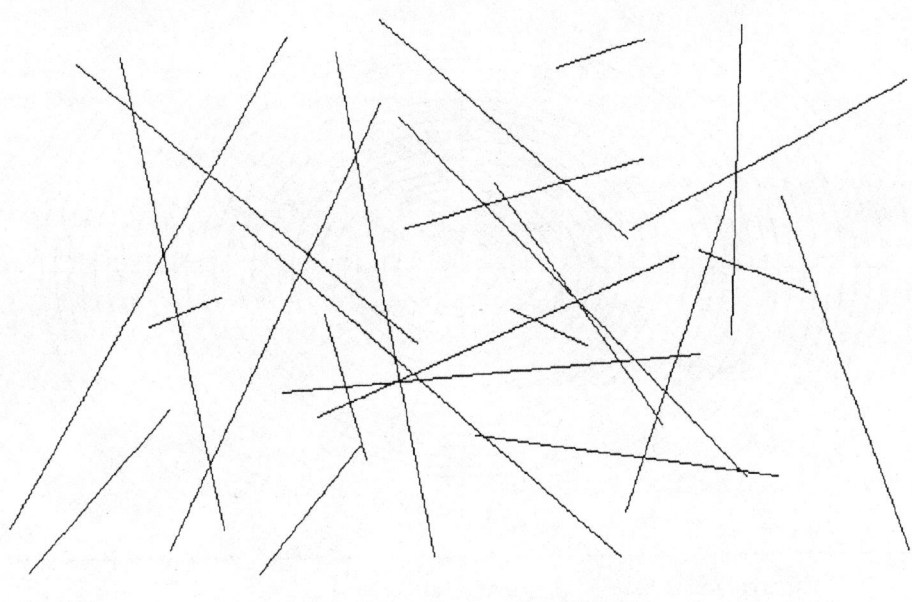

Figure 15-2.   Drawing lines in Graphics mode

Returning to the example, the statement

```
Circle(MaxX Div 2, MaxY Div 2, 10);
```

draws a circle at the center of the screen with a radius of ten horizontal pixels. You can increase the size of the radius to a point where parts of the circle run off the edge of the screen. When this occurs, the image is *clipped,* or truncated, to protect you from writing into memory outside that allocated for graphic images.

The example program listed here demonstrates the use of the **Line** and **Circle** procedures as well as some other important graphics techniques. The program begins by drawing lines that intersect at the center of the screen and then draws concentric circles from the edge of the screen toward the center (see Figure 15-3). Next, the program saves a rectangular area

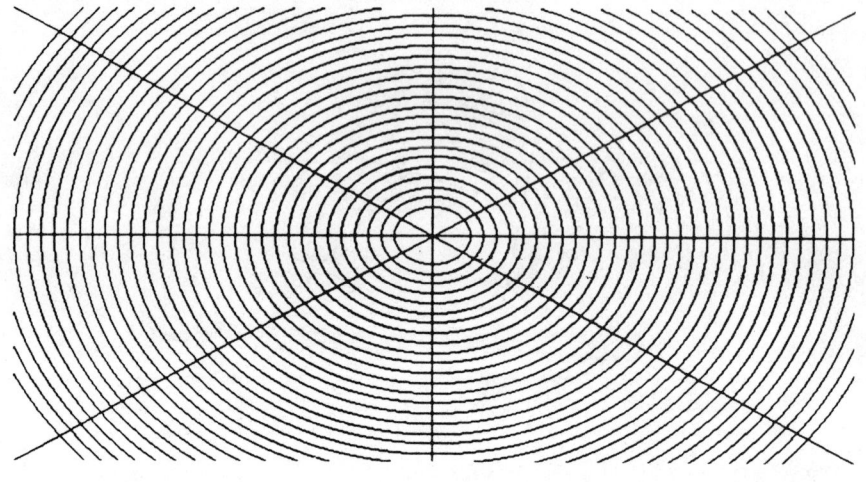

Figure 15-3.   Drawing lines and circles

around the center of the screen and flashes it in reverse and normal colors. Finally, the program fills the sectors of the circle with a random selection of colors and patterns (see Figure 15-4).

```
Program CircleDemo;
Uses CRT, GRAPH;
Var
  Palette : PaletteType;
  MaxX,
  MaxY,
  i,
  ErrorCode,
  GraphMode,
  GraphDriver : Integer;
  Size : Word;
  P : Pointer;

Begin
GraphDriver := Detect;
InitGraph(GraphDriver,GraphMode,'D:\TP5');
ErrorCode := GraphResult;
If ErrorCode <> grOK Then
```

```
   Begin
   WriteLn('Graphics error: ',GraphErrorMsg(ErrorCode));
   Halt;
   End;

MaxX := GetMaxX;
MaxY := GetMaxY;

(* Draw lines on screen *)
Line(MaxX Div 2, 0, MaxX Div 2, MaxY);
Line(0, MaxY Div 2, MaxX, MaxY Div 2);
Line(0, 0, MaxX, MaxY);
Line(MaxX, 0, 0, MaxY);

(* Draw concentric circles *)
i := MaxY;
While i > 20 Do
  Begin
  Circle(MaxX Div 2, MaxY Div 2, i);
  i := i - 10;
  End;

(* Save a portion of the screen *)
Size := ImageSize(Round(MaxX * 0.25),
                  Round(MaxY * 0.25),
                  Round(MaxY * 0.75));
GetMem(P, Size);
GetImage(Round(MaxX * 0.25),
         Round(MaxY * 0.25),
         Round(MaxX * 0.75),
         Round(MaxY * 0.75),P^);

(* Flash a portion of the screen *)
For i := 1 To 6 Do
  Begin
  PutImage(Round(MaxX * 0.25),
           Round(MaxY * 0.25),
           P^,NotPut);

  GetImage(Round(MaxX * 0.25),
           Round(MaxY * 0.25),
           Round(MaxX * 0.75),
           Round(MaxY * 0.75),P^);
  End;

GetPalette(Palette);

(* Fill in portions of the graphic image *)
  Repeat
  SetFillStyle(Random(9),Random(Palette.Size)+1);
  FloodFill(Random(MaxX),Random(MaxY),White);
  Until KeyPressed;

ReadLn;
CloseGraph;
End.
```

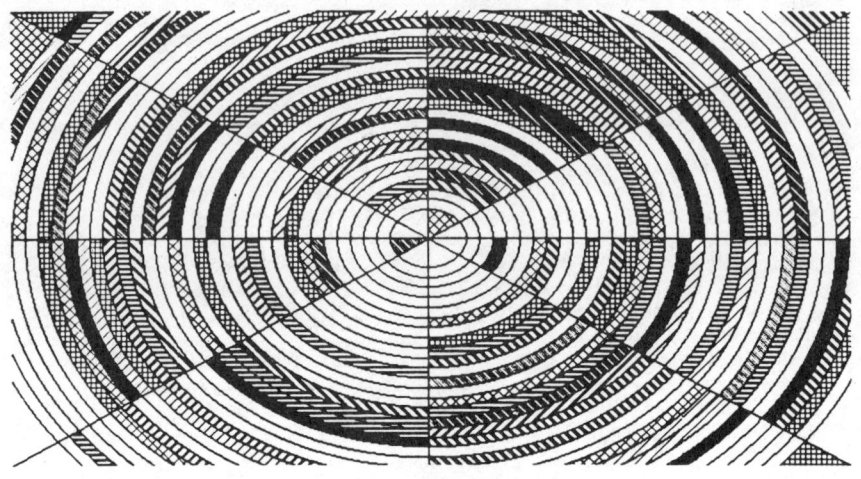

Figure 15-4.   Filling with colors and patterns

Saving and Changing the Image

The example program just given demonstrates how you can save a portion of a graphic screen and redisplay it in an altered form. The process of saving a graphic image requires three steps:

1. Determine how much memory you will need to store the graphic image.

2. Allocate a buffer of that size.

3. Save the image in the buffer.

This is accomplished with the following code:

```
Size := ImageSize(Round(MaxX * 0.25),
                  Round(MaxY * 0.25),
                  Round(MaxX * 0.75),
                  Round(MaxY * 0.75));
GetMem(P, Size);
GetImage(Round(MaxX * 0.25),
         Round(MaxY * 0.25),
         Round(MaxX * 0.75),
         Round(MaxY * 0.75),P^);
```

The first statement uses the function **ImageSize** to calculate the amount of memory required to store a rectangular image defined by two coordinate pairs defining upper left and lower right points on the screen. The amount of memory will vary dramatically with the display adapter and graphics mode in use, but cannot exceed 64K. The **GetMem** procedure then allocates memory from the heap to **pointer** variable **P**. Finally, the procedure **GetImage** moves the image defined by the coordinate pairs to the buffer that **P** points to.

Once you have saved a graphic image, you can retrieve it at any time. In the example program, this is done with the procedure **PutImage**:

```
PutImage(Round(MaxX * 0.25),
         Round(MaxY * 0.25),
         P^,NotPut);
```

PutImage takes four parameters. The first two are a coordinate pair that indicate where the upper left corner of the saved image should appear on the screen. The third parameter is the pointer to the buffer where the image is stored. The fourth parameter is the most interesting because it determines how the image will appear. The example above uses the constant **NotPut**, which uses a bit-wise negation process (in which the value of individiual bits is reversed) to reverse the colors of the image, producing a reverse video effect.

The last part of the program fills the graphic with different colors and patterns. This process begins with the **GetPalette** procedure, which returns information about the color capabilities of the current graphics driver and mode.

```
GetPalette(Palette);

(* Fill in portions of the graphic image *)
  Repeat
  SetFillStyle(Random(9),Random(Palette.Size)+1);
  FloodFill(Random(MaxX),Random(MaxY),White);
  Until KeyPressed;
```

GetPalette takes a single parameter of type **PaletteType**, which is defined as follows:

```
Type
  PaletteType = Record
    Size : Byte;
    Colors : Array[0..MaxColors] of ShortInt;
```

The **Size** field contains the number of colors currently available, and **Colors** contains the numeric codes that correspond to the colors. With a single call to **GetPalette** you know exactly what you have to work with in terms of graphic colors.

The procedures that do the hard work—drawing different patterns in varying colors—are **SetFillStyle** and **FloodFill**. The GRAPH unit defines 12 different patterns to use as filler in graphics. The procedure **SetFillStyle** lets you choose the pattern you want to use and the color you want to display it in. **FloodFill** "paints" the inside of a polygon or circle using the pattern and color you defined using **SetFillStyle**. To do its job, **FloodFill** needs two pieces of information: (1) the location of a pixel inside the area to fill and (2) the color of the boundary of the area. The boundary color is the only way **FloodFill** can determine where to stop filling.

Dragging an Image

The **PutImage** procedure was used in an earlier example to produce a reverse video effect. It can also be used to "drag" an image across the screen. The important quality of dragging an image is that when the image moves, it does not disturb the pixels "underneath" the image. Anyone who has worked with desktop publishing or other "paint" programs is familiar with the dragging concept.

   To drag an image, you must do two things. First, the image to be dragged must be stored in a buffer separate from the underlying image. Second, you must use the procedure **PutImage** with **XORPut** as the third parameter. The following sample program demonstrates how this is done. It saves the image of a circle, draws lines on the screen, and then drags the circle around the screen (see Figure 15-5).

```
Program CircleDemo2;
Uses CRT, GRAPH;
Var
   Direction : (up,down,right,left);
   XX,YY,
   MaxX,
   MaxY,
   ErrorCode,
   GraphMode,
   GraphDriver : Integer;
   Size : Word;
   P : Pointer;

Begin
GraphDriver := Detect;
InitGraph(GraphDriver,GraphMode,'D:\TP5');
ErrorCode := GraphResult;
If ErrorCode <> grOK Then
   Begin
   WriteLn('Graphics error: ',GraphErrorMsg(ErrorCode));
   Halt;
   End;

MaxX := GetMaxX;
MaxY := GetMaxY;


(* Draw a circle, save it, and clear the screen. *)

Circle(MaxX Div 2, MaxY Div 2, 20);

XX := Round(MaxX * 0.45);
YY := Round(MaxY * 0.45);
Size := ImageSize(XX, YY,
                  Round(MaxX * 0.55),
                  Round(MaxY * 0.55));
GetMem(P, Size);
GetImage(XX,YY,
         Round(MaxX * 0.55),
         Round(MaxY * 0.55),P^);
```

```
    ClearViewPort;

    (* Draw lines on screen *)
    Line(MaxX Div 2, 0, MaxX Div 2, MaxY);
    Line(0, MaxY Div 2, MaxX, MaxY Div 2);
    Line(0, 0, MaxX, MaxY);
    Line(MaxX, 0, 0, MaxY);

    (* Start dragging the circle. *)

    Direction := down;
    PutImage(XX, YY, P^,XORPut);

      Repeat
      PutImage(XX, YY, P^,XORPut);

        Case Direction Of

        Down :
          Begin
          YY := YY + 5;
          If YY > (MaxY * 0.75) Then
            Direction := Left;
          End;

        Left :
          Begin
          XX := XX - 5;
          If XX < (MaxX * 0.25)  Then
            Direction := Up;
          End;

        Up :
          Begin
          YY := YY - 5;
          If YY < (MaxY * 0.25)  Then
            Direction := Right;
          End;

        Right :
          Begin
          XX := XX + 5;
          If XX > (MaxX * 0.75)  Then
            Direction := Down;
          End;
        End;

      PutImage(XX, YY, P^,XORPut);

      Until KeyPressed;

    CloseGraph;
    End.
    list 15-15
```

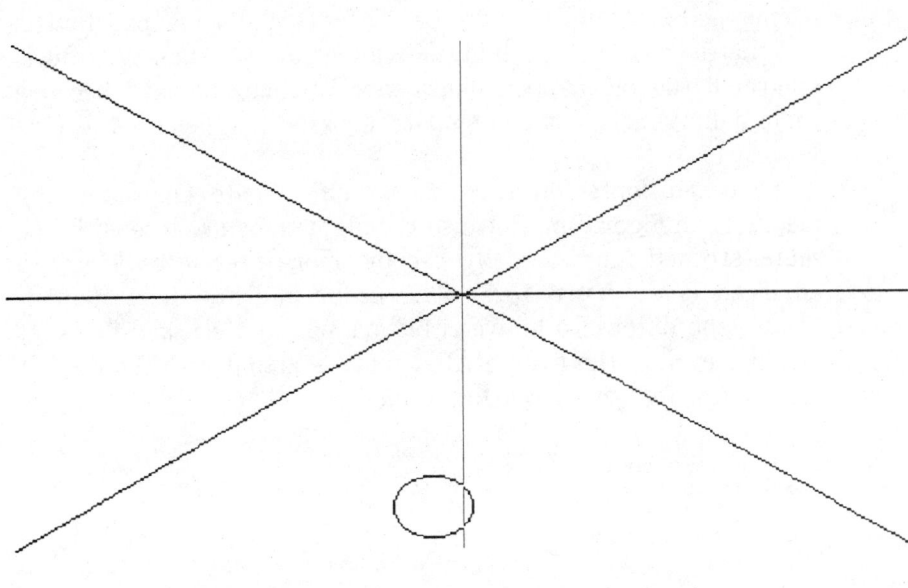

Figure 15-5.   Dragging a circle in Graphics mode

The dragging is accomplished with the statement

```
PutImage(XX, YY, P^,XORPut);
```

This statement is used twice for each step in the movement. The first time it is used, **PutImage** erases the circle; the second time, it redraws it at the new location. As the circle moves around the screen, the lines are left undisturbed. An important point in using this technique is to define the smallest possible buffer to store the dragged image—the larger the buffer, the longer it takes to update the image, and the slower the dragging will seem.

Graphic Text

Graphics wouldn't be much use without text. The ability to combine text and graphics is the foundation of the desktop publishing industry. The GRAPH unit contains five fonts: one bit-mapped font and four "stroked" fonts. A bit-mapped font is one that is created from a static number of elements. When it is enlarged, the bit-mapped characters become "blocky" because their definition is not changed to match their larger size (see Figure 15-6).

Stroked fonts, on the other hand, create characters by means of an algorithm. Because the algorithms are insensitive to scale, stroked fonts actually become more precise as they are enlarged (see Figure 15-7). The program listed here demonstrates the difference between bit-mapped and stroked fonts. It displays each of the five GRAPH fonts, starting with the default bit-mapped font, in increasing size.

```
Program TextDemo;
Uses CRT, GRAPH;
Const
  CharType : Array [0..4] of String[20] =
             ('Default','Triplex','Small','Sans Serif','Gothic');
Var
  S : String;
  MaxX,
  MaxY,
  i,j,k,
  ErrorCode,
  GraphMode,
  GraphDriver : Integer;

Begin
GraphDriver := Detect;
InitGraph(GraphDriver,GraphMode,'D:\TP5');
GraphMode := GetMaxMode;
InitGraph(GraphDriver,GraphMode,'D:\TP5');
ErrorCode := GraphResult;
If ErrorCode <> grOK Then
  Begin
  WriteLn('Graphics error: ',GraphErrorMsg(ErrorCode));
  Halt;
  End;

MaxX := GetMaxX;
MaxY := GetMaxY;

For i := 0 To 4 Do
  Begin
  k := 0;
  For j := 1 To 10 Do
    Begin
    SetTextStyle(i,HorizDir,j);
    OutTextXY(j*20,k,CharType[i]);
```

```
      k := k + TextHeight(CharType[i]) + 10;
      End;

   SetTextStyle(0,HorizDir,2);
   S := 'Press ENTER...';
   OutTextXY(MaxX - TextWidth(S),MaxY - TextHeight(S),S);
   ReadLn;
   ClearDevice;
   End;

CloseGraph;
End.
```

To select a font, use the procedure **SetTextStyle**, which takes three parameters. The first parameter is the font, and can range from 0 (default) to 4 (Gothic). The second parameter is the direction in which the text is to be written. You have two choices here: 0 (horizontal) or 1 (vertical). The third parameter controls the size of the characters. The normal font size is 1 for the default font and 4 for the stroked fonts, but these can be increased to ten times the normal size.

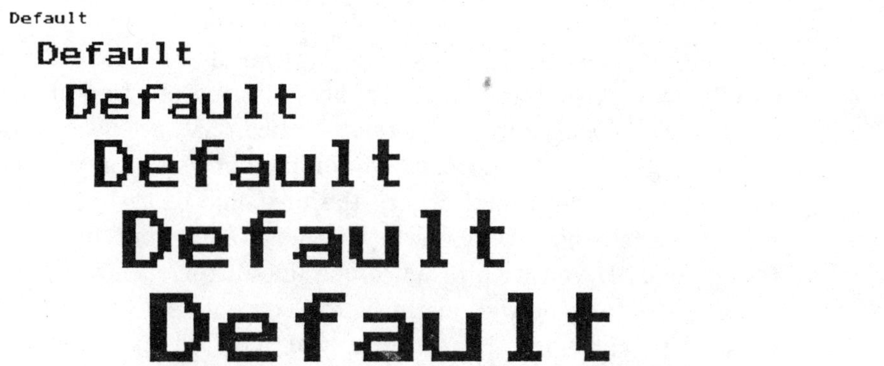

Figure 15-6.   A bit-mapped font

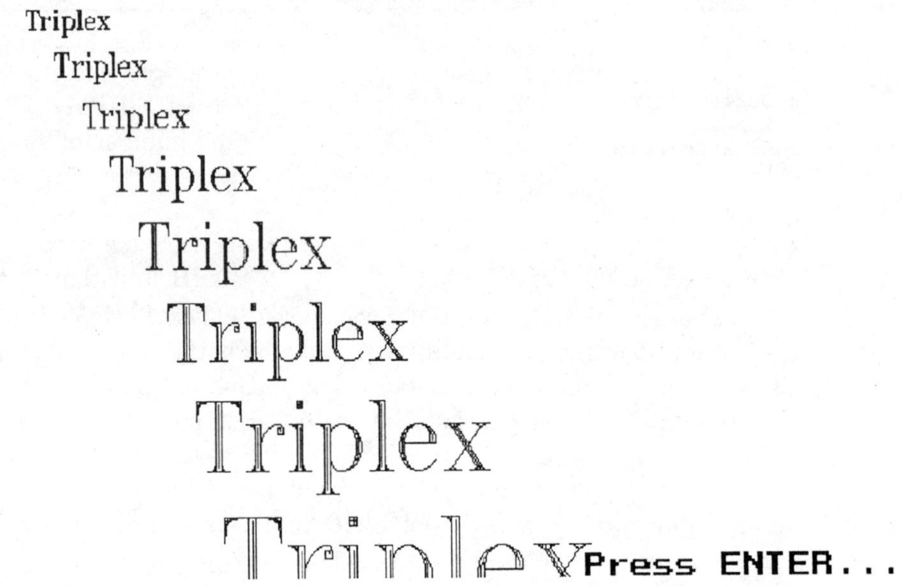

Triplex
  Triplex
    Triplex

Triplex

Triplex

Triplex

Triplex

Triplex **Press ENTER...**

Figure 15-7.   A stroked font

Once you have selected a font, you can display text with the **OutTextXY** procedure, which displays a string starting at coordinates you supply as parameters. Notice that in the example program, **OutTextXY** is used in conjunction with the function **TextHeight** to determine where the next line of text should be placed. **TextHeight** is necessary because each font has a different scale. If you wish to place one line of text below another, you must determine the height of the current text and use that number to calculate the distance you have to move down in order to write the next line. In the program, the statement

```
k := k + TextHeight(CharType[i]) + 10;
```

moves the next line of text down by the size of the current line plus ten pixels. As you can see, using text in the Graphics mode is not easy, even when the fonts are defined for you.

More on Colors

To round out the discussion on Turbo Pascal graphics, let's consider the use of color with a procedure named **FillPoly**. The **FillPoly** procedure creates a polygon with any number of sides and fills it with a color and pattern you define with the **SetFill-Style** procedure.

To use **FillPoly** you must first define a variable array of **PointType**, a record type defined in the GRAPH unit that contains an x and y coordinate. The following example program shows how this is done.

```
Program ColorDemo;
Uses CRT, GRAPH;

Type
  TriType = Array [1..3] of PointType;

Var
  Tri : TriType;
  S : String;
  MaxX,
  MaxY,
  x1,y1,
  i,j,k,
  ErrorCode,
  GraphMode,
  GraphDriver : Integer;

  Palette : PaletteType;

Begin
GraphDriver := Detect;
InitGraph(GraphDriver,GraphMode,'D:\TP5');
GraphMode := GetMaxMode;
InitGraph(GraphDriver,GraphMode,'D:\TP5');
ErrorCode := GraphResult;
If ErrorCode <> grOK Then
  Begin
  WriteLn('Graphics error: ',GraphErrorMsg(ErrorCode));
  Halt;
  End;

MaxX := GetMaxX;
MaxY := GetMaxY;

GetPalette(Palette);
SetFillStyle(3,3);
```

```
While Not Keypressed Do
  Begin
    SetFillStyle(Random(13),Random(Palette.Size)+1);

    Tri[1].X := Random(MaxX);
    Tri[1].Y := Random(MaxY);
    Tri[2].X := Random(MaxX);
    Tri[2].Y := Random(MaxY);
    Tri[3].X := Random(MaxX);
    Tri[3].Y := Random(MaxY);

    FillPoly(3,Tri);
    Delay(100);

    x1 := x1 + (MaxX Div 12);
    y1 := y1 + (MaxY Div 12);
    End;

ReadLn;
CloseGraph;
End.
```

The example program uses **FillPoly** to draw triangles. Since a triangle is completely defined by three points, the following definition is sufficient:

```
Type
  TriType = Array [1..3] of PointType;
```

A variable named **Tri** is declared as **TriType**. To create a triangle, the program first defines the three coordinate pairs in **Tri**. The call to **FillPoly** passes the number of points in the polygon (three in this case) and the variable **Tri**, which contains the coordinates. As the following listing shows, the triangle's coordinates are determined randomly.

```
Tri[1].X := Random(MaxX);
Tri[1].Y := Random(MaxY);
Tri[2].X := Random(MaxX);
Tri[2].Y := Random(MaxY);
Tri[3].X := Random(MaxX);
Tri[3].Y := Random(MaxY);

FillPoly(3,Tri);
```

For each triangle drawn, colors and patterns are also selected randomly using **SetFillStyle**, as shown here:

```
SetFillStyle(Random(13),Random(Palette.Size)+1);
```

This statement randomly selects one of the 12 fill patterns defined in the GRAPH unit and also randomly selects a color from the Video mode palette (see Figure 15-8). Thus, when you run this program, you will see randomly generated triangles with randomly selected patterns and colors.

The graphics potential of the PC is great, but tapping into it is a challenge for even the most experienced programmer. For the beginner, Turbo Pascal's GRAPH unit provides an easy way to learn about graphics programming. For the professional programmer, the GRAPH unit's rich set of routines and data structures provides the building blocks for sophisticated applications. If you are interested in learning more about graphics programming, consider Borland's Graphix Toolbox, which provides even more power and functions.

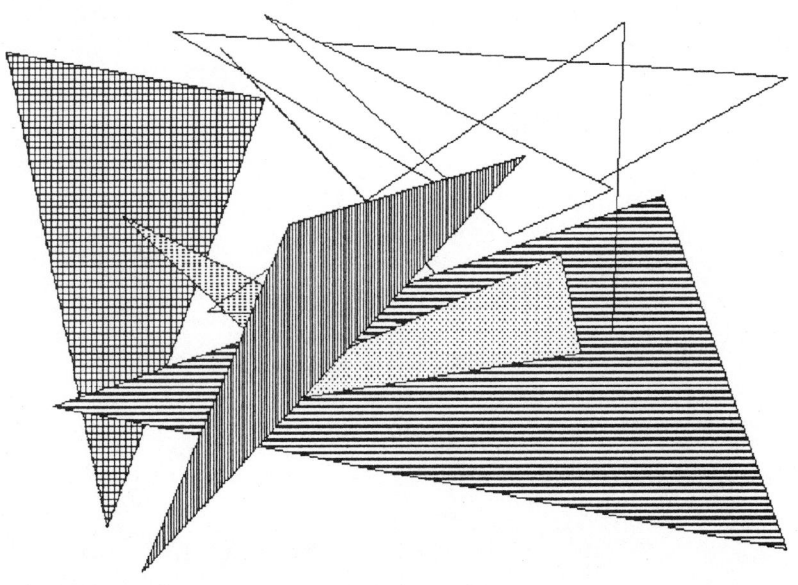

Figure 15-8.   Filling triangles with color and patterns

Interrupts, Telecommunications, and Memory-Resident Programs

Using Interrupts
Writing the Interrupt Handler
Memory-Resident Programs

Life is full of interruptions—and so is computing. In computer programming, interruptions are called *interrupts*. If you own a telephone, you will understand the concept of an interrupt. When your telephone rings, you stop what you are doing, answer the phone, and resume working when your conversation is over. In a way, computers have little telephones ringing inside the microprocessor that make it stop and do something else for a moment.

This chapter introduces the concept of interrupts and how they are used in Turbo Pascal. Interrupts are fundamental to the operation of your computer; and if you want to tap the full power of the personal computer, you must understand them. Because telecommunications commonly use interrupt programming, the concepts will be illustrated with examples from a Turbo Pascal communications program that is listed at the end of this chapter.

Using Interrupts

Do you occasionally find it inconvenient when your telephone rings? Imagine how inconvenient it would be to have a telephone that does not ring. You would have to pick up the receiver from time to time to see if anyone were calling. Not only would this waste time, but you would run the risk of missing a call if someone called and hung up before you picked up the receiver.

Of course, our phones do ring, and so we can do other things and answer the telephone only when we know someone is calling. In similar fashion, interrupts allow your computer to work until something happens that requires your computer's attention.

One interrupt controls your computer's internal clock. About 18 times each second, this interrupt stops your microprocessor and asks it to increment the DOS time and date. You do not notice this because it happens so quickly. Other interrupts occur when you press a key on your keyboard or data comes into a serial port. In fact, interrupts occur all the time, but you do not notice them because they generally require the microprocessor-to do very little work.

Hardware and Software Interrupts

Interrupts are of two types: hardware and software. *Hardware interrupts,* generated by such actions as pressing a key, a tick of the system clock, or data entering a serial port, originate in the computer's circuitry and are controlled by a special chip, the 8259 interrupt controller. When a hardware interrupt occurs, this chip acts as a traffic cop, making sure the interrupt goes in the correct direction. The 8259 receives an interrupt request, evaluates its priority, and routes the request to the procedure it needs.

Software interrupts are generated by programs that request special BIOS and DOS services. In Turbo Pascal, the commands **Intr** and **MsDos** create software interrupts (see Chapter 12). Whether hardware or software, however, all interrupts use the *interrupt vector table.*

The Interrupt Vector Table

The interrupt vector table is an array of memory addresses located at the lowest part of the PC's memory. The array is 1024 bytes long and contains the addresses of all the routines that are triggered by interrupts. Because an address requires 4 bytes, the 1024-byte interrupt vector table can hold a maximum of 256 interrupt addresses.

An interrupt, when initiated, fetches an address from the interrupt vector table, jumps to that memory location, and executes the routine located there. Each address in the interrupt vector table is used exclusively by a single interrupt. For example, Interrupt 8, the clock timer, always fetches the address at offset 0020h. Table 16-1 contains the PC's eight hardware interrupts, numbers 8 through 15, and their offsets in the interrupt vector table.

Of the hardware interrupts, the most useful to program are the clock tick (number 8), the keyboard interrupt (number 9), and the COM1 serial port (number 12). Interrupt 12 is used for serial communications with other computers. Interrupts 8 and 9 are used for many purposes, including pop-up terminate-stay-resident (TSR) programs.

Replacing Interrupts

Each time you start your computer, DOS fills the interrupt vector table with addresses to standard interrupt routines. As soon as the computer is running, however, you can change

| Interrupt | | | |
Dec	Hex	Offset	Purpose
8	8	0020h	System clock tick
9	9	0024h	Keyboard interrupt
10	A	0028h	Not used
11	B	002Ch	Second serial port (COM2)
12	C	0030h	First serial port (COM1)
13	D	0034h	Hard-disk interrupt
14	E	0038h	Floppy-disk interrupt
15	F	003Ch	Printer interrupt

Table 16-1.   Location of Hardware Interrupts in the Interrupt Vector Table

addresses in the interrupt vector table to point to interrupt handling procedures that you have written; the interrupt will then execute your procedure instead of the default procedure. In short, by changing addresses in the interrupt vector table, you can usurp DOS and BIOS and take charge of your computer's basic functions.

Although programmers are not usually interested in altering the addresses of software interrupts, they are interested in changing hardware interrupt addresses. By changing the keyboard interrupt address, for example, a memory-resident program can intercept a keystroke and interpret it before it ever gets to the main program. This is how memory-resident programs such as SuperKey and SideKick work.

An interrupt address can be changed in two ways: by changing the interrupt vector table directly or by using a DOS service to do it for you. To change memory directly, you must overlay an array of addresses on the interrupt vector table, as follows:

```
Var
  AsyncVector : Pointer;

  InterruptVector : Array [0..$FF] of Pointer
                    Absolute $0000:$0000;
```

The example code just given uses the **pointer** data type. **Pointers** are 4-byte data types that hold a segment and offset that together constitute a memory address. The variable **InterruptVector**, an array of 256 (0oh through FFh) addresses, is declared absolute at the very beginning of RAM, where the interrupt vector table resides. Since **InterruptVector** and the table share the same space, when you change a value in one, you also change it in the other. To change an address in the interrupt vector table, use the following statements:

```
AsyncVector := InterruptVector[$0C];
InterruptVector[$0C] := @AsyncInt;
```

The first statement stores the vector for Interrupt 12 (0C in hexadecimal) in the variable **AsyncVector**. Saving the original address is important since you will need to restore it eventually. The second statement replaces the original vector with the address of a Turbo Pascal procedure named **AsyncInt**.

The Turbo Pascal operator @ returns a four-byte address (segment and offset) of the procedure **AsyncInt**. The address is then loaded into the interrupt vector table. Now, when Interrupt **0Ch** is triggered by data arriving at the serial port, **AsyncInt** will execute instead of the normal procedure.

When you are done using the interrupt vector, you must restore the original address that you saved in the **pointer** variable **AsyncVector**. If you do not restore the address, you may crash your computer and have to reboot. This single line of code is all you need to restore the original interrupt vector address:

```
InterruptVector[$0C] := AsyncVector;
```

With the interrupt vector now restored to its original value, your computer will operate normally.

It is simple to change interrupt addresses directly, but it is safer to use DOS services, which apply to a wider range of computers. DOS service **35h** reports a vector's contents, and service **25h** changes an address in the interrupt vector table. Fortunately, the Turbo Pascal DOS unit provides two routines— **GetIntVec** and **SetIntVec**—that do exactly what is needed. Both procedures take two parameters: the interrupt number (for example, **0Ch**) and a **pointer** variable. The process of saving an interrupt vector and replacing it with a new vector is shown here:

```
GetIntVec($0C,AsyncVector);
SetIntVec($0C,@AsyncInt);
```

When you are done using the interrupt, you can restore the old interrupt address, as shown here:

```
SetIntVec($0C,AsyncVector);
```

Using the procedures from the DOS unit is safer than directly altering the interrupt vector table. But, now that you know how to change a vector to point to your own procedure, what does that procedure look like?

Writing the Interrupt Handler

Interrupt handler is a term that refers to the code that executes as the result of an interrupt. In the previous examples, the handler was a Turbo Pascal procedure named **AsyncInt**, which was attached to Interrupt **0Ch**. Interrupt handlers are different from other types of procedures because you do not always control when they will execute. For example, Interrupt **0Ch** is triggered when a byte is ready in COM1. You have no way of knowing when that will occur, so your interrupt handler must be extra cautious so as not to disturb the normal processing of the computer. In other words, a well-written interrupt handler is like a cat burglar: it enters when you least expect it, steals some computing time, and leaves without a trace.

The trick to writing interrupt handlers is leaving without a trace. To do this, the handler must save all the CPU's registers before executing and restore them when done. (The handler need not save the CS, IP, or Flags registers because DOS saves these for you prior to calling the interrupt.) But saving the CPU registers alone is not enough—you must also conquer the problem presented by the data segment.

Restoring the Data Segment

When an interrupt handler is invoked, only the code segment (CS) and instruction pointer (IP) registers are correctly set to the values your handler needs. The data segment (DS) register, on the other hand, contains the value used by the procedure being interrupted and may not contain the correct value for the interrupt handler. Without the correct data segment, your handler cannot refer to its own global variables. Your interrupt handler must, therefore, store its DS value someplace in the code segment, so that the correct DS can be set.

Turbo Pascal Interrupt Support

While all of this may seem a bit intimidating, Borland comes to the rescue. Turbo Pascal lets you write interrupt handler procedures that automatically save all registers, set up the DS register, and restore all registers when done. To declare a procedure as an interrupt handler, you need only append the **Interrupt** directive to the end of the procedure declaration, as shown here:

```
Procedure IntHandler; Interrupt;
```

The **Interrupt** directive instructs Turbo Pascal to insert the appropriate code to save registers, set up the DS register, restore registers, and issue an **IRET** command to terminate the procedure. You may optionally declare in your handler a list of pseudo-variables that represent the CPU registers:

```
Procedure IntHandler(Flags,CS,IP,AX,BX,CX,DX,SI,DI,DS,ES,BP);
         Interrupt;

Procedure IntHandler(SI,DI,DS,ES,BP); Interrupt;
```

As you can see in the preceding listing, the parameter list can include all the CPU registers (Flags through BP) or a subset of the registers (for example, SI through BP). There are, however, two restrictions. First, you cannot change the order of the parameters. Second, if you delete parameters, you may only do so from the left. For example, if you want only the SI and DS registers, you must include SI, DI, DS, ES, and BP in your parameter list, in that order.

When your interrupt handler executes, you will have access to all the pseudo-parameters that you listed in the procedure heading. The values in the parameters will represent the contents of the CPU registers *prior to the interrupt*.

Note that the SP and SS registers are not included as pseudo-parameters. This means that your interrupt handler will be using the stack of the program it interrupted. This is a bit risky since you have no idea how large the stack of the interrupted program is. The safest approach is to avoid as much as possible using the stack in your interrupt handler. The next section of this chapter demonstrates how an interrupt handler can be used to create a telecommunications program.

PC Telecommunications

Telecommunications, the transmission of data from one computer to another via telephone lines, is simple in concept, but complicated in practice. In concept, the computer sends a byte to a serial port, which sends it on to the modem. The modem translates the bits into tones and sends the tones to another modem, which translates them back into bits. The translated bits are sent to the receiving serial port where they wait to be picked up by the software.

In practice, writing a program to do all these things is not so simple. The complexity is partly due to the number of hardware elements you must control: the RS-232 serial port, the INS8250 universal asynchronous receiver transmitter (UART), the 8259 interrupt controller, and the modem itself. In addition, there are many variations of modem speed, parity, stop bits, data bits, which serial port to use, and so on.

The Telecommunications Program

The following program, called **AsyncCommunications**, provides simple telecommunications capability using Interrupt 12. The program assumes you have a Hayes-compatible modem connected to your first serial port. Before you run the program, set the values in procedure **SelectModemSet** to those of the remote computer you want to call.

```
Program CommX;
{$S-,R-,I-,V-,F+}
Uses CRT, DOS;
Type
  ModemSetType = Record
```

```
                ComPort,
                BPS,
                DataBits,
                StopBits        : Integer;
                Parity          : Char;
                PhoneNumber     : String;
                End;

        Const
          MainDseg : Integer = 0;
          MaxBufLen  = 1024;
          CR         = #13;

          (*******************************\
          (* ISN8250 UART Registers.       *)
          (*******************************)
          DataPort = $03F8;
          (* Contains 8 bits to transmit or receive.      *)
          IER       = $03F9;
          (* Enables the serial port when set equal to 1. *)
          LCR       = $03FB;
          (* Sets communications parameters.              *)
          MCR       = $03FC;
          (* Bits 1, 2 and 4 are turned on to ready modem.*)
          LSR       = $03FD;
          (* When bit 6 is on, it is safe to send a byte. *)
          MDMMSR    = $03FE;
          (* Initialized to 80h when starting.            *)

          ENBLRDY = $01;     (* Initial value for Port[IER].    *)
          MDMMOD  = $0B;     (* Initial value for Port[MCR].    *)
          MDMCD   = $80;     (* Initial value for Port[MDMMSR]. *)

          INTCTLR = $21;     (* Port for 8259 Interrupt Controller. *)

        Var
          ModemSet        : ModemSetType;
          AsyncVector     : Pointer;
          Regs            : Registers;
          Buffer          : Array [1..MaxBufLen] Of Char;
          I,
          CharsInBuf,
          CircOut,
          CircIn          : Word;
          Orig            : Char;

        (**********************************************************)

        Procedure ClearBuffer;
        Begin
        CircIn := 1;
        CircOut := 1;
        CharsInBuf := 0;
        FillChar(Buffer,SizeOf(Buffer),0);
        End;
```

```
(*****************************************************************)

Procedure SelectModemSet;
Begin
With ModemSet Do
  Begin
  ComPort    := 1;              (* Must be 1 in this program. *)

    Repeat
    Write('BPS (300,1200): ');
    ReadLn(BPS);
    Until (BPS = 300) Or (BPS =1200);

    Repeat
    Write('Data bits (7,8): ');
    ReadLn(DataBits);
    Until DataBits in [7,8];

    Repeat
    Write('Stop bits (0,1): ');
    ReadLn(StopBits);
    Until StopBits in [0,1];

    Repeat
    Write('Parity (N,E,O): ');
    ReadLn(Parity);
    Parity := UpCase(Parity);
    Until Parity in ['N','E','O'];

  Write('Phone number: ');
  ReadLn(PhoneNumber);
  End;
End;

(*****************************************************************)

Procedure AsyncInt; Interrupt;
Begin
Inline($FB);        (* STI *)

If (CharsInBuf < MaxBufLen) Then
  Begin
  Buffer[CircIn] := Char(Port[DataPort]);
  If (CircIn < MaxBufLen) Then
    Inc(CircIn,1)
  Else
    CircIn := 1;
  Inc(CharsInBuf,1);
  End;

Inline($FA);        (* CLI *)

Port[$20] := $20;
End;

(*****************************************************************)
```

```
Procedure SetSerialPort(ComPort,
                        BPS,
                        StopBits,
                        DataBits: Integer;
                        Parity : Char);
Var
  Regs : Registers;
  Parameter : Byte;
Begin
  Case BPS Of
  300  : BPS := 2;
  1200 : BPS := 4;
  End;

If StopBits = 2 Then
  StopBits := 1
Else
  StopBits := 0;

If DataBits = 7 Then
  DataBits := 2
Else
  DataBits := 3;

Parameter := (BPS Shl 5) + (StopBits Shl 2) + DataBits;

  Case Parity Of
  'E' : Parameter := Parameter + 8;
  'O' : Parameter := Parameter + 24;
  End;

With Regs Do
  Begin
  DX := ComPort - 1;
  AH := 0;
  AL := Parameter;
  Flags := 0;
  Intr($14,Regs);
  End;
End;

(*******************************************************)

Procedure EnablePorts;
Var
  B : Byte;
Begin
MainDseg := Dseg;
ClearBuffer;
GetIntVec($0C,AsyncVector);
SetIntVec($0C,@AsyncInt);

B := Port[INTCTLR];
B := B And $0EF;
Port[INTCTLR] := B;
```

```
B := Port[LCR];
B := B And $7F;

Port[LCR] := B;
Port[IER] := ENBLRDY;
Port[MCR] := $08 Or MDMMOD;
Port[MDMMSR] := MDMCD;
Port[$20] := $20;
End;

(**********************************************************)

Function GetCharInBuf : Char;
Begin
If CharsInBuf > 0 Then
  Begin
  GetCharInBuf := Buffer[CircOut];
  If CircOut < MaxBufLen Then
    Inc(CircOut,1)
  Else
    CircOut := 1;
  Dec(CharsInBuf,1);
  End;
End;

(**********************************************************)

Function CarrierDetected : Boolean;
Var
  Ch : Char;
  Timer  : Integer;
Begin
CarrierDetected := False;
Timer:=40;
While (Port[MDMMSR] And $80) <> $80 Do
  Begin
  If KeyPressed Then
    Begin
    Ch := ReadKey;
    If Ch = #27 Then
      Exit;
    End;
  If (CharsInBuf > 0) Then
    Begin
    Ch := GetCharInBuf;
    Write(Ch);
    If Ch = CR Then
      WriteLn;
    End;
  If Timer = 0 Then
    Exit
  Else
    Begin
    Dec(Timer,1);
    Delay(1000);
```

```
      End;
    End;
  CarrierDetected := True;
  End;

  (**********************************************************)

  Procedure SendChar(B: Byte);
  Begin
  While ((Port[LSR] And $20) <> $20) Do
    Begin
    End;
  Port[Dataport] := B;
  End;

  (**********************************************************)

  Procedure StringToPort(S : String);
  Var
    I : Integer;
  Begin
  For I := 1 To Length(S) Do
    SendChar(Ord(S[I]));
  SendChar(Ord(CR));
  End;

  (**********************************************************)

  Procedure DisablePorts;
  Var
    B : Byte;
  Begin
  (* Turn off carrier signal. *)
  StringToPort('ATC0');

  (* Turn off the communication interrupt for COM 1. *)
  B := Port[INTCTLR];
  B := B Or $10;
  Port[INTCTLR] := B;

  (* Disable 8250 Data Ready Interrupt. *)
  B := Port[LCR];
  B := B And $7F;
  Port[LCR] := B;
  Port[IER] := $0;

  (* Disable OUT2 on 8250. *)
  Port[MCR] := $0;

  Port[$20] := $20;

  SetIntVec($0C,AsyncVector);

  MsDos(Regs);
  End;

  (**********************************************************)
```

```pascal
Function SuccessfulConnect(PhoneNumber : String) : Boolean;
Var
  S : String;
Begin
(* ATDT assumes touch-tone dial. *)
S := 'ATDT'+PhoneNumber;
StringToPort(S);
Delay(300);
If CarrierDetected Then
  SuccessfulConnect:=True
Else
  Begin
  Write('Error: Unable To Connect.');
  StringToPort('ATC0'); (* Turn off carrier signal. *)
  SuccessfulConnect:=False;
  End;
End;

(*********************************************************)

Procedure SetHayesModem;
Begin
StringToPort('ATC0');      (* Turn off carrier signal.      *)
Delay(1000);               (* Wait a second.                *)
StringToPort('ATZ');       (* Reset modem to cold-start.    *)
Delay(1000);               (* Wait a second.                *)
StringToPort('ATF1');      (* Full Duplex.                  *)
Delay(1000);               (* Wait a second.                *)
StringToPort('ATE0');      (* Do not echo in command state. *)
Delay(1000);               (* Wait a second.                *)
StringToPort('ATV1');      (* Verbal result codes.          *)
Delay(1000);               (* Wait a second.                *)
StringToPort('ATQ0');      (* Send result codes.            *)
Delay(1000);               (* Wait a second.                *)
End;

(*********************************************************)

Procedure StartCommunicating;
Var
  OutChar,
  InChar : Char;
Begin
ClearBuffer;

  Repeat
  If (CharsInBuf > 0) Then
    Begin
    InChar := GetCharInBuf;
    If InChar in [#32..#126] Then
      Write(InChar)
    Else If (InChar = CR) Then
      WriteLn;
    End;
```

```
    If KeyPressed Then
      Begin
      OutChar := ReadKey;
      If (OutChar <> #27) Then
        Begin
        SendChar(Ord(OutChar));
        If OutChar = CR Then
          WriteLn
        Else
          Write(OutChar);
        End;
      End;
    Until OutChar = #27;
End;

(**********************************************************)

Begin
ClrScr;

SelectModemSet;

With ModemSet Do
  SetSerialPort(ComPort,BPS,StopBits,DataBits,Parity);

EnablePorts;

SetHayesModem;

If SuccessfulConnect(ModemSet.PhoneNumber) Then
  StartCommunicating;

WriteLn;
Write('Logging off...');
StringToPort('ATZ');        (* Reset modem to cold-start.  *)
Delay(1000);                (* Wait a second.              *)
DisablePorts;
End.
```

The main block of this program calls several procedures and functions, and outlines the steps necessary to establish asynchronous communications. The first procedure called is **SelectModemSet**, which allows the user to specify the communications port to use, the bits per second, the number of stop and data bits, the parity, and the telephone number. (Note that this program is designed to use communications port number 1 (COM1) only.) These data items are stored in a record of type **ModemSetType**, which is defined in the following listing.

```
Type
  ModemSetType = Record
    ComPort,
    BPS,
    DataBits,
    StopBits      : Integer;
    Parity        : Char;
    PhoneNumber   : String;
  End;
```

After this record is initialized, its contents are passed to the procedure **SetSerialPort**, which uses BIOS Interrupt **14h** to set the serial port to your parameters. To use this interrupt, you

7	6	5	4	3	2	1	0

Parameter	Bits Used	Bit Pattern	Meaning
Data Bits	Bits 0-1	00	5 data bits
		01	6 data bits
		10	7 data bits
		11	8 data bits
Stop Bits	Bit 2	0	1 stop bit
		1	2 stop bits
Parity	Bits 3-4	00	No parity
		01	Odd parity
		10	No parity
		11	Even parity
Speed (BPS)	Bits 5-7	000	100 BPS
		001	150 BPS
		010	300 BPS
		011	600 BPS
		100	1200 BPS
		101	2400 BPS
		110	4800 BPS
		111	9600 BPS

Table 16-2.   Contents of AL Register for BIOS Interrupt 14h

must set AH to 0, which tells BIOS to initialize a serial port, set AL to a parameter byte whose bits contain the communications settings, and set DX to 0 for COM1 or 1 for COM2.

The most difficult part of using Interrupt 14 is setting the bits in the parameter byte. Table 16-2 shows the definitions of each bit in this byte.

Once the modem has been set, the interrupt is installed by procedure **EnablePorts**. This procedure saves the old interrupt vector address, installs the address of procedure **AsyncInt**, and prepares the INS8250 UART chip for communications.

The final step in preparation is to initialize the modem to the proper settings with the **SetHayesModem** procedure. While there are many modems available, the Hayes Smartmodem is the commonly accepted standard for personal computers. The modem commands used here should work on any modem compatible with the Hayes Smartmodem. Table 16-3 lists the commands available for the Hayes Smartmodem. For a full explanation of the internal operation of the Hayes Smartmodem, see the *Smartmodem 1200 Hardware Reference Manual* by Hayes Microcomputer Products, Inc. If you use an incompatible modem, change this procedure to match your modem.

Now that the serial port is set, the interrupt is installed, and the modem is initialized, it is time to begin communications. The Boolean function **SuccessfulConnect(ModemSet.Phone-Number)** dials the phone number passed to it and waits for a carrier-detect signal from the modem, indicating that the connection has been established, in which case the function returns TRUE, and communications begin. If no carrier-detect signal is obtained, the function returns FALSE and the program ends.

After the carrier-detect signal is received, control is passed to the procedure **StartCommunicating**, which transmits the characters you type and displays the characters received from the remote computer. This procedure continues until you press ESC, which produces an ASCII code 27.

The **DisablePorts** procedure, the final step in the program, installs the original interrupt in the interrupt vector table and resets the UART chip.

Command	Parameters	Description
A	None	Modem answers a telephone call without waiting for a ring. This is used to change from Voice mode, where you speak to someone, to Data mode, where two computers communicate
A/	None	Repeats the last command
Cn	0,1	Transmitter off. When $n = 1$, the modem calls, answers, or connects to another modem. All other times, $n = 0$
,(Comma)	None	Causes a two-second delay when dialing a telephone number
Ds	Number	Puts the modem in the Originate mode and dials the telephone number represented by s
En	0,1	When $n = 0$, the modem in the command state does not echo back characters. When $n = 1$, characters are echoed
Fn	0,1	When $n = 0$, the modem operates in half-duplex; when $n = 1$, the modem operates in full-duplex
Hn	0,1,2	This command controls your telephone's dial tone. When $n = 0$, the modem is "on-hook" and no dial tone is present. When $n = 1$, the modem is "off-hook" and the dial tone is present. The parameter 2 is used for special applications using amateur radio equipment
In	0,1	This command requests the Smartmodem's three-digit product code. The first two digits indicate the product (for example, 12 indicates a Smartmodem 1200) and the third digit represents the revision number
Mn	0,1,2	The **M** command controls the speaker. When $n = 0$, the speaker is always off. When $n = 1$, the speaker is on until a carrier is detected. When $n = 2$, the speaker is always on

Table 16-3.   Hayes Smartmodem Commands

Command	Parameters	Description
O	None	When the modem is on-line, the **O** command returns the modem to the Command state. In the Command state, any of the modem commands can be initiated
P	None	Tells the modem to dial the telephone using pulses rather than tones
Qn	0,1	The modem can send result codes that report the modem's status. The command **Q0** tells the modem to send status codes. **Q1** turns this feature off
R	None	Put **R** at the end of a telephone number when calling an originate-only modem
Sr?	1..16	Reads the contents of one of the 16 modem registers, specified by **r**
Sr=n	r = 1..16	Sets modem register **r** to the value **n**
;	None	Places a semicolon at the end of the dial command to force the modem back to the Command state after the modem connects with the remote modem
T	None	Tells the modem to dial in Tone mode rather than Pulse mode
Vn	0,1	The modem can return codes in numbers or words. **V0** selects numeric codes; **V1** selects words
Xn	0,1	The modem can return a basic set of codes or an extended set. **X0** selects the basic set; **X1** selects the extended set
Z	None	Sets the modem to its cold-start configuration, which is like turning the modem off and on

Table 16-3.   Hayes Smartmodem Commands (*continued*)

The Circular Input Buffer

The *circular input buffer* is one of the central elements of an interrupt-driven communications program. Because data can arrive at the serial port at any time, the interrupt handler must be able to capture and process that data while the computer is busydoing something else. If the interrupt does not store the character in a buffer, the character will be lost before the program has time to capture it.

A circular buffer, which is an array of characters, resolves this problem by storing characters temporarily until your computer has time to catch up with the stream of input characters. The circular buffer is controlled by three **Integer** variables: **CircIn**, **CircOut**, and **CharsInBuf**. **CircIn** points to the next character that the interrupt routine puts into the input buffer, and **CircOut** points to the next character to be taken out of the buffer. **CharsInBuf** is the number of characters waiting in the buffer.

When no characters are in the input buffer, **CircIn** and **CircOut** are equal and **CharsInBuf** is zero. When data comes into the serial port, the interrupt routine adds the incoming characters to the buffer and increments both **CircIn** and **CharsInBuf**. Note that when the end of the buffer is reached, **CircIn** is set to 1, the beginning of the buffer. This is why the buffer is called circular.

The procedure **GetCharInBuf** checks whether **CharsInBuf** is greater than zero, which indicates that characters are present in the buffer. If **CharsInBuf** is greater than zero, the character in the buffer is removed, **CharsInBuf** is decremented, and **CircOut** is incremented. Thus, **CircOut** is constantly chasing **CircIn** to make sure that there are no characters in the input buffer.

Generally, your computer communicates at either 300 or 1200 bits per second. This is fairly slow compared to the speed at which the 8088 processes data. Therefore, the circular buffer should never be full. The **AsyncCommunications** program uses a 1K buffer, which should be more than enough for most communications purposes.

Memory-Resident Programs

When Borland's SideKick program burst onto the software market in 1984, it seemed like magic. Anytime, anywhere, a key stroke could call up a notepad, calculator, and other useful utilities. SideKick could do this because it is a memory-resident program, that is, one that locks itself in memory and is always there even when you run other programs.

Now, years later, memory-resident programs are fairly common. Even so, they remain a mystery to most programmers. This section explains how you can write limited-function memory-resident programs using Turbo Pascal.

The Reentrance Issue

Memory-resident programs are often referred to as TSRs because they terminate but stay resident in your computer's memory. Locking a program into memory is easy; getting it to do something useful once it is there can be terribly complicated. Most of the problems have to do with the fact that DOS is not reentrant. If you are not familiar with the term *reentrant*, don't be too concerned; it's a technical term with a simple explanation.

DOS provides a rich set of services to the programmer. These services are used for disk I/O, controlling the video display, keyboard input, and more. The problem is that a DOS service will not work if it is interrupted by another DOS service. Normally, this will never occur because DOS executes only one program at a time. With TSRs, however, the picture becomes more complicated. Consider this scenario: a program calls a DOS service to retrieve some data from a disk file. The DOS service begins executing, and at that moment, a TSR executes another DOS service. In short, the first DOS service is interrupted by the second. The result is disaster—the two DOS services collide and, most likely, your system crashes. That's what reentrance is all about.

There are two ways to deal with reentrance. The first approach is the easiest: make sure that your TSR never uses any DOS services. The second approach is more complicated: make sure that your TSR never executes a DOS service while another

DOS service is active. With the second approach, your TSR has the full power of the PC at its disposal, but requires some very complex programming. This chapter will limit its scope to the easy way, avoiding the use of DOS services at all times. If you are interested in writing more powerful TSRs, you will find a complete discussion and examples in *Turbo Pascal: Advanced Programmer's Guide* by this author (Berkeley, Calif.: Borland-Osborne/McGraw-Hill, 1988).

Going Resident

Included in the Turbo Pascal DOS unit is a procedure named **Keep**, which terminates your program but keeps it resident. **Keep** takes a single **Word** parameter, which is passed to DOS as an exit code. With the **Keep** procedure, making your program resident is the easiest, and last, step of the TSR process. Much has to be done before you get to the **Keep** command. For one thing, you have to decide how to activate your TSR once it's resident. You also have to install the interrupt handlers that will do the work of the TSR. Once you understand some basic concepts, you will be surprised how straightforward a TSR can be.

Activating the TSR

For a TSR to do anything, it has to be triggered. If you use SideKick, you know that the trigger is pressing the hot keys. In that case, the keyboard is the trigger. The computer's clock timer is another good trigger—one that is pulled about 18 times a second. In fact, the keyboard and the timer are the triggers used most often to activate TSRs. The one you select will depend on the application. The timer interrupt is great if you need to constantly check for something, like a value of a flag. The keyboard is better suited to TSRs that need to respond at the user's request. The program example given here uses both the timer and the keyboard to create a TSR that blanks your computer's screen after a certain amount of time has passed without keyboard activity. Pressing a key instantly restores the screen. Screen-blanking programs protect your monitor from "burn in," a problem that occurs when computers are left on, but unused, for long periods.

```
{$M 2000,0,0}
{$R-,S-,I-,D+,F+,V-,B-,N-,L+ }
Program ScreenSaver;
Uses
  DOS, CRT;

Const
  TimerInt = $08;          (* Timer interrupt *)
  KbdInt   = $09;          (* Keyboard interrupt *)
  TimeLimit : Word = 5460; (* Wait 5 minutes before blanking *)

Var
  Regs       : Registers;

  Cnt        : Word; (* Counts timer ticks          *)
  PortNum    : Word; (* Port used to disable video *)
  PortOff    : Word; (* Value to disable video      *)
  PortOn     : Word; (* Value to enable video       *)

  OldKbdVec   : Pointer;
  OldTimerVec : Pointer;

  i    : Real;
  Code : Word;

(***********************************************************)

Procedure STI;
InLine($FB);

(***********************************************************)

Procedure CLI;
InLine($FA);

(***********************************************************)

Procedure CallOldInt(Sub:Pointer);
Begin
InLine($9C/              { PUSHF                    }
       $FF/$5E/$06);  { CALL DWORD PTR [BP+6] }
End;
```

```
(*************************************************************)

Procedure Keyboard(Flags,CS,IP,AX,BX,CX,DX,
                   SI,DI,DS,ES,BP : Word); Interrupt;
Begin
CallOldInt(OldKbdVec);        (* Call original interrupt *)

If (Cnt >= TimeLimit) Then    (* Restore screen, if disabled *)
  Port[PortNum] := PortOn;
Cnt := 0;                     (* Reset counter *)
STI;
End;


(*************************************************************)

Procedure Clock(Flags,CS,IP,AX,BX,CX,DX,
                SI,DI,DS,ES,BP : Word); Interrupt;
Begin
CallOldInt(OldTimerVec);      (* Call original interrupt *)

If (Cnt > TimeLimit) Then     (* If timer limit is reached, *)
  Port[PortNum] := PortOff    (* disable video              *)
Else
  Inc(Cnt,1);                 (* Otherwise, increment counter *)
STI;
End;


(*************************************************************)

Begin
(* If user entered a number parameter, *)
(* compute the delay factor.           *)

If ParamCount = 1 Then
  Begin
  Val(ParamStr(1),i,code);
  If (Code = 0) and (i > 0) and (i < 11) Then
    TimeLimit := Trunc(i*18.2*60);
  End;

Regs.AH := $0F;               (* Determine the type of video *)
Intr($10,Regs);               (* adapter in use (Mono or CGA) *)

If Regs.AL = 7 Then           (* Mono adapter *)
  Begin
  PortNum := $3B8;
  PortOff := $21;
  PortOn  := $29;
  End
Else                          (* Color adapter *)
  Begin
  PortNum := $3D8;
  PortOff := $25;
  PortOn  := $2D;
  End;
```

```
(* Save original interrupts *)
GetIntVec(KbdInt, OldKbdVec);
GetIntVec(TimerInt, OldTimerVec);

(* Install new interrupts *)
SetIntVec(TimerInt, @Clock);
SetIntVec(KbdInt, @Keyboard);

Cnt := 0;   (* Initialize counter *)
Keep(0);    (* Terminate and stay resident *)
End.
```

Notice that the listing just given begins with the following compiler directive:

{$M 2000,0,0}

This directive limits the stack segment to 2000 bytes and allocates space for the heap. You must limit the amount of memory your TSR will use, especially the heap. If you do not limit the heap, your TSR will grab all available memory and leave none for any other programs.

Blanking the Screen

The TSR just given relies on a useful feature found on monochrome and CGA video adapters. This feature allows you to turn the video display off and on, without affecting the contents of the display. The function is accessed through a port: writing a specific value to the port turns the video off, another value turns it on. Unfortunately, the port address and the off/on values differ depending on the adapter in use (see Table 16-4). When the TSR starts, it must determine which adapter is in use and select the appropriate port address and off/on values.

How the TSR Works

Once installed, the TSR starts counting seconds. When the elapsed time passes a limit, the TSR blanks the screen. Time is

	Monochrome	CGA
Port Address	3B8h	3D8h
Turn Off	21h	25h
Turn On	29h	2Dh

Table 16-4. Video On/Off Control Values

counted from the last keystroke. Thus, if the limit is two minutes, the screen will go blank two minutes after the last keystroke. Once the screen is blank, pressing any key restores the screen, and the TSR begins counting time again.

This process depends on a counter that is continuously incremented. When a keystroke is detected, the counter is set back to zero and begins incrementing again. When the counter reaches a limit defined by the programmer, the TSR blanks the screen.

The Interrupt Handlers

The TSR relies on two interrupt handlers—**Keyboard** and **Clock**. The program attaches **Keyboard** to the keyboard interrupt ($09), so that anytime a key is pressed, **Keyboard** is activated. Likewise, **Clock**, the handler attached to the timer interrupt ($08), executes with every tick of the system clock. Notice that both handlers start out by calling the original interrupt (the one they replaced). This point is critical—your TSR must never interfere with the normal functioning of the keyboard and clock interrupts. The procedure **CallOldInt** is designed specifically for executing interrupts.

```
Procedure Keyboard(Flags,CS,IP,AX,BX,CX,DX,
                   SI,DI,DS,ES,BP : Word); Interrupt;
Begin
CallOldInt(OldKbdVec);          (* Call original interrupt *)

If (Cnt >= TimeLimit) Then      (* Restore screen, if disabled *)
  Port[PortNum] := PortOn;
Cnt := 0;                       (* Reset counter *)
STI;
End;
```

```
(*************************************************************)
Procedure Clock(Flags,CS,IP,AX,BX,CX,DX,
                SI,DI,DS,ES,BP : Word); Interrupt;
Begin
CallOldInt(OldTimerVec);      (* Call original interrupt *)

If (Cnt > TimeLimit) Then     (* If time limit is reached, *)
  Port[PortNum] := PortOff    (* disable video             *)
Else                                                       *)
  Inc(Cnt,1);                 (* Increment counter *)
STI;
End;
```

The **Clock** handler performs two tasks. First, it checks to see if the counter has passed the time limit. If so, the handler blanks the screen; if not, it increments the counter. The **Keyboard** handler does just the opposite. If the counter has passed the time limit, the handler restores the screen. In any case, the counter is reset to zero. As you can see, TSRs need not be complicated to be useful.

Installing the TSR requires four simple steps:

1. Save the original interrupts for the keyboard and timer.

2. Install your interrupt handlers.

3. Initialize the counter to zero.

4. Call **Keep** to terminate and stay resident.

```
(* Save original interrupts *)
GetIntVec(KbdInt, OldKbdVec);
GetIntVec(TimerInt, OldTimerVec);

(* Install new interrupts *)
SetIntVec(TimerInt, @Clock);
SetIntVec(KbdInt, @Keyboard);

Cnt := 0;    (* Initialize counter *)
Keep(0);     (* Terminate and stay resident *)
```

The example TSR sets the default time limit at 5460, about five minutes. When loading the TSR, the user can override the default by adding a number to the command line. The number indicates the number of minutes to wait before blanking the screen. For example, the command

```
SCRSAVE 1.5
```

sets the time interval to 90 seconds (1.5 minutes). You can specify any time limit up to ten minutes.

Interrupt processing is one of the most useful and challenging aspects of PC programming. With Turbo Pascal, you can easily write interrupt handlers for use in telecommunications and memory-resident programs. Though the concept of interrupts may be new to you, it is an area well worth exploring, for mastery of the use of interrupts is a sign of a well-versed programmer.

Turbo Pascal Procedure and Function Library

Fundamental Routines
Buffered String Input
Large String Procedures
Arithmetic Functions
File Encryption

Good programmers are pack rats; they store every function and procedure they come across because they know that sooner or later they will use them. Putting together a good library of procedures and functions takes years of coding, testing, and swapping information with other programmers. You can get a head start on your library with the procedures and functions in this chapter.

Fundamental Routines

Certain routines are so generally useful that you include them in almost all programs. Some of the most valuable ones write directly to screen memory, control the PC's sound generator, and center a string on the screen.

FastWrite

The fastest way to display text is to write directly to video memory. When you do so, you must use either an external assembler procedure or inline code; otherwise your procedure will create snow on the screen. This inline procedure writes a string to coordinates x and y in the colors you specify. The parameter **stype** must contain either "M" for monochrome displays or "C" for color displays.

```
Procedure FastWrite( x, y : Integer;
                     Var S : String;
                     fg, bg : Integer;
                     stype : Char);
Var
  i, b : Byte;
Begin
If UpCase(Stype) = 'M' Then
  Begin
  b := (bg Shl 4) + fg;
  x := ((x-1)*2) + ((y-1)*160);
  For i := 1 To Length(S) Do
    Begin
    Mem[$B000:X] := Byte(s[i]);
    Mem[$B000:X+1] := b;
    Inc(x,2);
    End;
  End
Else
Inline($50/              (* PUSH    AX        *)
       $53/              (* PUSH    BX        *)
       $51/              (* PUSH    CX        *)
       $52/              (* PUSH    DX        *)
       $1E/              (* PUSH    DS        *)
       $06/              (* PUSH    ES        *)
       $57/              (* PUSH    DI        *)
       $56/              (* PUSH    SI        *)
       $8B/$5E/<x/       (* MOV     BX,x      *)
       $8B/$46/<y/       (* MOV     AX,y      *)
       $4B/              (* DEC     BX        *)
       $48/              (* DEC     AX        *)
       $B9/$50/$00/      (* MOV     CX,0050   *)
       $F7/$E1/          (* MUL     CX        *)
       $03/$C3/          (* ADD     AX,BX     *)
       $B9/$02/$00/      (* MOV     CX,0002   *)
       $F7/$E1/          (* MUL     CX        *)
       $8B/$F8/          (* MOV     DI,AX     *)
       $8B/$5E/<bg/      (* MOV     BX,bg     *)
       $8B/$46/<fg/      (* MOV     AX,fg     *)
       $B9/$04/$00/      (* MOV     CX,0004   *)
       $D3/$E3/          (* SHL     BX,CL     *)
       $03/$D8/          (* ADD     BX,AX     *)
       $86/$DF/          (* XCHG    BL,BH     *)
       $BA/$DA/$03/      (* MOV     DX,03DA   *)
       $B8/$00/$B8/      (* MOV     AX,B800   *)
       $8E/$C0/          (* MOV     ES,AX     *)
       $C5/$76/<s/       (* LDS     SI,s      *)
       $8A/$0C/          (* MOV     CL,[SI]   *)
       $80/$F9/$00/      (* CMP     CL,00     *)
       $74/$15/          (* JZ      2E06      *)
       $FC/              (* CLD               *)
```

```
      $46/                (* INC      SI                *)
      $8A/$1C/            (* MOV      BL,[SI]           *)
      $EC/                (* IN       AL,DX             *)
      $A8/$01/            (* TEST     AL,01             *)
      $75/$FB/            (* JNZ      2DF5              *)
      $FA/                (* CLI                        *)
      $EC/                (* IN       AL,DX             *)
      $A8/$01/            (* TEST     AL,01             *)
      $74/$FB/            (* JZ       2DFB              *)
      $8B/$C3/            (* MOV      AX,BX             *)
      $AB/                (* STOSW                      *)
      $FB/                (* STI                        *)
      $E2/$EC/            (* LOOP     2DF2              *)
      $5E/                (* POP      SI                *)
      $5F/                (* POP      DI                *)
      $07/                (* POP      ES                *)
      $1F/                (* POP      DS                *)
      $5A/                (* POP      DX                *)
      $59/                (* POP      CX                *)
      $5B/                (* POP      BX                *)
      $58/                (* POP      AX                *)
      $E9/$00/$00/        (* JMP      2E11              *)
      $8B/$E5/            (* MOV      SP,BP             *)
      $5D/                (* POP      BP                *)
      $C2/$0E/$00);       (* RET      000E              *)
End;
```

GetScreenType

To use **FastWrite** and many other routines in this chapter, you must know what type of display adapter the computer uses. This information is reported by the procedure **GetScreenType**, shown here. **GetScreenType** uses BIOS interrupt **10h** with register AH set to **0Fh**, which returns the current video mode. If the returned mode is 7, the screen is monochrome.

```
Procedure GetScreenType(Var stype : Char);
Var
  Regs : Registers;
Begin
Regs.AH := $0F;
Intr($10,Regs);
If Regs.AL = 7 Then
  stype := 'M'
Else
  stype := 'C';
End;
```

Controlling the Cursor

The following three procedures control the size of the cursor, making it small or large, and also turn it off. The parameter **stype** contains the type of adapter in use ("M" or "C"). The color screen uses up to 8 lines for the cursor, while the monochrome screen uses as many as 14.

```
Procedure Cursor_Off(Stype : Char);
Var
  Regs : Registers;

Begin
With Regs Do
  Begin
  AH :=$01;
  CH :=$20;
  CL :=$20;
  END
Intro($10, Regs);
End;


(*********************************************)

Procedure Cursor_Small(Stype : Char);
Var
  Regs : Registers;

Begin
  Case Stype Of
  'M' :
    Begin
    With Regs Do
      Begin
      AH := $01;
      CH := 12;
      CL := 13;
      End;
    End;

  'C' :
    Begin
    With Regs Do
      Begin
      AH := $01;
      CH := 6;
      CL := 7;
```

```
        End;
      End;
    End;
    Intr($10, Regs);
End;


(*******************************************)

Procedure Cursor_Big(Stype : Char);
Var
  Regs : Registers;

Begin
  Case Stype Of
   'M' :
     Begin
     With Regs Do
       Begin
       AH := $01;
       CH := 0;
       CL := 13;
       End;
     End;

    'C' :
     Begin
     With Regs Do
       Begin
       AH := $01;
       CH := 0;
       CL := 7;
       End;
     End;
   End;
  Intr($10, Regs);
  End;
```

Centering Text

Center displays a string in the middle of a screen line you specify. The syntax of the command is just like that of the **FastWrite** command, except that no x coordinate is specified. Instead, the procedure calculates which x coordinate will properly center the string.

```
Procedure Center(y : Integer;
                 s : String;
                 fg,
                 bg : Integer;
                 stype : Char);
Var
    x : Integer;

Begin
x := 40 - (Length(s) Div 2);
FastWrite(x, y, s, fg, bg, Stype);
End;
```

Generating Sound

The Turbo Pascal commands **Sound** and **NoSound** control the PC's sound generator. **Sound** takes an **Integer** parameter that specifies the pitch of the tone. The tone continues until you issue the **NoSound** command. By using the **Delay** command, you can produce a tone that lasts a specified amount of time. The procedure **Beep**, presented here, uses these three commands to create a tone of a certain pitch and duration. The parameter **Freq** determines the pitch, and **Time** specifies the duration in milliseconds.

```
Procedure Beep(Freq, Time : Integer);
Begin
Sound(Freq);
Delay(Time);
NoSound;
End;
```

Buffered String Input

Turbo Pascal's input procedures **Read** and **ReadLn** are quite limited. When entering data, you can only delete backward with the BACKSPACE key. There is also no direct way to know if a function key has been pressed. The two procedures in this section, **InKey** and **InputStringShift**, extend your ability to control the keyboard.

InKey

Each time you press a function key, the PC generates a scan code along with a character. For example, function key F1 generates a scan code (#0) followed by ASCII character 59, the semicolon. The procedure **InKey** checks for the scan code when a key is pressed. If the code is present, **InKey** sets the parameter **FunctionKey** to TRUE.

InKey also allows you to control the cursor in two ways. The parameter **BeginCursor** determines the way the cursor looks when the procedure is waiting for a key to be pressed: "B" creates a big cursor, "S" a small cursor, and "O" no cursor. The parameter **EndCursor** tells **InKey** how it should leave the cursor after the key has been read.

Since keeping track of function-key codes is difficult, **InKey** sets a global scalar variable that refers to the function keys by name. This scalar is defined as shown here:

```
Type
  Keys = (NullKey, F1, F2, F3, F4, F5, F6, F7, F8, F9, F10,
         CarriageReturn, Tab, ShiftTab, Bksp, UpArrow,
         DownArrow, RightArrow, LeftArrow, DeleteKey,
         InsertKey, HomeKey, Esc, EndKey, TextKey,
         NumberKey, Space, PgUp, PgDn);

Var
  Key : Keys;
```

You can use this definition to easily program control loops by testing for a specific key, as shown here:

```
Repeat
InKey(Fk, Ch, 'O','O');
Until Key = F1;
```

In this example, the program keeps accepting keyboard input until you press the F1 key. The complete **InKey** procedure is shown here:

```
Procedure InKey(Var FunctionKey : Boolean;
                Var ch : Char;
                BeginCursor,
                EndCursor : Char);
Begin

  Case BeginCursor Of
  'B' : Cursor_Big(Stype);
  'S' : Cursor_Small(Stype);
  'O' : Cursor_Off(Stype);
  End;

FunctionKey := False;
ch := ReadKey;
If (ch = #0) Then
  Begin
  FunctionKey := True;
  ch := ReadKey;
  End;

If FunctionKey Then
  Case Ord(ch) Of
  15: (* shift Tab *)     key := ShiftTab;
  72: (* up arrow *)      key := UpArrow;
  80: (* down arrow *)    key := DownArrow;
  82: (* insert key *)    key := InsertKey;
  75: (* left arrow *)    key := LeftArrow;
  77: (* right arrow *)   key := RightArrow;
  73: (* pge up *)        key := PgUp;
  81: (* pge down *)      key := PgDn;
  71: (* home *)          key := HomeKey;
  79: (* End *)           key := EndKey;
  83: (* delete *)        key := DeleteKey;
  82: (* insert *)        key := InsertKey;
  59: (* F1 *)            key := F1;
  60: (* F2 *)            key := F2;
  61: (* F3 *)            key := F3;
  62: (* F4 *)            key := F4;
  63: (* F5 *)            key := F5;
  64: (* F6 *)            key := F6;
  65: (* F7 *)            key := F7;
  66: (* F8 *)            key := F8;
  67: (* F9 *)            key := F9;
  68: (* F10 *)           key := F10;
  End
Else
  Case Ord(ch) Of
   8: (* back Space *)    key := Bksp;
   9: (* Tab key *)       key := Tab;
  13: (* return *)        key := CarriageReturn;
```

```
27: (* escape *)          key := Esc;
32: (* Space bar *)       key := Space;

33..44, 47, 58..254:
  (* TextKey *)             key := TextKey;

45..46, 48..57:
  (* number key *)          key := NumberKey;
End;

Case EndCursor Of
'B' : Cursor_Big(Stype);
'S' : Cursor_Small(Stype);
'O' : Cursor_Off(Stype);
End;

End;
```

InputStringShift

A good input procedure allows you to use all the keys on the PC keyboard to delete characters with both the BACKSPACE and DEL keys, move back and forth with RIGHT and LEFT ARROW keys, and switch between Insert and Overwrite modes by pressing the INS key.

InputStringShift, provides your program with all these features. This procedure also lets you enter a string that is longer than the space on the screen you provided for input. For example, even if you set aside only 10 spaces on the screen for input, you still can accept strings as long as 255 characters. **InputStringShift** shifts the string back and forth in the input window as you type or use the arrow and DEL keys.

InputStringShift takes seven parameters, which are shown here:

```
Procedure InputStringShift(Var S : String;
                   WindowLength,
                   MaxLength,
                   X,Y : Integer;
                   FT : Char;
                   BackgroundChar : Integer);
```

S, a string variable, accepts the input; **WindowLength** specifies the size of the data-entry field (from 1 to 255); **MaxLength** is the maximum length of the string (from 1 to 255), and x and y are the screen coordinates of the first character of the input field. **FT** specifies the field type and can be either "T" for text or "N" for numeric. When the field is empty, blank spaces are filled with a character specified by the parameter **BackgroundChar**. Character 176 is a good choice because it creates a lightly shaded background.

```
Procedure InputStringShift(Var S : String;
                           WindowLength,
                           MaxLength,
                           X,Y : Integer;
                           FT : Char;
                           BackgroundChar : Integer);
Var
  xx, i, j, p : Integer;
  ch : Char;
  InsertOn,
  SpecialKey : Boolean;
  offset : Integer;
  TempStr : String;

Procedure XY(x, y : Integer);
Var
  Xsmall : Integer;
Begin
  Repeat
  Xsmall := x-80;
  If Xsmall > 0 Then
    Begin
    y := y+1;
    x := Xsmall;
    End;
  Until Xsmall <= 0;
GotoXY(x, y);
End;

(***********************************)

Procedure SetString;
Var
  i : Integer;
Begin
i := Length(s);
While s[i] = Char(BackgroundChar) Do
  i := i-1;
s[0] := Char(i);
cursor_small(stype);
End;

(***********************************)

Begin
j := Length(s)+1;
```

```
For i := j To MaxLength Do
  s[i] := Char(BackgroundChar);
s[0] := Char(MaxLength);

TempStr := Copy(s, 1, WindowLength);
FastWrite(x,y,TempStr,Yellow,Black,stype);
p := 1;
offset := 1;
InsertOn := True;

  Repeat
  xx := X+(p-offset);
  If (p-offset) = WindowLength Then
    xx := xx-1;

  XY(XX, Y);

  If InsertOn Then
    InKey(SpecialKey, ch, 'S', 'O')
  Else
    InKey(SpecialKey, ch, 'B', 'O');

  If (FT = 'N') Then
    Begin
    If (key = TextKey) Then
      Begin
      beep(100,250);
      key := NullKey;
      End
    Else If (ch = '-') And ((p > 1) Or (s[1] = '-')) Then
      Begin
      beep(100,250);
      key := NullKey;
      End
    Else If (ch = '.') Then
      Begin
      If Not((Pos('.', s) = 0) Or (Pos('.', s) = p)) Then
        Begin
        beep(100,250);
        key := NullKey;
        End
      Else If (Pos('.', s) = p) Then
        Delete(s, p, 1);
      End;
    End;

  Case key Of

    NumberKey,
    TextKey,
    Space :
      Begin
      If (Length(s) = MaxLength) Then
        Begin
        If p = MaxLength Then
          Begin
```

```
            Delete(s, MaxLength, 1);
            s := s+ch;
            If p = WindowLength+offset Then
              offset := offset+1;
            TempStr := Copy(s, offset, WindowLength);
            FastWrite(x,y,TempStr,Yellow,Black,stype);
            End
        Else
          Begin
          If InsertOn Then
            Begin
            Delete(s, MaxLength, 1);
            Insert(ch, s, p);
            If p = WindowLength+offset Then
              offset := offset+1;
            If p < MaxLength Then
              p := p+1;
            TempStr := Copy(s, offset, WindowLength);
            FastWrite(x,y,TempStr,Yellow,Black,stype);
            End
          Else        (* overwrite *)
            Begin
            Delete(s, p, 1);
            Insert(ch, s, p);
            If p = WindowLength+offset Then
              offset := offset+1;
            If p < MaxLength Then
              p := p+1;
            TempStr := Copy(s, offset, WindowLength);
            FastWrite(x,y,TempStr,Yellow,Black,stype);
            End;
          End;
        End
    Else
      Begin
      If InsertOn Then
        Begin
        Insert(ch, s, p);
        End
      Else
        Begin
        Delete(s, p, 1);
        Insert(ch, s, p);
        End;
      If p = WindowLength+offset Then
        offset := offset+1;
      If p < MaxLength Then
        p := p+1;

      TempStr := Copy(s, offset, WindowLength);
      FastWrite(x,y,TempStr,Yellow,Black,stype);
      End;
    End;

Bksp :
  Begin
```

```
    If p > 1 Then
      Begin
      p := p-1;
      Delete(s, p, 1);
      s := s+Char(BackgroundChar);
      If offset > 1 Then
        offset := offset-1;
      TempStr := Copy(s, offset, WindowLength);
      FastWrite(x,y,TempStr,Yellow,Black,stype);
      ch := ' ';
      End
    Else
      Begin
      beep(100,250);
      ch := ' ';
      p := 1;
      End;
    End;

LeftArrow :
  Begin
  If p > 1 Then
    Begin
    p := p-1;
    If p < offset Then
      Begin
      offset := offset-1;
      TempStr := Copy(s, offset, WindowLength);
      FastWrite(x,y,TempStr,Yellow,Black,stype);
      End;
    End
  Else
    Begin
    SetString;
    Exit;
    End;
  End;

RightArrow :
  Begin
  If (s[p] <> Char(BackgroundChar)) And (p < MaxLength)
    Then Begin
    p := p+1;
    If p = (WindowLength+offset) Then
      Begin
      offset := offset+1;
      TempStr := Copy(s, offset, WindowLength);
      FastWrite(x,y,TempStr,Yellow,Black,stype);
      End;
    End
  Else
    Begin
    SetString;
    Exit;
    End;
  End;
```

```
DeleteKey :
  Begin
  Delete(s, p, 1);
  s := s+Char(BackgroundChar);
  If ((Length(s)+1)-offset) >= WindowLength Then
    Begin
    TempStr := Copy(s, offset, WindowLength);
    FastWrite(x,y,TempStr,Yellow,Black,stype);
    End
  Else
    Begin
    TempStr := Copy(s, offset, WindowLength);
    FastWrite(x,y,TempStr,Yellow,Black,stype);
    End;
  End;

InsertKey :
  Begin
  If InsertOn Then
    InsertOn := False
  Else
    InsertOn := True;
  End;

Else If Not(key In [CarriageReturn, UpArrow, DownArrow,
                PgDn, PgUp, NullKey, Esc, Tab,
                F1, F2, F3, F4, F5, F6,
                F7, F8, F9, F10]) Then beep(100,250);

End;

Until (key In [CarriageReturn, UpArrow, DownArrow, PgUp,
            PgDn, Esc, Tab, F1, F3, F4, F5, F6, F7, F8,
            F9, F10]);

SetString;
End;
```

Large String Procedures

Turbo Pascal limits strings to a maximum of 255 characters.
While this is long enough for most strings, there are times when
you will need longer strings. The procedures in this section allow
you to define strings up to 32,767 characters long. The procedures assume a record type that includes an **Integer** field, which
keeps track of the string length, and an array of characters. An
example of this record type, **BigString**, follows:

```
Const
   MaxBigStrLen = 1000;
Type
   BigString = record
                   length : Integer;
                   ch : array [1..MaxBigStrLen] of Char;
                   End;
```

BigString can hold up to 1000 characters, and it can be easily extended by changing the value of **MaxBigStrLen**.

The procedures and functions in this section mimic the standard Turbo Pascal string commands; they use the same syntax and names, but begin with the word "Big." For example, the equivalent of Turbo Pascal's **Insert** command is the **BigInsert** command.

SetBigString

SetBigString initializes a big string, **st1**, to a value specified in parameter **s**.

```
Procedure SetBigString(Var st1 : BigString;s : String);
Var
   i : Integer;
Begin
For i := 1 To Length(s) Do
   st1.ch[i] := s[i];
st1.length := Length(s);
End;
```

BigConcat

Big strings cannot use the Turbo Pascal concatenation operator +. You can, however, simulate the **Concat** command, as shown in the procedure **BigConcat**, which concatenates **st2** to **st1**.

```
Procedure BigConcat(Var st1 : BigString;
                        st2 : BigString);
Var
   i : Integer;
Begin
Move(st2.ch[1],st1.ch[st1.length+1],st2.length);
st1.length := st1.length + st2.length;
End;
```

BigInsert

BigInsert inserts one **BigString** inside a target **BigString** starting at character **p**.

```
Procedure BigInsert(Var st1,st2 : BigString; p : Integer);
Var
  st3 : BigString;
  i,j : Integer;
Begin
Move(st2.ch[1],st3.ch[1],p-1);

Move(st1.ch[1],st3.ch[p],st1.length);

Move(st2.ch[p],st3.ch[p+st1.length],(st2.length-p)+1);

st3.length := st1.length + st2.length;
If st3.length > MaxBigStrLen Then
  st3.length := MaxBigStrLen;

Move(st3.length,st2.length,st3.length+2);
End;
```

BigDelete

BigDelete removes characters from a **BigString** starting at character **p**. It deletes as many characters as specified in the parameter **len**.

```
Procedure BigDelete(Var st1 : BigString; p,len : Integer);
Var
  st2 : BigString;

Begin
Move(st1.ch[1],st2.ch[1],p-1);
Move(st1.ch[(p+len)],st2.ch[p],(st1.length-(p+len))+1);
st2.length := (st1.length - len);
Move(st2.length,st1.length,st2.length+2);
End;
```

BigPos

The function **BigPos** returns the position of one **BigString** inside another **BigString**. To indicate the position, **BigPos** returns a positive number; if no match is found, it returns 0.

```
Function BigPos(Var st1,st2 : BigString) : Integer;
Var
  found : Boolean;
  i,j,StopFlag : Integer;
Begin
StopFlag := (st2.length - st1.length) + 1;
For i := 1 To StopFlag Do
  Begin
  found := True;
  j := 1;

    Repeat
    If st2.ch[i+j-1] <> st1.ch[j] Then
      found := False;
    j := j + 1;
    Until (Not found) Or (j = st1.length);

  If found Then
    Begin
    BigPos := i;
    Exit;
    End;
  End;
BigPos := 0;
End;
```

BigLength

The **BigLength** procedure returns an **Integer** with the length of a **BigString**.

```
Function BigLength(Var St1 : BigString) : Integer;
Begin
BigLength := st1.length;
End;
```

BigCopy

Because the Turbo Pascal string function **Copy** cannot be directly duplicated for large strings (Turbo Pascal cannot define a function using a **Record** data type) you must use **BigCopy**, which provides a result in the form of a procedure. **BigCopy** takes **len** characters from **st1**, starting from character **p**, and assigns them to **st2**.

```
Procedure BigCopy(Var st1,st2 : BigString; p,len : Integer);
Begin
Move(st1.ch[p],st2.ch[1],len);
st2.length := len;
End;
```

Arithmetic Functions

Most of the numerical procedures and functions your programs
need are available in Turbo Pascal. One thing these procedures
cannot do, however, is convert a fraction that is stored in a
string to a decimal equivalent or convert a decimal value into a
fraction. The two functions listed here, **Real _ To _ Frac** and
Frac _ To _ Real, do just that.

Real _ To _ Frac

Real _ To _ Frac accepts two parameters: **r**, the value to convert to decimal, and **d**, the denominator of the fraction. The
function returns a string that contains the integer portion of the
fraction, as well as the fractional portion. The two are separated
by a space.

```
Function Real_To_Frac(r : Real; d : Integer) : String;
Var
  is, ns, ds, s1, s2 : String[20];
  r1, r2, i, f : Real;
  code, p, n : Integer;

Begin
If r = 0 Then
  Begin
  Real_To_Frac := '0';
  Exit;
  End;

is := '0';
ds := '0';
ns := '0';

Str(r:0:8, s2);
p := Pos('.', s2);
If p > 0 Then
```

```
  s1 := Copy(s2, 1, p-1);

Delete(s2, 1, p-1);
Val(s1, i, code);
Str(i:0:0, is);

Val(s2, f, code);
If f > 0.0 Then
  Begin
  n := 0;
    Repeat
    n := n+1;
    r1 := n/d;
    Until r1 >= f;
  If (r1-f) > (1.0/(d*2.0)) Then
    n := n-1;

  While (Not Odd(n)) And (n > 0) Do
    Begin
    n := n DIV 2;
    d := d DIV 2;
    End;
    Str(n:0, ns);
    Str(d:0, ds);
    End;

If (ns = '1') And (ds = '1') Then
  Begin
  ns := '0';
  Val(is,r1,code);
  r1 := r1 + 1;
  Str(r1:0:0,is);
  End;

If (is = '0') And (ns = '0') Then
  Real_To_Frac := '0'
Else If ns = '0' Then
  Real_To_Frac := is
Else If is = '0' Then
  Begin
  If (ns = '1') And (ds = '1') Then
    Real_To_Frac := '1'
  Else
    Real_To_Frac := ns+'/'+ds;
  End
Else
  Real_To_Frac := is+' '+ns+'/'+ds
End;
```

Frac _ To _ Real

Frac _ To _ Real, a function of type **Real**, converts a string that contains a fraction into a real number. The procedure takes two parameters: **Frac**, the string that contains the fraction, and **code**, an integer that indicates an error in conversion. If **code** is equal to zero, no error occurred; if it is not equal to zero, an error did occur. The fraction is formed by an integer, a space, the numerator, a slash, and a denominator. The following are all legal fractions:

```
14 1/2
3/16
29
```

As you can see, both the whole number and the fractional portion are optional.

```
Function Frac_To_Real(Frac : String;
                      Var code : Integer) : Real;
Var
  n, d, i : Real;
  ns, ds, is : String[8];
  l,p,
  p_slash,
  p_space,
  j : Integer;

Begin
While (frac[1] = ' ') and (Length(frac) > 0) Do
  Delete(frac,1,1);
If frac = '' Then
  Begin
  Frac_To_Real := 0;
  Exit;
  End;

p_slash := Pos('/',frac);
p_space := Pos(' ',frac);

is := '';
ns := '';
ds := '';

If (p_slash > 0) Then
  Begin
  If (p_space > 0) Then
    Begin (* slash and space *)
    For j := 1 To (p_space-1) Do
      is := is + frac[j];
    For j := (p_space+1) To (p_slash-1) Do
      ns := ns + frac[j];
    For j := (p_slash+1) To Length(frac) Do
      ds := ds + frac[j];
```

```
        Val(is,i,code);
        Val(ns,n,code);
        Val(ds,d,code);

        Frac_To_Real := i + n / d;
        End
      Else
        Begin (* slash and no space *)
        For j := (p_space+1) To (p_slash-1) Do
          ns := ns + frac[j];
        For j := (p_slash+1) To Length(frac) Do
          ds := ds + frac[j];

        Val(ns,n,code);
        Val(ds,d,code);

        Frac_To_Real := n / d;
        End
      End
    Else
      Begin
      If (p_space > 0) Then
        Begin (* no slash and space *)
        For j := 1 To (p_space-1) Do
          is := is + frac[j];

        Val(is,i,code);
        Frac_To_Real := i;
        End
      Else
        Begin (* no slash and no space *)
        is := is + frac;
        Val(is,i,code);
        Frac_To_Real := i;
        End
      End;
    End;
```

File Encryption

Protecting letters, data, and programs is a common task. The only sure protection is to encode the file itself. The programs presented here do this, and offer some extra features as well.

Encode

The **Encode** program encrypts a file based on a password you provide. To encrypt a file, type

ENCODE FILENAME PASSWORD

If you enter the name of a file that does not exist, the program will abort with the message **File not found.** The program also checks to see whether the file was already encrypted. Files encrypted with **Encode** contain the word "LOCKED" in the first 6 bytes. When **Encode** finds these letters, it aborts and displays the message **File already locked.** This protection is necessary to keep you from encrypting the same file twice.

Note also that this program overwrites the original file with binary zeros and then erases the file. This keeps out snoopers who might browse through your disk with a special program for this purpose.

The password can be up to six characters long. It generates two seed values, which control the encryption. **Encode** stores these two seed values in the encrypted file so that the file can never be decoded with an incorrect password.

```
Program Encode;
Const
  MaxBuf = 30000;
Var
  password : String[6];
  seed1,
  seed2 : Byte;
  source,
  dest : File;
  buffer : Array [1..MaxBuf] Of Byte;
  BytesRead : Real;
  i : Integer;

(***********************************)

Procedure OpenFiles;
Const
  s : Array [1..6] Of Char = ('L','O','C','K','E','D');
Begin
Assign(source,ParamStr(1));
(*$I-*)
Reset(source,1);
(*$I+*)
If IOresult <> 0 Then
  Begin
  WriteLn('File not found.');
  Halt;
  End;

BlockRead(source,buffer,6);
```

```
If ((buffer[1] = ord('L')) And
    (buffer[2] = ord('O')) And
    (buffer[3] = ord('C')) And
    (buffer[4] = ord('K')) And
    (buffer[5] = ord('E')) And
    (buffer[6] = ord('D'))) Then
      Begin
      WriteLn('File already locked.');
      Halt;
      End;

Reset(source,1);
Assign(dest,'$$$$$.$$');
Rewrite(dest,1);
BlockWrite(dest,s,6);
BlockWrite(dest,seed1,1);
BlockWrite(dest,seed2,1);
End;

(************************************)

Procedure Getseed;
Var
  i,j : Integer;
Begin
seed1 := 0;
seed2 := 0;
password := ParamStr(2);

j := Length(password);
For i := 1 To Length(password) Do
  Begin
  seed1 := seed1 + (Ord(password[i]) * i);
  seed2 := seed2 + (Ord(password[i]) * j);
  j := j - 1;
  End;
End;

(************************************)

Procedure EncodeFile;
Var
  i1,i2 : Byte;
  rr : Integer;
Begin
i1 := seed1;
i2 := seed2;
BytesRead := 0;
BlockRead(source,buffer,MaxBuf,rr);
BytesRead := BytesRead + rr;
While rr > 0 Do
  Begin
  For i := 1 To rr Do
    Begin
    i1 := i1 - i;
    i2 := i2 + i;
```

```
    If odd(i) Then
      buffer[i] := buffer[i] - i1
    Else
      buffer[i] := buffer[i] + i2;
    End;
  BlockWrite(dest,buffer,rr);
  BlockRead(source,buffer,MaxBuf,rr);
  BytesRead := BytesRead + rr;
  End;
End;

(*************************************)

Procedure CloseFiles;
Var
  i : Integer;
Begin
Rewrite(source,1);
FillChar(buffer,MaxBuf,0);
While BytesRead > 0 Do
  Begin
  If BytesRead > MaxBuf Then
    BlockWrite(source,buffer,MaxBuf)
  Else
    Begin
    i := Trunc(BytesRead);
    BlockWrite(source,buffer,i);
    End;
  BytesRead := BytesRead - MaxBuf;
  End;
Close(source);
Close(dest);
Erase(source);
Rename(dest,ParamStr(1));
End;

(*************************************)

Begin
If Paramcount <> 2 Then
  Begin
  WriteLn('Syntax: ENCODEIT Filename password');
  Halt;
  End;
Getseed;
OpenFiles;
EncodeFile;
CloseFiles;
End.
```

Decode

Decode restores files that have been encrypted with the **Encode** program. The syntax for **Decode** is

DECODE FILENAME PASSWORD

Decode first checks to see if the file is locked; locked files have the letters "LOCKED" in the first 6 bytes. Next it uses the password to generate two seed values and compares those to the seed values stored in the encrypted file. If the seed values match, the program continues; if not, it displays the message **Wrong password** and stops.

```pascal
Program Decode;
Const
  MaxBuf = 30000;
Var
  password : String[6];
  source,
  dest     : File;
  buffer   : Array [1..MaxBuf] Of Byte;
  BytesRead : Real;
  seed1,
  seed1x,
  seed2,
  seed2x : Byte;
  i : Integer;

(************************************)

Procedure OpenFiles;
Const
  s : Array [1..6] Of Char = ('L','O','C','K','E','D');
Begin
Assign(source,ParamStr(1));
(*$I-*)
Reset(source,1);
(*$I+*)
If IOresult <> 0 Then
  Begin
  WriteLn('File not found.');
  Halt;
  End;
BlockRead(source,buffer,6);
If Not ((buffer[1] = ord('L')) And
        (buffer[2] = ord('O')) And
        (buffer[3] = ord('C')) And
        (buffer[4] = ord('K')) And
        (buffer[5] = ord('E')) And
        (buffer[6] = ord('D'))) Then
         Begin
         WriteLn('File not locked.');
         Halt;
         End;

BlockRead(source,seed1x,1);
```

```
  BlockRead(source,seed2x,1);

  If ((seed1 <> seed1x) Or (seed2 <> seed2x)) Then
    Begin
    WriteLn('Wrong password.');
    Halt;
    End;

  Assign(dest,'$$$$$.$$');
  Rewrite(dest,1);
  End;

(*************************************)

Procedure Getseed;
Var
  i,j : Integer;
Begin
seed1 := 0;
seed2 := 0;
password := ParamStr(2);

j := Length(password);
For i := 1 To Length(password) Do
  Begin
  seed1 := seed1 + (ord(password[i]) * i);
  seed2 := seed2 + (ord(password[i]) * j);
  j := j - 1;
  End;
End;

(*************************************)

Procedure DecodeFile;
Var
  i1,i2 : Byte;
  rr : Integer;
Begin
i1 := seed1;
i2 := seed2;
BytesRead := 0;
BlockRead(source,buffer,MaxBuf,rr);
BytesRead := BytesRead + rr;
While rr > 0 Do
  Begin
  For i := 1 To rr Do
    Begin
    i1 := i1 - i;
    i2 := i2 + i;
    If odd(i) Then
      buffer[i] := buffer[i] + i1
    Else
      buffer[i] := buffer[i] - i2;
    End;
  BlockWrite(dest,buffer,rr);
  BlockRead(source,buffer,MaxBuf,rr);
```

```pascal
    BytesRead := BytesRead + rr;
    End;
End;


(***********************************)

Procedure CloseFiles;
Var
  i : Integer;
Begin
Rewrite(source,1);
FillChar(buffer,MaxBuf,0);
While BytesRead > 0 Do
  Begin
  If BytesRead > MaxBuf Then
    BlockWrite(source,buffer,MaxBuf)
  Else
    Begin
    i := Trunc(BytesRead);
    BlockWrite(source,buffer,i)
    End;
  BytesRead := BytesRead - MaxBuf;
  End;
Close(source);
Close(dest);
Erase(source);
Rename(dest,ParamStr(1));
End;


(***********************************)

Begin
If ParamCount <> 2 Then
  Begin
  WriteLn('Syntax: DECODEIT Filename password');
  Halt;
  End;
Getseed;
OpenFiles;
DecodeFile;
CloseFiles;
End.
```

Optimizing Turbo Pascal Programs

At the very least, a program should be free from bugs. Users expect programs to work as advertised, from start to finish, day in and day out. But the fact that a program functions properly is not always enough: users also want programs that work quickly. Optimization is the process of making sure your program runs as fast as it can without compromising the basic functions it performs. This chapter suggests methods you can use to optimize your programs, streamline your code, and eliminate unnecessary bottlenecks.

Optimization: Perfection Versus Excellence

The cost of excellence is reasonable; the cost of perfection is exorbitant. Some programmers spend hours optimizing even unimportant sections of code. Good programmers, however, learn to select the code that can benefit most from optimization, and avoid wasting time on trivial improvements.

There are two criteria to consider when selecting the parts of a program to optimize. First, can the code be improved enough to make a difference? It's quite possible, especially if you are an experienced programmer, that you wrote the section optimally the first time. In most cases, however, even well-written sections can benefit from closer inspection.

Second, the improvements you make must be noticeable to the user. If the user will not notice the difference in speed, your efforts at optimization are wasted. If, however, you feel a section of code can be improved and that the improvement will be noticed by the user, start optimizing.

Approaches to Optimization

Speed is just one goal of optimization; others include minimizing code size and reducing the data space required. With RAM in plentiful supply, however, speed is by far the highest concern. Therefore, the suggestions presented in this chapter are directed to making your programs faster.

The most obvious way to speed up a program is to write sections in assembler and include them in your code as external procedures or inline code. This approach, discussed in Chapter 13, requires time and an extensive knowledge of assembler. Before going to this extreme, you can gain a lot of speed simply by using Turbo Pascal more efficiently. A well-written Turbo Pascal procedure can run quite fast and is much easier to write, debug, and maintain than assembler code.

Timing Program Execution

You cannot optimize without having a way to measure just how much you gain or lose when you change a section of code. You may be surprised to find that a minor change can lead to a substantial increase in speed, while larger changes may do little to increase speed.

The guideline you need is contained in the procedures **ClockOn** and **ClockOff**, listed as follows in a unit named **TIMER**.

```
Unit TIMER;
(********************************************************)
Interface
(********************************************************)
Uses DOS;

Procedure ClockOn;

Procedure ClockOff;

(********************************************************)
Implementation
(********************************************************)

Var
  h,m,s,s100 : Word;
  StartClock,
  StopClock : Real;

(********************************************************)

Procedure ClockOn;
Begin
GetTime(h,m,s,s100);
StartClock := (h * 3600) + (m * 60) + s + (s100 / 100);
End;

(********************************************************)

Procedure ClockOff;
Begin
GetTime(h,m,s,s100);
StopClock := (h * 3600) + (m * 60) + s + (s100 / 100);
WriteLn('Elapsed time = ',(StopClock - StartClock):0:2);
End;

End.
```

The **TIMER** unit uses the procedure **GetTime** from the
DOS unit to get the time from the system clock. The procedures
ClockOn and **ClockOff** both call **GetTime**; both use the result
to calculate the current time in seconds. **ClockOn** stores its
result in the variable **StartClock**, while **ClockOff** computes the
value of **StopClock**, subtracts **StartClock** from it, and reports
the elapsed time in seconds. The program named **TestLoop**
demonstrates how to use the procedures in the **TIMER** unit.

```
Program TestLoop;
Uses CRT, TIMER;
Var
  i,j : integer;

Begin
ClrScr;
```

```
j := 0;

ClockOn;  (* Initialize value of StartClock. *)

For i := 1 To MaxInt Do
  j := j + 1;

ClockOff; (* Display elapsed time. *)

WriteLn;
Write('Press ENTER...');
ReadLn;
End.
```

TestLoop times the execution of a simple **For-Do** loop by preceding it with a call to **ClockOn** and following it with a call to **ClockOff**. When you run this program, you will see the following message:

```
Elapsed time = 0.99

Press ENTER...
```

This message indicates that the **For-Do** loop took 0.99 seconds to execute. All timings reported in this chapter are based on a PC-compatible computer running at 4.77 MHz. Your timings may differ, depending on the computer you use. The specific time you get, however, is unimportant. The value of the timing procedures is to evaluate the relative speed of different procedures that produce the same result. The program listed here demonstrates how to compare the speed of two similar routines.

```
Program TestProcs;
Uses CRT, TIMER;
Const
  ArrLen = MaxInt;
Type
  ArrType = Array [1..ArrLen] Of Char;
Var
  a : ArrType;
  i : Integer;

(*********************************)

Procedure Init1(Var a : ArrType;
                    L : Integer);
Begin
FillChar(a,L,0);
End;
```

```
(********************************)

Procedure Init2(Var a : ArrType;
                    L : Integer);
Var
  i : Integer;
Begin
For i := 1 To L Do
  a[i] := #0;
End;

(********************************)

Begin
ClrScr;

ClockOn;
Init1(a,ArrLen);
ClockOff;

ClockOn;
Init2(a,ArrLen);
ClockOff;

WriteLn;
Write('Press ENTER...');
ReadLn;
End.
```

The program just given uses two procedures, **Init1** and **Init2**, both of which initialize an array of characters to all binary zeros. **Init1** uses the Turbo Pascal standard procedure **FillChar** to initialize the array, while **Init2** accomplishes the same goal with a **For-Do** loop.

The results of this program show that **Init1** takes 0.05 seconds to execute, while **Init2** requires 1.38 seconds. It is easy to see which is the better routine.

Optimizing Control Structures

When you optimize a program, control structures should be one of the first things you check. Because Turbo Pascal offers so many flexible control structures, it is easy to write control structures your first time through that are less than optimal.

Nested If-Then Statements

If-Then statements execute Boolean comparison statements, which can include numerous individual comparisons. When you optimize **If-Then** statements, the goal is to minimize the number of comparisons the computer executes. The procedure listed here demonstrates a very poor use of **If-Then** statements:

```
Procedure BooleanTest1;
Begin
If (i = 1) Then    (* Comparison number 1 *)
  Begin
  a := '1';
  End;
If (i = 2) Then    (* Comparison number 2 *)
  Begin
  a := '2';
  End;
If (i = 3) Then    (* Comparison number 3 *)
  Begin
  a := '3';
  End;
If (i = 4) Then    (* Comparison number 4 *)
  Begin
  a := '4';
  End;
If (i <> 1) and
   (i <> 2) and
   (i <> 3) and
   (i <> 4) Then   (* Comparison number 5 *)
  Begin
  a := 'X';
  End;
End;
```

This routine executes one of five branches, depending on the value of variable **i**. Notice that all five comparisons are executed each time the code section is processed. This process can be made far more efficient with the following code:

```
Procedure BooleanTest2;
Begin
If (i = 1) Then         (* Comparison number 1 *)
  Begin
  a := '1';
  End
Else If (i = 2) Then    (* Comparison number 2 *)
  Begin
  a := '2';
```

```
      End
Else If (i = 3) Then      (* Comparison number 3 *)
   Begin
   a := '3';
   End
Else If (i = 4) Then      (* Comparison number 4 *)
   Begin
   a := '4';
   End
Else                      (* Comparison number 5 *)
   Begin
   a := 'X';
   End;
End;
```

Here, the **Else-If** statement reduces the number of comparisons required. For example, if **i** equals 1, only one comparison is executed. At the other extreme, when **i** is less than 1 or greater than 4, all four comparisons are required.

While the **If-Then-Else** structure is clearly efficient, the **Case** control structure is even more efficient. This code section shows how the **Case** command would replace the **If-Then-Else** statements:

```
Procedure BooleanTest3;
Begin

   Case i Of

   1 :
      Begin
      a := '1';
      End;

   2 :
      Begin
      a := '2';
      End;

   3 :
      Begin
      a := '3';
      End;

   4 :
      Begin
      a := '4';
      End;

   Else
      Begin
```

```
      a := 'X';
    End;

  End;

End;
```

While the **Case** statement does not eliminate the number of potential comparisons, under certain circumstances, it does perform them a bit more efficiently. These three procedures were compared in the following program, which repeated each procedure 30,000 times.

```
Program BooleanTest;
Uses CRT, TIMER;
Var
  j,i : Word;
  a : Char;

(***************************************************)

Procedure BooleanTest1;
Begin
If (i = 1) Then    (* Comparison number 1 *)
  Begin
  a := '1';
  End;
If (i = 2) Then    (* Comparison number 2 *)
  Begin
  a := '2';
  End;
If (i = 3) Then    (* Comparison number 3 *)
  Begin
  a := '3';
  End;
If (i = 4) Then    (* Comparison number 4 *)
  Begin
  a := '4';
  End;
If (i <> 1) and
   (i <> 2) and
   (i <> 3) and
   (i <> 4) Then    (* Comparison number 5 *)
  Begin
  a := 'X';
  End;
End;

(***************************************************)

Procedure BooleanTest2;
Begin
If (i = 1) Then            (* Comparison number 1 *)
  Begin
```

```
    a := '1';
    End
Else If (i = 2) Then      (* Comparison number 2 *)
    Begin
    a := '2';
    End
Else If (i = 3) Then      (* Comparison number 3 *)
    Begin
    a := '3';
    End
Else If (i = 4) Then      (* Comparison number 4 *)
    Begin
    a := '4';
    End
Else                      (* Comparison number 5 *)
    Begin
    a := 'X';
    End;
End;


(******************************************************)

Procedure BooleanTest3;
Begin

    Case i Of

    1 :
       Begin
       a := '1';
       End;

    2 :
       Begin
       a := '2';
       End;

    3 :
       Begin
       a := '3';
       End;

    4 :
       Begin
       a := '4';
       End;

    Else
       Begin
       a := 'X';
       End;
    End;
End;


(******************************************************)
```

```
Begin
ClrScr;

WriteLn('Random values of i...');
WriteLn;
RandSeed := 0;
ClockOn;
For j := 1 To 30000 Do
  Begin
  i := Random(7);
  BooleanTest1;
  End;
ClockOff;

RandSeed := 0;
ClockOn;
For j := 1 To 30000 Do
  Begin
  i := Random(7);
  BooleanTest2;
  End;
ClockOff;

RandSeed := 0;
ClockOn;
For j := 1 To 30000 Do
  Begin
  i := Random(7);
  BooleanTest3;
  End;
ClockOff;

WriteLn;
WriteLn;
WriteLn('i = 1...');
WriteLn;

i := 1;
ClockOn;
For j := 1 To 30000 Do
  BooleanTest1;
ClockOff;

ClockOn;
For j := 1 To 30000 Do
  BooleanTest2;
ClockOff;

ClockOn;
For j := 1 To 30000 Do
  BooleanTest3;
ClockOff;

WriteLn;
WriteLn;
WriteLn('i = 5...');
```

```
WriteLn;

i := 5;
ClockOn;
For j := 1 To 30000 Do
  BooleanTest1;
ClockOff;

ClockOn;
For j := 1 To 30000 Do
  BooleanTest2;
ClockOff;

ClockOn;
For j := 1 To 30000 Do
  BooleanTest3;
ClockOff;

WriteLn;
Write('Press ENTER...');
ReadLn;

End.
```

This program produced the results shown in Table 18-1. Overall, the **If-Then-Else** statement is almost as efficient as the **Case** statement, but both are much more efficient than the **If-Then** statements.

Testing Values in Boolean Expressions

If-Then statements, Repeat-Until loops, and While-Do loops all require Boolean expressions, expressions that compare a variable to one or more test values. These tests can take several forms, from chained comparisons to set comparisons. Which one is most efficient?

	Random	Value of i 1	5
BooleanTest1	9.00	3.18	3.96
BooleanTest2	7.97	1.98	2.91
BooleanTest3	7.63	2.03	2.53

Table 18-1.   Results of Boolean Tests

Perhaps some will be surprised that set comparisons, while more compact to write, are far less efficient in operation. For example, the following **Set Inclusion** statement tests if a character variable **Ch** contains a letter in the set ['A','B','C']:

```
If Ch in ['A','B','C'] Then ...
```

The same comparison is performed far more efficiently with this chained comparison:

```
If (Ch = 'A') Or (Ch = 'B') Or (Ch = 'C') Then
```

If that surprises you, try tracing through both statements using the Turbo Debugger. You will find that the chained comparison requires far less code.

The program called **TestChar** demonstrates the difference in speed between a **Set Inclusion** statement and two similar forms of **If-Then** statements.

```
Program TestChar;
Uses CRT, TIMER;
Var
  i : Integer;
  Ch : Char;

Begin
ClrScr;
Ch := 'A';

(* Set Inclusion Statement. *)

ClockOn;
For i := 1 to MaxInt Do
  Begin
  If Ch in ['A','B','C'] Then
    Begin
    End;
  End;
ClockOff;

(* If-Then Statement *)

ClockOn;
For i := 1 To MaxInt Do
  Begin
  If (Ch = 'A') or (Ch = 'B') or (Ch = 'C') Then
    Begin
```

```
      End;
    End;
ClockOff;

(* Nested If-Then statement *)

ClockOn;
For i := 1 To MaxInt Do
  Begin
   If (Ch = 'A') Then
     Begin
     End
   Else If (Ch = 'B') Then
     Begin
     End
   Else If (Ch = 'C') Then
     Begin
     End;
  End;
ClockOff;

WriteLn;
WriteLn;
WriteLn;

Ch := 'C';

(* Set Inclusion Statement. *)

ClockOn;
For i := 1 To MaxInt Do
  Begin
   If Ch in ['A','B','C'] Then
     Begin
     End;
  End;
ClockOff;

(* If-Then Statement *)

ClockOn;
For i := 1 To MaxInt Do
  Begin
   If (Ch = 'A') or (Ch = 'B') or (Ch = 'C') Then
     Begin
     End;
  End;
ClockOff;

(* Nested If-Then statement *)

ClockOn;
For i := 1 To MaxInt Do
  Begin
   If (Ch = 'A') Then
     Begin
```

```
      End
    Else If (Ch = 'B') Then
      Begin
      End
    Else If (Ch = 'C') Then
      Begin
      End;
    End;
  ClockOff;
  WriteLn;
  Write('Press ENTER...');
  ReadLn;

End.
```

When the character in question is "A," the loop using the set-inclusion comparison requires 2.96 seconds to execute (Table 18-2), while the chained comparison and nested **If-Then-Else** statements require only 1.05 and 1.04 seconds, respectively. When the character is the last one tested (in this case the letter "C"), the results are similar, though the performance of the set-inclusion comparison degrades less than the other two.

Optimizing Arithmetic

The speed of your calculations depends largely on the type of variables involved (**Integer** or **Real**) and the type of operation involved (addition, subtraction, multiplication, or division). **Integer** computations always require much less time than computations with **Real** variables. The following program, **MathComp**,

	Value of Ch	
Comparison	**"A"**	**"C"**
Set inclusion	2.96	3.13 (Seconds)
Chained comparison	1.05	1.43
Nested If-Then-Else	1.04	1.54

Table 18-2.   Timings for Character Comparisons

compares the speed of integer and real computations for addition operations. You can change the program to test other operations.

```
Program MathComp;
Uses CRT,TIMER;
Var
  i,
  a, b, c : Integer;
  x, y, z : Real;

Begin
ClrScr;
a := 1;
b := 1;
ClockOn;
For i := 1 To 10000 Do
  Begin
  c := a + b;
  End;
ClockOff;

x := 1.0;
y := 1.0;
ClockOn;
For i := 1 To 10000 Do
  Begin
  z := x + y;
  End;
ClockOff;
WriteLn;
Write('Press ENTER...');
ReadLn;
End.
```

	Integer	Real
Addition	0.33	2.03
Subtraction	0.33	3.19
Multiplication	0.60	4.89
Division	0.66	13.02

Table 18-3.   Timing for Various Arithmetic Operations

Table 18-3 shows the execution times for **Integer**s and **Real**s for the four arithmetic operators. As you can see, **Integer** computations are almost ten times faster than **Real** computations across the board.

Division involving **Real** variables is the slowest of all the computations, requiring over twice as much time as multiplication operations and four times as much as addition or subtraction.

In general, avoid using **Real**s when **Integer**s will do. If you must use **Real**s, avoid division when possible. For example, the equation

$$X / 4.0$$

can be changed to

$$X * 0.25$$

which is far faster.

Some programs that use a lot of calculations contain many complicated formulas. In such programs, optimization should be second to readability. If, in the process of optimization, you make a subtle change to a complicated formula, you may never find your error.

Optimizing File Operations

Even when you use a hard disk, disk file input and output are slow operations. This is especially true for Turbo Pascal text files. You can speed up your text-file operations by specifying a text buffer for the file. The process is demonstrated in the program listed here:

```
Program TestTextBuf;
Uses CRT, TIMER;
Var
  Buf1 : Array [1..256] of Char;
  Buf2 : Array [1..1023] of Char;
  Buf3 : Array [1..1024] of Char;
```

```
   Buf4 : Array [1..4096] of Char;
   T : Text;

(***************************************************)

Procedure WriteFile;
Var
   s : String;
   i : Integer;
Begin
FillChar(s,SizeOf(s),'A');
s[0] := Chr(255);
For i := 1 To 100 Do
   WriteLn(T,s);
End;

(***************************************************)

Begin
ClrScr;
Assign(T,'TEST.X');

Rewrite(T);
ClockOn;
WriteFile;
ClockOff;

Rewrite(T);
SetTextBuf(T,Buf1);
ClockOn;
WriteFile;
ClockOff;

Rewrite(T);
SetTextBuf(T,Buf2);
ClockOn;
WriteFile;
ClockOff;

Rewrite(T);
SetTextBuf(T,Buf3);
ClockOn;
WriteFile;
ClockOff;

Rewrite(T);
SetTextBuf(T,Buf4);
ClockOn;
WriteFile;
ClockOff;

Close(T);
Erase(T);

WriteLn;
Write('Press ENTER...');
```

```
ReadLn;
End.
```

This program declares a text file named **T** and four buffers of different sizes: 256 bytes, 1023 bytes, 1024 bytes, and 4096 bytes. If you do not specify a buffer to a text file, Turbo Pascal assigns a default buffer of 128 bytes.

Generally speaking, the larger the buffer, the faster your input and output operations will be. This is not strictly the case with Turbo Pascal text files, as Table 18-4 shows.

Output to the default 128-byte buffer is fairly slow (5.38 seconds) as is output to a 200-byte buffer (5.16 seconds). Surprisingly, a 1023-byte buffer is actually slower than the default buffer. Yet, increasing the buffer by one byte, to 1024 bytes, cuts the elapsed time to just 2.20 seconds. Increasing the buffer to 4096 bytes brings the elapsed time down to 1.43 seconds.

As for the difference in time between the 1023-byte buffer and the 1024-byte buffer, why does adding one byte cause a significant increase in speed? Disks are organized into 512-byte sectors that are organized into clusters of 1024 bytes for floppy disk and from 2048 to 8192 bytes for hard disks. When a buffer's size is set equal to the size of a cluster, the disk drive does less work with each read and write. In general, the best buffer sizes are multiples of 1024 bytes.

Optimizing String Operations

The **String** data type is an important part of Turbo Pascal, largely due to the standard procedures provided for string ma-

Buffer size	Time
128 bytes (Default)	5.38
256 bytes	5.16
1023 bytes	6.87
1024 bytes	2.20
4096 bytes	1.43

Table 18-4.   Impact of Text Buffers of Various Sizes

nipulation. However, string procedures, especially concatenation, can be quite slow.

The program called **TestProcs** uses two procedures, each of which creates a string that contains 100 characters, all of which are "A's."

```pascal
Program TestProcs;
Uses CRT, TIMER;
Var
  i : Integer;

(*********************************)

Procedure Concat1;
Var
  i : Integer;
  s : String;
Begin
s := '';
For i := 1 To 100 Do
  s := s + 'A';
End;

(*********************************)

Procedure Concat2;
Var
  i : Integer;
  s : String;
Begin
For i := 1 To 100 Do
  s[i] := 'A';
s[0] := Chr(100); (* Set string length. *)
End;

(*********************************)

Begin
ClrScr;

ClockOn;
For i := 1 To 100 Do Concat1;
ClockOff;

ClockOn;
For i := 1 To 100 Do Concat2;
ClockOff;

WriteLn;
Write('Press ENTER...');
ReadLn;
End.
```

Procedure **Concat1**, which uses the Turbo Pascal concatenation operator, requires 6.32 seconds, while procedure **Concat2**, which uses an index to the string's characters, needs only 0.27 second.

The **Copy** command can also be replaced to increase speed, as demonstrated by the **CopyString** program:

```
Program CopyString;
Uses CRT, TIMER;
Var
  p,i,j : Integer;
  s1,s2 : String;

Begin
ClrScr;

s1 := 'ABCDEFGHIJKLMNOP';

ClockOn;
For i := 1 To 10000 Do
  s2 := Copy(s1,3,5); (* Using the Copy command. *)
ClockOff;

ClockOn;
For i := 1 To 10000 Do
  Begin
  Move(s1[3],s2[1],5); (* Using the Move command. *)
  s2[0] := Chr(5);      (* Set the length byte. *)
  End;
ClockOff;

WriteLn;
Write('Press ENTER...');
ReadLn;
End.
```

In **CopyString**, the command

```
    s2 := Copy(s1,3,5);
```

is replaced by the statements

```
    Move(s1[3],s2[1],5);
    s2[0] := Chr(5);
```

The **Move** command copies a portion of **s1** into **s2**, while the second statement correctly sets the length of **s2**. The **Copy** command requires 2.58 seconds for 10,000 iterations, compared with only 1.32 seconds for the optimized code.

Compiler Directives

Compiler directives control error checking features in Turbo Pascal. The three directives that have an impact on execution speed are the **R** directive, which checks the range of indexes; the **S** directive, which checks the stack errors; and the **B** directive, which enables short-circuit Boolean evaluation.

Range Checking

When enabled, the Range Checking (**R**) compiler directive adds code that checks for out-of-range conditions when assigning numeric values or accessing array elements. This additional code significantly increases overhead in your program, with noticeable results.

```
{$R+}
Program DirectiveTest;
Uses CRT, TIMER;
Var
  i,j : Integer;
  a : array [1..100] of Byte;

Begin
ClrScr;

Write('Range checking...');
ClockOn;
For i := 1 To 1000 Do
For j := 1 To 100 Do
  a[j] := 1;
ClockOff;

WriteLn;
Write('Press ENTER...');
ReadLn;
End.
```

When run with the **{$R+}** directive, this program takes 9.45 seconds; with **{$R−}**, it takes only 3.08 seconds. While range checking is essential during program development, you must disable this compiler directive to get the best performance for your program.

Stack Checking

The Stack Checking compiler directive (**{$S+}**) instructs the compiler to make sure that the stack has enough memory for local variables before calling a procedure. This is extremely important because stack errors are among the most difficult to trace. The program listed here demonstrates what effect stack checking can have on a program's performance.

```
Program DirectiveTest;
Uses CRT, TIMER;
Var
  i : Integer;
  s : String;

(********************************************************)

Procedure Proc;
Var
  x : array [1..5000] of Word;
Begin
End;

(********************************************************)

Begin
ClrScr;
s := 'AAAAAAAAAAAAAAAAAAAAAAAAAAAAAAAAAAAAAAAAAAAAAAAA';

Write('Stack checking...');
ClockOn;
For i := 1 To 10000 Do
Proc;
ClockOff;

WriteLn;
Write('Press ENTER...');
ReadLn;
End.
```

This program makes repeated calls to a procedure, **Proc**, that uses a large local array variable. When the stack checking directive is enabled ({$S+}), the program executes in 0.88 second; when disabled ({$S−}), it executes in just 0.49 second. As with range checking, stack checking is essential during program development and testing. Once completed, however, the directive should be turned off to maximize performance.

Boolean Evaluation

Turbo Pascal supports two types of Boolean evaluation: complete and short-circuit. Which one you choose can have a dramatic impact on the efficiency of your program. Consider the following Boolean evaluation:

```
If (a = 1) Or (a = 2) Or (a = 3) Then
```

If **a** is equal to 1, then there is no need to test any of the other conditions in the statement. Yet, under complete evaluation, that is exactly what happens. Short-circuit evaluation, as its name implies, jumps out of the Boolean expression as soon as a condition is met that assures a correct answer. The program listed here demonstrates the impact of Boolean evaluation on program performance.

```
{$B+}
Program DirectiveTest;
Uses CRT, TIMER;
Var
  a,i : Integer;

(***********************************************************)

Begin
ClrScr;

ClockOn;
a := 1;
For i := 1 To 10000 Do
  Begin
```

```
      If (a = 1) Or (a = 2) Or (a = 3) Then
        Begin
        End;
      End;
   ClockOff;

   WriteLn;
   Write('Press ENTER...');
   ReadLn;
   End.
```

When short-circuit evaluation is enabled ({$B −}), the program executes in 0.27 second; under complete evaluation ({$B +}), execution takes 0.71 second. Unless you have good reason to insist on complete evaluation, you should always select short-circuit evaluation for your programs.

Procedures and Functions

Pascal allows the programmer to break a program down into procedures and functions, providing a more orderly framework for the program. Unfortunately, every time a procedure is called, Turbo Pascal must perform housekeeping tasks to keep track of memory. You can easily increase the speed of a program by putting a procedure's code directly into the main body of another procedure or into the main program. The impact of declaring a separate procedure is demonstrated by **TestProc3**:

```
Program TestProc3;
Uses CRT, TIMER;
Var
   i,j : Integer;

(*********************************)

Procedure DemoProc;
Begin
j := 0;
j := 0;
j := 0;
j := 0;
End;

(*********************************)
```

```
Begin
ClrScr;

ClockOn;
For i := 1 To 30000 Do
  DemoProc;                        (* Procedure call. *)
ClockOff;

ClockOn;
For i := 1 To 30000 Do
  Begin
  j := 0;                          (* No procedure call. *)
  j := 0;
  j := 0;
  j := 0;
  End;
ClockOff;

WriteLn;
Write('Press ENTER...');
ReadLn;
End.
```

Procedure **DemoProc** in **TestProc3** sets the **Integer** variable **j** equal to zero four times. The same process is also repeated in the main program block. When you run the program, the procedure requires 2.26 seconds for 30,000 iterations compared with only 1.48 seconds for the code in the program block.

Clearly, calling a procedure adds to a program's overhead. However, putting the code directly in the program has several disadvantages. First, if the procedure is called several times in the program, you must duplicate its code each time, adding to your program's code size. Second, when you want to change the procedure, you have to change it in each place it occurs. You must weigh these disadvantages against the speed you gain by removing the procedure call.

Reference Parameters Versus Value Parameters

When Turbo Pascal passes a reference parameter to a procedure, it passes the variable's address, not the value of the variable. Value parameters, on the other hand, pass the entire contents of the variable. If the value parameter is a 4000-byte array, 4000 bytes are passed to the procedure, compared with only 4 bytes when Turbo Pascal passes an address.

As the program **TestParams1** demonstrates, it takes longer to pass value parameters:

```
Program TestParams1;
Uses CRT, TIMER;
Type
  AType = Array [1..2000] Of Integer;

Var
  a : AType;
  i,j : Integer;

(********************************)

Procedure a1(var a : AType);
Begin
End;

(********************************)

Procedure a2(a : AType);
Begin
End;

(********************************)

Begin
ClrScr;

ClockOn;
For i := 1 To 1000 Do
  a1(a);
ClockOff;

ClockOn;
For i := 1 To 1000 Do
  a2(a);
ClockOff;

WriteLn;
Write('Press ENTER...');
ReadLn;
End.
```

TestParams1 uses two procedures, **a1** and **a2**. Procedure **a1** accepts a reference parameter and **a2** accepts a value parameter. In both procedures, the parameter is an array of 2000 integers. When you run this program, you will find that procedure **a1** requires only 0.06 second for 1000 iterations, while **a2** requires 15.32 seconds to complete the same number of iterations. If you want to maximize the performance of your programs, try substituting reference parameters for value parameters. But, be careful—reference parameters retain any changes you make to them inside the procedure.

Performance is a concern for all programmers. Fortunately, Turbo Pascal produces some of the fastest, most efficient code of any compiler available. By using Turbo Pascal creatively, taking advantage of all its power, you can create programs that really fly. But remember that speed is just one consideration, and it can work to the detriment of maintainability. Optimized code often uses tricks and special logic that you might not remember a year later. If you must optimize, make sure that the benefits are worth the effort.

Turbo Pascal Database Toolbox

Toolbox Database Procedures
Database Low-Level Command Summary
Database High-Level Command Summary
The TAHIGH Database Routines
Database Toolbox Sort Routines

The Turbo Pascal Database Toolbox, the first of the Borland Toolboxes for Turbo Pascal, consists of two major parts: the database procedures and the sort procedures. With the database procedures, you can maintain and process large databases with remarkable speed. The sort routines let you order a file with a highly efficient sorting algorithm.

Toolbox Database Procedures

Database management is one of the most popular microcomputer applications. Some of the first programs available for micros were database managers, and even today they tend to be among the top sellers.

The main advantage of a database is its ability to use an index to speed up searches. Nondatabase files must be searched sequentially: each record is read one by one until the right one is found. As a file grows in size, sequential searches take too much time. Indexed searches, on the other hand, are far faster than sequential searches. In a file with thousands of records, an indexed search can locate the record you want in seconds.

An index contains entries that consist of a *key* and a record number. A key is a string that identifies a specific record. For example, a social security number can be used as a key to a database of personnel records. In the index, each social security number is matched to a record number. When you search the index for a social security number, the procedure returns the record number associated with that number. You then use the record number to retrieve the correct record from the database.

The indexed search process is illustrated in Figure 19-1, which shows an index file and a database file. The index file contains social security numbers matched with record numbers. The database contains personnel records that include the social security number. To retrieve the record for the individual with social security number 432-34-9987, first search the index. The index search finds the matching social security number and returns the record number, which is 2. Then retrieve record number 2 from the database file and process the information.

The B+tree Structure

It takes less time to search an index than to search a database because the index is organized into a special structure known as a *B+tree*. The B+tree structure makes it possible to find one key among thousands in only a few steps.

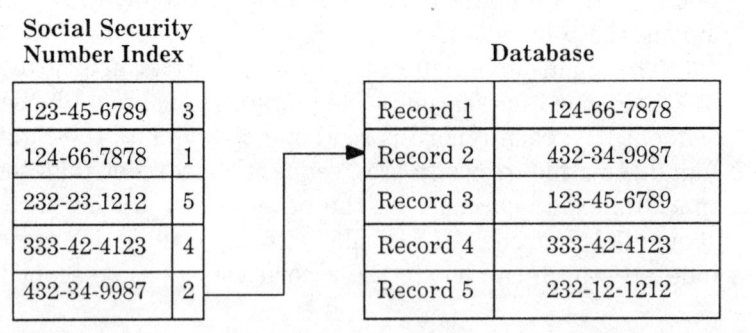

Figure 19-1. Index and database files

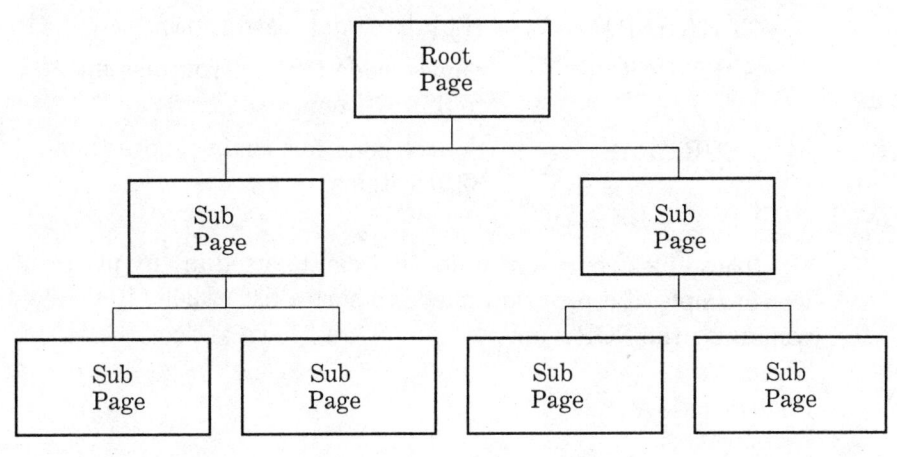

Figure 19-2.   B+tree structure

The basic building block of a B+tree index is a page. Each page contains many keys and record numbers. A B+tree index connects pages to each other in a pyramid-like structure that starts with a root page and grows larger with each successive level, as shown in Figure 19-2.

An index search starts at the root page of the B+tree and moves down into the lower levels as the search continues, stopping only when it finds a matching key. Because of the way the keys are ordered, only a small portion of the tree needs to be searched to find a match.

It is difficult to write routines that implement the B+tree concept. The routines must keep track of the amount of RAM available, rearrange the order of the keys as new keys are added, and report errors when they occur. The Database Toolbox does the programming for you, allowing you to concentrate on your application.

Turbo Pascal Database Toolbox Files

The Turbo Pascal Database Toolbox routines are contained in the following files on your distribution disks.

TACCESS.PAS	Database declarations and routines
TAHIGH.PAS	High-level database routines
SORT.PAS	Source code for sort routines up to 32,767 items
LSORT.PAS	Source code for sorting more than 32,767 items

These files represent units that can be used in any program. For example, if a program needs to sort a list of 2000 items, you would use the SORT unit:

```
Program DoSort;
Uses SORT;
```

The remaining programs on your distribution disks contain example programs that demonstrate how to use the Toolbox units, a program that helps you calculate the values you need to use the TACCESS unit most efficiently, and utilities that convert REFLEX data files to TACCESS data files, and vice versa.

Data Files, Index Files, and the Status Indicator

The TACCESS unit contains the following data types, which create database and index files.

The DataFile Data Type

The **DataFile** data type defines a Turbo Pascal Database Toolbox database file as follows:

```
DataFile  =  Record
                 F              : File;
                 FirstFree,
                 NumberFree,
                 Int1           : LongInt;
                 ItemSize       : Word;
                 NumRec         : LongInt;
             End;
```

Included in this data type is information about the database file, such as the total number of records in the file (**NumRec**), the number of deleted records (**NumberFree**), the number of the most recently deleted record (**FirstFree**), and the record size (**ItemSize**). The Int1 field is used by the Turbo Database Toolbox index routines. All of the information just mentioned is stored in the database *header record,* which is the first record of the database. When you open a database, TACCESS reads the header record in order to initialize the database.

You can add records to and delete records from a database. Naturally, as you add records to a database, the size of the disk file increases. Deleting records, however, does not decrease the size of the file. Rather, the space allocated to deleted records is left idle and then reused when new records are added to the database. TACCESS will always reuse all deleted record space before expanding the size of the physical disk file.

The IndexFile Data Type

IndexFile is a data type that declares indexes for databases. While the Database Toolbox provides the routines that manage the index, you are responsible for correctly using these routines. This means you must add a key to the index whenever you add a record to the database, delete a key when a record is removed from a database, and change a key when you update a record — and in the process, alter the value of the key.

Duplicate Keys

You can specify whether to allow duplicate keys in an index or not. An index of names, for example, should allow duplicate keys since two people can have the same name. In other cases, such as auto part numbers, duplicate keys should not be allowed since no two auto parts can have the same part number.

The OK Status Indicator

The Database Toolbox declares a global Boolean variable called **OK**, which reports errors in Toolbox operations. For example, if you attempt to find a key in an index and the key is not found, the Toolbox sets **OK** to FALSE. You should check the value of **OK** after most Toolbox operations to make sure your program handles error conditions properly.

Database Constant Declarations

Before you include the Database Toolbox files in your program, declare the following constants that control the amount of memory and disk space your files will require.

MaxDataRecSize   This constant determines the size of the buffer that holds database records. The buffer can be as small as 8 bytes and as large as 65,535 bytes. You can set **MaxDataRec-Size** to a value larger than the record size you use, but at no time can the size of your record exceed **MaxDataRecSize**. If your database uses two records, one containing 50 bytes and the other containing 100 bytes, **MaxDataRecSize** must be at least 100 to accommodate the larger record.

MaxHeight   This constant determines the maximum height of the B+tree. A B+tree consists of layers of pages. The first layer is the root page, the second layer is pages directly connected to the root page, and so forth. An index with large pages requires fewer levels than an index with small pages. Similarly, an index with only a small number of keys requires fewer levels than an index with a large number of keys.

You can calculate the correct value of **MaxHeight** for your database by using the following program:

```
Program CalcMaxHeight;
Uses CRT;
Var
  PageSize,
  MaxKeys : LongInt;

Begin
ClrScr;
Write('Enter maximum number of keys: ');
ReadLn(MaxKeys);
Write('Enter number of keys per page: ');
ReadLn(PageSize);
```

```
Write('MaxHeight = ',Ln(MaxKeys)/Ln(PageSize*0.5):0:0);
WriteLn;
Write('Press ENTER...');
ReadLn;
End.
```

As you can see from the **CalcMaxHeight** program, **Max-Height** increases as **MaxKeys** increases, and decreases as **PageSize** increases. Table 19-1 shows how the number of keys and page size affect the value of **MaxHeight**. With a page size of 40 and 1000 keys, **MaxHeight** is 2, but if the number of keys is increased to 60,000, **MaxHeight** increases to only 4. Even with a small page size of 10 and 60,000 keys, the index requires **Max-Height** to be only 7.

Larger page sizes require fewer levels in the B + tree, which can speed up your searches. Of course, large pages also use more memory, but the trade-off in speed is usually worth it. If you use a page size of 30 or more, a **MaxHeight** value of 5 should be sufficient.

MaxKeyLen   Index keys are **String** data types and so they can be up to 255 characters long. **MaxKeyLen** specifies the largest key allowed in your index files. If one index uses keys 6 characters long and another uses 10-character keys, **Max-KeyLen** must be set to at least 10. The larger the value of **MaxKeyLen**, the more memory your index will require.

Number of Keys	PageSize	MaxHeight
1,000	40	2
10,000	40	3
60,000	40	4
1,000	10	4
10,000	10	6
60,000	10	7

Table 19-1.   PageSize, MaxHeight, and Number of Keys in an Index

Order   This constant must be one-half the page size. The page size must, therefore, be an even number. The Database Toolbox uses **Order** to decide when a new branch needs to be added to the B+tree.

PageSize   This determines the number of keys per page in the index. The value of **PageSize** affects both the efficiency of the index and the amount of memory it will require. A large page size packs more keys into each page, thus increasing the likelihood that you will find a match on the page being searched. But as the page size grows, so does the amount of memory needed to store the index. The minimum page size is 4 and the maximum is 254, but normally page size ranges from 30 to 50.

PageStackSize   When Turbo Pascal needs to search an index page, it reads the page in from disk and stores it in RAM. The Database Toolbox also notes the pages it reads so that your program does not reread pages that are already in RAM. Once RAM is full, however, newly read pages must replace pages already stored in RAM, thereby slowing the index searches.

    PageStackSize controls how much RAM is devoted to storing index pages. If **PageStackSize** equals 3, then three pages can be held in RAM at one time. A larger **PageStackSize** value allows more pages to be stored in RAM, which increases the speed of index searches. But, if the **PageStackSize** value is too big, your program may not have enough memory to run. Borland suggests you set **PageStackSize** to any value from 16 to 32.

TACCESS.DEF

The TACCESS unit uses an include file, named TACCESS.DEF, that contains all the constant declarations mentioned previously. You can create your own TACCESS.DEF file using the Turbo Pascal editor. The contents of such a file might look like this:

```
Const
  MaxDataRecSize  = 100;
  MaxKeyLen       = 10;
  PageSize        = 30;
```

```
Order          = 15;
PageStackSize  = 5;
MaxHeight      = 5;
```

The problem most programmers encounter in creating a TAC-
CESS.DEF file is what values to assign to each constant. Fortunately, Borland provides a program, TABUILD.EXE, which not
only helps you calculate the values of the database constants,
but it also will compile the TACCESS unit based on your data
definitions. For example, consider the following data declarations:

```
Type
  DataKey = String[20];

  DataRec = Record
    Name : String[30];
    Age  : Word;
    Income : Real;
    End;

MaxDataType = DataRec;
MaxKeyType  = DataKey;
```

This code segment declares two data types—a data record and a
key record—and then assigns those types to **MaxDataType** and
MaxKeyType. Store these definitions in a text file (for example,
DATA.TYP) and, at the DOS prompt, simply type

```
TABUILD \W+ DATA.TYP
```

TABUILD will read the DATA.TYP file, compute the sizes of
the data and index keys, and display a worksheet that computes
memory requirements, disk space use, and other vital information. As the user, you can alter three values—the number of
records in the database, the number of keys on each index page
(**PageSize**) and the number of pages to be stored in RAM
(**PageStackSize**). As Table 19-2 demonstrates, changing the
values of the constants can have a big impact on performance. A
database with 1000 records, a maximum of 64 keys per page, and
5 pages in RAM requires 9305 bytes of RAM, 1.78 comparisons
per search, and completes 67% of its searches in RAM. Reducing

Database Records	Page Size	Page Stack Size	Page Stack RAM	Comparisons per Search	Searches Completed in RAM
1,000	64	5	9305	1.78	66.72%
10,000	64	5	9305	2.38	45.53%
1,000	20	5	2925	2.55	49.66%
1,000	64	10	18610	1.78	80.06%
100,000	30	20	17500	3.70	49.88%

Table 19-2.   Results from TABUILD Worksheet

the number of keys per page to 20 reduces the required RAM to 2925 bytes, but increases the comparisons per search to 2.55, and only 50% of all searches are completed in RAM.

The values you select for **PageSize** and **PageStackSize** will be determined by your application. Will your database have a large number of records? Is conserving RAM a high priority? Do you want to minimize search time as much as possible? You can weigh the pros and cons by using the TABUILD worksheet.

Once you have decided, using the TABUILD worksheet, on the values of **PageSize** and **PageStackSize**, you can press the F2 key to automatically create a TACCESS.DEF and compile the TACCESS unit. The values for **MaxDataRecSize** and **MaxKeyLen** are determined by the definitions found in DATA.TYP; **PageSize** and **PageStackSize** are the values you selected in the TABUILD worksheet; and the remaining constants, **Order** and **MaxHeight**, are calculated. Using TABUILD greatly simplifies the process of creating a database that is finely tuned to the specific application at hand.

Sample Declarations

The listing here demonstrates how to declare Database Toolbox constants in your program.

```
Program SampleDecs;
Uses TACCESS;
```

```
Var
  DatF : DataFile;
  IdxF : IndexFile;
  DatRef : LongInt;
```

DatF is a database file, **IdxF** is an index file, and **DatRef** is a variable used to hold record numbers. Record numbers are the links between a database and its index. For example, when you search an index for a name, the index routine returns the record number for that name (assuming a match is found). You then use this record number (**DatRef**) to retrieve the appropriate record from the database file.

Database Low-Level Command Summary

The Turbo Pascal Database Toolbox contains procedures and functions for both low-level and high-level use. Listed in this section are the low-level routines. This section is a quick reference guide, not a tutorial. For more detailed information on the Database Toolbox, please refer to the *Turbo Pascal Database Toolbox Owner's Handbook*.

AddKey

Syntax

Procedure AddKey (Var IdxF : IndexFile; Var DatRef :
                    LongInt; Var Key);

Usage   **AddKey** adds **Key** and its associated data record number **DatRef** to index file **IdxF**. **AddKey** usually follows **AddRec**, which adds a record to a database and returns a record number, **DatRef**.

When the key is successfully added to the index, **AddKey** sets **OK** to TRUE. If you attempt to add a duplicate key to an index that does not allow them, **AddKey** sets **OK** to FALSE. If the key is longer than the maximum length specified when the index was created or opened, the Database Toolbox truncates the key to the correct length.

Because the parameter **Key** is untyped, you can pass any data type through the variable without causing a Turbo Pascal error. The index, however, will work only with **Strings**. It is your responsibility to make sure that only **Strings** are used as keys.

AddRec

Syntax

Procedure AddRec(Var DatF : DataFile;
                    Var DatRef : LongInt; Var Buffer);

Usage   **AddRec** adds a record that is contained in **Buffer** to database file **DatF** and returns **DatRef**, the record number. **Buffer**, an untyped variable, can be any type of data record. If any records have been deleted from the database, **AddRec** will reuse them before expanding the file.

It is unnecessary to check the status of **OK** after a call to **AddRec**. The only errors that **AddRec** can cause are I/O errors such as no more room on your disk. When **AddRec** causes an I/O error, the procedure **TaIOCheck** takes over, displays an error message, and terminates the program.

ClearKey

Syntax

Procedure ClearKey(Var IdxF : IndexFile);

Usage   Returns the index file pointer for **IdxF** to the first entry in the index. Use this when you want to process an index sequentially from the beginning with the **NextKey** or **PrevKey**

commands. If you call **PrevKey** directly after **ClearKey**, the index file pointer will point to the last key in the index.

CloseFile

Syntax

Procedure CloseFile(Var DatF : DataFile);

Usage   **CloseFile** closes an open data file. All data files that are opened should be closed before the program ends.

CloseIndex

Syntax

Procedure CloseIndex(Var IdxF : IndexFile);

Usage   **CloseIndex** closes an open index file. All index files should be closed before a program ends.

DeleteKey

Syntax

Procedure DeleteKey (Var IdxF : IndexFile; Var DatRef : LongInt; Var Key);

Usage   **DeleteKey** purges a key and its related record number from an index file. If the index file does not allow duplicate keys, **DeleteKey** locates an index file entry by searching for a match for **Key**. If duplicates are allowed, **DeleteKey** attempts to match both **Key** and **DatRef**.

DeleteRec

Syntax

Procedure DeleteRec(Var DatF : DataFile; DatRef : LongInt);

Usage   **DeleteRec** destroys the contents of the record and adds the record number to the list of deleted records, which the Database Toolbox maintains. Afterward, when new records are added to the data file, the space taken up by the deleted records is reused by new records.

EraseFile

Syntax

Procedure EraseFile(Var DatF : DataFile);

Usage   **EraseFile** closes **DatF** and erases the file.

EraseIndex

Syntax

Procedure EraseIndex(Var IdxF : IndexFile);

Usage   **EraseIndex** closes **IdxF** and erases the file.

FileLen

Syntax

Function FileLen(Var DatF: DataFile) : LongInt;

Usage   **FileLen** returns a data file's size in terms of the number of records it contains. In its computations, **FileLen** includes active records, deleted records, and the record reserved by the Database Toolbox (record 0).

FindKey

Syntax

Procedure FindKey (Var IdxF : IndexFile; Var DatRef :
                  LongInt; Var Key);

Usage   **FindKey** searches and returns an index for a match to **Key**. If a match is found, **FindKey** returns the record number (**DatRef**) associated with the key and sets **OK** to TRUE. If a match is not found, **OK** is set to FALSE and **Key** is set to the value of the last key read from the index file.

FlushFile

Syntax

Procedure FlushFile(Var DatF : DataFile);

Usage   **FlushFile** writes out to disk all data stored in RAM buffers. Database file buffers are normally flushed when the file is closed. Flushing the file ensures that no data will be lost if the program should terminate without closing the database file.

FlushIndex

Syntax

Procedure FlushIndex(Var IdxF : IndexFile);

Usage   **FlushIndex** writes out to disk all data stored in RAM index buffers. Index file buffers are normally flushed when the index is closed. Flushing the file ensures that no data will be lost if the program should terminate without closing the index file.

GetRec

Syntax

Procedure GetRec(Var DatF : DataFile; DatRef : LongInt;
          Var Buffer);

Usage   **GetRec** retrieves a record number (**DatRef**) from data file **DatF** and places the contents in **Buffer**. **GetRec** does not affect the variable **OK**; any errors that occur are handled by **TaIOCheck** and result in termination of the program.

MakeFile

Syntax

Procedure MakeFile(Var DatF : DataFile; FileName :
          String; RecLen : Integer);

Usage   **MakeFile** creates a new data file **DatF** with the name **FileName**. The data file stores records of length **RecLen**. **MakeFile** sets **OK** to TRUE if the file is successfully created and to FALSE if an error occurred (for example, when a read-only file with the same name already exists).

MakeIndex

Syntax

Procedure MakeIndex (Var IdxF : IndexFile; FileName :
          String; KeyLen, Status : Integer);

Usage   **MakeIndex** creates index file **IdxF** with the name **FileName**. **KeyLen** defines the maximum key length allowed in the index, and **Status** determines whether duplicate keys are allowed. If **Status** equals 0, duplicate keys are not allowed in the index; if it equals 1, duplicates are allowed.
    If the index file is successfully created, **OK** is set to TRUE.

NextKey

Syntax

Procedure NextKey (Var IdxF : IndexFile; Var DatRef :
          Integer; Var Key);

Usage   **NextKey** advances the index file pointer to the next entry in the index and returns that entry's key and the record number. **NextKey** sets **OK** to TRUE unless the file pointer is positioned at the last key in the index. When this occurs, **OK** is set to FALSE and the file pointer remains positioned at the last key in the index. If **NextKey** is called again, the index file pointer points to the first key in the index.

OpenFile

Syntax

Procedure OpenFile(Var DatF : DataFile; FileName :
          String; RecLen : Integer);

Usage   **OpenFile** opens an existing data file. The value of **RecLen** must be the same as the value used when the file was created. If the file is successfully opened, **OK** is set to TRUE.

OpenIndex

Syntax

Procedure OpenIndex (Var IdxF : IndexFile; FileName :
                                String; KeyLen, Status : Integer);

Usage   **OpenIndex** opens an existing index file. **KeyLen** and **Status** must be the same values used when the index file was created. If the file is successfully opened, **OK** is set to TRUE.

PrevKey

Syntax

Procedure PrevKey (Var IdxF : IndexFile; Var DatRef :
                                LongInt; Var Key);

Usage   **PrevKey** moves the index file pointer to the previous entry in an index file and returns that entry's key and record number. If you use the **ClearKey** command, a call to **PrevKey** positions the index file pointer at the last key in the index.

    PrevKey sets **OK** to TRUE until it reaches the first record in the index, in which case **OK** is set to FALSE and the key and record number remain unchanged. An additional call to **PrevKey** moves the file pointer to the last entry in the index.

PutRec

Syntax

Procedure PutRec(Var DatF : DataFile; DatRef : LongInt;
                                Var Buffer);

Usage   **PutRec** replaces an existing record in a data file with the contents of **Buffer**. **DatRef** must be greater than 1 and less than **FileLen(DatF)**.

SearchKey

Syntax

Procedure SearchKey (Var IdxF : IndexFile; Var DatRef :
                        Integer; Var Key);

Usage   **SearchKey** locates the first key in an index that is equal to or greater than **Key**. When **SearchKey** finds such an index entry, it returns the key and record number of that entry and sets **OK** to TRUE. For example, if an index contains the three names Berman, McDonald, and Smith, and **Key** equals Brown, **SearchKey** returns McDonald.

   If none of the keys in the index is equal to or greater than **Key**, **OK** is set to FALSE, and the values of **DatRef** and **Key** remain unchanged.

UsedRecs

Syntax

Function UsedRecs(Var DatF : DataFile) : LongInt;

Usage   **UsedRecs** computes the number of active records in your data file. Deleted records and the reserved record used by the Database Toolbox are not included in this count.

Database High-Level Command Summary

This section describes the high-level routines included in the Turbo Pascal Database Toolbox and is designed to be a quick reference guide, not a tutorial. For more detailed information on the Database Toolbox, please refer to the *Turbo Pascal Database Toolbox Owner's Handbook*.

The DataSet Type

The routines in the Database Toolbox are very powerful, but some programmers find them difficult to use, especially when it comes to maintaining index files. Borland has simplified the process by supplying high-level database routines in a unit named TAHIGH. These routines allow easy maintenance of a database and a single index. Limiting a database to one index is not much of a problem for most database applications, and it greatly simplifies the task of updating index entries for a database.

The high-level database routines utilize a data type, **DataSet**, defined in the TAHIGH unit:

```
Type
  DataSet = Record
    Data : DataFile;
    Index : IndexFile;
    End;
```

DataSet very simply consists of a database file and an index file. Because the data file and index file are linked by a common record, it is impossible to update the wrong index or to get a record from the wrong database.

The TAHIGH Database Routines

TaClose

Syntax

Procedure TaClose(Var DatSet : DataSet);

Usage   Closes the **DatSet** database and index files.

TaCreate

Syntax

Procedure TaCreate(Var DatSet : DataSet; DatFName :
　　　　　　String; RecordLen : Integer;
　　　　　　IndexFName : String;
　　　　　　KeyLen : Integer);

Usage   Creates a database file (with name **DatFName**) and
an index file (with name **IndexFName**). The record length of the
database file is defined by **RecordLen**, and the length of the
index keys is defined by **KeyLen**.

TaDelete

Syntax

Procedure TaDelete(Var DatSet : DataSet; Var Key);

Usage   Deletes the database record and index entry for the
record identified by **Key**. If the key is not found in the index, **OK**
is set to FALSE.

TaErase

Syntax

Procedure TaErase(Var DatSet : DataSet);

Usage   Closes and erases the database and index files of
DatSet.

TaFlush

Syntax

Procedure TaFlush(Var DatSet : DataSet);

Usage   Flushes to disk the RAM buffers of the **DatSet** database and index files. Flushing the buffers ensures that data will not be lost if the program terminates without first closing the **DatSet** files.

TaInsert

Syntax

Procedure TaInsert(Var DatSet : DataSet; Var DataRec, Key);

Usage   Adds a record (**DataRec**) to the database and a key (**Key**) to the index file. The process is aborted if the key already exists in the index, in which case **OK** is set to FALSE.

TaNext

Syntax

Procedure TaNext(Var DatSet : DataSet; Var DataRec, Key);

Usage   Retrieves from the database the record that corresponds to the next key in the index. Upon return, **Key** is set to the value of the next key.

TaOpen

Syntax

Procedure TaOpen(Var DatSet : DataSet; DatFName :
        String; RecordLen : Integer;
        IndexFName : String; KeyLen : Integer);

Usage   Opens an existing database and index file with record
length **RecLen** and key length **KeyLen**.

TaPrev

Syntax

Procedure TaPrev(Var DatSet : DataSet; Var DataRec, Key);

Usage   Retrieves from the database the record that corresponds to the previous key in the index. Upon return, **Key** is set
to the value of the previous key.

TaRead

Syntax

Procedure TaRead(Var DatSet : DataSet; Var DataRec,
        Key; FindExact : Boolean);

Usage   Retrieves from the database the record that corresponds to **Key**. If **FindExact** is TRUE, then the procedure will
locate a record only if the key matches exactly. If **FindExact** is
FALSE, then the procedure will locate a record if the first part
of the keys match.

TaReset

Syntax

Procedure TaReset(Var DatSet : DataSet);

Usage   Moves the file pointer to the beginning of the data set. After calling **TaReset**, **TaNext** will retrieve the record that corresponds to the first key in the index.

TaUpdate

Syntax

Procedure TaUpdate(Var DatSet : DataSet; Var DataRec, Key);

Usage   Locates the record that corresponds to **Key** and updates the record with the data in **DataRec**. The key remains unchanged, but the data record is updated.

TaWrite

Syntax

Procedure TaWrite(Var DatSet : DataSet; Var DataRec, Key);

Usage   Writes a data record to the data file. **TaWrite** first attempts to locate **Key** in the index. If **Key** is found, **TaWrite** updates the existing record. If **Key** is not found, **TaWrite** adds **Key** to the index and creates a new database record in the database file.

Database Toolbox Sort Routines

A useful sorting procedure must be fast, able to sort files larger than can be held in RAM, and easy to implement in a variety of situations. The Database Toolbox procedures contained in the SORT unit provide all three qualities, simplifying even the most complicated sorting task. Another unit, LSORT, works just like the SORT unit, except that the routines in LSORT can sort more than 32,767 records. The names of the procedures and functions in LSORT are the same as those in SORT, except that an "L" is appended to the beginning of the name. Thus, the **SortEOS** function in the SORT unit becomes **LSortEOS** in the LSORT unit. While the LSORT unit is more powerful, it is less efficient than the SORT unit when sorting small amounts of data.

General Concepts

The **TurboSort** routine is a "black box" into which you read unsorted records and out of which comes sorted records. The process consists of three steps:

1. Release records to the sort routine.

2. Compare and rearrange records.

3. Return records from the sort routine.

While the Database Toolbox does all the hard work, you must write three simple procedures — **Inp**, **Less**, and **Outp** — on your own.

The Input Procedure

Inp, the **TurboSort** input procedure, releases data items to the **TurboSort** routine with the **SortRelease** command. The data items can be of any type from a character or integer to a complicated record structure. A typical **Inp** procedure is shown here:

```
{$F+}
Procedure Inp;
Begin
Assign(InFile,'TEMP.DAT');
Reset(InFile);
While Not Eof(InFile) Do
  Begin
  Read(InFile,DataRec);
  WriteLn(DataRec);
  SortRelease(DataRec);
  End;
Close(InFile);
End;
{$F-}
```

In the preceding procedure, records are read from a data file and released to the **TurboSort**. When **Inp** finishes, **TurboSort** advances to the sorting process, which uses a function named **Less**.

The Less Function

The function **Less** defines the method by which **TurboSort** orders data items. At its simplest, **Less** might look like this:

```
{$F+}
Function Less(Var x,y) : Boolean;
Var
  Rec1 : DataRecType Absolute x;
  Rec2 : DataRecType Absolute y;
Begin
Less := Rec1 < Rec2;
End;
{$F-}
```

Less declares two records of the type you are sorting (**DataRecType**). The first, **Rec1**, is declared absolute at **x**, and the second, **Rec2**, is declared absolute at **y**. In the body of the function, **Rec1** and **Rec2** are compared and the value of **Less** is set accordingly.

TurboSort continues to call **Inp** until all the data items are correctly sorted, at which point it calls the **OutP** procedure.

The Output Procedure

Outp, the sort output procedure, uses the **SortReturn** command to retrieve data items in their sorted order. **SortEOS,** a Boolean indicator that is TRUE when the last data item has been returned, is used to control loops. A typical **Outp** procedure looks like this:

```
{$F+}
Procedure Outp;
Begin
ClrScr;
WriteLn('Returning sorted records...');
WriteLn;
  Repeat
  SortReturn(DataRec);
  WriteLn(DataRec);
  Until SortEOS;
End;
{$F-}
```

The sorted records are retrieved and written to a new file, OUTFILE. When the procedure is done, the output file will contain the same information as the input file, but in sorted order.

Calling the TurboSort Routine

Once you define **Inp, Less,** and **Outp,** your program invokes the sort routine with a call to the **Integer** function **TurboSort,** which takes an **Integer** parameter that indicates the size of the data item being sorted. It is important to remember that **Inp, Less,** and **Outp** must be declared as far calls and cannot be nested. Here is an example of how **TurboSort** would be called to sort a file of integers:

```
Res := TurboSort(SizeOf(DataRec),@Inp,@Less,@Outp);
```

In this case, **TurboSort** is given the value 2 since integers contain two bytes. In addition, this statement writes out the

Code	Meaning	Action Required
0	Sort completed—no errors	None
3	Not enough RAM available for sort	Reduce memory usage of program through overlays or dynamic variables
8	The data item being sorted is too short—it must be at least 2 bytes long	Increase the size of the data item
9	More than **MaxInt** records were passed to **TurboSort**. (Does not apply to LSORT)	Break your file into smaller pieces, sort each piece separately, and then merge the files
10	Write error encountered. Disk may be full or damaged	Check disk for free space and possible damage
11	Read error encountered	Check disk for possible damage
12	File creation error	Check to see if your directory is full or whether you are trying to access a nonexisting directory

Table 19-3.   TurboSort Status Codes

value that **TurboSort** returns. This value is a status code that indicates how the sort went. The **TurboSort** status codes and their meanings are listed in Table 19-3.

Programming Examples

Your Database Toolbox disk provides example programs that demonstrate the **TurboSort** routines. The program called **Sort-Demo** creates a series of random integers, sorts them, and displays them on the screen.

```
Program SortDemo;
Uses CRT,SORT;
Type
  DataRecType = Word;

Var
  Res : Integer;
  OutFile,
```

```
  InFile : File of DataRecType;
  DataRec : DataRecType;

(************************************************************)

{$F+}
Procedure Inp;
Begin
ClrScr;
WriteLn('Reading input file...');
WriteLn;
Assign(InFile,'TEMP.DAT');
Reset(InFile);
While Not Eof(InFile) Do
  Begin
  Read(InFile,DataRec);
  WriteLn(DataRec);
  SortRelease(DataRec);
  End;
Close(InFile);

Write('All records released. Press ENTER to sort...');
ReadLn;
End;
{$F-}


(************************************************************)

{$F+}
Function Less(Var x,y) : Boolean;
Var
  Rec1 : DataRecType Absolute x;
  Rec2 : DataRecType Absolute y;
Begin
Less := Rec1 < Rec2;
End;
{$F-}


(************************************************************)

{$F+}
Procedure Outp;
Begin
ClrScr;
WriteLn('Returning sorted records...');
WriteLn;
  Repeat
  SortReturn(DataRec);
  WriteLn(DataRec);
  Until SortEOS;
End;
{$F-}


(************************************************************)
```

```
Procedure CreateFile;
Var
  i,j : Word;
Begin
Assign(OutFile,'TEMP.DAT');
Rewrite(OutFile);
For i := 1 To 15 Do
  Begin
  j := Random(100);
  Write(OutFile,j);
  End;
Close(OutFile);
End;

(*********************************************************)

Begin
CreateFile;
Res := TurboSort(SizeOf(DataRec),@Inp,@Less,@Outp);
WriteLn('Result of sort is: ',Res);

WriteLn;
Write('Press ENTER...');
ReadLn;
End.
```

Borland's Database Toolbox simplifies some of the most common, yet vexing programming problems—accessing and ordering data efficiently. With the routines the Toolbox provides, you can build highly efficient database programs with more flexibility, higher performance, and lower overhead than you could get in any of the database programs available on the market.

Turbo Pascal Graphix Toolbox

TWENTY

Graphix Toolbox Procedures
Screen Procedures
Graphics Windows
Graphics Clipping
World Coordinate System
Headers
Color
Plotting Commands
Text

While Turbo Pascal provides some built-in graphics capabilities, they do not come close to providing a complete graphics library. You could write your own graphics library, but for only a few dollars, you can buy Borland's Turbo Pascal Graphix Toolbox, which contains most of the routines you could ask for. The Graphix Toolbox reference manual, which accompanies the disks, describes all the features in great detail. This chapter serves as a quick reference to the graphics procedures contained in the Graphix Toolbox.

Graphix Toolbox Procedures

EnterGraphic

Syntax

Procedure EnterGraphic;

Usage   **EnterGraphic** clears the screen and sets the computer to Graphics mode. It does not initialize the graphics system.

Error

Syntax

Procedure Error(Proc, Code);

Usage   **Error** informs the user when an error occurs in a graphics procedure. The parameter **Proc** is the address of the procedure in which the error occurred, and **Code** indicates the type of error. The error will terminate the program if Break mode is enabled. The **SetBreakOn** command enables Break mode, and **SetBreakOff** disables it.

GetErrorCode

Syntax

GetErrorCode : Integer;

Usage   **GetErrorCode** returns the code of the error that occurred most recently. To use **GetErrorCode**, Break mode

Error Code	Meaning
−1	No error
0	Error message missing
1	Font file missing
2	Index out of range
3	Coordinates out of range
4	Too few array elements
5	Error opening file
6	Out of window memory
7	Value out of range

Table 20-1.   Graphics Error Codes

must be disabled with the **SetBreakOff** command. The error codes and their meanings are listed in Table 20-1.

HardCopy

Syntax

Procedure HardCopy(Inverse : Boolean; Mode : Byte);

Usage **HardCopy** prints the graphic displayed on the active screen. The **Inverse** parameter prints in reverse (dark background) when TRUE and prints standard (dark foreground) when FALSE. **Mode** determines the size and density of the printed graphic, as detailed in Table 20-2.

InitGraphic

Syntax

Procedure InitGraphic;

Usage **InitGraphic** initializes the graphics system. It must be called before any other graphics command, but **InitGraphic** can be called only once in a program. Among other things, this procedure checks that the appropriate hardware is present, loads the error message file and standard character set, sets the aspect ratio, and sets the vertical window movement step to the default value. The vertical window movement step is the number of pixels a window moves up or down in one step.

Mode	Points per Line	Epson Mode
0, 4, 5	640	4
1	960	1
2	960	2
3	1920	3
6	720	6

Table 20-2. Printing Density Using HardCopy

LeaveGraphic

Syntax

Procedure LeaveGraphic;

Usage   **LeaveGraphic** returns the system to Text mode.

SetBreakOff

Syntax

Procedure SetBreakOff;

Usage   **SetBreakOff** disables Break mode, in which error conditions cause a program to abort. After **SetBreakOff** is called, error checking becomes the programmer's responsibility.

SetBreakOn

Syntax

Procedure SetBreakOn;

Usage   **SetBreakOn** enables Break mode. Once enabled, Break mode causes a program to terminate when an error occurs.

SetMessageOff

Syntax

Procedure SetMessageOff;

Usage   **SetMessageOff** reduces error messages displayed by the Graphix Toolbox. When Break mode is enabled, **SetMessageOff** abbreviates error messages. When Break mode is disabled, **SetMessageOff** suppresses all error messages.

SetMessageOn

Syntax

Procedure SetMessageOn;

Usage   **SetMessageOn** tells the Graphix Toolbox to produce extended error messages. When Break mode is enabled, **Set-MessageOn** displays complete error messages and terminates the program. When Break mode is disabled, **SetMessageOn** causes the Graphix Toolbox to display an error message on line 24 of your monitor, but it does not halt execution.

Screen Procedures

ClearScreen

Syntax

Procedure ClearScreen;

Usage   **ClearScreen** clears the active screen.

CopyScreen

Syntax

Procedure CopyScreen;

Usage   **CopyScreen** transfers the image on the active screen to the inactive screen.

GetAspect

Syntax

Function GetAspect : Real;

Usage   **GetAspect** returns the current value of the aspect ratio.

GetScreen

Syntax

Function GetScreen : Integer;

Usage   **GetScreen** reports which screen is currently active: a value of 1 indicates the displayed screen is active, while 2 indicates the RAM screen is active.

GetScreenAspect

Syntax

Function GetScreenAspect : Real;

Usage   **GetScreenAspect** returns the current aspect ratio in terms of pixels.

InvertScreen

Syntax

Procedure InvertScreen;

Usage   **InvertScreen** reverses the displayed graphic by changing pixels from white to black and from black to white. This command also works when colors other than black and white are used.

LoadScreen

Syntax

Procedure LoadScreen(FileName : WrkString);

Usage   Loads a screen from file **FileName** into memory.

SaveScreen

Syntax

Procedure SaveScreen(FileName : WrkString);

Usage   **SaveScreen** stores a graphic display in a file named with the variable **FileName**.

SelectScreen

Syntax

Procedure SelectScreen(I : Integer);

Usage   The Graphix Toolbox allows you to display graphics on either the active screen (the screen you see) or on a RAM screen (a screen held in memory that is not displayed). Setting **I** equal to 1 selects the active screen, while a value of 2 selects the RAM screen.

SetAspect

Syntax

Procedure SetAspect(Aspect : Real);

Usage   When you initialize the Graphix Toolbox, the default aspect ratio is enabled. This ratio displays correctly proportioned circles and ellipses. **SetAspect** changes the aspect ratio by a multiplier, **Aspect**. For example, the command **SetAspect(2)** will display circles twice as tall as they are wide.

SetScreenAspect

Syntax

Procedure SetScreenAspect(Aspect : Real);

Usage   **SetScreenAspect** defines the aspect ratio in terms of pixels. **Aspect** is the aspect ratio defined in terms of pixels. For example, **SetScreenAspect(d1)** creates circles that have as many pixels vertically as they do horizontally.

SwapScreen

Syntax

Procedure SwapScreen;

Usage   **SwapScreen** exchanges the displayed screen and the RAM screen.

Graphics Windows

ClearWindowStack

Syntax

Procedure ClearWindowStack(N : Integer);

Usage   **ClearWindowStack** clears the window number **N**. Once erased with this procedure, the window cannot be restored by **RestoreWindow**.

CopyWindow

Syntax

Procedure CopyWindow(From, To : Byte; X, Y : Integer);

Usage   **CopyWindow** transfers the contents of the active screen to the RAM screen, or the contents of the RAM screen to the active screen. **From** and **To** indicate the source and destination: 1 indicates the displayed screen, 2 indicates the RAM screen. Coordinates **X:Y** indicate the screen location of the window.

DefineTextWindow

Syntax

Procedure DefineTextWindow(I, Left, Up, Right, Down,
                                Border : Integer);

Usage   **DefineTextWindow** defines an area of the screen in terms of text coordinates (80 × 25). The location of the window is determined by **Left, Up, Right,** and **Down,** which define the edges of window number **I. Border** determines the number of pixels that separate the text window from the rest of the screen.

DefineWindow

Syntax

Procedure DefineWindow(I, Xlow, Ylow, Xhi, Yhi : Integer);

Usage   **DefineWindow** declares a rectangular portion of the screen to be window number **I.** The window's location is determined by **Xlow:Ylow** for the upper left corner and **Xhi:Yhi** for the lower right corner, all of which are defined as world coordinates. The **X** coordinates represent 8-pixel chunks, which means the command

    DefineWindow(1,0,0,9,9)

creates a screen 10 pixels high and 80 pixels wide.

GetWindow

Syntax

Function GetWindow : Integer;

Usage   **GetWindow** returns the number of the window that is currently active.

InvertWindow

Syntax

Procedure InvertWindow;

Usage   **InvertWindow** changes the pixels in the active window from black to white and from white to black. If colors are used, they are reversed in similar fashion.

LoadWindow

Syntax

Procedure LoadWindow(N, X, Y : Integer;
                FileName :
                WrkString);

Usage   **LoadWindow** reads a window from a file named FILENAME, stores the contents in window **N**, and displays the window at coordinates **X:Y**.

LoadWindowStack

Syntax

Procedure LoadWindowStack(FileName : WrkString);

Usage   **LoadWindowStack** reads in two files—FILENAME.STK and FILENAME.PTR—which contain a window stack that was stored previously.

RedefineWindow

Syntax

Procedure RedefineWindow(I, Xlow, Ylow,
                              Xhi, Yhi : Integer);

Usage   **RedefineWindow** changes the dimensions of window
I. Coordinates **Xlow:Ylow** determine the position of the upper
left corner and **Xhi:Yhi** determine the lower right corner. The **X**
coordinates represent 8 pixels each, as in the **DefineWindow**
command.

ResetWindows

Syntax

Procedure ResetWindows;

Usage   **ResetWindows** sets all the windows to the size of the
screen and selects Window 1 as the active window. In addition,
all headers are removed. While the graphic currently displayed
remains unchanged, all further graphics are drawn according to
absolute screen coordinates.

ResetWindowStack

Syntax

Procedure ResetWindowStack;

Usage   **ResetWindowStack** discards all the windows stored
on the window stack and frees the memory.

RestoreWindow

Syntax

Procedure RestoreWindow(N, X, Y : Integer);

Usage　　**RestoreWindow** takes window **N** from the window stack and displays it on the screen at coordinates **X:Y**.

SaveWindow

Syntax

Procedure SaveWindow(N : Integer;
　　　　　　　　　　FileName : WrkString);

Usage　　**SaveWindow** stores window **N** in a disk file with the name FILENAME.

SaveWindowStack

Syntax

Procedure SaveWindowStack(FileName : WrkString);

Usage　　**SaveWindowStack** stores all the windows currently on the window stack in two files, one named FILENAME.STK and the other named FILENAME.PTR. Since the Graphix Toolbox automatically adds the extensions, do not specify an extension for FILENAME.

SelectWindow

Syntax

Procedure SelectWindow(N : Integer);

Usage　　**SelectWindow** makes window **N** the active window.

SetWindowModeOff

Syntax

Procedure SetWindowModeOff;

Usage   **SetWindowModeOff** permits you to create graphics using absolute coordinates only.

SetWindowModeOn

Syntax

Procedure SetWindowModeOn;

Usage   **SetWindowModeOn** enables Window mode, which is also the default mode. By calling **SetWindowModeOn**, you can draw graphics using world coordinates.

StoreWindow

Syntax

Procedure StoreWindow(N : Integer);

Usage   **StoreWindow** saves window **N** on the window stack. Before the window is saved, the Graphix Toolbox checks to see if the window stack has enough memory to store the window. If there is too little memory, an error occurs and the window is not saved.

WindowMode

Syntax

Function WindowMode : Boolean;

Usage   **WindowMode** returns TRUE if Window mode is currently enabled and FALSE if Window mode is disabled.

WindowSize

Syntax

Function WindowSize(N : Integer) : Integer;

Usage   **WindowSize** returns the memory required to store window **N** on the window stack. The amount is rounded up to the nearest kilobyte. This procedure is used to check if enough room remains on the window stack to save the window **N**.

WindowX

Syntax

Function WindowX(X : Real) : Integer;

Usage   **WindowX** accepts a world coordinate **X** and returns the equivalent absolute screen coordinate.

WindowY

Syntax

Function WindowY(Y : Real) : Integer;

Usage **Window Y** accepts a world coordinate **Y** and returns the equivalent absolute screen coordinate.

Graphics Clipping

Clipping

Syntax

Function Clipping : Boolean;

Usage **Clipping** returns TRUE if clipping is enabled and FALSE if it is disabled. When clipping is enabled, only the portion of the graphic that fits within the current window is displayed.

SetClippingOn

Syntax

Procedure SetClippingOn;

Usage **SetClippingOn** enables Clipping mode, in which drawings are limited to the boundaries of the active window. Any portion of the drawing that falls outside the active window is not drawn.

SetClippingOff

Syntax

Procedure SetClippingOff;

Usage   SetClippingOff disables Clipping mode, thus allowing drawings to extend beyond the boundaries of the active window.

World Coordinate System

DefineWorld

Syntax

Procedure DefineWorld(I : Integer; Xlow,
                      Ylow, Xhi, Yhi : Real);

Usage   **DefineWorld** defines the coordinate system for world **I**. **Xlow:Ylow** indicates the upper left corner of the screen and **Xhi:Yhi** indicates the lower right corner. Once the coordinates are defined, they are not enabled until you invoke the **Select-World** command.

SelectWorld

Syntax

Procedure SelectWorld(I : Integer);

Usage   **SelectWorld** selects world coordinate system **I**.

SetBackground

Syntax

Procedure SetBackground(Pattern : Byte);

Usage   SetBackground sets the background pattern with a byte that determines the pattern. Each bit in the byte corresponds to a pixel location; thus, the entire byte controls eight pixels. If a bit is on, its corresponding pixel is turned on; if off, the pixel is off. The Graphix Toolbox repeats the byte pattern throughout the active window.

SetBackground8

Syntax

Procedure SetBackground8(Pattern : BackgroundArray);

Usage   SetBackground8 creates a patterned background that is defined by **Pattern**, an array of eight bytes. Each byte in **Pattern** controls eight horizontal pixels. Together, the eight bytes define a portion of the screen that is 8 × 8 pixels.

When a bit in one of the bytes is on, the pixel is turned on, otherwise the pixel is turned off. The Graphix Toolbox repeats the pattern throughout the active window.

Headers

DefineHeader

Syntax

Procedure DefineHeader(I : Integer; Hdr : WrkString);

Usage   **DefineHeader** defines a header for window **I**. The header displays the contents of the string **Hdr**.

DrawBorder

Syntax

Procedure DrawBorder;

Usage   **DrawBorder** creates a border around the active window. The border can include a header at either the top or the bottom of the window.

GetVStep

Syntax

Function GetVStep : Integer;

Usage   **GetVStep** returns the number of vertical pixels a window will move in one step.

MoveHor

Syntax

Procedure MoveHor(Delta : Integer; FillOut : Boolean);

Usage   **MoveHor** moves the active window **Delta** the specified steps (at eight pixels per step) to the right or left. The window moves to the left when **Delta** is negative and to the right when it is positive. **FillOut** determines what happens to the space "underneath" the window after it is moved. When **FillOut** is set to FALSE, the area is set to the opposite of the current color. When **FillOut** is TRUE, the area underneath the window is replaced by the same area in the RAM screen. In short, you must keep a copy of the window in the RAM screen so that when the window moves, the newly exposed part of the screen can be filled in correctly.

MoveVer

Syntax

Procedure MoveVer(Delta : Integer; FillOut : Boolean);

Usage   **MoveVer** moves the active window up or down by **Delta** steps. A vertical step is one pixel (by default), but this can be changed by **SetVStep**. When **Delta** is positive, the window moves up; when negative, the window moves down. **FillOut** determines how the newly exposed portion of the screen is filled in (see **MoveHor**).

RemoveHeader

Syntax

Procedure RemoveHeader(I : Integer);

Usage   **RemoveHeader** removes a header definition from window **I**. Calling this command does not change the window displayed.

ResetWorlds

Syntax

Procedure ResetWorlds;

Usage   **ResetWorlds** initializes all the world coordinates to the coordinates of the absolute screen coordinates.

SetHeaderOff

Syntax

Procedure SetHeaderOff;

Usage   **SetHeaderOff** suppresses the display of window headers when the **DrawBorder** command is used.

SetHeaderOn

Syntax

Procedure SetHeaderOn;

Usage   **SetHeaderOn** enables the display of window headers when the **DrawBorder** command is used.

SetHeaderToBottom

Syntax

Procedure SetHeaderToBottom;

Usage   **SetHeaderToBottom** causes window headers to be displayed at the bottom of a window.

SetHeaderToTop

Syntax

Procedure SetHeaderToTop;

Usage   **SetHeaderToTop** causes window headers to be displayed at the top of a window.

SetVStep

Syntax

Procedure SetVStep(Step : Integer);

Usage   **SetVStep** sets the vertical distance that a window can be moved in one step. **Step,** a positive integer, determines the distance in terms of pixels.

Color

GetColor

Syntax

Function GetColor : Integer;

Usage   **GetColor** returns the value of the current drawing color. If **GetColor** returns 0, the current drawing color is the background color; if it equals 255, the current drawing color is the foreground color.

SetBackgroundColor

Syntax

Procedure SetBackgroundColor(Color : Integer);

Usage   **SetBackgroundColor** determines the color of background pixels. **Color** can be any value that is valid for your adapter.

SetColorBlack

Syntax

Procedure SetColorBlack;

Usage   **SetColorBlack** selects the current background color as the drawing color.

SetColorWhite

Syntax

Procedure SetColorWhite;

Usage   **SetColorWhite** tells the Graphix Toolbox to use the current foreground color as the current drawing color.

SetForegroundColor

Syntax

Procedure SetForegroundColor(Color : Integer);

Usage   **SetForegroundColor** determines the color of foreground pixels. **Color** can be any valid foreground color your adapter supports.

Plotting Commands

Bezier

Syntax

Procedure Bezier(A : PlotArray; N : Integer;
               Var B : PlotArray; M : Integer);

Usage   A Bezier polynomial curve connects the points on a graph in a smooth, curved line. Parameter **A** is an array of **X** and **Y** points, **N** is the number of points, and **B** is an array of **X** and **Y** points that are produced by the Bezier calculation. **M** controls the smoothness of the curve; the higher the value, the smoother the curve.

DrawAxis

Syntax

Procedure DrawAxis(XDensity, YDensity,
               Left, Top, Right, Bottom : Integer;
               XAxis, YAxis : Integer;
               Arrows : Boolean);

Usage   DrawAxis creates scaled horizontal and vertical axes for drawing polygons. **XDensity** and **YDensity** determine the density of the tick marks that appear on each axis. **Left**, **Top**, **Right**, and **Bottom** are the distances from each edge of the screen that determine the drawing area for the polygon. **XAxis** and **YAxis** determine the style of the axes: when either is a negative number, that axis is not drawn. When **Arrows** is TRUE, the axes will have arrows at each end.

DrawCartPie

Syntax

Procedure DrawCartPie(Xcenter, Ycenter, Xstart, Ystart,
               Inner, Outer : Real;
               A : PieArray;
               N, Option, Scale : Integer);

Usage   DrawCartPie draws a pie chart centered at coordinates **Xcenter:Ycenter** starting at **Xstart:Ystart**. The procedure uses values in parameter **A**. This parameter is of type **PieArray**, which is an array of real numbers and labels. **DrawCartPie** uses the numbers in **A** to compute the relative area of each segment of the pie. The string portions of **A** serve as labels for each segment of the pie. **N** is the number of segments in the pie, and **Inner, Outer, Option,** and **Scale** function as they do in **DrawCircleSegment**.

DrawCircle

Syntax

Procedure DrawCircle(X, Y, R : Real);

Usage   **DrawCircle** draws a circle at coordinates **X:Y** with radius **R**.

DrawCircleSegment

Syntax

Procedure DrawCircleSegment(Xcenter, Ycenter: Real;
                            Var Xstart, Ystart : Real;
                            Inner, Outer, Angle, Area : Real;
                            Text :WrkString;
                            Option, Scale : Byte);

Usage   **DrawCircleSegment** draws a circle or part of a circle. The circle's center is located at coordinates **Xcenter:Ycenter**, and the arc of the circle starts at coordinates **Xstart:Ystart**. This command also draws a line from inside the circle to the outside, and positions a label at the outer end of this line. The inner end of the line is determined by **Inner** and the outer end by **Outer**. Both **Inner** and **Outer** represent radius units; thus, a value of 0.5 means halfway between the center of the circle and the circumference.

Angle is the number of degrees in the angle of the arc that forms the circle segment. **Area** is a number that is displayed as part of the label if you select the appropriate option. **Text** contains the label you wish to display with the circle segment, and **Option** determines how the label or numbers are displayed, as follows:

Option	Meaning
0	No label
1	Text label
2	Text and number label
3	Number only label

Scale is a multiplier that increases or decreases the size of the label. When **Scale** equals 1, the label appears in its default size.

DrawHistogram

Syntax

Procedure DrawHistogram(A : PlotArray; N : Integer);

Usage   **DrawHistogram** is used to create bar charts. **A** is of type **PlotArray**, which is a two-dimensional array of integers. **DrawHistogram** uses only the first dimension in the array. This dimension contains values that determine the height of each bar in the histogram. **N** indicates the number of elements in **A** used to plot the histogram.

DrawLine

Syntax

Procedure DrawLine(X1, Y1, X2, Y2 : Real);

Usage   **DrawLine** draws a line from coordinates **X1:Y1** to **X2:Y2**. If Window mode is on, the coordinates are world coordinates; otherwise, they are absolute coordinates.

DrawLineClipped

Syntax

Procedure DrawLineClipped(X1, Y1, X2, Y2 : Real);

Usage   **DrawLineClipped** draws a line from absolute coordinates **X1:Y1** to **X2:Y2**. The line is clipped at the boundaries of the active window even when Window mode is turned off.

DrawPoint

Syntax

Procedure DrawPoint(X, Y : Real);

Usage   **DrawPoint** plots a single pixel at coordinates **X:Y**. If in Window mode, the coordinates are world coordinates; if not, they are absolute coordinates.

DrawPolarPie

Syntax

Procedure DrawPolarPie(Xcenter, Ycenter, Radius, Angle,
                Inner, Outer : Real;
                A : PieArray;
                N, Option, Scale : Integer);

Usage   **DrawPolarPie** operates in much the same manner as **DrawCartPie**, except that instead of using **Xstart** and **Ystart** to determine the coordinate at which the circumference begins, you use **Radius** and **Angle**. **Radius** is the radius of the pie in terms of world pixels, and **Angle** determines the starting point of the circumference expressed in degrees.

DrawPolygon

Syntax

Procedure DrawPolygon(A : PlotArray; First, Last, Code,
                    Scale, Lines : Integer);

Usage   **DrawPolygon** creates a line drawing with **A**, which is an array of x and y coordinates. **First** and **Last** indicate the beginning and ending points in the vertex to be plotted. **Code** specifies the type of symbol that is drawn at each plotted coordinate, and **Scale** is a multiplier that determines how large the symbol will appear. When **Scale** equals 1, the symbol is drawn to the default scale. **Lines** controls how filler lines appear on the graphic. When **Lines** is less than zero, filler lines are drawn from the Y-zero axis to the vertex; when **Lines** is greater than zero, lines are drawn from the bottom of the display to the vertex. When **Lines** equals zero, no lines are drawn.

DrawSquare

Syntax

Procedure DrawSquare(X1, Y1, X2, Y2 : Real;
                    Fill : Boolean);

Usage   **DrawSquare** draws any rectangular shape defined by world coordinates **X1:Y1** and **X2:Y2**. The square is drawn in the current line style, and when **Fill** is TRUE, the rectangle is filled with the current drawing color and pattern.

DrawStraight

Syntax

Procedure DrawStraight(X1, X2, Y : Integer);

Usage   **DrawStraight** draws only horizontal lines starting at absolute coordinates **X1:Y** and extending to **X2:Y**. **DrawStraight** is faster than **DrawLine**.

FindWorld

Syntax

Procedure FindWorld(I : Integer; A : PlotArray;
                    N : Integer;
                    ScaleX, ScaleY : Real);

Usage   **FindWorld** determines the proper world coordinates for world **I**, using **A**, the array of vertices, and **N**, the number of vertices. **ScaleX** and **ScaleY** are multipliers that can add additional scaling to the world coordinates. When both **Scalex** and **Scaley** are equal to 1, no additional scaling is added.

GetLineStyle

Syntax

Function GetLineStyle : Integer;

Usage   **GetLineStyle** returns an integer that indicates the current line style.

Hatch

Syntax

Procedure Hatch(X1, Y1, X2, Y2 : Real; Delta : Integer);

Usage   **Hatch** fills a rectangular portion of the screen, defined by coordinates **X1:Y1** and **X2:Y2**, with diagonal lines. The separation between the hatched lines is determined by **Delta**. When **Delta** is one, 100 % (1/1) of the rectangle is filled with solid color. When **Delta** is 2, 50% (1/2) of the rectangle is filled. A positive **Delta** draws hatched lines from upper left to lower right; a negative value draws lines from lower left to upper right.

The rectangle is drawn in absolute coordinates unless Window mode is on, in which case world coordinates are used.

PointDrawn

Syntax

Function PointDrawn(X, Y : Real) : Boolean;

Usage   **PointDrawn**, a Boolean function, returns TRUE if a point has been drawn at world coordinates **X:Y**.

RotatePolygon

Syntax

Procedure RotatePolygon(A: PlotArray; N : Integer;
                        Angle : Real);

Usage   **RotatePolygon** rotates the polygon defined by **A** and **N** by **Angle** degrees. The center of the rotation is calculated by the Graphix Toolbox.

RotatePolygonAbout

Syntax

Procedure RotatePolygonAbout(A: PlotArray; N : Integer;
                              Angle, X, Y : Real);

Usage   **RotatePolygonAbout** rotates the polygon defined by **A** and **N** by **Angle** degrees. The center of the rotation is determined by world coordinates **X** and **Y**.

ScalePolygon

Syntax

Procedure ScalePolygon(A : PlotArray; N : Integer;
                        Xfactor, Yfactor : Real);

Usage   **ScalePolygon** multiplies **N** x and y coordinates of **A** by **Xfactor** and **Yfactor**. This alters the proportions of the polygon when it is displayed.

SetLineStyle

Syntax

Procedure SetLineStyle(LS : Integer);

Usage   SetLineStyle determines the type of line the Graphix Toolbox draws. **LS** can be set to any of five predefined line styles:

0	Solid line
1	Dotted line
2	Dashes
3	Dashes and dots
4	Short dashes

Spline

Syntax

Procedure Spline(A : PlotArray; N : Integer; X1, Xm : Real;
                 Var B : PlotArray; m : Integer);

Usage   **Spline** interpolates a smooth curve around the points in a polygon defined by **A** and **N** and stores the result in **B**. **X1** and **Xm** represent the starting and ending points in **A**, and **m** is the number of points used to define the smooth curve.

TranslatePolygon

Syntax

Procedure TranslatePolygon(A : PlotArray; N : Integer;
                           DeltaX, DeltaY : Real);

Usage   **TranslatePolygon** moves a polygon defined by **A** and **N** by adding **DeltaX** to its x coordinates and **DeltaY** to its y coordinates.

Text

DefineHeader

Syntax

Procedure DefineHeader(I : Integer; Hdr : WrkString);

Usage **DefineHeader** uses **Hdr** to define the header for window **I**.

DefineTextWindow

Syntax

Procedure DefineTextWindow(I, Left, Up, Right, Down,
Border : Integer);

Usage **DefineTextWindow** defines window **I** with text coordinates (80 × 25). **Left, Up, Right,** and **Down** specify the text coordinates that define the edges of the window. **Border** specifies the number of pixels that separate the text portion of the window from the edges of the window.

DrawASCII

Syntax

Procedure DrawASCII(Var X,Y : Integer; Scale, Ch : Byte);

Usage **DrawASCII** displays character **Ch** at absolute coordinates **X:Y**. The size of the character is multiplied by **Scale**.

DrawText

Syntax

Procedure DrawText(X,Y,Scale : Integer;
                        Text : WrkString);

Usage   **DrawText** displays string **Text** at absolute coordinates **X:Y**. The size of the characters is multiplied by **Scale**.

DrawTextW

Syntax

Procedure DrawTextW(X,Y,Scale : Real; Text : WrkString);

Usage   **DrawTextW** displays string **Text** at world coordinates **X:Y**. The size of the characters is multiplied by **Scale**.

TextDown

Syntax

Function TextDown(TY, Boundary : Integer) : Integer;

Usage   **TextDown** returns the absolute coordinate of the
pixel located at text line **TY** plus the number of pixels specified
in **Boundary**.

TextLeft

Syntax

Function TextLeft(TX, Boundary : Integer) : Integer;

Usage   **TextLeft** returns the absolute coordinate of the pixel located at text column **TX** less the number of pixels specified in **Boundary**.

TextRight

Syntax

Function TextRight(TX, Boundary : Integer) : Integer;

Usage   **TextRight** returns the absolute coordinate of the pixel located at text column **TX** plus the number of pixels specified in **Boundary**.

TextUp

Syntax

Function TextUp(TY, Boundary : Integer) : Integer;

Usage   **TextUp** returns the absolute coordinate of the pixel located at text line **TY** less the number of pixels specified in **Boundary**.

Turbo Pascal Editor Toolbox

Aspects of Word Processing Programming
Editor Toolbox Procedures and Functions

All programmers use a word processor or text editor to write their programs. Yet to many the fundamental operations of a word processor remain a mystery. The Turbo Pascal Editor Toolbox sheds light on this topic by providing the source code you need to customize your own word processor and at the same time learn how these programs are written.

Aspects of Word Processing Programming

People use their computers for word processing more than for any other purpose. In many offices, word processors have replaced typewriters completely. The proliferation of word processing software has brought forth a wide range of software—some good, some bad, and much in between.

What makes a word processor good or bad depends to some degree on personal taste. One thing that everyone prefers, however, is speed. Slow word processors are more than an annoyance; they cost valuable time. The Turbo Pascal Editor Toolbox routines are fast largely because they are well written, utilize a linked list buffer structure, and use as much RAM as possible to store documents as they are edited.

TWENTY ONE

Another characteristic people look for in a word processor is features—generally, the more a word processor has, the better. The Turbo Pascal Editor Toolbox provides a good range of features, from word wrapping and moving blocks of text, to windows and background printing.

The Editor Toolbox comes with three word processors: the binary editor, First-Ed, and MicroStar. The binary editor is a self-contained assembler language program that is easy to use, but offers little in the way of instruction to programmers. First-Ed, and its more advanced cousin, MicroStar, are written almost entirely in Turbo Pascal and contain a wealth of examples on good programming technique.

Editor Toolbox Procedures and Functions

The Editor Toolbox uses many specialized routines to perform different tasks. While many of these routines are tailored to the editing environment, you can learn much from them that can be applied to other programming situations.

CheckCurWinModified   [MSFILE.PAS]

Syntax

Function CheckCurWinModified : Boolean;

Description

If the current window has been modified, prompts the user to save it or else lose the changes.

EdAbandonFile   [EDFILE.PAS,MSFILE.PAS]

Syntax

Procedure EdAbandonFile(ExitEditor : Boolean);

Description

Closes, without saving, the file currently in the editor. After the file is closed, **EdShutWindow** is called to close the window.

EdAddTrailingBackslash   [MSSTRING.PAS]

Syntax

Function EdAddTrailingBackslash(Mask : Filepath) : Filepath;

Description

This function adds a trailing backslash (\) to a pathname when it needs one.

EdAddWindow   [EDMAIN.PAS,MSMAIN.PAS]

Syntax

Procedure EdAddWindow;

Description

This procedure adds a text window to the editor, gets a file for the window, reads the file, and makes the new window the active window.

EdAdjustColNo   [MSPTROP.PAS]

Syntax

Function EdAdjustColNo(P, Q : PlineDesc;
                        Col : Integer) : Integer;

Description

When you move up and down line by line, the cursor should remain in the same column. This gets complicated when the display fonts option is enabled because the displayed font codes are not counted when calculating columns. **EdAdjustColno** returns an integer that represents the effective column in a new line that matches the effective column in the current line.

EdAllocateWindow   [MSMEMOP.PAS,EDMEMOP.PAS]

Syntax

Function EdAllocateWindow(Top, Len, Cr, Cc : Integer;
                           Fn : Filepath) : PwinDesc;

Description

Allocates memory for a new text stream, initializes a window descriptor, and returns the address of that descriptor.

EdAppPromptLine   [MSUSER.PAS,EDUSER.PAS]

Syntax

Procedure EdAppPromptLine(S : VarString);

Description

This procedure is used to create flexible user prompts. It appends string **S** to **PromptLine** and updates **PromptCol** to point to the new end of line.

EdArg2Integer   [MSUSER.PAS]

Syntax

Procedure EdArg2Integer(Arg : String255;
                    Min, Max : Integer;
                    Var V);

Description

Converts string **Arg** to an integer value between **Min** and **Max**. Untyped variable **V** holds the resulting integer. If the value is below **Min**, the procedure returns the value of **Min**. If the value is above **Max**, the procedure returns the value of **Max**.

EdAskfor   [MSUSER.PAS,EDUSER.PAS]

Syntax

Procedure EdAskFor(Prompt : VarString;
              Xp, Yp, Wid : Integer;
              Var Rs : VarString);

Description

Pops up a window at coordinates **Xp:Yp** with a width of **Wid**. The window displays **Prompt** and accepts string **Rs** from the user.

EdAskforEditor   [EDUSER.PAS,MSUSER.PAS]

Syntax

Procedure EdAskForEditor(Xp, Yp, XSize, MaxLen : Byte;
                                            HaveWindow : Boolean;
                                                    Var Rs : Var-
                                                            String);

Description

Allows the user to edit string **Rs**, which is displayed at **Xp:Yp**.
This string is displayed to a maximum length of **XSize** characters, but may contain up to **MaxLen** characters. If **HaveWin-
dow** is TRUE, the keystrokes are coming from a macro.

EdBackPtr   [EDPTROP.PAS,MSPTROP.PAS]

Syntax

Procedure EdBackPtr(Var P);

Description

Returns a pointer of type **PlineDesc** or **PwinDesc** that points to
its backward link.

EdBackTab   [MSTABS.PAS]

Syntax

Procedure EdBackTab;

Description

Performs a back tab command. To do so, it must compute the
location of the previous tab position and move the cursor to that
position.

EdBackupCurLine   [MSPTROP.PAS,EDPTROP.PAS]

Syntax

Procedure EdBackupCurLine(W : PwinDesc);

Description

When the user reduces a window, the current text line might be cropped as the bottom of the window moves up. This procedure moves the cursor up to ensure that the cursor is always visible in the window.

EdBiosScroll   [EDSCRN2.PAS,MSSCRN2.PAS]

Syntax

Procedure EdBiosScroll;

Description

Uses the BIOS service to scroll a portion of the screen up or down. Using the BIOS service is faster than redrawing the screen.

EdBlockBegin   [EDPTROP.PAS,MSPTROP.PAS]

Syntax

Procedure EdBlockBegin;

Description

Sets the block begin marker to the cursor position.

EdBlockCopy   [MSBLOK.PAS,EDBLOK.PAS]

Syntax

Procedure EdBlockCopy;

Description

Processes the copy block command when valid block begin and block end markers have been set.

EdBlockDelete   [EDBLOK.PAS,MSBLOK.PAS]

Syntax

Procedure EdBlockDelete;

Description

Processes the delete block command when valid block begin and block end markers have been set.

EdBlockEnd   [EDPTROP.PAS,MSPTROP.PAS]

Syntax

Procedure EdBlockEnd;

Description

Sets the block end marker to the current cursor position.

EdBlockHide   [MSPTROP.PAS,EDPTROP.PAS]

Syntax

Procedure EdBlockHide;

Description

When you define a block, using **EdBlockBegin** and **EdBlock-End**, the characters in the block are displayed using different attributes. **EdBlockHide** hides the selected block by returning the display to normal attributes. This procedure acts as a toggle, hiding and unhiding the block in turn.

EdBlockInit   [MSFIND.PAS]

Syntax

Procedure EdBlockInit;

Description

When you perform a block search (a search for text within a defined block), this procedure positions the logical cursor at the beginning of the block (if search is forward) or at the end of the block (if the search is backward).

EdBlockMove   [MSBLOK.PAS,EDBLOK.PAS]

Syntax

Procedure EdBlockMove;

Description

Moves a defined block of text from its current location to the location of the cursor.

EdBlockRead   [MSUSER.PAS]

Syntax

```
Procedure EdBlockRead(Var F : File;
                      Var Buf;
                      Num : Word;
                      Var BytesRead);
```

Description

Reads **Num** bytes of text from file **F** into buffer **Buf**. Upon return, **BytesRead** contains the number of bytes actually read from the file. This procedure is merely a shell that calls the Turbo Pascal standard procedure **BlockRead** and then checks for I/O errors.

EdBlockWord   [EDPTROP.PAS, MSPTROP.PAS]

Syntax

```
Procedure EdBlockWord;
```

Description

Marks the word to the right of the cursor as a block.

EdBlockWrite   [MSUSER.PAS]

Syntax

```
Procedure EdBlockWrite(Var F : File;
                       Var Buf;
                       Num : Word);
```

Description

Writes **Num** bytes of text from buffer **Buf** into file **F**. This procedure is a shell that calls the Turbo Pascal standard procedure **BlockWrite** and then checks for I/O errors.

EdBottomScreen   [MSPTROP.PAS,EDPTROP.PAS]

Syntax

Procedure EdBottomScreen;

Description

Moves the logical cursor to the last line displayed in the current window.

EdBreathe   [EDUSER.PAS,MSUSER.PAS]

Syntax

Procedure EdBreathe;

Description

This procedure calls **EdKeyPressed**. Its purpose is to extract characters from the BIOS keyboard buffer and place them in the editor's larger buffer.

EdBrowseDirectory   [MSDIR.PAS]

Syntax

Procedure EdBrowseDirectory(Var W : WindowRec;
                            TotalFiles : Integer);

Description

Lets user scroll a window in which appear filenames for a selected directory. **TotalFiles** is the number of files in **Fname**, a pointer to a sorted array of filenames.

EdBufferCurrentLine   [EDPTROP.PAS,MSPTROP.PAS]

Syntax

Procedure EdBufferCurrentLine;

Description

Stores the current line so that the user can restore the line with the ^QL command.

EdBufferSize   [EDMEMOP.PAS,MSMEMOP.PAS]

Syntax

Function EdBufferSize(Ncols : Integer) : Integer;

Description

Calculates the amount of memory needed to store a line of text that uses **Ncols** columns.

EdBuildFontAttribute   [MSSCRN1.PAS]

Syntax

Procedure EdBuildFontAttribute(Var Fa : FontAttributeArray);

Description

This procedure initializes **Fa** to the display attributes corresponding to each combination of fonts.

EdCalcMemory [MSMEMOP.PAS,EDMEMOP.PAS]

Syntax

Function EdCalcMemory : VarString;

Description

Returns, in the form of a string, the amount of memory available on the heap.

EdCenterLine [MSTABS.PAS]

Syntax

Procedure EdCenterLine;

Description

Centers the current line in margins.

EdChangeAttribute [MSSCRN1.PAS,EDSCRN1.PAS]

Syntax

Procedure EdChangeAttribute(Number, Row,
                    Col, Attr : Integer);

Description

Starting at coordinates **Row** and **Col**, this procedure sets the video attribute of the next **Number** characters to **Attr**.

EdChangeCase   [MSTEXT.PAS]

Syntax

Procedure EdChangeCase(Mode : CaseChange);

Description

Toggles the case of a single character or a block of characters. Uppercase letters become lowercase, and vice versa.

EdChangeFlag   [EDPTROP.PAS,MSPTROP.PAS]

Syntax

Procedure EdChangeFlag(P : PlineDesc;
                       FlagVal : Boolean;
                       FlagPos : Word);

Description

Each line contains a flag, the individual bits of which indicate different statuses. If **FlagVal** is not zero, **EdChangeFlag** sets the flag of line **P** according to the **FlagPos** map; if **FlagVal** equals zero, **EdChangeFlag** clears the flag of line **P** according to the **FlagPos** map.

EdChangeStatus   [MSPTROP.PAS]

Syntax

Procedure EdChangeStatus(NewVal : Word;
                         Var StoreLoc : Word);

Description

Sets flag **StoreLoc** equal to **NewVal**.

EdChangeStreamName   [EDPTROP.PAS, MSPTROP.PAS]

Syntax

Procedure EdChangeStreamName(Fname : Filepath);

Description

Changes name of text stream in the current window to **Fname**.

EdCheckNoMarker   [EDPTROP.PAS, MSPTROP.PAS]

Syntax

Procedure EdCheckNoMarker;

Description

After a deletion operation, **EdCheckNoMarker** determines if any block markers point to text that no longer exists. If this occurs, **EdCheckNoMarker** sets the block pointers to **Nil**.

EdChooseAppending   [MSTEXT.PAS]

Syntax

Procedure EdChooseAppending(Var Choice : Integer);

Description

Displays a menu asking the user to choose between overwriting a specified file or appending text to the file.

EdClassifyInput   [MSMAIN.PAS,EDMAIN.PAS]

Syntax

Procedure EdClassifyInput;

Description

Retrieves next character from the typeahead buffer and either inserts the character into the current text stream or, if the character is a control character, routes the request to the appropriate routine.

EdCleanFileName   [MSSTRING.PAS,EDSTRING.PAS]

Syntax

Procedure EdCleanFileName(Var Fname : Filepath);

Description

This procedure accepts a filename, **Fname**, converts the string to uppercase letters, removes blank spaces, expands the file path, and performs some error checking.

EdClearBuffer   [MSUSER.PAS]

Syntax

Procedure EdClearBuffer;

Description

Clears the editor typeahead keyboard buffer.

EdClearString   [EDSTRING.PAS,MSSTRING.PAS]

Syntax

Procedure EdClearString(Var S);

Description

Sets string S to a null string.

EdCloneAttrFlags   [MSPTROP.PAS]

Syntax

Procedure EdCloneAttrFlags(P, Q : PlineDesc;
                                            Col : Integer);

Description

Determines the attribute that is active in column **Col** of line **P**, and applies that attribute to line **Q**.

EdCloneModifiedFlags   [MSBACK.PAS,EDBACK.PAS]

Syntax

Procedure EdCloneModifiedFlags;

Description

The editor allows you to view the same text stream in more than one window. **EdCloneModifiedFlags** makes sure that any flags that are modified in one window are modified in the other window.

EdClrFlag   [EDPTROP.PAS,MSPTROP.PAS]

Syntax

Procedure EdClrFlag(P : PlineDesc;
                               Mask : Word);

Description

Clears the flags for line **P** depending on the value of **Mask**.

EdCmdAccessible   [MSSCRN2.PAS]

Syntax

Function EdCmdAccessible(Menu : Menuptr;
                                      Sub : Byte) : Boolean;

Description

When no text window is open, many menu functions are not available. **EdCmdAccessible** returns TRUE when choice **Sub** of menu **Menu** is accessible. If it returns FALSE, the editor will not allow you to select that function.

EdCommandKeys   [EDCMDS.PAS,MSCMDS.PAS]

Syntax

Function EdCommandKeys(C : CommandType;
                                   P : CommandPriority) :
                                   CommandString;

Description

This procedure retrieves from command list **CmdList** a series of keystrokes that correspond to command **C**. The contents of **CmdList** are defined in MSCMDS.ASM, which is linked to MicroStar and used as data space.

EdCompress   [MSPTROP.PAS]

Syntax

Procedure EdCompress(P : PlineDesc;
                     Lmargin : Integer;
                     Var Col, Len : Integer);

Description

When right justification is on, spaces are added within a line to make the line flush with the right margin. **EdCompress** removes these added blanks.

EdComputeEffectiveColNo   [MSPTROP.PAS]

Syntax

Function EdComputeEffectiveColNo(Attribs : Boolean;
                                 P : PlineDesc;
                                 Col : Integer) : Integer;

Description

Returns the column number **Col** for line **P**. When **Attribs** is TRUE, the function returns the effective column number, adjusted for control characters. If **Attribs** is FALSE, the function returns the original value of **Col**.

EdControlFilter   [EDSTRING.PAS,MSSTRING.PAS]

Syntax

Function EdControlFilter(Ch : Char) : Char;

Description

Returns the control character equivalent of character **Ch**. For example, **EdControlFilter('L')** returns CTRL-L.

EdCursorInBlock   [MSPTROP.PAS,EDPTROP.PAS]

Syntax

Function EdCursorInBlock(Q : PlineDesc;
                        C : Integer;
                        EndMarkOn : Boolean) : Boolean;

Description

Searches the text buffer from the beginning of the marked block to determine if column **C** of line **Q** is within the defined block. If **EndMarkOn** is FALSE, the function will also return FALSE if position **Q:C** happens to be the location of an end block marker.

EdDefaultExtension   [EDSTRING.PAS,MSSTRING.PAS]

Syntax

Procedure EdDefaultExtension(Ext : VarString;
                            Var Fname : Filepath);

Description

If **Fname** does not include an extension, **Ext** is appended to it.

EdDeleteAllText   [MSMEMOP.PAS,EDMEMOP.PAS]

Syntax

Procedure EdDeleteAllText(W : PwinDesc);

Description

Deletes an entire text stream.

EdDeleteLeadingBlanks   [MSSTRING.PAS]

Syntax

Procedure EdDeleteLeadingBlanks(Var S : String);

Description

Removes leading blanks from string S.

EdDeleteLeftChar   [MSEDIT.PAS,EDEDIT.PAS]

Syntax

Procedure EdDeleteLeftChar;

Description

Processes the command that deletes the character to the left of the cursor.

EdDeleteLine   [MSEDIT.PAS,EDEDIT.PAS]

Syntax

Procedure EdDeleteLine;

Description

Processes the command that deletes the current line. The deleted line is stored in the undo buffer.

EdDeleteLineNoRecourse   [MSTEXT.PAS]

Syntax

Procedure EdDeleteLineNoRecourse;

Description

Deletes a line but does not store it in the undo buffer.

EdDeleteLineRight   [MSEDIT.PAS,EDEDIT.PAS]

Syntax

Procedure EdDeleteLineRight;

Description

Deletes all text on the current line to the right of the cursor.

EdDeleteRightChar   [EDEDIT.PAS,MSEDIT.PAS]

Syntax

Procedure EdDeleteRightChar;

Description

Processes the command that deletes the character to the right of the cursor.

EdDeleteRightWord   [EDEDIT.PAS,MSEDIT.PAS]

Syntax

Procedure EdDeleteRightWord;

Description

Processes the command that deletes the word to the right of the cursor.

EdDeleteTrailers   [MSSTRING.PAS]

Syntax

Procedure EdDeleteTrailers(Var S : String);

Description

Deletes any characters following the first word in string S.

EdDesTextDesc   [MSMEMOP.PAS, EDMEMOP.PAS]

Syntax

Procedure EdDesTextDesc(P : PlineDesc);

Description

Releases memory from both P^.Txt, the line text buffer, and P^, effectively eliminating this line from the text stream.

EdDirectory   [MSFILE.PAS]

Syntax

Procedure EdDirectory;

Description

Displays a file directory and allows the user to browse through it.

EdDisplayCommandBuffer   [MSUSER.PAS, EDUSER.PAS]

Syntax

Procedure EdDisplayCommandBuffer;

Description

While awaiting a completed command, displays the partial command on the screen. For example, displays ^K when waiting for complete command ^KD.

EdDisplayPromptWindow   [MSUSER.PAS,EDUSER.PAS]

Syntax

Procedure EdDisplayPromptWindow(Msg : VarString;
                                Yp : Integer;
                                OKset : Charset;
                                Var Ch : Char;
                                BoxAttr : BoxType);

Description

Displays a one-line message **Msg** centered on line **Yp** and waits for a character to be entered. Acceptable characters are defined by **OKset**, and **BoxAttr** defines the characteristics of the box and message.

EdDosPathDelim   [MSSTRING.PAS]

Syntax

Function EdDosPathDelim(Ch : Char) : Boolean;

Description

Returns TRUE if **Ch** is a legal DOS path delimiter (that is, \, :, or Null).

EdDownLine   [MSEDIT.PAS,EDEDIT.PAS]

Syntax

Procedure EdDownLine;

Description

Processes the command that moves the cursor down one line.

EdDownPage   [MSEDIT.PAS,EDEDIT.PAS]

Syntax

Procedure EdDownPage;

Description

Processes the command that moves the cursor down one page.

EdDrawBox   [MSUSER.PAS]

Syntax

Procedure EdDrawBox(Border : BorderChars;
                    XPosn, YPosn, XSize, YSize : Byte;
                    BoxAttr : BoxType);

Description

Draws a box with upper left corner at **XPosn:YPosn**. The size of the box is **XSize** horizontal characters and **YSize** vertical characters. The characters used to draw the border are contained in **Border**, and the type of box is defined by **BoxAttr**.

EdDrawItem   [MSSCRN2.PAS]

Syntax

Procedure EdDrawItem(Menu : Menuptr;
                     Sub : Byte);

Description

Displays the choices in the main and pull-down menus.

EdDrawMenu   [MSSCRN2.PAS]

Syntax

Procedure EdDrawMenu(Menu : Menuptr);

Description

Draws a menu and any child menus that are currently selected.

EdDrawSolidCursor   [MSSCRN1.PAS]

Syntax

Procedure EdDrawSolidCursor;

Description

Creates a solid cursor.

EdEditKeyWindow   [MSMACRO.PAS]

Syntax

Procedure EdEditKeyWindow(Msg : VarString;
                    Xmin, Ymin, Xmax, Ymax,
                    MaxLen : Integer;
                    Var Keys : MacroString);

Description

Sets up a window that is used to edit macros and printer setup strings.

EdEditMacro [MSMACRO.PAS]

Syntax

Procedure EdEditMacro;

Description

Used to edit a command macro.

EdEditTabLine [MSTABS.PAS]

Syntax

Procedure EdEditTabLine;

Description

Allows user to edit the tab spacing on the ruler line.

EdEndOfPath [EDSTRING.PAS,MSSTRING.PAS]

Syntax

Function EdEndOfPath(Path : Filepath) : Filepath;

Description

Accepts a full path and filename and returns only the filename part.

EdEraseMenuHelp   [MSUSER.PAS]

Syntax

Procedure EdEraseMenuHelp;

Description

Removes a help message from the prompt line.

EdEraseMenus   [MSSCRN2.PAS]

Syntax

Procedure EdEraseMenus;

Description

Removes all menus from the screen.

EdEraseSolidCursor   [MSSCRN1.PAS]

Syntax

Procedure EdEraseSolidCursor;

Description

Hides the cursor before scrolling, to make scrolling less distracting.

EdErrorMsg   [EDUSER.PAS,MSUSER.PAS]

Syntax

Procedure EdErrorMsg(Msgno : Integer);

Description

Displays error message **Msgno** and clears the typeahead buffer.

EdExistFile   [EDFILE.PAS,MSFILE.PAS]

Syntax

Function EdExistFile(Fname : Filepath) : Boolean;

Description

Returns TRUE if file **Fname** exists.

EdFastWrite   [EDSCRN1.PAS,MSSCRN1.PAS]

Syntax

Procedure EdFastWrite(St : String;
                      Row, Col, Attr : Integer);

Description

Displays string **St** at coordinates **Col:Row** in using video attribute byte **Attr**. This procedure displays without snow.

EdFileError   [MSUSER.PAS]

Syntax

Function EdFileError : Boolean;

Description

Returns TRUE if an error occurred during a file operation.

EdFileHasExtension   [EDSTRING.PAS,MSSTRING.PAS]

Syntax

Function EdFileHasExtension(Fname : Filepath;
                            Var DotPos : Integer) : Boolean;

Description

Returns TRUE when file **Fname** has an extension. **DotPos** returns the position of the period in **Fname**.

EdFileWrite   [EDFILE.PAS,MSFILE.PAS]

Syntax

Procedure EdFileWrite(Fname : Filepath;
                      Quitting : Boolean);

Description

Saves current text stream to file **Fname**. If **Quitting** is TRUE, then the program is ending.

EdFind   [MSFIND.PAS,EDFIND.PAS]

Syntax

Procedure EdFind;

Description

Processes the find-pattern command.

EdFindNext   [MSMAIN.PAS,EDMAIN.PAS]

Syntax

Procedure EdFindNext;

Description

Looks for the next occurrence of the last match found.

EdFindReplace   [EDFIND.PAS]

Syntax

Procedure EdFindReplace;

Description

Processes the command that locates a pattern in the text stream
and replaces it with another pattern.

EdFindWinDesc   [EDPTROP.PAS,MSPTROP.PAS]

Syntax

Function EdFindWinDesc(Wno : Byte) : PwinDesc;

Description

Returns the window descriptor for window number **Wno**.

EdFindWindow   [EDPTROP.PAS,MSPTROP.PAS]

Syntax

Function EdFindWindow(T : PlineDesc) : PwinDesc;

Description

Returns the window containing line **T**.

EdFirstLetter   [MSSTRING.PAS]

Syntax

Function EdFirstLetter(S : String) : Char;

Description

Returns the first nonblank character of string **S**.

EdFixBaseLine   [EDPTROP.PAS,MSPTROP.PAS]

Syntax

Procedure EdFixBaseLine(WindFrom : PwinDesc);

Description

Redefines **Topline** and **Curline** in window **WindFrom** before a block operation deletes them.

EdFixBlockInsertedLine   [MSPTROP.PAS,EDPTROP.PAS]

Syntax

Procedure EdFixBlockInsertedLine(ThisL, NextL : PlineDesc;
                                 BreakCol : Integer;
                                 Delta : Integer);

Description

This procedure is called when a line is broken in two. **ThisL** is the portion of the original line, and **NextL** is the portion moved to the next line. **BreakCol** is the column at which the break occurs, and **Delta** is subtracted from the **Col** field in **ThisL**.

EdFixBlockInsertedSpace   [MSPTROP.PAS,EDPTROP.PAS]

Syntax

Procedure EdFixBlockInsertedSpace(P : PlineDesc;
                                  Start : Integer;
                                  Num : Integer);

Description

Called when characters are added or deleted from line **P**. **Start** is the column at which the operation begins. **Num** is the number of characters added or, if negative, deleted.

EdFixMarkInsertedLine   [EDPTROP.PAS,MSPTROP.PAS]

Syntax

Procedure EdFixMarkInsertedLine(ThisL, NextL : PlineDesc;
                                       BreakCol : Integer;
                                       Delta : Integer);

Description

When **ThisL** is broken into two lines, creating **NextL**, this procedure adjusts the text markers and **InMark** flags. **BreakCol** is the column in **ThisL** at which the break occurs. When a text marker is part of the text moved to **NextL**, the procedure subtracts **Delta** from the new line's **Col** field.

EdFixMarkInsertedSpace   [EDPTROP.PAS,MSPTROP.PAS]

Syntax

Procedure EdFixMarkInsertedSpace(P : PlineDesc;
                                         Start : Integer;
                                         Num : Integer);

Description

Updates the text markers in line **P** after characters have been inserted or deleted. **Start** is the starting column, and **Num** is the number of characters inserted or, if negative, deleted.

EdFixUpWindowSpan   [EDPTROP.PAS,MSPTROP.PAS]

Syntax

Procedure EdFixUpWindowSpan(P : PlineDesc);

Description

When the user deletes line **P** from a window, this procedure checks to see if **P** is either at the top of the window or is the line on which the cursor is located. If either is true, the window has to be updated to reflect new lines in these positions.

EdFlagExit   [EDEDIT.PAS]

Syntax

Procedure EdFlagExit;

Description

When the user exits from the editor, this procedure shuts down the background printing and sets **RunDown** to TRUE.

EdFlagSet   [EDPTROP.PAS,MSPTROP.PAS]

Syntax

Function EdFlagSet(P : PlineDesc;
                   Mask : Word) : Boolean;

Description

Returns TRUE if the mask flag in line **P** is set.

EdFlushUndo   [MSTEXT.PAS]

Syntax

Procedure EdFlushUndo;

Description

Deletes the contents of the undo buffer.

EdForceMessage   [MSUSER.PAS]

Syntax

Procedure EdForceMessage(Msg : VarString);

Description

Turns off **IntrFlag** to ensure that a message is displayed quickly.

EdFwdPtr   [MSPTROP.PAS,EDPTROP.PAS]

Syntax

Procedure EdFwdPtr(Var P);

Description

Changes **P** (**PlineDesc** or **PwinDesc**) to its forward link.

EdGenLineNo   [MSBACK.PAS,EDBACK.PAS]

Syntax

Procedure EdGenLineNo;

Description

Calculates the current line and byte count for each visible window.

EdGenLineOne   [MSBACK.PAS]

Syntax

Procedure EdGenLineOne(W : PwinDesc);

Description

Calculates line numbers and the byte count of the cursor position for window **W**.

EdGetAnyChar   [MSUSER.PAS,EDUSER.PAS]

Syntax

Function EdGetAnyChar : Char;

Description

Returns a character from internal keyboard buffer.

EdGetCursorCommand   [MSUSER.PAS]

Syntax

Function EdGetCursorCommand(CmdSet : Charset) : Char;

Description

Waits for a valid cursor key to be pressed and returns the command as a WordStar-style character command (for example, ^E).

EdGetCustomMenuChoice   [MSMENU.PAS]

Syntax

Procedure EdGetCustomMenuChoice(Var Menu : Custom-
                                           MenuRec;
                                Var Choice : Integer);

Description

Displays a custom menu and returns the user's choice.

EdGetDefaultExtension   [MSSET.PAS,EDFILE.PAS]

Syntax

Procedure EdGetDefaultExtension;

Description

Asks the user to enter a new default file extension.

EdGetFileName   [EDFILE.PAS,MSFILE.PAS]

Syntax

Function EdGetFileName(Prompt, DefExt : VarString;
                    Row, Attr : Byte;
                    Var LastFname : Filepath) : Filepath;

Description

Displays **Prompt** on **Row** using **Attr** and expects user to enter a filename. If the filename has no extension, **DefExt** is appended. Returns a filename to use.

EdGetInput   [MSUSER.PAS,EDUSER.PAS]

Syntax

Function EdGetInput : Char;

Description

Returns the next character from typeahead buffer.

EdGetMacroNumber   [MSMACRO.PAS]

Syntax

Procedure EdGetMacroNumber(Msgno : Integer;
                        Var Macronum : Integer);

Description

Lets the user select a macro from a menu. **Msgno** refers to the message displayed on the prompt line when using the menu. The number of the macro is returned in **Macronum**.

EdGetMenuChoice   [MSMENU.PAS]

Syntax

Procedure EdGetMenuChoice(Var Cmd : CommandType;
                        Var ExitMenu : Boolean);

Description

Displays a menu. Upon return, **Cmd** contains the command to execute. If **ExitMenu** is TRUE, the menu system is removed from the screen.

EdGetMessage   [MESSAGE.PAS]

Syntax

Function EdGetMessage(Msgno : Integer) : String;

Description

Returns message number **Msgno** from the packed message buffer.

EdGetNumber   [MSUSER.PAS,EDUSER.PAS]

Syntax

Function EdGetNumber(Prompt : VarString;
                        Default : Integer) : Integer;

Description

Prompts user to enter a number using **Prompt**, offering **Default** as a choice.

EdGetOptions   [MSFIND.PAS]

Syntax

Procedure EdGetOptions(Xp, Yp, Width, MaxLen : Integer;
                        HaveWindow : Boolean);

Description

Prompts the user to enter the search options for a find-and-replace operation.

EdGetPageNum   [MSPTROP.PAS]

Syntax

Function EdGetPageNum(P : PlineDesc) : Integer;

Description

Returns the page number on which line **P** is located.

EdGetScreenMode   [MSSCRN1.PAS]

Syntax

Procedure EdGetScreenMode;

Description

Determines which video adapter is in use.

EdGetSearchString   [MSFIND.PAS]

Syntax

Procedure EdGetSearchString(Xp, Yp, Width, MaxLen :
                            Integer;
                            HaveWindow : Boolean;
                            Var SearchStr : VarString);

Description

Prompts user to enter a string to search for.

EdGetWindowToDivide   [EDPTROP.PAS,MSPTROP.PAS]

Syntax

Function EdGetWindowToDivide : Byte;

Description

Determines which window would be best to split and returns that window's number.

EdGlobalInit   [MSFIND.PAS]

Syntax

Procedure EdGlobalInit;

Description

Positions cursor at the beginning of the text stream (or the end, for a backward search) prior to a global search.

EdGotoColumn   [MSPTROP.PAS,EDPTROP.PAS]

Syntax

Procedure EdGotoColumn(Cno : Integer);

Description

Moves the cursor to column **Cno** on current line.

EdGotoLine   [MSPTROP.PAS,EDPTROP.PAS]

Syntax

Procedure EdGotoLine(Lno : Integer);

Description

Moves the cursor to line **Lno** of current window.

EdGotoPage   [MSEDIT.PAS]

Syntax

Procedure EdGotoPage(Pno : Integer);

Description

Moves the cursor to page **Pno**. This assumes that pagination is on.

EdGotoXY   [MSUSER.PAS,EDUSER.PAS]

Syntax

Procedure EdGotoXY(C, R : Byte);

Description

Moves the cursor to column **C** in row **R**.

EdHasWildCards   [MSSTRING.PAS]

Syntax

Function EdHasWildCards(Fname : Filepath) : Boolean;

Description

Returns TRUE if **Fname** contains wildcards.

EdHelpMenu   [MSTEXT.PAS]

Syntax

Procedure EdHelpMenu;

Description

Lets user select a help section from a menu.

EdHelpWindow   [MSUSER.PAS]

Syntax

Procedure EdHelpWindow(Cmd : CommandType);

Description

Displays a help window for command **Cmd**.

EdHighlightScreen   [MSSCRN2.PAS,EDSCRN2.PAS]

Syntax

Procedure EdHighlightScreen(Col1, Col2 : Integer;
                            Attr : Byte;
                            WaitForKey : Boolean);

Description

When a string match is located using the find feature, this procedure highlights the string using **Attr**. If **WaitForKey** is TRUE, then the procedure waits for the user to press a key.

EdHscroll   [EDBACK.PAS,MSBACK.PAS]

Syntax

Procedure EdHScroll;

Description

Scrolls windows horizontally.

EdHscrollOne   [MSBACK.PAS,EDBACK.PAS]

Syntax

Procedure EdHScrollOne(W : PwinDesc);

Description

Scrolls window **W** horizontally.

EdInitialize   [MSMAIN.PAS,EDMAIN.PAS]

Syntax

Procedure EdInitialize;

Description

Initializes editor variables and data structures.

EdInitMenus   [MSMENU.PAS]

Syntax

Procedure EdInitMenus;

Description

Initializes the dynamic data structures used in the menu system.

EdInitPrintState   [MSPRTM.PAS]

Syntax

Procedure EdInitPrintState;

Description

Sets up default printing values.

EdInitWindowSettings   [MSPTROP.PAS,EDPTROP.PAS]

Syntax

Procedure EdInitWindowSettings(W : PwinDesc);

Description

Sets fields in window **W** to default values.

EdInsertCtrlChar   [MSEDIT.PAS,EDEDIT.PAS]

Syntax

Procedure EdInsertCtrlChar;

Description

Inserts a control character into the text stream. This procedure, called when the user presses CTRL-P, forces the next character that is typed to be inserted into the text as a control character.

EdInsertLine   [EDEDIT.PAS,MSEDIT.PAS]

Syntax

Procedure EdInsertLine;

Description

Processes the insert-line command.

EdInsertLinePrimitive   [MSMEMOP.PAS,EDMEMOP.PAS]

Syntax

Procedure EdInsertLinePrimitive(M : BlockMarker;
                                Var P : PlineDesc);

Description

Inserts a new line after marker **M**. Returns a pointer, **P**, to new line.

EdInsertMacro   [MSMACRO.PAS]

Syntax

Procedure EdInsertMacro(MacNum, Ntimes : Integer);

Description

Put characters from macro **MacNum** into the typeahead buffer.
The macro will be inserted **Ntimes** times.

EdInsertPrintFormat   [MSTEXT.PAS]

Syntax

Procedure EdInsertPrintFormat(Ch : Char);

Description

Inserts print font toggles surrounding current cursor or marked
block.

EdInsertSpace   [EDMEMOP.PAS,MSMEMOP.PAS]

Syntax

Function EdInsertSpace(P : PlineDesc;
                    Start : Integer;
                    Num : Integer) : Boolean;

Description

Inserts **Num** spaces at position **Start** of line **P**.

EdInsertUndoBuffer   [MSTEXT.PAS]

Syntax

Procedure EdInsertUndoBuffer;

Description

Inserts the entire undo buffer at the current cursor location.

EdINT24Off   [INT24.PAS]

Syntax

Procedure EdINT24Off;

Description

Restores critical error handler saved previously.

EdINT24On   [INT24.PAS]

Syntax

Procedure EdINT24On;

Description

Installs our own critical error handler.

EdINT24Result   [INT24.PAS]

Syntax

Function EdINT24Result : Word;

Description

Returns the latest result from the critical error handler you installed.

EdInterruptibleDelay   [EDSCRN2.PAS, MSSCRN2.PAS]

Syntax

Procedure EdInterruptibleDelay(Time : Integer);

Description

Repeats a loop until either **Time** seconds have elapsed or the user presses a key.

EdInvokeDOS   [MSINVOKE.PAS]

Syntax

Procedure EdInvokeDOS;

Description

Starts a DOS shell.

EdJoinLine   [MSMEMOP.PAS,EDMEMOP.PAS]

Syntax

Procedure EdJoinLine;

Description

Joins two lines and updates block markers if required.

EdJoinLinePrimitive   [MSMEMOP.PAS,EDMEMOP.PAS]

Syntax

Procedure EdJoinLinePrimitive(P : PlineDesc;
                              LenP : Integer);

Description

Joins line **P** at column **LenP** with the next line.

EdJumpLastPosition   [MSTEXT.PAS]

Syntax

Procedure EdJumpLastPosition;

Description

Moves the cursor to its previous position in the text stream.

EdJumpMarker   [EDEDIT.PAS,MSEDIT.PAS]

Syntax

Procedure EdJumpMarker(M : BlockMarker);

Description

Moves cursor to marker **M**.

EdKeyInterrupt   [MSUSER.PAS,EDUSER.PAS]

Syntax

Function EdKeyInterrupt : Boolean;

Description

Returns TRUE if global variable **IntrFlag** is set to **Interrupt**, which means that background processes may be interrupted.

EdKeyPressed   [EDUSER.PAS,MSUSER.PAS]

Syntax

Function EdKeyPressed : Boolean;

Description

Returns TRUE if input is available in the typeahead buffer.

EdLeftChar   [EDEDIT.PAS,MSEDIT.PAS]

Syntax

Procedure EdLeftChar;

Description

Processes the left character command.

EdLeftLine   [EDEDIT.PAS,MSEDIT.PAS]

Syntax

Procedure EdLeftLine;

Description

Positions cursor at the left-most edge of the line.

EdLeftWord   [EDEDIT.PAS,MSEDIT.PAS]

Syntax

Procedure EdLeftWord;

Description

Moves cursor to the beginning of the word to the left of the cursor.

EdLineIndent   [EDPTROP.PAS,MSPTROP.PAS]

Syntax

Function EdLineIndent(P : PlineDesc) : Integer;

Description

Returns the indent of line **P** or 0 if the line is empty.

EdLinkBuffer   [MSPTROP.PAS,EDPTROP.PAS]

Syntax

Procedure EdLinkBuffer(P, Q : PlineDesc);

Description

Links line **Q** to follow line **P**.

EdLinkedWindow   [EDPTROP.PAS,MSPTROP.PAS]

Syntax

Function EdLinkedWindow(W : PwinDesc) : Boolean;

Description

Returns TRUE if window **W** is linked to any others.

EdLocase   [MSSTRING.PAS]

Syntax

Procedure EdLocase(Var S : String);

Description

Converts uppercase letters in **S** to lowercase.

EdLogDrive   [EDFILE.PAS,MSFILE.PAS]

Syntax

Procedure EdLogDrive(NewPath : Filepath);

Description

Lets the user select a new drive or directory.

EdLongPosBack   [MSSTRING.PAS,EDSTRING.PAS]

Syntax

Function EdLongPosBack(Var Buffer;
                       Start : Integer;
                       Var Pattern : VarString) : Integer;

Description

Searches backward, starting at **Start**, looking for a match to **Pattern**. When a match is found, returns the location as an offset from **Buffer**. If no match is found, returns zero.

EdLongPosFwd   [MSSTRING.PAS,EDSTRING.PAS]

Syntax

Function EdLongPosFwd(Var Buffer;
              Start, Size : Integer;
              Var Pattern : VarString) : Integer;

Description

Operates the same as **EdLongPosBack**, except that this procedure searches forward. This procedure will search a maximum of
Size bytes.

EdLongUpcase   [EDSTRING.PAS,MSSTRING.PAS]

Syntax

Procedure EdLongUpcase(Var Buffer;
              Size : Integer);

Description

Uses external procedure to convert **Size** characters in **Buffer** to
all uppercase.

EdMainMenu   [MSMAIN.PAS,EDMAIN.PAS]

Syntax

Procedure EdMainMenu;

Description

Captures command-line parameters and sets up the editor.

EdMakeBakFile   [MSFILE.PAS]

Syntax

Procedure EdMakeBakFile(Fname : Filepath);

Description

Creates a backup of file **Fname**. The backup file will have the .BAK extension.

EdMakTextDesc   [MSMEMOP.PAS,EDMEMOP.PAS]

Syntax

Function EdMakTextDesc(Ncols : Integer) : PlineDesc;

Description

Creates and returns a new text descriptor record. Checks to see that **Ncols** is not greater than the maximum number of characters per line.

EdMarkBlock   [EDBACK.PAS,MSBACK.PAS]

Syntax

Procedure EdMarkBlock;

Description

Sets line descriptors within a marked block.

EdMemAvail   [MSPTROP.PAS,EDPTROP.PAS]

Syntax

Function EdMemAvail(Size, Margin : Word) : Boolean;

Description

Returns TRUE if the amount of contiguous memory existing on heap exceeds the sum of **Size** and **Margin**.

EdMoveCursorIntoLine   [EDPTROP.PAS,MSPTROP.PAS]

Syntax

Procedure EdMoveCursorIntoLine;

Description

Moves cursor into new line, but does not allow the cursor to extend beyond the end of the line.

EdMoveFromScreen   [MSSCRN1.PAS,EDSCRN1.PAS]

Syntax

Procedure EdMoveFromScreen(Var Source, Dest;
                        Length : Integer);

Description

Moves **Length** words from **Source** (video memory) to **Dest** (video buffer) without snow.

EdMoveToBegin   [MSTEXT.PAS]

Syntax

Procedure EdMoveToBegin;

Description

Moves cursor to prior line with indentation equal to current line.

EdMoveToEnd   [MSTEXT.PAS]

Syntax

Procedure EdMoveToEnd;

Description

Moves cursor to following line with indentation equal to current line.

EdMoveToScreen   [MSSCRN1.PAS,EDSCRN1.PAS]

Syntax

Procedure EdMoveToScreen(Var Source, Dest;
                    Length : Integer);

Description

Moves **Length** words from **Source** (video buffer) to **Dest** (video memory) without snow.

EdNewLine   [MSEDIT.PAS,EDEDIT.PAS]

Syntax

Procedure EdNewLine;

Description

Processes a carriage return.

EdNewLinePrimitive   [MSMEMOP.PAS,EDMEMOP.PAS]

Syntax

Procedure EdNewLinePrimitive;

Description

Creates a new line at the cursor position and moves the text to
the right as necessary.

EdNewStream   [MSPTROP.PAS,EDPTROP.PAS]

Syntax

Function EdNewStream : Word;

Description

Returns the current value of **NextStream** and then increments
the variable.

EdNewTextStream   [MSMEMOP.PAS]

Syntax

Function EdNewTextStream(W : PwinDesc) : Boolean;

Description

Creates a new text stream in window **W** and returns TRUE if successful.

EdNextSentence   [MSTEXT.PAS]

Syntax

Procedure EdNextSentence;

Description

Advances cursor to start of next sentence.

EdNoBlock   [EDPTROP.PAS,MSPTROP.PAS]

Syntax

Function EdNoBlock : Boolean;

Description

Returns TRUE if no block is marked and visible.

EdOffBlock   [MSPTROP.PAS,EDPTROP.PAS]

Syntax

Procedure EdOffBlock;

Description

Turns off the **Inblock** bit for every line of a text stream in every window.

EdPadEntry   [MSSTRING.PAS]

Syntax

Function EdPadEntry(F : String;
                    Width : Byte) : String;

Description

Returns string **F**, padded with one blank on the left and as many blanks on the right as to increase the length to **Width**.

EdPickDir   [MSDIR.PAS]

Syntax

Function EdPickDir(Mask : Filepath;
                   Msgno : Integer;
                   Attr : Byte;
                   ReturnFile : Boolean) : Filepath;

Description

Lets user select a filename from a directory listing.

EdPickDirectory   [MSDIR.PAS]

Syntax

Function EdPickDirectory(Var W : WindowRec;
                         TotalFiles : Integer;
                         Mask : FilePath) : FilePath;

Description

Pops up window **W**, which displays the directory with **To-talFiles** entries that conform to **Mask**. The function returns the full path and filename for the file selected.

EdPrevSentence   [MSTEXT.PAS]

Syntax

Procedure EdPrevSentence;

Description

Positions cursor at start of the previous sentence.

EdPrintExit   [MSUSER.PAS]

Syntax

Procedure EdPrintExit;

Description

Shuts down background printing.

EdPrintFile   [MSMAIN.PAS]

Syntax

Procedure EdPrintFile;

Description

Performs necessary tasks to prepare a file for printing.

EdPrintNext   [MSUSER.PAS]

Syntax

Procedure EdPrintNext(PrintChars : Integer);

Description

Instructs background printing process to print the next **Print-Chars** characters of the file to be printed.

EdPrintSetDefaults   [MSPRTM.PAS]

Syntax

Procedure EdPrintSetDefaults(PrtDefFile : Filepath);

Description

Sets up defaults for printing system by reading their values from file **PrtDefFile**.

EdPrintSetup   [MSPRTM.PAS]

Syntax

Function EdPrintSetup : Boolean;

Description

Lets user set up for printing by selecting options from a menu. The function returns TRUE if printing is to begin.

EdProcessCommand   [MSMAIN.PAS,EDMAIN.PAS]

Syntax

Procedure EdProcessCommand(C : CommandType);

Description

This routine is the main command processor for the editor. This procedure executes functions based on the value of C.

EdProcessText   [MSEDIT.PAS,EDEDIT.PAS]

Syntax

Procedure EdProcessText(Ch : Char;
                        ImmediateUpdate : Boolean);

Description

Processes text input by adding **Ch** to the text stream. When Immediate Update is TRUE, the remainder of the screen will be updated as soon as it is possible.

EdPromptGotoCol [MSTEXT.PAS,EDTEXT.PAS]

Syntax

Procedure EdPromptGotoCol;

Description

Processes the Goto Col #n command.

EdPromptGotoLine [EDTEXT.PAS,MSTEXT.PAS]

Syntax

Procedure EdPromptGotoLine;

Description

Processes Goto Line #n command.

EdPromptGotoPage [MSTEXT.PAS]

Syntax

Procedure EdPromptGotoPage;

Description

Goes to page specified by user.

EdPromptGotoWindow   [MSTEXT.PAS]

Syntax

Procedure EdPromptGotoWindow;

Description

Goes to window specified by user.

EdPromptJumpMarker   [MSTEXT.PAS]

Syntax

Procedure EdPromptJumpMarker;

Description

Uses a menu to select and then jump to a text marker.

EdPromptLogDrive   [EDMAIN.PAS,MSMAIN.PAS]

Syntax

Procedure EdPromptLogDrive;

Description

Prompts the user for a new directory and then logs that as the current directory.

EdPromptMacroInsert   [MSMACRO.PAS]

Syntax

Procedure EdPromptMacroInsert;

Description

Prompts user to select a macro and then executes the macro once.

EdPromptSetMarker   [MSTEXT.PAS]

Syntax

Procedure EdPromptSetMarker;

Description

Uses a menu to choose and set a text marker.

EdPromptWriteBlock   [EDFILE.PAS]

Syntax

Procedure EdPromptWriteBlock;

Description

Asks user for a filename and then writes a block of text to the file.

EdPtrIsNil   [MSPTROP.PAS,EDPTROP.PAS]

Syntax

Function EdPtrIsNil(Var P) : Boolean;

Description

Returns TRUE if pointer **P** is nil.

EdPtrNotNil   [EDPTROP.PAS,MSPTROP.PAS]

Syntax

Function EdPtrNotNil(Var P) : Boolean;

Description

Returns TRUE if pointer **P** is not nil.

EdPushPrintString   [MSUSER.PAS]

Syntax

Procedure EdPushPrintString(S : PrintCommand);

Description
Pushes command string **S** onto print stack.

EdPushUndo   [MSMEMOP.PAS,EDMEMOP.PAS]

Syntax
Procedure EdPushUndo(Var P : PlineDesc);

Description
Saves deleted line **P** on the undo stack.

EdPushWindowStack   [MSMEMOP.PAS,EDMEMOP.PAS]

Syntax
Procedure EdPushWindowStack(W : PwinDesc);

Description
Puts window descriptor **W** on the window free list.

EdReadFile   [EDFILE.PAS,MSFILE.PAS]

Syntax
Procedure EdReadFile(Fname : Filepath);

Description

Checks and opens text file **Fname** for editing.

EdReadMacroFile   [MSMACRO.PAS]

Syntax

Procedure EdReadMacroFile(Fname : Filepath);

Description

Read macro file **Fname**.

EdReadTextFile   [EDFILE.PAS,MSFILE.PAS]

Syntax

Procedure EdReadTextFile(Fname : Filepath;
                         ReadingBlock : Boolean);

Description

Read text file **Fname** into current window. If **ReadingBlock** is TRUE, then the file is read in as a marked block; if FALSE, the file is read in as a new text stream.

EdRealign [MSPTROP.PAS,EDPTROP.PAS]

Syntax

Procedure EdRealign;

Description

Realigns windows over text streams.

EdRealignOne [MSPTROP.PAS]

Syntax

Procedure EdRealignOne(W : PwinDesc);

Description

Realigns window **W**.

EdReformBlock [MSTEXT.PAS]

Syntax

Procedure EdReformBlock;

Description

Reformats marked block.

EdReformParagraph   [MSTEXT.PAS]

Syntax

Procedure EdReformParagraph;

Description

Reformats the current paragraph.

EdRepaginate   [MSBACK.PAS]

Syntax

Procedure EdRepaginate;

Description

Repaginates all windows.

EdRepaginateOne   [MSBACK.PAS]

Syntax

Procedure EdRepaginateOne(W : PwinDesc);

Description

Repaginates window **W**.

EdResetPageLine   [MSPTROP.PAS]

Syntax

Procedure EdResetPageLine(W : PwinDesc);

Description

Sets the **PaginationDone** flag to FALSE after an edit operation occurs.

EdResetPromptLine   [MSUSER.PAS,EDUSER.PAS]

Syntax

Procedure EdResetPromptLine;

Description

Clears the command line of partial commands.

EdResetTempMargin   [MSPTROP.PAS]

Syntax

Procedure EdResetTempMargin(W : PwinDesc;
                            FullReset : Boolean);

Description

Sets temporary margin back to fixed left margin when appropriate.

EdResetWindow   [MSMEMOP.PAS]

Syntax

Procedure EdResetWindow(W : PwinDesc);

Description

When user opens a new window, resets the window descriptor.

EdResetWindowPrimitive   [MSPTROP.PAS]

Syntax

Procedure EdResetWindowPrimitive(W : PwinDesc);

Description

Low-level routine for resetting window.

EdRestoreCurrentLine   [MSEDIT.PAS,EDEDIT.PAS]

Syntax

Procedure EdRestoreCurrentLine;

Description

Restores text and flags of current line.

EdRestoreScreenMode   [EDSCRN1.PAS,MSSCRN1.PAS]

Syntax

Procedure EdRestoreScreenMode;

Description

Cleans up screen upon exit.

EdRestoreTextWindow   [MSUSER.PAS]

Syntax

Procedure EdRestoreTextWindow(W : WindowRec);

Description

Given a pointer to a **WindowRec**, restores the contents of the window.

EdRestoreWindow   [MSUSER.PAS]

Syntax

Procedure EdRestoreWindow(Var W : WindowPtr;
                          XPosn, YPosn, XSize, YSize :
                          Byte);

Description

Given a pointer to a **WindowRec**, restores the contents of the window.

EdRightChar   [EDEDIT.PAS,MSEDIT.PAS]

Syntax

Procedure EdRightChar;

Description

Processes right character command.

EdRightJustify   [MSEDIT.PAS]

Syntax

Procedure EdRightJustify(P : PlineDesc;
                              Lmargin, Rmargin : Integer);

Description

Inserts spaces in line to make it fill to **Rmargin**.

EdRightLine   [MSEDIT.PAS,EDEDIT.PAS]

Syntax

Procedure EdRightLine;

Description

Moves cursor to right edge of line.

EdRightWord   [EDEDIT.PAS,MSEDIT.PAS]

Syntax

Procedure EdRightWord;

Description

Advances cursor to next word.

EdSaveDefaults   [MSSET.PAS]

Syntax

Procedure EdSaveDefaults;

Description

Writes the current default settings to disk.

EdSaveFile   [EDMAIN.PAS,MSMAIN.PAS]

Syntax

Procedure EdSaveFile;

Description

Saves the current text stream to disk and continues in Edit mode.

EdSaveTabLine   [MSTABS.PAS]

Syntax

Procedure EdSaveTabLine;

Description

Writes current tab line into text.

EdSaveTextWindow   [MSUSER.PAS]

Syntax

Procedure EdSaveTextWindow(Border : BorderChars;
                           Title : VarString;
                           XLow, YLow, XHigh, YHigh :
                           Byte;
                           Var W : WindowRec);

Description

Saves existing screen and sets up a new text window.

EdScanCmdList   [EDCMDS.PAS,MSCMDS.PAS]

Syntax

Function EdScanCmdList(CmdPtr : Byte;
                       Var CmdCode : CommandType) :
                       CmdMatchType;

Description

Sees if current command buffer matches any installed commands.

EdScanPattern   [MSFIND.PAS]

Syntax

Function EdScanPattern(Q : PlineDesc;
                        Pattern : VarString;
                        Var C : Integer) : PlineDesc;

Description

Scans for pattern, returning **PlineDesc** and column **C** if found.

EdSchedule   [MSMAIN.PAS,EDMAIN.PAS]

Syntax

Procedure EdSchedule;

Description

Edits schedule.

EdScrollDown   [MSEDIT.PAS,EDEDIT.PAS]

Syntax

Procedure EdScrollDown;

Description

Processes scroll down command.

EdScrollUp   [EDEDIT.PAS,MSEDIT.PAS]

Syntax

Procedure EdScrollUp;

Description

Processes scroll up command.

EdSetAttributes   [MSBACK.PAS]

Syntax

Procedure EdSetAttributes;

Description

Sets line flags for on-screen font attributes.

EdSetAttrOne   [MSBACK.PAS]

Syntax

Procedure EdSetAttrOne(W : PwinDesc;
                        EndLine : PlineDesc);

Description

Sets font attributes for one window.

EdSetBotMargin   [MSSET.PAS]

Syntax

Procedure EdSetBotMargin;

Description

Prompts for and sets the bottom margin of the current window.

EdSetColors   [MSSET.PAS]

Syntax

Procedure EdSetColors;

Description

Customizes editor colors.

EdSetCursor   [EDSCRN1.PAS,MSSCRN1.PAS]

Syntax

Procedure EdSetCursor(ScanLines : Word);

Description

Changes the scan lines of the hardware cursor.

EdSetCursorOff   [MSSCRN1.PAS]

Syntax

Procedure EdSetCursorOff;

Description

Turns off the hardware cursor when appropriate.

EdSetEga25LineMode   [MSSCRN1.PAS]

Syntax

Procedure EdSetEga25LineMode;

Description

Switches EGA card back into normal 25-line display.

EdSetEga43LineMode   [MSSCRN1.PAS]

Syntax

Procedure EdSetEga43LineMode;

Description

Switches EGA card into 43-line display.

EdSetEvenTabs   [MSPTROP.PAS]

Syntax

Procedure EdSetEvenTabs(Var Tabs : TabArray);

Description

Sets the tab array to even tabs on the current default spacing.

EdSetFlag   [MSPTROP.PAS,EDPTROP.PAS]

Syntax

Procedure EdSetFlag(P : PlineDesc;
                    Mask : Word);

Description

Sets the line flag.

EdSetInsertMode   [MSUSER.PAS]

Syntax

Procedure EdSetInsertMode(Inserting : Boolean);

Description

Keeps the cursor appearance and BIOS keyboard flag up to date.

EdSetLeftMargin   [MSSET.PAS]

Syntax

Procedure EdSetLeftMargin;

Description

Sets up a new left margin.

EdSetMarker   [MSTEXT.PAS,EDTEXT.PAS]

Syntax

Procedure EdSetMarker(M : Byte);

Description

Processes set text marker command.

EdSetNumber   [MSUSER.PAS,EDUSER.PAS]

Syntax

Procedure EdSetNumber(Var Num;
                 Msg, Min, Max : Integer;
                 Var Empty : Boolean);

Description

Prompts for and sets an integer value in range **Min . . Max**.

EdSetPageLength   [MSSET.PAS]

Syntax

Procedure EdSetPageLength;

Description

Prompts for and saves the page length of the current window.

EdSetPageNum   [MSPTROP.PAS]

Syntax

Procedure EdSetPageNum(P : PlineDesc;
                       Num : Integer);

Description

Sets the page number of the line.

EdSetPtrNil   [EDPTROP.PAS,MSPTROP.PAS]

Syntax

Procedure EdSetPtrNil(Var P);

Description

Initializes pointer **P** to nil.

EdSetRightMargin   [MSSET.PAS]

Syntax

Procedure EdSetRightMargin;

Description

Sets up a new right margin.

EdSetStartCol   [MSFIND.PAS]

Syntax

Function EdSetStartCol(Colno : Integer) : Integer;

Description

Sets cursor to appropriate starting position.

EdSetSupportPath   [MSSET.PAS]

Syntax

Procedure EdSetSupportPath;

Description

Defines the path or drive for all the editor support files.

EdSetTabLine   [MSTABS.PAS]

Syntax

Procedure EdSetTabLine;

Description

Sets the tabs by reading the current line.

EdSetTabSize   [MSSET.PAS]

Syntax

Procedure EdSetTabSize;

Description

Prompts for and sets a new default tab size.

EdSetTempAtCursor   [MSTABS.PAS]

Syntax

Procedure EdSetTempAtCursor;

Description

Sets the temporary margin to the cursor column.

EdSetTempMargin   [MSTABS.PAS]

Syntax

Procedure EdSetTempMargin;

Description

Sets a temporary left margin based on tab position.

EdSetTextNo   [EDPTROP.PAS,MSPTROP.PAS]

Syntax

Procedure EdSetTextNo(W : PwinDesc);

Description

Sets the **FirstTextNo** of a window.

EdSetTopMargin   [MSSET.PAS]

Syntax

Procedure EdSetTopMargin;

Description

Prompts for and sets the top margin of the current window.

EdSetUndoLimit   [EDTEXT.PAS,MSSET.PAS]

Syntax

Procedure EdSetUndoLimit;

Description

Prompts for and sets the global undo limit.

EdSetupKeyLength   [MSCMDS.PAS]

Syntax

Procedure EdSetupKeyLength(Var AsciiLength,
                    ExtendedLength : LengthArray);

Description

Defines lengths of text-key representations.

EdSetupWindow   [MSUSER.PAS]

Syntax

Function EdSetupWindow(Border : BorderChars;
            XLow, YLow, XHigh, YHigh : Byte;
            BoxAttr : BoxType) : WindowPtr;

Description

Saves current screen and sets up a new window.

EdShowMemory   [EDTEXT.PAS,MSTEXT.PAS]

Syntax

Procedure EdShowMemory;

Description

Shows free memory for text.

EdShowMenuHelp   [MSUSER.PAS]

Syntax

Procedure EdShowMenuHelp;

Description

Puts the menu help into the prompt line.

EdShutWindow   [MSFILE.PAS,EDFILE.PAS]

Syntax

Procedure EdShutWindow(ExitEditor : Boolean);

Description

Shuts the current window, sets **Rundown** to TRUE if last one
and ExitEditor are TRUE.

EdSizeLine   [EDMEMOP.PAS,MSMEMOP.PAS]

Syntax

Function EdSizeLine(P : PlineDesc;
                    Ncols : Integer;
                    Init : Boolean) : Boolean;

Description

Expands line size to accommodate **Ncols** characters.

EdSizeWindow   [EDEDIT.PAS,MSTEXT.PAS]

Syntax

Procedure EdSizeWindow;

Description

Interactively sizes the current window.

EdSpellingCheck   [MSSPELL.PAS]

Syntax

Procedure EdSpellingCheck;

Description

Checks spelling of block or file using Turbo Lightning.

EdString2Integer   [MSUSER.PAS]

Syntax

Procedure EdString2Integer(Src : VarString;
                                                Var R);

Description

Converts string to integer. If **R** returns with the value of 0, check the value of **GetError** to see if an error occurred.

EdStringEmpty   [EDSTRING.PAS,MSSTRING.PAS]

Syntax

Function EdStringEmpty(Var S) : Boolean;

Description

Returns TRUE if string is empty.

EdSysInfo   [EDEDIT.PAS,MSTEXT.PAS]

Syntax

Procedure EdSysInfo;

Description

Displays editor information.

EdTab   [EDTEXT.PAS,MSTABS.PAS]

Syntax

Procedure EdTab;

Description

Processes tab command.

EdTextLength   [MSPTROP.PAS,EDPTROP.PAS]

Syntax

Function EdTextLength(P : PlineDesc) : Integer;

Description

Returns the length of line text, 0 if all blank.

EdTextRepresentation   [MSCMDS.PAS]

Syntax

Function EdTextRepresentation(Keys : String;
                              Var Kptr : Integer;
                              Var Special : Boolean) : String;

Description

Returns a text representation of command keystrokes.

EdToggleBoolean   [MSPTROP.PAS, EDPTROP.PAS]

Syntax

Procedure EdToggleBoolean(Var B : Boolean);

Description

Toggles a Boolean.

EdToggleCompressWrap   [MSSET.PAS]

Syntax

Procedure EdToggleCompressWrap;

Description

Processes CompressWrap toggle command.

EdToggleEga43Line   [MSSET.PAS]

Syntax

Procedure EdToggleEga43Line;

Description

Toggles 43-line Display mode.

EdToggleFixedTabs   [MSSET.PAS]

Syntax

Procedure EdToggleFixedTabs;

Description

Processes fixed-tab toggle command.

EdToggleInitZoomState   [MSSET.PAS]

Syntax

Procedure EdToggleInitZoomState;

Description

Toggles default zoom state.

EdToggleJustify   [MSSET.PAS]

Syntax

Procedure EdToggleJustify;

Description

Processes justification toggle command.

EdToggleMacroRecord   [MSMACRO.PAS]

Syntax

Procedure EdToggleMacroRecord;

Description

Toggles whether keystrokes are being recorded for use in macros.

EdTogglePaginate   [MSSET.PAS]

Syntax

Procedure EdTogglePaginate;

Description

Toggles display/computation of page numbers.

EdToggleRetraceMode   [MSSET.PAS]

Syntax

Procedure EdToggleRetraceMode;

Description

Toggles snow control.

EdToggleSolidCursor   [MSSET.PAS]

Syntax

Procedure EdToggleSolidCursor;

Description

Toggles block cursor.

EdToggleTabLine   [MSSET.PAS]

Syntax

Procedure EdToggleTabLine;

Description

Toggles display of tab lines.

EdToggleTextMarker   [EDPTROP.PAS,MSPTROP.PAS]

Syntax

Procedure EdToggleTextMarker;

Description

Toggles visibility of text markers.

EdToggleWordWrap   [MSSET.PAS]

Syntax

Procedure EdToggleWordWrap;

Description

Changes state of word wrap.

EdTopofStream   [MSPTROP.PAS,EDPTROP.PAS]

Syntax

Function EdTopofStream(W : PwinDesc) : PlineDesc;

Description

Returns pointer to first line in stream.

EdTopScreen   [MSPTROP.PAS,EDPTROP.PAS]

Syntax

Procedure EdTopScreen;

Description

Moves cursor to top of screen.

EdUndo   [MSEDIT.PAS, EDEDIT.PAS]

Syntax

Procedure EdUndo;

Description

Processes undo command.

EdUndrawMenu   [MSSCRN2.PAS]

Syntax

Procedure EdUndrawMenu(Menu : Menuptr);

Description

Removes the menu and its children from the screen.

EdUpcase   [MSSTRING.PAS]

Syntax

Procedure EdUpcase(Var S : String);

Description

Converts lowercase letters in string to uppercase.

EdUpdateCmdLine   [EDUSER.PAS,MSUSER.PAS]

Syntax

Procedure EdUpdateCmdLine;

Description

Updates the message line.

EdUpdateCursor   [MSUSER.PAS,EDUSER.PAS]

Syntax

Procedure EdUpdateCursor;

Description

Moves the cursor to the right spot.

EdUpdateFont   [MSPTROP.PAS]

Syntax

Procedure EdUpdateFont(C : PrintCommandtype;
                       Var FontByte : Byte);

Description

Toggles appropriate bit of packed font byte.

EdUpdateLine [MSSCRN2.PAS,EDSCRN2.PAS]

Syntax

Procedure EdUpdateLine(P : PlineDesc;
                          Row, Leftedge, Leftcol : Integer;
                          Attribs : Boolean);

Description

Updates one row of the screen.

EdUpdateScreen [MSSCRN2.PAS,EDSCRN2.PAS]

Syntax

Procedure EdUpdateScreen;

Description

Updates physical screen.

EdUpdateStatusLine [EDSCRN2.PAS,MSSCRN2.PAS]

Syntax

Procedure EdUpdateStatusLine(W : PwinDesc);

Description

Updates window status line for specified window.

EdUpdateWindow   [MSSCRN2.PAS]

Syntax

Procedure EdUpdateWindow(W : PwinDesc);

Description

Updates a single window on the screen.

EdUpLine   [MSEDIT.PAS,EDEDIT.PAS]

Syntax

Procedure EdUpLine;

Description

Processes up-line command.

EdUpPage   [MSEDIT.PAS,EDEDIT.PAS]

Syntax

Procedure EdUpPage;

Description

Processes up-page command.

EdUserPush [MSUSER.PAS,EDUSER.PAS]

Syntax

Procedure EdUserPush(S : String255);

Description

Pushes string onto typeahead buffer.

EdWait [MSUSER.PAS,EDUSER.PAS]

Syntax

Procedure EdWait;

Description

Displays a wait signal.

EdWaitForKey [MSUSER.PAS]

Syntax

Procedure EdWaitForKey;

Description

Tight loop waiting for keystroke.

EdWhatFont   [MSTEXT.PAS]

Syntax

Procedure EdWhatFont;

Description

Displays the font type of the character at the cursor.

EdWindow   [MSSCRN1.PAS]

Syntax

Procedure EdWindow(Xmin, Ymin, Xmax, Ymax : Byte);

Description

Sets current window coordinates without compiler's range checking.

EdWindowBottomFile   [MSEDIT.PAS,EDEDIT.PAS]

Syntax

Procedure EdWindowBottomFile;

Description

Moves cursor to bottom of file.

EdWindowCreate   [EDMEMOP.PAS,MSMEMOP.PAS]

Syntax

Procedure EdWindowCreate(Wno : Byte);

Description

Creates new window by splitting window **Wno** in two.

EdWindowDelete   [MSMEMOP.PAS,EDMEMOP.PAS]

Syntax

Procedure EdWindowDelete(Wno : Byte);

Description

Performs delete window command processing.

EdWindowDown   [EDPTROP.PAS,MSPTROP.PAS]

Syntax

Procedure EdWindowDown;

Description

Processes down-window command.

EdWindowGoto   [EDPTROP.PAS,MSPTROP.PAS]

Syntax

Procedure EdWindowGoto(Wno : Byte);

Description

Moves cursor into window **Wno**, counted from top of screen.

EdWindowNumber   [EDPTROP.PAS,MSPTROP.PAS]

Syntax

Function EdWindowNumber : Byte;

Description

Returns the window number of the current window.

EdWindowTopFile   [EDPTROP.PAS,MSPTROP.PAS]

Syntax

Procedure EdWindowTopFile;

Description

Goes to top of window.

EdWindowUp [EDPTROP.PAS,MSPTROP.PAS]

Syntax

Procedure EdWindowUp;

Description

Processes up-window command.

EdWriteBlock [MSFILE.PAS]

Syntax

Procedure EdWriteBlock(Fname : Filepath;
                    Exists, Appending : Boolean);

Description

Writes or appends marked block to file.

EdWriteMacroFile [MSMACRO.PAS]

Syntax

Procedure EdWriteMacroFile(Fname : Filepath);

Description

Writes a new macro file.

EdWriteNamedFile   [MSFILE.PAS]

Syntax

Function EdWriteNamedFile : Boolean;

Description

Gets filename, saves current text stream to it, and changes stream names.

EdWriteOrAppendBlock   [MSMAIN.PAS]

Syntax

Procedure EdWriteOrAppendBlock;

Description

Writes or appends a marked block of text to a disk file.

EdWritePromptLine   [EDUSER.PAS,MSUSER.PAS]

Syntax

Procedure EdWritePromptLine(S : VarString);

Description

Writes a new message line to the screen.

EdWrLine   [EDSCRN1.PAS,MSSCRN1.PAS]

Syntax

Procedure EdWrLine(Row : Integer);

Description

General-purpose text write—no character translation.

EdWrLineCtrl   [EDSCRN1.PAS,MSSCRN1.PAS]

Syntax

Procedure EdWrLineCtrl(Row : Integer);

Description

General-purpose text write—control characters translated.

EdYcenterWindow   [MSUSER.PAS]

Syntax

Function EdYcenterWindow(Rows : Byte) : Byte;

Description

Returns a legal row number centered in the current window.

EdYesNo   [MSUSER.PAS,EDUSER.PAS]

Syntax

Function EdYesNo(Prompt : VarString) : Boolean;

Description

Returns TRUE for Yes, FALSE for No.

EdZapPromptLine   [MSUSER.PAS,EDUSER.PAS]

Syntax

Procedure EdZapPromptLine;

Description

Zaps message line, leaving it blank.

EdZoomWindow   [MSPTROP.PAS]

Syntax

Procedure EdZoomWindow(FixCurline : Boolean);

Description

Makes the current window fill the entire screen.

EscapeSequence   [ESCSEQ.PAS]

Syntax

Function EscapeSequence(Ch : Char) : String;

Description

Returns the text name corresponding to scan code **Ch**.

ExecShrink   [INVOKE.PAS]

Syntax

Function ExecShrink(Command : String) : Integer;

Description

Runs any DOS command. Call with Command = '' for a new shell.

Numerical Methods Toolbox

Roots to Equations in One Variable
Interpolation
Numerical Differentiation
Numerical Integration
Matrix Routines
Eigenvalues and Eigenvectors
Initial Value and Boundary Value Methods
Least-Squares Approximation
Fast Fourier Transform Routines

Engineers, statisticians, mathematicians, and other number crunchers were among the first to appreciate the power of the computer. But transforming a mathematical formula into a usable computer program was no simple task. The Turbo Pascal Numerical Methods Toolbox provides a complete set of the most popular numerical algorithms. This chapter serves as a reference guide to the algorithms the Toolbox contains.

Roots to Equations in One Variable

Root of a Function Using the Bisection Method (BISECT.INC)

Description   Bisect calculates the root of the real continuous function contained in **TNTargetF**.

Syntax

```
Procedure Bisect (LeftEnd   : Real;
                  RightEnd  : Real;
                  Tolerance : Real;
                  MaxIter   : Integer;
              Var Answer    : Real;
              Var fAnswer   : Real;
              Var Iter      : Integer;
              Var Error     : Byte);
```

Input Parameters

LeftEnd	Left end of the interval
RightEnd	Right end of the interval
Tolerance	Tolerance of solution
MaxIter	Maximum number of iterations

Output Parameters

Answer	Approximated root of **TNTargetF**	
fAnswer	Value of function at approximated root	
Iter	Number of iterations performed	
Error	0	No error
	1	**Iter > MaxIter**
	2	Endpoints are of the same sign
	3	**LeftEnd > RightEnd**
	4	**Tolerance <= 0**
	5	**MaxIter < 0**

User-Defined Function

```
Function TNTargetF(x : Real) : Real;
```

Root of a Function Using the Newton-Raphson Method (RAPHSON.INC)

Description   Newton _ Raphson determines the root of function **TNTargetF**. The function **TNDerivF** contains the derivative of the function in **TNTargetF**.

Syntax

```
Procedure Newton _ Raphson  (Guess      : Real;
                             Tolerance : Real;
                             MaxIter    : Integer;
                         Var Root       : Real;
                         Var Value      : Real;
                         Var Deriv      : Real;
                         Var Iter       : Integer;
                         Var Error      : Byte);
```

Input Parameters

Guess	Approximation of root
Tolerance	Tolerance of solution
MaxIter	Maximum number of iterations

Output Parameters

Root	Approximated root
Value	Value of function at approximated root
Deriv	Value of derivative at approximated root
Iter	Number of iterations performed
Error	0 No error
	1 **Iter > MaxIter**
	2 Slope = 0
	3 **Tolerance <= 0**
	4 **MaxIter < 0**

User-Defined Function

```
Function TNTargetF(x : Real) : Real;
Function TNDerivF(x : Real) : Real;
```

Root of a Function Using the Secant Method (SECANT.INC)

Description   **Secant** calculates the root of the function **TNTargetF** given two initial approximations.

Syntax

```
Procedure Secant  (Guess1    : Real;
                    Guess2    : Real;
                    Tolerance : Real;
                    MaxIter   : Integer;
               Var  Root      : Real;
               Var  Value     : Real;
               Var  Iter      : Integer;
               Var  Error     : Byte);
```

Input Parameters

Guess1	First approximation of the root
Guess2	Second approximation of the root
Tolerance	Tolerance of solution
MaxIter	Maximum number of iterations

Output Parameters

Root	Approximated root	
Value	Value of function at approximated root	
Iter	Number of iterations performed	
Error	0	No error
	1	**Iter > MaxIter**
	2	Slope $= 0$
	3	**Tolerance $< = 0$**
	4	**MaxIter < 0**

User-Defined Function

Function TNTargetF(x : Real) : Real;

Real Roots of a Real Polynomial Equation Using the Newton-Horner Method with Deflation (NEWTDEFL.INC)

Description   Newt_Horn_Defl uses an initial guess to estimate several roots of a user-specified polynomial.

Syntax

Procedure Newt_Horn_Defl (InitDegree : Integer;
                                        InitPoly   : TNvector;
                                        Guess   : Real;
                                          Tolerance : Real;
                                          MaxIter   : Integer;
                    Var Degree   : Integer;
                    Var NumRoots : Integer;
                    Var Poly   : TNvector;
                    Var Root   : TNvector;
                    Var Imag   : TNvector;
                    Var Value   : TNvector;
                    Var Deriv   : TNvector;
                    Var Iter   : TNIntVector;
                    Var Error   : Byte);

Input Parameters

InitDegree	Degree of user-defined polynomial
InitPoly	Coefficients of user-defined polynomial
Guess	Initial approximation of root
Tolerance	Tolerance of solution
MaxIter	Maximum number of iterations

Output Parameters

Degree	Degree of the deflated polynomial
NumRoots	Number of approximated roots
Poly	Coefficients of deflated polynomial
Root	Real part of approximated roots

Imag	Imaginary part of all approximated roots
Value	Value of polynomial at each approximated root
Deriv	Value of the derivative at each approximated root
Iter	Number of iterations performed
Error	0 No error
	1 **Iter > MaxIter**
	2 Slope = 0
	3 **Degree <= 0**
	4 **Tolerance <= 0**
	5 **MaxIter < 0**

User-Defined Types

TNvector = Array [0..TNArraySize] Of Real;
TNIntVector = Array [0..TNArraySize] Of Integer;

Complex Roots of a Complex Function Using Müller's Method (MULLER.INC)

Description   **Muller** approximates the complex root of function **TNTargetF**.

Syntax

```
Procedure Muller  (Guess      : TNcomplex;
                   Tolerance  : Real;
                   MaxIter    : Integer;
              Var  Answer     : TNcomplex;
              Var  yAnswer    : TNcomplex;
              Var  Iter       : Integer
              Var  Error      : Byte);
```

Input Parameters

Guess   Initial guess for root of complex function
Tolerance   Tolerance of solution
MaxIter   Maximum number of iterations

Output Parameters

Answer   Approximated root of the function
                  TNTargetF
yAnswer   Value of function **TNTargetF** at
                  approximated root
Iter   Number of iterations performed
Error   0   No error
                  1   **Iter > MaxIter**
                  2   Parabola could not be formed
                  3   **Tolerance $<=0$**
                  4   **MaxIter <0**

User-Defined Type

TNcomplex = Record
    Re,
    IM : Real;
    End;

User-Defined Function

Procedure TNTargetF(x : TNcomplex; Var y : TNcomplex);

Complex Roots of a Complex Polynomial Using Laguerre's Method and Deflation (LAGUERRE.INC)

Description   **Laguerre** finds the roots of a complex polynomial. The roots may be complex themselves.

Syntax

```
Procedure Laguerre (Var  Degree      : Integer;
                    Var  Poly        : TNCompVector;
                         InitGuess   : TNcomplex;
                         Tolerance   : Real;
                         MaxIter     : Integer;
                    Var  NumRoots    : Integer;
                    Var  Roots       : TNCompVector;
                    Var  yRoots      : TNCompVector;
                    Var  Iter        : TNIntVector;
                    Var  Error       : Byte);
```

Input Parameters

Degree	Degree of the polynomial
Poly	Coefficients of the polynomial
InitGuess	Initial guess at root of polynomial
Tolerance	Tolerance of solution
MaxIter	Maximum number of iterations

Output Parameters

Degree	Degree of the deflated polynomial
Poly	Coefficients of the deflated polynomial
NumRoots	Number of approximated roots
Roots	Approximated roots of the polynomial
yRoots	Value of the polynomial at the approximated root
Iter	Number of iterations performed
Error	0 No error
	1 **Iter > MaxIter**
	2 **Degree <= 0**
	3 **Tolerance <= 0**
	4 **MaxIter < 0**

User-Defined Types

```
TNcomplex = Record
   Re,
```

```
    Im : Real;
    End;
TNIntVector = Array [0..TNArraySize] Of Integer;
TNCompVector = Array [0..TNArraySize] Of TNcomplex;
```

Interpolation

Polynomial Interpolation Using Lagrange's Method (LAGRANGE.INC)

Description   **Lagrange** computes a polynomial to fit data points x and y and interpolates the y data points for the x data points in **XInter**.

Syntax

```
Procedure Lagrange  (NumPoints : Integer;
                Var XData      : TNvector;
                Var YData      : TNvector;
                    NumInter   : Integer;
                Var XInter     : TNvector;
                Var YInter     : TNvector;
                Var Poly       : TNvector;
                Var Error      : Byte);
```

Input Parameters

NumPoints	Number of data points
XData	The x data points
YData	The y data points
NumInter	Number of interpolations desired
XInter	x data points at which interpolation is to take place

Output Parameters

YInter	Interpolated y data points
Poly	Coefficients of the interpolating polynomial
Error	0 No error
	1 Duplicates found among x data points
	2 **NumPoints** < 1

User-Defined Types

TNvector = Array [0. .TNArraySize] Of Real;
TNmatrix = Array [0. .TNArraySize] Of TNvector;

Interpolation Using Newton's Interpolary Divided-Difference Method (DIVDIF.INC)

Description   **Divided _ Difference** interpolates y data points for given x data points using arrays of x and y data points.

Syntax

```
Procedure Divided _ Difference (NumPoints : Integer;
                        Var  XData     : TNvector;
                        Var  YData     : TNvector;
                             NumInter  : Integer;
                        Var  XInter    : TNvector;
                        Var  YInter    : TNvector;
                        Var  Error     : Byte);
```

Input Parameters

NumPoints	Number of data points
XData	The x data points
YData	The y data points
NumInter	The number of interpolations
XInter	The x data points at which interpolation is to take place

Output Parameters

YInter	The interpolated y data points
Error	0 No error
	1 Duplicates found among x data points
	2 **NumPoints** < 1

User-Defined Types

TNvector = Array [0..TNArraySize] Of Real;
TNmatrix = Array [0..TNArraySize] Of TNvector;

Free Cubic Spline Interpolation (CUBE—FRE.INC)

Description   **CubicSplineFree** produces a smooth curve through a set of data points.

Syntax

```
Procedure CubicSplineFree (NumPoints : Integer;
              Var  XData      : TNvector;
              Var  YData      : TNvector;
                   NumInter   : Integer;
              Var  XInter     : TNvector;
              Var  Coef0      : TNvector;
              Var  Coef1      : TNvector;
              Var  Coef2      : TNvector;
              Var  Coef3      : TNvector;
              Var  YInter     : TNvector;
              Var  Error      : Byte);
```

Input Parameters

NumPoints	Number of data points
XData	The x data points
YData	The y data points
NumInter	The number of interpolations

| XInter | The x data points at which interpolation is to take place |

Output Parameters

Coef0	Coefficient of the constant term
Coef1	Coefficient of the linear term
Coef2	Coefficient of the squared term
Coef3	Coefficient of the cubed term
YInter	Interpolated y data points Error

0	No error
1	Duplicate x values found
2	x values not in ascending order
3	**NumPoints** < 2

User-Defined Type

TNvector = Array[0. .TNArraySize] Of Real;

Clamped Cubic Spline Interpolation (CUBE_CLA.INC)

Description   **CubicSplineClamped** produces a series of interpolated y data points for given x data points. The resulting x and y data points create a smooth curve through the original x and y data points. The line is continuous, and the first and second derivatives are also continuous.

Syntax

```
Procedure CubicSplineClamped  (NumPoints : Integer;
                          Var  XData      : TNvector;
                          Var  YData      : TNvector;
                               DerivLE    : Real;
                               DerivRE    : Real;
                               NumInter   : Integer;
```

Var	XInter	: TNvector;
Var	Coef0	: TNvector;
Var	Coef1	: TNvector;
Var	Coef2	: TNvector;
Var	Coef3	: TNvector;
Var	YInter	: TNvector;
Var	Error	: Byte);

Input Parameters

NumPoints	Number of data points
XData	The x data points
YData	The y data points
DerivLE	Derivative of the function at the left endpoint
DerivRE	Derivative of the function at the right endpoint
NumInter	Number of y data points to interpolate
XInter	The x data points at which interpolation is to take place

Output Parameters

Coef0	Coefficient of the constant term	
Coef1	Coefficient of the linear term	
Coef2	Coefficient of the squared term	
Coef3	Coefficient of the cubed term	
YInter	Interpolated values	
Error	0	No error
	1	Duplicates found among x data points
	2	x data points not in ascending order
	3	**NumPoints** < 2

User-Defined Type

TNvector = Array [0. .TNArraySize] Of Real;

Numerical Differentiation

First Differentiation Using Two-Point, Three-Point, or Five-Point Formulas (DERIV.INC)

Description   **First_Derivative** approximates the first derivative of function y = f(x) using an array of x data points and an array of y data points.

Syntax

Procedure First_Derivative (NumPoints : Integer;
                      Var   XData   : TNvector;
                      Var   YData   : TNvector;
                      Point   : Byte;
                      NumDeriv : Integer;
                      Var   XDeriv   : TNvector;
                      Var   YDeriv   : TNvector;
                      Var   Error   : Byte);

Input Parameters

NumPoints	Number of data points
XData	The x data points
YData	The y data points
Point	Number of points. Must equal 2, 3, or 5
NumDeriv	Number of points at which the derivative is to be approximated
XDeriv	The x data points at which the derivative is to be approximated

Output Parameters

YDeriv	The y data points approximated for each x data point in **XDeriv**

Error   0   No error
                         1   Not all derivatives were computed
                         2   Duplicates found among x data points
                         3   x data points not in ascending order
                         4   Insufficient data
                         5   **Point** is not equal to 2, 3, or 5
                         6   x data points not evenly spaced for
                             five-point formula

User-Defined Type

TNvector = Array [1..TNArraySize] Of Real;

Second Differentiation Using Three-Point or Five-Point Formulas (DERIV2.INC)

Description   Second_Derivative approximates the second derivative of function y = f(x).

Syntax

Procedure Second_Derivative (NumPoints : Integer;
                          Var   XData   : TNvector;
                          Var   YData   : TNvector;
                                Point   : Byte;
                                NumDeriv   : Integer;
                          Var   XDeriv   : TNvector;
                          Var   YDeriv   : TNvector;
                          Var   Error   : Byte);

Input Parameters

NumPoints   Number of data points
XData   The x data points
YData   The y data points
Point   Number of points. Must be 3 or 5

| NumDeriv | Number of points at which the derivative is to be approximated |
| XDeriv | The x data points at which the approximation is to take place |

Output Parameters

YDeriv	The y data points approximated using the x data points in **XDeriv**	
Error	0	No error
	1	Not all derivatives were computed
	2	Duplicates found among x data points
	3	x data points not in ascending order
	4	Insufficient data
	5	**Point** is not equal to 3 or 5
	6	x data points not evenly spaced

User-Defined Type

TNvector = Array[1..TNArraySize] Of Real;

Differentiation with a Cubic Spline Interpolant (INTERDRV.INC)

Description   Interpolate_Derivative approximates the first and second derivatives of a function y = f(x).

Syntax

```
Procedure Interpolate_Derivative (NumPoints : Integer;
                          Var  XData     : TNvector;
                          Var  YData     : TNvector;
                               NumDeriv  : Integer;
                          Var  XDeriv    : TNvector;
                          Var  YInter    : TNvector;
```

```
Var  YDeriv      : TNvector;
Var  YDeriv2     : TNvector;
Var  Error       : Byte);
```

Input Parameters

NumPoints	The number of data points
XData	The x data points
YData	The y data points
NumDeriv	The number of x points at which the derivative is to be approximated
XDeriv	The x data points at which derivatives will be approximated

Output Parameters

YInter   The approximated y values corresponding to the x data points in **XDeriv**

YDeriv   The approximation to the first derivative at the x data points in **XDeriv**

YDeriv2   The approximation to the second derivative at the x data points in **XDeriv**

Error
0	No error
1	Duplicates found among x data points
2	x data points not in ascending order
3	**NumPoints** < 2

User-Defined Type

TNvector = Array[1..TNArraySize] Of Real;

Differentiation of a User-Defined Function (DERIVFN.INC)

Description   **FirstDerivative** uses a set of x data points to approximate the first derivative for the function y = f(x).

Syntax

```
Procedure FirstDerivative (NumDeriv : Integer;
                      Var  XDeriv    : TNvector;
                      Var  YDeriv    : TNvector;
                           Tolerance : Real;
                      Var  Error     : Byte);
```

Input Parameters

NumDeriv	Number of points at which the derivative is to be approximated
XDeriv	The x data points at which the derivative is to be approximated
Tolerance	The accuracy of the solution

Output Parameters

YDeriv	Approximation to the first derivative at the x data points in **XDeriv**	
Error	0	No error
	1	**Tolerance < TNNearlyZero**

User-Defined Function

Function TNTarget(x : Real) : Real;

User-Defined Type

TNvector = Array[1..TNArraySize] Of Real;

Second Differentiation of a User-Defined Function (DERIV2FN.INC)

Description   **SecondDerivative** uses an array of x data points to approximate the second derivative of a function y = f(x).

Syntax

Procedure SecondDerivative (NumDeriv : Integer;
                                        Var XDeriv   : TNvector;
                                        Var YDeriv   : TNvector;
                                               Tolerance : Real;
                                        Var Error   : Byte);

Input Parameters

NumDeriv	Number of points used to approximate the derivative
XDeriv	The x data points used to approximate the derivative
Tolerance	The accuracy of the solution

Output Parameters

YDeriv	Approximation to the second derivative of the x data points in **XDeriv**	
Error	0	No error
	1	**Tolerance < TNNearlyZero**

User-Defined Function

Function TNTargetF(x : Real) : Real;

User-Defined Type

TNvector = Array[1. .TNArraySize] Of Real;

Numerical Integration

Integration Using Simpson's Composite Algorithm (SIMPSON.INC)

Description   **Simpson** computes the integral for the user-defined function using a range of **LowerLimit** to **UpperLimit**.

Syntax

```
Procedure Simpson  (LowerLimit  : Real;
                    UpperLimit  : Real;
                    NumIntervals : Integer;
               Var  Integral    : Real;
               Var  Error       : Byte);
```

Input Parameters

LowerLimit	Lower limit of integration
UpperLimit	Upper limit of integration
NumIntervals	Number of intervals used in approximation

Output Parameters

Integral	Approximation of the integral function
Error	0 No error
	1 **NumIntervals** < 1

User-Defined Function

```
Function TNTargetF(x : Real) : Real;
```

Integration Using the Trapezoid Composite Rule (TRAPZOID.INC)

Description   **Trapezoid** computes the integral for the user-defined function using a range of **LowerLimit** to **UpperLimit**.

Syntax

```
Procedure Trapezoid (LowerLimit  : Real;
                     UpperLimit  : Real;
```

```
                        NumIntervals : Integer;
              Var  Integral      : Real;
              Var  Error         : Byte);
```

Input Parameters

LowerLimit	Lower limit of integration
UpperLimit	Upper limit of integration
NumIntervals	Number of intervals used in approximation

Output Parameters

Integral	Approximated integral of the function	
Error	0	No error
	1	**NumIntervals** $< = 0$

User-Defined Function

Function TNTargetF(x : Real) : Real;

Integration Using Adaptive Quadrature and Simpson's Rule (ADAPSIMP.INC)

Description   **Adaptive_Simpson** approximates the integral of a function and allows the user to specify the level of accuracy desired by setting the value of **Tolerance**.

Syntax

```
Procedure Adaptive_Simpson (LowerLimit   : Real;
                            UpperLimit   : Real;
                            Tolerance    : Real;
                            MaxIntervals : Integer;
                       Var  Integral     : Real;
                       Var  NumIntervals : Integer;
                       Var  Error        : Byte);
```

Input Parameters

LowerLimit	Lower limit of integration
UpperLimit	Upper limit of integration
Tolerance	Accuracy of the solution
MaxIntervals	The maximum number of intervals allowed

Output Parameters

Integral	The approximated integral of the function	
NumIntervals	The actual number of intervals used	
Error	0	No error
	1	**Tolerance <= 0**
	2	**MaxIntervals <= 0**
	3	**NumIntervals >= MaxIntervals**

User-Defined Function

Function TNTargetF(x : Real) : Real;

Integration Using Adaptive Quadrature and Gaussian Quadrature (ADAPGAUS.INC)

Description   Adaptive_Gauss_Quadrature approximates the integral of function y = f(x) over a specified interval.

Syntax

```
Procedure
Adaptive_Gauss_Quadrature (LowerLimit    : Real;
                           UpperLimit    : Real;
                           Tolerance     : Real;
                           MaxIntervals  : Integer;
                       Var Integral      : Real;
```

```
                              Var   NumIntervals : Integer;
                              Var   Error        : Byte);
```

Input Parameters

LowerLimit	Lower limit of integration
UpperLimit	Upper limit of integration
Tolerance	Accuracy of the result
MaxIntervals	The maximum number of intervals to use

Output Parameters

Integral	The approximated integral of the function	
NumIntervals	The maximum number of intervals used	
Error	0	No error
	1	**Tolerance** $< = 0$
	2	**MaxIntervals** $< = 0$
	3	**NumIntervals** $> =$ **MaxIntervals**

User-Defined Function

Function TNTargetF(x : Real) : Real;

Integration Using the Romberg Algorithm (ROMBERG.INC)

Description   Romberg approximates the integral of **TN-TargetF**.

Syntax

```
Procedure Romberg (LowerLimit : Real;
                   UpperLimit : Real;
                   Tolerance  : Real;
                   MaxIter    : Integer;
               Var Integral   : Real;
```

```
Var  Iter        : Integer;
Var  Error       : Byte);
```

Input Parameters

LowerLimit   Lower limit of integration
UpperLimit   Upper limit of integration
Tolerance   Accuracy of solution
MaxIter   The maximum number of iterations
                    allowed

Output Parameters

Integral   The approximated integral of function f(x)
Iter   The number of iterations performed
Error   0   No error
                    1   **Tolerance <= 0**
                    2   **MaxIntervals <= 0**
                    3   **Iter >= MaxIter**

User-Defined Function

Function TNTargetF(x : Real) : Real;

Matrix Routines

Determinant of a Matrix (DET.INC)

Description   **Determinant** computes the determinant of an
N × N matrix.

Syntax

```
Procedure Determinant (Dimen : Integer;
                       Data   : TNmatrix;
                  Var  Det    : Real;
                  Var  Error  : Byte);
```

Input Parameters

Dimen	The dimension of the data points
Data	The square matrix

Output Parameters

Det	Determinant of the data matrix	
Error	0	No error
	1	**Dimen** < 1

User-Defined Types

```
TNvector = Array[1..TNArraySize] Of Real;
TNmatrix = Array[1..TNArraySize] Of TNvector;
```

Inverse of a Matrix (INVERSE.INC)

Description   **Inverse** produces the inverse of an N × N matrix.

Syntax

```
Procedure Inverse (Dimen : Integer;
                   Data   : TNmatrix;
              Var  Inv    : TNmatrix;
              Var  Error  : Byte);
```

Input Parameters

Dimen	Dimension of the data matrix
Data	The elements of the square matrix

Output Parameters

Inv	The inverse of the data matrix	
Error	0	No error
	1	**Dimen** < 1
	2	No inverse exists

User-Defined Types

TNvector = Array[1..TNArraySize] Of Real;
TNmatrix = Array[1..TNArraySize] Of Real;

Solving a System of Linear Equations with Gaussian Elimination (GAUSELIM.INC)

Description   Gaussian_Elimination produces the solution to a system of N linear equations.

Syntax

```
Procedure Gaussian_Elimination (Dimen        : Integer;
                                Coefficients : TNmatrix;
                                Constants    : TNvector;
                           Var  Solution     : TNvector;
                           Var  Error        : Byte);
```

Input Parameters

Dimen	Dimension of the coefficients matrix
Coefficients	The square matrix containing the coefficients of the equation
Constants	The constant term of each equation

Output Parameters

Solution   Solution to the set of equations
Error   0   No errors
                           1   **Dimen** < 1
                           2   Coefficients matrix is singular; no
                                unique solution exists

User-Defined Types

TNvector = Array[1..TNArraySize] Of Real;
TNmatrix = Array[1..TNArraySize] Of TNvector

Solving a System of Linear Equations with Gaussian Elimination and Partial Pivoting (PARTPIVT.INC)

Description   Partial_Pivoting produces the solution to a
system of N × N linear equations.

Syntax

```
Procedure Partial_Pivoting (Dimen      : Integer;
                            Coefficients : TNmatrix;
                            Constants  : TNvector;
                     Var    Solution   : TNvector;
                     Var    Error      : Byte);
```

Input Parameters

Dimen   Dimension of the coefficients matrix
Coefficients   The square matrix containing the
                           coefficients of the equations
Constants   The constant term of each equation

Output Parmeters

Solution	Solution to the set of equations
Error	0 No error
	1 **Dimen** < 1
	2 Coefficients matrix is singular; no unique solution exists

User-Defined Types

TNvector = Array[1..TNArraySize] Of Real;
TNmatrix = Array[1..TNArraySize] Of TNvector;

Solving a System of Linear Equations with Direct Factoring (DIRFACT.INC)

Description   To solve a system of N linear expressions using direct factoring, two Numerical Toolbox procedures are used: **LU_Decompose** and **LU_Solve**. **LU_Decompose** decomposes the matrix into an upper and lower triangle. **LU_Solve** then solves the linear equations.

Syntax

```
Procedure LU_Decompose (Dimen      : Integer;
                        Coefficients : TNmatrix;
                   Var  Decomp     : TNmatrix;
                   Var  Permute    : TNmatrix;
                   Var  Error      : Byte);
```

Input Parameters

Dimen	Dimension of the coefficients matrix
Coefficients	Square matrix containing the coefficients of the equations

Output Parameters

Decomp	The LU decomposition of the coefficients matrix
Permute	A permutation matrix that records the effects of pivoting
Error	0 No error
	1 **Dimen** < 1
	2 The coefficients matrix is singular

User-Defined Types

TNvector = Array[1. .TNArraySize] Of Real;
TNmatrix = Array[1. .TNArraySize] Of TNvector;

Syntax

```
Procedure LU _ Solve  (Dimen      : Integer;
                 Var   Decomp     : TNmatrix;
                       Constants  : TNvector;
                 Var   Permute    : TNmatrix;
                 Var   Solution   : TNvector;
                 Var   Error      : Byte);
```

Input Parameters

Dimen	Dimension of the coefficients matrix
Decomp	The lower and upper triangle decomposition of the coefficients matrix
Constants	The constant terms of each equation
Permute	A permutation matrix that records the effects of pivoting

Output Parameters

Solution	Solution to each system of equations
Error	0 No error
	1 **Dimen** < 1

User-Defined Types

TNvector = Array[1. .TNArraySize] Of Real;
TNmatrix = Array[1. .TNArraySize] Of TNvector;

Solving a System of Linear Equations with the Iterative Gauss-Seidel Method (GAUSSIDL.INC)

Description   **Gauss_Seidel** produces the solution to N linear equations with N unknowns.

Syntax

```
Procedure Gauss_Seidel (Dimen       : Integer;
                        Coefficients : TNmatrix;
                        Constants    : TNvector;
                        Tolerance    : Real;
                        MaxIter      : Integer;
                    Var Solution     : TNvector;
                    Var Iter         : Integer;
                    Var Error        : Byte);
```

Input Parameters

Dimen	Dimension of the coefficients matrix
Coefficients	The square matrix containing the coefficients of the equations
Constants	The constant terms of the equation
Tolerance	The tolerance of the solution
MaxIter	The maximum number of iterations allowed

Output Parameters

Solution		Solution to the set of equations
Iter		The number of iterations performed
Error	0	No error

1   **Iter** > **MaxIter** and matrix is not
    diagonally dominant
2   **Iter** > **MaxIter** and matrix is
    diagonally dominant
3   **Dimen** < 1
4   **Tolerance** < 0
5   **MaxIter** < 0
6   Zero on the diagonal of the matrix of
    coefficients
7   Sequence is diverging

User-Defined Types

TNvector = Array[1..TNArraySize] Of Real;
TNmatrix = Array[1..TNArraySize] Of TNvector;

Eigenvalues and Eigenvectors

Real Dominant Eigenvalue and Eigenvector of a Real Matrix Using the Power Method (POWER.INC)

Description   **Power** calculates a matrix's dominant eigen-value and its associated eigenvector.

Syntax

```
Procedure Power (Dimen:       Integer;
            Var  Mat          : TNmatrix;
            Var  GuessVector  : TNvector;
                 MaxIter      : Integer;
                 Tolerance    : Real;
            Var  Eigenvalue   : Real;
            Var  Eigenvector  : TNvector;
            Var  Iter         : Integer;
            Var  Error        : Byte);
```

Input Parameters

Dimen	Dimension of matrix **Mat**
Mat	The matrix
GuessVector	Initial approximation to the eigenvector
MaxIter	The maximum number of iterations allowed
Tolerance	The accuracy of the solution

Output Parameters

Eigenvalue	Approximation of the matrix's dominant eigenvalue
Eigenvector	Approximation of the dominant eigenvalue's eigenvector
Iter	The number of iterations performed
Error	0 No error
	1 **Dimen** $< = 1$
	2 **Tolerance** $< = 0$
	3 **MaxIter** $< = 0$
	4 **Iter** $> =$ **MaxIter**

User-Defined Types

TNvector = Array[1..TNArraySize] Of Real;
TNmatrix = Array[1..TNArraySize] Of TNvector;

Real Eigenvalue and Eigenvector of a Real Matrix Using the Inverse Power Method (INVPOWER.INC)

Description   InversePower converges to the eigenvalue closest to a value supplied by the user.

Syntax

```
Procedure InversePower (Dimen       : Integer;
                        Mat         : TNmatrix;
                    Var GuessVector : TNvector;
                        ClosestVal  : Real;
                        MaxIter     : Integer;
                        Tolerance   : Real;
                    Var Eigenvalue  : Real;
                    Var Eigenvector : TNvector;
                    Var Iter        : Integer;
                    Var Error       : Byte);
```

Input Parameters

Dimen	Dimension of matrix **Mat**
Mat	The matrix
GuessVector	The initial estimate of the eigenvector
ClosestVal	The approximate eigenvalue
MaxIter	The maximum number of iterations allowed
Tolerance	The accuracy of the solution

Output Parameters

Eigenvalue	Approximation of the eigenvalue closest to **ClosestVal**	
Eigenvector	The approximated eigenvector associated with eigenvalue	
Iter	The number of iterations performed	
Error	0	No error
	1	**Dimen** < = 1
	2	**Tolerance** < = 0
	3	**MaxIter** < = 0
	4	**Iter** > = **MaxIter**
	5	**Eigenvalue/ Eigenvector** not calculated

User-Defined Types

TNvector = Array[1..TNArraySize] Of Real;
TNmatrix = Array[1..TNArraySize] Of TNvector;

Real Eigenvalues and Eigenvectors of a Real Matrix Using the Power Method and Wielandt's Deflation (WIELANDT.INC)

Description   **Wielandt** approximates each eigenvalue and the associated eigenvector of a matrix.

Syntax

```
Procedure Wielandt (Dimen        : Integer;
                    Mat          : TNmatrix;
               Var  GuessVector  : TNvector;
                    MaxEigens    : Integer;
                    MaxIter      : Integer;
                    Tolerance    : Real;
               Var  NumEigens    : Integer;
               Var  Eigenvalues  : TNvector;
               Var  Eigenvectors : TNmatrix;
               Var  Iter         : TNIntVector;
               Var  Error        : Byte);
```

Input Parameters

Dimen	Dimension of the matrix **Mat**
Mat	The matrix
GuessVector	Initial estimate of the eigenvector
MaxEigens	The number of eigenvalues and eigenvectors to find
MaxIter	The maximum number of iterations allowed
Tolerance	The accuracy of the solution

Output Parameters

NumEigens   The number of eigenvectors returned
Eigenvalues   The first **NumEigens** eigenvalues of the
                    matrix
Eigenvectors   The eigenvectors associated with each
                    eigenvalue
Iter   The number of iterations performed
Error   0   No error
                    1   **Dimen** < = 1
                    2   **Tolerance** < = 0
                    3   **MaxIter** < = 0
                    4   **MaxEigens** < = 0, **MaxEigens** >
                         Dimen
                    5   **Iter** > = **MaxIter**
                    6   The last two eigenvalues are not real

User-Defined Types

TNvector = Array[1. .TNArraySize] Of Real;
TNmatrix = Array[1. .TNArraySize] Of TNvector;
TNIntVector = Array[1. .TNArraySize] Of Integer;

The Complete Eigensystem of a Symmetric Real Matrix Using the Cyclic Jacobi Method (JACOBI.INC)

Description   **Jacobi** estimates the eigensystem for a symmetric matrix.

Syntax

Procedure Jacobi (Dimen   : Integer;
                  Mat   : TNmatrix;
                  MaxIter   : Integer;
                  Tolerance   : Real;
              Var Eigenvalues : TNvector;
              Var Eigenvectors : TNmatrix;
              Var Iter   : Integer;
              Var Error   : Byte);

Input Parameters

Dimen	Dimension of matrix **Mat**
Mat	The matrix
MaxIter	The maximum number of iterations allowed
Tolerance	The accuracy of the solution

Output Parameters

Eigenvalues	Approximated eigenvalues of the matrix	
Eigenvectors	The eigenvectors associated with the eigenvalues	
Iter	The number of iterations performed	
Error	0	No error
	1	**Dimen** $<= 1$
	2	**Tolerance** $<= 0$
	3	**MaxIter** $<= 0$
	4	**Mat** is not symmetric
	5	**Iter** $>=$ **MaxIter**

User-Defined Types

TNvector = Array[1..TNArraySize] Of Real;
TNmatrix = Array[1..TNArraySize] Of TNvector;

Initial Value and Boundary Value Methods

Solution to an Initial Value Problem for a First-Order Ordinary Differential Equation Using the Runge-Kutta Method (RUNGE_1.INC)

Description   **InitialCond1stOrder** computes the approximate solution for a first-order ordinary differential equation with a specified initial condition.

Syntax

```
Procedure InitialCond1stOrder  (LowerLimit   : Real;
                                UpperLimit   : Real;
                                XInitial     : Real;
                                NumReturn    : Integer;
                                NumIntervals : Integer;
                          Var   TValues      : TNvector;
                          Var   XValues      : TNvector;
                          Var   Error        : Byte);
```

Input Parameters

LowerLimit	Lower limit of interval
UpperLimit	Upper limit of interval
XInitial	Value of x at lower limit
NumReturn	Number of (t,x) pairs returned from the procedure
NumIntervals	Number of subintervals used in the calculations

Output Parameters

TValues	Values of t between the limits	
XValues	Values of x approximated at the values in **TValues**	
Error	0	No error
	1	**NumReturn** < 1
	2	**NumIntervals** < **NumReturn**
	3	**LowerLimit** = **UpperLimit**

User-Defined Function

TNTargetF(t, x : Real) : Real;

User-Defined Type

TNvector = Array[1..TNArraySize] Of Real;

Solution to an Initial Value Problem for a First-Order Ordinary Differential Equation Using the Runge-Kutta-Fehlberg Method (RKF_1.INC)

Description   **RungeKuttaFehlberg** approximates a solution to a first-order ordinary differential equation within a specified tolerance. The equation must have a specified initial condition.

Syntax

```
Procedure RungeKuttaFehlberg (LowerLimit : Real;
                              UpperLimit : Real;
                              XInitial   : Real;
                              Tolerance  : Real;
                              NumReturn  : Integer;
                          Var TValues    : TNvector;
                          Var XValues    : TNvector;
                          Var Error      : Byte);
```

Input Parameters

LowerLimit	Lower limit of interval
UpperLimit	Upper limit of interval
XInitial	Value of x at **LowerLimit**
Tolerance	Accuracy of solution
NumReturn	Number of (t, x) values to be returned

Output Parameters

TValues	Values of t at which x was approximated
XValues	Approximated values of x at the values in **TValues**
Error	0 No error
	1 **Tolerance** $<= 0$
	2 **NumReturn** $<= 0$
	3 **LowerLimit** = **UpperLimit**
	4 **Tolerance** not reached

User-Defined Function

Function TNTargetF(t, x : Real) : Real;

User-Defined Type

TNvector = Array[1. .TNArraySize] Of Real;

Solution to an Initial Value Problem for a First-Order Ordinary Differential Equation Using the Adams-Bashforth/Adams-Moulton Predictor/Corrector Scheme (ADAMS — 1.INC)

Description   **Adams** approximates the solution to a first-order ordinary differential equation with a specified initial condition.

Syntax

```
Procedure Adams  (LowerLimit    : Real;
                  UpperLimit    : Real;
                  XInitial      : Real;
                  NumReturn     : Integer;
                  NumIntervals : Integer;
             Var  TValues        : TNvector;
             Var  XValues        : TNvector;
             Var  Error          : Byte);
```

Input Parameters

LowerLimit   Lower limit of interval
UpperLimit   Upper limit of interval
XInitial   Initial value of x at **LowerLimit**
NumReturn   Number of (t, x) values to be returned
NumIntervals   Number of subintervals to be used in
                 calculations

Output Parameters

TValues	Values of t between the limits
XValues	Values of x approximated at values in **TValues**
Error	0 No error
	1 **NumReturn** < 1
	2 **NumIntervals** < **NumReturn**
	3 **LowerLimit** = **UpperLimit**

User-Defined Function

Function TNTargetF(t, x : Real) : Real;

User-Defined Type

TNvector = Array[1..TNArraySize] Of Real;

Solution to an Initial Value Problem for a Second-Order Ordinary Differential Equation Using the Runge-Kutta Method (RUNGE_2.INC)

Description   **InitialCond2ndOrder** computes the solution to a second-order ordinary differential equation with a specified initial condition.

Syntax

```
Procedure InitialCond2ndOrder  (LowerLimit    : Real;
                                UpperLimit    : Real;
                                InitialValue  : Real;
                                InitialDeriv  : Real;
                                NumReturn     : Integer;
                                NumIntervals  : Integer;
                           Var  TValues       : TNvector;
```

```
Var  XValues      : TNvector;
Var  XDerivValues : TNvector;
Var  Error        : Byte);
```

Input Parameters

LowerLimit	Lower limit of interval
UpperLimit	Upper limit of interval
InitialValue	Initial value of x at **LowerLimit**
InitialDeriv	Derivative of x at **LowerLimit**
NumReturn	Number of (t, x) values to be returned
NumIntervals	Number of subintervals used in calculations

Output Parameters

TValues	Values of t between the limits
XValues	Values of x approximated using values in **TValues**
XDerivValues	The first derivative of approximated x values
Error	0 No Error
	1 **NumReturn** < 1
	2 **NumIntervals** < **NumReturn**
	3 **LowerLimit** = **UpperLimit**

User-Defined Function

Function TNTargetF(t, x, xprime : Real) : Real;

User-Defined Type

TNvector = Array[1..TNArraySize] Of Real;

Solution to an Initial Value Problem for an nth-Order Ordinary Differential Equation Using the Runge-Kutta Method (RUNGE_N.INC)

Description   **InitialCondition** integrates an nth-order ordinary differential equation with specified initial conditions.

Syntax

```
Procedure InitialCondition  (Order        : Integer;
                             LowerLimit    : Real;
                             UpperLimit    : Real;
                             InitialValues : TNvector;
                             NumReturn     : Integer;
                             NumIntervals  : Integer;
                         Var SolutionValues : TNmatrix;
                         Var Error          : Byte);
```

Input Parameters

Order	Order of the differential equation
LowerLimit	Lower limit of interval
UpperLimit	Upper limit of interval
InitialValues	Initial value of x and its derivatives at **LowerLimit**
NumReturn	Number of t and x values returned from the procedure
NumIntervals	Number of subintervals used in the calculations

Output Parameters

SolutionValues	Values of t, x, and the derivatives of x between the limits
Error	0 No error

1   **NumReturn** < 1
2   **NumIntervals** < **NumReturn**
3   **Order** < 1
4   **LowerLimit** = **UpperLimit**

User-Defined Function

Function TNTargetF(V : TNVector) : Real;
where
    V[0] is t;
    V[1] is x;
    V[2] is the first derivative of x;
    V[3] is the second derivative of x;
and so forth

User-Defined Types

TNvector = Array[1..TNRowSize] Of Real;
TNmatrix = Array[1..TNColumnSize] Of TNvector;

Solution to an Initial Value Problem for a System of Coupled First-Order Ordinary Differential Equations Using the Runge-Kutta Method (RUNGE_S1.INC)

Description   **InitialConditionSystem** integrates a system of first-order ordinary differential equations with specified initial conditions.

Syntax

Procedure InitialCondition System (NumEquations: Integer;
                                     LowerLimit   : Real;
                                     UpperLimit   : Real;
                                     InitialValues : TNvector;
                                     NumReturn   : Integer;

```
                                    NumIntervals  : Integer;
                          Var SolutionValues : TNmatrix;
                          Var Error          : Byte);
```

Input Parameters

NumEquations	Number of first-order differential equations
LowerLimit	Lower limit of interval
UpperLimit	Upper limit of interval
InitialValues	Initial values of x at **LowerLimit**
NumReturn	Number of t and x values to be returned
NumIntervals	Number of subintervals to be used in calculations

Output Parameters

SolutionValues	Values of t and x between the limits	
Error	0	No error
	1	**NumReturn** < 1
	2	**NumIntervals** < **NumReturn**
	3	**NumEquations** < 1
	4	**LowerLimit** = **UpperLimit**

User-Defined Function

One function for each differential equation:

Function TNTargetF1(V : TNvector) : Real;
Function TNTargetF2(V : TNvector) : Real;
.
.
.

Function TNTargetFN(V : TNvector) : Real;

User-Defined Types

TNvector = Array[1..TNRowSize] Of Real;
TNmatrix = Array[1..TNColumnSize] Of TNvector;

Solution to an Initial Value Problem for a System of Coupled Second-Order Ordinary Differential Equations Using the Runge-Kutta Method (RUNGE_S2.INC)

Description   **InitialConditionSystem2** integrates a system of second-order ordinary differential equations with specified initial conditions.

Syntax

Procedure InitialCondition System2 (NumEquations : Integer;

          LowerLimit   : Real;
          UpperLimit   : Real;
          InitialValues   : TNvector;
          NumReturn   : Integer;
          NumIntervals   : Integer;
     Var SolutionValues   : TNmatrix;
     Var Error   : Byte);

Input Parameters

NumEquations	Number of second-order differential equations
LowerLimit	Lower limit of interval
UpperLimit	Upper limit of interval
Initial Values	Values of x and the first derivative of x at **LowerLimit**
NumReturn	Number of values of t, x, and the first derivative of x to be returned
NumIntervals	The number of subintervals to be used in the calculations

Output Parameters

SolutionValues	Values of t, x, and the first derivative of x between the limits	
Error	0	No error
	1	**NumReturn** < 1

2	**NumIntervals < NumReturn**
3	**NumEquations < 1**
4	**LowerLimit = UpperLimit**

User-Defined Functions

One function for each differential equation used:

Function TNTargetF1(V : TNvector) : Real;
Function TNTargetF2(V : TNvector) : Real;
.

.

.

Function TNTargetFN(V : TNvector) : Real;

User-Defined Type

TNData = Record
    x : Real;
    xDeriv : Real;
    End;
TNvector = Array[0. .TNRowSize] Of TNData;
TNmatrix = Array[0. .TNColumnSize] Of TNvector;

Solutions to a Boundary Value Problem for a Second-Order Ordinary Differential Equation Using the Shooting and Runge-Kutta Methods (SHOOT2.INC)

Description   **Shooting** approximates the solution to a second-order ordinary differential equation with specified boundary conditions.

Syntax

Procedure Shooting (LowerLimit   : Real;

```
                            UpperLimit    : Real;
                            LowerInitial  : Real;
                            UpperInitial  : Real;
                            InitialSlope  : Real;
                            NumReturn     : Integer;
                            Tolerance     : Real;
                            MaxIter       : Integer;
                            NumIntervals : Integer;
                  Var  Iter              : Integer;
                  Var  XValues           : TNvector;
                  Var  YValues           : TNvector;
                  Var  YDerivValues : TNvector;
                  Var  Error             : Byte);
```

Input Parameters

LowerLimit   Lower limit of interval
UpperLimit   Upper limit of interval
LowerInitial   Value of y at **LowerLimit**
UpperInitial   Value of y at **UpperLimit**
InitialSlope   Approximation of slope at **LowerLimit**
NumReturn   Number of values of x, y, and first
                    derivative of y to be returned
Tolerance   Accuracy of solution
MaxIter   Maximum number of iterations to be
                    performed
NumIntervals   Number of subintervals used in
                    calculations

Output Parameters

Iter   Number of iterations performed
XValues   Values of x between limits
YValues   Values of y approximated for values in
                    XValues
YDerivValues   Values of the first derivative of y
                    approximated for values in **XValues**
Error   0   No error

1   **NumReturn** < 1
2   **NumIntervals** < **NumReturn**
3   **LowerLimit** = **UpperLimit**
4   **Tolerance** <= 0
5   **MaxIter** <= 0
6   **Iter** > **MaxIter**
7   Convergence is not possible

User-Defined Function

Function TNTargetF(x, y, yPrime : Real) : Real;

User-Defined Type

TNvector = Array[1..TNArraySize] Of Real;

Solution to a Boundary Value Problem for a Second-Order Ordinary Linear Differential Equation Using the Linear Shooting and Runge-Kutta Methods (LINSHOT2.INC)

Description   **LinearShooting** approximates the solution to a second-order ordinary differential equation with specified boundary conditions.

Syntax

```
Procedure LinearShooting (LowerLimit   : Real;
                          UpperLimit   : Real;
                          LowerInitial : Real;
                          UpperInitial : Real;
                          NumReturn    : Integer;
                          NumIntervals : Integer;
                    Var   XValues      : TNvector;
                    Var   YValues      : TNvector;
```

       Var   YDerivValues : TNvector;
       Var   Error   : Byte);

Input Parameters

LowerLimit	Lower limit of interval
UpperLimit	Upper limit of interval
LowerInitial	Initial value y at **LowerLimit**
UpperInitial	Initial value y at **UpperLimit**
NumReturn	Number of values of x, y, and the first derivative of y to be returned
NumIntervals	Number of subintervals to use in calculations

Output Parameters

XValues	Values of x between the limits
YValues	Values of y approximated using values in **XValues**
YDerivValues	Values of the first derivative of y approximated using values in **XValues**
Error	0 No error
	1 **NumReturn** < 1
	2 **NumIntervals** < **NumReturn**
	3 **LowerLimit** = **UpperLimit**
	4 Equation is not linear

User-Defined Function

Function TNTargetF(x, y, yPrime : Real) : Real;

User-Defined Type

TNvector = Array[1..TNArraySize] Of Real;

Least-Squares Approximation

Least-Squares Approximation (LEAST.INC)

Description   **LeastSquares** finds the least-squares approximation for a series of x and y data points.

Syntax

Procedure Least Squares		(NumPoints	: Integer;
	Var	XData	: TNColumnVector;
	Var	YData	: TNColumnVector;
	Var	NumTerms	: Integer;
	Var	Solution	: TNRowVector;
	Var	YFit	: TNColumnVector;
	Var	Residuals	: TNColumnVector;
	Var	StandardDeviation	: Real;
	Var	Error	: Byte);

Input Parameters

NumPoints	Number of data points
XData	X coordinates of data points
YData	Y coordinates of data points
NumTerms	Number of terms in least-squares approximation

Output Parameters

Solution	Coefficients of the basis vectors
YFit	Values of the least-squares fit at the **XData** values
Residuals	Difference between **YData** and **YFit** values

StandardDeviation	Square root of the variance	
Error	0	No errors
	1	**NumPoints** < 2
	2	**NumTerms** < 1
	3	**NumTerms** > **NumPoints**
	4	Least-squares solution does not exist

User-Defined Types

TNColumnVector = Array[1..TNColumnSize] Of Real;
TNRowVector = Array[1..TNRowSize] Of Real;
TNMatrix = Array[1..TNColumnSize] Of TNRowVector;
TNSquareMatrix = Array[1..TNRowSize] Of TNRowVector;
TNString40 = String[40];

Fast Fourier Transform Routines

Description   The Fast Fourier Transform (FFT) routines are divided into two groups. The first group contains four alternative FFT methods for calculating discrete Fourier transforms (FFTB2.INC, FFTB4.INC, FFT87B2.INC, FFT87B4.INC). The remaining procedures are routines that use FFT to produce various results.

User-Defined Types

The Fast Fourier Transform routines require the following data types:

TNvector = Array[0..TNArraySize] Of Real;
TNvectorPtr = ^TNvector;

Fast Fourier Transform Routines (FFTB2.INC, FFTB4.INC, FFT87B2.INC, FFT87B4.INC)

Syntax

```
Procedure FFT (NumberOfBits : Byte;
               NumPoints     : Integer;
               Inverse       : Boolean;
           Var XReal         : TNvectorPtr;
           Var XImag         : TNvectorPtr;
           Var SinTable      : TNvectorPtr;
           Var CosTable      : TNvectorPtr);
```

Input Parameters

NumberOfBits	Number of data points as a power of 2 or 4, depending on the routine being used
NumPoints	Number of data points
Inverse	FALSE indicates forward transform; TRUE indicates inverse transform
XReal	Pointer to real values of the data points
XImag	Pointer to imaginary values of the data points
SinTable	Table of sine values
CosTable	Table of cosine values

Output Parameters

XReal	Pointer to real values of the discrete Fourier transform of the input data
XImag	Pointer to imaginary values of the discrete Fourier transform of the input data

In-Place Transformation of Complex Data (COMPFFT.INC)

Syntax

```
Procedure ComplexFFT (NumPoints : Integer;
                      Inverse   : Boolean;
```

```
                    Var  XReal      : TNvectorPtr;
                    Var  XImag      : TNvectorPtr;
                    Var  Error      : Byte);
```

Input Parameters

NumPoints	Number of data points
Inverse	FALSE indicates forward transform; TRUE indicates inverse transform
XReal	Pointer to real values of data points
XImag	Pointer to imaginary values of data points

Output Parameters

XReal		Pointer to real values of the discrete Fourier transform of the input data
XImag		Pointer to imaginary values of the discrete Fourier transform of the input data
Error	0	No error
	1	**NumPoints** < 2
	2	**NumPoints** not a power of 2 or 4

In-Place Transformation of Real Data (REALFFT.INC)

Syntax

```
Procedure RealFFT (NumPoints : Integer;
                   Inverse   : Boolean;
              Var  XReal      : TNvectorPtr;
              Var  XImag      : TNvectorPtr;
              Var  Error      : Byte);
```

Input Parameters

NumPoints	Number of data points

Inverse	FALSE indicates forward transform; TRUE indicates inverse transform
XReal	Pointer to real values of the data points

Output Parameters

XReal		Pointer to real values of the Fourier transform of the input data
XImag		Pointer to imaginary values of the Fourier transform of the input data
Error	0	No errors
	1	**NumPoints** < 4
	2	**NumPoints** not a power of 2 or twice a power of 4

Calculation of the Convolution of Two Complex Vectors (COMPCNVL.INC)

Syntax

```
Procedure ComplexConvolution (NumPoints : Integer;
                        Var  XReal     : TNvectorPtr;
                        Var  XImag     : TNvectorPtr;
                        Var  HReal     : TNvectorPtr;
                        Var  HImag     : TNvectorPtr;
                        Var  Error     : Byte);
```

Input Parameters

NumPoints	Number of data points
XReal	Pointer to real values of the first set of data points
XImag	Pointer to imaginary values of the first set of data points

HReal	Pointer to real values of the second set of data points
HImag	Pointer to imaginary values of the second set of data points

Output Parameters

XReal	Pointer to imaginary values of the convolution of **XReal**, **XImag** and **HReal**, **XImag**
XImag	Pointer to imaginary values of the convolution of **XReal**, **XImag** and **HReal**, **XImag**
Error	0 No error
	1 **NumPoints** < 2
	2 **NumPoints** not a power of 2 or 4

Calculation of the Convolution of Two Real Vectors (REALCNVL.INC)

Syntax

```
Procedure RealConvolution (NumPoints : Integer;
                      Var  XReal    : TNvectorPtr;
                      Var  XImag    : TNvectorPtr;
                      Var  HReal    : TNvectorPtr;
                      Var  Error    : Byte);
```

Input Parameters

NumPoints	Number of data points
XReal	Pointer to real values of the first set of data points
HReal	Pointer to real values of the second set of data points

Output Parameters

XReal	Pointer to the real values of the convolution of **XReal** and **HReal**
XImag	Pointer to the imaginary values of the convolution of **XReal** and **HReal**
Error	0 No error
	1 **NumPoints** < 2
	2 **NumPoints** not a power of 2 or 4

Calculation of the Correlation of Two Complex Vectors (COMPCORR.INC)

Syntax

```
Procedure ComplexCorrelation (NumPoints : Integer;
                        Var  Auto      : Boolean;
                        Var  XReal     : TNvectorPtr;
                        Var  XImag     : TNvectorPtr;
                        Var  HReal     : TNvectorPtr;
                        Var  HImag     : TNvectorPtr;
                        Var  Error     : Byte);
```

Input Parameters

NumPoints	Number of data points
Auto	FALSE for cross-correlation; TRUE for autocorrelation
XReal	Pointer to real values of the first set of data points
XImag	Pointer to imaginary values of the first set of data points
HReal	Pointer to real values of the second set of data points (for cross-correlation)
HImag	Pointer to imaginary values of the second set of data points (for cross-correlation)

Output Parameters

XReal   Pointer to real values of the correlation of
                       XReal, XImag and **HReal, HImag** (or the
                       autocorrelation of **XReal, XImag** if **Auto**
                       is TRUE)
XImag   Pointer to imaginary values of the
                       correlation of **XReal, XImag** and **HReal,
                       HImag** (or the autocorrelation of **XReal,
                       XImag** if **Auto** is TRUE)
Error   0   No error
                       1   **NumPoints** < 2
                       2   **NumPoints** not a power of 2 or 4

Calculation of the Correlation of Two Real Vectors (REALPCORR.INC)

Syntax

```
Procedure RealCorrelation (NumPoints : Integer;
                    Var   Auto      : Boolean;
                    Var   XReal     : TNvectorPtr;
                    Var   XImag     : TNvectorPtr;
                    Var   HReal     : TNvectorPtr;
                    Var   Error     : Byte);
```

Input Parameters

NumPoints   Number of data points
Auto   FALSE for cross-correlation; TRUE for
                       autocorrelation
XReal   Pointer to real values of the first set of
                       data points
HReal   Pointer to real values of the second set of
                       data points (for cross-correlation)

Output Parameters

XReal	Pointer to real values of the correlation of **XReal** and **HReal** (or the autocorrelation of **XReal** if **Auto** is TRUE)
XImag	Pointer to imaginary values of the correlation of **XReal** and **HReal** (or the autocorrelation of **XReal** if **Auto** is TRUE)
Error	0 No error
	1 **NumPoints** < 2
	2 **NumPoints** not a power of 2 or 4

Debugging

As a general rule, programs do not run correctly the first time. Unfortunately, they often don't run correctly the tenth time, either. Tracking down and fixing program bugs can be time-consuming, painful, and unproductive. Fortunately, Turbo Pascal now includes an integrated debugger that can help you spot problems in seconds and can make your programming more rewarding.

The Integrated Debugger

Debuggers have been around for a long time. One of the first, DEBUG.COM, was included with the PC operating system. With DEBUG, a programmer could trace through a program one assembly-language instruction at a time, view segments of memory, and uncover bugs through a painstaking process. While useful in its own right, DEBUG suffered from several shortcomings. First, you could only see your program in assembler, a real limitation if you wrote the program in C, Pascal, or another high-level language. Second, variables were shown as addresses and offsets. Tracing a specific variable throughout a program was difficult, to say the least.

TWENTY THREE

Programmers needed a better debugger—one that showed variables by name and could match source code to the underlying assembler instructions. Microsoft packaged a symbolic debugger—SYMDEB—with their assembler, and other software developers soon offered products of their own with additional desirable features. Recently, Borland introduced its own standalone debugger, Turbo Debugger, with a wide array of powerful features. Yet, as powerful as they are, all of these debuggers have one disadvantage—you have to get out of Turbo Pascal to use them.

While it lacks the advanced features you will find in Turbo Debugger, Turbo Pascal's integrated debugger does provide an easy-to-use way to track down all but the most subtle software bugs. Best of all, you don't need to leave the integrated development environment to use it. Even if you've never used a debugger before, you'll find the integrated debugger a pleasure. With it you can watch how variables change as you move through your program a line at a time, or you can set break points and jump from place to place in your program. The integrated debugger, combined with fast compilation, makes Turbo Pascal perhaps the most productive programming environment available.

Getting Ready to Debug

Before you debug a program, there are several things you must do. First, you must enable the **D** compiler directive either by adding the compiler directive {$D+} to your source code, or by enabling the **Debug Information** selection on the Options/ Compiler menu. This tells Turbo Pascal to store program information that links a program's source code to its object code. If your program uses local variables, you should also enable the **L** compiler by either including the {$L+} compiler directive to your source code or by enabling the **Local Symbols** selection on the Options/Compiler menu. When this directive is enabled, Turbo Pascal stores information about local variables, allowing you to view them by name.

Finally, before you compile your program, you must be sure to enable the **Integrated Debugging** selection on the Debug menu. Enabling this option reserves RAM used to store debugging information. If you do not intend to debug a program and you need extra RAM, disable this feature. With these details attended to, you can proceed to debug your program.

Debugger Features

Now that you know how to prepare to debug a program, what can you do next? The answer is nearly anything you want to. The integrated debugger gives you complete control over the execution of your program. You can set break points, trace from line to line, watch variables change, and more. The important point is that you'll never have to guess what your program is doing—you'll be able to watch every step.

The Execution Bar

When you are debugging a program, the *execution bar* highlights the program statement that will execute next. You can move the cursor around the source file, and even load other source files into the editor, but the integrated debugger will always keep track of the execution bar. The execution bar remains active until the program terminates or until you end the debugging session by selecting the **Program Reset** option on the Run menu.

Go to Cursor (F4)

The **Go to Cursor** feature lets you specify a temporary stopping point for your program. To use this feature, place the cursor on a line of code in your program and press F4. Turbo Pascal will execute your program until it reaches the program line containing the cursor, at which point control will be returned to you.

This feature is especially handy if you want to go directly, rather than step by step, to a spot deep within your program.

To see how **Go to Cursor** works, consider the program shown in Figure 23-1. The execution bar is the first **Begin** statement in the program, and the cursor is four lines down. When you press F4, the program executes the first two statements, skips the blank line, and halts execution at the line where the cursor is (see Figure 23-2).

While **Go to Cursor** is like a break point, it is less restrictive. Break points have to be set and remain set until removed, while **Go to Cursor** relies only on the current position of the cursor. Note, however, that when you use this feature, the program will return control only if it reaches the line you selected. If, on the other hand, your program never executes that line, you will not receive control.

```
 File     Edit     Run     Compile     Options     Debug     Break/watch
                                       Edit
     Line 18     Col 1     Insert Indent              Unindent     C:TEST.PAS

Function RemoveBlanks(s : String) : String;
Begin
While s[1] = ' ' Do
  Delete(s,1,1);
RemoveBlanks := s;
End;


(**************************************************)

Begin
s := '        A';
s := RemoveBlanks(s);

s := '        ';
s := RemoveBlanks(s);
End.
                                     Watch

 F1-Help  F5-Zoom  F6-Switch  F7-Trace  F8-Step  F9-Make  F10-Menu
```

Figure 23-1.   Program at start of execution

```
  File    Edit    Run    Compile   Options   Debug    Break/watch
 ────────────────────────────── Edit ───────────────────────────
     Line 22    Col 1    Insert Indent          Unindent   C:TEST.PAS

 Function RemoveBlanks(s : String) : String;
 Begin
 While s[1] = ' ' Do
   Delete(s,1,1);
 RemoveBlanks := s;
 End;

 (*******************************************************)

 Begin
 s := '       A';
 s := RemoveBlanks(s);

 s := '      ';
 s := RemoveBlanks(s);
 End.
 ──────────────────────────── Watch ─────────────────────────────


 F1-Help  F5-Zoom  F6-Switch  F7-Trace  F8-Step  F9-Make  F10-Menu
```

Figure 23-2.   After using Go to Cursor

Trace Into (F7)

A fundamental feature of any debugger is the ability to execute
one statement at a time. The **Trace Into** feature, activated by
the F7 key, executes the statement highlighted by the execution
bar, moves the bar to the next statement, and returns control to
you. If the execution bar is a function or procedure call, **Trace
Into** will jump to that part of the program and continue executing from there. In Figure 23-3, the execution bar is located on
the statement that calls the function **RemoveBlanks**. When F7 is
pressed, the debugger traces into the **RemoveBlanks** function
(see Figure 23-4).

If you are not interested in tracing into a procedure call,
but wish to execute the procedure and move to the next line, use
the **Step Over** feature.

Step Over (F8)

Like **Trace Into**, the **Step Over** feature executes one line of code
at a time. **Step Over**, however, will not trace into function or

```
  File    Edit    Run    Compile    Options    Debug    Break/watch
══════════════════════════════ Edit ════════════════════════════
      Line 20    Col 1    Insert Indent          Unindent   C:TEST.PAS
While s[1] = ' ' Do
  Delete(s,1,1);
RemoveBlanks := s;
End;

(***************************************************)

Begin
s := '       A';
s := RemoveBlanks(s);

s := '        ';
s := RemoveBlanks(s);
End.


──────────────────────────── Watch ────────────────────────────
•s: '       A'

F1-Help  F5-Zoom  F6-Switch  F7-Trace  F8-Step  F9-Make  F10-Menu
```

Figure 23-3.   Before executing a function

```
  File    Edit    Run    Compile    Options    Debug    Break/watch
══════════════════════════════ Edit ════════════════════════════
      Line 10    Col 1    Insert Indent          Unindent   C:TEST.PAS

(***************************************************)

Function RemoveBlanks(s : String) : String;
Begin
While s[1] = ' ' Do
  Delete(s,1,1);
RemoveBlanks := s;
End;

(***************************************************)

Begin
s := '       A';
s := RemoveBlanks(s);

s := '        ';
s := RemoveBlanks(s);
──────────────────────────── Watch ────────────────────────────
•s: 'ABC'

F1-Help  F5-Zoom  F6-Switch  F7-Trace  F8-Step  F9-Make  F10-Menu
```

Figure 23-4.   After tracing into a function

procedure calls. Instead, it executes the procedure or function as a single statement, moves the execution bar to the next statement, and returns control to you at that point. This feature is useful for avoiding procedures and functions that do not need to be debugged.

To see how this works, consider Figure 23-3, where the execution bar is positioned on the statement that calls the function **RemoveBlanks**. When you press F8, the debugger executes the entire statement, including the function call, at one time and moves the bar forward to the next statement (see Figure 23-5).

Evaluate (CTRL-F4)

Pressing CTRL-F4 pops up the *Evaluate window,* a special window that lets you evaluate expressions and modify values of variables. The Evaluate window contains three boxes—Evaluate, Result, and New value (see Figure 23-6). In the Evaluate box

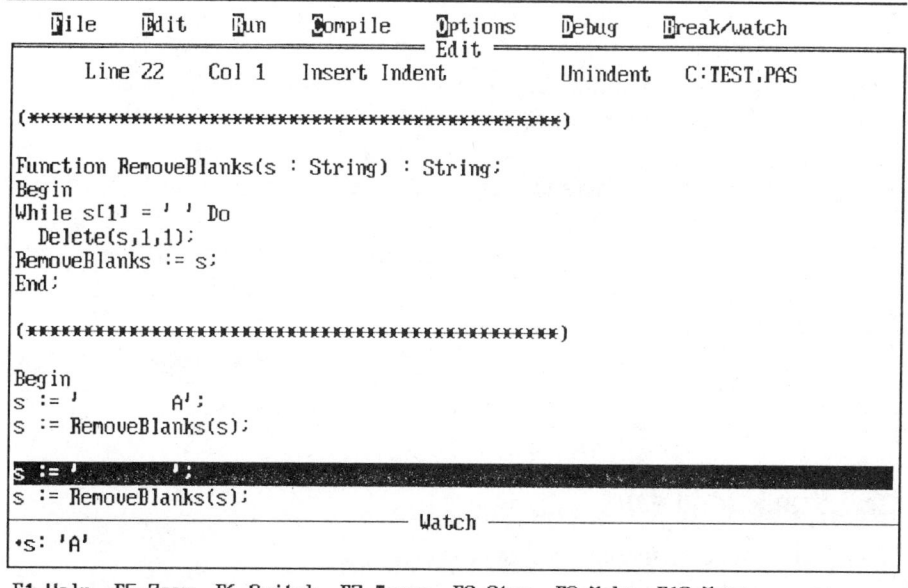

Figure 23-5.   After stepping over a function

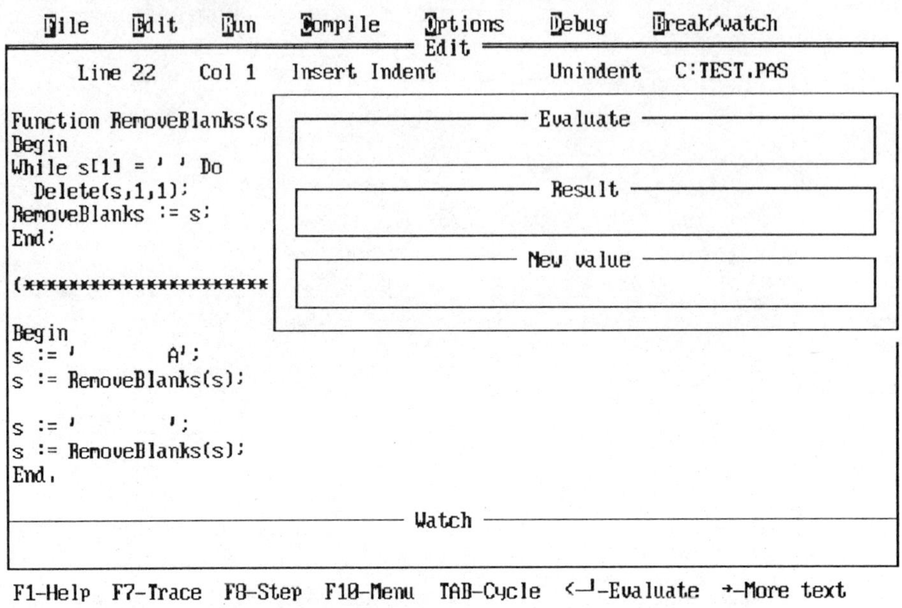

```
 File    Edit    Run    Compile   Options   Debug    Break/watch
                                  Edit
      Line 22    Col 1    Insert Indent        Unindent    C:TEST.PAS

Function RemoveBlanks(s        ┌──────────── Evaluate ───────────┐
Begin                         │                                 │
While s[1] = ' ' Do           └─────────────────────────────────┘
  Delete(s,1,1);              ┌──────────── Result ─────────────┐
RemoveBlanks := s;            │                                 │
End;                          └─────────────────────────────────┘
                              ┌──────────── New value ──────────┐
(*************************    │                                 │
                             └─────────────────────────────────┘
Begin
s := '       A';
s := RemoveBlanks(s);

s := '       ';
s := RemoveBlanks(s);
End,

                         ──────────── Watch ────────────

 F1-Help  F7-Trace  F8-Step  F10-Menu  TAB-Cycle  <─┘-Evaluate  →-More text
```

Figure 23-6.   The Evaluate window

you type the name of a variable, an expression, or a numeric value. For example, if you enter a hexadecimal number in the Evaluate box and press ENTER, the decimal equivalent will appear in the Result box (see Figure 23-7). You can also use the Evaluate window to modify the value of a variable. For example, in Figure 23-8, the string variable s is found to contain only space characters. In the New value box, the variable's contents have been changed to **ABC**. Modifying the value of a variable is an easy way to test how your program reacts to a variety of situations.

Call Stack (CTRL-F3)

In large programs it is easy to lose track of the function and procedure calls that preceded a particular point in the program. The **Call Stack** function provides an easy way to find out how you got to the current location. When you press CTRL-F3 (or select

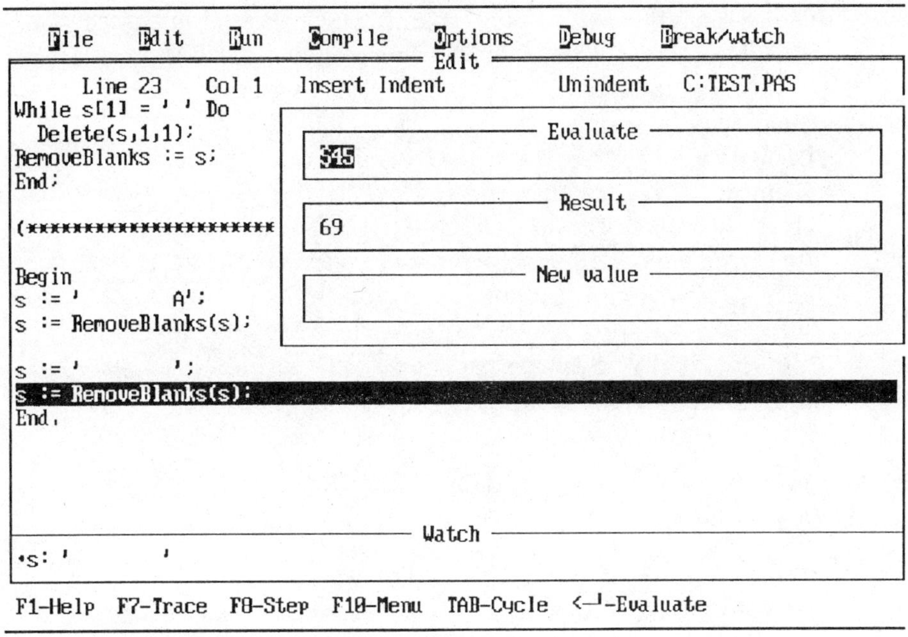

```
  File    Edit    Run    Compile   Options   Debug    Break/watch
========================================== Edit ==========================================
        Line 23    Col 1    Insert Indent          Unindent    C:TEST.PAS
While s[1] = ' ' Do
  Delete(s,1,1);                 +---------------- Evaluate -----------------+
RemoveBlanks := s;               | $45                                       |
End;                             |                                           |
                                 +---------------- Result -------------------+
(***********************         | 69                                        |
                                 |                                           |
Begin                            +---------------- New value ----------------+
s := '      A';                  |                                           |
s := RemoveBlanks(s);            |                                           |
                                 +-------------------------------------------+
s := '    ';
s := RemoveBlanks(s);
End.




                          ====== Watch =======
•s: '        '
```
F1-Help F7-Trace F8-Step F10-Menu TAB-Cycle <─┘-Evaluate

Figure 23-7.   Converting a hexadecimal value

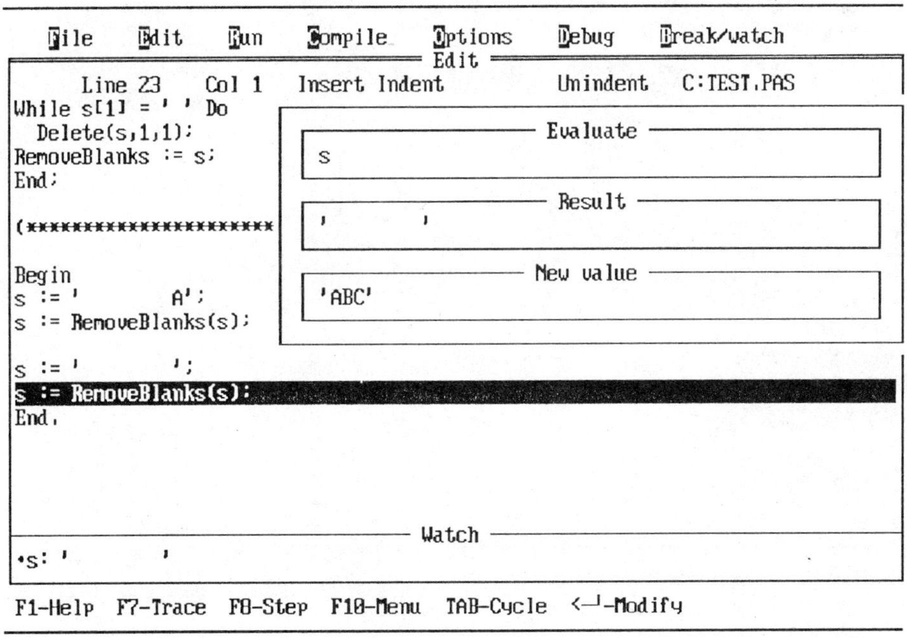

```
  File    Edit    Run    Compile   Options   Debug    Break/watch
========================================== Edit ==========================================
        Line 23    Col 1    Insert Indent          Unindent    C:TEST.PAS
While s[1] = ' ' Do
  Delete(s,1,1);                 +---------------- Evaluate -----------------+
RemoveBlanks := s;               | s                                         |
End;                             |                                           |
                                 +---------------- Result -------------------+
(***********************         | '        '                                |
                                 |                                           |
Begin                            +---------------- New value ----------------+
s := '      A';                  | 'ABC'                                     |
s := RemoveBlanks(s);            |                                           |
                                 +-------------------------------------------+
s := '    ';
s := RemoveBlanks(s);
End.




                          ====== Watch =======
•s: '        '
```
F1-Help F7-Trace F8-Step F10-Menu TAB-Cycle <─┘-Modify

Figure 23-8.   Modifying a variable

Call Stack from the Debug menu) Turbo Pascal opens the Call Stack window, which lists in reverse order all previous procedure and function calls. For example, in Figure 23-9, the Call Stack window shows four entries—PROC3, PROC2, PROC1, REMOVEBLANKS, and BUG, which is the name of the program itself. Notice that the REMOVEBLANKS entry also displays the value of the parameter passed to the routine.

Inside the Call Stack window, you can use the cursor keys to highlight any of the entries. If you press ENTER, Turbo Pascal will take you to the source code location of the highlighted routine. Now you can be certain of what events brought you to your current position in the program.

Add Watch (CTRL-F7)

The ability to watch variables is one of the most important features of the integrated debugger. A program bug is almost

```
 File    Edit    Run    Compile    Options    Debug    Break/watch
═══════════════════════════════════════ Edit ═══════════════════
     Line 11    Col 7    Insert Indent         Unindent * C:TEST.PAS
Begin                              ┌───────── Call Stack ─────────┐
End;                               │ PROC3                        │
                                   │ PROC2                        │
(********************************) │ PROC1                        │
                                   │ REMOVEBLANKS('        A')    │
Procedure Proc2;                   │ BUG                          │
Begin                              └──────────────────────────────┘
Proc3;
End;


(********************************)

Procedure Proc1;
Begin
Proc2;
End;


(********************************)
────────────────────────── Watch ───────────────────────────────

F1-Help  ↑↓→←-Scroll   <─┘-View call
```

Figure 23-9.   The Call Stack window

always related to or signaled by an unexpected value in a variable. The Watch window appears at the bottom of your screen. (If you do not see the Watch window, press F5.) To add a variable to the Watch window, press CTRL-F7 (or select **Add watch** from the Break/watch menu) and type in the name of the variable (see Figure 23-10). Alternately, place the cursor on a variable and press CTRL-F7 and then press ENTER to add that variable to the Watch window. When you enter a variable name and press ENTER, the variable will appear in the Watch window (see Figure 23-11). As you trace through your program, you can see how the variable changes. If the variable changes in a way that you don't expect, you may have found a bug.

Another way to add variables to the Watch window is to press F6, which activates the Watch window, and press INS. The Add Watch box pops up, and in it you type the name of the variable you wish to add. Press ENTER to complete the process, and then press F6 again to return to the Edit window.

```
  File      Edit      Run      Compile      Options      Debug      Break/watch
================================================== Edit ==================
       Line 28    Col 1    Insert Indent          │ Add watch          Ctrl-F7
  p : Pointer;                                     │ Delete watch
  s : String;                                      │ Edit watch
                                                   │ Remove all watches
(*************************************************
                                                   │ Toggle breakpoint  Ctrl-F8
                      ── Add Watch ──              │ Clear all breakpoints
Function │ S                                       │ View next breakpoint
Begin    │
While s[1] = ' ' Do
  Delete(s,1,1);
RemoveBlanks := s;
End;

(*********************************************)

Begin
s := '        A';
s := RemoveBlanks(s);
──────────────────────────────────── Watch ────────────────────────────

 F1-Help  F5-Zoom  F6-Switch  F7-Trace  F8-Step  F9-Make  F10-Menu  ←-More text
```

Figure 23-10.   Adding a variable to the Watch window

```
    File    Edit    Run    Compile    Options    Debug    Break/watch
 ══════════════════════════════════════ Edit ═════════════════════════════
       Line 20    Col 1    Insert Indent          Unindent    C:TEST.PAS
    p : Pointer;
    s : String;

 (*************************************************)

 Function RemoveBlanks(s : String) : String;
 Begin
 While s[1] = ' ' Do
   Delete(s,1,1);
 RemoveBlanks := s;
 End;

 (*************************************************)

 Begin
 s := '       A';
 s := RemoveBlanks(s);
 ═══════════════════════════════════ Watch ═══════════════════════════════
 •s: '       A'
```

F1-Help F5-Zoom F6-Switch F7-Trace F8-Step F9-Make F10-Menu

Figure 23-11.   A variable in the Watch window

```
    File    Edit    Run    Compile    Options    Debug    Break/watch
 ══════════════════════════════════════ Edit ═════════════════════════════
       Line 20    Col 1    Insert Indent          Unindent    C:TEST.PAS
    s : String;

 (*************************************************)

 Function RemoveBlanks(s : String) : String;
 Begin
 While s[1] = ' ' Do
   Delete(s,1,1);
 RemoveBlanks := s;
 End;

 (*************************************************)

 Begin
 s := '       A';
 s := RemoveBlanks(s);
 ═══════════════════════════════════ Watch ═══════════════════════════════
 •s[1]: ' '
  s: '       A'
```

F1-Help F5-Zoom F6-Switch F7-Trace F8-Step F9-Make F10-Menu

Figure 23-12.   Two variables in the Watch window

When you add a variable to the Watch window, a dot appears to the left of the variable's name (see Figure 23-12). This dot identifies which of the variables in the Watch window is selected. When you edit or delete a variable from the Watch window, the selected variable will be the one affected. To change the selected variable, press F6 to activate the Watch window, use the cursor keys to highlight another variable, and press F6 again to return to the Edit window.

Delete Watch

As you add variables to the Watch window, the window grows upward. At some point, the window stops growing, and excess variables will be pushed off the screen. At this point you may wish to delete variables from the Watch window. To delete the currently selected variable, choose **Delete watch** from the Break/watch menu. To delete another variable, press F6 to activate the Watch window, use the cursor keys to highlight the desired variable, and press DEL. When you are done, press F6 again to return to the Edit window.

Edit Watch

You can edit variable names in the Watch window to correct misspellings or to alter the way the variable is defined. To edit the currently selected variable, choose **Edit watch** from the Break/watch menu. When the Edit watch window pops up, make your changes and press ENTER. Alternatively, you can edit a variable by pressing F6 to activate the Watch window, highlighting the variable you want, and pressing ENTER.

Remove All Watches

If you want to remove all variables from the Watch window, select **Remove all watches** from the Break/watch menu.

Toggle Breakpoint (CTRL-F8)

A break point is a flag attached to a line of source code that tells Turbo Pascal to stop execution when it reaches that line. Using break points can be more efficient than tracing when you have a good idea of the location of the bug. You can set up to 21 break points within a program by simply positioning the cursor on the line to break at and pressing CTRL-F8 or by selecting **Toggle breakpoint** from the Break/watch menu.

Always set break points on lines that contain an executable statement. Do not set break points on blank lines, comment lines, compiler directives, data declarations, or other non-executable parts of your program.

Once a break point has been set for a line, it can be removed by repeating the same sequence used to set it; place the cursor on the line with the break point and press CTRL-F8. Break points are also cleared when you end your debugging session, and they are not made part of the .EXE program file.

Clear All Breakpoints

To clear all the break points you have set in a program, choose **Clear all breakpoints** from the Break/watch menu.

View Next Breakpoint

If you use a lot of break points in a program, it is easy to lose track of them. To locate break points, select **View next breakpoint** from the Break/watch menu. Turbo Pascal will find the next break point, load the appropriate source file, and position the cursor on the line at which the break point has been set.

CTRL-BREAK

You can halt your program's execution at any point by pressing CTRL-BREAK, which halts the program and positions the execution bar at the next statement to be executed. When you break a program from the outside, you cannot always be sure where you will be placed in the program. Still, this technique is useful for jumping in and out of a program at random points and is especially good for terminating endless loops.

Debugging: An Example

As with most things, debugging is best learned by example. To see how the debugger can help uncover subtle errors in program code, consider the following program that consists of a unit (UNIT1.PAS) and a main program file (BUG.PAS). But, before you read on, take a look at the following listing and see if you can find the two bugs contained in it.

```pascal
Unit Unit1;
{$D+,L+}
Interface

Procedure Proc1;

Implementation

Procedure Proc1;
Var
  i : Integer;
Begin
WriteLn('This is Proc1');
While i < 2 Do
  Begin
  WriteLn('i = ',i);
  Inc(i,1);
  End;
End;

End.

(*******************************************************)

Program Bug;
{$D+,L+}
Uses CRT, Unit1;
Var
  w : Integer;
  r1,r2 : Real;

Begin
ClrScr;

Proc1;

r1 := 1.0E+38;
For w := 1 To 10 Do
  Begin
  r2 := r1 + 1.0;
  WriteLn(r1,' + 1.0 = ',r2);
  r1 := r2;
  End;
```

```
WriteLn;
Write('Press ENTER...');
ReadLn;
End.
```

If you couldn't find the bugs, don't be too concerned. That's why we have debuggers in the first place. In fact, after using a debugger for a while, you will become much more adept at avoiding bugs in the first place.

Starting Up

Type in and compile the program and unit just given. (Before compiling, check the Debug menu to be sure that integrated debugging is on.) When you are ready, load the main program file into the editor, place the cursor on the call to **Proc1**, and press F4. Turbo Pascal will begin executing your program (performing a **Make** first, if needed) and stop with the execution bar highlighting the call to **Proc1** (see Figure 23-13). At this point, you can do several things. You can press F8 to step over the call

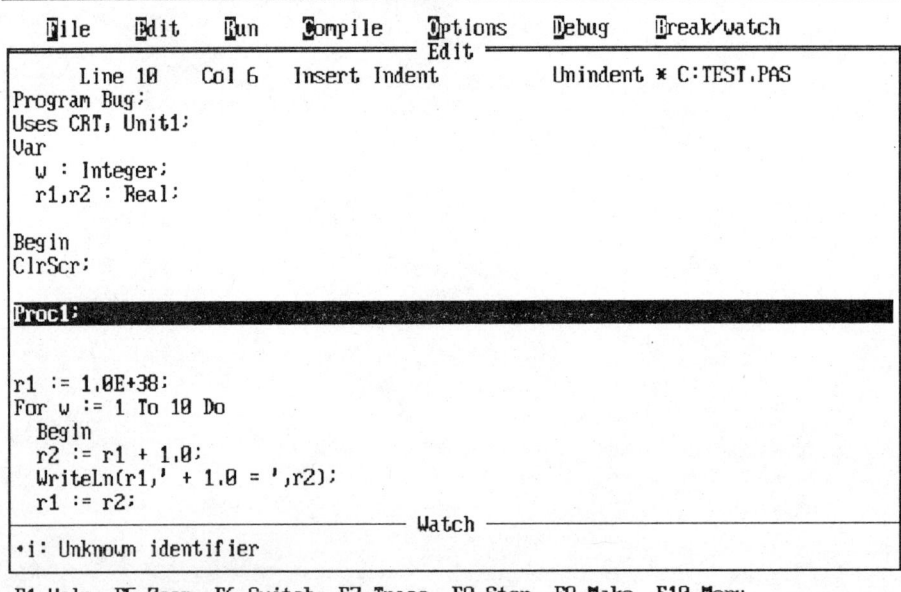

Figure 23-13.   Starting a debugging session

to **Proc1**; you can press F7 to trace into **Proc1**; you can go to
another point in the program and press F4 again; you can press
CTRL-F2 to reset the program to the beginning; or you can press
CTRL-F9 to let the program run. Let's press F7 to trace into **Proc1**.

Adding Watch Variables

When you trace into **Proc1**, the execution bar is placed on the
first **Begin** (see Figure 23-14). Notice that the variable **i** has
been added to the Watch window and that it has a value of
30468. By now you may have spotted the bug in this procedure.
As the following listing shows, the procedure assumes that **i** will
start out at a value less than two.

```
While i < 2 Do
  Begin
  WriteLn('i = ',i);
  Inc(i,1);
  End;
```

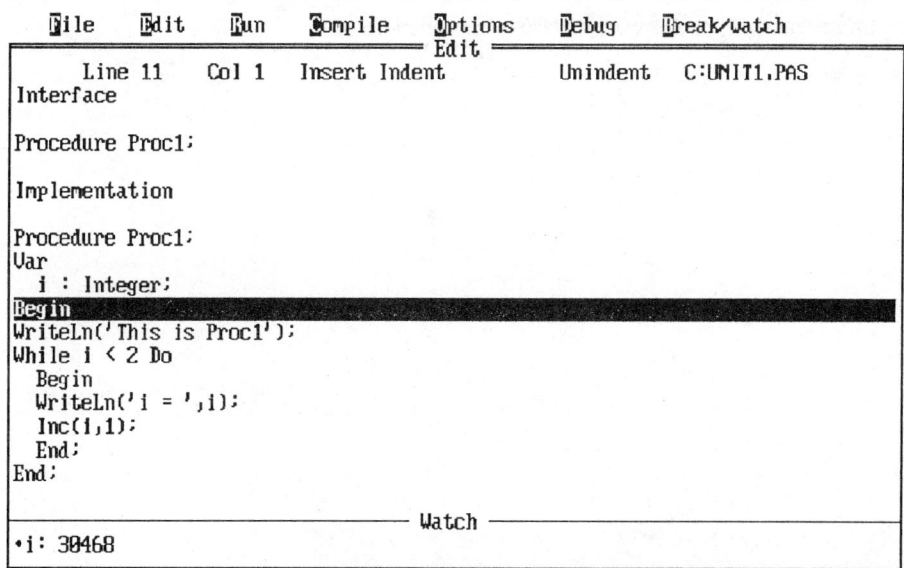

Figure 23-14.   Tracing into Proc1

Notice that **i** is never initialized, so you cannot know in advance
what value **i** will have when the procedure executes. In this case,
i has a value far above 2, so the loop will not execute at all.
Without the ability to watch the value of **i**, you might spend a lot
of time tracking down this little bug.

More on the Watch Window

Continue pressing F7 until you are back at the main program file.
Position the cursor on the **WriteLn** statement and press F4 (see
Figure 23-15). At the bottom you can see that the Watch window
now has three variables—**i**, **r1**, and **r2**. Notice that **i** is now
called an unknown identifier. Why? The variable **i** was local to
procedure **Proc1**. We are now outside that procedure and beyond the scope of the variable, which is why the identifier is
unknown.

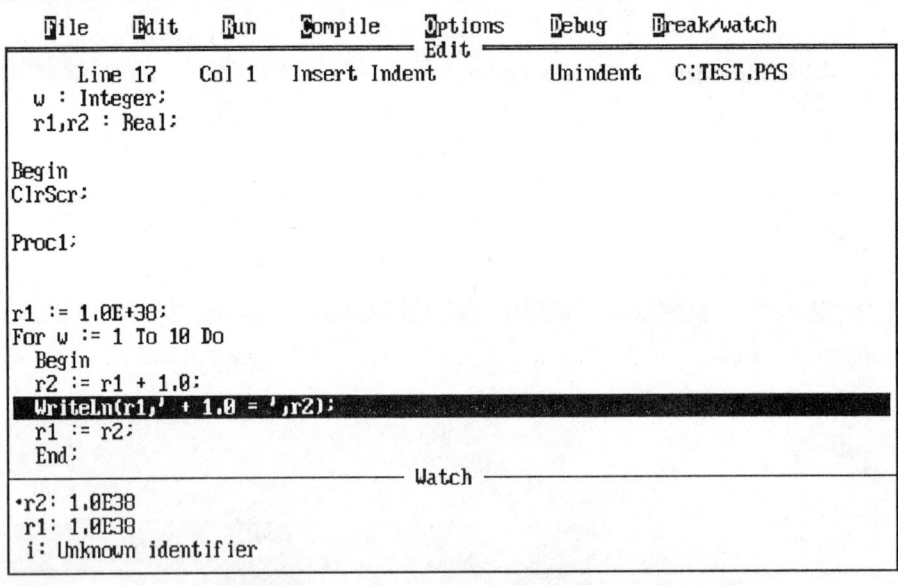

Figure 23-15.   Checking variables in the Watch window

If, on the other hand, a global variable **i** had been declared, the Watch window would reflect the value of the global variable. The Watch window can display the value of variables only within the variable's scope.

Looking at the Watch window, you might have been surprised to find that **r1** and **r2** have the same value, despite the fact that **r2** was assigned the value of **r1** plus 1.0. What happened? Floating-point variables retain only a fixed number of significant digits. When the number gets large, it will not reflect additions of small values. So, while you might expect **r1** to increase in value with each loop, the Watch window shows that this is not the case.

Display Format

You can use the Watch window to display the contents of any data type. If you do not specify otherwise, data is displayed in a default format (see Table 23-1). The Watch window, however, allows you to use format specifiers that alter the way the data is displayed. For example, you can view a value in hexadecimal format or as a raw memory dump. Table 23-2 lists the format specifiers and describes how they work.

Data Type	Default Display Format
Bytes, Integers, Words	Numeric scalars are displayed as their decimal value
Reals	Floating-point variables are displayed in decimal format without exponents, if possible
Characters	Characters from ASCII code 32 and up are displayed as themselves. Control characters, ASCII codes 0 to 31, are displayed as decimal values preceded by the # sign
Booleans	Displayed as either TRUE or FALSE

Table 23-1.   Default Display Formats

Data Type	Default Display Format
Pointers	Pointers are displayed as segments and offsets. If the segment portion matches the code segment or data segment, the CSEG or DSEG specifier will be displayed. Addresses are displayed in hexadecimal format
Strings	Strings are displayed as concatenated characters, enclosed in quotes. Control characters are displayed as decimal numbers preceded by the # sign
Arrays	Array contents are displayed within parentheses, separated by commas. If the array is multidimensional, nested parentheses are used
Records	The contents of records are displayed as lists surrounded by parentheses. Elements in the record are separated by commas. Nested records are shown as nested lists

Table 23-1.   Default Display Formats (*continued*)

Format Specifier	Result
$, H, X	Displays scalars
C	Displays special characters as their ASCII graphic value instead of as decimal values
D	Displays scalars as decimal values
Fn	Displays a floating-point number with **n** significant digits. The value of **n** can range from 2 to 18; the default is 11
M	Displays a memory dump of a variable as hex bytes. Adding the **D** specifier causes the dump to be shown in decimal, and the **C** or **S** specifier displays the dump as a string of ASCII and special characters

Table 23-2.   Watch Window Format Specifiers

Format Specifier	Result
P	Displays pointers in segment-and-offset format with both values in four-digit hex format
R	Displays the record's field names along with their values
S	Displays a string using ASCII and special characters. Normally, special characters are shown as decimal values

Table 23-2.   Watch Window Format Specifiers (*continued*)

Using format specifiers is fairly simple. When you add a variable to the Watch window, simply add a comma and list the format specifiers you want to use. For example, if you want to view an integer **i** in hexadecimal format, you would enter **i, X**. The following example program declares a variety of data types. Figure 23-16 shows how these variables look when displayed using format specifiers. Notice in the figure that a typecast is used to display the **ch** variable as a decimal value. Using typecasts in the Watch window is a powerful method of viewing your data in a variety of ways.

```
Program BugTest;
Uses CRT;

Var
  Rec : Record
    i : Integer;
    b : Byte;
    End;

  ch : Char;
  i : Integer;
  r : Real;
  s : String;
  p : Pointer;
  d : (Zero, One, Two, Three);

Begin
ClrScr;

r := 123;
i := 123;
ch := 'A';
```

```
s := '123' + #1 + 'ABC';
p := @ch;
Rec.i := 1;
Rec.b := 2;
FillChar(d,SizeOf(d),1);

WriteLn;
Write('Press ENTER...');
ReadLn;
End.
```

Programming for Debugging

When writing your program, keep in mind that the integrated debugger can only debug one statement per line. For example, Turbo Pascal allows you to write the following line of code:

```
s := 1 * z; z := i Div Trunc(Sqrt(s)); s := z Div 0;
```

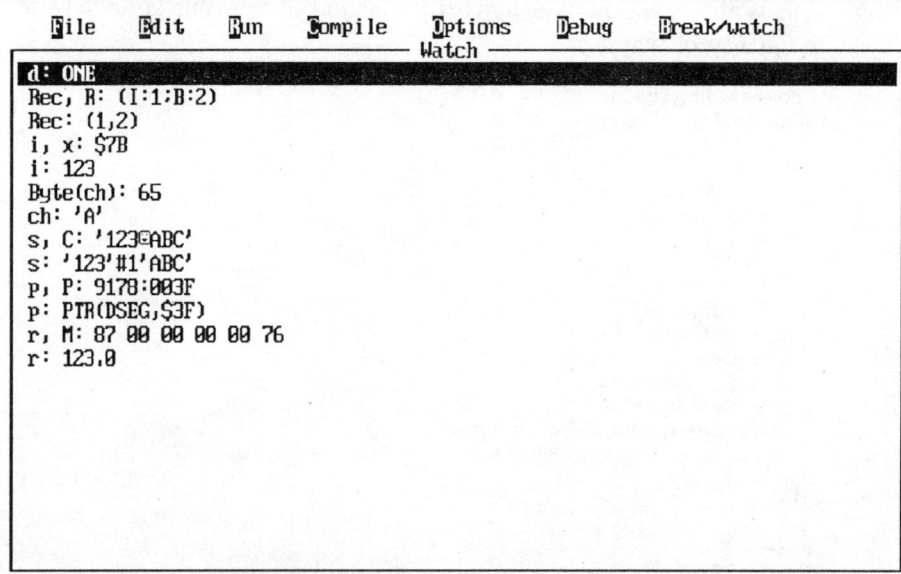

Figure 23-16.   The Watch window

This single line contains three statements. If an error occurs in any of the three, the integrated debugger will not be able to tell you which statement caused the error. In this case, it would be better to code as follows:

```
s := 1 * z;
z := i Div Trunc(Sqrt(s));
s := z Div 0;
```

Now when an error occurs, you will know exactly which statement caused the error.

On the other hand, if you have sections of code that you are certain are correct, you might consider lumping them into one line to save time when tracing through the program. For example, the following code is efficient because you can trace past it in one step instead of four:

```
s := 1; x := 2; i := 3; j := 4;
```

Another important programming point is not to get sloppy just because you have the integrated debugger. It's always better to avoid problems by using proper programming techniques than to catch the problems afterward with the debugger. As much as is possible and practical, break up programs into modules, rely on parameters rather than on global variables, and test modules as much as possible before integrating them into your programs.

Memory Requirements

The integrated debugger requires memory and, with large programs, you might find that too little is left over to run a debugging session. You can maximize the use of memory through several techniques. First, if you have expanded memory installed in your computer, make sure that at least 64K is available; Turbo Pascal will use this memory to store the editor file,

If your program allocates more stack-and-heap memory than it uses, you can reduce the size of these data areas, freeing memory for the debugger. Removing RAM-resident programs, like SideKick, will also give the debugger more memory to work with.

When you compile your program, turn off error-checking compiler directives, such as the **S** and **R** directives. These directives increase the size of your programs. Where local symbols will not be watched, use the {$L −} compiler directive to reduce the size of the local symbol table. Likewise, where debugging is unnecessary, use the {$D −} compiler directive to conserve memory.

You can also save memory by organizing your program into overlays. This will slow down your program, but give you more memory for debugging. As much as possible, test procedures and functions separately from the main program. This will speed up your testing and provide memory for debugging.

Finally, you can gain memory by modifying the TURBO .TPL file. Use the TPUMOVER program to remove any unused units from TURBO.TPL. This method, however, is a bit drastic and should be used only as a last resort.

Debugger Limitations

While the integrated debugger is powerful, it does have some limitations. It will not, for example, trace into any of the standard Turbo Pascal units (**CRT, DOS, GRAPH, GRAPH3, PRINTER, SYSTEM,** and **TURBO3**). Of course, these units are supplied by Borland and do not require any debugging.

The integrated debugger will not trace into external procedures, interrupt procedures, procedures that are written entirely in inline code, any procedure not compiled with the {$D +} compiler directive, any procedure for which the source code is not available, or any procedure set up as an exit procedure. In short, the integrated debugger will help you in 99% of the situations most programmers run into. If, however, you absolutely need to trace through every part of your program, consider purchasing the Turbo Debugger, which is more powerful than the integrated debugger built into Turbo Pascal.

Bugs are a natural part of programming. No matter how carefully you code, you simply can't avoid errors in logic. Tracking down and correcting bugs used to be time-consuming and clumsy. With its built-in debugger, Turbo Pascal greatly increases your programming productivity and will help you produce better programs.

Object Oriented Programming

An Object Lesson
Inheritance
Encapsulization
Static and Virtual Methods
Object Type Compatibility
Dynamic Allocation of Objects

Over the past few years, object oriented programming (OOP) has been making headlines in programming circles. With version 5.5, Borland brings OOP to Turbo Pascal. While OOP is a dramatically new approach to programming, one that breaks the traditional separation between code and data, it is easy to master with a little effort. And once you understand it, OOP can make your programs easier to write and maintain.

Contrary to popular belief, you need not relearn programming to understand OOP; everything you know about Turbo Pascal today still applies. OOP does, however, add a few new and powerful concepts. Turbo Pascal lets you use OOP techniques as little or as much as you like.

An Object Lesson

As its name implies, object oriented programming relies heavily on the concept of the object. In our daily lives, we are familiar with all kinds of objects — televisions, lamps, checkbooks, and so on. But when we turn on a television, we don't distinguish between its physical elements (the tuning dial, the picture tube, the antenna) and its behavior (providing an image and sound). We simply turn it on and select a channel.

Like the television, objects make programs more accurately conform to the way we deal with the real world. To gain this quality, objects depend on three main concepts: (1) combining code and data, (2) inheritance, and (3) encapsulation.

Code + Data = Object

As a Pascal programmer, you are used to defining data structures to hold information and defining procedures and functions to manipulate information. In OOP, data and procedures are combined into *objects*. An object contains both the characteristics of an entity (its data) and its behavior (its procedures). By melding these characteristics and behaviors, an object knows everything it needs to do its work.

To understand objects, it is useful to think in terms of metaphors. An airplane can be described in physical terms — the number of passengers it can hold, the amount of thrust it generates, its drag coefficient, and so on. Alternatively, an airplane can be described in functional terms — it takes off, it ascends and descends, it turns and lands, and so on. Yet neither the physical description nor the functional description alone captures the essence of what the airplane is — you need both.

In traditional programming, you would define an airplane's physical characteristics as a data structure, such as this:

```
Type
  Airplane = Record
    AirSpeed : Word;
    Altitude : Word;
    Flaps    : (Up, Down);
    End;
```

You would separately define the airplane's behaviors as procedures and functions:

```
Procedure Accelerate;
Begin
{...}
End;

Procedure Decelerate;
Begin
```

```
{...}
End;

Procedure FlapsUp;
Begin
{...}
End;

Procedure FlapsDown;
Begin
{...}
End;
```

In OOP, characteristics (data) and behaviors (procedures) are combined into a single entity known as an object. An airplane defined as an object might look like this:

```
Type
  Airplane = Object
    AirSpeed : Word;
    Altitude : Word;
    Flaps    : (Up, Down);
    Procedure Init;
    Procedure Accelerate;
    Procedure Decelerate;
    Procedure Ascend;
    Procedure Descend;
    Procedure FlapsUp;
    Procedure FlapsDown;
    End;
```

The object just given contains declarations for both data and procedures. In the language of OOP, procedures and functions declared within an object are known as *methods*. Notice that the object defines only the methods header; the actual code for the methods is specified separately, like this:

```
Procedure Airplane.Init;
Begin
Flaps := Down;
AirSpeed := 0;
Altitude := 0;
End;

Procedure Airplane.FlapsUp;
Begin
Flaps := Up;
End;
```

Notice that the method is defined by both the object name (**Airplane**) and the procedure name (**FlapsUp**), just as you would refer to a field in a record. In fact, you can think of an object as a record that contains both data fields and method declarations.

Within these methods, the data field Flaps is referred to without specifying the object name. Specifying **Airplane.** in the procedure declaration acts like a **With** statement for the body of the procedure.

Once an object has been defined, you can declare variables using the object's name, as shown here:

```
Var
  A : Airplane;
```

In your program, you can now write statements like these:

```
With A Do
  Begin
  Init;
  FlapsUp;
  Accelerate;
  Ascend;
  End;
```

Now you can begin to see the advantages of OOP—all actions affecting an object can be made by referring to the object itself. There can be no confusion about which data structure procedure **FlapsUp** will use. Turbo Pascal 5.5 does not, however, keep you from accessing object fields directly. For example, it is perfectly legal to write

```
A.Flaps := Up;
```

As you become better acquainted with OOP, you will learn that accessing an object's fields directly is both unnecessary and undesirable. The responsibility for good programming style is entirely yours.

Inheritance

While objects contain data and procedures of their own, they can also inherit the same from other objects. Inheritance in OOP is similar to the familiar Turbo Pascal technique of nesting records. Consider the following record definitions:

```
Type
  Movement = Record
    Direction    : 0..360;    (* Compass degrees *)
    Speed        : 0..400;    (* Miles per hour *)
    SpeedChange  : -10..10;   (* MPH per second *)
    End;

  AirStatus = Record
    Mvmt         : Movement;
    Altitude     : 0..35000;  (* Feet *)
    AltChange    : -100..100; (* Feet per second *)
    End;
```

The record **Movement** contains fields used to determine speed and direction. The second record, **AirStatus**, declares **Mvmt**, which contains the fields in the **Movement** record. This type of nesting allows you to build increasingly complex record structures.

In OOP, object inheritance replaces the need for nested records and simplifies the process of adding complexity. The following listing shows how to use objects to replace nested record declarations:

```
Type
  Movement = Object
    Direction    : 0..360;    (* Compass degrees *)
    Speed        : 0..400;    (* Miles per hour *)
    SpeedChange  : -10..10;   (* MPH per second *)
    Procedure Init;
    End;

  AirStatus = Object(Movement)
    Altitude     : 0..35000;  (* Feet *)
    AltChange    : -100..100; (* Feet per second *)
    Procedure Init;
    End;
```

Unlike record declarations, the objects contain method declarations. Notice how the declaration of **AirStatus** includes a reference to **Movement**:

    AirStatus = Object(Movement)

By this declaration, **AirStatus** inherits everything contained in **Movement** — data and methods. In OOP terminology **Movement** is an *ancestor type* and **AirStatus** is a *descendant type*. An object can have more than one ancestor type. In the example just given, **Movement** is the *immediate ancestor* of **AirStatus** and **AirStatus** is the *immediate descendent* of **Movement**. The overall lineage of ancestors and descendents is known as the *object hierarchy*.

You might have noticed that both **Movement** and **AirStatus** contain a method named **Init**. When a method in a descendent object is given a name that is identical to one in an ancestor object, the descendent method takes precedence. Thus, to call the **Init** procedure from within the **AirStatus** object, you would need to specify the call as **Movement.Init;**. Note, however, that while inherited methods can share the same name, inherited data fields cannot. Once an object's data field is named, no data field in any descendent object can share that field's name.

Inheritance is a complex subject with many ramifications, which will be dealt with in detail over the remainder of this chapter. While at first these complexities make OOP appear difficult to use, with practice you will find that they are easily mastered.

Encapsulization

One of the overriding goals of OOP is *encapsulization*, the creation of objects that function as complete units. One of the rules of encapsulization is that the programmer need never directly access the data fields within an object. Instead, methods should be defined within the object to take care of all data manipulation. Consider the following object definition:

```
Movement = Object
   Direction    : Word;     (* Compass degrees *)
   Speed        : Word;     (* Miles per hour *)
   SpeedChange  : Integer;  (* MPH per second *)
   Procedure Init;
   Function GetDirection      : Word;
   Function GetSpeed          : Word;
   Function GetSpeedChange    : Integer;
   Procedure SetDirection(NewDirection : Word);
   Procedure SetSpeed(NewSpeed : Word);
   Procedure SetSpeedChange(Change : Integer);
   Procedure Accelerate;
   Procedure Decelerate;
   End;
```

The object just listed contains only three data fields: Direction, Speed, and SpeedChange. To provide access to these three fields, the object defines nine methods, each of which either reports or alters the value of a field. By encapsulizing an object, you can eliminate side effects caused by unauthorized access to an object's data.

Encapsulization is code intensive. Not only are extra procedures added, but also every access to a data field requires a function or procedure call. This means that your programs may be larger and slower. But the advantages of clearer code and easier maintenance may well outweigh the disadvantages.

Static and Virtual Methods

OOP allows two types of methods: static methods and virtual methods. Static methods are less complicated, require less memory, and execute more quickly, but they do not give you the full benefit of object oriented programming. Virtual methods, on the other hand, provide an unprecedented level of flexibility in the use of objects. You are free to use both static and virtual methods in your programs, but you should understand the use of both to understand when each is appropriate.

Static Methods

The examples given thus far in this chapter use static methods, and their definition and use should be fairly clear. What might not be clear is why virtual methods should be necessary.

Problems with static methods develop when different objects share the same name. This is best shown by an example. The following program contains three objects: **Location**, **Ch**, and **St**. Both **Ch** and **St** contain a method named **Show**, which is called by the method **MoveTo** located in **Ch**.

```
Program Static;
Uses CRT;
(**************************************************)
(* OBJECT: Location                             *)
(**************************************************)
Type
  Location = Object
    X,Y : Byte;
    Procedure Init;
    Procedure Position(NewX, NewY : Byte);
    End;

Procedure Location.Init;
Begin
X := 1;
Y := 1;
End;

Procedure Location.Position(NewX, NewY : Byte);
Begin
X := NewX;
Y := NewY;
End;

(**************************************************)
(* OBJECT: Ch                                   *)
(**************************************************)

Type
  Ch = Object(Location)
    C : Char;
    Procedure Init;
    Procedure Show;
    Procedure SetC(NewC : Char);
    Procedure MoveTo(NewX, NewY : Byte);
    End;

Procedure Ch.Init;
Begin
Location.Init;
```

```
C := 'A';
End;

Procedure Ch.Show;
Begin
Write(C);
End;

Procedure Ch.SetC(NewC : Char);
Begin
C := NewC;
End;

Procedure Ch.MoveTo(NewX, NewY : Byte);
Begin
X := NewX;
Y := NewY;
GotoXY(X,Y);
Show;
End;

(***********************************************)
(* OBJECT: St                                *)
(***********************************************)

Type
  St = Object(Ch)
    S : String;
    Procedure Init;
    Procedure Show;
    Procedure SetS(NewS : String);
    End;

Procedure St.Init;
Begin
Ch.Init;
S := '';
End;

Procedure St.Show;
Begin
Write(S);
End;

Procedure St.SetS(NewS : String);
Begin
S := NewS;
End;

Var
  S : St;

Begin
ClrScr;

With S Do
```

```
Begin
Init;
SetS('THIS IS A STRING');
MoveTo(10,10);
 End;
ReadLn;
End.
```

The version of **MoveTo** in the **St** object displays a string, while
the version in **Ch** displays a character. A variable named **S** is
declared to be of type **St**. The program initializes the **S** object,
initializes the string, and then executes the **MoveTo** method.
What happens? Instead of displaying the string, the program
displays the character in the **Ch** object. In short, the program
executed the wrong version of **Show**. How did this occur?

The answer lies in the object hierarchy. The method **Move-
To** resides in the **Ch** object, so the statement **S.MoveTo** causes
Turbo Pascal to trace backward from the **St** object into the **Ch**
object to locate the method. Once **MoveTo** executes, it encounters a call to a method named **Show**. With no other information,
Turbo Pascal executes the closest version of **Show**, the one that
resides in the **Ch** object (see Figure 24-1). So instead of displaying a string, the program displays a character.

This is an example of *early binding*. When the program is
compiled, Turbo Pascal resolves the call to **Show** by pointing to

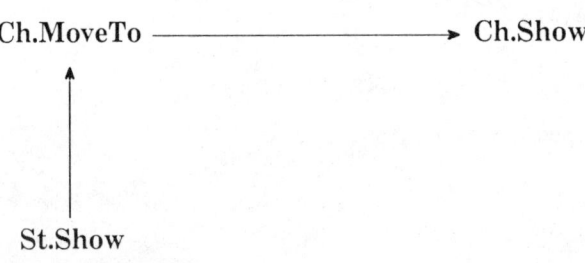

Figure 24-1.   Path of static method calls

the procedure located in **Ch**. This binding is termed "early" because it is defined at compile time. (Virtual methods, by contrast, use late binding, which will be discussed shortly.)

How can this error be avoided? The static solution is to redefine the method **MoveTo** within the **St** object. But that solution runs counter to the philosophy of OOP, which strives to reduce redundant code. The OOP solution to errors produced by early binding is the use of virtual methods.

Virtual Methods

The name *virtual* does little to describe how virtual methods function. Simply stated, virtual methods keep track of where in the object hierarchy a method call originated. This means that method calls can move in both directions in the object hierarchy. Using the example given earlier, a call to **St.Show** would trace back to **Ch.MoveTo** as before. But, when **Ch.MoveTo** encounters a call to **Show**, it executes the version in the calling object **St**, not **Ch** (see Figure 24-2).

This is an example of late binding. *Late binding* simply means that the exact path of execution is determined at run time, not at compile time. This is accomplished using a *virtual*

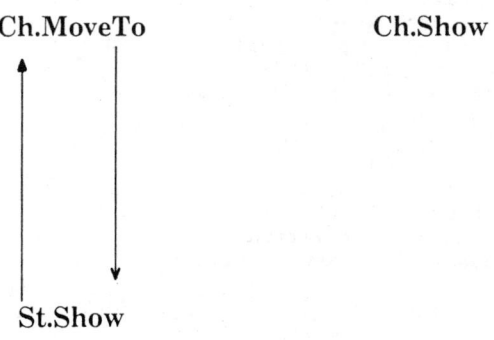

Figure 24-2.   Path of dynamic method calls

method table (VMT), a jump table that Turbo Pascal sets up for every object type that *contains or inherits* a virtual method.

The Virtual Method Table

A VMT is a table of addresses that point to procedures and functions. By maintaining a table of addresses for each object type, Turbo Pascal can determine a path of execution that would be impossible to determine at compile time.

The structure of the VMT begins with two words. The first word contains the size of the object using the VMT; the second word contains the negative value of the first word and is used as a means of validating that the VMT has been properly initialized. When virtual call validation is enabled with the {$R+}, Turbo Pascal tests to see if the sum of the first two words of the VMT equals zero. If it does not, Turbo Pascal generates run-time error 210.

Using Virtual Methods

To declare a method virtual, simply add the reserved word **Virtual** to the method declaration in the object definition, as shown here:

```
Type
  Ch = Object(Location)
    C : Char;
    Constructor Init;
    Procedure Show; Virtual;
    Procedure SetC(NewC : Char);
    Procedure MoveTo(NewX, NewY : Byte);
    End;

  St = Object(Ch)
    S : String;
    Constructor Init;
    Procedure Show; Virtual;
    Procedure SetS(NewS : String);
    End;
```

In the listing just given, the method **Show** has been declared virtual in both the **Ch** and **St** object types. Three rules govern the declaration of virtual methods. First, once a method has been declared virtual in an object, the same method in any descendent object must also be declared virtual. Because **Show** is virtual in **Ch**, it must also be declared virtual in **St**, a descendent of **Ch**.

The second rule is that once a virtual method has been declared, its header cannot change in any subsequent declaration; you cannot change a virtual method from a procedure to a function or alter the parameter list.

The third rule of virtual methods is that any object that contains virtual methods must also declare a *constructor method* prior to the virtual methods.

Constructor Methods

Constructor methods, which play a critical role in late binding, are declared by substituting the word **Constructor** for **Procedure,** as demonstrated in the previous listing. Turbo Pascal uses constructors to initialize the VMT. The rule on constructor methods is that they must be called before any virtual methods are called. This makes sense, since you cannot execute a virtual method without a properly initialized VMT. In the following example program, utilizing virtual methods and constructors resolves the problem encountered in the program using static methods.

```
Program Static;
Uses CRT;
(**************************************************)
(* OBJECT: Location                              *)
(**************************************************)
Type
  Location = Object
    X,Y : Byte;
    Procedure Init;
    Procedure Position(NewX, NewY : Byte);
    End;

Procedure Location.Init;
Begin
X := 1;
Y := 1;
End;
```

```
Procedure Location.Position(NewX, NewY : Byte);
Begin
X := NewX;
Y := NewY;
End;

(**************************************************)
(* OBJECT: Ch                                   *)
(**************************************************)

Type
  Ch = Object(Location)
    C : Char;
    Constructor Init;
    Procedure Show; Virtual;
    Procedure SetC(NewC : Char); Virtual;
    Procedure MoveTo(NewX, NewY : Byte);
    End;

Constructor Ch.Init;
Begin
Location.Init;
C := 'A';
End;

Procedure Ch.Show;
Begin
Write(C);
End;

Procedure Ch.SetC(NewC : Char);
Begin
C := NewC;
End;

Procedure Ch.MoveTo(NewX, NewY : Byte);
Begin
X := NewX;
Y := NewY;
GotoXY(X,Y);
Show;
End;

(**************************************************)
(* OBJECT: St                                   *)
(**************************************************)

Type
  St = Object(Ch)
    S : String;
    Constructor Init;
    Procedure Show; Virtual;
    Procedure SetS(NewS : String);
    End;

Constructor St.Init;
```

"Sorry, Sue, darling; I didn't really mean to say 'Yes' and 'No' at the same time. But did you mean that time we sat here on that day before I left the Castle, or that other day – I think it was just about a year ago – when we were sitting here remembering that day – I mean, the first day?"

"I meant the morning of the day before you had to leave us," said Susan. "I know that day holds very special memories for you."

"Oh, it does – it does!" said Jim. "And memories of that day are flooding back into my mind now, Sue, because it was a day very like this – warm and sunny, I mean, and with the cherry blossom on the trees!" I mustn't let Sue know what I was *really* thinking about! he thought.

"Listen!" said Susan suddenly. "They're coming! I can hear voices!"

Jim listened, and heard the sound of the perambulator being pushed across the footbridge, and people talking, and someone (probably Ailean) making cooing noises to the baby. Bother! he said to himself. Now there'll be no more peace for me to continue my happy daydreams!

Mrs. Middleton appeared on the lawn, pushing Julia in her perambulator, and close beside her was Ailean. Then, a little way behind them, they saw Samantha coming, carrying a tray with the coffee things on it.

"Here we are!" said Ailean. "This is the Private Lawn."

"My goodness – what a beautiful place this is!" said Mrs. Middleton. "Thank you, my Lady, for inviting us to come out here!"

"It'll be a nice place on days like this for Julia to play in, when she gets a little older," said Susan.

"Hello, everybody!" said Samantha as she arrived with her tray and set it down on the table.

A few minutes later cups of coffee had been poured out, and they were all sitting around the garden table. Ailean had taken the chair to the left of Mrs. Middleton so that she could be as near as possible to Julia; it was obvious that she was fascinated by the baby, and kept turning round to look into the perambulator to smile or make faces for her. Julia, for her part, was now old enough to recognize a face when someone was talking to her, and she would respond by smiling, making little noises, and waving her arms about, as she was now doing.

"You're getting on splendidly with Julia, Ailean!" remarked Susan, watching the communication between the two of them.

"She's a lovely little thing, isn't she?" said her nanny, Mrs. Middleton.

"Oh, but she's absolutely *sweet!*" said Ailean enthusiastically.

Jim was watching them, but he said nothing. He was sitting with Susan on his left, and Samantha on his right, so that he was nearly opposite to Ailean on the round garden table (Ailean had Samantha to her left). For once Ailean isn't interested in me right now, he thought, when he had tried, but failed to catch her eye. No, she's much more interested in Julia than in me! He was surprised to find that the realization that this was so provoked in him a feeling which was very close to being a feeling of jealousy. So I'm annoyed, am I, that she's giving all of her attention to Julia, and none to me? Yes, I am annoyed! It may be very foolish of me to be thinking and feeling like this but, really, I don't think I can help it!

Jim did not hear very much of the conversation that was going on around him until Ailean asked a question about Julia.

"How old is she?"

"Oh!" said Susan. "She's... let me think... what's the date today?"

"It's the second of May today, ma'am," said Mrs. Middleton, "so I think that means that Julia is exactly three months old today."

"So it does!" said Susan. "Julia was born on the second of February - Candlemas - wasn't she? Fancy me forgetting that!"

Jim wondered whether Susan could really have forgotten how old Julia was, or whether she was simply pretending to have forgotten. Anyway, it doesn't matter, he told himself. But Ailean was absolutely right when she said that Julia is "absolutely sweet" - oh, yes, she most certainly is - and she's my darling little daughter, and I'm very fond of her, and growing fonder every day! I think I'm getting used now to the idea of being a father, and having a little daughter to love as well as my wife. It's quite a different kind of love, of course, from what I feel for my darling, Sue - who is uniquely precious to me - but it certainly is love none the less. It's a funny thing, I suppose, that when I married Sue it never occured to me that love could be like this - that it *should* be like this - that it should be a family thing, as it were. It never occured to me that we might have children some day, and that the two of us might become three, or four, or more...

Now Jim heard almost nothing of the conversation that was going on around him while his very active train of thoughts pursued aspects of love within the wider family, but it surprised him to discover that he had never given this subject serious consideration before. I suppose it's because we've been just the two of us for a long time, but now there are three of us.

But, of course, there was Rachel. Almost exactly a year ago she came into my life so, in a way, there were three of us then. No, but Rachel doesn't count, and Ailean won't count either, even if I fall madly in love with her, because they're not part of my family as Sue and Ju are.

Then Jim remembered that it had been almost exactly a year ago that he had sat with Susan in almost the very same spot where they were sitting now. But the year had now come full circle. On that day one year ago he had been thinking about many things, but he had been thinking a great deal about his love for Susan. Now, a year and eight months after his wedding, Jim Sandy was feeling, more or less, that marriage was indeed turning out to be the blissful experience that he had hoped it would be...

THE END

Lightning Source UK Ltd.
Milton Keynes UK
UKOW02f2145240516

274891UK00002B/339/P

```
Begin
Ch.Init;
S := '';
End;

Procedure St.Show;
Begin
Write(S);
End;

Procedure St.SetS(NewS : String);
Begin
S := NewS;
End;

Var
  S : St;
  C : Ch;

Begin
ClrScr;
C.Init;
With S Do
  Begin
  Init;
  SetS('THIS IS A STRING');
  MoveTo(10,10);
  End;
ReadLn;
End.
```

Inside Virtual Methods

Objects that contain virtual methods are provided a VMT field. The VMT field contains the 16-bit offset into the data segment at which the object's VMT is located. All variables of the same object type point to the same VMT. The VMT field is invisible to the programmer and provides a link between the object variable and the VMT. In the example program just given, variables of type **Location, Ch,** and **St** would have the structures shown in Figure 24-3. Since **Location** contains no virtual methods, variables of this type contain no VMT field. The **Ch** object, on the other hand, does contain virtual methods and, therefore, is provided a VMT field following the data fields. The **St** object also uses virtual methods, but because it inherits a VMT field from **Ch,** Turbo Pascal does not add one. Instead, **St**'s data field is

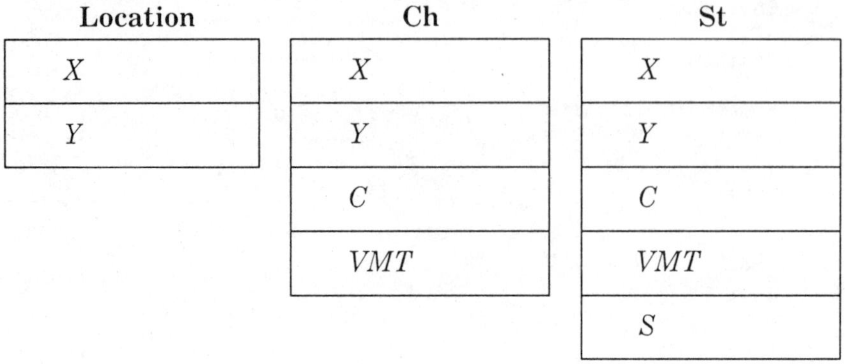

Location	Ch	St
X	X	X
Y	Y	Y
	C	C
	VMT	VMT
		S

Figure 24-3. Internal structure of object variables

simply appended to those inherited from **Ch**. Remember that the VMT field is not part of the object, but part of variables of an object type.

The compiler sets up an object's VMT in the data segment *only if a call to the constructor method is made somewhere in the program.* If you do not call the constructor method, a VMT will not be set up, and any calls to other virtual methods in the object will result in program failure. If you are using objects with virtual methods, be sure to initialize the object by calling its constructor at the beginning of the program.

The VMTs for the program just given are shown in Figure 24-4. Notice that only those methods defined as virtual are included in the VMT. The **St** VMT includes the inherited procedure **Ch.SetC**, whose address is the same as in the **Ch** VMT. The method **Show**, however, has different addresses in **Ch** and **St** because the **St** object redeclared it. In effect, the version of **Show** in **St** overrides the version in **Ch**.

When a virtual method is called, Turbo Pascal passes the address of the calling variable on the stack of the virtual method. Thus, when calling **S.Show**, the address of **S** is passed on the stack. This address is known as the *self parameter,* and it is always the last item passed on the stack. Using this address, the method picks up the VMT address from the variable and

Ch VMT
$0005
$FFFB
Ch.Show 71A3:004F
Ch.SetC 71A3:007E

St VMT
$0105
$FEFB
St.Show 71A3:010E
Ch.SetC 71A3:007E

Figure 24-4.   Virtual method tables

executes the appropriate method by using the address found in
the VMT. In other words, the variable passes a pointer to itself
to the method, the method uses that pointer to locate the VMT,
and the VMT tells the method which code to execute.

Object Type Compatibility

Object variables follow slightly different compatibility rules than
do normal Turbo Pascal variables. The primary difference is that
an ancestor type is compatible with a descendent type, but the
reverse is not true. For example, in the program given previously, the statement

```
C := S;
```

would be legal, but

```
S := C;
```

would not. The reasoning is that, through inheritance, **S** contains
everything in **C**, but **C** does not (or probably does not) contain
everything in **S**. The statement **C := S** assigns to **C** all values

that it shares in common with **S**. Similarly, a procedure that accepts a **Ch** object variable as a **Var** parameter can also accept a variable of type **St**. Thus a procedure declared

```
Procedure ChangeValue(Var C : Ch);
Begin
End;
```

could be called as

```
ChangeValue(S);
```

The flexibility of object type compatibility may seem unimportant at first, but it makes possible a powerful feature of OOP: *polymorphism.* Polymorphism is just a fancy way of saying that a procedure is willing to accept a wide range of object types, *even if it is unaware of them at compile time.* As long as the parameter variable is a descendent of the **Var** parameter type, the procedure will accept it. You could define 10 (or 100) different ancestors to **Ch**, and the **ChangeValue** procedure would not only accept them, but would use them as you intended.

Polymorphism has another important implication. If the procedure that accepts the polymorphic variable gets its information about that variable at run time, you will be able to define compatible objects *without recompiling the unit that contains the procedure.* This adds the important quality of *extensibility.* You can compile a unit of routines that accept polymorphic variables, distribute the compiled unit without the source code, and the users will be able to create their own objects to work with the compiled procedures. In other words, you don't have to think of everything in advance—the end users can add what they want!

Dynamic Allocation of Objects

By now you probably are beginning to sense the value of OOP. But there is one last topic that requires considerable explanation—dynamic allocation. Dynamic object variables require special care. To allocate dynamic object variables, you must follow special rules regarding allocation, deallocation, and the use of the destructors.

Destructors

You have already learned how constructor methods are vital to using virtual methods. Similarly, destructor methods are crucial to the use of dynamic allocation. When a dynamic object variable is allocated, memory is taken from the heap for use by the variable.

When it comes time to deallocate the variable, however, how can Turbo Pascal determine how much memory to release? The answer is to use the VMT, which contains the size of the variable. Thus, a primary function of the destructor method is to provide access to the VMT, so that the correct amount of memory may be released. In fact, a destructor method may have no code at all, serving only as a link to the VMT. In other cases, the destructor method will contain cleanup routines that may deallocate other dynamic variables, close disk files, and so on. Consider the following example, which modifies an object defined in earlier program examples:

```
Type
  BufferType = Array[1..1000] Of Byte;
  St = Object(Ch)
    S : String;
    F : Text;
    FileOpen : Boolean;
    Buffer : ^BufferType;
    Constructor Init;
    Destructor Done; Virtual;
    Procedure Show; Virtual;
    Procedure SetS(NewS : String);
    Procedure OpenFile(Fname : String);
    End;

Constructor St.Init;
Begin
Ch.Init;
S := '';
FileOpen := FALSE;
```

```
New(Buffer);
End;

Destructor St.Done;
Begin
Dispose(Buffer);
If FileOpen Then
   Close(F);
End;
```

The object **St** now contains pointer variable **Buffer**, text file **F**, and Boolean variable **FileOpen**. A destructor method named **Done** has also been added. The constructor method **Init** has been expanded to allocate the **Buffer** variable and to initialize **FileOpen** to FALSE. The destructor method **Done** performs two major tasks: it deallocates the **Buffer** variable and closes the disk file, if it is open. With these definitions, variables of type **St** are ready to be allocated.

Allocating and Deallocating the Object Variable

Turbo Pascal 5.5 extends the traditional use of the **New** and **Dispose** standard procedures. Now both routines can take two parameters—a dynamic variable and a procedure name. To allocate a dynamic variable, the procedure call is straightforward. Given variable **S1** of type **St**, the syntax would be

```
New(S1,Init);
```

which tells Turbo Pascal to allocate the object variable **S1** and execute its constructor method **Init**. Performing both tasks at once ensures that the variable will be allocated correctly. Once allocated, the variable is used as any other object variable, except that a ^ must follow the variable name.

Dynamic deallocation is a mirror image of allocation. The **Dispose** command to deallocate **S1** would be

```
Dispose(S1,Done);
```

which executes the shutdown procedures in **Done** and deallocates its memory from the heap. You could use the following code to accomplish the same thing

```
New(S1)
S1^.Init;
{...}
S1^.Done;
Dispose(S1);
```

but it is safer and easier to use the extended versions of **New** and **Dispose**. The following program offers a complete example of the use of dynamically allocated virtual object data types.

```
Program DynamicObject;
Uses CRT;
(************************************************)
(* OBJECT: Location                           *)
(************************************************)
Type
  Location = Object
    X,Y : Byte;
    Procedure Init;
    Procedure Position(NewX, NewY : Byte);
    End;

Procedure Location.Init;
Begin
X := 1;
Y := 1;
End;

Procedure Location.Position(NewX, NewY : Byte);
Begin
X := NewX;
Y := NewY;
End;

(************************************************)
(* OBJECT: Ch                                 *)
(************************************************)

Type
  Ch = Object(Location)
    C : Char;
    Constructor Init;
    Procedure Show; Virtual;
    Procedure SetC(NewC : Char);
    Procedure MoveTo(NewX, NewY : Byte);
    End;
```

```
Constructor Ch.Init;
Begin
Location.Init;
C := 'A';
End;

Procedure Ch.Show;
Begin
Write(C);
End;

Procedure Ch.SetC(NewC : Char);
Begin
C := NewC;
End;

Procedure Ch.MoveTo(NewX, NewY : Byte);
Begin
X := NewX;
Y := NewY;
GotoXY(X,Y);
Show;
End;

(***********************************************)
(* OBJECT: St                                  *)
(***********************************************)

Type
  BufferType = Array[1..1000] Of Byte;
  St = Object(Ch)
    S : String;
    F : Text;
    FileOpen : Boolean;
    Buffer : ^BufferType;
    Constructor Init;
    Destructor Done; Virtual;
    Procedure Show; Virtual;
    Procedure SetS(NewS : String);
    Procedure OpenFile(Fname : String);
    End;

Constructor St.Init;
Begin
Ch.Init;
S := '';
FileOpen := FALSE;
New(Buffer);
End;

Destructor St.Done;
Begin
Dispose(Buffer);
If FileOpen Then
  Close(F);
End;
```

```
Procedure St.Show;
Begin
Write(S);
End;

Procedure St.SetS(NewS : String);
Begin
S := NewS;
WriteLn(F,NewS);
End;

Procedure St.OpenFile(Fname : String);
Begin
Assign(F,Fname);
Rewrite(F);
FileOpen := TRUE;
End;

(**************************************************)

Var
  S1,S2 : ^St;

Begin
ClrScr;
New(S1,Init);
New(S2,Init);

With S1^ Do
  Begin
  OpenFile('ST1.LOG');
  SetS('THIS IS STRING 1');
  MoveTo(10,10);
  End;
With S2^ Do
  Begin
  OpenFile('ST2.LOG');
  SetS('THIS IS STRING 2');
  MoveTo(10,11);
  End;

Dispose(S1,Done);
Dispose(S2,Done);

GotoXY(1,24);
Write('Press ENTER...');
ReadLn;
End.
```

While object oriented programming has been around for years, it is still new to most programmers. Its concepts require a rethinking of what programming is, what problems it can solve, and how a solution should be structured. For very complex programming tasks, its power can mean the difference between success and failure. With Turbo Pascal 5.5 you can learn the elements of OOP in a friendly way. It will take time, but in the end, your scope as a programmer will be greatly increased.

Turbo Pascal Error Codes

Compiler Error Messages
Run-time Error Messages

Compiler Error Messages

Compiler error messages refer to problems in your code or programming environment that prevent Turbo Pascal from producing an executable file. In the integrated development environment, Turbo Pascal will attempt to locate the source-code location of the error.

1	Out of memory
2	Identifier expected
3	Unknown identifier
4	Duplicate identifier
5	Syntax error
6	Error in real constant
7	Error in integer constant
8	String constant exceeds line
9	Too many nested files
10	Unexpected end of file
11	Line too long
12	Type identifier expected
13	Too many open files

14	Invalid filename
15	File not found
16	Disk full
17	Invalid compiler directive
18	Too many files
19	Undefined type in pointer definition
20	Variable identifier expected
21	Error in type
22	Structure too large
23	Set base type out of range
24	File components may not be files
25	Invalid string length
26	Type mismatch
27	Invalid subrange base type
28	Lower bound greater than upper bound
29	Ordinal type expected
30	Integer constant expected
31	Constant expected
32	Integer or real constant expected
33	Type identifier expected
34	Invalid function result type
35	Label identifier expected
36	Begin expected
37	End expected
38	Integer expression expected
39	Ordinal expression expected
40	Boolean expression expected
41	Operand types do not match operator
42	Error in expression
43	Illegal assignment
44	Field identifier expected

45	Object file too large
46	Undefined external
47	Invalid object-file record
48	Code segment too large
49	Data segment too large
50	Do expected
51	Invalid Public definition
52	Invalid Extrn definition
53	Too many Extrn definitions
54	Of expected
55	Interface expected
56	Invalid relocatable reference
57	Then expected
58	To or Downto expected
59	Undefined forward
60	Too many procedures
61	Invalid typecast
62	Division by zero
63	Invalid file type
64	Cannot read or write variables of this type
65	Pointer variable expected
66	String variable expected
67	String expression expected
68	Circular unit reference
69	Unit name mismatch
70	Unit version mismatch
71	Duplicate unit name
72	Unit file format error
73	Implementation expected
74	Constant and case types do not match
75	Record variable expected

76	Constant out of range
77	File variable expected
78	Pointer expression expected
79	Integer or real expression expected
80	Label not within current block
81	Label already defined
82	Undefined label in preceding statement part
83	Invalid @ argument
84	Unit expected
85	";" expected
86	":" expected
87	"," expected
88	"(" expected
89	")" expected
90	"=" expected
91	":=" expected
92	"[" or "(." expected
93	"]" or ".)" expected
94	"." expected
95	".." expected
96	Too many variables
97	Invalid For control variable
98	Integer variable expected
99	Files are not allowed here
100	String length mismatch
101	Invalid ordering of fields
102	String constant expected
103	Integer or Real variable expected
104	Ordinal variable expected
105	Inline error
106	Character expression expected

107	Too many relocation items
112	Case constant out of range
113	Error in statement
114	Cannot call an interrupt procedure
116	Must be in 8087 mode to compile this
117	Target address not found
118	Include files are not allowed here
120	Nil expected
121	Invalid qualifier
122	Invalid variable reference
123	Too many symbols
124	Statement part too long
126	Files must be Var parameters
127	Too many conditional symbols
128	Misplaced conditional directive
129	ENDIF directive missing
130	Error in initial conditional defines
131	Header does not match previous definition
132	Critical disk error
133	Cannot evaluate this expression
134	Expression incorrectly terminated
135	Invalid format specifier
136	Invalid indirect reference
137	Structured variables are not allowed here
138	Cannot evaluate without SYSTEM unit
139	Cannot access this symbol
140	Invalid floating-point operation
141	Cannot compile overlays to memory
142	Procedure or function variable expected
143	Invalid procedure or function reference
144	Cannot overlay this unit

Run-time Error Messages

A run-time error is an error condition that occurs while your program is running. When such an error occurs, Turbo Pascal displays this message:

Run-time error nnn at xxxx:yyyy

where **nnn** is the numeric code for the run-time error, **xxxx** is the program segment in which the error occurred, and **yyyy** is the offset of the location of the error.

DOS Errors

2	File not found
3	Path not found
4	Too many open files
5	File access denied
6	Invalid file handle
12	Invalid file access code
15	Invalid drive number
16	Cannot remove current directory
17	Cannot rename across drives

I/O Errors

100	Disk read error
101	Disk write error
102	File not assigned
103	File not open
104	File not open for input

105	File not open for output
106	Invalid numeric format

Critical Errors

150	Disk is write-protected
151	Unknown unit
152	Drive not ready
153	Unknown command
154	CRC error in data
155	Bad drive request structure length
156	Disk seek error
157	Unknown media type
158	Sector not found
159	Printer out of paper
160	Device write fault
161	Device read fault
162	Hardware failure

Fatal Errors

200	Division by zero
201	Range check error
202	Stack overflow error
203	Heap overflow error
204	Invalid pointer operation
205	Floating-point overflow
206	Floating-point underflow
207	Invalid floating-point operation
208	Overlay manager not installed
209	Overlay file read error

ASCII Codes for the PC

ASCII Value	Character	ASCII Value	Character
0	Null	12	Form-feed
1	☺	13	Carriage return
2	☻	14	♫
3	♥	15	☼
4	♦	16	►
5	♣	17	◄
6	♠	18	↕
7	Beep	19	‼
8	◘	20	¶
9	Tab	21	§
10	Linefeed	22	▬
11	Cursor home	23	↨

Table B-1.   ASCII Codes for the PC

795

ASCII Value	Character	ASCII Value	Character
24	↑	58	:
25	↓	59	;
26	→	60	<
27	←	61	=
28	Cursor right	62	>
29	Cursor left	63	?
30	Cursor up	64	@
31	Cursor down	65	A
32	Space	66	B
33	!	67	C
34	"	68	D
35	#	69	E
36	$	70	F
37	%	71	G
38	&	72	H
39	'	73	I
40	(	74	J
41	)	75	K
42	*	76	L
43	+	77	M
44	,	78	N
45	-	79	O
46	.	80	P
47	/	81	Q
48	0	82	R
49	1	83	S
50	2	84	T
51	3	85	U
52	4	86	V
53	5	87	W
54	6	88	X
55	7	89	Y
56	8	90	Z
57	9	91	[

Table B-1.   ASCII Codes for the PC (*continued*)

ASCII Value	Character	ASCII Value	Character
92	\	126	~
93	]	127	⌂
94	^	128	Ç
95	–	129	ü
96	'	130	é
97	a	131	â
98	b	132	ä
99	c	133	à
100	d	134	å
101	e	135	ç
102	f	136	ê
103	g	137	ë
104	h	138	è
105	i	139	ï
106	j	140	î
107	k	141	ì
108	l	142	Ä
109	m	143	Å
110	n	144	É
111	o	145	æ
112	p	146	Æ
113	q	147	ô
114	r	148	ö
115	s	149	ò
116	t	150	û
117	u	151	ù
118	v	152	ÿ
119	w	153	Ö
120	x	154	Ü
121	y	155	¢
122	z	156	£
123	{	157	¥
124	¦	158	Pt
125	}	159	ƒ

Table B-1.   ASCII Codes for the PC (*continued*)

ASCII Value	Character	ASCII Value	Character
160	á	194	┬
161	í	195	├
162	ó	196	─
163	ú	197	┼
164	ñ	198	╞
165	Ñ	199	╟
166	ª	200	╚
167	º	201	╔
168	¿	202	╩
169	⌐	203	╦
170	¬	204	╠
171	½	205	═
172	¼	206	╬
173	¡	207	╧
174	«	208	╨
175	»	209	╤
176	░	210	╥
177	▒	211	╙
178	▓	212	╘
179	│	213	╒
180	┤	214	╓
181	╡	215	╫
182	╢	216	╪
183	╖	217	┘
184	╕	218	┌
185	╣	219	█
186	║	220	▄
187	╗	221	▌
188	╝	222	▐
189	╜	223	▀
190	╛	224	α
191	┐	225	β
192	└	226	Γ
193	┴	227	π

Table B-1.   ASCII Codes for the PC (*continued*)

ASCII Value	Character	ASCII Value	Character
228	Σ	242	$\geq$
229	σ	243	$\leq$
230	μ	244	$\lceil$
231	τ	245	J
232	ϕ	246	$\div$
233	θ	247	$\approx$
234	Ω	248	$\circ$
235	δ	249	$\bullet$
236	∞	250	$\cdot$
237	$\emptyset$	251	$\sqrt{}$
238	ϵ	252	n
239	$\cap$	253	2
240	$\equiv$	254	$\blacksquare$
241	$\pm$	255	(blank 'FF')

Table B-1.   ASCII Codes for the PC (*continued*)

The PC Keyboard

The computer keyboard produces codes that are associated with letters and symbols. One key, however, can produce a different set of codes when you press other keys at the same time. For example, the A key normally produces the letter "a" (ASCII code 97), but when pressed along with the SHIFT key, it produces the letter "A" (ASCII code 65). Two other keys—CTRL and ALT—produce even more codes.

Some keys, such as the function keys (F1 through F10), produce two codes: a scan code (#0) and another code that indicates the key pressed. To read keys that produce scan codes, use the following procedure:

```
Procedure Inkey(Var  ch : Char;
                Var fk : Boolean);
Begin
fk := False;
ch := ReadKey;
If ch = #0 Then
  Begin
  fk := True;
  ch := ReadKey;
  End;
End;
```

This procedure uses **ReadKey**, which is found in the CRT unit. When **fk** is TRUE, a scan-code key has been pressed and the ASCII code for that key is returned in **ch**. When **fk** is FALSE, a normal key has been pressed and the value is contained in **ch**.

The following table lists the keys on the PC keyboard and the codes they return.

Key	Normal		SHIFT		CTRL		ALT	
F1	0	59	0	84	0	94	0	104
F2	0	60	0	85	0	95	0	105
F3	0	61	0	86	0	96	0	106
F4	0	62	0	87	0	97	0	107
F5	0	63	0	88	0	98	0	108
F6	0	64	0	89	0	99	0	109
F7	0	65	0	90	0	100	0	110
F8	0	66	0	91	0	101	0	111
F9	0	67	0	92	0	102	0	112
F10	0	68	0	93	0	103	0	113
←	0	75		52	0	115		none
→	0	77		54	0	116		none
↑	0	72		56		none		none
↓	0	80		50		none		none
HOME	0	71		55	0	119		none
END	0	79		49	0	117		none
PGUP	0	73		57	0	132		none
PGDN	0	81		51	0	118		none
INS	0	82		48		none		none
DEL	0	83		46	0	255		none
ESC		27		27		27		none
BACKSPACE		8		8		127		none
TAB		9	0	15		none		none
ENTER		13		13		10		none
A		97		65		1	0	30
B		98		66		2	0	48
C		99		67		3	0	46
D		100		68		4	0	32
E		101		69		5	0	18
F		102		70		6	0	33
G		103		71		7	0	34
H		104		72		8	0	35
I		105		73		9	0	23
J		106		74		10	0	36
K		107		75		11	0	37

Key	Normal	SHIFT	CTRL		ALT	
L	108	76		12	0	38
M	109	77		13	0	50
N	110	78		14	0	49
O	111	79		15	0	24
P	112	80		16	0	25
Q	113	81		17	0	16
R	114	82		18	0	19
S	115	83		19	0	31
T	116	84		20	0	20
U	117	85		21	0	22
V	118	86		22	0	47
W	119	87		23	0	17
X	120	88		24	0	45
Y	121	89		25	0	21
Z	122	90		26	0	44
[	91	123		27		none
\	92	124		28		none
]	93	125		29		none
'	96	126		none		none
0	48	41		none	0	129
1	49	33		none	0	120
2	50	64	0	3	0	121
3	51	35		none	0	122
4	52	36		none	0	123
5	53	37		none	0	124
6	54	94		30	0	125
7	55	38		none	0	126
8	56	42		none	0	127
9	57	40		none	0	128
*	42	none	0	114		none
Keypad +	43	43		none		none
Keypad −	45	45		none		none
=	61	43		none	0	131
/	47	63		none		none
;	59	58		none		none
−	45	95		31	0	130

Turbo Pascal Reserved Words

The following are Turbo Pascal reserved words.

Absolute   Declares a variable that resides at a specific memory location. For example:

```
Var
  R : Real;
  X : Integer Absolute R;      (* X shares memory with R *)
  Y : Integer Absolute 0000:0000; (* Y is located at segment 0
                                     at offset 0 *)
```

And   Combines two Boolean expressions such that both must be true for the entire expression to be true. For example:

```
If (A > B) And (C > D) Then ...
```

And   Also compares two bytes or integers and returns a third byte or integer. A bit in the resulting integer is turned on only if both bits in the same position are on in the first and second integers.

Array   Defines a data type that repeats its structure a specified number of times. For example:

```
Var
  i : Array [1..20] Of Integer;
```

defines a data item that consists of 20 integers.

Begin   Indicates the beginning of a block of code.

Case   A control structure that branches conditionally based on the value of a scalar. For example:

```
Var
  i : Integer;

  Case I Of
  1 :
    Begin
    { Statements }
    End;

  2..3 :
    Begin
    { Statements }
    End;

  4 :
    Begin
    { Statements }
    End;

  Else
    Begin
    { Statements }
    End;

  End;
```

Const   Defines a data item as either a typed or untyped constant. For example:

```
Const
  i = 100;              (* Untyped constant *)
  j : Integer = 100; (* Typed constant *)
```

Div   Performs integer division.

Do   Used with looping control structures. For example:

```
For i := 1 To 10 Do ...

While i < 11 Do ...
```

DownTo   Used in For-Do loops where the counter is decremented. For example:

```
For i := 100 DownTo 1 Do ...
```

Else   Executes a block of code when an **If-Then** statement is FALSE. For example:

```
If (A < B) Then
  Begin
  { Statements }
  End
Else
  Begin
  { Statements }
  End;
```

End   Denotes the end of a block of code, the end of a case statement, the end of a record definition, or the end of a program.

External   Tells Turbo Pascal to look in an object file for the executable code for a procedure. For example:

```
{$L ASM_PROC}
Procedure ExtProc; External;
```

File   A data type that stores data on a disk.

For   Used in For-Do loops. For example:

```
For i := 1 To 100 Do ...
```

Forward   Declares the heading of a procedure before the actual procedure is defined. The full heading is declared in the **Forward** statement. Later, when the body of the procedure is declared, only the procedure name is used. For example:

```
Procedure X(i,j : Integer) : Forward;

{ Statements }

Procedure X;
```

```
Begin
{ Statements }
End;
```

Function   Declares a subroutine to be a function. Functions return values of a specific data type. For example:

```
Function Add(a,b : Integer) : Integer;
Begin
Add := a + b;
End;
```

Goto   Transfers control to the location of the label contained in the **Goto** statement. For example:

```
Label
  EndProc; (* Label declaration *)

Begin
For i := 1 To 1000 Do
  Begin
  j := j + 1;
  If j > 1000 Then
    Goto EndProc;
  End;

EndProc;
End;
```

If   Used in **If-Then** statements. For example:

```
If (A < B) Then ...
```

Implementation   Indicates the beginning of the implementation section of a unit.

In   Tests for set inclusion. For example:

```
Var
  Ch : Char;

If Ch In ['A'..'Z'] Then ...
```

Inline   Tells Turbo Pascal to treat the code that follows as machine-language instructions. For example:

```
Inline($1E/$06/$07/$1F);
```

Interface   Defines the beginning of the interface section of a unit.

Interrupt   Defines a procedure as an interrupt procedure. Interrupt procedures are used for writing interrupt service routines.

Label   Declares labels used with **Goto** statements (see **Goto**).

Mod   Returns the remainder of integer division.

Nil   May be assigned to any pointer variable. Used in comparisons to test whether a pointer has a valid value. For example:

```
Type
  Aptr = ^Arecord;
  Arecord = Record
    i : Integer;
    Next : Aptr;
    End;
Var
  A : Aptr;

Begin
New(A);
If (A^.Next = Nil) Then ...
```

Not   Reverses the result of a Boolean expression. For example, if

```
(A > B)
```

is true, then

```
Not (A > B)
```

is false.

Of   Used in the **Case** statement (see **Case**) and in declaration of a set or array data type.

Or   Combines Boolean expressions such that the entire expression is true if either condition is true. For example:

```
If (A > B) Or (C > D) Then ...
```

is true if either the first or the second comparison (or both) is true.

Or   Also compares two bytes or integers and returns a third byte or integer. A bit in the resulting integer is turned on if either or both bits in the same position are on in the first and second integers.

Packed   Declares arrays such that the arrays use less memory than they normally would. Turbo Pascal supports this reserved word, but it has no effect since all Turbo Pascal arrays are stored in packed format.

Procedure   Defines a block of code as belonging to a procedure.

Program   Defines a block of code as belonging to a program. This is the first statement in a program.

Record   Defines a complex data type that combines several simple or complex data types. For example:

```
Type
  Student = Record
    Name : String[20];
    Age : Integer;
    End;

  Class = Record
    Students : Array [1..30] Of Student;
    RoomNumber : Integer;
    End;
```

Repeat   Used in **Repeat-Until** control structures. For example:

```
i := 1;
  Repeat
  { Statements }
  i := i + 1;
  Until i > 100;
```

Set   Defines a set variable. For example:

```
Var
  Letters : Set Of Char;
```

Shl   Shifts the bits in a byte or integer one position to the left and sets the right-most bit to zero.

Shr   Shifts the bits in a byte or integer one position to the right and sets the left-most bit to zero.

String   Defines a **String** data type. A string can be defined from 1 to 255 characters long. If no length is specified, the length defaults to 255 characters. For example:

```
Var
  s : String; (* Maximum 255 characters *)
```

Then   Used in **If-Then** statements (see **If**).

To   Used in For-Do loops (see **For**).

Type   Defines data types that can then be used to define variables. For example:

```
Type
  PersonType = Record
    Name : String[20];
    Address : String[50];
    Income : Real;
    End;
Var
  Person1, Person2 : PersonType;
```

Unit   Declares the source file to be a Turbo Pascal unit.

Until   Used in Repeat-Until loops (see **Repeat**).

Uses   Declares the use of one or more units. For example:

```
Program Test;
Uses CRT, DOS;
```

Var   Defines variables. For example:

```
Var
  i : Integer;
  s : String;
```

While   Used in While-Do loops. For example:

```
i := 0;
While i < 100 Do
  Begin
  { Statements }
  i := i + 1;
  End;
```

With   Used for implicit reference to a record variable. For example:

```
Var
  Person : Record
    Name : String;
    Age : Integer;
    End;

Begin
With Person Do
  Begin
  ReadLn(Name);
  ReadLn(Age);
  End;
```

Xor   Combines Boolean expressions such that the entire expression is true if only one of two conditions is true. For example:

```
If (A > B) Xor (C > D) Then ...
```

is true if the first comparison is true or the second comparison is true, but not if both are true.

Xor   Also compares two bytes or integers and returns a third byte or integer. A bit in the resulting integer is turned on if either, but not both, bits in the same position are on in the first and second integers.

Turbo Pascal Procedure and Function Reference

The following are Turbo Pascal standard procedures.

Abs

Syntax

Function Abs(r : Real) : Real;
Function Abs(i : Integer) : Integer;

Description   **Abs** returns the absolute value of the parameter passed to it. The function result is the same type (**Real** or **Integer**) as the parameter.

Addr

Syntax

Function Addr(Var Variable) : Pointer;

Description   **Addr** returns the address of a variable, typed constant, or procedure. The result is a **Pointer** type.

Append

Syntax

Procedure Append(Var F: Text);

Description   **Append** opens a text file for writing and positions the file pointer at the end of the file.

Arc   [GRAPH Unit]

Syntax

Procedure Arc(x, y : Integer;
                StAngle,
                EndAngle,
                Radius : Word);

Description   **Arc** draws a circle around coordinates **x:y** with a radius of **Radius**. The circle begins drawing clockwise from **StAngle** and stops at **EndAngle**.

ArcTan

Syntax

Function ArcTan(R: Real) : Real;

Description   **ArcTan** returns the arctangent of the parameter passed to it.

Assign

Syntax

Procedure Assign(Var F: File; Name : String);

Description   **Assign** links file variable **F** to the file named in **Name**.

AssignCrt   [CRT Unit]

Syntax

Procedure AssignCrt(Var F : Text);

Description   **AssignCrt** allows the user to send output to the video display by writing to file **F**.

Bar   [GRAPH Unit]

Syntax

Procedure Bar(x1, y1, x2, y2 : Integer);

Description   **Bar** draws a filled-in rectangular area of the screen.

Bar3D   [GRAPH Unit]

Syntax

Procedure Bar3D(x1, y1, x2, y2 : Integer;
                    Depth : Word;
                    Top : Boolean);

Description   **Bar3D** draws a filled-in three-dimensional rect-angular area of the screen. The rectangle is drawn **Depth** pixels deep. If **Top** is TRUE, the procedure draws a three-dimensional top on the rectangle.

BlockRead

Syntax

Procedure BlockRead(Var F: File;
                    Var B: Type;
                    NumRecs: Integer;
                    Var RecsRead: Integer);

Description   **BlockRead** attempts to read **NumRecs** records from untyped file **F** into buffer **B**. **RecsRead** indicates the number of records actually read. Note that the **RecsRead** parameter is supported only in PC/MS-DOS versions.

BlockWrite

Syntax

Procedure BlockWrite(Var F: File;
                    Var B: Type;
                    NumRecs: Integer);

Description   **BlockWrite** writes **NumRecs** records from buffer **B** to untyped file **F**.

ChDir

Syntax

Procedure ChDir(S: String);

Description   **ChDir** changes the current directory to that in **S**.

Chr

Syntax

Function Chr(I: Integer);

Description   **Chr** returns the ASCII character that corresponds to **I**.

Circle   [GRAPH Unit]

Syntax

Procedure Circle(x, y : Integer;
                    Radius : Word);

Description   **Circle** draws a circle with a radius of **Radius** around the coordinate **x:y**.

ClearDevice   [GRAPH Unit]

Syntax

Procedure ClearDevice;

Description   **ClearDevice** clears the graphics screen.

ClearViewPort   [GRAPH Unit]

Syntax

Procedure ClearViewPort;

Description   **ClearViewPort** clears the current viewport.

Close

Syntax

Procedure Close(Var F: File);

Description   **Close** flushes the buffer for file **F** and then closes the file.

CloseGraph   [GRAPH Unit]

Syntax

Procedure CloseGraph;

Description   CloseGraph restores the video display to the mode that existed prior to entering graphics mode. The procedure also frees memory used by the graphics system.

ClrEol   [CRT Unit]

Syntax

Procedure ClrEol;

Description   ClrEol clears the current screen line from the cursor position to the right edge of the screen.

ClrScr   [CRT Unit]

Syntax

Procedure ClrScr;

Description   ClrScr clears the screen and positions the cursor at location (1,1) on the screen.

Concat

Syntax

Function Concat(S1, S2, . . ., Sn) : String;

Description   **Concat** combines any number of strings and returns them as a single string. If the length of the concatenated string is greater than 255, Turbo Pascal generates a run-time error.

Copy

Syntax

Function Copy(S: String; P, L: Integer) : String;

Description   **Copy** returns a portion of string **S**, which starts at character number **P** and contains **L** characters.

Cos

Syntax

Function Cos(R: Real) : Real;

Description   **Cos** returns the cosine of **R**.

Cseg

Syntax

Function Cseg : Word;

Description   Cseg returns the segment address of the program's code segment.

Dec

Syntax

Procedure Dec(Var x : Scalar;
                n : LongInt);

Description   Dec decrements variable **x** by **n**. If you omit **n**, **x** will be decremented by 1.

Delay   [CRT Unit]

Syntax

Procedure Delay(ms : Word);

Description   **Delay** halts program execution for **ms** milliseconds.

Delete

Syntax

Procedure Delete(S: String; P, L: Integer);

Description   **Delete** removes **L** characters from string **S** starting with character number **P**.

DelLine   [CRT Unit]

Syntax

Procedure DelLine;

Description   **DelLine** deletes the screen line on which the cursor is located. Lines below the deleted line scroll up one line.

DetectGraph   [GRAPH Unit]

Syntax

Procedure DetectGraph(Var GD, GM : Integer);

Description   **DetectGraph** returns the detected graph driver (**GD**) and graphics mode (**GM**) for the display adapter installed.

DiskFree   [DOS Unit]

Syntax

Function DiskFree(Drive : Word) : LongInt;

Description   **DiskFree** returns the amount of free disk space, in bytes, on drive **Drive** (1 = A, 2 = B, 0 = Default drive).

DiskSize   [DOS Unit]

Syntax

Function DiskSize(Drive : Word) : LongInt;

Description   **DiskSize** returns the size, in bytes, of drive **Drive** (1 = A, 2 = B, 0 = Default drive).

Dispose

Syntax

Procedure Dispose(P: Pointer);

Description   **Dispose** frees heap memory allocated to a **pointer** variable. **Dispose** is used in conjunction with the **New** command.

DosExitCode   [DOS Unit]

Syntax

Function DosExitCode : Word;

Description   **DosExitCode** returns the exit code of a subprocess (0 = normal termination, 1 = termination by CTRL-C, 2 = termination by device error, 3 = termination by **Keep** procedure).

DosVersion   [DOS Unit]

Syntax

Function DosVersion : Word;

Description   **DosVersion** returns the version of the operating system. The major release number is in the high-order byte, and the minor version number is in the low-order byte.

DrawPoly   [GRAPH Unit]

Syntax

Procedure DrawPoly(NumPoints : Word;
                   Var PolyPoints);

Description   **DrawPoly** draws a polygon defined by **NumPoints** points. The array **PolyPoints** contains the coordinates for the points of the polygon.

Dseg

Syntax

Function Dseg : Word;

Description   **Dseg** returns the segment address of the program's data segment.

EnvCount   [DOS Unit]

Syntax

Function EnvCount : Integer;

Description   **EnvCount** returns the number of strings defined in the DOS environment.

EnvStr   [DOS Unit]

Syntax

Function EnvStr(i : Integer) : String;

Description   **EnvStr** returns environment string number **i**.

Eof

Syntax

Function Eof(F: File) : Boolean;

Description   **Eof** returns TRUE when the file pointer in **F** reaches the end of the file.

Eoln

Syntax

Function Eoln(F: File) : Boolean;

Description   **Eoln** returns TRUE when the file pointer in **F** reaches either the end of a line (indicated by a carriage return and line feed) or the end of the file.

Erase

Syntax

Procedure Erase(F: File);

Description   **Erase** deletes disk file **F** and removes its information from the directory.

Exec   [DOS Unit]

Syntax

Procedure Exec(Path, CmdLine : String);

Description   **Exec** executes the file named in **Path** with command-line parameters defined in **CmdLine**. For example, in this program

```
{$M 2000,0,0}
Program TestExec;
Uses DOS;
Begin
Exec ('TESTPROG.EXE','A B C');
ReadLn;
Exec ('\COMMAND.COM','');
End.
```

the first **Exec** statement executes the program TESTPROG. EXE with command-line parameters A, B, C. The second **Exec** statement invokes the DOS COMMAND.COM file with no parameters; this creates a DOS shell from which you can run other programs. You can escape from the DOS shell by typing **EXIT** at the DOS prompt. Note that the program limits the amount of memory allocated to the heap in order to leave room for the program being executed.

Exit

Syntax

Procedure Exit;

Description   **Exit** causes a program to leave the block currently being executed.

Exp

Syntax

Function Exp(R: Real) : Real;

Description   **Exp** returns the exponential of **R**.

FExpand   [DOS Unit]

Syntax

Function FExpand(P : PathStr);

Description   **FExpand** accepts a filename **P** and returns the filename with its complete path structure, including drive.

FilePos

Syntax

Function FilePos(F: File) : Integer;

Description   **FilePos** returns the record number at which the file pointer in **F** is located.

FileSize

Syntax

Function FileSize(F: File) : Integer;

Description   **FileSize** returns the number of records currently contained in **F**.

FillChar

Syntax

Procedure FillChar(Variable: Type; I, Code: Scalar);

Description   **FillChar** fills **I** bytes of memory with the value **Code**, which may be of any scalar type, starting at the address of **Variable**.

FillEllipse   [GRAPH Unit]

Syntax

Procedure FillEllipse(x, y : Integer;
                      XRadius,
                      YRadius : Word);

Description   **FillEllipse** draws an ellipse centered at coordinates x:y with a vertical radius of **YRadius** and a horizontal radius of **XRadius**. The ellipse is filled with the current fill color and fill style, and the border is drawn with the current color.

FillPoly [GRAPH Unit]

Syntax

Procedure FillPoly(NumPoints : Word
                   Var PolyPoints);

Description   **FillPoly** draws a polygon with **NumPoints** points. The array **PolyPoints** contains the coordinates for the points of the polygon.

FindFirst [DOS Unit]

Syntax

Procedure FindFirst(Path : String;
                    Attr : Word;
                    Var S : SearchRec);

Description   **FindFirst** returns information on the first file found in directory **Path** whose attributes match **Attr**. The standard values of **Attr** are

```
Const
  ReadOnly      = $01;
  Hidden        = $02;
  SysFile       = $04;
  VolumeId      = $08;
  Directory     = $10;
  Archive       = $20;
  AnyFile       = $3F;
```

The **SearchRec** data type is defined as

```
Type
  SearchRec = Record
    Fill : Array [1..21] Of Byte;
    Attr : Byte;
```

```
Time : LongInt;
Size : LongInt;
Name : String[12];
End;
```

If the search is successful, the value of **DosError** will be zero.

FindNext   [DOS Unit]

Syntax

Procedure FindNext(Var S : SearchRec);

Description   **FindNext** returns information on the next file found in the directory **Path** defined in **FindFirst** whose attributes match those used in **FindFirst**. If the search is successful, the value of **DosError** will be zero.

FloodFill   [GRAPH Unit]

Syntax

Procedure FloodFill(x, y : Integer;
                    Border : Word);

Description   **FloodFill** fills an enclosed area of the graphics display with the current color and pattern. The area must be completely enclosed by the color **Border**, and the **x:y** coordinates must lie within the area to be filled.

Flush

Syntax

Procedure Flush(Var F : Text);

Description   **Flush** sends to disk all buffered output for file **F**.

Frac

Syntax

Function Frac(R: Real) : Real;

Description   **Frac** returns the noninteger portion of **R**.

FreeMem

Syntax

Procedure FreeMem(Var P: Pointer; I: Integer);

Description   **FreeMem** frees **I** bytes of heap memory associated with variable **P**, which must have been previously allocated by **GetMem**.

FSearch   [DOS Unit]

Syntax

Function FSearch(Path : PathStr;
                 DirList : String) : PathStr;

Description   **FSearch** searches in the list of directories included in **DirList** for a filename that matches **Path**. If the file is found, the result is returned as a string. If not found, the function returns an empty string.

FSplit   [DOS Unit]

Syntax

Procedure FSplit(Path : PathStr;
                 Var Dir : DirStr;
                 Var Name : NameStr;
                 Var Ext : ExtStr);

Description   **FSplit** accepts a filename **Path** and returns its components. The following types are used:

```
Type
  PathStr = String[79];
  DirStr  = String[67];
  NameStr = String[8];
  ExtStr  = String[4];
```

GetArcCoords   [GRAPH Unit]

Syntax

Procedure GetArcCoords(Var ArcCoords : ArcCoordsType);

Description   GetArcCoords returns the coordinates used by the most recently used **Arc** or **Ellipse** command. The structure of **ArcCoordsType** is as follows:

```
Type
  ArcCoordsType = Record
    x, y : Integer;
    Xstart, Ystart : Integer;
    Xend, Yend : Integer;
    End;
```

GetAspectRatio   [GRAPH Unit]

Syntax

Procedure GetAspectRatio(Var Xasp, Yasp : Word);

Description   GetAspectRatio returns in **Xasp** and **Yasp** the effective resolution of the graphics screen. The aspect ratio is computed as **Xasp** divided by **Yasp**.

GetBkColor   [GRAPH Unit]

Syntax

Function GetBkColor : Word;

Description   GetBkColor returns the index for the current palette of the current background color.

GetCBreak   [DOS Unit]

Syntax

Procedure GetCBreak(Var Break : Boolean);

Description   **GetCBreak** returns the current state of CTRL-BREAK checking in DOS. When **Break** is FALSE, DOS checks for CTRL-BREAK during console, printer, or serial I/O. When it is TRUE, DOS checks for CTRL-BREAK at every system call.

GetColor   [GRAPH Unit]

Syntax

Function GetColor : Word;

Description   **GetColor** returns the current drawing color in the graphics mode.

GetDate   [DOS Unit]

Syntax

Procedure GetDate(Var Year,
                Month,
                Day,
                DayOfWeek : Word);

Description   **GetDate** returns the date as determined by the system clock.

GetDefaultPalette   [GRAPH Unit]

Syntax

Procedure GetDefaultPalette(Var Pal : PaletteType);

Description   **GetDefaultPalette** returns in **Pal** the default palette for the current graphics driver. The structure of **Palette Type** is as follows:

```
Type
  PaletteType = Record
    Size : Byte;
    Colors : Array [0..MaxColor] Of ShortInt;
    End;
```

GetDir

Syntax

Procedure GetDir(d: Byte; Var s: String);

Description   **GetDir** gets the directory for the drive specified by **d**. The directory is returned in **s**. If **d** is zero, **GetDir** searches the default drive.

GetDriverName   [GRAPH Unit]

Syntax

Function GetDriverName : String;

Description   **GetDriverName** returns the name of the current graphics driver.

GetEnv   [DOS Unit]

Syntax

Function GetEnv(EnvVar : String) : String;

Description   **GetEnv** returns the environment string for the environment variable specified in **EnvVar**.

GetFAttr   [DOS Unit]

Syntax

Procedure GetFAttr(Var F; Var Attr : Word);

Description   **GetFAttr** returns the file attribute for file **F**. Before calling this procedure, **F** must be assigned but not opened.

GetFillPattern   [GRAPH Unit]

Syntax

Procedure GetFillPattern(Var FP : FillPatternType);

Description   GetFillPattern returns in **FP** the definition of the current fill pattern. The structure of **FillPatternType** is

```
Type
   FillPatternType = Array [1..8] Of Byte;
```

GetFillSettings   [GRAPH Unit]

Syntax

Procedure GetFillSettings(Var FS : FillSettingsType);

Description   GetFillSettings returns in **FS** the current fill pattern and color. The structure of **FillSettingsType** is

```
Type
   FillSettingsType = Record
      Pattern : Word;
      Color : Word;
      End;
```

GetFTime   [DOS Unit]

Syntax

Procedure GetFTime(Var F; Var Time : LongInt);

Description   GetFTime returns in **Time** the time stamp for file **F**. File **F** must be assigned and opened before using this procedure. The variable **Time** is a packed value and must be unpacked with the **UnPackTime** procedure.

GetGraphMode   [GRAPH Unit]

Syntax

Function GetGraphMode : Integer;

Description   **GetGraphMode** returns the current graphics mode. The numeric value of the graphics mode must be interpreted in combination with the graphics driver.

GetImage   [GRAPH Unit]

Syntax

Procedure GetImage(x1, y1, x2, y2 : Integer;
            Var BitMap);

Description   **GetImage** stores a rectangular portion of a graphics screen, defined by **x1:y1** and **x2:y2** in **BitMap**.

GetIntVec   [DOS Unit]

Syntax

Procedure GetIntVec(IntNo : Byte;
            Var : Vector : Pointer);

Description   **GetIntVec** returns in **Vector** the current contents of interrupt vector number **IntNo**.

GetLineSettings   [GRAPH Unit]

Syntax

Procedure GetLineSettings(Var LST : LineSettingsType);

Description   **GetLineSettings** returns in **LST** the current settings for line style, pattern, and thickness. The structure of **LineSettingsType** is

```
Type
  LineSettingsType = Record
    LineStyle : Word;
    Pattern : Word;
    Thickness : Word;
    End;
```

GetMaxColor   [GRAPH Unit]

Syntax

Function GetMaxColor : Word;

Description   **GetMaxColor** returns the highest value that represents a color in the current palette.

GetMaxMode   [GRAPH Unit]

Syntax

Function GetMaxMode : Word;

Description   **GetMaxMode** returns a value that indicates the highest-resolution graphics mode for the installed adapter.

GetMaxX   [GRAPH Unit]

Syntax

Function GetMaxX : Integer;

Description   **GetMaxX** returns the maximum horizontal co-ordinate for the current graphics mode.

GetMaxY

Syntax

Function GetMaxY : Integer;

Description   **GetMaxY** returns the maximum vertical coor-dinate for the current graphics mode.

GetMem

Syntax

Procedure GetMem(Var P: Pointer; I: Integer);

Description   **GetMem** reserves **I** bytes on the heap and stores the starting address in variable **P**.

GetModeName   [GRAPH Unit]

Syntax

Function GetModeName(ModeNumber : Word) : String;

Description   **GetModeName** returns a string describing the graphics mode denoted in **ModeNumber**.

GetModeRange   [GRAPH Unit]

Syntax

Procedure GetModeRange(GraphDriver : Integer;
                            Var LoMode,
                            HiMode : Integer);

Description   **GetModeRange** returns the highest (**HiMode**) and lowest (**LoMode**) resolution modes for the graphics driver denoted by **GraphDriver**.

GetPalette   [GRAPH Unit]

Syntax

Procedure GetPalette(Var P : PaletteType);

Description   **GetPalette** returns in **P** the current palette. The structure of PaletteType is

```
Const
  MaxColors = 15;
Type
  PaletteType = Record
    Size : Byte;
    Colors : Array [0..MaxColors] Of ShortInt;
    End;
```

GetPaletteSize   [GRAPH Unit]

Syntax

Function GetPaletteSize : Word;

Description   GetPaletteSize returns the maximum number of palette entries that the current graphics mode can support.

GetPixel   [GRAPH Unit]

Syntax

Function GetPixel(x, y : Integer);

Description   GetPixel returns the color of the pixel at coordinates x:y.

GetTextSettings   [GRAPH Unit]

Syntax

Procedure GetTextSettings(Var TS : TextSettingsType);

Description   GetTextSettings returns in **TS** the current text settings. The structure of **TextSettingsType** is

```
Type
  TextSettingsType = Record
    Font : Word;
    Direction : Word;
    CharSize : Word;
    Horiz : Word;
    Vert : Word;
    End;
```

GetTime   [DOS Unit]

Syntax

Procedure GetTime(Var Hour,
                Minute,
                Second,
                Sec100 : Word);

Description   GetTime returns the time according to the system clock.

GetVerify   [DOS Unit]

Syntax

Procedure GetVerify(Var Verify : Boolean);

Description   **GetVerify** returns the status of write-verification in DOS. When **Verify** is TRUE, DOS verifies all disk writes.

GetViewSettings   [GRAPH Unit]

Syntax

Procedure GetViewSettings(Var VP : ViewPortType);

Description   **GetViewSettings** returns in **VP** the current viewport settings. The structure of **ViewPortType** is

```
Type
  ViewPortType = Record
    x1, y1, x2, y2 : Integer;
    Clip : Boolean;
    End;
```

GetX   [GRAPH Unit]

Syntax

Function GetX : Integer;

Description   **GetX** returns the horizontal coordinate of the current position.

GetY   [GRAPH Unit]

Syntax

Function GetY : Integer;

Description   **GetY** returns the vertical coordinate of the current position.

GotoXY   [CRT Unit]

Syntax

Procedure GotoXY(x, y: Integer);

Description   GotoXY places the cursor at screen coordinates X:Y.

GraphDefaults   [GRAPH Unit]

Syntax

Procedure GraphDefaults;

Description   **GraphDefaults** resets the graphics settings to their default values.

GraphErrorMsg   [GRAPH Unit]

Syntax

Function GraphErrorMsg(Code : Integer) : String;

Description   **GraphErrorMsg** returns an error message corresponding to the error condition denoted by **Code**.

GraphResult   [GRAPH Unit]

Syntax

Function GraphResult : Integer;

Description   **GraphResult** returns an error code for the last graphics procedure.

Halt

Syntax

Procedure Halt;

Description   **Halt** terminates a program.

Hi

Syntax

Function Hi(I: Integer) : Byte;

Description   **Hi** returns the high-order byte from integer **I**.

HighVideo   [CRT Unit]

Syntax

Procedure HighVideo;

Description   **HighVideo** enables the high-intensity video display.

ImageSize   [GRAPH Unit]

Syntax

Function ImageSize(x1, y1, x2, y2 : Integer);

Description   ImageSize returns the number of bytes required to store the bit map for the portion of the screen defined by **x1:y1** and **x2:y2.**

Inc

Syntax

Procedure Inc(Var x; n : LongInt);

Description   Inc increments the value of scalar **x** by **n.** If **n** is omitted from the parameter list, **x** is incremented by 1.

InitGraph   [GRAPH Unit]

Syntax

Procedure InitGraph(Var GraphDriver : Integer;
                    Var GraphMode : Integer;
                    DriverPath : String);

Description   InitGraph initializes the graphics environment to the graphics driver **GraphDriver** and mode **GraphMode.** If **GraphDriver** is zero, the procedure automatically detects the display adapter and sets the mode to the highest resolution. The procedure will look for .BGI files in the path defined by **DriverPath.**

Insert

Syntax

Procedure Insert(Source : String;
                 Var Target : String;
                 Index : Integer);

Description   **Insert** inserts string **Source** into string **Target** at position **Index**.

InsLine   [CRT Unit]

Syntax

Procedure InsLine;

Description   **InsLine** inserts a blank line on the screen at the current cursor position.

InstallUserDriver   [GRAPH Unit]

Syntax

Function InstallUserDriver(Name : String;
                          AutoDetectPtr : Pointer) :
                          Integer;

Description   **InstallUserDriver** installs a non-Borland graphics driver. **Name** contains the name of the file that contains the driver, and **AutoDetectPtr** is a pointer to an optional autodetect function. The driver must be in .BGI format.

InstallUserFont   [GRAPH Unit]

Syntax

Function InstallUserFont(FontFileName : String) : Integer;

Description   **InstallUserFont** lets the user install a non-Borland font. The file named by **FontFileName** contains the font information.

Int

Syntax

Function Int(R: Real) : Integer;

Description   **Int** returns the integer portion of **R**.

Intr   [DOS Unit]

Syntax

Procedure Intr(Func : Byte; Var Regs : Registers);

Description   **Intr** calls BIOS interrupt **Func** with registers defined by **Regs**.

IOresult

Syntax

Function IOresult : Word;

Description   **IOresult** reports an error code when input/output operations are performed. If **IOresult** is not equal to zero, an error occurred.

Keep   [DOS Unit]

Syntax

Procedure Keep(ExitCode : Word);

Description   **Keep** terminates the program, but keeps it resident. The procedure passes **ExitCode** as a standard DOS error code.

KeyPressed   [CRT Unit]

Syntax

Function KeyPressed : Boolean;

Description   **KeyPressed** returns TRUE when a key has been pressed.

Length

Syntax

Function Length(S: String) : Integer;

Description   **Length** returns the length of string S.

Line   [GRAPH Unit]

Syntax

Procedure Line(x1, y1, x2, y2 : Integer);

Description   **Line** draws a line from **x1:y1** to **x2:y2**.

LineRel   [GRAPH Unit]

Syntax

Procedure LineRel(Dx, Dy : Integer);

Description   **LineRel** draws a line from the current pointer to a point defined by **Dx** and **Dy**. For example, if the current pointer is positioned at 1:2, then the command **LineRel(100,100)** will draw a line from 1:2 to 101:102.

LineTo   [GRAPH Unit]

Syntax

Procedure LineTo(x, y : Integer);

Description   **LineTo** draws a line from the current pointer to **x:y.**

Ln

Syntax

Function Ln(Var R: Real) : Real;

Description   **Ln** returns the natural logarithm of **R.**

Lo

Syntax

Function Lo(I: Integer) : Byte;

Description   **Lo** returns the low-order byte of integer **I.**

LowVideo   [CRT Unit]

Syntax

Procedure LowVideo;

Description   **LowVideo** sets the video display to low intensity.

Mark

Syntax

Procedure Mark(P: Pointer);

Description   **Mark** stores the current top-of-heap address in pointer **P**.

MaxAvail

Syntax

Function MaxAvail: LongInt;

Description   **MaxAvail** returns the size of the largest block of unallocated memory on the heap.

MemAvail

Syntax

Function MemAvail: LongInt;

Description   **MemAvail** returns the total amount of unallocated memory on the heap.

MkDir

Syntax

Procedure MkDir(S: String);

Description   **MkDir** makes a directory with the name stored in string **S**.

Move

Syntax

Procedure Move(Var V1, V2; I: Integer);

Description   **Move** copies **I** bytes of memory from the location of variable **V1** to the location of variable **V2**.

MoveRel   [GRAPH Unit]

Syntax

Procedure MoveRel(Dx, Dy : Integer);

Description   **MoveRel** moves the current pointer to a position **Dx** pixels horizontally and **Dy** pixels vertically, relative to the current cursor position.

MoveTo   [GRAPH Unit]

Syntax

Procedure MoveTo(x, y : Integer);

Description   **MoveTo** positions the current pointer on pixel x:y.

MsDos   [DOS Unit]

Syntax

Procedure MsDos(Var Regs : Registers);

Description   **MsDos** executes DOS services using the values set in **Regs**.

New

Syntax

Procedure New(Var P: Pointer);

Description   New allocates memory on the heap for pointer P. After memory is allocated, the variable is referred to as **P^**.

NormVideo   [CRT Unit]

Syntax

Procedure NormVideo;

Description   **NormVideo** restores the default screen attributes to those that were present at the cursor position when the program started.

NoSound   [CRT Unit]

Syntax

Procedure NoSound;

Description   **NoSound** stops any tone currently being generated by the PC's speaker.

Odd

Syntax

Function Odd(I: Integer) : Boolean;

Description   **Odd** returns TRUE when **I** is odd and FALSE when **I** is even.

Ofs

Syntax

Function Ofs(<Variable, Procedure, or Function>) : Integer;

Description   **Ofs** returns the memory-address offset for any variable, procedure, or function.

Ord

Syntax

Function Ord(S: Scalar) : Integer;

Description   **Ord** returns the integer value of any scalar variable.

OutText   [GRAPH Unit]

Syntax

Procedure OutText(TextString : String);

Description   **OutText** displays the string **TextString** using the current settings for fonts, justification, height, and width.

OutTextXY   [GRAPH Unit]

Syntax

Procedure OutTextXY(x, y : Integer; TextString : String);

Description   **OutTextXY** displays the string **TextString** at position **x:y** using the current settings for fonts, justification, height, and width.

OvrClearBuf   [OVERLAY Unit]

Syntax

Procedure OvrClearBuf;

Description   **OvrClearBuf** empties the overlay buffer, requiring all overlays to be read from disk.

OvrGetBuf   [OVERLAY Unit]

Syntax

Function OvrGetBuf : LongInt;

Description   OvrGetBuf returns the size of the overlay buffer.

OvrInit   [OVERLAY Unit]

Syntax

Procedure OvrInit(FileName : String);

Description   OvrInit initializes the overlay manager. **File Name** contains the name of the overlay file.

OvrInitEMS   [OVERLAY Unit]

Syntax

Procedure OvrInitEMS;

Description   OvrInitEMS loads the overlay file into expanded memory if enough memory is available.

OvrSetBuf   [OVERLAY Unit]

Syntax

Procedure OvrSetBuf(BufSize : Integer);

Description   **OvrSetBuf** allocates **BufSize** bytes to the overlay buffer. **BufSize** must not be smaller than the default overlay buffer.

PackTime   [DOS Unit]

Syntax

Procedure PackTime(Var DT : DateTime;
                    Var Time : LongInt);

Description   **PackTime** accepts the variable **DT**, which contains date and time information, and returns **Time**, which contains the same information in packed form.

ParamCount

Syntax

Function ParamCount: Word;

Description   **ParamCount** returns the number of command-line parameters entered.

ParamStr

Syntax

Function ParamStr(I: Word: String);

Description   **ParamStr** returns parameters that were entered on the command line. For example, **ParamStr(1)** returns the first parameter. In DOS 3.x, **ParamStr(0)** returns the path and filename of the executed file.

Pi

Syntax

Function Pi : Real;

Description   **Pi** returns the value of the mathematical constant **Pi**. The precision of the number depends on whether 8087 mode is activated.

PieSlice   [GRAPH Unit]

Syntax

Procedure PieSlice(x, y : Integer;
                StAngle, EndAngle, Radius : Word);

Description   **PieSlice** draws a slice of a pie chart centered at x:y, with radius **Radius**, starting at **StAngle** and ending at **EndAngle**.

Pos

Syntax

Function Pos(SubS, S : String) : Integer;

Description   **Pos** returns the position of SubS in S. If SubS is not found in **S**, **Pos** returns 0.

Pred

Syntax

Function Pred(Var S: Scalar): Integer;

Description   **Pred** decrements any scalar variable.

Ptr

Syntax

Function Ptr(Segment, Offset: Integer) : Pointer;

Description   **Ptr** accepts two integers that contain a segment and an offset and returns a single 32-bit pointer value.

PutImage   [GRAPH Unit]

Syntax

Procedure PutImage(x, y : Integer;
　　　　　　　　Var BitMap;
　　　　　　　　BitBlt : Word);

Description   **PutImage** displays the contents of **BitMap** starting at **x:y**. **BitBlt** specifies the process to use to display the bit map, and can take the following values:

```
Const
  CopyPut   = 0;
  XORPut    = 1;
  OrPut     = 2;
  AndPut    = 3;
  NotPut    = 4;
```

PutPixel   [GRAPH Unit]

Syntax

Procedure PutPixel(x, y : Integer; Pixel : Word);

Description   **PutPixel** plots a single point of color, defined by **Pixel**, at position **x:y**.

Random

Syntax

Function Random(I: Word): Word;
Function Random: Real;

Description   **Random** returns a number randomly generated by Turbo Pascal. If you pass an integer parameter, **Random** returns an integer greater than or equal to zero and less than the parameter. Without an integer, **Random** returns a real value greater than or equal to zero and less than 1.

Randomize

Syntax

Function Randomize;

Description   **Randomize** initializes the seed value of the random-number generator. The seed value is stored in a **Long-Int** variable **RandSeed**.

Read (ReadLn)

Syntax

Procedure Read({Var F: File,} Parameters);
Procedure ReadLn({Var F: File,} Parameters);

Description   **Read** receives input from either the standard input device or the file specified by **F**. **ReadLn**, which can be used only on text files, receives input in the same way that **Read** does, but after reading in the data, **ReadLn** moves the file pointer forward to the next carriage return/line feed delimiter.

ReadKey [CRT Unit]

Syntax

Function ReadKey : Char;

Description   **ReadKey** reads a character from the keyboard without echo. If the result is #0, then a special key has been pressed and you must call **ReadKey** again to capture the second part of the key code.

Rectangle [GRAPH Unit]

Syntax

Procedure Rectangle(x1, y1, x2, y2 : Integer);

Description   **Rectangle** draws a rectangle with its upper-left corner at **x1:y1** and lower-right corner at **x2:y2**.

RegisterBGIdriver [GRAPH Unit]

Syntax

Function RegisterBGIdriver(Driver : Pointer) : Integer;

Description   **RegisterBGIdriver** allows the user to load a BGI driver file (read from disk onto the heap or linked into the program using BINOBJ) and register the driver with the graphics system. **Driver** is a pointer to the location of the BGI driver. If an error occurs, the function returns a value less than zero; otherwise, it returns the assigned driver number.

RegisterBGIfont   [GRAPH Unit]

Syntax

Function RegisterBGIfont(Font : Pointer) : Integer;

Description   **RegisterBGIfont** allows the user to load a BGI font driver file (read from disk onto the heap or linked into the program using BINOBJ) and register the font with the graphics system. **Font** is a pointer to the location of the BGI driver. If an error occurs, the function returns a value less than zero; otherwise, it returns the assigned font number.

Release

Syntax

Procedure Release(Var P: Pointer);

Description   **Release** reclaims memory that has been since allocated since the **Mark** command. Used to store the top-of-heap address in **P**.

Rename

Syntax

Procedure Rename(Var F: File; S: String);

Description   **Rename** changes the name of file **F** to that contained in **S**.

Reset

Syntax

Procedure Reset(Var F: File {; I: Integer});

Description   **Reset** opens file **F** for reading. If the file is untyped, you can specify the record size in **I**.

RestoreCRTMode   [GRAPH Unit]

Syntax

Procedure RestoreCRTMode;

Description   **RestoreCRTMode** restores the video display to the mode that existed before graphics was initialized.

Rewrite

Syntax

Procedure Rewrite(Var F: File {; I: Integer});

Description   **Rewrite** prepares a file to be written. If the file does not exist, Turbo Pascal creates it. If the file does exist, its contents are destroyed. If the file is untyped, you can specify the record size in **I**.

RmDir

Syntax

Procedure RmDir(S: String);

Description   **RmDir** removes the directory specified in S.

Round

Syntax

Function Round(R : Real) : LongInt;

Description   **Round** returns the rounded integer value of **R**.

RunError

Syntax

Procedure RunError;
Procedure RunError(ErrorCode : Word);

Description   **RunError** halts program execution and generates a run-time error. If **ErrorCode** is included, Turbo Pascal will interpret this as the type of run-time error that occurred.

Sector   [GRAPH Unit]

Syntax

Procedure Sector(x, y : Integer;
         StAngle, EndAngle, XRadius, YRadius :
         Word);

Description   **Sector** draws a sector centered at **x:y**, starting at **StAngle**, ending at **EndAngle**, with horizontal radius **XRadius** and vertical radius **YRadius**.

Seek

Syntax

Procedure Seek(Var F: File; P: Integer);

Description   **Seek** moves the file pointer to the beginning of record number **P** in file **F**.

SeekEof

Syntax

Function SeekEof(Var F: File) Boolean;

Description   **SeekEof** is similar to EOF, except that it skips blanks, tabs, and end-of-line markers (CR/LF) sequences before it tests for an end-of-file marker. The type of result is Boolean.

SeekEoln

Syntax

Function SeekEoln(Var F: File): Boolean;

Description   **SeekEoln** is similar to **Eoln**, except that it skips blanks and tabs before it tests for an end-of-line marker. The type of the result is Boolean.

Seg

Syntax

Function Seg(Var Variable) : Word;
Function Seg(<Procedure or Function>) : Word;

Description   **Seg** returns the segment address of a variable, procedure, or function.

SetActivePage   [GRAPH Unit]

Syntax

Procedure SetActivePage(Page : Word);

Description   **SetActivePage** selects the graphics video display page to make active.

SetAllPalette   [GRAPH Unit]

Syntax

Procedure SetAllPalette(Var Palette);

Description   **SetAllPalette** changes all palettes to the definition contained in **Palette**.

SetAspectRatio   [GRAPH Unit]

Syntax

Procedure SetAspectRatio(Xasp, Yasp : Word);

Description   **SetAspectRatio** changes the aspect ratio used to display graphics to **Xasp** divided by **Yasp**.

SetBkColor   [GRAPH Unit]

Syntax

Procedure SetBkColor(Color : Word);

Description   **SetBkColor** sets the default background color for the graphics mode using entry **Color** of the current palette.

SetCBreak   [DOS Unit]

Syntax

Procedure SetCBreak(Break : Boolean);

Description   **SetCBreak** turns CTRL-BREAK on (when **Break** is TRUE) or off (when **Break** is FALSE).

SetColor   [GRAPH Unit]

Syntax

Procedure SetColor(Color : Word);

Description   **SetColor** sets the current drawing color to entry **Color** of the palette.

SetDate   [DOS Unit]

Syntax

Procedure SetDate(Year, Month, Day : Word);

Description   **SetDate** updates the system clock to the date passed as parameters. For example, the command **SetDate** (**1990,12,1**) sets the date to December 1, 1990.

SetFAttr   [DOS Unit]

Syntax

Procedure SetFAttr(Var F; Attr : Word);

Description   **SetFAttr** sets the attribute byte of file **F** to **Attr**. File **F** must be assigned but not opened before calling this procedure.

SetFillPattern   [GRAPH Unit]

Syntax

Procedure SetFillPattern(Pattern : FillPatternType;
                   Color : Word);

Description   **SetFillPattern** defines the graphic pattern used to fill portions of the screen with commands such as **Fill-Poly** and **FloodFill**.

SetFillStyle   [GRAPH Unit]

Syntax

Procedure SetFillStyle(Pattern : Word;
                  Color : Word);

Description   **SetFillStyle** sets the pattern used to fill areas of a graphic display.

SetFTime   [DOS Unit]

Syntax

Procedure SetFTime(Var f; Time : LongInt);

Description   **SetFTime** sets the time stamp of file **f** to the value of **Time**, which is a packed representation of the time and date. **Time** is created with the procedure **PackTime**.

SetGraphBufSize   [GRAPH Unit]

Syntax

Procedure SetGraphBufSize(BufSize : Word);

Description   **SetGraphBufSize** sets the size of the graphics buffer.

SetGraphMode   [GRAPH Unit]

Syntax

Procedure SetGraphMode(Mode : Integer);

Description   **SetGraphMode** sets the current graphics mode to that specified by **Mode**.

SetIntVec   [DOS Unit]

Syntax

Procedure SetIntVec(IntNo : Byte; Vector : Pointer);

Description   **SetIntVec** places the value of **Vector** at interrupt **IntNo** in the interrupt vector table.

SetLineStyle   [GRAPH Unit]

Syntax

Procedure SetLineStyle(LineStyle : Word;
                     Pattern : Word;
                     Thickness : Word);

Description   **SetLineStyle** determines the style, pattern, and thickness of lines drawn in Graphics mode.

SetPalette   [GRAPH Unit]

Syntax

Procedure SetPalette(ColorNum : Word; Color : ShortInt);

Description   **SetPalette** sets color number **ColorNum** of the active palette to **Color**.

SetRGBPalette   [GRAPH Unit]

Syntax

Procedure SetRGBPalette(ColorNum,
                        RedValue,
                        GreenValue,
                        BlueValue : Integer);

Description   **SetRGBPalette** sets palette entry **ColorNum** to consist of any combination of red, green, and blue.

SetTextBuf

Syntax

Procedure SetTextBuf(Var f : Text; Var Buf);
Procedure SetTextBuf(Var f : Text; Var Buf; Size : Word);

Description   **SetTextBuf** assigns text file **f** to buffer **Buf**. If size is not specified, the buffer's size is that of **Buf**. **Size** can be used to override the default buffer size.

SetTextJustify   [GRAPH Unit]

Syntax

Procedure SetTextJustify(Horiz, Vert : Word);

Description   **SetTextJustify** defines the display format used by **OutText** and **OutTextXY**.

SetTextStyle   [GRAPH Unit]

Syntax

Procedure SetTextStyle(Font : Word;
                       Direction : Word;
                       CharSize : Word);

Description   **SetTextStyle** determines how characters will be displayed in Graphics mode. The characteristics include the font, the direction in which the writing takes place, and the size of the characters.

SetTime   [DOS Unit]

Syntax

Procedure SetTime(Hour, Minute, Second, Sec100 : Word);

Description   **SetTime** sets the system clock according to the values passed as parameters.

SetUserCharSize   [GRAPH Unit]

Syntax

Procedure SetUserCharSize(MultX, DivX, MultY, DivY : Word);

Description   **SetUserCharSize** changes the width and height proportions for stroked fonts. For example, if **MultX** is 1 and **DivX** is 2, then characters will be displayed with one-half the width they would normally have.

SetVerify   [DOS Unit]

Syntax

Procedure SetVerify(Verify : Boolean);

Description   **SetVerify** turns disk-write verification on (when **Verify** is TRUE) or off (when **Verify** is FALSE).

SetViewPort   [GRAPH Unit]

Syntax

Procedure SetViewPort(x1, y1, x2, y2 : Integer;
                          Clip : Boolean);

Description   **SetViewPort** selects a rectangular portion of the graphics screen to use as the active screen. When clipping is TRUE, drawings are clipped at the borders of the viewport.

SetVisualPage   [GRAPH Unit]

Syntax

Procedure SetVisualPage(Page : Word);

Description   **SetVisualPage** selects the graphics page to display.

SetWriteMode   [GRAPH Unit]

Syntax

Procedure SetWriteMode(WriteMode : Integer);

Description   **SetWriteMode** selects one of two modes for drawing lines. In **CopyPut** mode (0) lines are drawn using the assembler MOV command. In **XORPut** mode (1) lines are drawn using the XOR command.

Sin

Syntax

Function Sin(R: Real) : Real;

Description   **Sin** returns the sine of **R**.

SizeOf

Syntax

Function SizeOf(Var Variable) : Word;

Description   **SizeOf** returns the number of bytes required by a variable or a data type.

Sound   [CRT Unit]

Syntax

Procedure Sound(Freq: Word);

Description   **Sound** generates a tone from the PC's speaker at a frequency specified by **Freq**. The tone continues until the **NoSound** command is issued.

SPtr

Syntax

Function SPtr : Word;

Description   **SPtr** returns the current value of the stack pointer (SP) register.

Sqr

Syntax

Function Sqr(R: Real) : Real;

Description   **Sqr** returns the square of **R**.

Sqrt

Syntax

Function Sqrt(R: Real) : Real;

Description   Sqrt returns the square root of **R**.

SSeg

Syntax

Function SSeg : Word;

Description   SSeg returns the current value of the stack segment (SS) register.

Str

Syntax

Procedure Str(I: Integer; [:Length,] Var S: String);
Procedure Str(R: Real; [:Length:Decimals,] Var S: String);

Description   Str converts a real or integer number into a string.

Succ

Syntax

Function Succ(S: Scalar): Integer;

Description   Succ advances by one the value of any scalar.

Swap

Syntax

Function Swap(I: Integer) : Integer;

Description   Swap reverses the positions of the low- and high-order bytes in an integer. For example, if **I** equals 00FFh, **Swap** returns FF00h.

SwapVectors   [DOS Unit]

Syntax

Procedure SwapVectors;

Description   SwapVectors exchanges the current values of the interrupt vector table with those that were saved when the program started executing.

TextBackground   [CRT Unit]

Syntax

Procedure TextBackground(Color: Byte);

Description   **TextBackground** changes the default background color to that specified by **Color**.

TextColor   [CRT Unit]

Syntax

Procedure TextColor(Color: Byte);

Description   **TextColor** changes the default foreground color to that specified by **Color**.

TextHeight   [GRAPH Unit]

Syntax

Function TextHeight(TextString : String) : Word;

Description   **TextHeight** determines how much vertical space **TextString** will require given the current font and multiplication factor.

TextMode   [CRT Unit]

Syntax

Procedure TextMode(Mode : Word);

Description   **TextMode** activates one of the text modes supported by Turbo Pascal. These include

```
Const
    BW40    =      0; (* 40 x 25 black & white / color adapter *)
    CO40    =      1; (* 40 x 25 color / color adapter *)
    C40     = CO40; (* For 3.0 compatibility *)
    BW80    =      2; (* 80 x 25 black & white / color adapter *)
    CO80    =      3; (* 80 x 25 color / color adapter *)
    C80     = CO80; (* For 3.0 compatibility *)
    MONO    =      7; (* 80 x 25 monochrome adapter *)
    Font8x8 =    256; (* EGA and VGA 43-and 50-line mode *)
```

TextWidth   [GRAPH Unit]

Syntax

Function TextWidth(TextString : String);

Description   **TextWidth** returns the width in pixels required to display **TextWidth** given the current font and multiplication factor.

Trunc

Syntax

Function Trunc(R: Real) : Integer;

Description Trunc   returns the integer portion of **R**. The result must be within the legal range of an integer.

Truncate

Syntax

Procedure Truncate(Var f);

Description   **Truncate** forces end of file at the current position of the file pointer. Contents of the file beyond the file pointer are lost.

UnPackTime   [DOS Unit]

Syntax

Procedure UnPackTime(Time : LongInt;
                     Var DT : DateTime);

Description   **UnPackTime** decodes the variable **Time** and returns the results in **DT**. The structure of **DateTime** is

```
Type
  DateTime = Record
    Year, Month, Day, Hour, Min, Sec : Word;
    END;
```

Upcase

Syntax

Function Upcase(C : Char) : Char;

Description   **Upcase** returns the uppercase value of **C** if **C** is a lowercase letter.

Val

Syntax

Procedure Val(S: String; Var R: Real; Var Code: Integer);
Procedure Val(S: String; Var I: Integer; Var Code: Integer);

Description   **Val** attempts to convert **S** into a numerical value (**R** or **I**). If the conversion is successful, Turbo Pascal sets **Code** equal to zero. If unsuccessful, **Code** contains an integer that represents the character in the string at which the error occurred.

WhereX   [CRT Unit]

Syntax

Function WhereX: Byte;

Description   **WhereX** returns the column in the current window at which the cursor is located.

WhereY [CRT Unit]

Syntax

Function WhereY : Byte;

Description   **WhereY** returns the row in the current window at which the cursor is located.

Window [CRT Unit]

Syntax

Procedure Window(x1,y1,x2,y2 : Byte);

Description   **Window** restricts the active screen to the rectangle defined by coordinates **x1:y1** (upper left) and **x2:y2** (lower right). Turbo Pascal treats the upper-left corner of the window as coordinates 1:1.

Write (WriteLn)

Syntax

Procedure Write({Var F: File,} Parameters);
Procedure WriteLn({Var F: File,} Parameters);

Description   **Write** accepts a list of parameters, which it writes to the default output device. When the first parameter is a file variable, output is directed to that file. **WriteLn**, which can be used only on text files, operates in the same way as **Write**, but it adds a carriage return and line feed at the end of the output.

Hayes®	Hayes Microcomputer Products
IBM®	International Business Machines Corporation
Intel®	Intel Corporation
MicroStar™	Borland International, Inc.
SideKick®	Borland International, Inc.
Smartmodem™	Hayes Microcomputer Products
SuperKey®	Borland International, Inc.
Turbo Assembler®	Borland International, Inc.
Turbo Debugger®	Borland International, Inc.
Turbo Pascal®	Borland International, Inc.
Turbo Pascal Database Toolbox®	Borland International, Inc.
Turbo Pascal Editor Toolbox®	Borland International, Inc.
Turbo Pascal Graphix Toolbox®	Borland International, Inc.
Turbo Pascal Numerical Methods Toolbox™	Borland International, Inc.
WordStar®	MicroPro International Corporation
Z80®	Zilog, Inc.

TRADEMARKS

The manuscript for this book was prepared and submitted
to Osborne/McGraw-Hill in electronic form.
The acquisitions editor for this project was Jeffrey Pepper,
the technical reviewer was Steve Wood,
and the project editor was Dusty Bernard.

Text design by Judy Wohlfrom, using Century Expanded for
text body and Eras Demi for display.

Color separation and cover supplier,
Phoenix Color Corporation. Screens produced with
InSet from Inset Systems, Inc.
Book printed and bound by
R.R. Donnelley & Sons Company,
Crawfordsville, Indiana.